CRISIS AND CONTINUITY IN WORLD POLITICS

Edited by

GEORGE A. LANYI Oberlin College
AND
WILSON C. MC WILLIAMS Livingston College, Rutgers University

Consulting Editor: Inis L. Claude, Jr.

A Random House Book in International Relations

CRISIS AND CONTINUITY IN WORLD POLITICS

READINGS IN INTERNATIONAL RELATIONS

Second Edition

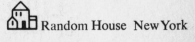

Random House New York

Copyright © 1966, 1973 by Random House, Inc.

All rights reserved under International and Pan-American Copyright Conventions. Published in the United States by Random House, Inc., and simultaneously in Canada by Random House of Canada Limited, Toronto.

Library of Congress Cataloging in Publication Data

Lanyi, George A.   ed.
　　Crisis and continuity in world politics.

　　Includes bibliographical references.
　　1. International relations—Addresses, essays, lectures. 2. World politics—Addresses, essays, lectures. I. McWilliams, Wilson C., joint ed. II. Title.
JX1308.L3   1972　　　　327′.08　　　　72–4372

Typography by James M. Wall

Manufactured in the United States of America.　Composed, printed, and bound by Kingsport Press, Inc., Kingsport, Tennessee.

Second Edition

9 8 7 6 5 4 3 2 1

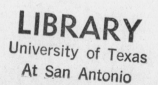

PREFACE

The years since the first edition of this book was published have been dominated by the war in Vietnam, and foreign policy has moved to the center of the stage in American politics. Passionate dissent has replaced the uneasy acquiescence and the patriotic zealotry of the Cold War years. The public has learned to doubt the experts and the experts, it is to be hoped, have learned to doubt themselves.

We have tried to give due attention to such new developments. But we have also tried to avoid two dangers created by the deep feelings associated with the struggle over policy in Vietnam. The first is the tendency of many Americans to ignore international politics out of a narrower concern for Vietnam, or worse, to develop theories and images of the international order which forget that it is Vietnam which is a part of world politics, not the reverse. The second is the temptation, too easily encouraged by the fascination with scientificity, to develop a new orthodoxy to replace the old, one no less bound in culture and in time. The mistaken pride of officialdom has not taught its opponents humility; it has only added fuel to their arrogance. That result, however, is part of an old pattern and one of the many continuities in world politics. Possibly, this book may help new students of international affairs to gain some perspective—in time and space—which will enable a clearer vision of the present and future.

Our earlier debts remain unpaid, and to them we have added obligations to Isebill V. Gruhn of the University of California at Santa Cruz, to Henry Plotkin of Rutgers University, to William I. Jones and Robert W. Tufts of Oberlin College for advice and criticism, to our new editors at Random House, Barry Rossinoff, for many suggestions, and Lynne Farber, who guided this revision, to Mrs. Vera Alferio for typing and pasting, and last but not least, to Susan Lanyi and Nancy McWilliams for insight, inspiration, and the tolerant reminder that procrastination never transforms good intentions into deeds.

Oberlin, Ohio   G. A. L.
New Brunswick, New Jersey   W. C. McW.

PREFACE TO THE FIRST EDITION

Every age is in some sense an age of crisis. Indeed, the life of man may best be envisioned as a series of crises connecting past and future, birth and death. Besieged by the dilemmas of their own time, men are perennially tempted to view their own problems—and their own wisdom—as unparalleled in history. To succumb to the temptation is to become, for the moment, an avant-garde, yet to be seen as an anachronism by the moment that is to come. In truth, the crisis of each age is unique and its own. We hope that we have paid due attention to the specific problems, and the ideas for coping with them, that have arisen in our time. Yet in a more fundamental sense, the drama is perpetual as man himself, the constant actor and the permanent spectator of the crisis in history. Knowledge of the past, Thucydides said, will be essential to those who seek to know the future, "which in the course of things human, must resemble if it does not reflect the past"; and he who writes rightly the history of his own times (said the Athenian) writes of and for all times.

We have no such high purpose. We will be well content if this book fulfills its modest objective: to serve as an introduction to the study of the crises and continuities of international political life. The book itself, we hope, will be useful as collateral reading or as a basic text for courses in international politics. In selecting material, we have tried to balance commentary and analysis with documentary materials. Controversy, we hope, is a feature of the book: in a science which still gropes in the dark corners of its subject matter, there has been too much consensus in the study of international politics. As much as possible, we have avoided reprinting materials already made available by eagle-eyed anthologists, but some classic essays must, inevitably, overlap with the selections of others. We have also attempted to avoid presenting excessively abridged selections, which all too often obscure or violate the intentions and argument of the original author, for whose purposes the editors feel some reverence. Our introductions to each chapter are intended to serve several purposes: to "introduce" the topic, to place the selections in the context of discussion, and to raise questions relating to the topic. If we accomplish the last purpose, it will have been our proudest claim, for the future of the discipline depends on the questions posed, and the answers sought, by the students now "introduced" to the subject.

Our thanks go to Charles Lieber, formerly of Random House, who suggested the book. Early in its genesis Wilfrid Knapp of St. Catherine's, Oxford, contributed useful advice. We are grateful for special suggestions to our colleague and chairman, John D. Lewis of Oberlin College. The chapter on "Arms and War" owes a special debt to David Lewis, and to Thornton Read, who put at our disposal a yet-unpublished paper on nuclear strategies. Our other debts are many: for research assistance and criticism to Dennis

Bathory; for typing to Miss June Wright, Mrs. Lois Wasem, and Mrs. Claudia Braxton. Above all we owe an irredeemable debt to Mrs. Susan Lanyi, who typed most of the manuscript, helped in proofreading and other tasks, and kept both the editors at their work with encouragement and, when required, with a prod of conscience.

Finally, we owe special thanks to Inis L. Claude, Jr., editorial consultant, for cogent criticism and constructive suggestions, and to Anne Dyer Murphy, who on behalf of Random House guided the manuscript through all the painful processes of revision, editing, and proofreading.

Oberlin, Ohio

G. A. L.
W. C. McW.

CONTENTS

I. THEORIES OF WORLD POLITICS

Is the study of international relations an independent discipline? And if so, how should it be approached? The reasons why such questions are asked at all, even by seasoned social scientists in America and Europe, are partly historical and lie partly in the nature of international relations.

Historically, it is certainly true that the study of political societies—the Greek city-state, the medieval *respublica christiana,* the modern commonwealth—has resulted in justly famed, systematic, often highly sophisticated treatises that even today are of relevance to us. There is no such illustrious sequence of great books on the relationship between more or less independent political societies. Historically, relations among nations have been approached by turning a scholarly searchlight on one or another aspect. Thus a great body of writing has accumulated on such topics as "the law of nations," international trade, the art and science of war, and how the "compleat diplomat" should behave. Yet when we look for overall principles and rules, concepts and processes that could be found in the actual conduct of political relations between independent political units, we will find enlightening generalizations in books that are only incidentally concerned with understanding political relations between nations as they actually existed.

Yet no one would deny that there have always been independent political units, that governmental power over the surface of the earth was always fragmented, that not even the mightiest empire succeeded in ruling all the peoples of the world. And at no time within written history were the governments of individual states completely isolated from all intercourse with the governments of neighboring states. It is undoubtedly true that the *nature* of these relations varied and changed from age to age, from civilization to civilization, and even within a particular civilization; but at all times and places international relations were characterized by one fact of overwhelming significance: namely, that relations among these states were conducted without reference to a common government. In this lies the second reason why philosophers, historians, or constitutional lawyers found it so difficult to submit international affairs to rigorous analysis. Some of them, indeed, threw up their hands and regarded such relations as mere anarchy, similar to the mythical state of nature in which individuals coexisted without common authority and common laws.

Even people who belonged to the same culture, such as the Greeks of antiquity, were aware that though something of a system had developed in the relations between Greek city-states, this was less well ordered, less subject to systematic discussion, less guided by clear and elaborate principles and rules than life within the *polis*. But discerning Greeks were also quite aware that these relations differed from relations between any Greek state and an "outsider" such as Persia.

Today it is impossible to deny that, because of the singular nature of international relations, they must be studied differently. Yet many have been acutely disturbed by the fact that the study of international relations seems to be without strong traditions and that scholars are just beginning to find out *how* politics among independent states was regarded in the past. Such studies usually confine themselves to the so-called modern state system, which emerged in sixteenth-century Europe and is traditionally regarded as having been solidly established by the Treaty of Westphalia (1648). It has also become not unusual to distinguish broadly between two theoretical approaches to world politics, the Machiavellian and the Kantian.[1] While writers and practicing statesmen would hardly ever follow one or the other tradition faithfully, it has seemed helpful for the sake of analysis to classify them as tending toward one or the other pole. Machiavelli in *The Prince* professes to look at the world as it is and believes that any theory of international relations must be, in our contemporary language, a policy science, an adjustment of the individual government's behavior to the opportunities and dangers the existing system offers. Kant, on the other hand, asserts that instead of accepting the world, which contains so few comforts to men who want to live a better and more moral life, we must try to transform it into a vastly better one. Machiavelli teaches his Prince "to learn how not to be good" and to use this knowledge according to the requirements of *necessità*. The supreme value for him, then, is the strength and survival of the individual principality or state; for the defense of the state, actions that in ordinary life would be regarded as evil are not only legitimate but, provided they are effective, imperative. Friedrich Meinecke, the German historian of Machiavellianism, regards the passage from the *Discourses* on the "defense of one's country" (quoted below, page 6) as the most powerful early statement in modern history of the concept of *raison d'état* (or *Staatsraison*), which elevates the "purpose of the state" above all other moral considerations. Kant, however, hopes that when properly organized states form a "league of nations," the defense of the individual state will be safeguarded by international law, in which case the whole concept of *raison d'état* will either disappear or, at worst, will become a last resort.

Modern Machiavellians continue to start from the individual state, trying to make the best of a far from pleasant world, while modern Kantians believe that the best kind of individual political units—Western democracies for some, socialist states for others—*could* (and some would say *will*) become the building-stones for an international system that would eliminate war and usher in a brave new world. Naturally it is an oversimplification to picture the learned and sophisticated Immanuel Kant as a naïve idealist gazing into Utopia, but

[1] We owe some debt here to Martin Wight's as yet unpublished lectures delivered at the London School of Economics and Political Science in 1960–1961.

then Karl Marx remarked once that he was certainly not a *Marxian*. It has also been pointed out that Machiavelli wrote his *Discourses on Livy* in a different frame of mind than *The Prince,* but this is debatable. Moreover, it seems a matter of historical fact that it was *The Prince* that shaped the outlook of many later writers, statesmen, and diplomats; and that international relations are affected by the way in which those who make foreign policy regard them can hardly be denied.[2]

The modern dichotomy, which was probably most persuasively expounded by E. H. Carr and which distinguishes between "realists" and "utopians," by and large follows this distinction. The realist will never cease to find stimulation from Machiavelli and his successors, while the utopian is still engrossed by Kant's *Perpetual Peace*. "Reality," however, can be variously observed, depending on what particular facts are used and what methods and concepts order and classify these facts. Forgetting that the world is in constant flux, the hardboiled realist, fearful of peering too far into the future, may actually look steadfastly into the past; and more than one of our contemporary realists has been caught indulging in a nostalgic contemplation of his own idealized version of the eighteenth or nineteenth century. Nor are utopians all brothers under the skin; on the contrary, one can hardly imagine a less congenial dialogue than one between a good Wilsonian and a staunch Leninist. And as Carr rightly observed, the most fruitful theory probably comes from a blending of the two approaches, which might lead to the building of "relevant utopias," to use Stanley Hoffmann's words.

The years since World War II have produced more soul-searching and more fresh suggestions about the ways and means of studying international relations than any other period. This is particularly true of the United States, where theoreticians proper were joined first by the more sophisticated publicists and finally by the seasoned practitioners of the Department of State in developing theoretical outlooks, principles, and observations intended to bring out "reality" in broad relief and liberate the educated public from the utopian illusions of the period between the two great wars. At the same time, however, a rival outlook on world politics, which challenged not only our world view but also the traditionally accepted values of our civilization, emerged from the Soviet Union.

In the face of this new, fearful challenge that threatened to bifurcate or even destroy our whole world, more and more scholars in the West were moved to find entirely new foundations for international relations. Some promised a "Copernican revolution" as soon as all the social and natural sciences could be scanned for facts, methods, and theoretical generalizations that could be used in various innovative ways for a completely new understanding of international relations. Whereas in the 1950s great academic debates raged around the claims of the realists and their denigration of the utopians, the 1960s saw multiple attacks against all those who followed traditional (sometimes called "classicist") approaches to international relations. The "scientific innovators" regarded themselves as a part of the "behavioral revolution" within the discipline of political science, a revolution—if this term can be applied at all to a

---

[2] The "dialogue" between Machiavelli and Kant is resumed in Chapter VII, where the role of morality in international relations is discussed.

highly academic school of social science—that came relatively slowly to the study of international relations.

The prebehavioral approach, as Hedley Bull stated, "derives from philosophy, history and law, and is characterized above all by explicit reliance upon judgment and by the assumptions that if we confine ourselves to strict standards of verification and proof there is very little of significance that can be said about international relations," and that, therefore, "general propositions about this subject must derive from a scientifically imperfect process of perception or intuition and that these general propositions cannot be accorded anything more than the tentative and inconclusive status appropriate to their doubtful origin." [3]

Those who follow the new behavioral approach assert, on the other hand, that by making their assumptions explicit, by developing logically consistent models, by stating clear hypotheses on how their models will operate, they are developing much more workable theories with which to conduct empirical research. Behavioral scholars believe, moreover, that their empirically verified theories will be not only more precise but also more valid than anything the traditionalists have achieved and that such theories will make it possible to predict political behavior with reasonable accuracy. The real test of science, they maintain, is prediction rather than mere understanding.

In order to construct new models and advance hypotheses for empirical research, the behavioral school has freed itself from the traditional disciplines and borrows imaginatively from the findings and the vocabulary of general systems theory, cybernetics, various psychological and sociological schools, anthropology, game theory, and so on. However, in studying international relations, just as in studying other branches of political science, behavioral innovators are by no means in agreement on how to proceed, what questions to ask, and what methods to use. While it is possible, as Michael Banks has done, to explain what distinguishes the behavioral school from the traditionalists, it is rather hard to provide an exhaustive and clearly arranged taxonomy of the various subschools, which at times look at one another with a sectarian hostility not uncommon among certain radical political groups.

Undoubtedly the behavioral school has increased opportunities for imaginative and enthusiastic scholars and has at the same time compelled the more traditionally inclined writers to state their theoretical assumptions with more clarity and rigor. But the proliferation of theoretical research has its dangers. We can move simultaneously in too many directions, become entangled in the problems of too many specialized disciplines, such as psychoanalysis or cybernetics. We can enrich our search with so many facts that the burden will completely overwhelm us. Or we can become used to moving on such high levels of abstraction that we lose the connection with world politics as it unfolds around us. Moreover—and this seems even more dangerous—we can begin to look at the world through such highly refined and esoteric perspectives that whatever we see and deduce will have little in common with the more down-to-earth ways in which the responsible statesman, the influential politician, or the practicing diplomat sees it. International strategy, for instance, can become

[3] "International Theory: the Case for a Classical Approach," *World Politics* (April 1966), p. 361.

most intriguingly complex and yet altogether logical and consistent when seen through the eyes of the highly trained game theorist; but as these ways of thinking are still alien to the practitioner, one may doubt whether such theories can ever become operational—in which case they neither help us to understand what is nor point the way to what could or should be.

Professor Hoffmann argues that we must try to relate all worthwhile efforts in the study of international relations in some kind of meaningful manner. We must try to clarify the values we would like to see promoted in the world, but in order to do so we must conduct more systematic empirical research into the past and present, or else we will become modern utopians. We should, he thinks, be cautious about rushing into theories that have the main purpose of becoming cookbooks for our policymakers. We must, he believes, connect our "sky-bound theories," while being constantly wary of rushing up tempting avenues that lead to futile logical exercises and sterile abstractions.

One may agree with Prof. Kenneth Waltz that those who have inquired into the causes of war have usually tried to find them in the nature of man, in the nature of states, or in the international system of states. Yet, Waltz concludes, accurate understanding of international relations requires some combination of all three approaches.[4] One might, however, remark that as there are no states without men and no international systems without states, "human nature" will remain, if not the basis, at least the starting point of all theories of politics. If so, in our outlook on world politics, we will always find ourselves between our infinite imagination, leaping forward and upward toward utopian possibilities, and our finite being, pointing out the necessary limitations set by the sobering realities of the present and the past.

[4] *Man, the State and War, passim.*

Niccolò Machiavelli

THE REAL TRUTH OF THE MATTER

It now remains to be seen what are the methods and rules for a prince as regards his subjects and friends. And as I know that many have written of this, I fear that my writing about it may be deemed presumptuous, differing as I do, especially in this matter, from the opinions of others. But my intention being to write something of use to those who understand, it appears to me more proper to go to the real truth of the matter than to its imagination; and many have imagined republics and principalities which have never been seen or known to exist in reality; for how we live is so far removed from how we ought to live, that he who abandons what is done for what ought to be done, will rather learn to bring about his own ruin than his preservation. A man who wishes to make a profession of goodness in everything must necessarily come to grief among so many who are not good. Therefore it is necessary for a prince, who wishes to maintain himself, to learn how not to be good, and to use this knowledge and not use it, according to the necessity of the case. . . .

ONE'S COUNTRY MUST BE DEFENDED,
WHETHER WITH GLORY OR WITH SHAME;
IT MUST BE DEFENDED ANYHOW

. . . [T]he Legate Lentulus said, "That for the purpose of saving the country no propositions ought to be rejected. The safety of Rome depended upon that army, and he maintained that it ought to be saved at any price; that the defense of their country was always good, no matter whether effected by honorable or ignominious means. That if the army were saved, Rome would in time be able to wipe out that disgrace; but if the army were lost, even if they died most gloriously, Rome and her liberties would also be lost." This advice of Lentulus was followed; and the case deserves to be noted and reflected upon by every citizen who finds himself called upon to counsel his country. For where the very safety of

Reprinted by permission of the publisher from *The Prince* (1513), Luigi Ricci, trans., revised by E. R. P. Vincent (London: Oxford University Press, 1935), Chapter XV.

Reprinted from *Discourses on the First Ten Books of Titus Livius,* Christian E. Detmold, trans. (Boston: James R. Osgood and Co., 1882), Third Book, Chapter XLI.

the country depends upon the resolution to be taken, no considerations of justice or injustice, humanity or cruelty, nor of glory or shame, should be allowed to prevail.   But putting all other considerations aside, the only question should be, What course will save the life and liberty of the country?   The French follow this maxim by words and deeds in defending the majesty of their king and the greatness of France; for nothing excites their impatience more than to hear any one say that such or such a thing is discreditable to the king.   For they say that their king can suffer no shame from any resolutions he may take, whether in good or in ill fortune; for whether he be victor or vanquished is a matter that only concerns the king.

Immanuel Kant

PERPETUAL PEACE
The Definitive Articles for Perpetual Peace Among States

The state of peace among men who live side by side is not the state of nature (*status naturalis*), it is rather a state of war.   This does not always mean actual war but a constant threat of war.   Therefore, a state of peace must be established; because the mere absence of a threat of war does not yet mean security from it, and unless this security is pledged to him by his neighbor (which can only happen in a state of law) man may treat his neighbor as an enemy. . . .

1. THE CIVIL CONSTITUTION IN EACH STATE
   SHALL BE REPUBLICAN

A republican constitution is based on three principles: first, on the principle of *freedom* of the members of a society as men; secondly, on the principle of *dependence* of all upon a single, common legislature as subjects; and thirdly, on the principles of *equality* of all *citizens*.   This is the only constitution which derives from the idea of the original contract upon which all rightful legislation of a people must be based. . . .   Is it also the one which can lead to perpetual peace?

Translated by the editor from *Zum ewigen Frieden. Ein philosophischer Entwurf* (1795).   Collected Works, ed. E. Cassirer (Berlin: B. Cassirer, 1925), VI, 433–446. For recent editions in English see C. J. Friedrich, *Inevitable Peace* (Cambridge, Mass.: Harvard University Press, 1948), and L. W. Beck, *Perpetual Peace*, The Library of Liberal Arts (Indianapolis: Bobbs-Merrill, 1957).

The republican constitution . . . offers the hope for the desired purpose, i.e., perpetual peace . . . because when the consent of the citizens is required in order to decide whether there should be war or not, nothing is more natural than that those who would have to decree for themselves all the deprivations of war, will think long before they will begin such an evil game. There are, after all, many deprivations: having to fight, having to pay the costs of war from their own possessions, having to repair painfully the devastation left behind by war, and to top it all, having to carry the burden of debts which can never be paid off because of the approach of new wars. On the other hand, in a constitution, where the subject is not a citizen and which is therefore not republican, it is the easiest thing in the world to decide to go to war, because the top leader is not a citizen but the owner of the state who does not sacrifice any of his banquets, his hunting parties, country houses, court festivities, and the like. He, therefore, will resolve on war for quite insignificant reasons as if it were a kind of pleasure party, and for propriety's sake, will leave the justifications with perfect indifference to the always willing diplomatic corps.

* * *

2. THE LAW OF NATIONS SHALL BE BASED ON A LEAGUE OF FREE STATES

Nations may be considered like individual men who in their state of nature hurt each other by their mere coexistence. Each of them for the sake of his own security, may and should demand that the others enter with him into a constitution similar to the civil constitution where the right of each can be secured. This would be a *league of nations,* which would not have to be a *state of many nations.* A state of many nations implies a contradiction because every state involves a relationship between a (legislating) *superior* and an (obeying) *inferior,* i.e., the subject people, and many nations in one state would constitute only one nation which is contradictory to our presupposition, as we are considering here the right of nations towards each other, as they constitute different states and are not amalgamated into one state.

* * *

In view of the evil nature of man which is clearly observable in the uncontrolled relation among nations (while in a civil-legal state it is heavily veiled by governmental coercion), it is astonishing that the word *law* has not yet been completely banished from the politics of war as mere pedantry, and that no state has been bold enough to declare itself publicly to this view. . . .

The homage which each state pays (at least verbally) to the concept of law proves, nevertheless, that there is in men an even greater moral disposition, even though at present dormant, to master eventually the undeniable evil element in him and to hope for the same from others. Otherwise, the word *law* would never be uttered by states which want to fight each other, unless it would be used mockingly, as in the case of the Gallic prince who declared: 'It is the advantage nature has given the stronger that the weaker should obey him.'

. . . [T]here must be a league of a particular kind which may be called the *league of peace* (*foedus pacificum*), which would be distinguished from a *peace treaty* (*pactum pacis*), as the latter tries to end only *one* war, while the former tries to end *all* wars forever. This league does not tend to assume any of the state's powers, but merely maintains and secures the freedom of the state itself and at the same time that of the other allied states, without subjecting themselves (as men do in the state of nature) to civil laws and their enforcement. . . .

3. THE LAW OF WORLD CITIZENSHIP SHALL BE LIMITED TO CONDITIONS OF UNIVERSAL HOSPITALITY

We speak here, as in the preceding articles not of philanthropy but of *law*. Therefore, *hospitality* means the right of a foreigner not to be treated with hostility when he arrives in the land of another. One may refuse to receive him when this can be done without his perishing, but as long as he remains peaceful, one may not treat him hostilely. It is not the right to be a permanent visitor which the foreigner may demand, because a special, beneficial contract would be needed to make him a fellow inhabitant for a certain period. It is only a right to visit which belongs to all men—the right of all men to offer their society because of their right to possess in common the surface of the globe over which they cannot disperse themselves indefinitely but where eventually they just have to tolerate each other. Originally, no man had more right to a particular place on earth than any other.

*   *   *

Since the narrower or wider community of all nations of the earth has already progressed so far that the violation of lawful rights in *one* place is felt in all *others,* the idea of a law of world citizenship is not a fantastic and exaggerated notion of law, but a necessary supplement to the unwritten code of constitutional and international law, and above all to the public law of mankind, and thus to perpetual peace. . . .

E. H. Carr

UTOPIA AND REALITY

The antithesis of utopia and reality—a balance always swinging towards and away from equilibrium and never completely attaining it—is a fundamental antithesis revealing itself in many forms of thought. The two methods of approach—the inclination to ignore what was and what is in contemplation of what should be, and the inclination to deduce what should be from what was and what is—determine opposite attitudes towards every political problem. "It is the eternal dispute," as Albert Sorel puts it, "between those who imagine the world to suit their policy, and those who arrange their policy to suit the realities of the world.". . .

FREE WILL AND DETERMINATION

The antithesis of utopia and reality can in some aspects be identified with the antithesis of Free Will and Determination. The utopian is necessarily voluntarist: he believes in the possibility of more or less radically rejecting reality, and substituting his utopia for it by an act of will. The realist analyses a predetermined course of development which he is powerless to change. For the realist, philosophy, in the famous words of Hegel's preface to his *Philosophy of Right,* always "comes too late" to change the world. By means of philosophy, the old order "cannot be rejuvenated, but only known." The utopian, fixing his eyes on the future, thinks in terms of creative spontaneity: the realist, rooted in the past, in terms of causality. All healthy human action, and therefore all healthy thought, must establish a balance between utopia and reality, between free will and determinism. The complete realist, unconditionally accepting the causal sequence of events, deprives himself of the possibility of changing reality. The complete utopian, by rejecting the causal sequence, deprives himself of the possibility of understanding either the reality which he is seeking to change or the processes by which it can be changed. The characteristic vice of the utopian is naivety; of the realist, sterility.[1]

Reprinted by permission of the publishers from *The Twenty Years Crisis, 1919–1939: An Introduction to the Study of International Relations,* 2nd ed. (New York: St. Martin's Press, and London: Macmillan & Company, Ltd., 1946), pp. 11–21.

[1] The psychologist may be interested to trace here an analogy—it would be dangerous to treat it as more—with Jung's classification of psychological types as "introverted" and "extroverted" (Jung, *Psychological Types*) or William James' pairs of opposites: Rationalist-Empiricist, Intellectualist-Sensationalist, Idealist-Materialist, Optimistic-Pessimistic, Religious-Irreligious, Free-willist–Fatalistic, Monistic-Pluralistic, Dogmatical-Sceptical (W. James, *Pragmatism*).

THEORY AND PRACTICE

The antithesis of utopia and reality also coincides with the antithesis of theory and practice. The utopian makes political theory a norm to which political practice ought to conform. The realist regards political theory as a sort of codification of political practice. The relationship of theory and practice has come to be recognised in recent years as one of the central problems of political thought. Both the utopian and the realist distort this relationship. The utopian, purporting to recognise the interdependence of purpose and fact, treats purpose as if it were the only relevant fact, and constantly couches optative propositions in the indicative mood. The American Declaration of Independence maintains that "all men are created equal," Mr. Litvinov [2] that "peace is indivisible," and Sir Norman Angell [3] that "the biological division of mankind into independent warring states" is a "scientific ineptitude." Yet it is a matter of common observation that all men are not born equal even in the United States, and that the Soviet Union can remain at peace while its neighbours are at war; and we should probably think little of a zoologist who described a man-eating tiger as a "scientific ineptitude." These propositions are items in a political programme disguised as statements of fact; and the utopian inhabits a dream-world of such "facts," remote from the world of reality where quite contrary facts may be observed. The realist has no difficulty in perceiving that these utopian propositions are not facts but aspirations, and belong to the optative not to the indicative mood; and he goes on to show that, considered as aspirations, they are not *a priori* propositions, but are rooted in the world of reality in a way which the utopian altogether fails to understand. Thus for the realist, the equality of man is the ideology of the under-privileged seeking to raise themselves to the level of the privileged; the indivisibility of peace the ideology of states which, being particularly exposed to attack, are eager to establish the principle that an attack on them is a matter of concern to other states more fortunately situated; the ineptitude of sovereign states the ideology of predominant Powers which find the sovereignty of other states a barrier to the enjoyment of their own predominant position. This exposure of the hidden foundations of utopian theory is a necessary preliminary to any serious political science. But the realist, in denying any *a priori* quality to political theories, and in proving them to be rooted in practice, falls easily into a determinism which argues that theory, being nothing more than a rationalisation of conditioned and predetermined purpose, is a pure excrescence and impotent to alter the course of events. While therefore the

[2] Soviet Minister of Foreign Affairs (1930–1939). [Eds.]

[3] English writer on international relations and winner of the Nobel Prize for Peace (1933). [Eds.]

utopian treats purpose as the sole ultimate fact, the realist runs the risk of treating purpose merely as the mechanical product of other facts.   If we recognise that this mechanisation of human will and human aspiration is untenable and intolerable, then we must recognise that theory, as it develops out of practice and develops into practice, plays its own transforming role in the process.   The political process does not consist, as the realist believes, purely in a succession of phenomena governed by mechanical laws of causation; nor does it consist, as the utopian believes, purely in the application to practice of certain theoretical truths evolved out of their inner consciousness by wise and farseeing people.   Political science must be based on a recognition of the interdependence of theory and practice, which can be attained only through a combination of utopia and reality.

THE INTELLECTUAL AND THE BUREAUCRAT

A concrete expression of the antithesis of theory and practice in politics is the opposition between the "intellectual" and the "bureaucrat," the former trained to think mainly on *a priori* lines, the latter empirically.   It is in the nature of things that the intellectual should find himself in the camp which seeks to make practice conform to theory; for intellectuals are particularly reluctant to recognise their thought as conditioned by forces external to themselves, and like to think of themselves as leaders whose theories provide the motive force for so-called men of action.   Moreover, the whole intellectual outlook of the last two hundred years has been strongly coloured by the mathematical and natural sciences.   To establish a general principle, and to test the particular in the light of that principle, has been assumed by most intellectuals to be the necessary foundation and starting-point of any science.   In this respect, utopianism with its insistence on general principles may be said to represent the characteristic intellectual approach to politics.   Woodrow Wilson, the most perfect modern example of the intellectual in politics, "excelled in the exposition of fundamentals. . . . His political method . . . was to base his appeal on broad and simple principles, avoiding commitment upon specific measures."   Some supposedly general principle, such as "national self-determination," "free trade" or "collective security" (all of which will be easily recognised by the realist as concrete expressions of particular conditions and interests), is taken as an absolute standard, and policies are adjudged good or bad by the extent to which they conform to, or diverge from, it.   In modern times, intellectuals have been the leaders of every utopian movement; and the services which utopianism has rendered to political progress must be credited in large part to them.   But the characteristic weakness of utopianism is also the characteristic weakness of the political intellectuals—failure to understand existing reality and the way in which their own standards are rooted in it.   "They could give to their political aspirations," wrote Meinecke of the role of intellectuals in German politics, "a spirit of purity and independence, of philosophical idealism and of elevation above the concrete play of interests . . . but through their defective feeling for the realistic interests of actual state life they quickly descended from the sublime to the extravagant and eccentric."

*   *   *

The bureaucratic approach to politics is, on the other hand, fundamentally empirical. The bureaucrat purports to handle each particular problem "on its merits," to eschew the formulation of principles and to be guided on the right course by some intuitive process born of long experience and not of conscious reasoning. "There are no general cases," said a French official, acting as French Delegate at an Assembly of the League of Nations; "there are only specific cases." In his dislike of theory, the bureaucrat resembles the man of action. "On s'engage, puis on voit" is a motto attributed to more than one famous general. The excellence of the British civil service is partly due to the ease with which the bureaucratic mentality accommodates itself to the empirical tradition of British politics. The perfect civil servant conforms closely to the popular picture of the English politician as a man who recoils from written constitutions and solemn covenants, and lets himself be guided by precedent, by instinct, by feel for the right thing. This empiricism is itself, no doubt, conditioned by a specific point of view, and reflects the conservative habit of English political life. The bureaucrat, perhaps more explicitly than any other class of the community, is bound up with the existing order, the maintenance of tradition, and the acceptance of precedent as the "safe" criterion of action. Hence bureaucracy easily degenerates into the rigid and empty formalism of the mandarin, and claims an esoteric understanding of appropriate procedures which is not accessible even to the most intelligent outsider. "Expérience vaut mieux que science" is the typical bureaucratic motto. "Attainments in learning and science," wrote Bryce, voicing a widely felt prejudice, "do little to make men wise in politics." When a bureaucrat wishes to damn a proposal, he calls it "academic." Practice, not theory, bureaucratic training, not intellectual brilliance, is the school of political wisdom. The bureaucrat tends to make politics an end in themselves. It is worth remarking that both Machiavelli and Bacon were bureaucrats.

*   *   *

LEFT AND RIGHT

The antithesis of utopia and reality, and of theory and practice, further reproduces itself in the antithesis of radical and conservative, of Left and Right, though it would be rash to assume that parties carrying these labels always represent these underlying tendencies. The radical is necessarily utopian, and the conservative realist. The intellectual, the man of theory, will gravitate towards the Left just as naturally as the bureaucrat, the man of practice, will gravitate towards the Right. Hence the Right is weak in theory, and suffers through its inaccessibility to ideas. The characteristic weakness of the Left is failure to translate its theory into practice—a failure for which it is apt to blame the bureaucrats, but which is inherent in its utopian character. "The Left has reason (*Vernunft*), the Right has wisdom (*Verstand*)," wrote the Nazi philosopher, Moeller van den Bruck. From the days of Burke onwards, English conservatives have always strongly denied the possibility of deducing political practice by a logical process from political theory. "To follow the syllogism alone is a short cut to the bottomless pit," says Lord Baldwin [4]—a phrase which may suggest that he practises as well as preaches abstention from rigorously logical modes of thought. Mr. Churchill refuses to believe that "extravagant logic in doctrine" appeals to the British elector. A particularly clear definition of different attitudes towards foreign policy comes from a speech made in the House of Commons by Neville Chamberlain [5] an answer to a Labour critic:

What does the hon. Member mean by foreign policy? You can lay down sound and general propositions. You can say that your foreign policy is to maintain peace; you can say that it is to protect British interests, you can say that it is to use your influence, such as it is, on behalf of the right against the wrong, as far as you can tell the right from the wrong. You can lay down all these general principles, but that is not a policy. Surely, if you are to have a policy you must take the particular situations and consider what action or inaction is suitable for those particular situations. That is what I myself mean by policy, and it is quite clear that as the situations and conditions in foreign affairs continually change from day to day, your policy cannot be stated once and for all, if it is to be applicable to every situation that arises.

The intellectual superiority of the Left is seldom in doubt. The Left alone thinks out principles of political action and evolves ideals for statesmen to aim at. But it lacks practical experience which comes from close contact with reality.[6] In Great Britain after 1919, it was a serious misfortune that the Left, having enjoyed office for negligible periods, had little experience of administrative realities and became more and more a party of pure theory, while the Right, having spent so little time in opposition, had few temptations to pit the perfection of theory against the imperfections of practice. In Soviet Russia, the group in power is more and more discarding theory in favour of practice as it loses the memory of its revolutionary origin. History everywhere shews that, when Left parties or politicians are brought into contact with reality through the assumption of political office, they tend to abandon their "doctrinaire" utopianism and move to-

[4] British Prime Minister (1924–1929, 1935–1937). [Eds.]
[5] British Prime Minister (1937–1940). [Eds.]
[6] This was written in 1939. [Eds.]

wards the Right, often retaining their Left labels and thereby adding to the confusion of political terminology.

ETHICS AND POLITICS

Most fundamental of all, the antithesis of utopia and reality is rooted in a different conception of the relationship of politics and ethics. The antithesis between the world of value and the world of nature, already implicit in the dichotomy of purpose and fact, is deeply embedded in the human consciousness and in political thought. The utopian sets up an ethical standard which purports to be independent of politics, and seeks to make politics conform to it. The realist cannot logically accept any standard value save that of fact. In his view, the absolute standard of the utopian is conditioned and dictated by the social order, and is therefore political. Morality can only be relative, not universal. Ethics must be interpreted in terms of politics; and the search for an ethical norm outside politics is doomed to frustration. The identification of the supreme reality with the supreme good, which Christianity achieves by a bold stroke of dogmatism, is achieved by the realist through the assumption that there is no good other than the acceptance and understanding of reality.

Michael Banks

TWO MEANINGS OF THEORY

In January 1966, over fifty scholars met in London at the Tenth United Kingdom . . . Conference on the University Teaching of International Relations. . . .

. . . One group took the view that the most appropriate way to approach theory was in conformity with the axioms of the allegedly universal method of science, and thus to build models and count data in the manner of what are now coming to be called the "behavioural sciences." [1] The

Reprinted by permission of the publishers from *The Year Book of World Affairs* (London: Stevens and Stevens and Sons, 1966), pp. 220–240.

[1] The term "behavioural science" is used here . . . because no other seems quite to fill the need. "Scientific" and "systematic" do not seem to be wholly accurate, and in any case invite prefixes like "semi-," "quasi-" or "pseudo-" which would make them just as unnecessarily pejorative as other labels like "scientistic." "Modern" and "contemporary" are useless because they ignore the key point, that two quite different types of theory are being employed contemporaneously.

other group insisted that the subject should retain its traditional methods, methods which have been successfully employed to establish the present status of the subject and which by now perhaps deserve the name of "classical." [2] The classical method stresses not science but judgment, intuition and impression, and has been succinctly described by Arnold Wolfers as the art of "mustering all the evidence that history, personal experience, introspection, common sense and the gift of logical reasoning put at [one's] disposal." [3]

*　　*　　*

This article . . . sets out to explore a few of the characteristics of the two schools of thought, with main emphasis on the behavioural, and to suggest—though not necessarily with merely eirenical motives—that they are by no means incompatible. To write in a brief space of such a large issue requires that two qualifications be made. The first concerns the use of labels. It would be nonsense to suggest that all scholars of International Relations are committed to one school or the other. . . . Furthermore, as a matter of principle, few scholars like to be regarded as belonging to schools of thought, especially in their role as teachers. They enjoy even less having their names attached to their alleged schools by writers other than themselves. To some, the distinction between the behavioural and the classical casts of mind may be acceptable and helpful; to others, it may appear misleading to take two "schools of thought" and to view each as consistent in itself and different from the other, when it might possibly be argued that differences between individual thinkers within each so-called "school" are more significant than any overall distinction between the "schools." All that is being suggested here, however, is that the labels "behavioural" and "classical" can usefully be juxtaposed as ideal types. . . .

THE DIFFICULTIES INVOLVED IN A
DISCUSSION OF "THEORY"

The second qualification is made with considerably more deference. It concerns the inherent difficulty of any discussion of theory. In the social sciences generally there is little consensus of what constitutes "theory" and little agreement even on the general objectives of the wide range of disciplines that the social sciences now include. . . . Ultimately the question of the appropriate methodology for the study of human affairs must be clarified and, hopefully, answered, if the social sciences are to develop

[2] The term "classical" was suggested for the traditional approach by H. N. Bull. . . . The term does not indicate only the study of the classic writers of political philosophy, law, history, strategy and philosophy of history, but refers also to present-day writing which is in the same mould.

[3] *Discord and Collaboration* (1962), pp. 236–237.

much beyond their present condition.   But until that question can be answered, it is presumably not possible to make any useful pronouncement upon the relative epistemological status of the different answers put forward to the question "What is theory?"   Fortunately, it is sufficient for the purpose here to sketch, briefly and crudely, the views of the behavioural and classical schools on the objectives of their theoretical exercises.

The issue of the aims of theory is perhaps the most basic of those dividing classicists from behaviouralists.   The behavioural school seems to have a fairly powerful, if undefined, vision of constructing, one day, a "general theory."   Such a theory would be revealing when applied to all human behaviour, including political behaviour, and it would be created without reference to the existing division of labour between the various subdisciplines of the social sciences.   The behavioural approach to theorising is, therefore, not so much "inter-disciplinary" as non-disciplinary in aspiration.   It follows that if such a theory were ever created, the section of it that explained International Relations would only be "partial" in relation to the whole of the theory.   The classical school, by contrast, concedes that theoretical progress may be made in limited fields on a piecemeal basis, as in the relatively advanced discipline of economics, but it contests on *a priori* grounds the claim that a universal theory is even conceivable, still less a practicable aim.   And on the narrower question of international theory, it seems to hold the view that although progress is possible, it must be slow and always limited in its explanatory power by the impossibility of measuring the infinity of variable factors or of putting the value aspects of political behaviour into any sort of scientific theory at all.   In short, the behavioural view of theory stresses the possibilities of future scientific development and sees the acquisition of knowledge as a cumulative process, which is building, generation by generation, a pyramid of knowledge even though the internal structure of the completed pyramid must still be unknown.   The classical view of theory stresses the volume of knowledge we already possess, and takes what it regards as the more realistic view of progress, that learning to walk must precede learning to run.   As H. J. Morgenthau has written, "there is a rational element in political action which makes politics susceptible to theoretical analysis, but there is also a contingent element in politics which obviates the possibility of theoretical understanding." [4]

---

[4] "The Intellectual and Political Functions of a Theory of International Relations" in H. V. Harrison (ed.), *The Role of Theory in International Relations* (1964), p. 108.   It may be argued that Morgenthau's own contribution, the single-factor explanation of international politics in terms of power, constitutes a "general theory." Behaviouralists would probably reject this claim, since the theory is not formulated in precise, falsifiable terms.

THE CHARACTER OF THE BEHAVIOURAL APPROACH

The behavioural approach is for the most part a product of the last decade or so, even in the United States where it mainly originated. . . . At its simplest, behaviouralism attempts, where possible, to apply scientific method to the subject-matter of the social sciences, and as a consequence it tries to look at problems in a way which ignores orthodox disciplinary boundaries.

In more detail, the approach may be distinguished from the classical in a number of ways. The first, already discussed, is by its ambition to create a general theory which would illuminate the study of society as a whole, a theory of which the international system would form a part, and the behaviour of individual States another part. A property of any mature theory, along with explanation, is prediction; and the aim of making predictive statements, often in the form of making "recommendations for policy" on the basis of purportedly behavioural studies, has tended to arouse critical reactions among classicists upon reading the behavioural literature. A second difference occurs in the concepts employed. International theory has always been somewhat eclectic in its collection of metaphors and concepts, but behavioural science ranges far beyond even the traditional repertoire, either to suggest new metaphors or to bring in a disconcerting conceptual array from many other disciplines of the natural, social and new communications sciences.

A third distinction, much the most important, lies in the fierce concentration of the behavioural approach on procedure, or methodology. It seeks to make assumptions explicit, to make hypotheses precise, to fit propositions together into logically consistent structures called "models," and to test these models rigorously against the facts of social and political life. Much of the actual work that results from this methodological preoccupation is daunting to a reader whose training has been in the classical approach. Behavioural scientists tend to make their theories extremely elaborate. Their concern for precision causes them to employ jargon (i.e., and e.g., "complex verbal formulations"), not as deliberate obscurantism, but in order to avoid the ambiguities with which virtually all writing about international politics has been burdened in the past. They frequently employ mathematics to clarify and expedite the logical analysis of interrelationships. They attempt to quantify wherever possible, and aspire to the emulation of the natural scientists by the use of experimental laboratories in the form of computer simulation and role-playing games.

Despite the fact that much behavioural writing is theoretical in tone almost to the point of becoming metaphysical, some exponents of the approach tend to regard their work as distinctively "empirical." If the word is taken to mean simply that all statements must be formulated in a way which makes them potentially falsifiable, then it does indicate a distinction between the behavioural and the classical approaches, for classical theory recognises that many statements about the relations of States must, if they are to be made at all, be put in a form which cannot be tested. If, alternatively, the term "empirical" implies strict attention to data, it hardly assists in distinguishing the behaviouralist from the classicist: both are concerned with precise statements about the real world though the statements are arrived at by a different route.

The deductive-inductive distinction is perhaps more helpful, because it draws attention to the means by which facts are assessed, rather than stressing the importance of the facts themselves. The classicist, drawing heavily on history for his methodology—in so far as a classicist would admit to possessing a "methodology" at all—would probably describe himself as an inductivist, while any behaviouralist would claim that his interest in factual material occurs only in the light of theory: he is engaged in testing propositions arrived at deductively, not expecting the data to fall into shape for him by themselves, as he surveys them with an open mind.

THE SCOPE OF BEHAVIOURALISM

As an intellectual movement, behaviouralism is both much wider than the discipline International Relations, and, in some senses and at its present stage of development, narrower. Its widest sense comes from its most extreme definition of scope, which holds that it covers all systems of behaviour, including, say, the subject-matter of biochemistry, or of human geography. A slightly less wide view of its scope, and perhaps the most generally accepted, is that given by D. Easton, who regards its central aim as the attempt to discover "fundamental units of analysis relating to human behaviour out of which generalisations can be formed and (which) may provide a common base on which the specialised sciences of men in society could be built." [5]   The necessary implication is that any researcher using this approach must be at home in several branches of social science simultaneously and in the "core" disciplines of sociology, psychology and anthropology especially. It is a traditional plea of those who wished to develop International Relations as a subject that its specialists should verse themselves thoroughly in related disciplines, but until behaviouralism arrived the disciplines selected were different—mainly history, law and philosophy.

To date there is no apparent consensus on just what Easton's "fundamental units of analysis" are to be: "culture," "exchange," "will," "role," "power," "function," "action," "choice," "the group," and "participation" are some of the basic concepts upon which large- or small-scale attempts have already been made to build conceptual systems of social and political life. Of these, "function" has commanded a persuasively large following in anthropology and now in the comparative study of government, and

[5] *A Framework for Political Analysis* (1965), pp. 14–15.

"power" has had by far the longest run in the study of world politics: it is still the reigning basis of international theory as taught in most universities. Lately the fashion has turned towards the concepts employed in the new behavioural sciences of communication theory (subdivided into cybernetics, information theory and sign-behaviour); general systems theory; and preferential behaviour (subdivided into game theory, decision-making and value inquiry). These conceptual schemes have in common the advantage that they avoid the traps of personifying collectivities and of painting static pictures of life in society, which is self-evidently dynamic. They view collectivities as systems of behaviour, operating within a distinct environment, with the parts of the system being operationally defined as sets of variables, responding both to the actions of each other and to stimuli flowing in from the environment.

Behaviouralism can be regarded as being narrower than classical international theory because it does not, as yet, pretend to be able to discuss within its own standards of scientific rigour the full scope of problems of International Relations. Classical theory puts forward empirical generalisations, all of a tentative character, about the whole range of problems of the relations between States. Behaviouralism deliberately avoids, in the first instance, the more daunting aspects of this subject-matter, the elements of contingency, the baffling shifts and turns of political events which can make anyone—classicist or behaviouralist—despair, at times, of ever making sense of human affairs. To the classicist, most of all to the historian, these aspects are something not to be ignored but to be taken into account, and particularly to be borne in mind as an inducement to modesty when making claims for the fruitfulness of one's research. To the behaviouralist, they must simply, for the time being, be left unexplained or treated within the framework of classical theory. Behavioural research, therefore, tends to concentrate, in international theory as in other parts of social analysis, on what seem to be, prima facie, the more theoretically rewarding starting-points contained in the repetitions, regularities and habitual symptoms of behaviour: the recidivism of criminals, the monogamous marriage, the activities of pressure-groups, the correlation of arms races with the outbreaks of war.

But the statement that behavioural theory cannot yet explain contingency is not intended to suggest that it is regarded as unimportant, nor that behaviouralists feel that it will never succumb to scientific analysis. The approach seems to be feeling its way towards what may become a useful theoretical distinction which may throw some new light on the ancient, intractable problem of determinism versus free will in human conduct. The study of recurrent patterns of behaviour may give us a clearer picture of those fixed, immutable aspects of the international system which require State action to be "necessitous" in the sense that it must fall within the limited zone dictated by the restrictive limits of the possible. To explain action within those limits, different sorts of analysis seem to be required. Efforts are being made, for example in attempts to devise applications for the abstract ideas of game theory, to clarify the problems of choice facing governments in these situations. This analysis is necessarily formal in the extreme, relying as it does on assumptions of rationality and of maximum available information about alternative strategies of action. Such assumptions are certainly not fulfilled in the real world. Most behaviouralists are as dubious of the value of game theory *per se* as classicists tend to be, but they are strongly in sympathy with the spirit of the exercise. Clearly some model is needed for situations where "free will" appears to be operative, where the future is quite clearly unpredictable in the light of existing knowledge, and where policy might take any one of a number of different paths. If at the moment the "explanation" consists of nothing more than an abstract model of what rational behaviour might look like, under various assumptions about objectives and possibilities, then that at least is a beginning for the process of understanding. Later it might be possible to fit the bewildering jigsaw of a real historical incident into the formal model, piece by piece: the structure of States, the limitations of communication both within and between State actors, the "irrational" or psychological effects of the multitude of human relationships involved in an international crisis, and the rest. This field of inquiry is the most challenging yet tackled in the study of international society, and progress of any significance has yet to be registered.

The relative narrowness of the behavioural approach may further be seen in its attitude to the dimension of time. In the work of the historian, time gives perspective: temporal detachment is essential to the exercise of judgment, and through time processes may be seen to be "working themselves out." Likewise in classical theory, especially in those sections of it which draw on philosophies of history or on the organismic images of society provided by some political philosophers, the dimension of time is an integral part of the process of analysis. Behavioural scientists, in contrast, either limit their historical attention to trends or sequences somewhat narrowly defined and selected, or seek to build models of a non-temporal character, of a kind which could be applied to any situation of a particular type at any point in history. This attitude is strongly reinforced by the desire to see propositions verified or tested. Since the new models tend to include a much wider range of factors, including psychological ones, than are adequately covered in existing studies of the past, the process of testing has to be directed to contemporary conditions, with the effect of the past regarded simply as one "given" in the situation.

THE PROBLEM OF VALUES IN
INTERNATIONAL THEORY

Behaviouralism is also somewhat narrower than classical theory in its treatment of value questions. The classical approach insists that it is not only
impossible to separate the process of making judgments about the relations
between States from the moral dispositions of the mind which makes those
judgments, but that it is also not desirable or efficient to attempt the separation, because an intuitive feeling for the moral dilemmas of statesmanship
is necessary to the understanding of the decisions made. One critic of
both schools even goes farther, to argue that theorists of all kinds depend,
in their attempt to create theory at all, on a basic value judgment, namely,
the belief in progress; and he seems to deduce from this that if that value
judgment is mistaken, then all attempts to create theory must fail.[6]

But the behaviouralist, while aware of the pitfalls in this most difficult
of aspects to the study of politics, nevertheless insists that an effort must be
made to maintain the scientific "value" of detachment. He struggles to
overcome the subjectivity of his hypotheses. In particular, ethical judgments are rigidly distinguished from explanatory statements, a point which
sets behavioural scientists sharply apart from the long tradition of classical
writing which usually tends to mix together the process of explanation,
judgments regarding what is good or bad and policy recommendations in
an inextricable blend. In so far as the behavioural scientist is interested
in moral questions, he tries to stand outside them . . . : what is of interest is the implications of the preferences and biases people hold, not
whether it is right or wrong for them to be held.

SUBSTANTIVE BEHAVIOURAL THEORIES
OF INTERNATIONAL SOCIETY?

In considering whether behaviouralists have yet contributed a body of international theory comparable in stature to the classical theory, it is essential to remember that this is *not* what most of them are trying to do, for
the reasons which have already been given. Classical theory consists of a
large body of inter-related propositions, or empirical generalisations, about
the nature of international society and its institutions, about the patterns
of relations between the member-States, and about the characteristics of
the foreign policies of the States. So far, behavioural theory has not attempted to replace this body of "conventional wisdom" with an alternative
set of propositions equally comprehensive in scope. What it has sought to
do is to challenge, or re-think, the assumptions on which the propositions
of classical theory are based; to introduce the more stimulating ideas pro-

[6] Martin Wight, "Why Is There No International Theory?," 2 *International Relations* (1960), pp. 35–48.

duced by other disciplines; and to try to demonstrate the relevance of new techniques for research and teaching. In brief, the contributions of behaviouralism might be summarised under these three headings: general conceptual schemes (as distinct from "general theory" as defined above); partial or small-field theories, usually empirically or logically based; and techniques. The short survey which follows is designed only to suggest the wealth of material which is available to exemplify the behavioural approach. Not all of it is predominantly behavioural in strict terms, but it is believed that most of it illustrates fairly well the spirit of the behavioural movement.

General conceptual schemes have been provided in their grandest form by studies in systems analysis exemplified by the major works of M. A. Kaplan [7] and D. Easton,[8] both of the University of Chicago. Each employed the basic ideas of communication and general systems theory, Kaplan with specific reference to the international situation, and Easton with even broader reference to all political systems. Partial theories are much more numerous, including those of equilibrium, alliances and coalitions;[9] of decision-making and the theory of foreign policy;[10] of diplomacy, bargaining and negotiation;[11] and of processes of integration.[12] These might be broadly regarded as contributions of partial theory from within the discipline. Others have come from outside it, in the form of "conflict resolution" or "peace research,"[13] theories of functionalism drawn from the field of the comparative study of government;[14] sociological theories of bureaucracy and social structure;[15] and psychological theories of roles, image-formation and perception.[16] Suggested innovations in techniques

[7] *System and Process in International Politics* (1957).

[8] *Op. cit.*, and *A Systems Analysis of Political Life* (1965).

[9] W. H. Riker, *The Theory of Political Coalitions* (1962); G. Liska, *Nations in Alliance* (1962); *idem, International Equilibrium* (1957).

[10] J. Frankel: *The Making of a Foreign Policy* (1963); R. C. Snyder and others, *Foreign Policy Decision-Making* (1962); G. Modelski, *A Theory of Foreign Policy* (1962).

[11] F. C. Iklé, *How Nations Negotiate* (1964); T. C. Schelling, *The Strategy of Conflict* (1960); M. Shubik (ed.), *Game Theory and Related Approaches to Social Behavior* (1964); A. Rapoport, *Fights, Games and Debates* (1960).

[12] E. B. Haas, *Beyond the Nation State* (1964); K. W. Deutsch and others, *Political Community and the North Atlantic Area* (1957).

[13] K. E. Boulding, *Conflict and Defense* (1962); E. B. McNeil (ed.), *The Nature of Human Conflict* (1965); R. Fisher (ed.), *International Conflict and Behavioral Science* (1964); also the periodicals *Journal of Conflict Resolution* and *Journal of Peace Research*.

[14] G. A. Almond and J. S. Coleman (eds.), *The Politics of the Developing Areas* (1960).

[15] P. M. Blau, *Exchange and Power in Social Life* (1964); *idem, Formal Organisations* (1962); H. A. Simon, *Models of Man* (1957).

[16] H. C. Kelman (ed.), *International Behavior* (1965).

include both generalised ones, like the use of statistics and mathematics; specific ones, like content analysis (the use of a rigorous classificatory scheme based on explicit theory when analysing the facts of a problem); and the laboratory techniques of gaming or simulation.[17]

Even at this early stage, the contribution of behavioural theorising to the general understanding of International Relations has been considerable. Its main value is the heuristic one, a property which the behaviouralists themselves claim for their abstract models in relation to particular problems, and which the behavioural movement as a whole has brought to the classical theory in much the same manner. It draws attention to aspects left unexamined before; it stimulates intuitive insights much in the way that great political philosophy can, but the straightforward study of current events cannot; it offers the prospect of linking the separate social sciences in a fashion which once upon a time was taken for granted, but which has been lost to sight as the constricting barriers of departmental specialisation have been erected in the past half-century. In all these aspects behavioural theory offers a great deal of promise, but little to date in the way of theoretical fulfilment. However, the stimulus is refreshing, the promises are exciting, and already the tone of theorising in International Relations is changing in response to the suggestions of behavioural theory.

At the most obvious level, the language of classical international theory is altering to absorb bits and pieces of the behavioural terminology. . . . Phrases like "escalation," "decision-making," "security-community" and even "mutual responsiveness" once considered slightly barbaric jargon, are entering the everyday language of the subject because they are more accurate than any other, and to some extent represent a new focus on concepts not considered quite so important before. An even better example might soon be "feed-back," a crucial tool of much behavioural theory representing a distinct idea which was not isolated for separate consideration in traditional works of classical theory. One technique of behaviouralism, the role-playing game, is showing signs of distinct popularity as a teaching . . . tool.

ATTEMPTS TO CREATE A SYNTHESIS OF
BEHAVIOURAL THEORY

This outline has been intended to show why there is, as yet, no question of any author writing a grand synthesis of purely behavioural theory which could serve as a convincing "general theory" for International Relations. The principal message conveyed by the new literature as one reads through it is to stress what we still have to learn. Where behavioural theory is precise, it is very small-scale in application. Where it treats matters of

[17] H. A. Guetzkow and others, *Stimulation in International Relations* (1963).

broad scale and of some substantive importance to the conduct of international politics generally, it ceases to be even as "precise" as classical theory, and becomes not theory but conceptual framework, ways of looking at the subject-matter.   Attempts to apply even small parts of the theory to concrete case-studies become bogged down by the morass of detail and problems of interpretation with which classical theorists have long been so familiar.   In a recent effort of this kind J. N. Rosenau quotes a colleague's remark to the effect that "the subject of internal war has not been processed for theoretical examination and rigorous quantitative treatment: 'in consequence, social theorists confronted by the subject are understandably at sea—like shoe-makers working not on leather but an ox.' " [18]

Where studies have been written on particular aspects of International Relations, aiming at a partial theory and combining the methods of both the classical and behavioural approaches, which is true of much of the recent material cited, and strikingly so of Schelling's *Strategy of Conflict,* . . . it seems fairly clear that they are more successful than they might have been had their writers confined their attention only to classical theory. . . .

*   *   *

THE COMPATIBILITY OF BEHAVIOURAL AND
CLASSICAL THEORY

Probably the most important factor contributing to the rising interest in the behavioural approach to the study of world politics has been the frustrations of those who, either as students or teachers, found the classical approach unsatisfying.   Perhaps mistakenly, it seemed to these dissenters that there was little place in the classical view of theory for views of the international political system which were radical, not in the revolutionary sense of Kant or Lenin, but in the methodological sense with which this essay has been concerned.   Behavioural theory has filled this need, without in any way circumscribing the activities necessary in the continuing search for an effective, or illuminating, body of classical theory.   If the relations between the two emerging schools of thought can avoid the wastefulness of polemical exchange, there could be—to employ the language of cybernetics—constructive feed-back and response between them. Their inquiries are not contradictory, but proceed in parallel and complementary fashion.   As K. Deutsch argued on this same point some years ago, "it is vitally important to restore the unity in the study of politics," [19] because communication of concepts between them can help both; to take

[18] *International Aspects of Civil Strife* (1964), p. 3.

[19] "Toward an Inventory of Basic Trends and Patterns in Politics," 54 *American Political Science Review* (1960), p. 35.

the most crude examples, it is obvious that the behaviouralists need relevant insights from which to extrapolate their refined models, and conversely it will do classical theory no harm, and perhaps considerable benefit, if its empirical generalisations are based upon the concrete pedestals of whatever formal quantification hard work, content analysis and computers are able to provide. It is possible to see the division of international theorists into schools of thought not as the disintegration of a once-proudly homogeneous discipline, but as the fruitful division of labour of a group of vigorously inquisitive minds.

Stanley Hoffmann

THE LONG ROAD TO THEORY

I

. . . Arguments about the degree of autonomy of international relations, both as an area of human activity and as an intellectual discipline, can go on forever. . . . However, the three following points should be decisive. First, the field *can* be sufficiently isolated for analytical purposes. International relations take place in a milieu which has its own "coherence and uniqueness," its rules of the game which differ sharply from the rules of domestic politics, its own perspective. Secondly, since this prerequisite is met, the field *should* be treated as an autonomous discipline. . . . Thirdly, without wanting to sound like an imperialist for a relatively green science, I would argue that the architectonic role Aristotle attributed to the science of the Polis might well belong today to international relations, which have become the very condition of our daily life. If we were to put the primary emphasis in the study of politics on world affairs, and to treat domestic politics in the light of world affairs, instead of the reverse, we might produce a Copernican revolution even bigger than the change that transformed economics when macro-analysis replaced micro-analysis.

As an autonomous discipline, international relations is not in very good shape. . . .

. . . First, we find a multitude of contributions from other fields, a conglomeration of partial approaches. Most fields have something to offer. But a flea market is not a discipline. We must try to make these contributions relevant by asking the right questions. In other words, there

Reprinted by permission of the author and the editors of *World Politics*, from *World Politics*, 11 (April 1959), 346–377.

must be a core, which is missing at present.   One of the functions of theory in the social sciences is precisely to provide such a core. . . .

Secondly, however, when we look at theory in our discipline, and examine the questions that theory asks, we find a bewildering array.   Theories of international relations are like planes flying at different altitudes and in different directions.   There are, at the highest elevation, numerous speculative works concerned either with the proper place of ideals and moral standards in world affairs, or with master key explanations, or with advice on statecraft—evidence of the difficulty of keeping apart the three kinds of theory that can be distinguished analytically: normative (or "value") theory, empirical (or "causal") theory, and policy theory (or recipes for action).   At a lower altitude, we find more rigorous analyses of limited and unconnected areas within the field: theories of nationalism and imperialism, of international law and organization, systematic inquiries into the decision-making processes of certain nations, or into the nature and varieties of war.   Here the writers have been concerned mainly with empirical knowledge.   This survey reveals two facts.   First, progress in our discipline requires two efforts.   We must try to link and expand the scattered studies of the latter type, and we must try to connect those earth-bound theories with the sky-bound theories of the former type.   Secondly, what is particularly distressing in international relations is the state of systematic empirical theory.   I do not believe that it can be separated from value theory and from policy theory; but the inevitable cocktail made of all three includes at present very little of the first.

I would suggest that the first condition of improvement is a clear recognition of the scholar's purpose.   His duty is to seek knowledge and understanding for their own sake; and this implies that the main purpose of research should not be "policy scientism."   The fighting of crusades, the desire to advise policy-makers, the scholar's dedication to national or international causes can, and perhaps even should be, the occasion, but they should not be the purpose of theoretical research. . . .

II

. . . The theory which has occupied the center of the scene in this country during the last ten years is Professor Morgenthau's "realist" theory of power politics.   It tries to give us a reliable map of the landscape of world affairs, to catch the essence of world politics.   The master key is the concept of interest defined in terms of power.   The theory succeeds in focusing attention on the principal actors in world affairs: the states, and on the factors that account for the autonomy of international relations: the differences between domestic and world politics which thwart the operation in the latter of ideas and institutions that flourish in the former, the drastic imperatives of survival, self-preservation, and self-help which are both the causes and the products of such differences.

However, as a general theory, the realist analysis fails because it sees the world as a static field in which power relations reproduce themselves in timeless monotony. The map is inadequate for two main reasons. First, the realist analysis of power is a very debatable one. The decision to equate politics and the effects of man's "lust for power," and the tendency to equate power and evil or violence, mutilate reality. A "power monism" does not account for all politics, when power is so somberly defined. Furthermore, the extent to which power as a carrier of evil and violence expresses a basic human instinct is questionable, for much of the international (or domestic) evil of power is rooted not in the sinfulness of man but in a context, a constellation, a situation, in which even good men are forced to act selfishly or immorally. The discrimination between the inherent or instinctive aspects of the "power drive," and the situational or accidental ones, is an important task, neglected by the theory.

Also, it is dangerous to put in a key position a concept which is merely instrumental. Power is a means toward any of a large number of ends (including power itself): the quality and quantity of power used by men are determined by men's purposes. Now, the realist theory neglects all the factors that influence or define purposes. Why statesmen choose at times to act in a certain way rather than in another is not made clear. The domestic considerations that define national power are either left out or brushed aside. So is the role of internationally shared values and purposes. We get a somewhat mechanistic view of international affairs in which the statesmen's role consists of adjusting national power to an almost immutable set of external "givens." The realist world is a frozen universe of separate essences. . . .

There is a second reason for the inadequacy of the map. The clumsiness that comes from the timeless concept of power is compounded by the confusing use of other concepts that are dated in more ways than one, and which the theory applies to situations in which they do not fit. The model of the realists is a highly embellished ideal-type of eighteenth- and nineteenth-century international relations. This vision of the golden age is taken as a norm, both for empirical analysis, and for evaluation. A number of oddities of the theory are explained thereby. First, the lack of an adequate discussion of ends. For when all the actors have almost the same credo, it becomes easy to forget the effects of the common credo on the actors' behavior, and to omit from among the main variables of the theory a factor whose role seems constant. It is nevertheless an optical illusion to mistake a particular pattern for the norm of a scientific system. Secondly, the conception of an objective and easily recognizable national interest is one which makes sense only in a stable period in which the participants play for limited ends, with limited means, and without domestic kibitzers to disrupt the players' moves. In such a period, the survival of the main players is rarely at stake in the game, and a hierarchy can rather easily be established among the other and far less vital interests that are at stake.   Today, survival is almost always in question, and the most divergent courses of action can be recommended as choices for survival. . . .

Thirdly, the idea that the national interest carries its own morality is also one which makes sense only in a stable period. . . .   For it is in such a period that an international consensus assures at least the possibility of accommodation of national objectives: the conflicts of interests which are involved are not struggles between competing international moralities. The philosophical pluralism implicit in the realist theory (which purports to be both normative and empirical) is hardly tolerable in periods of "nationalistic universalism," and it is unnecessary in periods of stability and moderation, which bloom only because of a basic agreement on values. Fourth, the emphasis on the rationality of foreign policy and the desire to brush aside the irrational elements as intrusions or pathological deviations are understandable only in terms of cabinet diplomacy, where such deviations appear (especially with the benefit of hindsight) to have been rare. There, rationality seemed like the simple adjustment of means to stable and generally recognized ends.   These concepts are far less applicable to a period in which the political struggles involve primarily the determination of ends.   Thus, behind the claim to realism, we find a reactionary utopia.

The consequence of this inadequacy of the map is that the theory's usefulness as a general theory for the discipline is limited.   In the first place, from the point of view of systematic empirical analysis, the theory stresses the autonomy of international relations to the point of leaving beyond its pale the forces which work for change and which, cutting across the states, affect the states' behavior.   We are presented both with a single key to the closed room of politics among nations, and with a warning that the room is in a house whose key we cannot have, or whose opening must be left to the "workman-like manipulation of perennial forces."   We are not told what they are, or how they operate.   We reach at this point one of the most fundamental ambiguities of the theory.   The postulate of the permanence of power politics among nations as the core of international relations tends to become a goal.   The static qualities of the theory lead to confusion between the phenomenon of power conflicts and the transitory forms and institutions in which such conflicts have been taking place in recent centuries.   Why should the sound reminder that power is here to stay mean that the present system of nation-states will continue, or change only through forces that are of no concern to us?   Such an attitude is a double evasion: from the empirical duty of accounting for change, and from the normative task of assessing whether the present system should indeed continue. . . .

. . . [A] second limitation . . . concerns the usefulness of the scheme as a normative theory.   It is something of a success philosophy.   The criterion of a good foreign policy is its rationality, but the touchstone of ra-

tionality is success.   Unfortunately the standards of success and failure
are not made clear.   First, how will we distinguish between the follies of
straight utopianism and the fallacies of wrong realism—realism that did
not work?   Secondly, from what viewpoint shall we decide whether a
statesman has succeeded or failed? . . .

With such flaws and contradictions, the policy guidance which the realist
theory is able to afford is limited.   Realism allows us to eliminate those
policies that would foolishly forget the prerequisite of power; but it does
not go much further.   Too many factors are left out for realist advice to
avoid the dilemma of homilies and admonishments, or suggestions inappropriate for revolutionary periods. . . .

There are other attempts at providing us with a master key, and at explaining as large an amount of data as possible.   I refer to philosophies of
history, to which specialists in international relations have sometimes
turned and are likely to turn.   Like Hegel and Marx, Spengler and (especially) Toynbee are being adopted by political scientists after having been
repudiated by historians.   They fill many of the gaps of realism.   Whereas
realism is too much concerned with timeless propositions and permanent
necessities, the philosophers are rightly dealing with problems of time and
change, and with the effects of changes within the units of the world on
the relations among these units.   Whereas realism puts the state at the
center of its analysis, philosophies of history remind us that world politics
is more than the intersection of various foreign policies, and that these
policies often depend on whether the states address themselves to other
members of the same civilization or culture, or to complete outsiders.
These philosophies are useful also because of their method: the comparison of cultures or civilizations as if they were contemporary carries a lesson for international relations.   Finally, philosophers of history have a
disarming way of making explicit, and even central, assumptions about
man, society, and history which are often repressed but nevertheless
operating in all social scientists' schemes.   Such candor is to be commended.

However, we are once more in the presence of a short cut. . . .   First,
the net is too wide-meshed to catch all the main factors in world affairs, and
to account for the main forces at work in a given period.   Secondly, history is again ransacked for confirmation of a postulate, and facts that do
not fit are left out or thrown together under headings that are sometimes
tautological rather than explanatory; the difference from realism lies in
the nature of the postulate: organic metaphors or spiritual revelations replace the power drive.   Thirdly, success or survival frequently serves as a
criterion of fitness of civilizations or nations, for this is the only way out
of the impasse of a "normative pattern for the evaluation of laws derived
empirically."

. . . But this road ends in the sky, not in a theory of international relations.

III

There is another road which is supposed to end in theory. . . . We start with a central concept, or a set of central related concepts, which will allow us to ask the right questions and to analyze the data systematically. We should end with a refined set of laws and propositions "capable of refutation or confirmation by means of controlled experiment or systematic observation."

. . . There have been two main varieties: on the one hand, an attempt inspired by "general systems theory" (applied to international relations, interpreted in terms of "systems of action") as a first step toward a "system of theory"; on the other hand, attempts at using as a conceptual scheme one particular concept, supposedly strategic enough to allow the organization of the whole field around it. . . .

Systems theory has progressed mainly in social sciences other than those concerned with politics. It is a spectacular development of the behavioral sciences. Its advocate in international relations is primarily Morton Kaplan.[1] . . .

. . . The scientific purposes of the representatives of this trend . . . are: to discover laws, recurrent patterns, regularities, high-level generalizations; to make of predictability a test of science; to achieve as soon as possible the ideal of deductive science, including a "set of primitive terms, definitions and axioms" from which "systematic theories are derived." These objectives, it seems to me, are the wrong ones.

. . . The best we can achieve in our discipline is the statement of trends. Because the experimental methods available in the social sciences are "not capable of *demonstrating* any causal laws," we can only eliminate certain hypotheses (i.e., find "negative laws"), and thus define limits, within which certain trends can be suggested with "some degree of approximation" only. The reduction of our field to a system of laws, even if it could be done, would be an impoverishment. As Max Weber warned, the knowledge of social laws is not the knowledge of social reality, but merely an aid for attaining this end. The most general "laws" of international relations are bound to be fairly trivial generalizations, for in the social sciences "regularities are found only at the level of wholes," which must be broken up if we want to understand reality. . . .

Predictability is possible only in areas (such as military action) where the number of variables is limited and known in advance—two conditions which are rarely met in the social sciences, and never possible at the level of a general theory. . . . Accuracy of prediction should not become the touchstone of adequate theory.

. . . It seems to me that "systems scientism," even in its more concrete

[1] Cf. Kaplan's contribution in Chapter X. [Eds.]

or inductive aspects, uses totally inappropriate techniques. There are two sorts of aberrations. The first is a cocktail of methods borrowed from other sciences. Thus, Mr. Kaplan grafts concepts torn from sociology, economics, cybernetics, biology, and astronomy onto a very different subject—a strange method for a believer in "systems." The previous question, whether these concepts fit our field, has not been asked. Consequently, this interdisciplinary arsenal serves a pointless invasion of our field by uprooted foreign methods, rather than a guided raid into neighboring fields by a rigorous method of our own.

Another aberration is the mushrooming of mathematical models, supposed to account for large parts of the field. Now, either the scientist includes in his model only the variables that can be measured; in this case, he is likely to leave out some of the more decisive ones, and to put in satellite factors, which merely reflect, or result from, more important variables which are left out because they are not measurable. Hence, far from explaining reality, many such models seem only to give mathematical substance to shadows, and to drive research into the chase and measurement of shadows. Or else, the model builders try to measure all the important variables, but this involves some fantastic assumptions, such as the postulate that in our discipline quantification always entails a gain in precision rather than a possible loss, or that quantities measured independently can be added or combined meaningfully. The result is always a timeless and closed mathematical universe.

Not only are the purposes and methods of systems scientism open to criticism. The results achieved so far in international relations are also questionable, on three counts. First, the map these efforts produce does not allow us to recognize the landscape. Precisely because they aim at a high level of generality and use tools coming from other disciplines, these systems do not capture the stuff of politics. They are built on the shaky foundations of metaphors taken too seriously. The political patterns they study are always reduced to something else. Both in Mr. Kaplan's and in some of Karl Deutsch's earlier works, men and societies are reduced to communication systems, without much concern for the substance of the "messages" these networks carry. Maybe communication theory will prove to be the common framework for efforts that seek to interpret the behavior of all systems "from atomic particles to galaxies," from viruses to planets. But this is not what we are interested in here. . . .

. . . "[S]ociologism" operates here, too—in the most unlikely field. International systems are discussed as if they had a compulsive will of their own; the implicit God, Society, who gave its stuffy oppressiveness to the universe of Comte and Durkheim, is again at work, under the incognito of System. Each system assigns roles to actors; the structure of the system sets its needs, its needs determine its objectives, and "the objectives of a system are values for the system." The only processes discussed are processes of maintenance, integration, and disintegration; for the implied supreme value is stability: mechanical stability, since purposes and values other than preservation of the system are left out. It is the usual penalty for the double attempt to drive the consideration of values out of the subject matter, and to present a value-free theory: the *status quo* becomes an empirical and normative pivot. However, international systems are always open and moving—at least sufficiently to force us to abandon the model and the vocabulary of the closed system.

Secondly, the inadequacy of the results can be shown by pointing to their inability to *explain* world politics. On the one hand . . . the tendency to reduce politics to what it is not, entail[s] a loss of such vital elements as institutions, culture, and the action of individuals as autonomous variables rather than social atoms. As in the realist theory, Mr. Kaplan's emphasis on international systems also involves a neglect of the domestic determinants of the national actors, and his model of action leaves out the forces of change operating within or across the actors. On the other hand, the striving for total objectivity, the desire to retain mainly measurable elements, and the effort to build systems combine in the production of models in which many variables are interrelated, but where no hierarchy is established among the variables. The principle of "indeterminacy" is followed with rigorous scientism, as if it were compatible with the goal of predictability; it does not allow us to determine what variables will be submitted to the standard scientific methods of verification and validation which determine whether these variables will be included in or excluded from our scheme; nor does it allow us to decide later whether the correlations we have discovered are meaningful and relevant or not. We are told what happens when the variables reach a certain position, but never why they should reach it, or in what way. . . .

Thirdly, the inadequacy of the results of systems theory is also revealed, more indirectly but not less effectively, by the strange underground connection which links this theory to a most objectionable form of policy scientism. A view of the social universe as the interplay of impersonal forces, the procedural and mechanical analogies, the implied norm of stability leads the social scientist almost inevitably to a therapeutic and manipulative approach—to the belief that the control of the variables he has identified would push society in the direction that he (or social "elites") deems desirable. The connection between the cool and detached objectivity of the theorist and the "engagement" of the policy scientist is often made through another set of metaphors: metaphors about the health and sickness of societies and systems. . . .

Attempts at organizing the discipline around a central, unifying concept are less ambitious but not much more promising. First, as we have seen before, the field is too huge for even only its principal features to be subsumed under, or explained by, one key concept. Secondly, the choice of one central idea is inevitably based upon a postulate which is too debatable to serve as the single philosophical underpinning of a theoretical system.

*   *   *

IV

We have been engaged in a wrecking operation. Nevertheless, the need for conceptualization and theory remains. I would like to offer some suggestions for a far more modest and slow way of proceeding toward theory. They are based on postulates which are certainly as debatable as those I have discussed. But there is a difference: I do not claim that it is possible to squeeze the whole camel of international relations through the eye of one needle.

Indeed, my first assumption is one of relativism and pluralism. Each one of the approaches I have reviewed has something to contribute; none is the only right way of phrasing the question, or the only right answer. In every social science, and quite obviously here, the facts we can gather are too numerous, too open to conflicting interpretations, too "unstructured," to fit only one scheme of analysis. . . .

Secondly, when one tries to understand a field, there is no sounder method than that of drawing one's questions and concepts . . . from other disciplines only insofar as they deal with factors or units relevant to international relations. Furthermore, international relations, like other social relations, involve not mere impersonal forces, but men. It is through men's values and institutions, through the thoughts and acts of their leaders, that the basic factors of the material environment affect international relations. Therefore the consideration of men's values, beliefs, and emotions, of their purposes and ideas, is indispensable. . . .

Thirdly, because of the inevitable subjectivity and "problem-orientation" of the social scientist, and because of the presence of human beings in all the processes we want to study, the strict distinction between "purely scientific" and "normative" theory should be dropped. . . . Science which refuses to pronounce on value problems leads to a policy scientism which accepts the values set by the policy-makers—for pure empirical science cannot tell us what we should do—and then proceeds in the name of science to a task of engineering based on truncated premises; for as Mill stated, good policy advice presupposes both science and a teleology. Conversely, discussions of value problems in world affairs, divorced from a consideration of the special milieu and the special rules of the game, will produce only stale moralizing.

On the basis of the preceding postulates, I would like to suggest two kinds of systematic research. . . . The first attempt I want to suggest is what Raymond Aron has called "historical sociology." It is not a general theory. At this stage, there can be no more general theory here than in, let us say, sociology. It is a general approach based on the following ideas. The search for timeless propositions and the deductive method are, at present, disappointing. We must proceed *inductively* and, before we reach any conclusions about trends manifest throughout history, we should resort to systematic historical research, not in order to turn our discipline into history, but in order to accomplish the tasks which I will now try to describe in general terms.

Our starting point would be an analysis of what Raymond Aron calls "diplomatic constellations," or historical situations. By comparing the results of our analysis of various situations separated by fairly even time intervals, we would be able to delimit and describe historical systems of international relations . . . to discover the dynamics of change from one system to another. This stage would be similar to the description of domestic political systems. A second stage would be the comparison of historical systems; here . . . we should define types of international systems, each type being characterized by a feature or combination of features which determines its originality. Another sort of comparison of systems would lead us, at last, to some meaningful generalizations about aspects common to many systems: types of relations between the basic units (such as the balancing process or relations between units of a different nature: an empire and a city-state, or a multi-national state and a nation-state), types of foreign policies, or the role of selected factors. Finally, we could proceed to comparisons of domestic political systems and international ones, and of types of domestic and international systems. For there are many similar problems: the organization of and restraints on power, the balancing of interests, the development of consensus and legitimacy, the availability of procedures of change. I have mentioned before both the autonomy of each "milieu" and the unity of politics. Since many writers in our field have tended either to assume a rigid difference between domestic and international forms of political organization, or to treat the latter as if they were deviations from the former, such a comparative effort would be interesting. . . .

In addition to such systematic research, there is a need to undertake a different kind of task. I have mentioned earlier some of the permanent reasons for a political philosophy of world affairs. . . .

The two traditional tasks of political philosophy: the search for the proper relation among the individual, the community in which he lives, and the world, on the one hand, and concern for the best methods by which a desirable relation could be realized, on the other, have not been well performed in world politics. . . .

. . . Our first problem is the clarification of the values we would like to see promoted in the world—and, as I have suggested, we cannot do so if we do not start with a view of man as, at least in part, a community-building animal, making moral decisions among alternative courses of action which all involve the presence of some values and the sacrifice of others.   Secondly, we must relate these values to the world as it is, far more closely than we usually do.   There are many advocates of courses of action which obviously clash with the characteristic features of the present international system—either because the course belongs to a bygone system judged more satisfactory by the writer, or because the course would put on the road to a new and more progressive system a world obviously unable or unwilling until now to travel such a road.   These advocates should not only plead for the destination; they should tell us in detail how we can reach it.   Purely perfectionist ethics that brush aside the problem of the difficult and dirty means to utopia are as unhelpful as their opposite: policy scientism that plunges into roads to unexamined destinations or believes that what ought to be emerges from what is.   The range of value conflicts and the degree to which values are shared in world politics are not necessarily different from what they are in domestic affairs; but the fundamental differences in structure and institutions, justly emphasized by realism, oblige us to be very precise about the ways in which such conflicts can be reduced and such sharing promoted, if these are our objectives. For the burden of proving that the present pattern of power politics is compatible with the realization of an international morality remains on us, although—or rather precisely because—we do not accept the view that the divorce is inevitable.

SUGGESTED READINGS

Aron, Raymond, *Peace and War—A Theory of International Relations*, Garden City, N.Y.: Doubleday, 1966.

Hinsley, F. H., *Power and the Pursuit of Peace,* Cambridge, England, and New York: Cambridge University Press, 1963, Part I.

Hoffmann, Stanley (ed.), *Contemporary Theory in International Relations,* Englewood Cliffs, N.J.: Prentice-Hall, 1960.

Knorr, Klaus, and Rosenau, James N. (eds.), *Contending Approaches to International Politics,* Princeton: Princeton University Press, 1969.

McClelland, Charles A., *Theory and the International System,* New York: Macmillan, 1966.

Morgenthau, Hans J., *Scientific Man vs. Power Politics,* Chicago: University of Chicago Press, 1946.

Rosecrance, Richard N., *Action and Reaction in World Politics—International Systems in Perspective,* Boston: Little, Brown, 1963.

Rosenau, James N. (ed.), *International Politics and Foreign Policy, A Reader in Research and Theory,* rev. 2nd ed., New York: Free Press, 1969.

Singer, David J. (ed.), *Human Behavior and International Politics—Contributions from the Social-Psychological Sciences,* Chicago: Rand McNally, 1965.

Waltz, Kenneth N., *Man, the State and War—A Theoretical Analysis,* New York: Columbia University Press, 1959.

II. NATIONS AND NATIONALISM

Through the doctrines of nationalism, the "nation" has come to be one of the ruling ideas of modern politics. So normal is it to use "nation" and "state" as synonymous that we need Alfred Cobban's reminder that the two are separable, that the idea that the nation should be the basis of the state is a very modern one. To Shakespeare's Brabantio only sorcery could account for Desdemona's love for the foreigner Othello "in spite of nature, of years, of country, credit, everything, to love that which she feared to look upon." Yet the Doge of Venice replied with a fine traditional reproof to all those symbols of the nation when he called them "thin habits and poor likelihoods of modern seeming" in comparison to the facts of Othello's character and his service to the state. Yet in Shakespeare's play, as in the world, it is the nation, and not traditional ideas of individual allegiance, that prevail. For Joseph Mazzini, two and a half centuries later, the principle of the "nation-state" became the very essence of freedom, as well as the only principle that could give unity, harmony, and balance to Europe.

But what is a nation? Theorists have sought to define the nation in terms of "objective" factors such as race or language, and found that their definitions left some nations unaccounted for, or failed to explain the separate nationalities of people who shared one of the factors: Americans and Britons speak English; the "Teutonic" Alsatians are French patriots. To others, the failure of such explanations merely served to demonstrate that the basis of nationality is in individual decision and volition. "A nation," said Ernest Renan, "is a daily plebiscite." That view is deeply appealing to Americans, most of whose ancestors came to the United States by choice; yet the persistence of "hyphenated" Americans suggests that a man may change his allegiance by conscious decision, but it is not so easy to change his "nationality." W. S. Gilbert satirized the more extreme "voluntary" theory of nationality when he wrote:

> For he himself has said it,
> And it's greatly to his credit,
> That he is an Englishman . . .
> Yes, in spite of all temptations
> To belong to other nations,
> He remains an Englishman.

The ambiguities in the term nation led many writers to despair of finding a common definition. Others employed admittedly universal but useless statements, such as "A nation is a 'state of mind.' " But what kind of state of mind? And what causes it? Nationality certainly refers to *people* in a way that the abstract and legal term *state* does not. It makes a claim on the total personality of the individual, on emotions and sentiments as well as reason, on internal values as well as external behavior. All of the theorists in this chapter are agreed that a nation implies a common culture, common symbols, a particular view of the world which is distinct from other world views. What makes a nation different from other cultural groups, however, is that one of the symbols associated with its values and attitudes is a particular piece of *territory*. A "people," those who share a common culture, need not have territory as a critical symbol. A Zionist might be described as a member of the "Jewish nation," but an anti-Zionist Jew could hardly be included in the "nation," though he might be one of the "Jewish people." Again, it was proper for medievalists to speak of a Christian "republic" or "public," but no strain of the term would permit reference to a Christian nation.

The term may be made still more specific if we distinguish between two types of loyalty and attachment to particular lands or territories. We may speak, first, of that loyalty which exists among men in small communities where all citizens can see and form intimate associations with the whole territory. Such communities are often called "face-to-face" in terms of the relations between men, of a particularly intense bond between men involving almost all of their personality. The same intensity often extends to the land as such in all details, an intensity summarized in the word "patria" or "fatherland." This term, now applied to great states like Germany, was originally a very local and limited one.

Different from the *patria* is the "territorial state." A state is not logically associated with any specific territory, and the territory of states expands and contracts; but insofar as a core area exists which for long periods of time remains in the state, it becomes intimately associated with it. Surely France could not exist without Paris; and it was once as hard for Germans to conceive of Germany without Vienna as it is proving for them to conceive of it without Berlin.

What defines the boundaries of the state, however, are legal, political, military, and economic considerations. The "city-state" perished when a larger state was made necessary by the military and economic environment. European states were made up of diverse *patrias* originally held together in loose federations that grew more unified or were conquered as technology developed. The "natural frontier," a traditional phrase of political geography, refers to that feature of terrain which forms the natural line of military defense, or of administrative control, between states.

Especially in modern times, the "territorial state" has existed in an environment that has compelled organization on a scale far larger than the *patria*. (This, of course, was a major argument of *The Federalist* in favor of federation in America.) But that larger scale has meant that the individual citizen was drawn into political and economic relations with men he had not known from childhood, indeed with men he had never met at all, and was made part of a state of which he had seen, at best, a very small part. In such a world the average citizen felt less important and less certain than in a world composed only of his family and friends. He might be freer to move about, able to gain more wealth or power; but his new freedom included a dependence and an insecurity that, as Erich Fromm suggested, men have been tempted to "escape," seeking a social universe in which conditions are more stable, men more predictable, the individual's status and dignity more secure.[1] Men have sought to recapture in the expanded world of the territorial state the atmosphere of the *patria*.

Karl W. Deutsch in his seminal *Nationalism and Social Communication* has drawn attention to this fact. Urbanization, the growth of a commercial economy, the expansion of mass communications, all "mobilized" men, made them conscious of relations with each other and with the state. But they were "unassimilated," uncertain of their place in the new order. Unless the ruling groups in the state were able to assimilate them through education and such rewards as wealth and status, Deutsch argues, they would become conscious of cultural bonds that united them *in opposition* to these ruling groups, and a separate "nationalism" would emerge.

This thesis, however, is unfortunately close to the thesis of the German philosopher Johann von Herder (1744–1803) that "nations," the ultimate "monad" in human nature, would "emerge" when barriers between nationals were swept away. Even if ruling groups fail to "assimilate" the newly "mobilized," what develops is not always "nationalism." Karl Marx, for example, argued that what would "emerge" was a consciousness of shared *class* bonds, not national ties, and often this has been the case.

Here a distinction is necessary between a *group,* the members of which are conscious of membership, and a *social category,* a set of individuals who share some attribute whether they are conscious of it or not. Men find they share bonds with one another when the categories of which they are a part become *salient* and *meaningful* in their immediate environment; for example, a Bavarian and a Prussian who moved to America noticed their regional distinctions less than the fact that both spoke German. What makes a particular category salient is a complex matter, but it may be stated that it is always based on a distinction from some other group of individuals who seem important: the status of a "child" is more important in a society where parental authority is strong, "class" is significant in a society based on such distinctions, "nationality" where "foreigners" are an important part of the environment. Thus many have noted the "marginal" nationalism characteristic of men who live on frontiers, and all his types of nationalism suggest what Rupert Emerson affirms: that nationalism is always in part an "antifeeling."

Second, in an environment like that of the modern state, where men are tied to relatively few of their fellows by deep personal and emotional bonds, the categories that become salient will tend to be based on external factors that can be seen or heard rather than on values and attitudes that must be felt. Physical appearance, race, language, and clothing are among the most typical. Men are conscious, however, that appearance or clothing is not an adequate test of the feelings and attitudes of others; and since, by our hypothesis, men seek the emotional and personal security of the *patria,* they tend to look for more certain guides. The great importance of language is probably due to the fact that speech is a better index of sentiments and values than merely physical qualities.

[1] *Escape from Freedom,* New York: Rinehart, 1939.

It is always vital when we speak of the process of "communication" to remember that communication is the result of, or the search for, *communion* between men. This suggests one of the major appeals of nationalism, as opposed to doctrines stressing "class": namely that nationalism affirms the bond between the individual and all of those who normally inhabit his territory. If nationality is in one sense always negative, it is in another always "positive," both in that the "outsider" is on the whole far away and in that it encourages community rather than conflict in daily life.

Nations and nationalism may be part of a common human response to a similar social and technological process, but the content of nationalism and the nation will vary with the cultures in which they originate and the times in which they develop. Nationalism took many forms among European states; Emerson adds a discussion of the differences between European and non-Western "nationalism."

Several factors may be noted: first, in Western Europe, the accidental birthplace of the scientific and technological revolution, changes that were forced on social and political life were, or seemed, primarily a matter of choice. Moreover, the West's accidental advantage gave it relatively more time in which to "assimilate" the mass of the community to the new order of things. Technological and social changes came one by one, and the numbers "mobilized" at any one time were few; on the whole, the ability of the state to provide economic and social rewards kept pace with the demands of individuals for assimilation. In France the resistance of the ruling classes and the economic problems of the state might produce the Revolution of 1789, but the "nation" still seemed something based on individual choice and doctrine, to be realized through changes in institutions and legislation. In eastern, southern, and central Europe, however, changes were more involuntary, imposed from above by ruling elites compelled to respond to the challenges posed by the growing power of Western states. Hostility to foreigners played a greater role; the decisions of private citizens counted for less; and the unity that they discovered with their fellows seemed something "innate," not connected with institutions or conscious decisions but with a mystic "national will" or "spirit." In the West the state and the nation were inseparably connected and, as Cobban indicates, closely related to individual freedom. But in central and eastern Europe the nation seemed separate from institutions and individual decisions; "Germany" existed before a German state. The nation was thought to demand a state that would include those who were "objectively" part of the nation; for whatever an individual might think, he "was" or "was not" a part of the *Volk*.

Emerson recalls that development in Asia and Africa is even more closely associated with "outsiders," with changes imposed in response to external threats or by foreign conquerors. To this "antielement" has been added another: that only rarely has there been a preexisting national culture, created "by the state" or not, that might serve as a unifying bond between newly "mobilized" peoples. Hostility to imperial powers often unites those who share little else: those assimilated to the values of the West, who feel themselves excluded by Western nations; those "mobilized" but not assimilated; and the traditional, "unmobilized" tribes and clans.

Old resentments and new frustrations combine, as Harry Johnson indicates, to produce a "taste for discrimination" against foreigners, and since gratifying that preference also coincides with the interests of new elites, policies of economic nationalism become logical even if such policies result in a lower level of goods and services. But economic nationalism is not always enough. Especially when political leaders encounter problems in providing their people with the industrial and technological progress that the people expect—not only for the material gains that result but as a means to dignity—might they be tempted to engage in "irredentist nationalism," bellicosity, or messianic foreign policy.

Only rarely, however, are the gains from such policies great enough to eliminate the psychological appeals of "particularistic" nationalism. Non-Western states find it hard to assimilate their own newly mobilized groups, and these, in turn, sensing discrimination and exclusion, fall back on passionate devotion to tribes, regions, and older loyalties generally.

As Walker Connor's argument suggests, none of these tendencies is re-stricted to non-Western states. The great industrial states may offer their citizens material prosperity. Government in such states, however, seems to grow ever more impersonal and technocratic; the cold calculations of the ex-pert do not light the fires of patriotism. Rather, distant and impersonal rule creates feelings of indignity that kindle a smoldering resentment and encour-age citizens to cling to narrower ethnic and national loyalties. Felt discrimi-nation against such groups can spark a resurgence of a nationalism that had seemed to have disappeared, even when separatism seems to run counter to economic and material common sense.[2]

Assimilation in the industrial states, in other words, is more superficial than was once believed. The nation-state, always something of an artificial growth, was justified by the material rewards it made available. But even the great powers, today, cannot protect their citizens. Weapons of war and changes in technology are constant threats, and ecological disaster seems a possible by-product of the engine of progress. The gains from being a citizen are more balanced—and to some, outweighed—by the costs, precisely at a time when the psychological bonds of the nation-state grow less firm. "Particularistic" and "minority" nationalism are only one problem; "alienation" from the na-tion also occurs among those who, lacking older clans and peoples, must seek to create new ones.

But it is unlikely that the nation-state will consent to "wither away." New and resurgent conflicts inside the state have not eliminated fear of and hos-tility toward outsiders, the perennial negative basis of national solidarity. And those who would preserve the nation-state may attempt to raise the salience of such antifeelings once again. In any of its forms, nationalism may again follow the path from national self-assertion through expansionism to imperialism. That possibility, with all the perils it implies, is one that em-braces all the tribes and peoples of humankind.

[2] J. P. MacIntosh, M.P., "Scottish Nationalism," *Political Quarterly* (October–November 1967).

Alfred Cobban

NATIONAL SELF-DETERMINATION

The right of national independence, which came to be called, during the first World War, the principle of self-determination, is . . . the belief that each nation has a right to constitute an independent state and determine its own government. . . . [I]t is a theory about the relationship that should prevail between the nation and the state, the latter being understood as any separately governed political community. . . .

. . . The movement for national independence, or self-determination, falls into the same category as utilitarianism, communism or Jeffersonian democracy. It is . . . an ideal and no simple, unconscious national movement can be identified with it. Struggles such as the rising of the French under the inspiration of Joan the Maid or the Hussite Wars are fundamentally different from . . . national movements . . . because of the absence of a theory of national self-determination, which could only appear in the presence of a democratic ideology. Now, democracy, in the modern sense of the word, was born in the second half of the 18th century. . . . [W]ith the French Revolution democracy became something more than . . . the representation of individuals, much less of classes or corporations, in a parliament exercising a constitutional control over the government: the people itself became the supreme authority, the single active principle in the state. It passed from the role of subject to that of sovereign.

The post-medieval form of the theory of the Divine Right of Kings . . . was replaced by the Divine Right of the People. Under the influence of the new . . . democratic ideas, the people ceased to be an atomic dust of individuals: it took shape and form, became a *whole* and was called the *Nation,* endowed with sovereignty and identified with the state. The revolutionary theory that a people had the right to form its own constitution and choose its own government . . . easily passed into the claim that it had a right to decide whether to attach itself to one state or another, or constitute an independent state. . . . The effect . . . was to transfer the initiative in state-making from the government to the people. Nation-states had formerly been built up, in the course of centuries, from above, by the influence of government: henceforth they were to be made much more rapidly from below by the will of the people. The logical consequence of the democratization of the idea of the state . . . was the theory of national self-determination.

*   *   *

Reprinted by permission of the publisher from *National Self-Determination* (London: Oxford University Press, 1948), pp. 4–5, 49–53. Issued under the auspices of the Royal Institute of International Affairs.

In modern times the term "nation" has commonly been employed in the sense of the political state. At the same time, the word "nation" was used long before self-determination was thought of, and used very largely in a non-political sense. A nation was a community of language or culture which might, or which might not, possess common political ties or aspirations. . . . The critical moment in the history of nationality is that when hitherto distinguishable, if not entirely separate, ideas of the cultural nation and the political state moved together and merged in one single idea. . . .

*   *   *

. . . Self-determination, on this basis, is the process by which a cultural nation becomes a political state, and also that by which a political state becomes a cultural nation. . . . [T]he application of the principle in Western Europe—where states had already to a considerable extent achieved the ideal of a common culture—was only to confirm the existing order of things. But in Central and Eastern Europe, in the nineteenth century, most cultural nations were not yet states. The theory of self-determination involved an effort on the part of these cultural nations to become state-nations.

. . . Once the ideal identification of nation and state has been accepted, the state in its own defence tends to act as though it were a single and united nation . . . if in fact it is not this, it must endeavour to make the facts correspond to the ideal, regardless of the rights or liberties of those among its citizens who do not belong to the majority nation. On the other hand, every nation, or fraction of a nation which is not a national state must seek to become one. . . .

*   *   *

. . . Every separate national culture must, on this theory, be a state in embryo, and the ideal of every state should be to employ a single culture-nation. . . . [E]xcept in the rare cases where nation and state already fully coincide, the two tendencies . . . are bound to come into conflict. . . .

In historical fact, cultural unity has usually followed on and not preceded political unity. The cultural nation was more the creation than the creator of the political state in France and England, in the United States and in the British Dominions. . . . But the process by which . . . the state evolved a common national consciousness was generally a slow, and what might be called a natural process. The modern belief in the identity of nation and state, with its corollary that unless a state is also a cultural nation it is no legitimate state, has provided a strong incentive to hasten the process. . . . This results in an attempt by the state to compel all its members to identify themselves culturally with the ruling nation. It is an important element in the development of totalitarianism. . . .

The opposite view is that the nation is prior to the state. . . . The state is not allowed to have any nation-creating right or capacity.   If it is not a nation to begin with, it has no rights at all. . . .

              *   *   *

With the passing of the initiative from the political state to the cultural nation, the idea of nationality launches a general offensive all along the line on the world of states. . . .   If a nation is subject to some state other than its own national state it claims national emancipation.   When it has achieved freedom from alien control it agitates for the union to its own political state of any members of its cultural or linguistic community who still remain under foreign rule. . . .   There may be minorities to suppress or territories to which some historical claim is possible.   Nor does the process . . . stop at this.   Triumphant nationalism almost invariably tends . . . to swell into imperialism. . . .

The development of nationalism into a principle of aggression is stimulated by the conception of national culture as something inherent in the members of the nations . . . as opposed to the older territorial idea of the state, which made the actual physical extent of country occupied the essential element which defined and therefore limited the political community. . . .   The fact is that in being poured into the mould of the state the nation acquires all the characteristics of the state as a power-organization, and this is the ultimate result of the identification of cultural nationality with political statehood.

Rupert Emerson

NATIONALISM AND POLITICAL DEVELOPMENT

If it were necessary to select the most important single force behind the revolutionary drive of the rising peoples of Asia and Africa, the choice would inevitably go to nationalism.   For none of its potential rivals can an effective case be made. . . .   To the peoples newly asserting their claim to equal status in the world, nationalism is the essence of what they seek.

In the debates in the United Nations on the Covenants of Human Rights the right of self-determination has frequently been considered the foundation on which all other rights rest; self-determination denied, no other right can be secure.   It is in this light that peoples around the globe have

Reprinted by permission of the publisher from *The Journal of Politics* (February 1960).

viewed nationalism, assuming that the remaining goods they seek will flow from its attainment. . . .

The prime rival to nationalism as a driving force is presumed to be the desire for an improved standard of living. From time to time it is asserted that the ordinary poverty-stricken Asian and African is really interested only in seeing an end put to his poverty. . . .   The evidence indicates that he regards at least temporary economic privation as an appropriate price to pay for national salvation. . . .

However strong the urge toward better living conditions and economic development, it tends always to take second place to the political claims of nationalism. The individual who protects his economic position by refusing to undertake the sacrifices which patriotism demands reads himself out of the community of right-minded, nation-fearing men. As one of the standard phrases of nationalism has it: we would rather be governed like hell by ourselves than well by someone else. Furthermore, the issue between nationalism and material advancement here posed is seen as a quite unreal one since the nationalist creed normally embraces the belief that material improvement will surely follow in the wake of national self-realization. Both well-being and economic development are considered unattainable in the shadow of imperialism. Only when the national destiny is safely entrusted to national and not alien hands is it possible to move confidently ahead on the path which leads to wealth, strength, and modernity. . . .

Communism might be put forward as a contemporary threat to nationalism and undoubtedly, in certain cases, individuals and groups have given to the Party a priority which they deny to the nation. More frequently, however, and particularly in the revolt against imperialist domination, Communism is seen as an alternative means of reaching national goals. . . .   It has often been contended that the success of the Communists in Asian countries hinges upon their ability to identify themselves with the local nationalist cause.

*   *   *

It is a great deal easier to assert the priority given nationalism than to lay out with any measure of precision its content. Rarely does nationalism represent a coherent and positive body of doctrine and belief, reaching significantly beyond insistence on the establishment of an independent state. Freedom from partition or alien intrusion is normally a far better defined matter than are the uses to which freedom would be put. . . .   Nehru commented on the fact that a large element in nationalism is negative. "Nationalism is essentially an anti-feeling," he has written . . . "and it feeds and fattens on hatred and anger against other national groups, and especially against the foreign rulers of a subject country."

The negative or "anti"-character of nationalism in a colonial setting is simple enough to explain, but it is by no means unique to colonialism.

Everywhere the national "we" has been to a considerable degree defined by contrast to the alien and opposing "they," and in most instances no operationally significant statement of what the nation stands for can be expected. Indeed, this may be . . . a standard feature of all nationalism. . . . To demand that each nation have a single positive content . . . for nationalism is to ask that it select from a diverse history certain strands which alone will constitute its legitimate national heritage. Not far down this road lies the *Gleichschaltung* of the Nazis.

The new states are, however, peculiarly divided within themselves by the gaps which separate different elements in the population. Not only do they have as diverse and internally contradictory a history as do other peoples, but they are also afflicted by an unusual degree of distance between the bulk of the population and the newly arisen leadership. The most notable gap is the one which divides the active, Western-educated urban group from the inert, uneducated, tradition-bound mass mainly composed of the peasantry. It is the first group from which the heirs of empire have been drawn to constitute the new élite, putting its stamp on the states which it has been largely responsible for bringing into being. Here are the makings of a fundamental dilemma. It is arguable that any nation's claim to a distinctive place in the sun must be derived from the past which has shaped it in this peculiar national fashion, yet the entire leadership of the new states tends to be made up of those most removed from the traditional society of their ancestors. Nationalism has characteristically been the property of the constantly expanding but still relatively slight minority most influenced by the West.

The social structure in Asian and African nations, then, is that a newly fashioned élite, oriented toward the West and modernization despite its passionate repudiation of Western imperial control, has taken a predominant lead in societies the bulk of whose members are still close to their ancestral past. In such a circumstance the definition of the national purpose must evidently be a hazardous process. . . .

The existence of great gaps in the society of the new states raises a further question. How real is the solidarity of a nation when it is so profoundly divided within itself? . . .

The fact that a people can stage a consolidated anti-imperial movement conveys no assurance that it will be able to maintain political coherence once the imperial enemy has vanished. It is, of course, true that the mere carrying on of an extended and concerted struggle is in itself a significant factor in the creation of national sentiment, but a more basic identity is necessary if the national unity is to endure. The sense of belonging together through the experience of a common history and of facing a common destiny is not something which can be created overnight. . . . The mass has so far demonstrated only meager interest in taking an active part in day-to-day political life. The leaders, for their part, have often shown an inclination to see themselves as an élite, properly entrusted with the destinies of their untutored countrymen. . . . Nor have the mass of the people up to this point been inclined to challenge the élitist claim of their new leaders, although the military have presented a decisive challenge in several countries. Where democratic institutions survive for an extended time and the people come to feel that political power is actually in their hands, the present relationship between mass and élite may take on a quite different cast.

*   *   *

The social contract theorist, in his purer flights of fancy, pictured a world in which distinct atoms of human beings, impelled by reason and other pressures, came together to make a contract which brought state and government into being. In the contemporary scene, the nation-state, as the term indicates, assumes that the state is built upon, or is the institutional embodiment of, a community of men who are already joined by intimate and old-established links. The state is not the product of random particles arbitrarily joined in political co-operation, but the expression of the close prior bonds which has brought this "We" to a sense of difference from the alien "They." Society derives, so to speak, not from a contract but from natural and organic growth.

*   *   *

As it is the presumption that the modern state is built upon the nation, so it is also the presumption that the nationalist speaks on behalf of a nation already in existence. Members of the nation may need to be roused to awareness of their national identity, but national unity itself is taken for granted. To question its existence is almost an insult to intelligence, and is certainly an insult to political ambition. The relationships are, however, in some instances reversed. In a great many cases in the past, and not infrequently in the present, it is the state which appears to have been the determining element in the creation of the nation, and at least on some occasions the nationalists have had to play a significant role in bringing into being the nation whose cause they have espoused.

Over and over again, if the origin of a nation is traced, it will be found that there was a state structure, or at least a political system approximating a state, which coincided to a striking degree with the modern nation in terms of the territory and people it embraced. The regularity of this coincidence furnishes good evidence for the thesis that, more often than not, the nation is a deposit which has been left behind by the state—although this evades the query as to whether the original state itself was perhaps the product of prior ethnic unity. Where the state has survived for many generations reasonably intact within an approximation of the same frontiers . . . the argument is so obvious as to need no elaboration. . . . States which have vanished from the historical scene for longer or shorter periods of time . . . left behind them firmly established national precipitates.

Outside Europe the rôle of the state as the formative factor in the shaping of nations is at least as great. . . . In Latin America the boundaries of the states tend to have a high degree of coincidence with the provincial jurisdictions marked out by Spain and other ruling powers; and it is the successor states which have shaped the Latin American nations insofar as national entities have in fact been welded together out of the disparate human materials. . . .

Nowhere is the significance of the state in its capacity as nation-maker more inescapably evident than in the colonial sphere. In some cases, of course, such as those of the Burmese and Vietnamese, the peoples who have recently claimed nationhood had achieved a vigorous earlier communal identity, despite the presence of minorities, and could look back to long-lived state systems of their own. In other cases, such as those of the Philippines and Indonesia, the lines drawn on the map by the imperial power were the determining element in establishing the boundaries within which peoples have developed a sense of national awareness. Here the common government was a major instrument in pressing ethnic diversity into a common mold.

The rôle of government in bringing to peoples the experience of a common destiny is obviously immense, but the human material involved sharply limits the effect of the forces set in motion by the achievement of political unification. Integration is possible where peoples have an original similarity and may be totally or virtually excluded where they are divided by large-scale disparities in such basic elements as race, culture, religion and language. . . . The effectiveness of the state in forging a nation dwindles away to the vanishing point in such a situation as that of South Africa where the *apartheid* doctrine explicitly rejects any conception of building a single national community. . . .

*   *   *

The nation establishes the demographic and geographic frontiers of the state. For the survival of the state nationalism furnishes another vital element in that it supplies the emotional cement which holds the members of the state together when disagreements threaten to pull them apart. What the social contract sought to provide by engaging men in formal obligations to each other came to be provided in the contemporary world by the social-historical fact of being born, brought up, and educated within the close-knit and emotion-laden confines of the nation. In the theory of the national era the state exists in order to realize the purposes of the nation, and, short of external attack, it can maintain its unity as long as the "We" of the nation takes priority over all the divergent pulls which might distract and disrupt.

Does nationalism have a clear tendency to produce one or another type of political institution? The answer to this question must be a slightly hesitant "No"; slightly hesitant because nationalism has in it democratic elements which cannot be ignored even where it has turned in ruthlessly authoritarian directions.

. . . Reduced to its bare bones, nationalism is no more than the assertion that this particular community is arrayed against the rest of mankind. This sense of separate identity can by itself give no clue as to how the community may choose to manage its own affairs.

*   *   *

. . . [T]he argument linking democracy and nationalism would run something as follows. Nationalism is peculiarly a product of or a response to the distinctive forces which have gone into the shaping of the modern world. Those forces are inherently and inevitably "democratic" in the sense that they mobilize submerged elements and classes of society into new social rôles, eat away at traditional attachments and relationships, and work toward the building of a new great society into which, in principle, all men are actively drawn. Obviously what is involved here is by no means necessarily a democratic constitutional structure nor even an immediate approximation of a society striving toward egalitarianism, although both of these are likely to be present at least as active aspirations. Far more, it is the general conception, derived from the changing social scene, that the people, the mass of ordinary humans, are of consequence, that they are achieving a sense both of their own worth and of their right and ability to do something about it, and that the leaders must speak in their name. The national era comes to be an era of mass communications and mass production, inescapably headed toward mass politics.

. . . As the peoples themselves—or, at least, a significant new element among them—begin to come of age and to a new consciousness of themselves, they demand a new place in a society in process of transformation. One of the characteristic forms which this demand has taken is insistence upon the centrality of the national community and upon the latter's right to make the state the sovereign organ of its identity and will. The people, after all, compose the nation, and it is not beyond the bounds of reason to suggest the revolutionary importance of the fact that the social-political community which has come to occupy the center of the contemporary stage—taking over the state in its own name and establishing a new criterion of legitimacy—should, therefore, be defined in terms of the people. In the new dispensation the state could no longer be seen as made up of the ruler and those who happened to be his subjects, but became in principle the emanation and instrument of the nation. The forward thrust of the bourgeoisie in Europe and later of the masses, had its close overseas parallel in the awakening rebellion of colonial people, in roughly similar circumstances and under similar leadership.

*   *   *

A second line of interconnection is the immense prestige which democracy has achieved—even among those who have no serious intent of practicing it. Democracy is taken as an ultimate good to which all peoples must aspire, but which only the advanced peoples can hope to master. The imperial centers—Britain, France, the Low Countries, the United States— which have so largely set the tone for the world as it has evolved in the last century and more, have established the pattern of democratic supremacy, and have, at least until recently, made no effort to conceal their belief that the "lesser breeds of man" could not be trusted to manage a democratic system. The imperial powers themselves, properly democratic at home, must impose a benevolently autocratic rule on the peoples whose tutelage they had undertaken. For the nationalists struggling to win their equality with the imperial masters here was a challenge: democracy was the political system whose realization would serve as a symbol that the bonds of inferiority had been broken.

Nor was the striving for democratic institutions only a matter of prestige. Assuming the nationalist leaders to be in almost every instance the product of Western education at home or abroad, the political philosophy and political history with which they were imbued pointed to democracy as the form of government which represented man's highest achievement and as the form which modern man naturally adopted. . . .

Furthermore, a swing in the democratic direction was a matter of vital political necessity for the nationalists. Their legitimacy in the eyes of their imperial opponents, and, no doubt, in their own as well, rested in very considerable part on their ability to demonstrate that they had the mass of their people behind them. . . .

In these and other fashions nationalism works to promote democracy, but it also contains ingredients which can with the greatest of ease turn in undemocratic or anti-democratic directions. Wherever nationalism is the main driving force, there is the temptation to give priority to the attainment of national unity, strength, and independence. In such circumstances the liberalism of democratic nationalism may yield to the demand for unity put forward in the name of the nation itself. . . .

*   *   *

No great confidence can be placed in the general populace as the defender of threatened democratic institutions. Poverty-ridden peoples in a climate of rising expectations are not likely to make their first concern the preservation of political forms and liberties whose meaning is obscure to them and whose promise appears of less significance than other prospects that are held out to them. If democracy fails to produce results with adequate speed and if authoritarian methods seem to hold the remedy, the masses cannot be counted on to rise to the defense of unfamiliar political machineries. . . .

*   *   *

In the West nationalism is now often denounced as being a divisive and anachronistic force—bad enough at any time and intolerable in the atomic era. . . .

*   *   *

In the newly rising countries nationalism has functions to perform which it has largely exhausted in the West.   While in the West the nation has come to represent the actual outer boundaries of communal allegiance for most men or has set limits which are already found too confining, in Asia and Africa it constitutes a great potential widening of the social and political horizons of most of the people.   Far from forcing men to live within restricted quarters, it opens new doors and windows.   Where men's lives have traditionally been bounded by family, tribe, or caste, by village, market town, or petty state, the emergence of nationalism creates pressures which force men into larger communities, as nationalism is itself a response to similar pressures. . . .

. . . All the agitation and propaganda associated with nationalist parties and upheavals dramatize the issues and serve to make the nation a living reality for people who have had no consciousness of its existence. To the extent that the new concept is grasped, the peasant isolated in his village becomes a citizen of a nation which takes its place in the world's councils.   The nation is itself still far removed from meeting the needs of an age of jet planes, radio, and intercontinental ballistic missiles, but it is at least an advance in social magnitude over what preceded it.

Nationalism by itself gives the answer to virtually none of the particular problems arising from the ubiquitous demand for development and, indeed, to very few of the multitude of questions which confront peoples coming to independence.   Its most vital contribution is in the realms of the intangibles of the spirit: the restoration of self-respect, the building up of morale, and the stimulation of social solidarity.   It does not, however, determine the choice between alternative and often conflicting values, each legitimately put forward as embraced within the national destiny; it does not provide all the good things associated with independence; and it does not establish the institutions necessary for further advance. . . .

*   *   *

. . . [N]ationalism can be of immense assistance if it is wisely and skillfully used by those responsible for the guidance of the new states.   If it is used merely to inflame and obscure, its contribution can be disastrous.

Harry G. Johnson

ECONOMIC NATIONALISM IN NEW AND
DEVELOPING STATES

. . . [T]o the economist, nationalism appears on the one hand as a driving force responsible for the urge of less developed countries (of which the majority are new states) to accelerate their economic development by economic planning, and on the other hand as the major political influence responsible for the fact that many features of the policies, concepts, and methods of economic development planning in such countries either do not make economic sense, or else would make economic sense only in certain specific and rather exceptional economic circumstances the actual presence of which no one has felt it necessary to establish by empirical economic research.

This last point may be illustrated by a variety of examples. In the first place, both public pronouncements in developing countries and the literature on economic development are pervaded by an emphasis on industrialization as the necessary path to economic development, despite the fact that many economists, looking either to past economic history or to the current situation in the less developed countries, have concluded that the development of agriculture or of exports of certain natural resource products constitutes their logical path to economic development. Secondly, in regard to the choice of industries to be fostered by development policy, there is a marked tendency to regard certain industries as strategic, almost regardless of the size of the country, its location, or its available skills. Which industries these are depend in large part on the stage of development. In the earliest stages of development, a steel industry is generally regarded as the *sine qua non* of economic development, even though steel requires a massive investment of capital and the world steel industry has tended to suffer from chronic over-capacity rather than excessive pressure of demand. In more advanced countries, such as Canada, Australia, the Union of South Africa, Mexico, and Argentina, the *sine qua non* of development is a domestic automotive industry, even though the establishment of such an industry involves essentially the local production of American or European models at costs substantially above the prices of imports. In countries that are generally regarded as advanced, other than the United States, a comparable emphasis has been placed on the production of atomic energy, even though the commercial profitability of that form of power is not yet firmly established. As indicated, an economic justification for regarding the specific industrial activities mentioned as

Reprinted by permission of the publisher from *Political Science Quarterly*, 80 (June 1965), 169–185.

strategic is difficult to provide; instead, the selection of what activity is strategic seems to be governed by rivalry with and imitation of other nations that are regarded in some sense as superior.

A third example, different in nature, is the almost universal prevalence of a preference for public enterprise over private enterprise. Such a preference is not necessarily a question of nationalism—it may be a consequence of political philosophy—but it frequently seems to be dictated by nationalism rather than by socialist political principle. The problem for the economist here is to explain what, if any, advantage a country with limited managerial skills and limited administrative capacity derives from organizing industrial activities under governmental control rather than through reliance on the competitive market place.

Two other examples are drawn from the area of international economic relations. In commercial policy, developing countries generally place great emphasis on policies of substituting domestic production for imports, when the economics of the situation would indicate that economic efficiency would best be served by reliance on the principle of comparative advantage. And in almost all the developing countries and new nations, there is strong opposition to the investment of foreign capital and to the employment of foreign scientific, technical, and managerial personnel, even though capital and professional people are scarce and their scarcity frequently constitutes the major bottleneck in the process of economic development. Both phenomena are clearly derived from nationalism.

The problem these examples pose for the economist as social scientist is to explain the tenacity with which these policies are followed and the regularities of behavior that can be discerned among countries, in terms of an underlying logical connection running from nationalism to economic policy. The purpose of this article is to provide such an explanation, in the form of a theoretical model of economic nationalism in new and developing states. . . .

I

The theoretical model presented derives primarily from three recent applications of economic theory to problems hitherto not generally considered to fall within its range.

The first of these is Gary S. Becker's study of discrimination against Negroes in the United States.[1] The key concept of this work is the "taste for discrimination," the notion that people who discriminate are willing to sacrifice material gain—by paying higher prices or accepting lower prices in their economic transactions—in order to enjoy a psychological gain derived from avoiding contact with the group discriminated against. The model of nationalism presented here adopts from Becker's work the

[1] Gary S. Becker, *The Economics of Discrimination* (Chicago, 1957).

notion that individuals seek—in accordance with the postulates of economic theory—to maximize their satisfaction, but that this satisfaction includes enjoyment of both psychic income and material income; it simply substitutes for the taste for discrimination a taste for nationalism.

The second source of the model is Anthony Downs' application of economic theory to the processes and practices of democratic government.[2] Downs' basic hypothesis is that political parties seek to maximize their gains from office; but that they win office by catering to the preferences of the voters, and can only continue in office by satisfying the voters' preferences for various types and quantities of governmental activity. In other words, power is exchanged for desired policies in a political transaction between party and electorate. A strategic element in Downs' theory of the workings of democracy is the cost of acquiring information. Downs uses this cost to explain the reliance on persuasion in arriving at political decisions; the inequality of political influence; the role of ideology; electoral apathy; and the bias of democratic government toward serving producer rather than consumer interests.

The third source of the model is Albert Breton's analysis of the economics of nationalism.[3] Breton identifies nationality with ownership by nationals of various types of property, and regards it as a type of collective consumption capital that yields an income of utility and can be invested in by spending public funds on the acquisition of such capital. Using this framework, Breton produces a number of specific and testable propositions about nationalism: nationalist policy is mainly concerned with redistributing income rather than increasing it; specifically, the redistribution is from the working class to the middle class; consequently, where the working class is poor, there will be a tendency to resort to confiscation rather than purchase of property. Furthermore, nationalism will tend to favor investment in national manufacturing, since manufacturing jobs and ownership are preferred by the middle class; its collective nature will appeal to socialists; and its emergence will be correlated with the rise of new middle classes who have difficulty in finding suitable career opportunities.

II

The development of the model of economic nationalism starts from Downs' model of the working of democracy. It is posited that political parties are engaged in the business of exchanging governmental policies and services, from which a party in power derives benefits in the form of psychic and material gains of various kinds, for votes from the electorate. The

[2] Anthony Downs, "An Economic Theory of Political Action in a Democracy," *Journal of Political Economy*, LXVI (1957), 135–50, and *An Economic Theory of Democracy* (New York, 1957).

[3] Albert Breton, "The Economics of Nationalism," *Journal of Political Economy*, LXXII (1964), 376–86.

party's success in gaining and keeping power depends on its success in furnishing what the electorate desires from the government in exchange for its votes.   The main obstacle to efficiency in this exchange stems from ignorance on both sides about the prospective gains from the policies offered, and the cost of acquiring the information necessary to make the exchange efficient.   This obstacle forces the political party to depend for its information about voter preferences on pressure groups and lobbyists, and on the communications media.   Also, though Downs does not develop the point because he is primarily concerned with established democracies, this dependence gives the political parties a strong incentive to establish control over communications media as a means of establishing political control.

The average voter, however, is motivated by his own rational self-interest not to acquire much knowledge about the policies of political parties and their consequences for his economic welfare, because whether or not he is well informed he will have a negligible influence on which party is elected.   It is this that gives ideology a crucial role in political life. The establishment of a distinctive party ideology simplifies the party's problem of communicating to the electorate by enabling the party to summarize all of its policies in one general symbolism; and it simplifies the problem of the voter, who can vote by ideology instead of being obliged to weigh up each party's record and promises on the whole range of specific policy issues.   Parties will therefore compete largely through their ideologies.

*   *   *

Where democracy is not well established, there will be a strong incentive for a party to attempt to create a comprehensive and preclusive ideology to enable it to enjoy exclusive control of government; this will be especially so in an underdeveloped economy and society.   The change of office from party to party in a normal democracy is an economically wasteful process, and relies on the capacity of the socio-political and economic system to re-absorb ousted political office-holders without imposing great private losses on them.   In an economically underdeveloped country, the change of office between parties is likely to impose substantial economic losses on the individuals who have to wait their turn in office, by comparison with the power and the material gains they would enjoy if they controlled the government permanently.   The acceptance of normal democracy depends on acceptance of the rules of the game; but the acceptance rests not only on a democratic tradition but also on an economic and socio-political system that does not impose severe economic losses on political losers.

Nationalistic feeling provides a foundation for the establishment of a preclusive ideology as a prerequisite for one-party government; and there is an evident connection between the stridency of nationalism in the new nations and their propensity to establish one-party government.   Even where the two-party system is maintained, the competition in ideology would tend to make both parties stress nationalism and nationalistic policies if there were widespread nationalistic sentiment among the electorate. Only if there were a sharp division of voter preferences, some voters envisaging advantages in nationalistic policies and others envisaging serious disadvantages, would there be significant political division on the issue; and in this case the political stability of the country would be seriously threatened.

Finally, one of Downs' important conclusions is that the working of political democracy will display an asymmetry with respect to economic issues. This asymmetry arises from the concentration of producer interests and the dispersion of consumer interests, which makes it easy to organize lobbies for producer interests and difficult to organize them for consumer interests. The relevance of this asymmetry for nationalism is that nationalist policies tend to concentrate on specific producer interests, whereas their costs are dispersed thinly over the mass of consumers, so that it is not too difficult for nationalist policies to win political support on the basis of the producer gains they promise, even though the net benefits, taking consumers and producers together, are negative.

*   *   *

III

As an ideology or state of political feeling, nationalism can be conceived of, along the lines of the Becker analysis of discrimination against Negroes, as attaching utility or value to having certain jobs held or certain property owned by members of the national group rather than by non-members of the national group. . . . In this context, it is most useful to employ a broad definition of property ownership, one including in property not merely the ownership of physical or financial assets but also rights to certain kinds of jobs, since job opportunities are property in the sense of yielding a stream of income to the holder. Nationalism can accordingly be conceived of as a state of social psychology or political sentiment that attaches value to having property in this broad sense owned by members of the national group.

The question that immediately arises is, To what kinds of property does this utility of nationality become attached? Clearly, in some sense it is the "important" or prestigious or socially relevant kinds of property that acquire this added value. One such, obviously, is the result of cultural and artistic activities—the national literature, music, and drama. Another is positions of authority in the governmental apparatus and in the social structure. Still another comprises particular types of economic activity and economic roles that carry superior status (and usually superior income also).

A related question is, What determines which specific items of property acquire added value from nationalism? There seem to be two major ways in which nationalistic utility can be acquired. One is internal, through observation within the country of foreign operations there; the property yielding income and status to the foreigner becomes the property valued by the nationalists. This mechanism of generating nationalistic utility is particularly important in ex-colonial countries or countries where foreign investment and alleged "economic imperialism" have been significant, where nationalism seeks particularly to replace the officialdom of the colonial power and the executives and shareholders of the foreign enterprises with nationals. The other mechanism is external, through contact with and observation of other nations, which provides knowledge of what forms of property are highly regarded in such societies.

Both of these mechanisms involve the determination of the nationalistic values of specific forms of property by imitation or emulation of other countries, either of their actual practices or of the "image" of themselves they project abroad. . . .

IV

The next step in the analysis is to recognize that the benefits from the gratification of nationalist sentiment are of two sorts, particular and general, or tangible and intangible. The particular benefits are the incomes and prestige that accrue to those nationals who acquire the property rights or the offices and employment opportunities in which nationalism invests. The general benefits consist of the psychic satisfaction derived by the community at large from gratification of the taste for nationalism. It is important to notice here the concentration of the tangible benefits on the subgroup of nationals that is eligible to hold the property or to fill the positions, as distinguished from the dispersion of the intangible benefits, which presumably accrue to the whole national society in so far as its members share the taste for nationalism. It is the intangible benefits that give national ownership of property the character of a collective consumption good—one for which consumption by one individual does not preclude consumption by another—and for the economist raises the difficult problem of how to determine the optimal quantity to supply.

The tangible benefits are directly or indirectly economic, and are of considerable value to the individuals who may receive them; thus the bias of the democratic process toward producer interests becomes relevant. These individuals have an economic incentive to pursue these prospective benefits through the cultivation of nationalism. Further, given the mechanisms by which nationalistic utility becomes attached to specific items of property, these items will tend to be such as to yield tangible benefits primarily to the educated, the entrepreneurially qualified classes, some at least of the wealthy, and other elite groups, so that there is an inherent class slant to the economic interest in pursuing nationalism.

There is, moreover, a natural consilience of the strictly economic interests in nationalism and the cultural interests in nationalism. Both the intellectuals engaged in cultural activities and the owners and managers of communications media have an interest in nationalism, particularly when it can be combined with a linguistic difference, but even when it cannot, because nationalism creates a monopolistic barrier to competition from other countries' purveyors of the same sorts of cultural products. Thus cultural nationalism complements economic nationalism, both involving tangible benefits in the form of protection of the market for the services of individuals. This consideration suggests also that the strength of economic and cultural interests in nationalism will vary with the threat of competition and the need for protection of the market. One would expect to find nationalist sentiment strongest where the individuals concerned are most vulnerable to competition from foreign culture or from foreign economic activities; conversely, one would expect to find that the nations that are leading culturally and economically will tend to be internationalist and cosmopolitan in outlook, because this would tend to extend the market area for their cultural and economic products. These expectations accord broadly with experience.

V

We now turn from nationalism as a political ideology to nationalism as an economic program. As such, nationalism seeks to extend the property owned by nationals so as to gratify the taste for nationalism. . . .

One obvious method is confiscation, that is, the forced transfer of property from foreign owners to nationals. Here it is important to notice a certain ambiguity in the concept of confiscation, extremely useful to nationalists, which arises because what appears to be confiscation may not really be confiscation in the fundamental economic sense of the term. For example, nationalizing the civil service, or nationalizing the administrative and executive jobs in a particular enterprise, may appear to transfer property of value from the foreigners to the nationals. But in so far as the foreigners were receiving a fair price for their skilled qualifications, and nationalization involves replacing them with nationals of inferior skills at the same salaries, the effect is primarily to transfer income within the national group, toward the individuals favored with promotion at the expense of the general community which must bear the costs of poorer administration, inferior economic efficiency, or deterioration of the quality of the service that results.

The result of nationalizing jobs is not, of course, necessarily merely a transfer of income among nationals. If previously there has been genuine discrimination against nationals, for example, where the civil servants have been of a foreign nationality even though their jobs could be performed as efficiently or more efficiently by nationals available at lower salaries, there will be a genuine transfer of income from foreigners to nationals, since discrimination against nationals in employment gives foreigners a source of monopoly gain at the expense of nationals. It is always difficult to determine, however, whether the employment of non-nationals represents discrimination against nationals or reflects their inferior quality; under competitive conditions there is a presumption in favor of the latter assumption. . . . Genuine confiscation, which transfers valuable property from foreigners to nationals, is therefore largely confined to property in the narrow sense, that is, to the tangible wealth—cash, securities, real property, and enterprises—owned in the country by foreigners.

The alternative to confiscation is investment of resources or purchase, that is, the use of wealth or savings that otherwise would be available for other purposes to purchase material property or job opportunities for nationals. This may be effected directly through public investment, or indirectly through various policies influencing private investment. The public investment method includes both the nationalization of existing foreign enterprises with fair compensation and the use of development funds or public revenue to create new enterprises. The method of influencing private investment involves using tariffs and related policies to stimulate industries of the kind desired; these policies also entail public investment, in the sense that the use of the tariff, for example, involves imposing a tax on the consumer in the form of higher prices, the revenue from which goes to subsidize the creation of the protected enterprises by the private entrepreneurs who then receive the higher prices.

VI

It must be recognized, of course, that nationalism is not the only reason why a government may choose to adopt any of these policies. There are many economic arguments as to why such policies might be beneficial in terms of increasing the national income, rather than serving purely to gratify the taste for nationalism. . . . These arguments are frequently effective in attracting support for nationalistic policies from non-nationalists, and especially socialists, who are inclined to believe implicitly that competition is inherently inefficient and susceptible of improvement by governmental action. The real question, however, is whether the facts of the situation conform to the possibilities of theoretical reasoning. Typically, little or no effort is devoted to confirming that this is so, the theoretical possibilities being employed instead to provide a plausible and apparently scientific defense of policies that are adopted for essentially nationalistic reasons.

With respect to the method of nationalization, it is necessary to realize that, provided compensation is fair, there is no transfer of wealth from foreigners to nationals, and no net gain in national wealth, because fair compensation involves paying the previous owner the present value of the future income he would have earned from the enterprise. The only exception occurs when nationalization permits efficiency-increasing changes in production methods that the previous owner would not have introduced. The gain (or loss) from nationalization does not result from the mere fact of nationalization; instead, gains or losses are the result of changes in management methods and policies introduced after nationalization. In so far as the objective of nationalization is to provide jobs for nationals, presumably people are employed in larger numbers or are of a lower quality than previously were employed, and this obviously involves economic waste. Alternatively stated, potential national output is sacrificed in return for the psychic income obtained from greater employment of nationals. The same is true of public investment in the creation of new industries when such investment is influenced by the desire to provide high-income and high-status jobs for nationals.

The desire to provide more, and more worthy, jobs for nationals will influence the selection of industries for nationalization in certain ways, and this may incidentally provide a means of distinguishing nationalistic from socialistic nationalization. "Nationalistic" nationalization, aside from the obvious tendency to concentrate on industries employing a high proportion of foreigners, will tend to be aimed at industries with a well-established and fairly static technology, that can be managed by bureaucratic routine, and at industries that enjoy a monopolistic position in the domestic market rather than competing actively in the domestic or especially the foreign market, since these characteristics will permit the employment of larger total numbers, and the substitution of lower-quality nationals for higher-quality foreigners, without risking the breakdown and bankruptcy of the industry. In any case, public ownership of industry, whether achieved by nationalization or new investment, permits losses incurred in consequence of the pursuit of nationalistic policies to be underwritten, within limits, by the taxing and borrowing powers of the government.

The alternative to investment or purchase of industry is the use of tariffs, tax concessions, and special privileges to promote the establishment of the kinds of industries that are desired. This method involves a much more clearcut possibility of economic loss, through higher costs of production paid for by consumers in the form either of higher prices or of lost tax revenue that has to be made up either by other taxes or by reduced governmental services, and an overt transfer from the general consumer, who pays the higher prices or taxes or loses governmental services, to the favored producers who are given a protected position in the market. The use of the tariff or of tax concessions to induce the local establishment of particularly desired industries, however, frequently has the paradoxical result of increasing nationalist dissatisfaction rather than contributing to satisfaction, by inducing the foreign producer of a product previously imported to establish domestic production facilities in the country, with the result that the country exchanges the dissatisfaction of not having the industry in the country for the dissatisfaction of having its industry owned and staffed by foreign enterprises.[4]

VII

The major implications of the theory of nationalist economic policy presented in this article may now be briefly summarized.

One implication is that nationalism will tend to direct economic development policy along certain specific lines; these lines might represent economic optimality, and would do so if the conditions posited by some familiar economic arguments were present. Failing empirical validation of those arguments, however, the consequence will be a reduction of material production below the economy's potential.

In the first place, nationalist economic policy will tend to foster activities selected for their symbolic value in terms of concepts of "national identity" and the economic content of nationhood; in particular, emphasis will be placed on manufacturing, and, within manufacturing, on certain industries possessing special value symbolic of industrial competence (such as the steel and automotive industries). Secondly, nationalist economic policy will foster activities offering prestigious jobs for the middle class and/or the educated class; the nature of such activities varies with the stage of development, very underdeveloped countries favoring bureaucratic jobs offering steady incomes for routine work, more advanced countries favoring managerial and professional jobs suitable for the products of the educational system, fairly mature countries favoring jobs in higher education and research.[5] Thirdly, nationalism will tend to favor both extensive state control over and extensive public ownership of economic enterprises: state control provides employment for the educated directly, in the central control system, while both the control system and public ownership give the government social control over the allocation of jobs to nationals.

A second implication is that nationalism will tend to direct economic policy toward the production of psychic income in the form of nationalistic satisfaction, at the expense of material income. If attention is confined to material income alone, a third implication is that nationalism will tend to redistribute material income from the lower class toward the

---

[4] This consequence of the tariff has been an important factor in the exacerbation of nationalist sentiment in Canada in recent years. The formation of the European Economic Community similarly has fostered American investment within the Community's boundaries and thereby provoked nationalist complaints.

[5] The emphasis on education in contemporary development tends to produce a rat-race in which a country first invests a great deal of scarce capital in educating people, and then is obliged to invest a great deal more in providing suitable employment opportunities for them, the consequence being a double waste of resources. Sometimes needs both for more education and for better jobs for the educated are urged simultaneously, despite the implicit economic contradiction.

middle class, and particularly toward the educated middle class; in this respect, nationalism reinforces the trend of modern society toward the establishment of a class structure based on educational attainment.[6]

This last implication relates to material income only, and does not necessarily imply that the lower classes are worse off because of nationalism when both real and psychic income are reckoned into the account. It is quite possible that the psychic enjoyment that the mass of the population derives from the collective consumption aspects of nationalism suffices to compensate them for the loss of material income imposed on them by nationalistic economic policies, so that nationalistic policies arrive at a quite acceptable result from the standpoint of maximizing satisfaction. It may even be that nationalistic policies are the cheapest and most effective way to raise real income in less developed countries; in some cases, one suspects, the prospects for genuine economic growth are so bleak that nationalism is the only possible means available for raising real income.[7]

It would seem, however, from the economic analysis of government presented earlier, that the lower classes are unlikely to be net gainers from economic nationalism, due to the effects of ignorance and the costs of acquiring information in concentrating political power in the hands of pressure groups, and the general tendency for producer interests to dominate over consumer interests that results from the natural response of voters to the high cost and negligible value of acquiring political information. The tendency for the mass of the population to suffer losses from economic nationalism is probably reinforced in the new nations by the prevalence of systems of one-party government, in which the party is based largely on urban support and frequently exercises a virtual monopoly over the country's communications system.[8]

Even though nationalism may involve a substantial redistribution of real income toward the middle class at the expense of the mass of the popula-

[6] It is one of the paradoxes of modern social philosophy that redistribution of income from the intellectually poor to the intellectually rich is regarded as desirable and proper whereas redistribution from the materially poor to the materially rich is regarded as utterly inequitable.

[7] Field research by members of the Committee for the Comparative Study of New Nations suggests that this may in fact be the case in some of the new African nations. Nationalism may itself create such a situation, nationalistic economic policies blocking economic growth so effectively that it becomes necessary to resort to ever more extreme nationalistic sentiment and policy to maintain the illusion of economic development.

[8] Both dependence on urban support and control over communications media are logical consequences of the economic theory of government as applied to such countries. Dependence on urban support in turn reinforces the bias of development policy toward promotion of manufacturing, and in general fosters policies favoring the city-dweller at the expense of the agricultural population. A particular aspect of this, important especially in Latin America, is the maintenance of low urban transport rates by direct or indirect subsidization, which in its turn fosters urban population growth and increases the political importance of urban residents.

tion, this redistribution may perform a necessary function in the early stages of forming a nation, in the sense that the existence of a substantial middle class may be a prerequisite of a stable society and democratic government. In other words, an investment in the creation of a middle class, financed by resources extracted from the mass of the population by nationalistic policies, may be the essential preliminary to the construction of a viable national state. . . .

Walker Connor

SELF-DETERMINATION:
THE NEW PHASE

Can two or more self-differentiating culture-groups coexist within a single political structure? The question may well seem clearly settled by the overwhelming factual evidence of contemporary international politics, for it is indeed a truism that political and ethnic borders seldom coincide. Thus, the very existence of a host of multinational states . . . would appear to document an affirmative answer. On the other hand, a recent spate of political unrest within such geographically diverse and historically unrelated states as . . . Canada, Guyana, India, Uganda, Belgium, the Sudan, Burma, Yugoslavia, Cyprus, Rwanda, the United Kingdom, and Iraq, focuses attention on the common root cause of intrastate yet international conflict and again brings into question the assumptions of the multinational state.

These assumptions were never seriously challenged until the rise of *popular* national consciousness, and the issue is therefore of relatively recent origin. . . .

What lent political force to the growth of national consciousness was the ancillary doctrine that political self-expression was a necessary concomitant of cultural consciousness, a doctrine that seriously challenged, perhaps even totally denied, the legitimacy of the multistate structure. . . . The doctrine . . . became both a catalyst and a defense for independence movements throughout the world and was instrumental in the post–World War II recession of European power from Africa and Asia.

There was, however, a unique feature to the African and Asian independence movements. Although they had been conducted in the name

Reprinted by permission of the author and the editors of *World Politics* from *World Politics*, 20 (October 1967), 30–53.

of self-determination of nations, they were, in fact, demands for political independence not in accord with ethnic distributions, but along the essentially happenstance borders that delimited either the sovereignty or the administrative zones of the former colonial powers. This fact combined with the incredibly complex ethnic map of Africa and Asia to create, in the name of self-determination of nations, a host of multinational states. Now in turn, these new political structures, along with some of the older European states, are the targets of growing demands that self-determination be carried a further step toward its natural conclusion. And the leaders of these new states, though recent espousers of national self-determination, are now perforce the defenders of multinationalism.

*   *   *

Aside from the more philosophic question of what ought to be the incidence of identity between nations and sovereign political entities, there remain two questions, . . . both of which can be subjected to empirical investigation. The first involves the potentiality of the multination state to survive as an effective political form. Is it essentially an anachronism, albeit a tenacious one, whose death knell sounded with the first indications of popular national consciousness? The second question involves the relationship between the nation-state, on the one hand, and democratic principles and institutions on the other. Is it the single-nation state or the multination state that manifests the greater adherence to democracy? Political developments since World War II may well indicate the appropriate answers to these questions. . . . [T]he post–World War II experiences of multination states follow a remarkably uniform pattern . . . The pattern is particularly evident in relation to the question involving the potential for survival of the multination state.

*   *   *

Consider Asia: Reports persist that the Chinese Communist government is turning the Turkic peoples of Sinkiang Province into a minority by promoting an intensive migration of Chinese into the province in order to ensure the region's allegiance to Peking. Moreover, earlier Tibetan resistance to Chinese rule has led to the continuous military occupation of that region since 1959. On Taiwan there are rumblings of dissatisfaction on the part of the indigenous population, who tend to look upon the ruling group of mainland expatriates as aliens. Despite Indonesia's recent preoccupation with the question of internal communism, it should not be forgotten that regionalism underlay the rebellion waged between 1958 and 1961 and that common awareness of cultural distinctions remains a source of resistance to rule from Djakarta. In the case of Vietnam, the intra-Vietnamese (Annamese) struggles have tended to obscure an active "self-determination" movement on the part of tribal hill peoples who populate more than half of the country's territory. Popularly but mistakenly grouped under the single designation "Montagnards," they have made evident, by a number of open revolts against Vietnamese rule and by the creation of a liberation front, that the internal political problems of Vietnam would not terminate even with the highly unlikely creation of a government acceptable to all the ethnic Vietnamese. In Laos, the confused and many-sided civil war has in no small part been due to the absence of transcultural identification with the Laotian state on the part of the diverse population. In Thailand, the effectiveness of Bangkok's writ diminishes rapidly when one leaves the culturally compatible Chao Phraya Valley for the Lao-speaking northeast, for the Karen-populated hills of the west, or for the Malay- and Chinese-populated regions of the Malay Peninsula. In neighboring Malaysia, cohesion suffers from the antagonisms between the Malays and a strong Chinese minority, antagonisms that have already led to the expulsion of Singapore from the Federation. In the case of Burma, it has been estimated that Rangoon controls only half of its territory; the remaining territory is populated by dissident, non-Burmese groups such as Shans, Kachins, Karens, Chins, and Mons. Within East Pakistan, the inhabitants have long voiced strong dissatisfaction with their political ties to the peoples of West Pakistan from whom they are differentiable on practically every basis other than religion.[1] In Ceylon, state unity has been frustrated by the intense rivalry between Sinhalese and Tamils which has periodically manifested itself in riots. Indian history has been even more often marred by eruptions of violence caused by the dissatisfaction of linguistic and cultural groups, and major governmental concessions concerning the delineating of provincial borders and the recognition of official languages have been the price of a return to order. . . . Iraq is riven by the Kurdish movement for self-determination, a problem that cannot be dissociated from the continuation of Kurdish territory into neighboring Iran and Turkey. Perhaps the most publicized failure of multinationalism since World War II involves an Asian and a non-Asian people on Cyprus; the only noteworthy interlude to the communal warfare there between Greek and Turk coincided with the ill-fated attempt at transnational government in the period 1960–1963.

Sub-Sahara Africa's short history of broad-scale independence has also provided a number of challenges to the concept of the multiculture state. Indeed, there is very little evidence of the existence of supratribal allegiance to the new political entities that have been created south of the Sahara, and much contrary evidence, such as the entire anarchic history of the Congo. . . . Nor has the presence of "Europeans" been a necessary prerequisite for racial tensions. Thus, the now rather lengthy insurrection waged by the Negro peoples of southern Sudan against the politically dominant Arabs of the northern sector, the overthrow and expulsion of the ruling Arab minority on Zanzibar in early 1964, the almost total

---

[1] East Pakistan, with the assistance of Indian armed forces, became the independent state of Bangladesh in 1972. [Eds.]

elimination within Rwanda of the formerly dominant Watusi by the Bahutu between 1959 and 1963, sporadic genocidal conflicts between the same two peoples for political control of neighboring Burundi, the revolt during 1966 of the important Buganda tribe against the centralization of rule in Uganda, the Somali irredentist movements in Ethiopia and northeastern Kenya, and the general resentment of East Coast Negroes toward settlers of Asian ancestry are all cases in which consciousness of race (in the minimal sense of readily visible distinctions) has proved antithetical to the concept of the multination state. Although less apparent a source of intrastate dissension than either tribalism or race, a third cultural division that seriously affects a number of states is that between the coastal and riverine people, who were most influenced by European ways and institutions during the period of colonialism, and the more isolated people of the interior. This bifurcation helps to explain, for example, the demise of the Mali Federation brought about by the withdrawal of Senegal in 1960, as well as the animosity between the Hausas and Ibos which threatens the survival of Nigeria. Yet a fourth division of Africa, which cuts across state lines and which appears to be growing in political significance, is that between Islamic and non-Islamic cultures. This distinction is perhaps the most important factor in an Eritrean movement for independence from Christian Ethiopia, and it is also a contributing element in Somali irredentism within Ethiopia and Kenya, in attitudes toward political independence within French Somaliland, and in the internal strife of both Nigeria and the Sudan.

The most warranted conclusion to be drawn from a review of recent developments throughout Africa and Asia would therefore appear to be that the concept of self-determination has proved more powerful than could be appreciated from the vantage point of the 1940's. If the evidence were limited to these two continents, a demurrer could be made on the ground that analysis had been limited to societies in which political institutions are in an inchoate and therefore ephemeral and inconclusive stage; it could be contended that analysis of long-range trends should logically give greater weight to the time-tested, modern states of Europe and of regions politically dominated by people of European background. However, the recent history of multinationalism in such cases does not differ appreciably from the Afro-Asian experience. . . .

Events have already furnished conclusive answers to the fate of . . . the Austro-Hungarian and the British empires. . . .

But what of those "Western" multinational states that are still in existence? . . . Alfred Cobban took exception to [Ernest] Barker's assertion that history indicated that democratic, multinational states could not survive. His empirical case on this point rested essentially upon the examples of Great Britain, South Africa, Canada, Belgium, and Switzerland.

The inclusion of Britain as an example of multinationalism is puzzling;

although Barker also acknowledged Britain to be an exception to his rule, it is an exception that cannot go unchallenged. Both Barker and Cobban had the transnationalism of the Scotch and Welsh in mind, but the view of most authorities holds that the self-identification of these people with London is the product of assimilation rather than of the continuing co-existence of prospering cultures. Indeed, authorities have customarily emphasized the remarkable homogeneity of Britain's major island.[2] More-over, when this homogeneity was challenged by the postwar influx of im-migrants from the West Indies and southern Asia, the result was racial friction and the passage of restrictive immigration legislation, antithetical to the concept of multinationalism. And in Northern Ireland, the attempts by the Catholic minority to express through the electoral process their long-standing discontent with political rule by a religiously and culturally distinct people, as well as the attempts of the moderate government to move toward equalization of opportunity for the minority, resulted in a series of violent reactions. . . .

As to the example of South Africa, it is assumed that this state would not have been included by Cobban could the subsequent governmental adherence to the policy of apartheid been prophesied. If, on the other hand, Cobban was referring solely to the relations between the two white minorities—Briton and Boer—it must be noted that fundamental differ-ences of attitude persist, even though currently suffused by the overriding issue of black-white relations. . . .

The examples of Canada and Belgium are more instructive because of the elongated period during which two distinct cultures have survived within their borders on an apparently harmonious basis. Thus, Cobban wrote that French and British Canadians "have achieved a common politi-cal nationality without abandoning their characteristic cultural differ-ences."[3] Tracing the unity of Canada back almost two hundred years to the French and Indian Wars, he credits its success to the wisdom of the British peace terms under which demands for compulsory anglicization were eschewed in favor of guarantees of cultural autonomy to the French community. Similarly, with regard to Belgium, Mill, although the propo-nent of the nation-state, acknowledged more than a century ago the existence of a common national consciousness shared by the Flemish and Walloons; and Cobban, as late as 1944, could detect "no reason at all"

---

[2] The degree of assimilation is evidenced by the fact that only a minority of Welshmen and an insignificant number of Scotsmen are able to converse in their original languages, and all but a handful of these are fluent also in English. In both regions there have been recent nationalist movements whose goals range from minor alterations in administrative forms and school curricula to total independence. How-ever, these movements are not considered to pose a serious challenge to "British nationalism," and, in any event, are a manifestation more of a resurgence of nation-alist particularism than of cooperative multinationalism.

[3] *National Self-Determination,* Chicago, 1949, p. 60.

for believing that cultural consciousness would lead to the disintegration of the state.[4] The contrast between these observations and recent events is striking. Contemporary relations between the two Belgian groups have been characterized more by street violence and demands for strict separation than by harmony. The breadth and fervor of the "Flanders for the Flemish" movement have been illustrated by broadly supported demands that French-speaking faculty members and students of Louvain University be forced to leave Flanders for Wallonia and by Flemish insistence on legislation that would preclude desirous Flemish parents from "denationalizing" their offspring by sending them to French schools. Canada, meanwhile, has been troubled by (1) separatist movements, (2) the insistence of the culturally French province of Quebec for increased independence of the central government and a greater share of governmental revenues, (3) demands for a balancing of opportunities between French and non-French people, (4) resistance to a governmental requirement that civil servants be bilingual, and (5) even by a question of the degree to which the traditional flag (since replaced) did and should symbolize the hegemony of "Anglo" culture.

Cobban's final example, Switzerland, is the most commonly employed illustration of a multinational "going concern." Here again, mid-nineteenth- and mid-twentieth-century assessments are in accord, for Mill perceived a powerful sentiment of Swiss nationality which "went beyond different races, different languages, and different religions". . . It is tempting to pass over Switzerland as a rule-proving exception attributable to the peculiarities of its size, location, topography, and special historical circumstances. And, admittedly, Swiss unity does not appear as seriously challenged by cultural cleavage as does that of Canada and Belgium. . . . It should be remembered that, as a result of Swiss neutrality, allegiance to Switzerland has not been severely tested against ethnic ties to Germany, France, or Italy. . . . [T]here is reason to speculate upon the degree of adherence that the central government could have expected had it elected to enter the Franco-Prussian War or either of the World Wars. . . . Vastly more significant, however, is the evidence that Switzerland has not been immune to the growing intrastate tensions . . . In Berne, the only canton with a substantial French-speaking minority . . . there has been an active secessionist movement in recent years, despite the fact that the boundaries of this canton were fixed more than 150 years ago.

In addition to the foregoing states, Cobban also referred to the Soviet Union as an example of successful multinationalism. . . . Cobban felt the inclusion justified because the Soviet Union was, in his opinion, at least more democratic and yet more cohesive than had been the tsarist regimes. No matter where one places the Soviet Union on the democratic-authoritarian spectrum, however, it cannot be accepted as an exemplar of

[4] *Ibid.*, p. 144.

cultural cooperation. Authorities may disagree on the level of assimilation that has been attained within the Soviet Union, but it is generally held
that the Soviet government has steadfastly followed a policy of russification. . . .

The elusiveness of a solution is illustrated by contrasting the experiences
of two other nondemocratic European states, Yugoslavia and Spain. Following the Soviet example, the Yugoslavian government has paid at least
limited homage to the concept of cultural autonomy. Thus, the ostensible
form of government is a federation of six ethnically delineated republics
and two autonomous areas, and the use of diverse languages and alphabets
is permitted. However, Yugoslavia has not been as successful as the Soviet
Union in preventing the public airing of intercultural enmity. The prevalence of ethnic tensions became a major issue in the mid-1966 purge
of Vice-President Rankovic and his followers. This group was accused of
"Great Serbian chauvinism," thereby intensifying the hostility that Croa-
tians, Slovenes, Albanians, . . . Macedonians, and the other minority
peoples felt toward the dominant Serbs. Even a year prior to these disclosures, the government had been forced to suppress a Crotian Liberation
Movement . . . It is evident, then, that the Yugoslav policy of granting
limited autonomy to culture groups has not furthered the cause of unity.

Franco's response to cultural division was enforced homogeneity. Although the Catalan and Basque minorities had enjoyed a short period of
linguistic autonomy under the Spanish Republic, Franco ordered that only
the Spanish language could be taught in the schools and used by the communications media. However, despite three decades of implementation,
the policy continued to meet strong resistance and the government has
recently retreated from its earlier position and become more permissive
toward the use of minority tongues. Thus, the Spanish attempt at forceful
eradication of minority cultures failed.

Additional evidence of European failure to accommodate multinationalism within a single state might include the often-expressed dissatisfaction
of the German-speaking people of the Italian Tyrol, the strained relations
between Rumanians and the Magyars of Rumanian Transylvania, and the
reappearance of the "Macedonian question," which involves minorities
within . . . Bulgaria, Greece, and Yugoslavia. . . .

The principal reason for the wide gap between anticipation and realization in matters involving self-determination is the universal tendency of
governments to render decisions upon the implicit assumption of the need
to preserve the entire political unit. As against a claim of the right of
self-determination, the government proclaims the right to stamp out rebellion and the duty to prevent secession. What is a self-evident truth to
those desiring independence is treason to those in custody of the government. This polarization in the attitudes of the "ins" and the "outs" toward self-determination is most evident in the about-face of those former

proponents of self-determination who led successful independence movements. . . . The African and Asian leaders who once castigated European domination as violative of the right of self-determination are not now prepared to recognize such a right on the part of their own minorities.

A survey of multinational states does not indicate that any particular form of government has solved this dichotomy between the need for unity and the fissiparous impact of ethnic consciousness. . . .

The prevalence of ethnic dissonance within so many authoritarian systems must be considered significant because authoritarianism does enjoy real advantages in combating nationalist movements. Among the more formidable weapons at the disposal of such governments are a clandestine reporting apparatus and the ability to intern leaders for long periods without bringing formal charges. Control of communications is also important, for, if effective, it permits the government to cut the leadership off from possible domestic and foreign support. Such a government, if it acknowledges at all the presence of a self-determination movement, will typically describe it as the activity of a few provocateurs or malcontents. In such cases, evaluation of the actual situation is difficult, perhaps impossible. . . . How strong, for example, is the Kashmiri desire for independence? How strong the movement within India for a Dravidistan? Tamilstan? Sikhistan? . . . In each of these instances, and the list could be greatly expanded, it is known that an ethnic movement does, in fact, exist, but lack of information prevents a valid assessment of its strength. However, it is safe to conclude that the political consciousness of various ethnic groups is even much more prevalent than we can document.

This trend obviously conflicts with the widely held opinion that nationalism has proved too parochial for the modern age and that its zenith is now well passed. This position has been lent credence by the postwar proliferation of multistate organizations, which ranged, in their original aims, from limited military or economic cooperation to complete unification. However, although the goals of a transstate organization may be contrary to national aspirations, they need not be so. One factor will be the degree of integration that is anticipated. There is nothing in military or economic cooperation that is inconsistent with extreme national consciousness, when the results of such cooperation are viewed as beneficial to the national interest. But the nearer one moves toward the erection of a multinationa¹ state, the sharper becomes the conflict between the organization and nationalism. For example, De Gaulle's nationalism does not blind him to the economic advantages that might flow to the French from regional economic cooperation under the EEC, but it explains his resistance to any proposed transfer of the decision-making power away from the individual states. Similarly, he supports limited military cooperation, but refuses to accept a position of national dependence concerning any aspect of military strategy. In short, there is nothing intrinsically incompatible between the growth of national consciousness and organizations of such limited goals as the European or Latin American Free Trade Associations. Significant, however, is the fact that in the case of those organizations whose goals have most clearly conflicted with nationalism, it is the organization that has been forced into retreat. . . . Similarly, the amazingly short-lived "Sino-Soviet bloc" foundered on the incompatibility of Chinese and Soviet national aspirations. Subsequent attempts by the Soviet Union to perpetuate the monolithic nature of the geographically more limited Eastern European multinational structure (including the Council for Mutual Economic Assistance and the Warsaw Pact) have experienced a series of major setbacks due to the rising nationalism of the Poles, Rumanians, Czechs, Bulgars, and other East European peoples. In interstate relations, as within the typical multinational state, the centrifugal forces of national aspirations are proving more powerful than the centripetal forces of transnationalism.

There is, moreover, considerable reason to expect a further proliferation of self-determination movements. For most people, ethnic consciousness still lies in the future. National consciousness presupposes an awareness of other culture-groups, but, to a majority of the world's population, the meaningful world still ends with the village. If the past and present are instructive, it can be expected that cultural and political consciousness will spread with increased communications and that the ethnic hodgepodges that are Asia and Africa will produce a host of new demands for the redrawing of political borders.

Should such demands for self-determination be met? The question can be viewed within two quite distinct contexts—the one, moral; the other, practical. If the question means whether each nationality, simply because it is a self-distinguishing culture-group, has a right to self-rule, then the question defies a provable conclusion. Axioms, such as "the right of self-determination," appear as moral imperatives until countered with opposing maxims. . . . A "principle" of self-determination can be countered by other "principles," such as the right of states to preserve themselves, to protect their territorial integrity, to maintain internal order, to legislate against treasonable acts, and so forth. If, on the other hand, the question is intended to ask whether it is reasonable or even possible to grant statehood to each nation, it is doubtful that even those who are most sympathetic to the principle of self-determination would answer in the affirmative. Mill and Barker, for example, were both prepared to acknowledge the impracticality of self-determination in the case of two or more groups who were so geographically intermingled as to preclude a clear-cut geographic separation. Another possible objection to self-determination is that the people in question are not prepared for self-rule. Other critics have raised the issue of minimum standards, maintaining that self-determination should be denied when the group is too small, or the territory too limited, or the possibility of maintaining a viable economy too remote.

The interesting point is that such practical considerations have seldom had much influence upon ethnic aspirations. Even the absence of a clear geographic base has not necessarily prevented self-determination movements from arising. In the case of the Greeks and Turks on Cyprus and that of the Hindus and Moslems in British India, there was a high degree of geographic suffusion of the two cultures, but this intermingling did not prevent intergroup violence in the first instance and actual partition in the second. So, too, the proposition that lack of readiness for self-rule is a legitimate bar to immediate independence . . . has been increasingly depicted as predicated upon bias and, consequently, is decreasingly heard in public debates concerning independence. With regard to criteria of size, it is again instructive to turn to Cobban in order to illustrate how self-determination has altered international affairs over the past two decades. In the course of emphasizing the impracticality of granting independence to each small nation, Cobban raised, as a *reductio ad absurdum,* the specter of granting independence to Malta and Iceland. The fact that these areas have been granted statehood and that they have been joined in this successful endeavor by such other tiny entities as Gambia, the Maldive Islands, Barbados, Trinidad-Tobago, and Western Samoa again illustrates that practical considerations are not apt to prove a match for the emotional power of self-determination in those cases in which the sentiments of the national group are decisive.

But are the sentiments of a national group apt to prove decisive? The last stages of the colonial era have produced a number of instances in which a realistic Britain and France took the initiative in ceding independence to overseas territories. Nevertheless, as Rupert Emerson has noted, history clearly establishes that governments are not apt to grant self-determination, and that cases in which it has been granted are rare indeed. But history also clearly indicates that the refusal to grant self-determination hardly eradicates the problem. The peacemakers of 1920 may have thought that they could dictate the proper limits of self-determination in Eastern Europe, stopping short of balkanization, but ferment for a furtherance of the self-determination principle plagues the area a half-century later. The appeal and the power of self-determination are quite independent of considerations of what a government ought to do or what it is apt to do. It is granted that the governments of multination states will continue to resist their minorities' requests for independence, but, in such cases, it is also expected that the states' existence will be increasingly challenged by secessionist-minded groups.

A quite natural response to this challenge is assimilation. If the coexistence of differing cultures appears incompatible with continued unity and yet partition is deemed unthinkable, policies to further homogeneity would seem to be in prospect. Moreover, this negative, albeit compelling, reason for instituting a policy of assimilation may be joined by positive considerations, in that marked heterogeneity represents an impediment to the statewide social and economic integration demanded by the modern state. This is particularly evident when linguistic differences are present. Certainly the Soviet Union must find a multiplicity of languages an efficiency-sapping nuisance, requiring countless oral and written translations of orders, blueprints, directions for the use of machinery, and so forth. So, too, a tendency for people to identify themselves with a particular culture and territory must constitute a most serious impediment to the mobility of labor. Aside, then, from the need to combat the divisiveness that springs from ethnic factionalism, the demands of modernization also exert pressure upon the government to eradicate its multinational character.

It would be a mistake, however, to underestimate the resistance to assimilation which governments can be expected to encounter. A number of governments have discovered belatedly that the enmity of groups toward acculturation represented a more formidable adversary than had been contemplated. Thus, the Indian and Pakistani governments have both been forced to backtrack on their plans for a single, official language; and Franco, by discarding many features of his assimilation program, has confessed failure to overcome Basque and Catalan resistance. On the other hand, the example of the American "melting pot" is often employed to illustrate that the assimilation of diverse cultures can be accomplished within a relatively short time. But it is highly questionable whether the experience of the United States is germane elsewhere. . . . Ethnic problems in the United States have not been primarily characterized by minorities resisting assimilation, but rather by the unwillingness of the dominant group to permit assimilation at the tempo desired by the minorities. Dealing with a proportionately small number of people who have voluntarily left their homeland to enter an existent cultural-political structure within which acceptance of the mores and language is a *sine qua non* of success is one matter; treating the relations between two large and neighboring ethnic groups, each possessing impressive title to its respective territory, is something quite different. . . .

The obvious point is that assimilation is even more of a natural foe to self-determination than is the multination state. The growing emotional power of ethnic consciousness, which threatens the multination state, also casts serious doubt upon the probable success of assimilation programs. Nonetheless, partly in resistance to the divisiveness of growing national consciousness and partly in response to the demands of modernization, an increased emphasis upon assimilation appears in prospect. As a consequence, the multination state faces a dual threat, consisting of demands for self-determination from below and governmental programs of assimilation from above.

*   *   *

On the other question . . . whether heterogeneity promotes authoritarianism or democracy—postwar developments indicate a link between multinationalism and pressure for nondemocratic actions. This is not to say that one can predict the form of government simply by the degree of cultural homogeneity within a state. Most of the governments of the multinational states merit, on balance, characterization as authoritarian. But so, too, did the prewar governments of highly homogeneous Germany and Japan, as well as the present governments of most of the Arab states. It is evident, then, that there are many factors that combine in a varying and unpredictable mixture to determine form of government. However, the aforementioned tendency of governments to stress their political and territorial integrity has not been conducive to democratic responses to the growing problem of cultural-political consciousness.

There is a logical relationship between the *self*-determination of nations and the democratic concept that popular opinion should determine political allegiance. It is therefore ironic that while so many governments pay lip service to self-determination, the instances in which a government has permitted a democratic process to decide a question of self-determination within its own territory are rare indeed. The general position of African governments with respect to Rhodesia during 1965 and 1966 offers a striking illustration of this inconsistency. Motivated by the pragmatic desire to rid Africa of "white rule," they insisted that British cession of independence, prior to the instituting of popular government, would be a travesty of the self-determination principle. Yet, at the same time, these governments were not prepared to permit the popular will to determine the political allegiance of segments of their own territories.

The natural repugnance of governments toward democratic solutions to questions involving the political allegiance of minorities has been underlined by instances of the refusal to grant plebiscites despite prior promises. India, for example, has suffered years of international embarrassment rather than honor its promises concerning a vote for the Kashmiri. . . . It seems clear that governments believe that questions involving the political allegiance of groups residing within the sovereign territory are much too important to be left to popular opinion.

The methods by which governments have combated national movements have, in the main, been coercive. Where expedient, governments have shown little hesitancy in conducting military campaigns against such movements. Present or recent cases in point include Algeria (the Berbers), Burma, Burundi, mainland China (Tibet), the Congo, Cyprus, India (Mizos, Nagas), Indonesia, Iraq, Nigeria, Rwanda, South Vietnam (the "Montagnards"), and Uganda. Moreover, as indicated earlier, the leaders of self-determination movements have seldom been accorded the legal safeguards that would be deemed minimal to meet democratic requirements. Often their only choices have been to live in exile, . . . to be committed periodically to long terms of imprisonment without legal process. Viewing self-determination movements as threats to survival, governments have tended to react violently and to justify the cruelest of treatment accorded to implicated leaders by branding them as rebels or traitors and therefore something worse than criminals. . . . [M]ultination states have tended to become less democratic in response to the growing threat of nationalistic movements.

Political developments since World War II clearly establish that national consciousness is not on the wane as a political force, but is quite definitely in the ascendancy. Its force is currently being felt throughout sub-Sahara Africa and Asia, as ethnic consciousness demands political recognition, in place of the present political division that reflects colonial patterns. Moreover, the influence of nationalism is expected to increase greatly throughout these continents as the multitude of ethnic groups, many of whom are not yet cognizant of their identity, further acquire national awareness. The multination states of Europe and of areas settled by Europeans are also experiencing an increase in nationalistic orientations.

No multinational structure has been immune to this surge of nationalism. Authoritarian and democratic, Communist and non-Communist societies have been similarly affected. Nor does the postwar proliferation of transstate organizations and blocs repudiate the influence of nationalism; indeed, recent interstate developments further attest to the increasing tendency to think in nationalistic terms.

No government of a multination state has found the solution to the dilemma posed by the goal of state unity on the one hand and the centrifugal tendencies of growing national consciousness on the other. Motivated both by the desire to prevent partition and by the demands of modernization, such governments can be expected to resist nationalistic movements, with coercive methods if need be, while concurrently promoting assimilation.

The outcome of such programs is unpredictable, but the proven tenacity and emotional power of nationalism make this abstraction a most formidable opponent. In any event, that pernicious and perhaps unrealistic principle termed "self-determination of nations" is far from spent as a significant force in international politics.

SUGGESTED READINGS

Deutsch, Karl W., *Nationalism and Social Communication*, New York: Technology Press (Massachusetts Institute of Technology and John Wiley), 1953.

————, and Foltz, William J. (eds.), *Nation-Building*, New York: Atherton, 1963.

Doob, Leonard W., *Patriotism and Nationalism*, New Haven: Yale University Press, 1964.

Emerson, Rupert, *From Empire to Nation—The Rise to Self-Assertion of Asian and African Peoples*, Cambridge, Mass.: Harvard University Press, 1960.

Fanon, Frantz, *The Wretched of the Earth*, New York: Grove Press, 1963.

Hayes, Carlton J. H., *The Historical Evolution of Modern Nationalism*, New York: Richard Smith, 1931.

Huntington, Samuel P., *Political Order in Changing Societies*, New Haven: Yale University Press, 1968.

Kohn, Hans, *The Idea of Nationalism*, New York: Macmillan, 1961.

Minogue, K. R., *Nationalism*, New York: Basic Books, 1967.

Pye, Lucian W., and Verba, Sidney (eds.), *Political Culture and Political Development*, Princeton: Princeton University Press, 1965.

Znaniecki, Florian, *Modern Nationalities*, Urbana: University of Illinois Press, 1952.

III. IMPERIALISM AND AFTER

The word "empire" was once among the most honored terms in the vocabulary of politics. It suggested the rule of law, civility, and peace extended to many nations. Around it gathered all the historic associations of Rome: Roman peace and Roman law. The great historic fiction of the Holy Roman Empire of the Germanic Nation endured until the age of Napoleon, and Napoleon himself called his "new order" an empire. Innumerable testaments can be found to bear witness to the lasting appeal of those ancient symbols and institutions to men of more modern times.[1]

In fact, well into the nineteenth century, the traditional admiration for empire was closely associated with faith in progress. Empire implied the extension of modern, rational, scientific civilization and government to "backward" peoples, as a part of the inevitable forward movement of humanity. It is almost forgotten that Karl Marx and Friedrich Engels held such a belief. To be sure, they saw a negative side to empire; Marx acknowledged that it was "sickening . . . to human feeling" to see the misery of India subjected to foreign rule, her ancient and "idyllic" village culture disrupted, her traditional public services abandoned. Yet, Marx argued, the old culture had itself been the foundation of a stagnant and brutal despotism; the pains of British rule were only the pains of transition; a brighter world than that which she had lost awaited India in the future. Engels, for his part, seemed even more delighted with the extension of French rule in North Africa.

Toward the close of the nineteenth century, however, a wide range of European observers began to find the negative side of empire more important, the hope for progress less certain. Increasingly "empire" and "imperialism" became pejorative terms. The violent conquest of unwilling peoples, the ruthless commercial exploitation of areas like the Congo Free State, rivalries among the colonial powers themselves, all combined to associate imperialism with rapacity, tyranny, injustice, and war. Poets like Rudyard Kipling might strive to discern the atmosphere of the older *imperium* in the modern empire; they only served, even for themselves, to illustrate how great was the difference between the two:

[1] Richard Koebner, *Empire,* New York: Grosset and Dunlap, 1965.

For heathen heart that puts her trust
In reeking tube and iron shard,
All valiant dust that builds on dust,
And guarding, calls not Thee to guard,
For frantic boast, and foolish word—
Thy mercy on Thy People, Lord!

Social and political analysts, trying to explain imperialism and its attendant evils, looked for some malfunction of institutions, some pathology of life or spirit, in the imperialist nations themselves. Logically enough, such critical examination began with Liberals and Marxists, determined to discover how nations could have strayed from the path of progress that their theorists had foreseen. Typically, they found their explanations in economic institutions and the logic of industrial and financial development. Though their prescriptions varied, Liberals like Hobson and Marxists like Lenin were convinced that if the maladjustments of the economic order were corrected, the evils of imperialism, indeed imperialism itself, would pass away.

Yet as D. K. Fieldhouse points out, such explanations failed to account for many aspects of imperialism: the fact that empire did not "pay," that imperialism was deeply illogical and irrational in many respects, that the leaders of the industrial and economic order themselves were frequently its opponents.

Joseph Schumpeter sought to avoid these problems by seeing the cause of imperialism in class relations, in an "atavistic" survival of warrior ethics and the desire for objectless and limitless expansion. Thorstein Veblen, examining the politics of World War I, came to the same conclusion regarding "Imperial Germany": that her military and feudal classes had not been displaced by the industrial revolution.

Yet this thesis was found to be no more adequate than that of the Liberals and Marxists. The atavistic classes themselves were frequently the strongest opponents of imperialism; Bismarck, for example, commented that Germany had no interest in the Near East "worth the bones of a Pomeranian grenadier." In her *Origins of Totalitarianism,* Hannah Arendt has pointed out that only when the traditional upper classes of European society began to lose control of the government of states did imperialism become a general and accepted policy.

Only too rarely did analysts of imperialism give heed to the arguments of proimperialist writers. Their arguments, most often based on Darwinist theses, contended that "struggle" was the law of nations no less than of individuals, and that a nation must "expand or die." The implication of grim alternatives was strengthened by the fact that such theorists almost always saw their own nation as losing and declining in the "struggle for existence," and empire appeared as the only alternative to decay and defeat. What such arguments suggest is that nineteenth-century imperialism was founded on a massive insecurity, a fear of weakness in the face of a nature whose only law was growth or death, an effort to overcome such fears by conquering nature and, insofar as they were part of nature, by conquering men.

Such fear is not so much atavistic as it is permanent in men, part of the nature of human beings who do not control the conditions of their life or the facts of age and death. Each of the classic theories of imperialism had its element of truth. Schumpeter was right to seek a cause more permanent and deeply rooted in man than the effects of industrial economic institutions. Yet Marxists and Liberals were equally right to examine those institutions. Herbert Lüthy was right to argue that "colonialism" is inseparable from the "colonization" that was coeval with modernity and that has united the world.[2] The industrialization of the world and the technological revolution placed unheard-of power in man's hands. They also destabilized the world, making it subject to constant change, amid which to stand still was to decline; moreover, they bound each state to the destiny of others, creating an interdependent world in which national self-sufficiency and autarchy became impossible. The world of politics became too complex for most men to understand, too large and too rapidly changing for them to control. Great impersonal forces, like technology, began to shape life. Much depended on the decisions of governments and peoples far away and neither known nor understood. Retreat from such a world was attractive, and some states like America attempted it; but the passing of time made such withdrawals less and less possible. Conquest was the only guarantee against being conquered. When Woodrow Wilson proclaimed that the world must be "made safe for democracy," part of his argument rested on the proposition that America must take up the sword and make the world over in her own image if American institutions were to be safe at home.

The processes that encouraged the development of modern imperialism have not disappeared with the end of European empires. The hard core of the theory of "neocolonialism" lies in the fact that self-government seems hollow and legal sovereignty no more than a sham. Political independence does not destroy dependence born of weakness and want; in the contemporary world, in fact, even affluence and power do not allow the great powers to escape from dependence on others, and the new states lack those cushions and comforts.

Many in the new states, and others in the industrial powers who sympathize with them, find it comforting and convincing to blame their status as neo-colonies on the dynamics of capitalism, following the argument of present-day Leninists like L. Goncharov. Yet as Hugh Seton-Watson demonstrates, the imperialism and colonialism of the Soviet Union have not even taken "new" forms. The rhetoric of "socialist internationalism" does not make the invasion of Czechoslovakia any less evident a case of imperialist policy.

As Henry M. Pachter indicates, the new imperialism is more than a policy of states. Smaller powers may struggle for "independence," while great powers strive to attain "security"; the goals are much the same. Meanwhile, great international corporations and organizations that scorn dependence on national frontiers grow in response to the logic of modern technology and economics. Political structures seem unable to deal with the "imperial" forces that rule our lives, and there will be pressure to expand or combine governments until we have some sense of control over our existence. All this has happened before; the nation succeeded the city or province, and in America the federal government replaced the states as the center of power when local regimes lost the ability to govern markets and organizations that moved in a wider orbit. And it may happen again.

But human beings resent dependence on an ever-widening circle of others

[2] Herbert Lüthy, "Colonization and the Making of Mankind," *Journal of Economic History,* 21 (December 1961), pp. 483–495.

—made only slightly more tolerable by being called "interdependence"—and the insecurity of a world of constant change. That resentment spells resistance and also the possibility that states and peoples may seek to find security and dignity through the domination and humiliation of others. The words of the Nazi leader Hermann Goering have a broader appeal than his ideology: "Better a terrible end than an endless terror."

Even without the industrialism and technology of modernity, moreover, men have sought to provide themselves with the illusion of omnipotence through the subjugation of others. Knowledge of that fact is part of the oldest wisdom of humanity. When Schumpeter saw a common thread connecting the Assyrian Empire with British *raj* or Pan-Germanism, he merely carried forward the argument of Saint Augustine's *City of God*. The problem of imperialism will not be "solved" merely by changing economic institutions or by destroying old empires. Such attempts, in the past, have merely replaced old empires with new ones that have not always been preferable to those they succeeded. The ending of imperialism demands answers both more basic and more complex than any yet proposed.

Karl Marx

THE BRITISH RULE IN INDIA

* * *

There cannot . . . remain any doubt but that the misery inflicted by the British on Hindustan is of an essentially different and infinitely more intensive kind than all Hindustan had to suffer before. I do not allude to European despotism, planted upon Asiatic despotism, by the British East India Company, forming a more monstrous combination than any of the divine monsters startling us in the temple of Salsette. This is no distinctive feature of British colonial rule, but only an imitation of the Dutch, and so much so that in order to characterise the working of the British East India Company, it is sufficient to literally repeat what Sir Stanford Raffles, the *English* governor of Java, said of the old Dutch East India Company:

"The Dutch Company, actuated solely by the spirit of gain and viewing their subjects with less regard or consideration than a West India planter formerly viewed a gang [of slaves] upon his estate, because the latter had paid the purchase money of human property, which the other had not, employed all the existing machinery of despotism to squeeze from the people their utmost mite of contribution, the last dregs of their labour, and thus aggravated the evils of a capricious and semi-barbarous government, by working it with all the practiced ingenuity of politicians, and all the monopolising selfishness of traders."

All the civil wars, invasions, revolutions, conquests, famines, strangely complex, rapid and destructive as the successive action in Hindustan may appear, did not go deeper than its surface. England has broken down the entire framework of Indian society, without any symptoms of reconstitution yet appearing. This loss of his old world, with no gain of a new one, imparts a particular kind of melancholy to the present misery of the Hindu and separates Hindustan, ruled by Britain, from all its ancient traditions, and from the whole of its past history.

There have been in Asia, generally, from immemorial times, but three departments of government: that of finance, or the plunder of the interior; that of war, or the plunder of the exterior; and, finally, the department of public works. Climate and territorial conditions, especially the vast tracts of desert, extending from the Sahara, through Arabia, Persia, India and Tartary, to the most elevated Asiatic highlands, constituted artificial irrigation by canals and waterworks, the basis of Oriental agriculture. As in Egypt and India, inundations are used for fertilising the soil in Mesopotamia, Persia, etc.; advantage is taken of a high level for feeding irrigative canals. This prime necessity of an economical and com-

Written in English for the *New York Tribune,* June 25, 1853.

mon use of water, which in the Occident drove private enterprise to voluntary association, as in Flanders and Italy, necessitated in the Orient, where
civilisation was too low and the territorial extent too vast to call into life
voluntary association, the interference of the centralising power of government.   Hence an economical function devolved upon all Asiatic governments, the function of providing public works.   This artificial fertilisation
of the soil, dependent on a central government and immediately decaying
with the neglect of irrigation and drainage, explains the otherwise strange
fact that we now find whole territories barren and desert that were once
brilliantly cultivated, as Palmyra, Petra, the ruins in Yemen, and large
provinces of Egypt, Persia and Hindustan; it also explains how a single war
of devastation has been able to depopulate a country for centuries, and to
strip it of all its civilisation.

Now, the British in East India accepted from their predecessors the department of finance and of war, but they have neglected entirely that of
public works.   Hence the deterioration of an agriculture which is not capable of being conducted on the British principle of free competition, of
laissez-faire and *laissez-aller*.   But in Asiatic empires we are quite accustomed to see agriculture deteriorating under one government and reviving
again under some other government.   There the harvests correspond to
good or bad government, as they change in Europe with good or bad sea-
sons.   Thus the oppression and neglect of agriculture, bad as it is, could
not be looked upon as the final blow dealt to Indian society by the British
intruder, had it not been attended by a circumstance of quite different importance, a novelty in the annals of the whole Asiatic world.   However
changing the political aspect of India's past must appear, its social condition has remained unaltered since its remotest antiquity, until the first
decennium of the nineteenth century.   The hand-loom and the spinning
wheel, producing their regular myriads of spinners and weavers, were the
pivots of the structure of that society.   From immemorial times, Europe
received the admirable textures of Indian labour, sending in return for
them her precious metals, and furnishing thereby his material to the gold-
smith, that indispensable member of Indian society, whose love of finery is
so great that even the lowest class, those who go about nearly naked, have
commonly a pair of golden earrings and a gold ornament of some kind
hung round their necks. . . .   It was the British intruder who broke up
the Indian hand-loom and destroyed the spinning wheel.   England began
with driving the Indian cottons from the European market; it then introduced twist into Hindustan and, in the end inundated the very mother
country of cotton with cottons.   From 1818 to 1836 the export of twist
from Great Britain to India rose in the proportion of 1 to 5,200.   In 1824
the export of British muslins to India hardly amounted to 1,000,000 yards
while in 1837 it surpassed 64,000,000 of yards.   But at the same time the
population of Dacca decreased from 150,000 inhabitants to 20,000.   This
decline of Indian towns celebrated for their fabrics was by no means the

worst consequence. British steam and science uprooted, over the whole surface of Hindustan, the union between agricultural and manufacturing industry.

These two circumstances—the Hindu, on the one hand, leaving, like all Oriental peoples, to the central government the care of the great public works, the prime condition of his agriculture and commerce, dispersed, on the other hand, over the surface of the country, and agglomerated in small centres by the domestic union of agricultural and manufacturing pursuits —these two circumstances had brought about, since the remotest times, a social system of particular features—the so-called *village system,* which gave to each of these small unions their independent organisation and distinct life.

* * *

These small stereotype forms of social organism have been to the greater part dissolved, and are disappearing, not so much through the brutal interference of the British tax-gatherer and the British soldier, as to the working of English steam and English free trade. Those family communities were based on domestic industry, in that peculiar combination of hand-weaving, hand-spinning and hand-tilling agriculture which gave them self-supporting power. English interference having placed the spinner in Lancashire and the weaver in Bengal, or sweeping away both Hindu spinner and weaver, dissolved these small semi-barbarian, semi-civilised communities, by blowing up their economical basis and thus produced the greatest, and to speak the truth, the only *social* revolution ever heard of in Asia.

Now, sickening as it must be to human feeling to witness those myriads of industrious patriarchal and inoffensive social organisations disorganised and dissolved into their units, thrown into a sea of woes, and their individual members losing at the same time their ancient form of civilisation, and their hereditary means of subsistence, we must not forget that these idyllic village communities, inoffensive though they may appear, had always been the solid foundation of Oriental despotism, that they restrained the human mind within the smallest possible compass, making it the unresisting tool of superstition, enslaving it beneath traditional rules, depriving it of all grandeur and historical energies. We must not forget the barbarian egotism which, concentrating on some miserable patch of land, had quietly witnessed the ruins of empires, the perpetration of unspeakable cruelties, the massacre of the population of large towns with no other consideration bestowed upon them than on natural events, itself the helpless prey of any aggressor who deigned to notice it at all. We must not forget that this undignified, stagnatory, and vegetative life, that this passive sort of existence evoked on the other part, in contradistinction, wild, aimless, unbounded forces of destruction and rendered murder itself a religious rite in Hindustan. We must not forget that these little communities were contaminated by distinctions of caste and by slavery, that they subjugated man to external circumstances, instead of elevating man the sovereign of circumstances, that they transformed a self-developing social state into never changing natural destiny, and thus brought about a brutalising worship of nature, exhibiting its degradation in the fact that man, the sovereign of nature, fell down on his knees in adoration of *Kanuman,* the monkey, and *Sabbala,* the cow.

England, it is true, in causing a social revolution in Hindustan, was actuated only by the vilest interests, and was stupid in her manner of enforcing them. But that is not the question. The question is, can mankind fulfil its destiny without a fundamental revolution in the social state of Asia? If not, whatever may have been the crime of England she was the unconscious tool of history in bringing about that revolution.

Friedrich Engels

THE CONQUEST OF ALGERIA

Upon the whole it is, in our opinion, very fortunate that the Arabian chief [Abd-el-Kader] has been taken. The struggle of the Bedouins was a hopeless one, and though the manner in which brutal soldiers, like Bugeaud, have carried on the war is highly blamable, the conquest of Algeria is an important and fortunate fact for the progress of civilization. The piracies of the Barbaresque states, never interfered with by the English government as long as they did not disturb their ships, could not be put down but by the conquest of one of these states. And the conquest of Algeria has already forced the Beys of Tunis and Tripoli, and even the Emperor of Morocco, to enter upon the road of civilization. They were obliged to find other employment for their people than piracy, and other means of filling their exchequer than tributes paid to them by the smaller states of Europe. And if we may regret that the liberty of the Bedouins of the desert has been destroyed, we must not forget that these same Bedouins were a nation of robbers, whose principal means of living consisted of making excursions either upon each other or upon the settled villagers, taking what they found, slaughtering all those who resisted, and selling the remaining prisoners as slaves. All these nations of free barbarians look very proud,

Reprinted by permission of the editor from Lewis S. Feuer, ed., *Basic Writings on Politics and Philosophy: Karl Marx and Friedrich Engels* (Garden City, N.Y.: Anchor Books, Doubleday, 1959), pp. 450–451. From an article written for the English Chartist newspaper *Northern Star,* January 22, 1848.

noble, and glorious at a distance, but only come near them and you will find that they, as well as the more civilized nations, are ruled by the lust of gain, and only employ ruder and more cruel means.   And after all, the modern *bourgeois,* with civilization, industry, order, and at least relative enlightenment following him, is preferable to the feudal lord or to the marauding robber, with the barbarian state of society to which they belong.

D. K. Fieldhouse

ECONOMIC IMPERIALISM: A REVISION

It is now nearly sixty years since J. A. Hobson published *Imperialism: a Study,*[1] and thereby gave the word the connotation it still generally carries. His conception of the nature of "imperialism"[2] has, indeed, been almost universally accepted and, partly through the expository literature it has generated, may be said to have exercised a significant historical influence. Yet, for all its success, Hobson's argument has always been extremely vulnerable to criticism . . .   The aim of the present article is to draw together some of the more important arguments that have been put forward for and against his thesis, and to suggest that, on balance, the noes have it.

Hobson's own claim to importance and originality lies simply in his having induced British, and subsequently world, opinion to accept his own special definition of the word imperialism.   Professor Koebner has already examined the various meanings given to the word before 1902.[3]   He has suggested that, as used in England, it had two general connotations in the 1890's, both of which were morally neutral.   In one sense, it was being used of those who wished to prevent the existing British settlement colonies from seceding and becoming independent states, and was therefore a conservative factor.   In another, and increasingly common, sense, it was being used to indicate an expansionist and "forward" attitude towards problems connected with the future control of the "uncivilized" parts of the world, such as Africa, the Middle East and the Pacific. . . .   In the eyes of the anti-imperialists the sin of expansionism lay in the waste of money it

Reprinted by permission of the publisher from *The Economic History Review,* Second Series, 14, 2 (December 1961), 187–209.

[1] Published in 1902.   References are to the third edition (1954).

[2] When used in Hobson's sense, the word will be enclosed in quotation marks. [Eds.]

[3] R. Koebner, "The Concept of Economic Imperialism," *Economic History Review,* 2nd ser. II, no. 1.

entailed on armaments, in the cost of colonial governments, and in the danger of international conflicts over intrinsically unimportant territories which it would be wiser to leave alone.   As a rule no worse motive was attributed to the imperialists than "jingoism" or excessive concern with Britain's position as a great power.

But, between 1896 and 1902, imperialism, as a word, began to lose its innocence.   Koebner has shown that events in South Africa, and particularly the Jameson Raid, gave rise to a suspicion that, here at least, the expansive urge was motivated by something other than a concern for national greatness, by what Harcourt called "stock-jobbing imperialism"—based on the interests of financiers.   This was, of course, a special case; and a distinction remained between an honest, even if misguided, imperialism, and the debased variety to be seen on the Rand.   Yet the idea now gained ground that South Africa might not, after all, be a special case, but might exhibit in an extreme form a factor inherent in all expansionism. . . .

Hobson's *Imperialism* therefore came out at a time when British public opinion, disillusioned by the Boer war, was already profoundly suspicious about the motives behind recent imperial expansion. . . . Yet, paradoxically, Hobson was not primarily concerned with imperial problems: and *Imperialism* can only be properly understood on the basis that his interest, then and throughout his life, was with the social and economic problems of Britain.   In a sense, this book was primarily a vehicle for publicizing the theory of "underconsumption," which he regarded as his main intellectual achievement, and which he expressed more fully in *The Evolution of Modern Capitalism*. . . .   In brief, the theory, which was an alternative to the Marxist concept of surplus value as an explanation of poverty, saw excessive investment by the capitalist, with its concomitant of underconsumption by the wage-earner, as the root cause of recurrent slumps, of low interest rates, and of permanent under-employment.   Hobson thought there were only two answers to this problem.   The correct one—which would also be the answer to the "condition of England question"—was to increase the buying power of the workers by giving them a higher share of the profits of industry.   The wrong one, which was no answer to the social question, was to invest the surplus capital overseas, where it could earn a high interest rate, and thus sustain domestic rates of interest, without benefiting the British worker.   And this, he held, was what Britain had been doing since at least the middle of the nineteenth century.

To this point the economic theory, though highly vulnerable, has no apparent relevance to the phenomenon of overseas expansion, that is, to imperialism.   The key to Hobson's theory of "imperialism" lies in the connexion he makes between the two.

Overproduction in the sense of an excessive manufacturing plant, and surplus capital which could not find sound investments within the country, forced

Great Britain, Germany, Holland, France to place larger and larger portions of their economic resources outside the area of their present political domain, and then stimulate a policy of political expansion so as to take in the new area.[4]

Thus "imperialism," in the special sense used by Hobson, is an external symptom of a social malady in the metropolitan countries. Without this domestic pressure for investment overseas, there would be no effective impulse towards the acquisition of new colonies. Conversely, without colonies, capital would lack an outlet, and domestic rates of interest would sink. Thus the need to export capital and to make it politically secure overseas was what Mr. John Strachey has recently called the "prime mover for the modern imperialist process . . ." And "imperialism," on this assumption, is not variously "sound" or "stock-jobbing"; but, without exception, results from the special economic interests of the capitalist, and is therefore "economic imperialism."

It is not proposed at this stage to examine Hobson's theory in detail: but some comment must be made on the logical value of the argument he uses to demonstrate the historical truth of this hypothesis. Does he, in fact, supply any evidence to support the claim that colonies were the product of a demand either for new investment opportunities, or for security for existing investments? He begins with a straightforward account of the expansion of the European empires since 1870, printing a list of territories acquired by Britain. . . . Then, in chapter two, he demonstrates that the expansion of the British empire had been of little apparent value to British trade; that trade with these recent acquisitions was the least valuable part of intra-imperial trade; and that British trade with all colonies was declining in relation to trade with the rest of the world.[5] Clearly, then, "imperialism" was not good for trade. Nor was it good for emigration (which, in any case, he thought unnecessary), since these new tropical colonies were quite unsuited to white settlement. And his conclusion was that

The Imperialism of the last six decades is clearly condemned as a business policy, in that at enormous expense it has procured a small, bad, unsafe increase of markets, and has jeopardised the entire wealth of the nation in arousing the strong resentment of other nations . . .[6]

How then can a motive be found for this imperial expansion? The motive is to be seen if, alongside the list of territorial acquisitions, is placed a table

[4] Hobson, p. 80.

[5] Hobson based this conclusion on figures taken from Cd. 1761, p. 407, which are quoted in Hobson, p. 33. These were inaccurate. A. K. Cairncross (*Home and Foreign Investment 1870–1913*, Cambridge University Press, 1953), p. 189, shows that British exports to the empire increased from 24 per cent to 33.6 per cent of total British trade between 1870–2 and 1890–2, and imports from 21.9 per cent to 22.9 per cent in the same period. Both percentages continued to increase to 1910–12. But Hobson was right in saying that the new colonies contributed little to the increased volume of intra-imperial trade.

[6] Hobson, p. 46.

showing the increase of British overseas investments in the same period. It then becomes obvious that, during the period in which British possessions had increased by 4,754 m. square miles and by a population of 88 millions, British overseas investments had also increased enormously— from £144 m. to £1698 m. between 1862 and 1893 alone. Could there be any doubt that the two sets of figures were intimately connected as cause and effect? Hobson had no doubts about it: "It is not too much to say that the modern foreign policy of Great Britain has been primarily a struggle for profitable markets of investment." [7]

But it is immediately apparent that Hobson had in no sense proved that there was any connexion between the investments made overseas and the territory acquired contemporaneously. His table of investments makes no differentiation between the areas in which investment had taken place, beyond such classifications as "Foreign," "Colonial," "U.S.A." and "Various," and, in fact, he assumes quite arbitrarily that the new colonies had attracted a high proportion of the investment called "Foreign" (i.e. before they were annexed) or "Colonial" (subsequent to annexation). . . . To put the case bluntly, Hobson performed an intellectual conjuring trick. Convinced of the essential truth of his economic theory, he deceived the eye by the speed of his hand, creating the illusion that, of the two sets of statistics he held up, one was the cause of the other.

. . . Two additional points in his main argument must be mentioned because they were intrinsic to his definition of the origins and nature of "imperialist" expansion.

The first of these concerns the relationship between the financial interest and other "imperialists," and is therefore crucial to his theory. He was aware that, contrary to his argument, the obvious driving force of British expansion since 1870 appeared to lie in the explorers, missionaries, engineers, patriotic pressure groups, and empire-minded politicians, all of whom had evident influence, and had demonstrable interests, other than those of investment, in territorial acquisitions. And he was equally aware that if the impulse to expansion could be satisfactorily explained in the old-fashioned terms of their idealism, their ambition, or their concern with the status of Britain as a world power, rather than in terms of the self-interest of the capitalist, his own central thesis would collapse. It was therefore necessary that these men—the Lugards, the Milners, the Johnstons, and the Roseberys—should be shown to be mere puppets—the tools of "imperialism" rather than its authors. Hobson did this by falling back on what may be called the "faceless men" gambit:

Finance manipulates the patriotic forces which politicians, soldiers, philanthropists, and traders generate; the enthusiasm for expansion which issues from these sources, though strong and genuine, is irregular and blind; the financial interest has those qualities of concentration and clear-sighted calculation which

[7] Hobson, p. 53.

are needed to set Imperialism to work.   An ambitious statesman, a frontier soldier, an overzealous missionary, a pushing trader, may suggest or even initiate a step of imperial expansion, may assist in educating patriotic public opinion to the urgent need of some fresh advance, but the final determination rests with the financial power.[8]

In this ingenious way Hobson inverted the apparent relationship between the obvious "imperialists" and the investor.   Instead of the financier being induced to invest in new possessions, with more or less enthusiasm, once political control had been imposed for other reasons, he becomes the essential influence in the take-over itself.   Investment no longer follows the flag: it decides where it is profitable to plant it, and tells the government whether it is to follow the advice of men of action or of ideas in each particular case.   Thus, "imperialism" can never be interpreted as the spontaneous expression of the idealism, the chauvinism or the mere energy of a nation.   In its practical form it is the expression of the special interests of the financier behind the scenes, who decides whether it is worth his while to allow a dream to become a reality, and who alone will reap the benefits.

*   *   *

The other essential point in the theory of "imperialism" is the suggestion that the possession of colonies by individual capitalist states results automatically in the exploitation of the indigenous peoples of Africa and Asia. . . .   Hobson argued that exploitation, whether by appropriation of land, or by the use of cheap labour—forced or nominally free . . . had been a general feature of the colonies of all the European powers.   Hobson, in the British humanitarian tradition, thought such exploitation to be both wrong and inexpedient.   Economic development was good for undeveloped colonies and for the world as a whole.   The danger lay in allowing the financiers to use the political power of the imperial authority for their own purposes; and the solution was for international control of colonies —the germ of the later mandate concept—and patience in allowing normal economic forces to give the natives an inducement to work freely in European enterprises.   Sensible as his general attitude was, it is clear that Hobson had thus included in "imperialism" the suggestion that countries possessing colonies were almost certain to exploit them in their own interests; and this argument was to become a staple of later critics of "colonialism."

II

The theory of "imperialism" as it developed after the publication of Hobson's *Study* continued to be founded on the three main concepts outlined above.   Yet . . . it is clear that it was Lenin, writing in 1916, rather than Hobson himself, who gave "imperialism" its dogmatic coherence and

[8] Hobson, p. 59.

much of its eventual influence.   It is therefore necessary to consider briefly the extent to which Lenin modified Hobson's ideas.[9]

The greatest difference lies in the first and most important part of the argument; that is, in the nature of the internal pressure in the capitalist countries which forces them to expand their colonial possessions.   Hobson had explained this pressure in terms of "under-consumption": but Lenin naturally had a more orthodox theory to hand.   Capitalism as a system was approaching the apocalypse Marx had foretold.   Competitive capitalism had, in the late nineteenth century, been replaced by "monopoly capitalism," with its characteristic agencies, the cartels, trusts and tariffs.   It was no longer dynamic, but anxious only to maintain its profit margins by more intensive exploitation of limited and protected markets.   Moreover, the "finance-capitalists"—the banks and trusts—who now largely controlled capital itself, found that, under monopoly conditions, it was more profitable to employ surplus capital abroad than in domestic industry.   At home, it could only increase production, lower prices, and raise wages.   Abroad it could give a high interest return without any of these consequences.   But, to gain the highest return from overseas investment it was desirable to have some political control over the territory in which the investment was made.   This might be in the limited form of a "semi-colony," such as the Argentine.   But only in the colony proper could really comprehensive economic and political controls be imposed which would give investments their highest return.   The result had been the competition between the great powers to acquire new colonies after 1870, which would continue until the whole uncivilized world had come under imperial rule.   Then would follow the inter-imperial wars for the redivision of the empires, leading to proletarian revolutions in the "imperialist" states, the creation of "socialist" states, and so, automatically, to the end of "imperialism."

. . . Hobson was a doctor prescribing a remedy, Lenin a prophet forecasting catastrophe.   But, while they disagreed as to the precise causes, both maintained that there existed in the "capitalist" countries a tremendous pressure for overseas investment, and that this was the main factor in producing "imperialist" expansion after 1870.

On Hobson's second point—the control and influence exercised by "finance" over government and over the men who actually carved out the new empires—there is little difference between them.   Lenin, if anything, went further, ignoring the theory that in a democratic country like Britain Hobson's "imperialists" found it necessary to corrupt public opinion through the press; and assuming, on the basis of Marxist theory and German experience, that the financial power of the banks and trusts was now so great that governments virtually did as they were told by the "finance-capitalist."   Moreover, Lenin rejected entirely the possibility that the drive

[9] V. I. Lenin, *Imperialism, the Highest Stage of Capitalism* (1916).

behind imperialism might have been the natural product of nationalism in international politics. To him as a Marxist such arguments were superficial. The only true explanation must lie in the fundamental economic environment which dictates political interests. . . .

On Hobson's third point, Lenin had little explicit to say. As a Marxist he assumed it to be axiomatic that all workers were exploited by capital; so that a colony would differ from the metropolis only in the fact that the exploiting capitalist was an alien, and colonies merely added to the pool of labour from which he could extract "surplus value."

* * *

III

The central feature of the theory of "imperialism," by which it must stand or fall, is the assertion that the empires built up after 1870 were not an option but a necessity for the economically advanced states of Europe and America: that these capitalist societies, because of their surplus of domestically produced capital, were forced to export capital to the under-developed regions of the world: and that it was only this investment—prospective or existing—that supplied a motive for the acquisition of new colonies.

Faced with this theory, the historian who does not take its truth for granted is likely to be sceptical on at least three main grounds. First, his instinct is to distrust all-embracing historical formulas which . . . seek to explain complex developments in terms of a single dominant influence. Again, he is likely to suspect an argument that isolates the imperial expansion of the period after 1870 from all earlier imperial developments if only because he is aware of so many elements of continuity in the history of overseas empires over the past few centuries. But, above all, he must be aware that the theory simply does not appear to fit the facts of the post-1870 period as he knows them. Looking, for example, at Hobson's list of territories acquired by Britain after 1870, it seems, at first sight at least, difficult to believe that any considerable part of them were annexed either because British capitalists had already invested much of their surplus capital there, or because they regarded them as fields for essential future investment. In some cases, perhaps, it seems that a *prima facie* case could be made out on these lines—for Egypt, the Transvaal and Rhodesia, to take Hobson's three main examples. But, even in these, further consideration must arouse doubts. Surely the strategic importance of the Suez Canal was as good a reason for controlling Egypt in 1882 as the preservation of the interests of the bond holders in the Canal Company. Was it really necessary, on purely economic grounds, to annex the Transvaal in 1899 when the British mine-owners were making vast fortunes under Kruger's government, and had shown themselves so divided over the question of the Jameson Raid and the independence of the Republic? Again, granted that Rhodes and the British South Africa Company had excellent economic reasons for wanting British control over Rhodesia, was their anxiety really due to the pressure of British funds waiting for investment opportunity?

Doubts such as these concerning even the key examples chosen by Hobson inevitably stimulate further examination of his list: and this makes it clear that not even a *prima facie* case could be made out for most of the territories he includes.   To take a random selection, it would surely be ludicrous to suggest that Fiji, British New Guinea or Upper Burma were annexed in order to protect large British investments, or even as a field for subsequent investment.   In each case secular explanations seem fully to account for their annexation: the chaotic condition of a mixed society in the Pacific, the fears of Australia for her military security, and the frontier problems of India.   And even where, as in Malaya, large capital investment did take place after annexation, the time factor must be considered. Were the British investor and the government really so alert to the possible future need for fields for investment?   Or did annexation in fact take place for quite other reasons, being followed by investment when new conditions and new possibilities arose which were then totally unforeseen?

Yet, obvious though the weakness of the theory of "imperialism" may seem when applied in specific cases, it is also clear that it would be extremely difficult to invalidate Hobson's model by a process of piecemeal examination.   For the adherents of this, as of most comprehensive formulas, could counter, . . . as Professor Sweezy does, by calling all annexations that do not fit demonstrably into the pattern "protective and anticipatory," or based on "consideration of a strategic nature.". . . Moreover, if the theory is false, it should be possible to demonstrate that its premises are false also.   And, since the essential premise of "imperialism" is the belief that the drive to acquire colonies after 1870 was the direct and necessary result of the need of the capitalists to export capital, this proposition demands careful examination.

It has been seen that this theory of surplus capital being forced out into the undeveloped world was expressed differently by Hobson and Lenin, and it will be convenient to consider Lenin's theory first.   This was, it will be remembered, that the centrifugal force in the capitalist countries was the interest of the monopolistic "finance-capitalists" who stood only to lose by investment at home.

In this the fallacy is immediately obvious.   If it was true of any country, it was not true of Britain; for no one could maintain that British capital was then controlled by a few trusts or even cartels. . . .   British capital, whatever its tendencies, was still "competitive" on Lenin's definition: and he in fact admitted that in Britain "monopoly" must be taken to mean the reduction of the competing enterprises to "a couple of dozen or so."   This is hardly a satisfactory explanation of the need to export capital on a vast scale; so, presumably, Britain must have other reasons both for this and for territorial annexation.   But, for different reasons, other countries also

escape from the formula.   Germany was Lenin's main example of the
country dominated by trusts: but, as Professor Hancock has pointed out,[10]
the age of German cartels came only after about 1900, while the main
German grab for colonies had taken place during the previous twenty
years.   And America, which certainly had vast industrial and financial
combinations, proved, in spite of Roosevelt's attempt to create an expansionist movement, to be the least "imperialist" of all the capitalist states.   It
would therefore seem reasonable to conclude that Lenin's narrow explanation for the export of capital and the concurrent extension of European
political control overseas is unacceptable.

Yet, whatever reasons are assigned to it, the fact of vast capital exports
from the advanced countries in the period after 1870 remains. . . .
Hence, the important questions must be faced.   Was there in fact a vast
reservoir of capital, generated (for example) in Britain, which was available for overseas investment?   Why was it invested abroad rather than at
home?   And was it in fact invested in those areas which were annexed as
colonies after 1871?

The publication in 1953 of Professor A. K. Cairncross's *Home and Foreign Investment 1870–1913* has made it possible to approach these questions from a new and non-doctrinaire angle.   The key to his interpretation
lay in his rejection of Hobson's naive model of the British capitalist, em-
barrassed by an excess of capital, which could not be invested at home because of the "under-consumption" factor, sending it abroad into undeveloped tropical territories where it would produce a high rate of interest.
Instead, it is necessary to see that capital exports were not divorced from
the economy of Great Britain but were in fact a necessary concomitant of
the pattern of British trade and development.   It can be shown that in fact
the great majority of this capital went to the "new" countries—to the
United States, Canada, Argentine, Australasia and South Africa in particular—who were producing the primary materials that the British economy
needed, and who had to have capital to expand their production for British
consumption.   To invest in these countries was therefore, in one sense, to
invest in a primary sector of the British economy itself.   And the return to
Britain was not entirely, or even primarily, in a tribute of money, but in
cheap and plentiful raw materials and food.

Moreover, far from weakening the British economy and reducing the
living standards of the working class as both Hobson and Lenin thought
they did, these capital exports were essential to both.   Indeed, Cairncross
argues convincingly that, by creating a demand for British products, these
investments simultaneously kept up the level of profits at home, kept down
the level of unemployment, and maintained wage levels.   And, as the rate
of overseas investment seems to have been greatest when the terms of trade
were against Britain—the 1880's being an exceptional period when special

[10] W. K. Hancock, *The Wealth of Colonies* (Cambridge, 1950), pp. 11–12.

factors in the United States offset the general tendency—Cairncross concludes that "it was foreign investment that pulled Britain out of most depressions before 1914." [11]

Seen, therefore, from the point of view of Britain's part in the world economy, rather than in purely domestic terms, capital exports no longer seem to have been forced out of the British economy by the selfish interests of the capitalists to maintain artificially high interest rates, and become, as Professor Nurkse has described them, "a means whereby a vigorous process of economic growth came to be transmitted from the centre to the outlying areas of the world." [12]   That is to say that the force behind the export of capital was the pull exerted by urgent need for capital in the newly-developing countries, who, because of their higher potential productivity and because markets were available for their exports, could afford to pay higher rates of interest than were obtainable in Britain.   Yet, important though it was in explaining why the British and European investor chose to send his capital abroad, this differential in rates of interest should not be overestimated. . . .   In fact it can be said that the British investor did not choose to invest abroad simply to get high interest rates, but, by and large, to get a slightly higher rate than on an equivalent type of stock at home.   Above all, if he chose to invest in a British colony, it was not because he expected higher interest, but because he wanted greater security than he would get in an equivalent foreign investment.   If he wanted a "risk" investment—diamonds, copper, gold, nitrates, etc.—he went for it wherever the enterprise happened to be situated.   But, in proportion to the whole, investments of this type were very small in 1911.

But, for the present argument, the third and most important fact . . . is that Hobson was entirely wrong in assuming that any large proportion of British overseas investment went to those undeveloped parts of Africa and Asia which were annexed during the "imperialist" grab after 1870. As Professor Nurkse has remarked of Hobson:

Had he tried to do what he did for trade, that is, to show the geographical distribution of overseas investment, he would have found that British capital tended to bypass the primitive tropical economies and flowed mainly to the regions of recent settlement outside as well as inside the British Empire.[13]

. . . The bulk of British investment then lay in the United States, £688 m., South America, £587 m., Canada, £372 m., Australasia, £380 m., India and Ceylon, £365 m., and South Africa, £351 m.   By contrast, West Africa had received only £29 m., the Straits and Malay States, £22 m., and the remaining British possessions, £33 m. . . .   The sums invested in these tropical areas, whether newly annexed or not, were quite

[11] Cairncross, p. 188.

[12] R. Nurkse, *Patterns of Trade and Development* (Stockholm, 1959), p. 14.

[13] *Ibid*, p. 19.

marginal to the total overseas investment, and continued to be relatively very small in the years immediately before 1911.   Hence, to maintain that Britain had found it necessary to acquire these territories because of an urgent need for new fields for investment is simply unrealistic: and, with the rejection of this hypothesis, so ingeniously conjured up by Hobson, the whole basis of his theory that "imperialism" was the product of economic necessity collapses.

IV

But to suggest that Hobson and Lenin were mistaken in thinking that the need to export capital from Europe after 1870 was so intense that it made the colonization of most of Africa and the Pacific necessary as fields for investment is merely to throw the question open again.   The essential problem remains: on what other grounds is it possible to explain this sudden expansion of European possessions, whose motive force is called imperialism?

*   *   *

Looking broadly over the four centuries since the early Portuguese discoveries, it may be said that, although European motives for acquiring colonies were extremely complex, they fell into two general categories. First was the specifically economic motive, whose aim was to create a lucrative trade for the metropolitan country.   Its typical expression was the trading base or factory, secured by some form of agreement with the local ruler: but, where no commodities already existed for trade, it could result in territorial possessions, like the sugar islands of the Caribbean, or the spice islands of the East; the fur-producing parts of North America, and the silver mines of Peru.   The export of capital played no significant part in this economic activity, for Europe had little surplus capital before the nineteenth century, and investment was restricted to the immediate needs of trade itself, of the mines, sugar estates, etc.

By contrast, it is clear that from the earliest days of European expansion the margin between economic and other motives was small, and that many colonies were rather the product of political and military rivalries than of the desire for profit.   The mercantile practices followed by all European states were as much concerned with national power as with economic advantage, and tended, as Adam Smith pointed out, to subordinate opulence to the needs of security. . . .

If, then, a general view of pre-nineteenth century imperial policies shows the complexity of its aims—made still more complicated in the early nineteenth century by the important new element of humanitarianism—it must seem surprising that Hobson should have interpreted post-1870 imperialism in narrowly economic terms, and have ignored the possibility that strictly political impulses may once again have been of major importance. The reason would seem to be that the evolution of imperial practices since about 1815 appeared, at the end of the century, to have constituted a clear break with earlier methods; to have made both the economic and the political criteria of earlier times irrelevant; and thus to have made comparison pointless. With the independence of almost all the American colonies, and the subsequent adoption by Britain—the chief remaining colonial power—of the practices of free trade, the possession of colonies no longer offered any positive economic advantage. . . . On the political side also, colonies had ceased to play an important part in diplomacy. With the preponderance of Britain as a naval power, and the weakness of most European states, power politics were largely restricted to Britain, France and Russia. As between them competitive aggressiveness was recurrent: but, except briefly in the Pacific, and more frequently in the Near East and on the borders of India, their rivalry did not produce any major competition for new territory. And this seemed to imply that the end of mercantilism had been followed by the end also of political imperialism: which in turn suggested that the renewal of a general international desire for colonies after 1870 must have sprung from some new phenomenon—the unprecedented need to acquire openings for the safe investment of surplus capital.

It is mainly because Hobson's theory of "imperialism" in his own time was based on this theory of discontinuity in nineteenth century history that it must be regarded as fallacious. For there had, in fact, been no break in the continuity of imperial development; merely a short-term variation in the methods used, corresponding with a temporary change in world conditions. In the first place, the extension of the territorial possessions of the three surviving great powers continued intermittently throughout: and the list of British acquisitions between 1840 and 1871 alone bears comparison with those of the following thirty years. On what grounds, in this period of so-called "anti-imperialism," are these to be explained? Obviously no single explanation will serve. Hong Kong stood alone as a trading base with a specifically economic function. Queensland was the result of internal expansion in Australia, British Columbia of rivalry from the United States. But the rest—the Punjab, Sind, Berar, Oudh and Lower Burma on the frontiers of British India; Basutoland, Griqualand and (temporarily) the Transvaal on the Cape frontier; and small areas round existing trading bases in West Africa—stand as evidence that an existing empire will tend always to expand its boundaries. They were not the product of an expansive British policy, but of the need for military security, for administrative efficiency, or for the protection of indigenous peoples on the frontiers of existing colonies. Basically, they demonstrated the fact, familiar in earlier centuries, that colonies which exist in a power vacuum will tend always to expand slowly until they meet with some immovable political or geographical obstacle; and that a metropolitan government can do little more than slow down the speed of movement. . . . And, to this extent, late nineteenth century imperialism was merely the continuation of a process which had begun centuries earlier.

At the same time, it must be said that this "contiguous area" theory does not fully cover certain of the new British possessions on Hobson's list. For some of them, like East Africa, were not strictly contiguous to an existing British colony; and others, such as Nigeria or Rhodesia, were clearly annexed too suddenly and on too large a scale to be seen as the product of the domestic needs of Lagos or the Cape. These therefore suggest that some other factor was at work—competition for new colonies on political grounds—which will be considered later.

Again, in the sphere of economic policy, the antithesis between different parts of the nineteenth century [was] . . . greatly exaggerated and misunderstood by Hobson. The rejection of most of the mercantile devices for stimulating European trade had not meant that trade ceased to be a matter of national concern, or that governments ceased to use political means to support their men of business; the contrast with earlier centuries lay mainly in the methods now used. Hobson seemed to think that free trade had ended "economic imperialism" of the mercantile variety simply because political control was no longer regarded as a prerequisite for economic exploitation of an undeveloped area. But . . . "formal" control, as in a colony, was not the only way in which "economic imperialism" could operate; indeed, it now had two complementary features. On its specifically economic side it implied, as always, the control of the economic assets of some other country for the advantage of the metropolitan state. And the essential weapons of the European trader or financier were economic—the demand for his goods, his capital or his credit, and the effectiveness of the organization he built up in a country lacking business organization. The stranglehold he thus obtained differed only in detail from that held in the eighteenth century by British firms in the American colonies, transferred now to the similarly defenceless, though politically independent, states of South America, the Middle and Far East. By the end of the nineteenth century most of the world had been thus brought under the economic control of European, and now also United States, business enterprise: their trade was organized and carried by foreign merchants, their revenues mortgaged to the loans they had received. This indeed was "economic imperialism" in its purest form; cosmopolitan in outlook, unconcerned with political frontiers, showing no interest in the creation of "formal" colonies except where, as in China, the formula of the open door proved otherwise unworkable. Only in the absolute volume of its activity, and in the increasing competition between rivals from newly industrialized countries, did the character of "economic imperialism" change before 1914. And, while it remained thus strictly economic and cosmopolitan, the "division of the world among the international trusts," which Lenin prophesied, remained a possibility.

Yet, even in its classical form, "economic imperialism" required political support from governments at home: and, in view of developments after about 1870, it is important to define the nature of the support it received. Essentially the men of business needed only two things which their own enterprise could not supply: a minimum standard of political security at the periphery, and the solution of the quasi-political problems arising out of their relations with foreign rivals by diplomatic action at the centre. The first need was met by the network of treaties made for them with their client countries which secured equality of opportunity and reasonable tariffs, and was backed up, where necessary, by the use of threats and force. . . .

Second, and parallel with this, went the constant diplomatic work of the foreign offices of Europe in maintaining the balance between their nationals at the circumference. On the common assumption that it was to the general interest that competition should remain fair, that an artificial monopoly was to the advantage of none, and that such problems must not be allowed to harm international relations, diplomacy sought to settle these disputes without taking refuge in unilateral annexation of the area concerned. In this it was generally successful, where the will to succeed existed. . . .

It is now possible to place the imperialism of the period of Hobson's *Study* in its historical context, and to attempt a definition of the extent to which it differed from that of earlier years. The most obvious fact on which his theory was based was that, by contrast with the preceding half-century, vast areas of the world were quickly brought under European control for the first time: and it is now evident that this cannot be explained in terms of either of the two tendencies operating throughout the earlier nineteenth century. Although the break with the past was not as sharp as Hobson seemed to think, it remains true that many British annexations cannot be explained on the "contiguous area" theory: and the new possessions of France, Italy and Germany were quite definitely in a different category. But neither can these facts be explained on Hobson's theory: for, as has been said, the places now to be taken over had hitherto attracted little capital, and did not attract it in any quantity subsequently. Nor, again, can an explanation be found in the more general theory of "economic imperialism," for these places in the Pacific and in Africa for which the nations now competed were of marginal economic importance; and, on the assumptions of the past fifty years, governments might have been expected to reject demands by their nationals for annexation of territories whose administrative costs would be out of all proportion to their economic value to the nation. In sum, the most obvious facts of the new phase of imperialism cannot be explained as the logical continuation of the recent past, nor in Hobson's terms of a new economic factor. What, then, was the explanation?

An answer is not, of course, hard to find, and indeed emerges clearly from the vast literature now available. With the exception of the supporters of the "imperialism" thesis, the consensus of opinion is very marked. The new factor in imperialism was not something without precedent, certainly not anything uniquely economic, but essentially a throwback to some of the characteristic attitudes and practices of the eighteenth century. Just as, in the early nineteenth century, the economic interests had demanded effectively that imperial questions should no longer be decided on political grounds, demanding opulence in place of security, so, at the end of the century, the balance was again reversed. The outstanding feature of the new situation was the subordination of economic to political considerations, the preoccupation with national security, military power and prestige.

Again, reasons are not hard to find. The significant fact about the years after 1890 was that Europe became once again an armed camp. . . . Between Germany and France there stood the question of Alsace-Lorraine: and for both the primary consideration was now a system of alliances which would, on the German side, prevent French counter-attack, on the French side, make revenge possible. Inevitably the rest of Europe was drawn into the politics of the balance of power between them; and for all statesmen military strength became once again the criterion of national greatness. Inevitably too this situation, with its similarities to the politics of the eighteenth century, brought in its train a return to many of the attitudes of mercantilism. Emigration to foreign states, instead of being regarded as an economic safety valve, became once again a loss of military or manufacturing manpower; and population statistics became a measure of relative national strength. Protective tariffs came back also, with the primary aim of building up national self-sufficiency and the power to make war.

Under such circumstances it was only to be expected that colonies would be regarded once again as assets in the struggle for power and status: but in fact the attitude of the powers to the imperial question was not at first a simple one. Indeed, it cannot be said that the attitudes characteristic of "the imperialism of free trade" were seriously weakened until the mid-1880's; and until then it seemed possible that the colonial question might be kept clear of European politics. . . . For most of the men who then ruled Europe retained a realistic appreciation of the potential value to their countries of those parts of the world that were available for annexation. Bismarck in particular recognized that, as sources of raw materials, as fields for emigration or as spheres for trade, the areas available in Africa and the Pacific had little to offer Germany, whatever national advantages those with private interests there might claim. At best they might offer naval bases, a strictly limited trade, and bargaining counters for use in diplomacy. It is improbable that Bismarck ever really changed this opinion: and, while he held off, it was unlikely that any other power would feel strong enough to precipitate a rush for new colonies. . . .

It was, therefore, Bismarck's action in 1884–5, in announcing the formal control by Germany over parts of West and South West Africa, and of

New Guinea, that really began the new phase of political imperialism: and it is therefore important to consider his reasons for giving Germany a "colonial policy.". . . In 1884 Bismarck seems to have decided that it was time for him to stop playing the honest broker in the disputes of other powers over their own possessions—such as Egypt and the Congo—and that, on two counts, both essentially diplomatic, Germany should now stake her own claims to colonies. The first was that it was politically desirable to show France that his recent support for Britain on the Egyptian question did not imply a general hostility towards her, since he was now prepared to take action resented by Britain: the second that Britain should be made to see that German support for her in the colonial field must be repaid by closer co-operation in Europe.

In a narrow sense, then, the race for colonies was the product of diplomacy rather than of any more positive force. . . . Thereafter the process could not be checked; for, under conditions of political tension, the fear of being left out of the partition of the globe overrode all practical considerations. Perhaps Britain was the only country which showed genuine reluctance to take a share; and this was due both to her immense stake in the continuance of the *status quo* for reasons of trade, and to her continued realism in assessing the substantive value of the lands under dispute. And the fact that she too joined in the competition demonstrated how contagious the new political forces were. Indeed, until the end of the century, imperialism may best be seen as the extension into the periphery of the political struggle in Europe. At the centre the balance was so nicely adjusted that no positive action, no major change in the status or territory of either side was possible. Colonies thus became a means out of the impasse; sources of diplomatic strength, prestige-giving accessions of territory, hope for future economic development. New worlds were being brought into existence in the vain hope that they would maintain or redress the balance of the old.

This analysis of the dynamic force of the new imperialism has been stated in purely political terms. What part was played in it by the many non-political interests with a stake in the new colonies: the traders, the investors, the missionaries, and the speculators? For these were the most vociferous exponents of a "forward" policy in most countries: and to men like Hobson it seemed that their influence, if backed by that of the greater interest of the financier, was decisive in causing the politicians to act.

. . . In general terms the answer would seem to be that, while statesmen were very much aware of the pressure groups—conscious of the domestic political advantage of satisfying their demands, and often themselves sympathetic to the case they put up—they were not now, any more than earlier in the century, ready to undertake the burden of new colonies simply on their account. What made it seem as if these interests were now calling the tune was that the choice facing the statesman was no longer between annexation and the continued independence of the area in question:

it was now between action and allowing a rival to step in. Salisbury and Rosebery may well have been convinced by the argument of men like Lugard that, on humanitarian grounds, it would be desirable for Britain to bring law and order to Uganda. But it was the threat of German or French occupation of the key to the Nile and Egypt that decided them to act. Yet . . . it is also true that the very existence of these hitherto embarrassing pressure groups now became a diplomatic asset, since they were the obvious grounds on which valid claims could be made, an approximation to the principle of effective occupation.

Thus the relative importance of the concrete interests and demands of the various pressure groups, as compared with the political criteria of the statesmen, was the reverse of that assigned to them by Hobson . . . Yet, if the first, and territorially decisive, factor in the imperialism of the post 1870 period was this unemotional, almost cynical, policy of the statesmen, it cannot be said that it was the only new feature, nor, in the long run, the most important one. For by the time Hobson wrote in 1902, those who supported a "forward" policy were no longer the few diplomatic chessplayers, nor even the relatively small pressure groups, but millions of people for whom an empire had become a matter of faith. Indeed, the rise of this imperialist ideology, this belief that colonies were an essential attribute of any great nation, is one of the most astonishing facts of the period. It was, moreover, an international creed, with beliefs that seemed to differ very little from one country to another. Its basic ideas had been clearly expressed as early as 1879 by a German, Treitschke:

Every virile people has established colonial power . . . All great nations in the fulness of their strength have desired to set their mark upon barbarian lands and those who fail to participate in this great rivalry will play a pitiable role in time to come. The colonizing impulse has become a vital question for every great nation.[14]

By the end of the century, the "imperial idea," as it has significantly been called,[15] after twenty years of propaganda by such groups of enthusiasts as the German *Kolonialverein* and the British Imperial Federation League, had become dominant. The process of educating the public has now been examined in detail: and it is interesting to see that in each case the historian has found it necessary to deal almost entirely in ideas, rather than in concrete facts. This is no accident. The imperialism of the early twentieth century, although ironically the product of the power politics of the previous two decades, bore little resemblance to the ideas of men like Bismarck and Salisbury. It was the generation of Kaiser Wilhelm II, of Theodore Roosevelt and of Chamberlain (in his later years) that came to adopt for the first time this mystical faith in the value of an empire. . . .

[14] Quoted in M. E. Townsend, *Origins of Modern German Colonization, 1871–1885*, p. 27.

[15] By A. P. Thornton, *The Imperial Idea and its enemies.*

For, by that time, imperialism had been shown to be a delusion. It was already the common experience of all the countries that had taken part in the partition of Africa and the Pacific that, except for the few windfalls, such as gold in West Africa, diamonds in South West Africa, and copper in the Congo and Rhodesia, the new colonies were white elephants: and that only small sectional interests in any country had obtained real benefits from them. Whether German, French, British or Italian, their trade was minute . . . ; their attraction for investors, except in mines, etc., was negligible; they were unsuitable for large-scale emigration, and any economic development that had taken place was usually the result of determined efforts by the European state concerned to create an artificial asset. Moreover, in most cases, the cost of administration was a dead weight on the imperial power. By 1900 all these facts were apparent and undeniable. They were constantly pressed by opponents of colonial expansion in each country; and Hobson's book consisted primarily of an exposition of these defects. Yet public opinion was increasingly oblivious to such facts: the possession of colonies had become a sacred cow, a psychological necessity. While the financiers continued to invest their money, as they had done in the previous fifty years, in economically sound projects . . . remaining true to the criteria of true "economic imperialism" —the politicians, pressed on now by a public demand they could not control, even if they had wanted to, continued, with increasing bellicosity, to scrape the bottom of the barrel for yet more colonial burdens for the white man to carry.

V

The reassessment of so abstract a concept as "imperialism," particularly within the present limitations of space, cannot hope to prove or to disprove anything. At the most it may lead to the suggestion that an earlier synthesis does not appear to fit the facts. How far can it be said that the arguments put forward above make necessary a revision of the theory of "imperialism" which derives from Hobson and Lenin?

The general conclusion would seem to emerge that, as an historical interpretation of the expansion of European empires between 1870 and 1914, it is unacceptable. As an economic theory it is unsatisfactory because detailed investigations have shown that the alleged need of the European investor, monopolist or individual capitalist, to find outlets for his surplus capital had little or nothing to do with the division of Africa and the Pacific between the European powers. Again, as a theory of historical development, which makes this expansion seem to be a unique phenomenon, capable of being understood only in terms of the special methodology used by Hobson and Lenin, it ignores both the continuity of nineteenth century developments, and also its similarity to earlier periods of European imperialism. In most respects, indeed, there was no break in continuity after 1870. On the political side, many of the new annexations of territory, particularly those made by Britain, resulted from the situation of existing possessions: and, on the economic side, the rapid expansion of European commercial and financial influence throughout the world—the true "economic imperialism"—did not change its character after 1870; and was no more likely then than before to have resulted in significant acquisitions of land. The real break in the continuity of nineteenth century development—the rapid extension of "formal" control over independent areas of Africa and the East—was a specifically political phenomenon in origin, the outcome of fears and rivalries within Europe. The competition for colonies, being as characteristic of economically weak countries like Italy as of others which had large resources of capital available for overseas deployment, was indeed more obviously a throw-back to the imperialism of the eighteenth century than the characteristic product of nineteenth century capitalism in an advanced phase. And the ideological fervour that became the dominant feature of the imperial movement after about 1890 was the natural outcome of this fevered nationalism, not the artifact of vested economic interests.

Yet, in conclusion, a paradox must be noted. Hobson's analysis of "imperialism" was defective: but the fact that it was defective was probably the result of his having grasped one essential truth about the imperial movement—that it had become irrational. Seeing clearly that the new tropical colonies could not be justified in terms of their economic value to the metropolitan powers—the criterion a nineteenth century rationalist would naturally apply—he was forced back on the theory that they must have been of value to sectional interests at least; and that these had succeeded in hoodwinking a presumably sane public opinion. Seen in this light, Hobson's sinister capitalists and their "parasites" were nothing more than a hypothesis, a *deus ex machina,* to balance an equation between the assumed rationality of mankind and the unreasonableness of imperial policies: and the book was a plea for a return to a sane standard of values.

His mistake, then, was to think that the equation needed such artificial adjustment. For, in the second half of the twentieth century, it can be seen that imperialism owed its popular appeal not to the sinister influence of the capitalists, but to its inherent attractions for the masses. In the new quasi-democratic Europe, the popularity of the imperial idea marked a rejection of the sane morality of the account-book, and the adoption of a creed based on such irrational concepts as racial superiority and the prestige of the nation. Whether we interpret it, as did J. R. Schumpeter in 1919, as a castback to the ideas of the old autocratic monarchies of the *ancien régime,* or as something altogether new—the first of the irrational myths that have dominated the first half of the twentieth century—it is clear that imperialism cannot be explained in simple terms of economic theory and the nature of finance capitalism. In its mature form it can best be described as a sociological phenomenon with roots in political facts: and it can properly be understood only in terms of the same social hysteria that has since given birth to other and more disastrous forms of aggressive nationalism.

L. Goncharov

NEW FORMS OF COLONIALISM IN AFRICA

*   *   *

As shown by the experience of the countries which have gained political sovereignty in recent years, the break-up of the colonial system in Africa has affected mainly the political relations of the ex-colonies with their former metropolitan countries. Political power passed from the hands of the colonial administrators, who had carried out the instructions of the ruling classes of the colonial powers, into the hands of local national forces. Thus the second, auxiliary function of the imperialistic monopoly is being eliminated as the colonial system breaks up. The colonial powers, however, are striving to find at least a partial substitute for the direct political control which is slipping out of their hands, in order to retain their main function, economic exploitation. This is the most important feature of colonialism in its new forms, in contrast to the old, "classical" colonialism.

Describing colonial policy in the epoch of capitalist imperialism, V. I. Lenin said that

finance capital and its corresponding foreign policy . . . give rise to a number of transitional forms of stated dependence. Typical of this epoch are not only the two main groups of countries—those owning the colonies, and colonies—but also the diverse forms of dependent countries which, officially, are politically independent, but, in fact, are enmeshed into the net of financial and diplomatic dependence.[1]

During the current collapse of the colonial system, the transitional forms of dependence of the under-developed countries reflect their process of liberation from foreign rule. New forms of colonialism simply represent the strategy and tactics of the retreating imperialists. Neo-colonialism is spearheaded against countries which are gaining or have already gained political sovereignty. The liberation of the African peoples is taking

Reprinted by permission of the publisher from *The Journal of Modern African Studies*, 1, 4 (1963), 467–474.

[1] V. I. Lenin, *Selected Works* (Moscow, 1950), 1, pp. 520–1.

place under complex, varied, and contradictory circumstances. Difficult and thorny is also their path to genuine freedom, independence, and prosperity. The main obstacle blocking this path is colonialism in its new forms.

Upon losing direct political control over the colonial territories, the imperialist powers proclaim principles of friendship, co-operation, and "free association" with the young sovereign states of Africa. In practice, however, the realisation of these principles reduces itself to:

a. maintaining the domination of foreign capital in the economy of the new states, and preventing the break-up of the colonial structure of their economy;
b. maintaining strong political ties with the countries which have succeeded in liquidating their colonial status, either by involving them in political communities headed by former metropolitan countries, or by preserving such communities created earlier;
c. imposing co-operation agreements upon the young states to undermine their national sovereignty and independence;
d. maintaining strategic positions by means of troops and military bases in these countries;
e. using the administrative machinery inherited from the colonial régime as an instrument for implementing their policy;
f. maintaining ideological influences in the former colonies; and
g. using outdated legislation which hinders the development of political democracy in the struggle against progressive forces in African states.

Such a policy has been pursued in the majority of the former colonies of Western European powers in Africa. True, attempts to employ the traditional means of colonial policy, including direct violence, are still successful sometimes. However, thanks to the increasing struggle against colonialism on a world-wide scale, the possibilities for the employment of such methods have decreased drastically. The principal factor now is not direct violence, but the attempt to reach a compromise with African national forces, and thus to establish indirect control by more refined and veiled methods of colonial policy.

It is known with what persistence the western powers have striven to maintain their economic positions and political influence in the Congo Republic (Leopoldville). Three days before the proclamation of the country's independence the Belgian authorities dissolved the semi-state organisation, Comité spécial du Katanga, which had had the right to appoint four of the six members of the administrative council of the Union minière du Haut Katanga. The new State thus lost one of its most important levers of control over the biggest mining company in the country, since it would otherwise have acquired the rights of the Comité spécial after independence. After this dissolution, the number of votes in the

Union minière possessed by a private Belgian company, *Compagnie du Katanga,* increased at the expense of the Congolese State by 184,476, thus changing the general proportion of votes in favour of the private share-holders.

There is no need to dwell upon the details of the dramatic events that took place in the Congo after the proclamation of independence. The Congolese tragedy reflects the new policy of the imperialist powers towards African countries. The aim of this policy is, while recognising the sovereignty of these countries, to maintain indirect control over them and to continue their exploitation. Some political figures of Katanga were employed by the western powers in their so-called "remote control diplomacy." Events in the Congo showed, at the same time, that imperialism does not hesitate to employ such methods of colonial policy as direct intervention, organising military plots, or stirring up inter-tribal hatred. Closely interwoven new and old forms of colonialism represent a characteristic feature of the crisis provoked by the western powers. An important feature also is that despite rivalry in the matter of robbing the country they have agreed upon the main thing, i.e. striving to impede the truly independent development of the Congo Republic and to maintain control over the wealth of Katanga. In 1960 the chairman of the Brussels Stock Exchange made a characteristic statement:

The Congo has escaped from our hands, but we can still save Katanga with its copper, cobalt, tin, zinc, and uranium mines. If Katanga slips out too, the shares of the *Union minière du Haut Katanga* will go down. If the Belgians stay in the Congo . . . the shares will double in value.

Imperialists pay considerable attention to maintaining their positions in other African States as well, though the methods of their policy there do not look so blatant as in the Congo. France, for example, uses a system of contractual relations as one of the principal means of implementing her policy. In 1960–1 she signed agreements with her former colonies in West and Equatorial Africa, and the Malagasy Republic, on co-operation in foreign policy, finance, higher education, justice, defence, and so on. Behind the formal equality of the parties, each group of agreements conceals the tendency of France to impose on her partners obligations which would keep them within the orbit of her influence.

Thus, for example, foreign policy agreements between members of the French Community lay down the need to co-ordinate the points of view, positions, and actions of the contracting parties before taking any important decision. The administrative bodies for financial and economic co-operation are formed of an equal number of representatives of the particular country concerned and the French Government. Numerous conventions on signal communications, merchant navigation, civil aviation, and so on, call for co-ordination and consultation between the African authorities and the French representatives.

A great menace for African States lurks in the defence agreements. France's agreement with the Central African Republic, the Congo Republic (Brazzaville), and the Republic of Chad states for example:

Article 1. The Central African Republic, Chad, and Congo have agreed with the French Republic to form a common system for preparing and guaranteeing their own defence and the defence of the Community. . . .
Article 2. The contracting parties pledge themselves to render mutual assistance and constantly to co-ordinate their action in respect of defence.

The agreement also stipulates the right of France to maintain on these countries' territory armed forces which are under the jurisdiction of France but not of the African authorities. It is easy to see that, since France is a member of the N.A.T.O. military bloc, such agreements represent a menace to the neutrality of African States and may even involve them in a military conflict against their will.

*   *   *

. . . In order to prevent the new States from embarking on the wide road of truly independent development, the imperialist powers employ various methods to maintain the colonial structure of the African economies and to secure their position as mere appendages of the world capitalist system, producing primary commodities.

Under present conditions, however, the imperialists do not risk an open declaration in favour of the economic backwardness and abnormal economic specialisation of the former colonies. They apply more flexible forms and methods, pretending to be benefactors of the peoples who have just thrown off foreign political domination. State loans and grants are a significant form of imperialist expansion which had already begun before the winning of independence. Imperialist propaganda clamorously advertises this so-called "assistance" to the African countries, representing it as the most important factor in their economic and social development. It is characteristic, however, that among these loans and subsidies there is almost no place for financing measures which would favour comprehensive economic development, particularly those branches of the economy which would allow them to eliminate their harmful dependence on the world capitalist market.

. . . France grants her former colonies in Africa "assistance" to an annual average of 1,300 million NF through F.A.C. (the Fund for Aid and Co-operation, formerly known as F.I.D.E.S.). But the distribution of the "assistance" in different fields leaves no doubt that France is striving to retain the bias towards primary production in the economy of her former colonies. Thus in 1962 almost 20 per cent of the Fund's allocations to Cameroun was assigned for the development of agriculture, forestry, and fishery; over 40 per cent for the development of "infrastructure," i.e. railways, highways, bridges, ports, and so on; and about 15 per cent for various general expenditures. The aim of capital investment in infrastructure is to reduce the production and distribution costs of foreign companies operating in the country, and thus to favour the increase of their profits. Only about 20 per cent of the allocation is to be spent on public health and education. As for measures for creating the country's own national industrial base, they are ignored completely.

True, a number of African countries have mining and even manufacturing enterprises which are run as French state corporations. The control of these is, of course, in the hands of large foreign industrial and financial groups. For example, the joint-stock company *Compagnie minière de l'Ogoué* (Comilog) exploits manganese deposits in Gabon. The Mining Prospecting Bureau, an official French organisation, possesses 22 per cent of the shares in Comilog. The other shares are distributed between the *Compagnie du Mocta* (14 per cent), the *Société auxiliaire* (15 per cent), both being French companies, and the United States Steel Corporation (49 per cent). Comilog received big loans from the International Bank for Reconstruction and Development and from the French Government. And this is quite understandable: an imperialist state readily renders support to private-capital monopolies which facilitate the pumping of raw materials out of African countries and securing the one-sided structure of their economy. In the above-mentioned example, it would have been impossible to take manganese out of Gabon without large, long-term capital investment in the construction of a railway and a suspension cable-way in inaccessible areas, and for this state aid was essential. It is of interest also to point out that lately there has been an ever-increasing tendency of monopolistic groups in France, U.S.A., Great Britain, Holland, Belgium, Italy, and West Germany to merge, in order to intensify the exploitation of African resources. Thus, "collective colonialism" manifests itself vigorously in the attempts of foreign monopolies to hamper the break-up of the colonial economic structure of young African States.

*   *   *

Foreign monopolies occupy dominating positions in the economy of former British colonies, too. British state capital operates in these countries mainly through the Commonwealth (formerly Colonial) Development Corporation. The main objectives for C.D.C. capital investment are mining, plantation, and light industry—for example, a soap factory in Kenya. These are the same sort of activities as were developed in the colonial past. The only new element is that the Corporation serves as a cover for monopolistic concerns which are operating as its partners in a number of enterprises.

Striving, in every possible way, to hinder the elimination of the pernicious heritage of colonialism in the economy of the African States, the imperialists have recently focused attention on involving these States in the European Economic Community or Common Market. It is no exaggeration to say that the E.E.C. is the main tool of "collective colonialism" in

Africa, aiming especially to maintain the unequal position of young African States in the capitalist system of international division of labour.

What are the provisions of the recent Convention under which 18 States, all former colonies or trust territories of France, Belgium, and Italy in Africa, agreed to "associate" with the Common Market? First of all, they were granted customs preferences for selling their tropical products in E.E.C. markets. But it is a well-known fact that the orientation of their economy towards the export of a limited number of farm crops has been one of the main hindrances to their economic development, since it redoubles their dependence on fluctuations on the world market and does not allow them to extricate themselves from the clutches of foreign monopolies.

But this is not all. Members of the E.E.C. compelled the 18 African countries to consent to considerable cutting down of the above-mentioned preferences from the level originally contemplated. By way of compensation, they will be granted subsidies for traditional export crops and for introducing some new ones. In five years (1963-7) the total amount of these subsidies will reach $230 million, out of the total development fund of $730 million. By this device the members of E.E.C. have limited the ability of African countries to use their resources for strengthening their national economies. Cutting down the preferences will decrease the foreign currency obtained from exports, and this will reduce their ability to import the capital goods needed for the development of their own industry. The amount allotted as compensation is to be spent on agriculture, as already mentioned; and this will be according to a pattern determined by a body including representatives not only of the associated territories, but also of the European countries of E.E.C.

It should be borne in mind also that the size of this compensation is not nearly enough to make up for the losses of the associated territories from reduced preferences, because the terms of trade for African primary producing countries are becoming worse and worse. The weekly *France Observateur* has said: "Under existing conditions any change in the prices of single crops, any difficulty in their marketing, leads to a decrease of revenue which in its size exceeds any foreign financial assistance." To make matters worse, in exchange for the promise of highly doubtful benefits, the associated countries are to abolish customs duties and quantitative restrictions on the import of manufactured goods from the member countries of E.E.C. It is hardly necessary to explain what such "customs disarmament" will mean to the associated countries. Their young and embryonic industries will be faced with competition from the highly industrialised powers of Western Europe, which will nip in the bud the growth of any truly national industry.

Hugh Seton-Watson

MOSCOW'S IMPERIALISM

A certain predominance of Russians in a country where they form at least half the population and possess a more developed culture than the other peoples is of course inevitable. Russian must be the principal language of state, and this must mean that non-Russians seeking a career within the Soviet Union not only must learn Russian, but must constantly use it and, indeed, adapt themselves to Russian ways of thinking and living. But in, fact, the compulsory use of Russian has gone much further than the mere needs of efficient administration would require. I need only mention the imposition of the Cyrillic alphabet on languages which had used the Arabic or Latin alphabets, and the massive introduction of Russian words into the minority languages.

Again, since there were, at the beginning of the Soviet era, many more persons with modern skills or organizing ability among the Russians than among the minority peoples, it was inevitable that Russians should be disproportionately numerous in positions of responsibility in political and economic administration throughout the Union. But here, too, the ruling Communist Party of the Soviet Union went further than mere efficiency required, appointing Russians to key posts in non-Russian areas on a massive scale. Mr. Rywkin well describes how this works in Central Asia.[1] Similar facts could be quoted for the Baltic Republics (Estonia, Latvia and Lithuania), for Azerbaidjan, for Moldavia (a land of predominantly Rumanian population), and to a lesser extent for the Ukraine. In the regions inhabited by small and rather backward peoples in European Russia and Siberia, the control of all key posts by Russians is even more marked.

A third form of Russification is mass settlement of Russian peasants or workers in the countryside or cities of non-Russian regions. This began under the Tsars in Siberia and Central Asia, but was continued and intensified under the Communists. The most striking recent example is Mr. Khrushchev's "virgin lands" campaign in Kazakhstan. Today, the Kazakhs, Bashkirs, and some other smaller peoples are already minorities within their supposed homelands. Russians have also been settled at the expense of the indigenous Rumanians in Moldavia, and of the Estonians and Latvians in the Baltic coastal area.

Reprinted by permission of the publisher from *Problems of Communism* (January–February, 1964).

[1] Michael Rywkin, "Central Asia and the Price of Sovietization," *Problems of Communism* (January–February, 1964). [Eds.]

All this certainly deserves to be called "Russification." But I do not believe that it has ever been the purpose of the Soviet leaders to force non-Russians to become Russians. This *was* the aim of some Russian nationalist politicians in the reigns of Tsars Alexander III and Nicholas II, who thus pursued what they considered to be the interest of the Russian nation. The aim of the Soviet Communists is different: it is the triumph of communism, of a socio-political doctrine which they have sought to put into practice within their own state and which they believe will ultimately be established throughout the world. Of course, convinced Russian Communists have always thought that communism is good for the Russian people. But it has never been part of their purpose to make non-Russians into Russians.

The efforts of the Soviet Communists to achieve their ideal society have led to the construction of a totalitarian regime which has been imposed on all their subjects. One of the essential features of Soviet totalitarianism is extreme centralism. The efforts of the non-Russians to live their own lives in their own way were bound to be unacceptable to the Soviet rulers. Inevitably, they began to see the maintenance of distinct cultures as "bourgeois nationalism," territorial separatism, and treason. What the Moscow rulers objected to was not that the Ukrainians or Uzbeks or other nationalities were not Russians, but that they would not conform to the model prepared for all by the ideologists of the CPSU. What suppressed the non-Russian peoples was not the Russian nation but the totalitarian Moloch.

The Communist leaders are in fact perfectly willing that Kirghiz, Udmurts, White Russians or any other nation should use their own language, in public or in private, provided that they express only Communist ideas with it. The fact . . . that the Soviet peoples still use their native languages should not induce false optimism. It is much more difficult to judge how far the specific national cultures of these peoples have been preserved. How far can an Uzbek retain his national culture if he is cut off from the traditions which have played so important a part in the formation of that culture? How can the idea of an Armenian nation be divorced from the history and the faith of the Armenian Church? . . . The problems are very complex. More is involved than the survival of languages, and totalitarianism is something different from Russian nationalism—even when, as is probably often the case, many of the individual executors of totalitarian policy are themselves unconscious or even conscious Russian nationalists.

In my own view, we would do better to think, not in terms of Russification, but of imperialism—of totalitarian Soviet imperialism. The Soviet Communists are imposing their rule by force on nations which were once conquered by the Tsars. The legitimacy on which 19th-century imperialists took their stand was the might of their sovereign governments. The British ruled large parts of Asia and Africa in the name of Queen Victoria; the Russians ruled Central Asia in the name of Nicholas II. Since 1917, however, the basis of Soviet legitimacy has been a number of unproven ideological assertions. Thus, it is asserted in Moscow that it is the destiny of the whole human race to advance through socialism to communism; that this historical development can be achieved only by the victory of the industrial working class over other classes; that the will of the working class can be embodied only in a Marxist-Leninist party; that a Marxist-Leninist party is one which pursues policies decided by the leaders of the CPSU; and, consequently, that the leaders of the CPSU possess a monopoly of the supreme wisdom required to direct this cosmic struggle—a struggle on which the true interests of all workers, including the unborn, and of all nations, including those which possess virtually no industrial working class at all, depend. This claim, made on behalf of the Soviet leaders, is as arrogant and as incapable of rational proof as any claim to divine authority made by a medieval European monarch or Mongol khan. The right of the Moscow government to rule the Uzbeks has as much or as little validity as the right of Queen Victoria to rule the Burmese.

Soviet spokesmen are entitled to point to the great material progress achieved in Central Asia under Soviet rule. Other European colonizers also showed great accomplishments, in more difficult climatic conditions, and with a more unfavorable proportion between their own numbers and the numbers of their colonial subjects. Supporters of the Central African Federation have argued that it has brought economic benefits to the Africans, and that it would have brought more if it had been allowed to continue. They may be right. But they have missed the point, which is that the Africans of the Rhodesias and Nyasaland want to run their own countries. It may be that they will run them badly, but they want to be their own masters. The Soviet government uses essentially the same arguments as Sir Roy Welensky.[2] It has developed the resources of Uzbekistan. Some of the benefits of this development have gone to the Uzbeks, some to the Russians living in Uzbekistan, and some into the great maw of the totalitarian Leviathan in Moscow. But at no time has the Soviet Government been willing to consider for a moment allowing the Uzbeks to run their own country, allowing them to create an independent Uzbek state.

One of the favorite Soviet arguments is that the Russian people, as opposed to past Russian rulers, were always good friends of the Central Asian peoples. This is unfortunately not true. It is only fair to admit that the best Russian officers and administrators in the time of the Tsars showed real concern for their Asian subjects, therein resembling the best British and French colonial administrators (there were also, of course, bad British, French and Russian colonial officials). But the "Russian people" who met the Central Asian peoples in their homelands—that is, the peasant settlers in Turkestan, or the Russian railway workers in Tashkent—showed no such concern. On the contrary, the worst atrocities by Russians against

[2] Formerly Prime Minister of South Rhodesia. [Eds.]

Central Asians were committed by these peasants and workers during the Civil War and the Basmachi revolt—and committed, ironically enough, not in the name of Tsardom or Empire, but in the name of world socialist revolution. It is only fair to point out that Lenin was shocked by these atrocities and did his best to stop them. But he was only partly successful. The truth is that the hostility between Russians and Asians in Turkestan arose from economic and social conditions. The Russian settlers were in essentially the same situation as the French *colons* in Algeria; the Russian railway workers in essentially the same situation as the white mine workers in Northern Rhodesia. The hostility of the "poor white" worker and the white colonial farmer to the colonial peoples is a phenomenon well known to any student of Western colonialism in Africa. It exists in the Soviet empire, too.

*   *   *

In conclusion, let me insist that I am not arguing that Soviet imperialism is uniquely wicked, but only that it is one among many varieties of modern imperialism, which should be studied as such. It is obvious that nationalists in Africa, engaged in a struggle for independence, must choose their friends and allies according to the needs of their struggle. It is thus idle to expect, for example, that an Angolan nationalist should worry too much about the imperialism of the Soviet Union when Moscow is an enemy of Portugal. But it is one thing to view your enemy's enemy as a potential temporary friend, another to assume that because he is your enemy's enemy he must be a paragon of virtue. As for the political and intellectual leaders of Asian or African states which are already independent, they both can and must judge the members of the community of independent states by their past records. If one lives in the jungle, there is no need to go tiger-hunting. But it is well to observe how the tiger treats the goats who come his way before one follows in their steps.

Henry M. Pachter

IMPERIALISM AND NEOCOLONIALISM: A REEXAMINATION

THE QUESTION ASKED

Clearly a superpower which maintains bases and troops on foreign soil, wages war in faraway countries, provides others with arms worth $3 billion a year, and influences their foreign as well as domestic policies; a country, moreover, whose currency serves as monetary reserve for half of the world's currencies, whose capital export and foreign trade are the main sources of new investment in underdeveloped areas, and whose corporations influence economic policies even on the most advanced continent; a country whose consumption of raw materials amounts to more than half of total exports from a number of other countries and whose exports of manufactured articles and cultural goods determine and revolutionize the style of life in the rest of the world; finally, a country which defines its own foreign policy in terms of a world historic struggle with one or two other expansionist powers and on whose ambitions smaller countries rely for their own protection—clearly such a power must be called imperialist by any definition of that term.

Yet saying this we have not admitted much. Any structure as big as the United States, the Soviet Union, the People's Republic of China, or for that matter the Lever Brothers concern, the United Fruit Corporation, the Ford Foundation, the Catholic Church, and Metro-Goldwyn-Mayer is bound to engage others of its kind in a power play that affects the interests, and often the fate, of the bystanders. Bigness itself provides opportunities and engenders a dynamism of its own, expansion feeding further expansion. Hegemony, however, is a dubious asset. In their "partnership" the smaller nations will feel more dependent than the big one. The limited concerns of the small nations are distorted through their projection on the large screen of world politics, which is of much more vital interest to the larger nation. Such big-power supremacy is resented even when exercised without malice and intent—as Gulliver found out in Lilliput.

Still, we would not be satisfied with a definition explaining imperialism as a mere by-product of bigness. Imperialism must be understood as a deliberate, well-profiled policy, executed with powerful means and accompanied by an ideology that justifies the striving for empire and domination. Bigness with a direction, expansion with deliberate intent, interests defined

Adapted from a paper delivered at the New York State Political Science Association's meeting in Saratoga Springs, N.Y., March 1970, under the title "The United States as a World Power—Imperialism and Neocolonialism: a Reexamination." Fuller versions may be read in *Dissent* (September 1970 and September 1971).

in terms not of business but of power and influence—these are the characteristics of "imperialism."

Imperialism is a complex of political, diplomatic, military, financial, and economic strategies to secure the hegemony of one nation over others; overlapping with but distinct from imperialism, the term "colonialism" shall mean for the length of this paper the subjection of one nation by another for purposes of economic exploitation.   Our aim is precisely to determine the relationship of these two terms in the conduct of U.S. foreign affairs.

*   *   *

IMPERIALISM WITHOUT EMPIRE

The U.S. empire cannot be found on any map or globe and yet it is worldwide.   The United States has no colonies to speak of; the few bases it has retained serve strategic purposes.   Its policies have all the marks of bigpower rivalry, and their critics charge that they are influenced too much by military thinking.   Yet, the U.S. is being accused of "financial" or "neo" colonialism.   Moreover, the loudest outcry against American domination does not come from underdeveloped countries whose raw materials we buy but from highly industrialized nations, which have practiced imperialism and colonialism in the recent past—France and Japan.   Jean-Jacques Servan-Schreiber—editor of *L'Express*—has charged that through superior techniques of management U.S. corporations can "use our own money to dominate our industries."   Also, political pressure helps U.S. corporations to infiltrate the allied economies and to exploit them in subtle, and often not so subtle, ways.   One might speak here of a "superimperialism" inasmuch as U.S. interests are milking or at least directing nations that themselves are colonial powers or are using this new technique of neocolonialism to dominate the economies of independent countries.

We may distinguish the following types:

1. Territorial imperialism: old-fashioned rule over conquered nations.
2. Naval colonialism: exploitation of less developed nations by settlers or managers.
3. Neocolonialism: domination of independent countries by investors or traders.
4. Superimperialism: domination of developed economy by imperial powers, with indirect exploitation of others.

On this tableau the United States is in very distinguished company. Ancient Athens certainly was an imperial power, though she owned no territory beyond the barren rocks of Attica.   Medieval Venice ruled the waves and financed the Crusades—which always ended up in places where the Venetians needed trading posts.   For, of course, all these big naval powers—Athens, Venice, the U.S., Genoa, and we even might add the Phoenicians—were commercial republics and they were ruled by the rich. The Athenians also were democratic at home; but they spoke harshly to their allies and they dealt brutally with defectors.   Here is how they lectured the unhappy citizens of Melos: "Of the Gods we believe and of men we know that by a necessary law of nature they rule wherever they can.   We did not invent this law, we are only following it. . . .   If you are well advised you will not think it dishonorable to submit to the greatest city in Hellas when it makes you the modest offer to become its ally without ceasing to enjoy the country that belongs to you."

A third characteristic these maritime republics have in common: they fight ideological wars—against dictatorships, against the barbarians, against the infidels, against backwardness, for free trade.   Democracy, freedom, humanism are ideas that claim universality precisely because they are not nationalistic.   Indivisible freedom cannot tolerate areas of servitude.   It was natural for Athens to fight for the freedom of cities in Asia, for Venice to fight against the closed society of the Moslem Turks.   The United States fought for Freedom of the Seas and proclaimed the principle of the Open Door against those imperial powers that conceived of their empires as fenced-in territories.   Woodrow Wilson fought for collective security; Franklin D. Roosevelt first quarantined the dictators and then fought for the Four Freedoms and the Atlantic Charter.

Does this perhaps sound suspicious?   Are these democracies imperialistic because they are commercial?   Open door has meant that a new imperialism tried to pry open some doors that older imperialisms held closed.   It has even been said that the Monroe Doctrine was proclaimed to fence South America in as a preserved hunting ground for U.S. capital. The trouble with this theory is that in 1823 the United States had little to sell to the Latin republics and no capital to invest.   All documents of the time show that the doctrine was a purely diplomatic move, designed to assert the independence of U.S. policies, and that "open door" was as much in China's interest as in America's.

DOLLAR DIPLOMACY

The Open Door policy in China was to stop the Russo-Japanese partition of Manchuria; the State Department asked the ill-famed railroad tycoon, Edward Harriman, to save Manchuria by investing a few million dollars there.   But Harriman and Morgan found the proposition unprofitable and asked for a government guarantee.   When Woodrow Wilson came to power, he refused to endorse the scheme.   Only thirty miles of railway were built—not in Manchuria but far to the south in Fukien; not a dollar was invested in Manchuria.   The total of U.S. investments in Asia and

Africa then was $200 million, in South America $400 million—nothing to compare with the $7 billion investment of foreigners in the United States. Yet the imperialist phase of U.S. policies coincides with this period.

It was Jefferson, by the way, who talked of annexing Cuba—no representative of finance he! But as the Louisiana Purchase showed, Jefferson had a strong sense of geopolitical realities; he was pursuing power politics, and the other presidents after him who coveted the Isthmus of Panama or moved to build a canal and deployed the Marines to protect it also were thinking in terms of strategy. We may call Jefferson an imperialist in the older sense, but not in Lenin's and Hobson's.[1]

Nor was it the dollar that called in the big stick. Rather, it was President Taft who desired to replace the big stick by subtler means. He defined "the purpose of the present Administration" as being the encouragement of "the use of American capital in the development of China by the promotion of essential reforms." He promised to "remove countries in this hemisphere from the jeopardy involved by heavy foreign debt and from the danger of internal complications due to disorder at home." And his secretary of state, Philander Knox, sounds almost modern when he said that he "could imagine no better use for American dollars than to replace insecurity by stability in neighboring states." And again: "The malady of revolution and financial collapse is most acute precisely in the region where it is most dangerous to us. It is here that we seek to apply the remedy." Taft and Knox called the technique they were using "dollar diplomacy"—meaning the deliberate, purposeful exploitation of commercial and financial interests in order to bind other countries to the United States, to further strategic projects, to counteract imperialistic designs of other powers.

Dollars were mobilized to serve diplomatic ends. Received wisdom has it the other way round: that diplomacy had to follow the initiative of the greedy dollar. Actually, American bankers complained that they did not have enough dollars to do the job the President asked them to do.

Alas, we all know what later on Taft's lofty resolutions came to: outright intervention by Marines in Nicaragua, Honduras, Mexico, Santo Domingo—and this under Woodrow Wilson, of all Presidents, who had begun his administration by repudiating dollar diplomacy in China! The United States was talking to her neighbors as Athens had talked to Melos. There is no doubt that her concern with the Caribbean area, her solicitude for the safety of the Panama Canal, her fear of foreign intervention on this continent generated naval and financial imperialism. Inevitably we established five protectorates—states that remained nominally independent but were governed by U.S. commissars—and interests of a commercial and financial nature were grafted upon this empire.

Before World War I this must still be called hemisphere imperialism.

[1] See D. K. Fieldhouse's article earlier in this chapter. [Eds.]

America was not yet a world power. She played no role in the rivalries that led to the catastrophe of 1914; and as we have seen, her imperialism was not motivated primarily by economic interests. To repeat: her trade with the Latin American countries was minimal, her investments there negligible; above all, being poor in capital she had no need to export it. The compulsion to expand was not economic but strategic. Financial imperialism, the so-called dollar diplomacy, was a tool, one of the means available to an overall policy; but this tool was soon to dominate the scene. In trying to develop techniques of humane, peaceful intervention, Knox created precisely those financial interests which Hobson and Lenin denounced as the roots of imperialism; the seeds he had planted sprouted as dragons' teeth.

This leads to the second observation about means, ends, and intentions. We have found that intentions don't really count. The attempt to stay out of the power game leads straight into it. The Open Door policy required meddling in the affairs of China; the design to stave off foreign intervention called for intervention; the wish to substitute dollars for bullets ended in more bullets. Worse: motives and ends initially seem to permit a wide choice of means—some of them even, in the beginning and in the intention, quite humane; but the means then take over and tend to determine the ends.

DILEMMAS OF POWER POLITICS

When we nominated ourselves tutors and guardians of the smaller American republics, we established exactly the kind of preserved hunting ground we pretended we had to deny the Russians and Japanese in Manchuria. When we created a safety zone in this hemisphere, we provided for American capital precisely those opportunities that then, in turn, had to be protected by the Marines.

In opposing imperialism abroad the United States needed to develop the weapons imperialists used: a two-ocean navy, a military establishment, the draft, a propaganda agency. It occupied bases abroad and tried to influence, nay to dominate other governments. Even if we grant that all this was not done for imperialistic motives, the means certainly were imperialistic, and the pacifist-isolationist fear was vindicated: in resisting evil one must do evil; in fighting the totalitarians, Americans lost some of their own values. This is the tragedy of all politics, the tragedy of power: it becomes absolute, independent of its purposes.

The United States has found it expedient, for example, to do business with dictators who are repugnant to our sensibilities—Trujillo, Batista, Somoza, Chiang Kai-shek, Diem, Franco. Some say that such alliances disclose the true reactionary nature of U.S. imperialism. Is guilt revealed by association? The charge is mistaken, for we do not "support" Franco; he is extorting an exorbitant price for a piece of real estate the Navy thinks it needs.   For similar reasons of self-interest we have "supported" Tito, Nasser, Sukarno, and other heroes of the Left.   The CIA even supported Ho Chi Minh and worked against Diem; we caused the downfall of Trujillo and Batista by withdrawing support from them; we offered to support Castro's farm reform.   Thirdly, and this may be decisive: The record is not consistent and clear at all but shows a frequent wavering between extremes.   For a while we would not recognize any Latin American dictator; then we decided to give the *abrazo* to any leader who actually was in possession of a country.   Often American interests pulled in different directions, with the CIA, the Army, the ambassador, business lobbies, and the State Department backing different contenders.

THE RATIONALE OF U.S. INTERVENTIONS

It is often said that we support dictators because they protect American business.   Some do protect American business interests; but the conjunction "because" is erroneous.   The national interest, or what the State Department defines as national interest, is not to protect individual American firms but to preserve a system of business which the American public identifies with its way of life and which the American government considers the alternative to the rival system of communism.   As the U.S. International Cooperation Administration declared, "The United States is convinced that private ownership and operation of industrial and extractive enterprises contribute more effectively than public ownership and operation to the general improvement of the economy of a country. . . . It is therefore a basic policy of the ICA to employ U.S. assistance to aid-receiving countries in such a way as will encourage the development of the private sectors of their economies."

In this the American government agrees with Stalin, who said: "Whoever conquers a territory introduces his own economic system into it." The American empire expresses its presence and exercises its influence through the capitalistic mode of operation for which it keeps as much of the world "open" as possible.   It also prefers democratic governments which guarantee the free exchange of goods and ideas.

The same enlightened self-interest was behind the Marshall Plan and the containment policy of the late forties—the twin weapons of the so-called cold war.   No doubt it was in the interest of both the American and the European democracies to keep the Soviet armies at bay and to avert the danger of a communist take-over.   To do that, the European economies had to be rebuilt and the reconstruction site had to be shielded.   These policies not only helped to restore a capitalist world market.   The interests of all parties also demanded a restoration of democracy in those countries of Europe that had lost it; democracy of necessity became the watchword of the Western coalition.   This was the ideology of the so-called cold war, the strategy that prevented a hot war.

In Europe we found democratic forces we were able to work with; we collaborate with such forces and institutions wherever they are available. Unfortunately there are not many of them, especially in the third world—and some whom we mistook for democrats, like Diem, disappointed us. Yet we gave $7 billion to Nehru despite his very pronounced anti-Americanism; we loyally supported the socialist Adoula in the Congo against Tshombe, an avowed puppet of the colonialists. We tried to defend democracy in Argentina against the dictator—without success, but not for want of trying. In Peru we supported the Acción Popular, with President Belaunde, and even Haya de la Torre, the venerable leader of the APRA (American Popular Revolution Alliance); in Bolivia we supported Paz Estenssero and his National Revolutionary Movement; when Mexico nationalized the oil companies, FDR arranged for a low compensation award, part of which was paid by the U.S. Treasury. [In Chile we are negotiating with Allende (added 1971).] The French even accused the CIA of aiding the Algerian rebels. Incidentally the General Ovando who seized power in Bolivia and the General Velasquez who possessed himself of Peru—both acclaimed by the Left as "anti-imperialists"—were the ones who on earlier occasions bloodily crushed miners' uprisings.

WHERE U.S. BUSINESS COMES IN

Clearly American and other business interests find a more favorable climate under republican governments than under populist-nationalist generals like Perón, Torres, Nasser. But while such pseudorevolutionary leaders incite popular enthusiasm by threatening to nationalize foreign property, they do not tax their own nabobs and continue to solicit American investments. As in all countries entering the industrial age, labor is being exploited, by native even more cruelly than by foreign capitalists. But what is actually a *social* question is made to appear as a racial or national question; class war is being deflected into "war of national liberation." Paul Baran and Herbert Marcuse therefore have characterized the pseudoprogressive, national-revolutionary governments as "the last and most dangerous disguise of business rule" over underdeveloped nations. Libya throws the Americans out only to call the French in, and Western firms can do business with dictators of the Left as well as of the Right. American firms were prepared to work for Castro until he forced the showdown, and only after he had opted for the Russian orbit did Eisenhower break with him. We allowed Ceylon and Indonesia to expropriate oil firms as long as they did not fall into the Russian or Chinese orbit. We did not invoke the Hickenlooper Amendment against Peru because we hoped that the revolutionary government would continue to do business with us.

These pragmatic policies have paid dividends that could hardly have been expected by the policymakers. When the Marshall Plan stopped the Russians in Europe, American capitalists would not bet their own money on European recovery; today American direct investments in Europe amount to $18 billion, in Canada and Australia to $21 billion—together four times as much as all our investments in all countries twenty years ago. U.S. firms also own $10 billion in Latin America, $7 billion in Africa, Asia and the Near East.   Seventeen billion dollars are invested in the oil industry; they produce the highest profits.   Five billion dollars are invested in mining, $24 billion in manufacturing, $13 billion in construction, finance, commerce, shipping, utilities, etc.   But if we disregard oil and mining, American investments in the third world are neither as substantial nor as profitable as those in the highly industrialized countries.

The benefits have been distributed very unevenly; they are concentrated in a few industries and a limited number of large corporations.   The Aluminum Corporation of America generates two-thirds of its total income in its foreign subsidiaries; Colgate-Palmolive, three-quarters.   Nearly half of the hundred biggest corporations in the United States depend for a sizable part of their dividends on foreign sources.   Vice versa, foreigners own $10 billion worth of plants in this country.   But if we count all assets, including stocks and bonds, the relationship is more balanced: Americans have invested $93 billion abroad, and the U.S. government has claims to $23 billion; foreigners own $70 billion of U.S. assets.

In recent years something new has been added to the economic structure of the West: the international corporation.   Books are already being written about these new corporations, which know no frontiers and no nationality.   They may establish themselves for production purposes in one country, for tax purposes in another.   They may be owned by nationals of one country and managed by nationals of another.   They know no government and no fatherland but are international freebooters, following their interests to any place that might suit them.   They even are planning across the national frontiers.   German firms are building chemical plants in South Carolina and electric power plants in South America with World Bank financing.   Mutual funds overseas also sell shares in U.S. corporations.

The importance of international corporations in world trade is staggering.   The gross value of goods produced by United States owned firms or affiliates abroad alone is $40 billion a year—twice our export of manufactured goods and the equivalent of total consumer expenditure in a good-sized country like Italy.   In another context A. A. Berle has indeed compared the new corporations to nations.   They account for a certain percentage of world trade; part of their product is reexported to the United States, another part elsewhere.   Prof. Harry Magdoff has pointed out—in the Maoist *Monthly Review*—that in certain industries, such as rubber, chemicals, and transportation equipment, the foreign plants export more than the mother company.   But Magdoff wishes to add those $40 billion to the volume of U.S. exports.   That would be very misleading for the labor and materials were bought in the countries of operation, and they

export to the United States.   In Latin America, U.S. firms employ 1,230,-
000 people, and nine out of ten in managerial positions were hired locally.
In fact these corporations are vitally concerned with finding and training
local talent.

The planning of such a large firm is now global.   Its loyalties are
determined by the political situation in each of the continents where it
operates.   Often the profits have to be reinvested locally, so the companies
are Arab in the Middle East, Pan-European in the countries of the Common Market, South American in Latin America.   What matters is not
where the profit goes but where the power resides; while financial control
may remain in New York, the thinking of the corporation assumes a
"colonial" coloration, and something similar to the managerial revolution
might be in the making, eroding the prerogatives of ownership and substituting for it the preponderance of functional criteria.

PROFITS WITHOUT A FATHERLAND

These new corporations constitute the opposite of Imperialism, which is
always tied to the policies of one country.   The term makes no sense if
one cannot point to a government that is pursuing these imperialist or
economic interests.   An international corporation knows no exports or
imports; whether its policies are good or bad, progressive or reactionary,
coinciding or colliding with any government interest, they cannot be
identical with "American imperialism."

On balance, of course, more U.S. managers operate abroad than foreigners do here; more U.S. citizens draw income from overseas sources
than vice versa.   U.S. private income from investments abroad is about $7
billion, whereas foreigners draw about $3 billion from dividends and interest
in this country.   This community of new arrangements to protect cur-
rencies; the International Monetary Fund and the World Bank, international cartels, and trade agreements constitute an international directorate of banking, industry, and commerce.   Walther Rathenau wrote, sixty
years ago, that the world was ruled by two hundred people who know
each other; his hyperbole might come true now in half of the world at
least, with interlocking directorates extending into many countries.

If the international corporations have lost their identification with the
country of their origin, their nations no longer identify their interests with
those of their corporations.   President Harding still considered U.S. corporations in Mexico quasi-extraterritorial; Presidents Eisenhower and
Nixon recognized the right of any country to nationalize corporations in its
territory.   On the other hand, the corporations often act in flagrant contradiction to national policy or even become spokesmen for the country
in which they operate.   American oil companies which once thought they
had the sheiks in their pockets now plead with President Nixon to change
America's Near East policy in favor of the Arabs.

Even at a time when the U.S. government considered itself the errand-boy of U.S. business, frequent misunderstandings often prevented agreement on what the national interest was.   When the State Department tried to mediate a quarrel between Chile and Peru over the Tacna-Arica territory, an arms manufacturer complained that it was "interfering perniciously with legitimate business."   While the government was internationalist, business remained isolationist; while Presidents seek to make the country defense conscious, the stock exchange has consistently given defense industries a lower rating than other firms and in recent years has responded to peace rumors with bullish behavior.   The *Wall Street Journal* and the right wing of the Republican party were isolationist and anti-interventionist through two world wars, the cold war, and even in Vietnam.   They all think it is bad business to spend $30 billion a year to protect a piddling few millions of trade and investments in Southeast Asia—never mind anticommunism and big-power aspirations.

NEOCOLONIALISM

If business is no longer patriotic, it may still display a "colonialist" stance vis-à-vis the underdeveloped countries.   At international conferences like UNCTAD, many charge that the rich get richer and the poor, poorer, that the producers of raw materials enrich the makers of machinery, the debtors feed the creditors.   Yet they ask for new loans.   But most U.S. capitalists would rather invest in highly developed countries.   Contrary to the Lenin-Hobson theory, capital is not anxious to flow to areas of low-wage levels; the U.S. government vainly implores U.S. business to help industrialize countries suffering from underdevelopment.

Likewise, our foreign trade is directed toward the developed countries. In 1968 we exported $23 billion worth of goods to industrial countries but only $11 billion to underdeveloped countries.   We imported $24 billion of merchandise from Western industrialized countries, but less than half that much—$9 billion—from communist *and* underdeveloped ones. We buy Volkswagens and Sony radios, but we pay low prices for our coffee.   We buy less bauxite, magnesia, and chromium because in many utensils metal is being replaced by plastic materials; and unfortunately for our friends in Manila, Du Pont is producing fibers that replace sisal.

Brazil, Ghana, Columbia, and a few more countries have an agreement on coffee, but they have not been able to stabilize their price.   Industrial countries limit their production when prices fall; in backward countries, farmers respond to price falls not by cutting production but by increasing it, thus making the problem worse.   As a result we have the phenomenon of the "scissors," i.e., industrial goods fetch ever-rising prices while farm products and others which underdeveloped countries must export are constantly depressed.   They lose in these exchanges.   Moreover they are far more dependent on exports and imports than we are.   They produce an excess of certain goods which they must exchange in order to satisfy their other needs, especially if they wish to industrialize. Now, unfortunately, our economy is so big that the 3 percent of gross national product constituting our imports, for other countries constitutes almost half of the world trade. When our imports decline by an ever so small percentage point, their exports decline catastrophically. But by the same token, a small concession on our part might mean a big help for them. Were we to pay better prices for primary commodities, many countries would not need our grants-in-aid.

However, the problem lies deeper. In order to modernize and industrialize themselves, the backward nations must cast off their traditional ways. If they wish to make effective use of our capital and know-how, they must adopt the businesslike attitudes of Western men. If these are laid down in the conditions of a loan, we often appear to impose our ways on them. This is resented as exploitation or as an attempt to appoint ourselves the guardians of nations that used to be sovereign. Our monetary and financial institutions—which discipline us as well as them—are experienced as enforcing agents of a foreign master. Especially the old ruling classes in underdeveloped countries see our development schemes as a double threat to their way of life and to the survival of their caste system. They have been unwilling and unable to create modern industries; but they resent the foreigners who develop their country's resources.

The foreign companies, especially those in the oil and mining businesses, make enormous profits. But where are these profits realized? We must distinguish between two very different cases. One is utilities, railways, and most manufacturing industries: there the profits are made off the natives and unless they are reinvested, which often is required by law, the money is taken out of the country—an absolute loss; these nations would be better off if such companies were nationalized and profits retained and used for development. Brazil now has a law making it obligatory for all companies to be owned at least 51 percent by nationals, though to profit from American know-how they may have a management contract with an American firm. On the whole this is a good arrangement.

Quite a different case concerns the extractive industries—mines, oil, bananas, timber. These companies produce a commodity that cannot be consumed by the natives. They must sell it to industrialized countries, above all the United States. Only here can the profit be realized. This is true of bananas just as well as of oil. The local powers in South America or Arabia may raise wage rates, ground rent, or royalty; they may write new laws or make new contracts; but neither the United Fruit Corporation nor ESSO will suffer. They will just raise prices and the American consumer will pay. But the world market sets limits to the return on commodities, as coffee and cocoa producers found out. Even though no United Fruit Corporation stands between them and the American consumer, their national and international cartels were unable to stabilize prices.

Thirdly, we have the case of U.S. businesses that have been transferred to a low-wage, no-tax country.   These runaway businesses reexport into the United States or other countries, and the AFL-CIO has charged, not without reason, that they are taking thousands of jobs from American workers, especially from minority people and those in hard-core poverty areas. When State Department officials are confronted with Latin American demands for lower tariffs, they actually are dealing with front men for international corporations.   Nevertheless it remains U.S. policy to encourage private investment abroad; for governmental and international development aid cannot nearly provide an adequate substitute for the lacking formation of new capital in the underdeveloped countries themselves.

AID IMPERIALISM

The charge of colonialism has been leveled even against development aid. Of course such aid is given for the same selfish reason a rich man has in cleaning up a slum.   He may impose his sanitary standards on neighbors who cannot afford them.   We also attach strings to our aid.   John F. Kennedy told the Latin Americans: No reform, no money.   The ruling classes down under, who would not part with their tax privileges or their hold on the land, duly brought the *Alianza para el Progreso* down.   I regret that we did not insist, and also that we did not attach another string to our grants, threatening to stop all aid to governments that bought heavy arms. All of this is "dollar diplomacy": the use of economic means for political ends.

Foreign aid is common currency in buying votes at the United Nations or political favors abroad.   In the World Bank Report for 1962, Eugene Black complained that often aid was given for no economic reasons at all or even against economic reason.   Nevertheless it is realistic to recognize this form of influence; those who condemn it or resent the strings have the option of refusing the gift—or they may repudiate the strings, as India has done frequently with immunity.   But who would expect Golda Meir to condemn our war in Vietnam?   Or Castro to condemn the invasion of Prague?

Passing from grants to loans: the term "aid" here is clearly a euphemism for export financing.   Loans usually are tied to the purchase of certain goods, require firm guarantees which often are burdensome, and may also call for reforms and controls bordering on receivership.   Such conditions are apt to turn an attempt at friendly cooperation into a situation of resentful dependence.   What to us appears as a reasonable arrangement is experienced by a weak partner as an instrument of control.

A THEORY AND A PROPOSAL

America is a conservative power. Its interest is the protection of the status quo; its policy is to strengthen all governments which guarantee a favorable environment to its influence. It maintains its hegemony through the deployment of a vast arsenal of political, strategic, economic, financial, and diplomatic weapons. These are often seen as a complex whole where one flying buttress supports the other. Just as often we find our political, strategic and economic agents working at cross-purposes.

While we encourage private investments abroad and tell underdeveloped countries to "earn" more by exporting, we also raise tariffs against the newly created industries. While the secretary of state is trying to place development goals before the backward nations, the banks impose on them conditions that make even modest reforms illusory. While the President tells his ambassadors to offer the U.S.A. in a "low profile," U.S. corporations hit the drum in ostentatious displays. While it would help our diplomacy if the United States were to abandon rights acquired through unequal treaties with corrupt governments, Congress answers every challenge of such rights with threatening gesticulations. Since much of the uneasiness in the third world, as we found, stems from the lopsidedness of our bilateral relations, we ought to handicap ourselves in negotiating with its representatives. But at every international conference our negotiators not only bring to bear the full weight of our strategic, political, and economic power; they also seem to think that we may lose our hegemony if we concede more than we have to.

Overbearing agents of U.S. corporations and government are responsible for much of the anti-Americanism which once spoke the language of fascism but recently has adopted the vocabulary of Marxism and Maoism. Ideologies tend to be all embracing and monolithic; moreover, capitalism and imperialism, U.S. power and U.S. business may appear as virtually one to people whose experience with the big power has been confined to its local representatives.

No such facile projection is possible to an observer whose vantage point permits him to see the manifold interests and pressures which influence the makers of U.S. policy, or who studies the variety of decisions which result and often wonders why they are so contradictory. He sees particular colonial interests which are at variance with the interests of U.S. business as a whole, and U.S. political interests which differ from both. He sees occasional coincidence of political and economic interests, but no necessary connection between them. To exemplify: Certain interests would like to punish Chile and Peru for nationalizing U.S. property; U.S. business on the whole would suffer from a trade war; the U.S. State Department should not be committed either way before it starts negotiating. Definitely, the time is gone when Lord Palmerston placed the Empire behind the interest of a Maltese Jew who happened to be Her Majesty's subject. Several

American Presidents have clearly stated that U.S. firms can no longer count on their automatic support.

We might divorce U.S. power still more visibly from private business interests by a gesture for which Franklin D. Roosevelt's settlement of the Mexican oil conflict provides the precedent: The U.S. Treasury could buy up the holdings of overseas mining and oil properties by U.S. citizens or corporations and transfer them to an international agency, as we proposed to do for uranium and fission products in the famous Baruch Plan in 1946.

Such a plan would not solve the problems of hunger, poverty, and over-population in the underdeveloped countries; it would not close the gap between them and the industrially advanced countries. Nor can any economic measures abolish the "Gulliver complex"—the dependence of backward and weak nations on rich and powerful ones. It is the fate of big powers that they are expected to provide leadership, but if they do, to appear as interventionist.

SUGGESTED READINGS

Fieldhouse, D. K., *The Theory of Capitalist Imperialism*, New York: Barnes & Noble, 1967.

Koebner, Richard, and Schmidt, H. D., *Imperialism: The Story and Significance of a Political Word, 1840–1960*, Cambridge, England: Cambridge University Press, 1964.

Langer, William L., *The Diplomacy of Imperialism*, rev. ed., New York: Knopf, 1951.

Mason, Philip, *Patterns of Dominance*, London and New York: Oxford University Press, 1970.

Niebuhr, Reinhold, *The Structure of Nations and Empires*, New York: Scribner's, 1959.

Schumpeter, Joseph, *Imperialism and Social Classes*, New York: Meridian, 1955.

Strachey, John, *The End of Empire*, New York: Random House, 1960.

Thornton, A. P., *Doctrines of Imperialism*, New York: John Wiley, 1965.

Wesson, Robert G., *The Imperial Order*, Berkeley and Los Angeles: University of California Press, 1967.

Williams, William A., *The Roots of the Modern American Empire*, New York: Random House, 1969.

IV. THE ROLE OF IDEOLOGY

Statesmen, publicists, and intellectuals have often asserted that a "conflict of ideologies" lies at the root of the contemporary international struggle. Social scientists have been more sceptical if, indeed, they have conceded that ideology plays any role at all. Political "realists" have often equated ideology with the word-spinnings of "utopians" and "idealists," seeing it as the moral costume in which, more or less consciously, political leaders dress up their quest for power. Political behavioralists sometimes identify ideology with moral values as a kind of political analysis irrevocably tainted by nonscientific "value judgments." Other political scientists have been less universal in their definitions, regarding ideology as essentially a form of moral fanaticism. Thus, for William Ebenstein, the "major conflict of our age" has been the struggle between "aggressive totalitarianism . . . a fanatical ideology that brooks no compromise" and "the free way of life." [1] And Marx and Engels saw ideology as any abstract, metaphysical doctrine as distinguished from their own, materialist science.[2] Ideology, it would seem, is always an illusion and always what one's opponent believes.

There are, in fact, two major conceptions of ideology. For Karl Mannheim, ideology was a set of beliefs and values, a "pattern of basic political symbols" that are implicit in the culture and way of life of a given social group and are made coherent and articulate only when the group is threatened or otherwise involved in challenging conflict.[3] As the life situation of the group changes, the character and meaning of its political doctrines change as well. Excluded from power, a group develops a "utopia," a savage indictment of the existing order that promises a radical transformation in the direction of a more perfect justice; the excuses of rulers for their failures are brushed aside as the camouflage of self-interest or evil intent. But once a utopian group takes power, Mannheim argued, its doctrine gradually becomes an ideology, a justification of its rule that seeks to explain its failures away. (E. H. Carr, obviously,

[1] *Today's Isms,* Englewood Cliffs: Prentice-Hall, 1955, p. vii.

[2] Friedrich Engels, *Anti-Dühring,* Moscow: Foreign Languages Press, 1962, p. 134.

[3] *Ideology and Utopia,* New York: Harcourt, Brace and World, 1951.

made this analysis the core of his own theory.) [4]   Fearing that ideologies might grow ever more rigid in an escalating cycle of challenge and response, Mannheim urged intellectuals—more alienated, as he saw them, from other social groups—to "unmask" the highly relative and self-interested character of ideologies. This might make the adherents of political doctrines less certain and fervent and might make it possible to arrange compromises that would permit coexistence or even consensus between erstwhile antagonists.

In the late 1950s a large number of social scientists influenced by Mannheim were encouraged by what they felt to be the "end of ideology." [5]   Growing disillusionment with the pretensions of ideology produced by a generation of intellectual and political unmasking, social change that undermined old classes and groups, and the affluence of industrial states that raised contentment and lessened desperation were thought to have produced a new, pragmatic spirit of bargaining and compromise.

Such ideas must seem bizarre today, given the proliferation of new, militant ideologies on all sides of the political spectrum. And doubt about our domestic political ability to arrange compromises between mutually exclusive political programs must cause some uneasiness about the hopes, which the end of ideology thesis aroused, for international coexistence.

The argument that ideology was ending, however, had an important element of truth. The solidarity of older social groups, and with it, the coherence of ideology, was collapsing as mobility, communication, and new forms of organization penetrated and divided what had once been isolated spheres. Nations felt that strain no less than social classes, as more than one political scientist pointed out.[6]

But the collapse of older groups left men with the sense of loneliness and isolation, a desperate insecurity in a world of great power and massive scale. And while many sought to withdraw from so terrifying a condition, others sought for new bonds and loyalties that could provide security and a sense of identity. Trained in the Marxian tradition and concerned with the more or less stable societies of prewar Europe, Mannheim had slighted the role of ideology in *creating* groups where none had existed before.

Religious or philosophic doctrines may appeal to human beings for many reasons other than their content. The mere fact that they seem to provide an "answer," whatever it is, may attract those who cannot endure confusion. Solidarity, on whatever basis, holds appeal for the lonely. The personal past of an individual, while always important, is often too disordered in times of rapid change or social decay to guide, much less "determine," his new affiliations. In fact, joining an ideological movement is often likened to a kind of "rebirth," and movements and parties frequently try to strengthen that sense of a new life. Unconsciously or by design, ideological movements adopt distinctive styles of dress, speech, and personal relations. Common doctrines in such cases are the foundation rather than the reflection of a social group, and it is in such groups that ideology is likely to be most militant and dogmatic.

[4] See Chapter I.

[5] Daniel Bell, *The End of Ideology,* New York: Collier, 1962.

[6] John Herz, *International Politics in the Atomic Age,* New York: Columbia University Press, 1962, pp. 96–108.

In both this sense of the term and Mannheim's, however, ideology is associated with the lack of secure moral standards of conduct. Humans are moral
animals and seek justification and guidance if only for personal security and
self-esteem; by becoming identified with such motives, moral norms affect our
conduct. The need for elaborate justification, however, arises only when we
are in doubt or under attack and no way seems morally safe. That uncertainty, as Guglielmo Ferrero made clear, lay behind Napoleon's efforts to find
some moral basis for his own power.[7] His inability to do so left him the prisoner of his own fears and suspicions and drove him to an eventually self-
defeating policy of aggression.

Such anxiety, however, has hardly been limited to Napoleon. The rapid,
semiautonomous growth of power and the almost unpredictable pace of change
makes older moral ideas—or ideas themselves—seem feeble and perpetually
outdated, neither sources of security nor guides to the future. One response
has been an ideology that prescribes an almost plastic "adjustment" to power
and change, which is the basis of many "realistic" theories. In the extreme
case, as Alan Bullock indicated in relation to Hitler, fear of and reverence for
power may create an ideology that seeks to moralize force itself, striving to
ally with cruelty and violence in the desperate quest for safety.[8] Hitler was
not alone in advocating the "ethics of the jungle"; he stands out because, as
Bullock argues, he was a perverted but undeniable political genius who made
the horror of such doctrines clear and unambiguous. And hopefully, he provided some kind of warning to contemporary men.

Not all ideologies, however, reflect a desperation as deep as Hitler's and
some doctrines are a source of security. As both R. N. Carew Hunt and
Richard Lowenthal suggest, doctrine is not only an important element in Soviet policy, but a significant element in Soviet willingness to reach compromises
with the West. Marxist-Leninism, after all, predicts an ultimately certain victory over capitalism. Beset by internal and external "contradictions," capitalism must eventually reach final crisis and collapse. As Nikita Khrushchev
recognized, however, nuclear war might radically upset the course of history,
setting humanity back in time or even permitting a defeat of socialism. While
socialist countries must be prepared to fight to defend what they have gained,
"peaceful competition" is a surer, more constructive path to success.

Of course, Marxist "optimism" can have quite different results. Stalin, for
example, found it impossible to believe that capitalist states, sensing their
eventual doom, would not try to extinguish Soviet socialism by war. Khrushchev's departure from Stalinism reflected, not simply his different personality,
but a stronger Soviet position of military security.

Similarly, the ideological side of the Soviet conflict with China is partly due
to the fact that Mao took power through guerrilla conflict and has a naturally
greater concern for Asia and non-Western areas generally than do his more
orthodox Russian counterparts. Mao has been more eager to preserve revolutionary zeal and commitment, partly due, one suspects, to China's lesser
ability to provide material rewards to its people. Even here, one must be

[7] *Principles of Power,* New York: Putnam, 1942, pp. 106–110.

[8] *Hitler: A Study in Tyranny,* rev. ed., New York: Harper & Row, 1964, especially, pp. 805–808.

careful not to exaggerate the differences between China and the Soviet Union. Russian leaders—including Khrushchev—have often focused on military factors and on "socialist solidarity" out of a doubt that they could, at present, win a "peaceful competition" with the West. (This fear, for example, appears to have been a major element in both the 1948 and 1968 seizures of power in Czechoslovakia.) [9] Yet Maoism, however bellicose the statements of Chinese leaders, has been prudent in practice. As Tang Tsou makes clear, Mao's China, weaker and more threatened than the Soviet Union, must be prepared to run more risks (or more able to convince others she will do so) if she is to avoid a hopeless passivity and dependence. Nonetheless Marxian optimism has helped provide Maoists with a greater willingness to wait, to show caution and even accommodation, than was ever possible for Germany in the grip of Nazism's frenzied desperation. In fact the greatest fear of Soviet and Chinese leaders alike has been the anxiety that the West, losing faith in itself, will unleash a holocaust to avoid disaster. Western ideological confidence, however mistaken socialists may imagine it to be, is paradoxically an important element in the security of the communist world.

Americans have tended to associate "ideological politics" with their opponents, but as Whittle Johnston maintains, America was the first nation founded on the basis of an ideology. American liberalism, as Louis Hartz has argued, is not the doctrine of a party, but an "irrational Lockeanism" so deeply planted in American culture as to be characteristic of almost all American political thought.[10]

Liberalism, which grew up in the moral uncertainty that accompanied the fragmenting of the Christian order and the beginnings of modern technology, suspected all moral claims on the individual that did not result from his own free consent. Early liberalism began, as Locke did, with man in a "state of nature," an isolated and independent being endowed with "natural rights." However liberal theorists accounted for the origin of government, or however far they strayed from the early doctrines, the freedom of the individual was a central first premise. Aggression, the violation of the individual's rights, was the primary, even the sole human crime. And quite naturally liberal theorists transferred such ideas to states and to international politics.

Hence, for John Locke, any measures are justified in punishing an aggressor, for aggression is bestial and less than human. No state, however, may use aggression as a pretext for punishing noncombatants, for interfering with their "self-determination," or for annexing their land, for such actions would be aggressive themselves and would serve as just grounds for future war. Little imagination is required to see these ideas (like those of Kant) in the policies Woodrow Wilson advocated at Versailles.

In an increasingly interdependent world, however, ideas of self-determination and nonintervention became more difficult to maintain. John Stuart Mill, defending these principles, felt forced to make several exceptions. It was legitimate, he felt, to intervene when dealing with "uncivilized" peoples who did not understand "advanced" moral standards and who, in any case, could

---

[9] See *The "Brezhnev Doctrine"* in Chapter X.
[10] *The Liberal Tradition in America,* New York: Harcourt, Brace and World, 1955.

not maintain their independence in the face of progress. (Locke, incidentally, had argued that one might take lands from those who "wasted" them, like the American Indians; in a world of scarcity, waste conferred no rights.) Moreover, Mill argued, a nation might support its ideological sympathizers when menaced by a foreign coalition and might intervene in one state to forestall or defeat intervention by another.

In Mill's argument lay the germs of much of postwar American foreign policy, even the official defenses of American intervention in Vietnam. Dean Acheson spells out many of the recent implications of Mill's liberalism, and it is notable that he justifies propaganda and ideological war, a "burning and fighting faith" in freedom, as part of America's *defense*. But of course, for liberalism as for Marxism, the threat of thermonuclear war adds new complications to old doctrines. The thesis that we must be prepared to destroy civilization in order to save it may well be valid, yet the absurdity of the argument makes the search for some "third alternative" morally and politically imperative.

But, as Johnston demonstrates, not all alternatives are wise or viable. The decline of the old state system, he contends, is itself responsible for the growth of international ideologies seeking some form of organization broader than the nation-state. Haunted, like all ideologies, by uncertainty and the "fears of illegitimate power," American liberalism has an aggressive side. But, as Johnston points out, the desire to withdraw from the world is only the other side of the coin, a response to the same fear. Withdrawal, in other words, is as ideological as "arrogance," and quite as impossible.

The hope for withdrawal, in fact, is based on a liberal doctrine that has been widely and ably criticized: the belief that *not helping* is also *not hurting*. If one refrains from beating a starving man, after all, one has not necessarily exhausted one's moral duties toward him—a criticism that has often been applied to theories of "nonviolence." [11] But nonviolent resistance, as a third alternative, has other limitations. It is, in fact, a theory of nonphysical resistance, which hopes to overcome the aggressor by damaging his sense of superiority, injuring his self-esteem, and awakening his moral conscience. Obviously such resistance is often practicable in political affairs. To use it, however, those who resist nonviolently must matter to those who assail them; the nonviolence of flies does not damage one's sense of superiority. And if I believe that greater force *is* the proof of my superiority—unlike the British in India—nonviolence may have the opposite effect its protagonists hope for. As Morgenthau argued, it is hard to believe, given recent events, that the "difficulty of digesting" conquered peoples deters any potential aggressor among the major powers.

Despite the importance of Gandhism in India, moreover, no state in the "third world" has adopted nonviolence in foreign policy. Quite the contrary, "nonalignment" in any of its forms, as George Liska suggests, has been a new form of the balance of power adapted by weak states, situated between opposing blocs, that seek to win the maximum benefits and political space for domestic development. The generous hopes of a Julius Nyerere for a "third

---

[11] George Orwell, "Reflections on Gandhi," in *A Collection of Essays,* Garden City, N.Y.: Anchor Books, 1954, pp. 177–186.

way" center on the ability of African nations to develop in peace an example that may influence the world. But such a policy requires not only a clever manipulation of the great powers: it demands that they be hostile. A peaceful world might destroy all the calculations of the nonaligned.

There are similarities between Nyerere's "communitary" alternative and the doctrines of the New Left that David Esmond describes. Certainly, New Left theorists have been aware of the perils of loneliness, weakness, and anxiety in world affairs. But that sense of danger caused the early New Left theorists, as David Esmond observes, to treat foreign policy as somehow secondary or completely dependent on the domestic policies of the United States. Such neglect of the autonomous nature of international politics may, in fact, be responsible for the growing frustrations that have developed in relation to Vietnam. And the difficulty of developing community is attested to by the increasing ideological fragmentation of the New Left.

William Pfaff doubtlessly speaks for many in urging a union of reasonable men against "romanticism," a division he sees as more contemporary than the decaying distinction between Right and Left.[12] Perhaps that is our best hope. But not only is Pfaff's argument much like Mannheim's, it has its own dangers. *Rationalism* is not "reason," but an ideology about reason. Those who do not understand that romance, sentiment, and affection—the stern joys of sacrifice and patriotism included—have their rightful place in human nature run the risk of repeating the errors of the liberal West after World War I. Reason without warmth and states without community leave too much space for "masters of the irrational" like Hitler and his imitators. The causes of ideology will remain with us and so will ideology itself. But the greatest error of all ideologists has been in creating definitions of human nature that are too narrow and too simple. Mankind, which Mark Twain once called "the scandal of the universe," is not easily captured in the walls of doctrine.

[12] See *Commonweal,* March 11, 1966, pp. 654–656.

R. N. Carew Hunt

THE IMPORTANCE OF DOCTRINE

The term ideology is one which is more often used than defined. As the present study will be concerned with what the Russian Communists, and Communists in general, mean by it, a definition taken from a Soviet source is in order. The *Filosoficheskii Slovar* (Philosophical Dictionary, 1954 ed.), calls ideology "a system of definite views, ideas, conceptions and notions adhered to by some class or political party," and goes on to say that it is always "a reflection of the economic system predominant at any given time.". . .

Such a summation, albeit neat, is not altogether satisfactory. Broadly speaking, Marx was right in contending that the ideology of a society—the complex of ideas which determine its "way of life"—will be that of its dominant class. . . . But this sociological fact applies equally to the Soviet Union, where the party certainly constitutes such a class and indeed is assigned the duty of fertilizing the masses with its ideas. Undoubtedly the current Soviet ideology is intended to strengthen the party and reinforce its claim to rule. But one must probe further to explain why the party should have adopted the particular body of doctrine that it has. . . .

* * *

. . . Its basic principles are to be found in Marx's revolutionary doctrine, the implications of which were spelled out by Lenin and Stalin when confronted with the practical problem of setting up the type of social order Marx had advocated. Communist literature and propaganda have made us familiar with the doctrine, and there is no need to analyze it here even if space permitted. The issue to be decided is what role ideology plays today, and how far it influences Soviet policy.

Virtually all analysts would agree that in the years of struggle before the October Revolution the Bolsheviks took the theory which lay behind their movement in deadly earnest; there is also general agreement that in the

Reprinted by permission of the publisher from *Problems of Communism* (March–April 1958).

1920's the doctrine acted as a stimulus to the workers, who took pride in building up their country. In the 1930's, however, the situation changed. Stalin assumed absolute power. The machinery of state and of the secret police was greatly strengthened, and all prospect of establishing a genuine classless society disappeared. With the Stalin-Hitler Pact, if not before, the Soviet Union entered an era which can plausibly be represented as one of naked power politics, perpetuated after World War II in the aggressive and obstructive policies pursued by the regime. Hence it is sometimes argued that Communist ideology has now ceased to possess any importance; that it is simply a top-dressing of sophistries designed to rationalize measures inspired solely by Soviet interests; and that apart from a few fanatics, such as may be found in any society, no one believes in the doctrine any longer, least of all the leaders themselves.

Yet such unqualified assertions are erroneous. Consider, first, the outlook of the ordinary Soviet citizen *vis-à-vis* the ideology. Day in, day out, he is subjected to intensive and skillfully devised propaganda through every known medium, designed to demonstrate that the ideology on which the Soviet Union is based makes it the best of all possible worlds, and that on this account it is encircled with jealous enemies bent on its destruction. The Soviet leadership has always considered it essential that every citizen possess as deep an understanding of Communist principles as his mind is capable of assimilating, and those holding positions of consequence are obliged recurrently to pass through carefully graded schools of political instruction.

It is significant that whenever the leaders feel themselves in a tight corner . . . their invariable reaction is to intensify indoctrination in an attempt to refocus public attention on "first principles." As hard-headed men they would certainly not attach such importance to indoctrination if they did not know that it paid dividends—and experience has proved that the persistent repetition of a body of ideas which are never challenged is bound to influence the minds of their recipients. Of course, the present generation does not react to the formal ideology with the same fervor as did its forebears who made the revolution, and there are doubtless those who view official apologetics with a large degree of cynicism. But between total commitment and total disillusionment there are many intermediate positions; it is quite possible for a man to regard much of what he is told as nonsense while still believing that there is something of value behind it, especially if he identifies that "something" with the greatness of his country as "the first socialist state" and believes in its historic mission.

More significant, in the present context, than the attitude of the ordinary citizen is that of the ruling elite which is responsible for policy. What its top-ranking members believe is a question which no one, of course, can answer positively. But before surmising, as do some analysts, that the Soviet leadership cannot possibly believe in the myths it propounds, we should remind ourselves that no class or party ever finds it difficult to persuade itself of the soundness of the principles on which it bases its claim to rule.

The Soviet leaders are fortified in this conviction by the very nature of their creed. They have been nurtured in it from birth, and it would be strange indeed if they had remained unaffected. It has become second nature to these men to regard history as a dialectical process—one of incessant conflict between progressive and reactionary forces which can only be resolved by the victory of the former. The division of the world into antagonistic camps, which is an article of faith, is simply the projection onto the international stage of the struggle within capitalistic society between the bourgeoisie, which history has condemned, and the proletariat, whose ultimate triumph it has decreed. The leaders seem to be confident that history is on their side, that all roads lead to communism, and that the contradictions of capitalism must create the type of situation which they can turn to their advantage.

Democratic governments desirous of recommending a certain policy normally dwell upon its practical advantages. But in the Soviet Union this is not so. Any important change of line will be heralded by an article in *Pravda,* often of many columns, purporting to show that the new policy is ideologically correct because it accords with some recent decision of a party congress, or with Lenin's teaching, or with whatever other criterion may be adopted. How far the policy in question will have been inspired by considerations of ideology as opposed to others of a more mundane nature can never be precisely determined. This, however, is not an exclusive feature of the Communist system; in politics, as for that matter in personal relations, it is seldom possible to disentangle all the motives which determine conduct. The policies of any part or government are likely to reflect its political principles even if they are so framed as to strengthen its position, and there is no reason why the policies adopted by the Soviet leaders should constitute an exception.

Analysts of the "power politics" school of thought hold that the Kremlin leaders are concerned solely with Soviet national interest, and merely use the Communist movement to promote it. Yet here again the difficulty is to disengage factors which are closely associated. The future of the Communist movement cannot be disassociated from the fortunes of the Soviet Union. . . .

The quarrel between the Soviet and the Yugoslav Communist parties— which an intergovernmental agreement of June 1956 has failed to resolve— is a good example of the interpenetration of ideological and non-ideological factors in policy determinations. The immediate occasion of the quarrel was Tito's unwillingness to allow the spread of Soviet influence through the presence of Soviet military officers and technological experts on Yugoslav soil. As a result Stalin determined to crush Tito, and resorted to various political and economic measures in an unsuccessful attempt to do so. It was at least a year before the struggle was extended to the ideological plane. But that it should have been was inevitable. One may well sympathize with Tito's desire for independence and hope that other national leaders will follow his example. Yet from the Communist point of view, if the movement is to be an international one, it must have an international center, and upon historical grounds alone Moscow has a strong claim to the mantle. . . .

. . . The official Soviet position is best expressed in an article in *New Times,* March 1956, which states that "while *serving as an example* to other working class parties, the CPSU *draws upon their experience and formulates it in general theoretical principles* for the benefit of all working class parties."

Clearly the Soviet leaders are on the defensive in this matter. They recognize that concessions must be made, but will make no more than they can help. The desire to perpetuate their own power doubtless influences their stand, but considering the fact that communism professes to be a world movement, it would be unreasonable to conclude that either national or personal interests are the sole factors motivating them.

. . . [T]he attitude of the Soviet leaders *must* be attributed, at least in part, to the theoretical principles which distinguish Communist regimes from other forms of dictatorship. Certainly the leaders shape and phrase their domestic and foreign policies to fit the general framework established by these principles, and the latter often do not allow much room for maneuver. . . .

*   *   *

. . . Poland affords a good example. With the country at its mercy after World War II, the Soviet regime decided, among other measures, to integrate the Polish economy with its own. Now had Poland been regarded merely as a colony to be exploited, the operation would have been viewed primarily as a business proposition, and due attention would have been paid to such questions as the nature of the country's resources and the aptitudes of its people. The need to proceed with caution was very evident. The traditional hostility of the Poles to everything Russian should have been taken into account, as well as the fact that the Polish Communist Party had no public support (due in part to the liquidation of its established leaders during the Great Purges). Yet it was decided that the country must pass through, in shorter time intervals, precisely those stages of development which the Soviet Union had traversed. The result was a serious disruption of the economy through the erection of a top-heavy industrial structure on the basis of a depressed agriculture. This policy cannot be attributed to Stalin alone as it was continued after his death. It proved disastrous, and is only intelligible on the assumption that it was primarily motivated by ideological considerations.

The argument can be carried further. By its behavior throughout its history, the Soviet Union has incurred the hostility, or at least the suspicion, of the entire free world. Yet there was no practical reason why it should have done so. After the October Revolution the Bolshevik regime was faced with appalling domestic problems, and it had nothing to gain by courting the animosity of the West. The Soviet leaders might well have built up their country in accordance with the principles to which they were committed without exciting such widespread hostility. What governments do at home is commonly regarded as their own affair. . . .

What no country will tolerate is the attempt, deliberately engineered by a foreign power, to overthrow its form of government; this has been the persistent aim and effort of the Soviet regime in defiance of its express diplomatic guarantees of non-interference. It is hard to see how this strategy has assisted the development of Soviet Russia, and that it has never been abandoned cannot be dissociated from those messianic and catastrophic elements in the Communist creed which influence, perhaps impel, the Soviet drive for world power.

In conclusion, it is frequently stated that communism has created an ideological cleavage between the West and the Soviet bloc. Yet this statement would be meaningless if the issue today were, as some believe, simply one of power politics. An ideology is significant only if it makes those who profess it act in a way they would not otherwise do. The fact that large numbers of persons accept communism would not constitute a danger if it did not lead them to support policies which threaten the existence of those who do not accept it. . . .

*   *   *

. . . Communists claim a theoretical justification for the basic principles in which they believe. But these principles must be translated into appropriate action; and action, if directed by the rulers of a powerful country like the Soviet Union, will take the form of *Realpolitik*. There is no yardstick which permits a measure of the exact relationship between power politics and ideology in the policies which result; but surely neither factor can be ignored.

Richard Lowenthal

THE LOGIC OF ONE-PARTY RULE

To what extent are the political decisions of the Soviet leadership influenced by its belief in an official ideology—and to what extent are they empirical responses to specific conflicts of interest, expressed in ideological terms merely for purposes of justification? The phrasing of the question at issue

Reprinted by permission of the publisher from *Problems of Communism* (March–April 1958).

suggests the two extreme answers which are *prima facie* conceivable—on the one hand, that ideology provides the Kremlin with a ready-made book of rules to be looked up in any situation; on the other hand, that its response to reality takes place without any reference to ideology. Yet any clear formulation of this vital issue will show that both extremes are meaningless nonsense.

A ready-made book of rules for any and every situation—an unvarying road-map to the goal of communism which the Soviet leaders must predictably follow—cannot possibly exist, both because the situations to be met by them are not sufficiently predictable, and because no government which behaved in so calculable a manner could conceivably retain power. On the other hand, empirical *Realpolitik* without ideological preconceptions can exist as little as can "empirical science" without categories and hypotheses based on theoretical speculation. Confronted with the same constellation of interests and pressures, the liberal statesman will in many cases choose a different course of action from the conservative—and the totalitarian Communist's choice will often be different from that of either.

*   *   *

. . . Either there are objective criteria of national interest, recognizable by the scholar—and then the view that these interests explain Soviet actions is capable of proof or refutation; or else it is admitted that different statesmen may interpret national interest in different but equally "legitimate" ways—and then the concept of a self-contained study of international relations collapses, because a consideration of the internal structures of different national communities and of the "ideologies" reflecting them becomes indispensable for an understanding of their foreign policies.

*   *   *

How, then, are we to distinguish those elements of Soviet ideology which are truly operative politically from those which are merely traditional scholastic ballast, linked to the operative elements by the historical accident of the founding fathers' authorship? The answer is to be found by going back to the original Marxian meaning of the term "ideology"—conceived as a distorted reflection of social reality in the consciousness of men, used as an instrument of struggle. The fundamental, distinctive social reality in the Soviet Union is the rule of the bureaucracy of a single, centralized and disciplined party, which wields a monopoly of political, economic and spiritual power and permits no independent groupings of any kind. The writer proposes as an hypothesis that the operative parts of the ideology are those which are indispensable for maintaining and justifying this state of affairs: "Marxism-Leninism" matters inasmuch as it expresses, in an ideologically distorted form, the logic of one-party rule.

*   *   *

We can expect, then, that Communist ideology will have an effective influence on the policy decisions of Soviet leaders when, and only when, it expresses the needs of self-preservation of the party regime. We can further expect that ideological changes and disputes within the Communist "camp" will offer clues to the conflicts and crises—the "contradictions"—which are inseparable from the evolution of this, as of any other, type of society. The fruitful approach, in this writer's view, consists neither in ignoring Communist ideology as an irrelevant disguise, nor in accepting it at its face value and treating it as a subject for exegesis, but in using it as an indicator of those specific drives and problems which spring from the specific structure of Soviet society—in regarding it as an enciphered, continuous self-disclosure, whose cipher can be broken by sociological analysis.

Let us now apply this approach to the doctrine of the "two camps" in world affairs. . . .

*   *   *

. . . [T]he "two camp" doctrine is the Communist version of what we have called the element of "collective paranoia" in totalitarian ideology—its need for a single, all-embracing enemy which is assumed to pull the wires of every resistance to the party's power. . . . The essential point is that in the nature of totalitarianism, any independent force—either inside or outside the state—is regarded as ultimately hostile; the concept of "two camps" and that of "unlimited aims" are two sides of the same phenomenon.

*   *   *

The peculiar forms taken by Moscow's suspicion of its wartime allies are too well known to need elaboration here; but it is less generally realized that such behavior was merely the reverse side of Soviet efforts to "strengthen" such temporary alliances where possible, by the use of party ties. Existence of the party channel has not, of course, been a *sine qua non* for Moscow's intragovernmental deals, as is shown by the examples of Russo-Turkish cooperation after World War I, the Stalin-Hitler pact, and perhaps also present Soviet cooperation with Egypt. But wherever Communist parties were tolerated by the partner, Soviet foreign policy has assigned to them a vital role. . . .

In the 1920's, Stalin's Chinese policy was openly run in double harness; diplomatic support for the Nationalist advance to the North was supplemented by an agreement of affiliation between the Chinese Communist Party and the Kuomintang, enabling the Communists to occupy influential political and military positions—an attempt no less serious for its ultimate total failure in 1927. In the 1930's, a variant of the same "dual policy" was evident when Moscow supported the League and "collective security," while Communist parties in France and Spain pursued "popular front" policies which soft-pedalled economic and social demands for the sake of influencing governmental foreign policy. In the Spanish case, the Communists, aided by the Republicans' dependence on Soviet supplies, ended up in virtual control of the Republic on the eve of its final collapse.

Again during World War II, Communists in the resistance movements and in the free Western countries were ordered to pursue the same tactics of social moderation and occupation of key positions as were practiced in China in the 1920's and Spain in the 1930's. Wartime military and political cooperation between "Soviet China" and Chiang Kai-shek was urged in the same spirit, with considerable success. All these are the foreign policy methods of a state *sui generis*—a one-party state enabled by its ideology to make use of a disciplined international movement organized for the struggle for power. . . .

The crucial example to illustrate the role of ideology in Soviet foreign policy, however, remains the history of the postwar division of Europe. . . . What matters in the present context is the different meaning attached by the Western and Communist leaders, including these agreements, to the concept of "spheres of influence," and the consequences of this "misunderstanding."

*   *   *

To Mr. Roosevelt and Mr. Churchill . . . these spheres of influence meant what they had traditionally meant in the relations of sovereign states—a gradual shading over from the influence of one power or group of powers to that of the other, a shifting relationship which might be loosely described in terms of "percentages of influence," ranging from 50/50 to 90/10. To the Soviets, "spheres of influence" meant something completely different in the framework of their ideology—the ideology of the single-party state. To them there could be no securely "friendly" government except a government run by a Communist party under their discipline; no sphere of influence but a sphere of Communist rule; no satisfactory percentage short of 100. Hence the consistent Soviet efforts, which began even before the end of the European war, to impose total control by Communist parties in every country on their side of the demarcation line—an effort that was finally successful everywhere but in Finland and Eastern Austria; hence also the indignant protests of the Western powers that the Soviets had broken the agreements on free elections and democratic development, and the equally indignant Soviet retort that they were only installing "friendly governments" as agreed, that theirs was the truly "democratic" system, and that they had kept scrupulously to the essential agreement on the military demarcation line.

*   *   *

If we now turn to interstate and interplay relations within the Communist camp, we seem at first sight to have entered an area where ideology is adapted quite unceremoniously to the changing requirements of practical politics. Lenin, having barely seized power in Russia and looking forward to an early spreading of Communist revolution, could talk airily enough about the sovereign equality and fraternal solidarity of sovereign "socialist" states. Stalin, having determined after the failure of short-term revolutionary hope to concentrate on "socialism in a single country," came to regard international communism as a mere tool of Soviet power, and to believe that revolutionary victories without the backing of Soviet arms were neither possible nor desirable; he wanted no sovereign Communist allies, only satellites, and he got them in postwar Eastern Europe.

*   *   *

Stalin's insistence on making the "leading role of the Soviet Union" an article of the international creed expressed not just the idiosyncrasies of a power-mad tyrant, but his perception of one side of the dilemma—the risk that a recognition of the sovereign equality of other Communist states might loosen the solidarity of the "camp" in its dealings with the non-Communist world, and weaken the ideological authority of the Soviet party leaders, with ultimate repercussions on their position in the Soviet Union itself. His successors disavowed him because his Yugoslav policy had failed, and because they perceived the other side of the dilemma—that rigid insistence on Soviet hegemony might break up the unity of the "camp" even more quickly, and might in particular lead to open conflict with China. But by going to Peiping and Belgrade and admitting the "mistakes" of Stalin's "Great Russian chauvinism" (as well as the "mistakes" of his internal terrorist regime), they precipitated the very crisis of authority which he had feared. . . .

*   *   *

Earlier in the paper, reference was made to some of the basic tenets which seem inseparably bound up with the preservation and justification of a Communist one-party regime. But within this unchanging framework, considerable variations in detail have taken place in the history of the Soviet Union. The appearance or disappearance of one of these "ideological variables" may be a valuable indicator of the kind of pressures which are exerted on the regime by the growing society and of the manner in which the leaders try to maintain control, sometimes by partly ceding to such pressures and seeking to canalize them, other times by a sharp frontal counterattack.

Among the most revealing of these variables are Soviet doctrines dealing with the economic role of the state and with the "class struggle" within Soviet society. The underlying reality is that a revolutionary party dictatorship, once it has carried out its original program and by this contributed to the emergence of a new privileged class, is bound to disappear sooner or later—to fall victim to a "Thermidor"—unless it prevents the new upper class from consolidating its position by periodically shaking up the social structure in a "permanent revolution from above." The ideological expression of this problem is the classical doctrine that the dictatorship of the proletariat should gradually "wither away" after it has succeeded in destroying the old ruling classes; thus, if continued dictatorship is to be justified, new goals of social transformation must be set and new "enemies" discovered.

In the early period of Stalin's rule, the new "goal" was the forced collectivization of the Russian countryside; the prosperous peasants—the *kulaks*—took the place of the former landowners and capitalists as the "enemy class" which had to be liquidated. . . .

The second step, also taken by Stalin in 1937, at the height of the great blood purge, consisted in proclaiming the doctrine that the "class struggle" in the Soviet Union was getting more acute as the "construction of socialism" advanced, because the "enemies" were getting more desperate. . . .

Stalin's final ideological pronouncement was contained in his political testament, "Economic Problems of Socialism," published in 1952. In this work he mapped out a program for the further revolutionary transformation of Soviet society, with the taking over of *kolkhoz* property by the state as its central element.

The first major renunciation of these Stalinist ideological innovations was made by Khrushchev in his "secret speech" at the Twentieth Congress.[1] Apart from his factual disclosures concerning Stalin's crimes, he denounced Stalin's doctrine of the sharpening class struggle with societal progress as dangerous nonsense, calculated to lead to the mutual slaughter of loyal Communists after the real class enemy had long been liquidated. This statement affords the master clue to the puzzle of why Khrushchev made the speech: it was a "peace offering" to the leading strata of the regime in the party machine, army, and managerial bureaucracy alike—a response to their pressure for greater personal security. But by his concession, Khrushchev reopened the problem which Stalin's doctrine and practice had intended to solve—that of preserving and justifying the party dictatorship by periodic major shake-ups of society.

By the spring and summer of 1957, Khrushchev showed his awareness of the practical side of the problem: his dismantling of the economic ministries, breaking up the central economic bureaucracy and strengthening the power of the regional party secretaries, was another such revolutionary shake-up. By November, he responded to the ideological side of the problem. First he repeated, in his solemn speech on the fortieth anniversary of the Bolshevik seizure of power, his rejection of Stalin's doctrine of ever-sharpening class struggle and ever-present enemies, thus indicating his wish to avoid a return to Stalin's terroristic revolution. Then he proceeded to develop his own alternative justification for maintaining the party dictatorship—a unique argument which identified the strengthening of party control with the "withering away of the state" predicted by Lenin.

Reviving this formula for the first time since it was buried by Stalin,

[1] February 1956. [Eds.]

Khrushchev explained that the military and police apparatus of the state would have to be maintained as long as a hostile capitalist world existed outside; but he added that the economic and administrative functions of the state bureaucracy would henceforth be steadily reduced by decentralization and devolution, thus strengthening the organs of regional self-government and of national autonomy within the various republics. At the same time, he quietly took steps to strengthen the control of the central party secretariat—his own seat of power—over the republican and regional party organs, thus following the old Leninist principle that the fiction of national autonomy must be balanced by the fact of centralized discipline within the ruling party.

In short, the same aim of maintaining the social dynamism of the party dictatorship and justifying its necessity, which Stalin achieved by exalting the economic role of the state, is pursued by Khrushchev by means of the reverse device of claiming that the state's economic functions have begun to "wither away." On the face of it, this doctrinal manipulation seems to reduce the role of ideology to that of ingenious trickery, obscuring rather than reflecting the underlying social realities. Yet, in fact, the very need for a change in the ideological argument reflects the change that is taking place in the underlying social situation—the resistance against a return to naked terrorism, the growing desire for a lessening of state pressure and a greater scope for local activity. Whether in industry or agriculture, in the control of literature or in relations with the satellite states, the basic conditions which the regime needs for its self-perpetuation have remained the same—but they can no longer be assured in the same way. That, too, is reflected in the variables of the official ideology.

Nikita S. Khrushchev

ON PEACEFUL COEXISTENCE

I have been told that the question of peaceful coexistence of states with different social systems is uppermost today in the minds of many Americans—and not only Americans. The question of coexistence, particularly in our day, interests literally every man and woman on the globe.

We all of us well know that tremendous changes have taken place in the world. Gone, indeed, are the days when it took weeks to cross the ocean from one continent to the other or when a trip from Europe to America.

Reprinted by permission of the publisher from *Foreign Affairs* (October 1959). Copyright by the Council on Foreign Relations, Inc., New York.

or from Asia to Africa, seemed a very complicated undertaking. The progress of modern technology has reduced our planet to a rather small place; it has even become, in this sense, quite congested. And if in our daily life it is a matter of considerable importance to establish normal relations with our neighbors in a densely inhabited settlement, this is so much the more necessary in the relations between states, in particular states belonging to different social systems.

You may like your neighbor or dislike him. You are not obliged to be friends with him or visit him. But you live side by side, and what can you do if neither you nor he has any desire to quit the old home and move to another town? All the more so in relations between states. It would be unreasonable to assume that you can make it so hot for your undesirable neighbor that he will decide to move to Mars or Venus. And vice versa, of course.

What, then, remains to be done? There may be two ways out: either war—and war in the rocket and H-bomb age is fraught with the most dire consequences for all nations—or peaceful coexistence. Whether you like your neighbor or not, nothing can be done about it, you have to find some way of getting on with him, for you both live on one and the same planet.

But the very concept of peaceful coexistence, it is said, by its alleged complexity frightens certain people who have become unaccustomed to trusting their neighbors and who see a double bottom in each suitcase. People of this kind, on hearing the word "coexistence," begin to play around with it in one way and another, sizing it up and applying various yardsticks to it. Isn't it a fraud? Isn't it a trap? Does not coexistence signify the division of the world into areas separated by high fences, which do not communicate with each other? And what is going to happen behind those fences?

The more such questions are piled up artificially by the cold-war mongers, the more difficult it is for the ordinary man to make head or tail of them. It would therefore be timely to rid the essence of this question of all superfluous elements and to attempt to look soberly at the most pressing problem of our day—the problem of peaceful competition.

*   *   *

From its very inception the Soviet state proclaimed peaceful coexistence as the basic principle of its foreign policy. It was no accident that the very first state act of the Soviet power was the decree on peace, the decree on the cessation of the bloody war.

What, then, is the policy of peaceful coexistence?

In its simplest expression it signifies the repudiation of war as a means of solving controversial issues. However, this does not cover the entire concept of peaceful coexistence. Apart from the commitment to non-aggression, it also presupposes an obligation on the part of all states to desist from violating each other's territorial integrity and sovereignty in any form and under any pretext whatsoever.   The principle of peaceful coexistence signifies a renunciation of interference in the internal affairs of other countries with the object of alerting their system of government or mode of life or for any other motives.   The doctrine of peaceful coexistence also presupposes that political and economic relations between countries are to be based upon complete equality of the parties concerned, and on mutual benefit.

It is often said in the West that peaceful coexistence is nothing else than a tactical method of the socialist states.   There is not a grain of truth in such allegations.   Our desire for peace and peaceful coexistence is not conditioned by any time-serving or tactical considerations.   It springs from the very nature of socialist society in which there are no classes or social groups interested in profiting by war or seizing and enslaving other people's territories.   The Soviet Union and the other socialist countries, thanks to their socialist system, have an unlimited home market and for this reason they have no need to pursue an expansionist policy of conquest in an effort to subordinate other countries to their influence.

It is the people who determine the destinies of the socialist states.   The socialist states are ruled by the working people themselves, the workers and peasants, the people who themselves create all the material and spiritual values of society.   And people of labor cannot want war.   For to them war spells grief and tears, death, devastation and misery.   Ordinary people have no need for war.

Contrary to what certain propagandists hostile to us say, the coexistence of states with different social systems does not mean that they will only fence themselves off from one another by a high wall and undertake the mutual obligation not to throw stones over the wall or pour dirt upon each other.   No!   Peaceful coexistence does not mean merely living side by side in the absence of war but with the constantly remaining threat of its breaking out in the future.   *Peaceful coexistence can and should develop into peaceful competition for the purpose of satisfying man's needs in the best possible way.*

We say to the leaders of the capitalist states: Let us try out in practice whose system is better, let us compete without war.   This is much better than competing in who will produce more arms and who will smash whom. We stand and always will stand for such competition as will help to raise the well-being of the people to a higher level.

The principle of peaceful competition does not at all demand that one or another state abandon the system and ideology adopted by it.   It goes without saying that the acceptance of this principle cannot lead to the immediate end of disputes and contradictions which are inevitable between countries adhering to different social systems.   But the main thing is ensured: the states which decided to adopt the path of peaceful coexistence repudiate the use of force in any form and agree on a peaceful settlement of possible disputes and conflicts, bearing in mind the mutual interests of the parties concerned. In our age of the H-bomb and atomic techniques this is the main thing of interest to every man.

* * *

The Communist Party of the Soviet Union at its Twentieth Congress made it perfectly clear and obvious that the allegations that the Soviet Union intends to overthrow capitalism in other countries by means of "exporting" revolution are absolutely unfounded. I cannot refrain from reminding you of my words at the Twentieth Congress: "It goes without saying that among us Communists there are no adherents of capitalism. But this does not mean that we have interfered or plan to interfere in the internal affairs of countries where capitalism still exists. Romain Rolland was right when he said that 'freedom is not brought in from abroad in baggage trains like Bourbons.' It is ridiculous to think that revolutions are made to order."

We Communists believe that the idea of Communism will ultimately be victorious throughout the world, just as it has been victorious in our country, in China and in many other states. . . . We may argue, we may disagree with one another. *The main thing is to keep to the positions of ideological struggle, without resorting to arms in order to prove that one is right.* The point is that with military techniques what they are today, there are no inaccessible places in the world. Should a world war break out, no country will be able to shut itself off from a crushing blow.

We believe that ultimately that system will be victorious on the globe which will offer the nations greater opportunities for improving their material and spiritual life. It is precisely socialism that creates unprecedentedly great prospects for the inexhaustible creative enthusiasm of the masses, for a genuine flourishing of science and culture, for the realization of man's dream of a happy life, a life without destitute and unemployed people, of a happy childhood and tranquil old age, of the realization of the most audacious and ambitious human projects, of man's right to create in a truly free manner in the interests of the people.

But when we say that in the competition between the two systems, the capitalist and the socialist, our system will win, this does not mean, of course, that we shall achieve victory by interfering in the internal affairs of the capitalist countries. Our confidence in the victory of Communism is of a different kind. It is based on a knowledge of the laws governing the development of society. Just as in its time capitalism, as the more progressive system, took the place of feudalism, so will capitalism be inevitably superseded by Communism—the more progressive and more equitable social system. We are confident of the victory of the socialist system because it is a more progressive system than the capitalist system. . . .

* * *

The problem of peaceful coexistence between states with different social systems has become particularly pressing in view of the fact that since the

Second World War the development of relations between states has entered a new stage, that now we have approached a period in the life of mankind when there is a real chance of excluding war once and for all from the life of society.   The new alignment of international forces which has developed since the Second World War offers ground for the assertion that a new world war is no longer a fatal inevitability, that it can be averted.

First, today not only all the socialist states, but many countries in Asia and Africa which have embarked upon the road of independent national statehood, and many other states outside the aggressive military groupings, are actively fighting for peace.

Secondly, the peace policy enjoys the powerful support of the broad masses of the people all over the world.

Thirdly, the peaceful socialist states are in possession of very potent material means, which cannot but have a deterring effect upon the aggressors.

Prior to the Second World War the U.S.S.R. was the only socialist country, with not more than 17 percent of the territory, 3 percent of the population, and about 10 percent of the output of the world.   At present, the socialist countries cover about one-fourth of the territory of the globe, have one-third of its population, and their industrial output accounts for about one-third of the total world output.

This is precisely the explanation of the indisputable fact that throughout the past years, hotbeds of war breaking out now in one and now in another part of the globe—in the Near East and in Europe, in the Far East and in Southeast Asia—have been extinguished at the very outset.

*   *   *

Of much importance, of course, is the fact that this policy has in our day merited not only the widest moral approval but also international legal recognition.   The countries of the socialist camp in their relations with the capitalist states are guided precisely by this policy.   The principles of peaceful coexistence are reflected in the decisions of the Bandung Conference of Asian and African countries.   Furthermore, many countries of Europe, Asia and Africa have solemnly proclaimed this principle as the basis of their foreign policy.   Finally, the idea of peaceful coexistence has found unanimous support in the decisions of the twelfth and thirteenth sessions of the United Nations General Assembly.

In our view, peaceful coexistence can become lasting only if the good declarations in favor of peace are supported by active measures on the part of the governments and peoples of all countries.   As far as the Soviet Union is concerned, it has already done a good deal in this respect, and I am able to share some experiences with you.

As far back as March 12, 1951, the Supreme Soviet of the U.S.S.R. adopted a "Law on the Defense of Peace," stating:

1. Propaganda for war, in whatever form it may be conducted, under-

mines the cause of peace, creates the menace of a new war and therefore constitutes the gravest crime against humanity.

2. Persons guilty of war propaganda should be brought to court and tried as heinous criminals.

Further, the Soviet Union has in recent years unilaterally reduced its armed forces by more than 2,000,000 men. The funds released as a result have been used to develop the economy and further raise the material and cultural living standards of the Soviet people.

The Soviet Union has liquidated its bases on the territories of other states.

The Soviet Union unilaterally discontinued the tests of atomic weapons and refrained from conducting them further until it became finally clear that the Western powers refused to follow our example and were continuing the explosions.

The Soviet Union has repeatedly submitted detailed and perfectly realistic proposals for disarmament, meeting the positions of the Western powers halfway. But to solve the disarmament problem it is necessary for our Western partners to agree and desire to meet us halfway too. This is just what is lacking.

When it became clear that it was very difficult under these conditions to solve the complex disarmament problem immediately, we proposed another concrete idea to our partners: Let us concentrate our attention on those problems which lend themselves most easily to a solution. Let us undertake initial partial steps on matters concerning which the views of the different parties have been brought closer together.

*   *   *

Attributing much importance to contacts and intercourse between statesmen of all countries, the Soviet Government a few years ago proposed that an East-West heads of government conference be convened in order to come to terms—taking into account present-day realities and guided by the spirit of mutual understanding—on concrete measures, the realization of which would help to relax international tension.

We also proposed that this conference consider those international questions for the settlement of which realistic prerequisites already existed. As a first step toward such a settlement, we proposed to the powers concerned that a peace treaty be concluded with Germany and that West Berlin be granted the status of a demilitarized free city. I want to emphasize particularly that we were guided primarily by the desire to put a final end to the aftermath of the Second World War. We regard the liquidation of the consequences of the Second World War and the conclusion of a peace treaty with the two German states—the German Democratic Republic and the German Federal Republic—as the question of questions.

*   *   *

As for Germany's unity, I am convinced that Germany will be united sooner or later. However, before this moment comes—and no one can foretell when it will come—no attempts should be made to interfere from outside in this internal process, to sustain the state of war which is fraught with many grave dangers and surprises for peace in Europe and throughout the world. The desire to preserve the peace and to prevent another war should outweigh all other considerations of statesmen, irrespective of their mode of thinking. The Gordian knot must be cut: the peace treaty must be achieved if we do not want to play with fire—with the destinies of millions upon millions of people.

* * *

We are prepared now as before to do everything we possibly can in order that the relations between the Soviet Union and other countries, and, in particular, the relations between the U.S.S.R. and the U.S.A., should be built upon the foundation of friendship and that they should fully correspond to the principles of peaceful coexistence.

I should like to repeat what I said at my recent press conference in Moscow: "Should Soviet-American relations become brighter, that will not fail to bring about an improvement in the relations with other states and will help to scatter the gloomy clouds in other parts of the globe also. Naturally, we want friendship not only with the U.S.A., but also with the friends of the U.S.A. At the same time we want to see the U.S.A. maintain good relations not only with us, but with our friends as well."

What, then, is preventing us from making the principles of peaceful coexistence an unshakable international standard and daily practice in the relations between the West and East?

Of course, different answers may be given to this question. But in order to be frank to the end, we should also say the following: *It is necessary that everybody should understand the irrevocable fact that the historic process is irreversible.* It is impossible to bring back yesterday. It is high time to understand that the world of the twentieth century is not the world of the nineteenth century, that two diametrically opposed social and economic systems exist in the world today side by side, and that the socialist system, in spite of all the attacks upon it, has grown so strong, has developed into such a force, as to make any return to the past impossible.

Real facts of life in the last ten years have shown convincingly that the policy of "rolling back" Communism can only poison the international atmosphere, heighten the tension between states and work in favor of the cold war. Neither its inspirers nor those who conduct it can turn back the course of history and restore capitalism in the socialist countries.

* * *

The well known British scientist, J. Bernal, recently cited figures to show that average annual expenditures for military purposes throughout the world between 1950 and the end of 1957 were expressed in the huge sum of about 90 billion dollars. How many factories, apartment houses, schools, hospitals and libraries could have been built everywhere with the funds now spent on the preparation of another war! And how fast could economic progress have been advanced in the underdeveloped countries if we had converted to these purposes at least some of the means which are now being spent on war purposes!

It is readily seen that the policy of peaceful coexistence receives a firm foundation only with increase in extensive and absolutely unrestricted international trade. It can be said without fear of exaggeration that there is no good basis for improvement of relations between our countries other than development of international trade.

If the principle of peaceful coexistence of states is to be adhered to, not in words, but in deeds, it is perfectly obvious that no ideological differences should be an obstacle to the development and extension of mutually advantageous economic contacts, to the exchange of everything produced by human genius in the sphere of peaceful branches of material production.

*   *   *

Striving for the restoration of normal trade relations with the United States, the Soviet Union does not pursue any special interests. In our economic development we rely wholly on the internal forces of our country, on our own resources and possibilities. All our plans to further economic development are drawn up taking into consideration the possibilities available here. As in the past, when we outline these plans we proceed only from the basis of our own possibilities and forces. Irrespective of whether or not we shall trade with Western countries, the United States included, the implementation of our economic plans of peaceful construction will not in the least be impeded.

However, if both sides want to improve relations, all barriers in international trade must be removed. Those who want peaceful coexistence cannot but favor the development of trade, economic and business contracts. Only on this basis can international life develop normally.

Peaceful coexistence is the only way which is in keeping with the interests of all nations. To reject it would mean under existing conditions to doom the whole world to a terrible and destructive war at a time when it is fully possible to avoid it.

Is it possible that when mankind has advanced to a plane where it has proved capable of the greatest discoveries and of making its first steps into outer space, it should not be able to use the colossal achievements of its genius for the establishment of a stable peace, for the good of man, rather than for the preparation of another war and for the destruction of all that has been created by its labor over many millenniums? Reason refuses to believe this. It protests.

*   *   *

The existence of the Soviet Union and of the other socialist countries is a real fact. It is also a real fact that the United States of America and the other capitalist countries live in different social conditions, in the conditions of capitalism. Then let us recognize this real situation and proceed from it in order not to go against reality, against life itself. Let us not try to change this situation by interferences from without, by means of war on the part of some states against other states.

I repeat, there is only one way to peace, one way out of the existing tension: peaceful coexistence.

Tang Tsou

MAO TSE-TUNG AND PEACEFUL COEXISTENCE

On December 30, 1963, in an interview on the French government-owned television network, Chou En-lai expressed his belief that "a world war opposing the Communist camp against the imperialist camp is not inevitable." But he went on to say that the risk of war remained because of the U.S. policy of "war and aggression." On the question of Sino-American relations, he declared that China sought a solution to differences with the United States; "in the first place a solution to the question of the retreat of American armed forces from Taiwan and the Taiwan Strait by peaceful means without recourse to force or threat of force." Some Western observers and news media immediately seized upon these remarks as an indication that Communist China was changing her position on the fateful question of the inevitability of war.

Actually, Chou merely reaffirmed the long-standing position of the Peking regime, and reiterated the views embodied in the 1957 Moscow Declaration of Communist Parties and the 1960 Statement—documents on which the Communist Party of China has established its line of "no retreat" and bases its counterattacks on the CPSU in the dispute over ideology and revolutionary strategy. While Chou's tour of Africa and Europe was a significant diplomatic foray, his remarks on the inevitability of war signify no change in the doctrinal position of the Chinese Communist Party (CCP). The superficial impression to the contrary merely reflects the widespread ignorance in the West about Communist China—in particular, the Chinese position on the question of war and peace.

Reprinted by permission of the publisher from *Orbis* (Spring 1964). *Orbis* is a quarterly journal of world affairs published by the Foreign Policy Research Institute of the University of Pennsylvania.

This ignorance and misunderstanding have been deepened by the Soviet propaganda drive which seeks to depict Communist Chinese leaders as madmen or maniacs bent on promoting world revolution through nuclear war. Whatever the motive behind this propaganda drive, it has had the effect of creating a Western image of a Soviet Union striving desperately to restrain the Chinese from precipitating a nuclear war. It has led some Western officials and scholars to think that Khrushchev's primary motive in seeking a *détente* with the West has been to counter the Chinese threat to the survival of mankind and to preserve the Soviet Union's economic achievements which would be destroyed in a nuclear holocaust. . . .

This reading of the Soviet motive is of doubtful validity: The Sino-Soviet dispute is not the primary motive for the Soviet search for a *détente* with the West. On the contrary, the Soviet search for a *détente* was itself the basic cause of the Sino-Soviet dispute. If the Soviet Union had not sought a *détente* with the West in opposition to China's view on revolutionary strategy and at the expense of China's interests, the dispute would not have arisen, or at least it would not have been intensified to such an extent. . . .

*   *   *

In order to make an objective analysis of Mao's views on war and peace, one must first of all understand Mao's views in his own terms. This is no easy task. For unlike political theorists in the West, Mao has not published any systematic writing on the questions of peaceful coexistence and the inevitability of war. But in the recent debate with Moscow, Peking has published a series of statements which provide a glimpse of Mao's views. Furthermore, Peking has published many of Mao's writings from the period between 1926 and 1949 which discuss the question of war and peace with the Nationalist Party. If one reads the recent statements from Peking in the light of Mao's earlier writings, and examines the latter in the light of the current political-military situation confronting Communist China, one can reach an understanding of Mao's view of these questions. . . . [H]is present views on the revolutionary strategy of the world communist movement have been shaped largely by his experience in the Chinese revolution. . . .

What are Mao's views on the questions of the inevitability of war and peaceful coexistence? How do they differ from Khrushchev's? In what sense do they agree with Khrushchev's? What is the source of the Sino-Soviet dispute? The basic and the original source of the Sino-Soviet conflict is a dispute over revolutionary strategy for the world communist movement. Naturally, this dispute involves both questions of ideology and national interests. But the world revolutionary strategy proposed by Peking is less influenced by China's national interest than by its revolutionary experience. It is, as a matter of fact, a direct projection to the international arena of Mao's political-military strategy in the struggle with

Generalissimo Chiang in the Chinese revolution.   In the present debate over the questions of peaceful coexistence and the inevitability of war, the Chinese arguments follow closely Mao's analysis of strategy and tactics in the period between 1937 and 1945, when an anti-Japanese united front existed between the Chinese Communist Party and the Nationalist Party. Mao's policy was to uphold the united front, or in other words, "peaceful coexistence" with Chiang, as a shield behind which he pushed forward his program of armed struggle against the Kuomintang.

By 1937 Mao had developed a strategy of surrounding the cities from the countryside, because the Kuomintang's hold on the cities was firm and incontestable while its control over the countryside was weak and vulnerable.   It is a new version of this strategy which Mao proposes to use to defeat the United States.   Mao realizes that the power of the West in the developed areas cannot be challenged successfully for the time being, but he believes its position in the underdeveloped areas is weak and vulnerable. His strategy calls for the world communist movement to concentrate its energy and resources on the underdeveloped areas of Asia, Africa and Latin America in order to promote national liberation movements and revolutionary civil wars.   Soviet leaders have had little experience and aptitude for this sort of warfare.   Their attention is centered on Eastern and Western Europe and the United States.   They attach less importance to the underdeveloped areas as an arena of struggle.

This controversy over priorities and the relative importance of the various parts of the world has taken the form of a debate over "the main contradictions of our time," and where these contradictions are concentrated. Soviet leaders charge that the CCP has put forward a "new theory."   They assert:

According to this new theory the main contradiction of our time is . . . contradiction not between socialism and imperialism, but between the national liberation movement and imperialism.   The decisive force in the struggle against imperialism . . . is not the world system of socialism, not the struggle of the international working class, but again the national liberation movement.[1]

In rebuttal, the Chinese argue that

Of course the contradiction between the socialist and capitalist camps is undoubtedly very sharp, but Marxist-Leninists must not regard the contradictions in the world as consisting solely and simply of the contradiction between the two camps. . . .   The fundamental contradictions in the contemporary world are the contradictions between the socialist camp and the imperialist camp, the contradiction between the proletariat and the bourgeoisie in the capitalist countries [so far so good from the Soviet point of view, but the Chinese add these other things], the contradiction between the oppressed nations and imperialism, and the contradictions among the imperialist countries and among the monopoly capitalist groups.

[1] *Peking Review,* October 25, 1963, p. 10.

Moreover, the Chinese add (and this is the significant point):

. . . the various types of contradictions in the contemporary world are *concentrated* in the vast areas of Asia, Africa, and Latin America; these are the most *vulnerable* areas under imperialist rule and the storm centers of world revolution dealing direct blows at imperialism. . . . In a sense, therefore, the whole cause of the international proletarian revolution *hinges* on the outcome of the revolutionary struggles of the people of these areas, who constitute the overwhelming majority of the world's population. . . . Today the national liberation revolutions in Asia, Africa, and Latin America are the *most important forces* dealing imperialism direct blows.[2]

This theory of the concentration of contradictions in the underdeveloped areas echoes Stalin's explanation of the success of the October Revolution. According to Stalin, although Russia was not a highly developed industrial society, all the contradictions in the era of imperialism found concentrated expression in Russia. Russia was the weakest link of imperialism.

*   *   *

Mao, of course, also sees the prospect that the arena of struggle will shift from the underdeveloped areas to the developed areas, just as the arena of struggle shifted from the countryside to the cities in the final phase of the Chinese revolution. An article by the editorial departments of the *People's Daily* and the *Red Flag,* commenting on the open letter of the Central Committee of the CPSU, declared:

The center of world contradictions, of world political struggles, is not fixed but shifts with changes in the international struggles and the revolutionary situation. We believe that, with the development of the contradiction and struggle between the proletariat and the bourgeoisie in Western Europe and North America, the momentous day of battle will arrive in these homes of capitalism and heartlands of imperialism. When that day comes, Western Europe and North America will undoubtedly become the center of world political struggles, of world contradictions.

This statement can best be understood in the light of Mao's belief that by waging national liberation wars and revolutionary civil wars in the underdeveloped areas, the revolutionary peoples are actually helping the proletariat in their struggle against the bourgeoisie.

Since Mao's global strategy is to encircle the developed areas from the underdeveloped areas, he must promote and support national liberation wars and revolutionary civil wars. The military-political strategy which Mao developed during the Chinese civil war and the Sino-Japanese War can be readily applied to these wars. The strategy of fighting guerrilla and mobile warfare with popular support does not depend for its success on modern weapons or vast financial resources, which the Communist Chinese lack. It depends rather on an ability to turn the nationalism of

---

[2] *Ibid.,* June 21, 1963, pp. 7, 9. (Italics added.)

the colonial or anti-colonial countries, and the nationalism of the newly independent countries, against the Western powers.   It relies on exploiting the political instability, economic chaos and social turmoil in these countries, manipulating the grievances of the oppressed classes, mobilizing the masses for political-military actions, organizing them into structured groups, offering them political leadership, and guiding them with a "correct" political-military strategy.   This expertise which the Chinese acquired in twenty years of struggle can be passed along through the training of new cadres.

The Chinese strongly emphasize that national liberation wars and revolutionary civil wars are just wars.   These wars are unavoidable.   It is the duty of communist parties to give them all necessary support.   Mao therefore upholds the doctrine of the inevitability of war insofar as this is applied to these two kinds of war.   "Revolutions are not possible without wars of national liberation or revolutionary civil war.   To say otherwise is opposed to revolutionary wars and to revolution." [3]

Until January 1961, Khrushchev's thesis was . . . that "the absence of war will not slow down the world revolutionary process, that in the future revolution will be possible without war." [4] He probably believed that a world communist victory could and would be achieved through non-military forms of struggle.   Khrushchev certainly feared that armed struggle, including revolutionary civil wars and national liberation wars, would escalate into a nuclear war.   In the spring of 1960, official Soviet statements contained a few hints suggesting that it would be undesirable for revolutionary struggles to be carried on so vigorously as to lead to a danger of world war.   Under attack by the Chinese, however, Soviet leaders conceded a point.   In January 1961, Khrushchev declared that national liberation wars are unavoidable.   He said: "Liberation wars will continue as long as imperialism exists; wars of this kind are revolutionary wars. Such wars are not only justified, they are inevitable, for the colonialists do not freely bestow independence on peoples." [5]

This concession did not halt the polemics.   To carry out his global strategy, Mao must energetically support national liberation wars and revolutionary civil wars—despite the danger that these wars could escalate into a major confrontation or local war between the two camps, and even into a world war.   Although they accept the inevitability of national liberation wars, Soviet leaders are more cautious than the Chinese in supporting them. . . .   Khrushchev stated that " 'local wars' in our time are very dangerous," and "we will work hard . . . to put out the sparks that may

[3] *Ibid.*, June 21, 1963, p. 13.

[4] Frederic S. Burin, "The Communist Doctrine of the Inevitability of War," *American Political Science Review,* June 1963, p. 352.

[5] G. F. Hudson, *et al., The Sino-Soviet Dispute* (New York: Praeger, 1961), pp. 211–213.

set off the flames of war." [6]   Khrushchev's formulations seem to suggest that he will support national liberation wars only so long as these wars do not lead to a local war between the two camps.   Khrushchev's reluctance to support revolutionary civil wars and national liberation wars was shown in Algeria, the Congo and even Vietnam.

The Chinese believe that Khrushchev's formula on the avoidability of local war is essentially "an attempt to oppose revolution in the name of safeguarding peace." [7]   They use the following argument against Khrushchev:

In recent years, certain persons have been spreading the argument that a single spark from a war of national liberation or from a revolutionary people's war will lead to a world conflagration destroying the whole of mankind . . . contrary to what these persons say, the wars of national liberation and the revolutionary people's wars that have occurred since World War II have not led to world war. . . .   The victory of these revolutionary wars has directly weakened the forces of imperialism and greatly strengthened the forces which prevent the imperialists from launching a world war and which defend world peace. [8]

Mao's revolutionary strategy of encircling the developed countries from the underdeveloped areas does not call for a world war or a nuclear war between the United States and the Soviet Union.   Far from proclaiming the inevitability of war between the two camps, the Chinese communists have consistently discounted the danger of a world war. [9]   As far back as 1946, when there was talk of a war between the Soviet Union and the United States, Mao minimized this possibility.   He indicated his belief to Anna Louise Strong that "the U.S. and the Soviet Union are separated by a vast zone which includes many capitalist, colonial and semi-colonial countries in Europe, Asia and Africa. . . .   Before the U.S. reactionaries have subjugated these countries, an attack on the Soviet Union is out of the question." [10]   By this remark, Mao meant that the immediate political-military struggle between the two camps would not take the form of a war between the United States and the Soviet Union but rather a struggle to control the intermediate zones.   This appraisal of U.S. intentions reflected his own concept of global strategy against the United States.   Mao uses the formula of the avoidability of world war to justify his strategy of pushing national liberation wars and revolutionary civil wars in the underdeveloped areas.   Again, he is projecting his past experience to the present. He reasons as follows: In spite of the fear of "certain people" over the out-

[6] Quoted in a Chinese statement, *Peking Review,* October 25, 1963, p. 9.

[7] *Ibid.*

[8] *Ibid.,* June 21, 1963, p. 14.

[9] Burin, *loc. cit.,* p. 348; *Peking Review,* November 2, 1963, pp. 9–10.

[10] Mao Tse-tung, *Selected Works* (Peking: Foreign Languages Press, 1961), p. 196.

break of a third world war, the Chinese communists fought and defeated the Nationalists in the period from 1946 to 1949. There is no reason why revolutionary wars in other underdeveloped areas against imperialists and their lackeys cannot be won even though there is again talk of a world war. To bolster his argument for militancy, Mao stresses the theme that by struggling against the imperialists, the working classes and the forces of peace can prevent the imperialists from launching a world war.

But Mao has a very complicated mind: what he says is not always exactly what he means. In spite of his professed belief in the possibility of avoiding a world war, Mao is aware of the fact that intensified struggle may increase the danger of a world war. Thus he argues that

while pointing to the possibility of preventing a new world war, we must also call attention to the possibility that imperialism may unleash a world war. Only by pointing to both possibilities, pursuing correct policies and preparing for both eventualities can we effectively mobilize the masses to wage struggle in defense of world peace. Only thus will the socialist countries and people and other peace-loving countries and people not be caught unawares and utterly unprepared should imperialism force a world war on people.[11]

* * *

Having admitted the possibility of a nuclear world war, Mao is concerned that the fear of a nuclear holocaust may lead to capitulation, or at least inhibit revolutionary actions in the underdeveloped areas. He apparently believes that he can dispel this fear by proclaiming the survival and triumph of the socialist system after the nuclear catastrophe. He also feels that by loudly proclaiming this view, he will also make it less likely that the United States will launch a nuclear war. It is in this context that he talks about half of mankind dying in a nuclear war, and the other half remaining to build socialism on the ruins of a world destroyed by a war launched by the imperialists.

If the imperialists dare to launch nuclear war and plunge mankind into such an unprecedented disaster, what should the international proletariat do? It is perfectly clear that there are two alternatives, either to resist imperialism firmly and bury it, or to be afraid of sacrifice and to capitulate. But some people believe that if nuclear war breaks out all mankind will perish. In reality, such talk amounts to saying there is no alternative to capitulation in the face of imperialist nuclear blackmail. Directing himself to this pessimistic and capitulationist talk, Comrade Mao Tse-tung pointed out that mankind will definitely not be destroyed even if the imperialists insist on a nuclear war with the possible sacrifice of hundreds of millions of people and impose it on mankind. The future of mankind will nevertheless be a bright one.[12]

[11] *Peking Review*, November 23, 1963, p. 10.

[12] *Ibid.*, July 26, 1963, p. 27. In November 1957 at the Moscow meeting of communist parties, Mao said: "The question has to be considered for the worst. The Political Bureau of our Party has held several sessions to discuss this question. . . . [I]f the worst came to the worst and half of mankind died, the other half would

In other words, Mao has gone much further than Herman Kahn in thinking the unthinkable. He has made the unthinkable thinkable by picturing the unthinkable as a bright future for socialism.

For all the talk about building a bright future on the ruins of a nuclear war, Mao does not think of nuclear weapons as offensive weapons. Peking has gone on record in opposition to a first strike: "A socialist country absolutely must not be the first to use nuclear weapons, nor should it in any circumstances play with them or engage in nuclear blackmail and nuclear gambling." [13] This last assertion is obviously an allusion to the Cuban affair. Nuclear weapons cannot be used to support people's revolutionary struggles or national liberation wars. Nor should a socialist country use them first against an imperialist country which wages a conventional war of aggression.[14] China wants to manufacture nuclear weapons as "the means of resisting U.S. nuclear blackmail." [15]

What, then, of the other side of the coin, that is, peaceful coexistence? To reconstruct Mao's views, we must again look at his revolutionary strategy, particularly during the period between 1937 and 1946. Mao's strategy throughout the whole period of the Chinese revolution was to encircle the city from the countryside. This strategy unfolded in three different phases during which the relations between Kuomintang (KMT) and the CCP underwent important changes. During the first phase, the CCP fought an all-out civil war with the KMT. When the CCP faced the possibility of total defeat, it sought peaceful coexistence with the KMT by proposing to form an anti-Japanese united front with the Nationalists.

During the second phase from 1937 to 1944, a united front (read for the term "united front," "peaceful coexistence") existed between the KMT and the CCP. . . . Under the protection of the policy of maintaining a united front with the KMT, the communists rapidly pushed forward their strategy of encircling the city from the countryside by expanding their control in the rural areas behind the Japanese lines. . . . Peking's present policy of peaceful coexistence bears a close resemblance to Mao's tactics of the united front during this period.

During the third phase from 1946 to 1949, the CCP won a revolutionary civil war against the KMT.

Mao's experience with the united front with the KMT has clearly influenced Peking's doctrine of peaceful coexistence as well as other questions in her debate with Moscow. It should be emphasized that, while Peking's statements on peaceful coexistence are made more frequently in

---

remain while imperialism would be razed to the ground and the whole world would become socialist; in a number of years there would be 2,700 million people again and definitely more." *Ibid.*, September 6, 1963, p. 10.

[13] *Ibid.*, November 23, 1963, p. 12.

[14] *Ibid.*, p. 13.

[15] *Ibid.*, September 6, 1963, p. 9.

discussing Peking's relations with the nonaligned countries than in discussing Sino-American relations, Mao does not completely reject the possibility of peaceful coexistence with the West, or even with the United States. But he does not envisage peaceful coexistence as a lasting state of affairs—just as he did not conceive of the united front with the KMT as anything more than a useful short-term policy. In this, his position is not so different from Khrushchev's as is commonly supposed. For Khrushchev has declared his intention to bury the capitalist system, and there cannot be peaceful coexistence between the corpse and those who bury it. The dispute arose with regard to the method of burying the West. In his pronouncements, Khrushchev emphasizes peaceful competition and economic progress, but in his actions he is not above making such military moves as placing missiles in Cuba, designed to improve the Soviet position in the balance of military power.

Mao emphasizes armed struggle in the underdeveloped areas to encircle the United States, but he is very cautious about taking any military action which might precipitate a direct confrontation with the United States. Despite his caution, Mao does not want peaceful coexistence to hinder in any way the development of revolutionary struggles in Asia, Africa and Latin America. Thus, Peking repeatedly has proclaimed that there cannot be peaceful coexistence between oppressed nations and oppressor nations, and that the condition for the success achieved by the national liberation movements after World War II was not peaceful coexistence between the two camps—as the Soviets maintain—but revolutionary struggle on the part of the oppressed peoples. . . . Moscow specifically denies Peking's charge that peaceful coexistence, according to Khrushchev's formula, applies to the relations between oppressed nations and oppressor nations. But Peking has challenged the Soviet prescription that the general line of the political program of the communist movement should be peaceful coexistence. For Mao fears that this formulation would inhibit revolutionary struggles. Peaceful coexistence with the West should not rule out armed struggles in the underdeveloped areas, which constitute a form of struggle against the United States, just as the united front with the KMT did not rule out local military clashes in the countryside.

In Mao's view, peaceful coexistence not only does not preclude conflict but it can be maintained only by waging struggle against the imperialists, just as the united front with the KMT not only did not preclude conflict, but could be maintained only by waging struggle. In this struggle, Peking's policy is

to unite all the forces that can be united in order to form a broad united front against U.S. imperialism and its lackeys. . . . It is possible for the socialist countries to *compel* one imperialist country or another to establish some sort of peaceful coexistence with them by relying on their own growing strength, the expansion of the revolutionary forces of the peoples, the united front with the nationalist countries and the struggle of all the peace-loving people, and by utilizing the internal contradiction of imperialism.[16]

In maintaining peaceful coexistence with the imperialist countries, it is necessary to enter into negotiations with them. "But it is absolutely impermissible to pin hopes for world peace on negotiations, spread illusions about them and thereby paralyze the fighting will of the peoples, as Khrushchev has done." [17]   Sometimes it is necessary for the socialist countries to reach compromises with the imperialists.   But "necessary compromises between the socialist countries and the imperialist countries do not require the oppressed peoples and nations to follow suit and compromise with imperialism and its lackeys." [18]

Peking continues to stress Lenin's view that the coexistence of socialism side by side with imperialism "for a long time is unthinkable," and that "one or the other must triumph in the end."   Presumably, this triumph would come about after the communists had gradually won over the underdeveloped areas and then carried the struggle to the developed areas by promoting conflict between the proletariat and monopoly capital.   To implement Mao's strategy it is not necessary to rely on a world war or a nuclear war.   But it is imperative, from Mao's viewpoint, that the imperialists be deterred from launching a nuclear war.   It is equally imperative that the communists not be paralyzed by the fear of nuclear war and thus fail to support national liberation wars and revolutionary civil wars.

[16] *Ibid.*, December 20, 1963, p. 10.   (Italics added.)
[17] *Ibid.*, September 22, 1963, p. 15.
[18] *Ibid.*, June 21, 1963, p. 15.

John Locke

OF CONQUEST

That the aggressor, who puts himself into the state of war with another and unjustly invades another man's right, can by such an unjust war never come to have a right over the conquered, will be easily agreed by all men, who will not think that robbers and pirates have a right of empire over whomsoever they have force enough to master or that men are bound by promises which unlawful force extorts from them. . . . The injury and the crime is equal, whether committed by the wearer of a crown or some petty villain. . . . The only difference is, great robbers punish little ones to keep them in their obedience but the great ones are rewarded with laurels and triumphs because they are too big for the weak hands of justice in this world. . . . [T]he conquered or their children have no court, no arbitrator on earth to appeal to. They may appeal, as Jeptha did, to heaven,[1] and repeat their appeal till they have recovered the native right of their ancestors, which was to have such a legislative over them as the majority should approve and freely acquiesce in. If it be objected that this would cause endless trouble, I answer, no more than justice does where she lies open to all that appeal to her. . . .

But supposing victory favors the right side, let us consider a conqueror in a lawful war,[2] and see what power he gets and over whom. . . .

[T]he conqueror gets no power but only over those who have actually assisted, concurred or consented to that unjust force that is used against him. For the people having given their governors no power to do an unjust thing, such as to make an unjust war (for they never had such a power in themselves), they ought not to be charged as guilty of the violence and

Excerpts from *Second Treatise on Civil Government* (1690), Chapter XVI.

[1] Ed. note. That is, they may appeal to force. See *Judges,* chapter 11. There is, at least, ambiguity in Locke's identification of divine justice with the result of battle, and it seems to imply that Locke, despite what he appears to argue, thought of force as the fundamental "law of nature."

[2] Ed. note. That is, a war fought to defend one's country or its rights against an aggressor.

injustice that is committed in an unjust war any further than they actually abet it, no more than they are to be thought guilty of any violence or oppression their governors should use upon the people themselves. . . . Conquerors, it is true, seldom trouble to make the distinction, [and] they willingly permit the confusion of war to sweep all together, but yet this alters not the right. . . .

The power a conqueror gets over those he overcomes in a just war is perfectly despotical; he has an absolute power over the lives of those, who by putting themselves in a state of war, have forfeited them; but he has not thereby a right and title to their possessions. This I doubt not but at first sight will seem a strange doctrine, it being quite contrary to the practice of the world. . . . But when we consider, the practice of the strong and powerful, how universal soever it may be, is seldom the rule of right. . . .

Though in all war . . . the aggressor seldom fails to harm the estate,[3] . . . it is the use of force only that puts a man into the state of war. For whether by force he begins the injury, or else having quietly and by fraud done the injury, he refuses to make reparation and by force maintains it (which is the same thing as at first to have done it by force), it is the unjust use of force that makes the war. . . . For quitting reason, which is the rule given between man and man, and using force, the way of beasts, he becomes liable to be destroyed by him he uses force against as any savage ravenous beast that is dangerous to his being.

But because the miscarriages of the father are no faults of the children, and they may be rational and peaceable notwithstanding the brutishness and injustice of the father, the father by his miscarriages and violence can but forfeit his own life, but involves not his children in his guilt or destruction. His goods, which nature that willeth the preservation of all mankind as much as possible, hath made to belong to the children to keep them from perishing, do still continue to belong to his children. For supposing them not to have joined in the war, either through infancy or choice, they have done nothing to forfeit them, nor has the conqueror any right to take them away . . . though perhaps he may have some right to them to repair the damages he has sustained by the war and the defense of his own right. . . . So that he that by conquest has a right over a man's person to destroy him if he pleases, has not thereby a right over his estate to possess and enjoy it. For it is the brutal force the aggressor has used that gives his adversary a right to take away his life and destroy him if he pleases as a noxious creature, but it is damage alone that gives him title to another man's goods. . . . The fundamental law of nature being that all, as much as may be, should be preserved, it follows that if there be not enough to fully satisfy . . . the conqueror's losses and the children's maintenance, he that hath and to spare must remit something of his full satis-

[3] Ed. note. That is, the land, crops and possessions of those he attacks.

faction and give way to the pressing and preferable title of those who are in danger of perishing without it.

But supposing the charge and damages of the war are to be made up to the conqueror to the utmost farthing; and that the children of the vanquished, spoiled of all their father's goods, are to be left to starve and perish; yet [this] . . . will scarcely give [the conqueror] a title to any country he shall conquer. For the damages of war can scarce amount to the value of any considerable tract of land in any part of the world where all the land is possessed and where none lies waste. . . . The conqueror will, indeed, be apt to think himself master; and it is the very condition of the subdued not to be able to dispute their right. But if that be all, it gives no title other than what bare force gives to the stronger over the weaker and, by this reason, he that is strongest will have a right to whatever he pleases to seize on. . . .

[T]he . . . conqueror never having had a claim to the land of that country, the people who are the descendants of, or claim under those who were forced to submit to the yoke of government by constraint, have always a right to shake it off and free themselves from the usurpation or tyranny which the sword hath brought in upon them, till their rulers put them under such a frame of government as they willingly and of choice consent to, which they can never be supposed to do till they either are put in a full state of liberty to choose their government and governors or at least till they have standing laws to which they have by themselves or their representatives given their free consent, and also till they are allowed their due property, which is so to be proprietors of what they have that nobody can take away any part of it without their own consent, without which men under any government are not in the state of freemen but are direct slaves under the force of war. And who doubts but that the Grecian Christians, descendants of the ancient possessors of that country, may justly cast off the Turkish yoke which they have so long groaned under, whenever they have a power to do it?

John Stuart Mill

ON NON-INTERVENTION

There is a country in Europe, equal to the greatest in extent of dominion, far exceeding any other in wealth, and in the power that wealth bestows, the declared principle of whose foreign policy is, to let other nations alone. No country apprehends, or affects to apprehend from it any aggressive designs. Power, from of old, is wont to encroach upon the weak, and to quarrel for ascendency with those who are as strong as itself. Not so this nation. It will hold its own, it will not submit to encroachment, but if other nations do not meddle with it, it will not meddle with them. Any attempt it makes to exert influence over them, even by persuasion, is rather in the service of others, than of itself: to mediate in the quarrels which break out between foreign states, to arrest obstinate civil wars, to reconcile belligerents, to intercede for mild treatment of the vanquished, or, finally, to procure the abandonment of some national crime and scandal to humanity, such as the slave-trade. Not only does this nation desire no benefit to itself at the expense of others, it desires none in which all others do not as freely participate. It makes no treaties stipulating for separate commercial advantages. If the aggressions of barbarians force it to a successful war, and its victorious arms put it in a position to command liberty of trade, whatever it demands for itself it demands for all mankind. The cost of the war is its own; the fruits it shares in fraternal equality with the whole human race. Its own ports and commerce are free as the air and the sky: all its neighbours have full liberty to resort to it, paying either no duties, or, if any, generally a mere equivalent for what is paid by its own citizens; nor does it concern itself though they, on their part, keep all to themselves, and persist in the most jealous and narrow-minded exclusion of its merchants and goods.

A nation adopting this policy is a novelty in the world; so much so, it would appear, that many are unable to believe it when they see it. By one of the practical paradoxes which often meet us in human affairs, it is this nation which finds itself, in respect of its foreign policy, held up to obloquy as the type of egoism and selfishness; as a nation which thinks of nothing but of outwitting and out-generalling its neighbours. . . .

Nations, like individuals, ought to suspect some fault in themselves when they find they are generally worse thought of than they think they deserve; and they may well know that they are somehow in fault when almost everybody but themselves thinks them crafty and hypocritical. It is not solely because England has been more successful than other nations in gaining what they are all aiming at, that they think she must be following after it with a more ceaseless and a more undivided chase. . . . They moreover

Reprinted from *Fraser's Magazine*, London (December 1859), pp. 766–776.

accept literally all the habitual expressions by which we represent ourselves
as worse than we are; expressions often heard from English statesmen, next
to never from those of any other country—partly because Englishmen, beyond all the rest of the human race, are so shy of professing virtues that
they will even profess vices instead; and partly because almost all English
statesmen, while careless to a degree which no foreigner can credit, respect-
ing the impression they produce on foreigners, commit the obtuse blunder
of supposing that low objects are the only ones to which the minds of their
non-aristocratic fellow-countrymen are amenable, and that it is always expedient, if not necessary, to place those objects in the foremost rank.

What is the sort of language held in every oration which, during the present European crisis, any English minister, or almost any considerable public
man, addresses to Parliament or to his constituents? The eternal repetition
of this shabby *refrain*—"We did not interfere, because no English interest
was involved;" "We ought not to interfere where no English interest is concerned." England is thus exhibited as a country whose most distinguished
men are not ashamed to profess, as politicians, a rule of action which no
one, not utterly base, could endure to be accused of as the maxim by which
he guides his private life; not to move a finger for others unless he sees his
private advantage in it. There is much to be said for the doctrine that a
nation should be willing to assist its neighbours in throwing off oppression
and gaining free institutions. Much also may be said by those who maintain that one nation is incompetent to judge and act for another, and that
each should be left to help itself, and seek advantage or submit to disadvantage as it can and will. But of all attitudes which a nation can take up on
the subject of intervention, the meanest and worst is to profess that it interferes only when it can serve its own objects by it. . . .

There is scarcely any necessity to say, writing to Englishmen, that this is
not what our rulers and politicians really mean. Their language is not a
correct exponent of their thoughts. They mean a part only of what they
seem to say. They do mean to disclaim interference for the sake of doing
good to foreign nations. They are quite sincere and in earnest in repudiating this. But the other half of what their words express, a willingness to
meddle if by doing so they can promote any interest of England, they do not
mean. The thought they have in their minds, is not the interest of England,
but her security. What they would say, is, that they are ready to act when
England's safety is threatened, or any of her interests hostilely or unfairly
endangered. This is no more than what all nations, sufficiently powerful
for their own protection, do, and no one questions their right to do. It is
the common right of self-defence. But if we mean this, why, in Heaven's
name, do we take every possible opportunity of saying, instead of this,
something exceedingly different? Not self-defence, but aggrandizement, is
the sense which foreign listeners put upon our words. Not simply to protect what we have, and that merely against unfair arts, not against fair rivalry; but to add to it more and more without limit, is the purpose for which

foreigners think we claim the liberty of intermeddling with them and their affairs. . . . Does it answer any good purpose to express ourselves as if we did not scruple to profess that which we not merely scruple to do, but the bare idea of doing which never crosses our minds? Of all countries which are sufficiently powerful to be capable of being dangerous to their neighbours, we are perhaps the only one whom mere scruples of conscience would suffice to deter from it. We are the only people among whom, by no class whatever of society, is the interest or glory of the nation considered to be any sufficient excuse for an unjust act; the only one which regards with jealousy and suspicion, and a proneness to hostile criticism, precisely those acts of its Government which in other countries are sure to be hailed with applause, those by which territory has been acquired, or political influence extended. Being in reality better than other nations, in at least the negative part of international morality, let us cease, by the language we use, to give ourselves out as worse.

*   *   *

There seems to be no little need that the whole doctrine of non-interference with foreign nations should be reconsidered, if it can be said to have as yet been considered as a really moral question at all. We have heard something lately about being willing to go to war for an idea. To go to war for an idea, if the war is aggressive, not defensive, is as criminal as to go to war for territory or revenue; for it is as little justifiable to force our ideas on other people, as to compel them to submit to our will in any other respect. But there assuredly are cases in which it is allowable to go to war, without having been ourselves attacked, or threatened with attack; and it is very important that nations should make up their minds in time, as to what these cases are. There are few questions which more require to be taken in hand by ethical and political philosophers, with a view to establish some rule or criterion whereby the justifiableness of intervening in the affairs of other countries, and (what is sometimes fully as questionable) the justifiableness of refraining from intervention, may be brought to a definite and rational test. Whoever attempts this, will be led to recognise more than one fundamental distinction, not yet by any means familiar to the public mind, and in general quite lost sight of by those who write in strains of indignant morality on the subject. There is a great difference (for example) between the case in which the nations concerned are of the same, or something like the same, degree of civilization, and that in which one of the parties to the situation is of a high, and the other of a very low, grade of social improvement. To suppose that the same international customs, and the same rules of international morality, can obtain between one civilized nation and another, and between civilized nations and barbarians, is a grave error, and one which no statesman can fall into, however it may be with those who, from a safe and unresponsible position, criticise statesmen. Among many reasons why the same rules cannot be applicable to situations so different, the two following are among the most important. In the first place, the rules of ordinary international morality imply reciprocity. But barbarians will not reciprocate. They cannot be depended on for observing any rules. Their minds are not capable of so great an effort, nor their will sufficiently under the influence of distant motives. In the next place, nations which are still barbarous have not got beyond the period during which it is likely to be for their benefit that they should be conquered and held in subjection by foreigners. Independence and nationality, so essential to the due growth and development of a people further advanced in improvement, are generally impediments to theirs. The sacred duties which civilized nations owe to the independence and nationality of each other, are not binding towards those to whom nationality and independence are either a certain evil, or at best a questionable good. The Romans were not the most clean-handed of conquerors, yet would it have been better for Gaul and Spain, Numidia and Dacia, never to have formed part of the Roman Empire? To characterize any conduct whatever towards a barbarous people as a violation of the law of nations, only shows that he who so speaks has never considered the subject. A violation of great principles of morality it may easily be; but barbarians have no rights as a *nation,* except a right to such treatment as may, at the earliest possible period, fit them for becoming one. The only moral laws for the relation between a civilized and a barbarous government, are the universal rules of morality between man and man.

A civilized government cannot help having barbarous neighbours: when it has, it cannot always content itself with a defensive position, one of mere resistance to aggression. After a longer or shorter interval of forbearance, it either finds itself obliged to conquer them, or to assert so much authority over them, and so break their spirit, that they gradually sink into a state of dependence upon itself: and when that time arrives, they are indeed no longer formidable to it, but it has had so much to do with setting up and pulling down their governments, and they have grown so accustomed to lean on it, that it has become morally responsible for all evil it allows them to do. This is the history of the relations of the British Government with the native States of India. It never was secure in its own Indian possessions until it had reduced the military power of those States to a nullity. But a despotic government only exists by its military power. When we had taken away theirs, we were forced, by the necessity of the case, to offer them ours instead of it. . . . But being thus assured of the protection of a civilized power, and freed from the fear of internal rebellion or foreign conquest, the only checks which either restrain the passions or keep any vigour in the character of an Asiatic despot, the native Governments either became so oppressive and extortionate as to desolate the country, or fell into such a state of nerveless imbecility, that every one, subject to their will, who had not the means of defending himself by his own armed followers, was the prey of anybody who had a band of ruffians in his pay. The British Government felt this deplorable state of things to be its own work; being the direct consequence of the position in which, for its own security, it had placed itself towards the native governments. Had it permitted this to go on indefinitely, it would have deserved to be accounted among the worst political malefactors. . . .

But among civilized peoples, members of an equal community of nations, like Christian Europe, the question assumes another aspect, and must be decided on totally different principles. It would be an affront to the reader to discuss the immorality of wars of conquest, or of conquest even as the consequence of lawful war; the annexation of any civilized people to the dominion of another, unless by their own spontaneous election. Up to this point, there is no difference of opinion among honest people; nor on the wickedness of commencing an aggressive war for any interest of our own, except when necessary to avert from ourselves an obviously impending wrong. The disputed question is that of interfering in the regulation of another country's internal concerns; the question whether a nation is justi-fied in taking part, on either side, in the civil wars or party contests of an-other; and chiefly, whether it may justifiably aid the people of another country in struggling for liberty; or may impose on a country any particular government or institutions, either as being best for the country itself, or as necessary for the security of its neighbours.

Of these cases, that of a people in arms for liberty is the only one of any nicety, or which, theoretically at least, is likely to present conflicting moral considerations. The other cases which have been mentioned hardly admit of discussion. Assistance to the government of a country in keeping down the people, unhappily by far the most frequent case of foreign intervention, no one writing in a free country needs take the trouble of stigmatizing. A government which needs foreign support to enforce obedience from its own citizens, is one which ought not to exist; and the assistance given to it by foreigners is hardly ever anything but the sympathy of one despotism with another. A case requiring consideration is that of a protracted civil war, in which the contending parties are so equally balanced that there is no probability of a speedy issue; or if there is, the victorious side cannot hope to keep down the vanquished but by severities repugnant to humanity and injurious to the permanent welfare of the country. In this exceptional case it seems now to be an admitted doctrine, that the neighbouring nations, or one powerful neighbour with the acquiescence of the rest, are warranted in demanding that the contest shall cease, and a reconciliation take place on equitable terms of compromise. Intervention of this description has been repeatedly practised during the present generation, with such general ap-proval, that its legitimacy may be considered to have passed into a maxim of what is called international law. . . .

With respect to the question, whether one country is justified in helping the people of another in a struggle against their government for free insti-tutions, the answer will be different, according as the yoke which the people are attempting to throw off is that of a purely native government, or of foreigners; considering as one of foreigners, every government which maintains itself by foreign support.   When the contest is only with native rulers, and with such native strength as those rulers can enlist in their defence, the answer I should give to the question of the legitimacy of intervention is, as a general rule, No.   The reason is, that there can seldom be anything approaching to assurance that intervention, even if successful, would be for the good of the people themselves.   The only test possessing any real value, of a people's having become fit for popular institutions, is that they, or a sufficient portion of them to prevail in the contest, are willing to brave labour and danger for their liberation.   I know all that may be said.   I know it may be urged that the virtues of freemen cannot be learnt in the school of slavery, and that if a people are not fit for freedom, to have any chance of becoming so they must first be free.   And this would be conclusive, if the intervention recommended would really give them freedom.   But the evil is, that if they have not sufficient love of liberty to be able to wrest it from merely domestic oppressors, the liberty which is bestowed on them by other hands than their own will have nothing real, nothing permanent.   No people ever was and remained free, but because it was determined to be so; because neither its rulers nor any other party in the nation could compel it to be otherwise.   If a people—especially one whose freedom has not yet become prescriptive—does not value it sufficiently to fight for it, and maintain it against any force which can be mustered *within* the country, it is only a question in how few years or months that people will be enslaved.   Either the government which it has given to itself, or some military leader or knot of conspirators who contrive to subvert the government, will speedily put an end to all popular institutions: unless indeed it suits their conveniences better to leave them standing, and be content with reducing them to mere forms; for, unless the spirit of liberty is strong in a people, those who have the executive in their hands easily work *any* institutions to the purposes of despotism.   There is no sure guarantee against this deplorable issue, even in a country which has achieved its own freedom; as may be seen in the present day by striking examples both in the Old and New Worlds: but when freedom has been achieved *for* them, they have little prospect indeed of escaping this fate.   When a people has had the misfortune to be ruled by a government under which the feelings and the virtues needful for maintaining freedom could not develop themselves, it is during an arduous struggle to become free by their own efforts that these feelings and virtues have the best chance of springing up.   Men become attached to that which they have long fought for and made sacrifices for; they learn to appreciate that on which their thoughts have been much engaged; and a contest in which many have been called on to devote themselves for their country, is a school in which they learn to value their country's interest above their own.

It can seldom, therefore—I will not go so far as to say never—be either judicious or right, in a country which has a free government, to assist, otherwise than by the moral support of its opinion, the endeavours of another to extort the same blessing from its native rulers. We must except, of course, any case in which such assistance is a measure of legitimate self-defence. If (a contingency by no means unlikely to occur) this country, on account of its freedom, which is a standing reproach to despotism everywhere, and an encouragement to throw it off, should find itself menaced with attack by a coalition of Continental despots, it ought to consider the popular party in every nation of the Continent as its natural ally: the Liberals should be to it, what the Protestants of Europe were to the Government of Queen Elizabeth. So, again, when a nation, in her own defence, has gone to war with a despot, and has had the rare good fortune not only to succeed in her resistance, but to hold the conditions of peace in her own hands, she is entitled to say that she will make no treaty, unless with some other ruler than the one whose existence as such may be a perpetual menace to her safety and freedom. These exceptions do but set in a clearer light the reasons of the rule; because they do not depend on any failure of those reasons, but on considerations paramount to them, and coming under a different principle.

But the case of a people struggling against a foreign yoke, or against a native tyranny upheld by foreign arms, illustrates the reasons for non-intervention in an opposite way, for in this case the reasons themselves do not exist. A people the most attached to freedom, the most capable of defending and of making a good use of free institutions, may be unable to contend successfully for them against the military strength of another nation much more powerful. To assist a people thus kept down, is not to disturb the balance of forces on which the permanent maintenance of freedom in a country depends, but to redress that balance when it is already unfairly and violently disturbed. The doctrine of non-intervention, to be a legitimate principle of morality, must be accepted by all governments. The despots must consent to be bound by it as well as the free States. Unless they do, the profession of it by free countries comes but to this miserable issue, that the wrong side may help the wrong, but the right must not help the right. Intervention to enforce non-intervention is always rightful, always moral, if not always prudent. Though it be a mistake to *give* freedom to a people who do not value the boon, it cannot but be right to insist that if they do value it, they shall not be hindered from the pursuit of it by foreign coercion. . . . The first nation which, being powerful enough to make its voice effectual, has the spirit and courage to say that not a gun shall be fired in Europe by the soldiers of one Power against the revolted subjects of another, will be the idol of the friends of freedom throughout Europe. That declaration alone will ensure the almost immediate emancipation of every people which desires liberty sufficiently to be capable of maintaining it: and the nation which gives the word will soon find itself at the head of an alliance of free peoples, so strong as to defy the efforts of any number of confederated despots to bring it down. The prize is too glorious not be snatched sooner or later by some free country; and the time may not be distant when England, if she does not take this heroic part because of its heroism, will be compelled to take it from consideration for her own safety.

Dean Acheson

THE FIRST LINE OF ACTION

*   *   *

We are faced with a threat—in all sober truth I say this—we are faced with a threat not only to our country but to the civilization in which we live and to the whole physical environment in which that civilization can exist. This threat is the principal problem that confronts the whole United States in the world today.

To understand this threat to our country and our civilization, we have to go back two hundred years and examine the ideas on which the United States was founded. We could go back more than two thousand years, to the very beginning of Western civilization. For more than two thousand years the ideas we inherited, and live by today, have been fought over, have been suppressed, and have been reborn in the minds of men.

The adventurous people who settled the eastern shores of North America in the seventeenth and eighteenth centuries brought with them certain ideas which had come down to them through the whole stormy history of civilization. The first of those ideas was freedom—freedom of the mind and spirit, the most dynamic and adventurous idea ever to seize the mind of man. It drove men—and it continues to drive men—to inquire into the relation between man and God; to study the nature of the universe; to explore the purpose of human society.

Every thought we have in our minds, every relationship we have in our private lives, every institution under which we live, all of modern science has been molded, and in many cases created, by the exercise of the freedom of the human mind.

The second principle on which this country was built is the idea of diversity. If you have freedom of the mind, you are bound to have diversity, and you are bound to welcome it. We welcome people who think differ-

Reprinted from the Department of State, *Strengthening the Forces of Freedom: Selected Speeches and Statements of Secretary of State Acheson,* February 1949–April 1950 (Washington, D.C., 1950), pp. 1–7. Address before a meeting of the American Society of Newspaper Editors, Washington, D.C., April 22, 1950.

ently from ourselves. We welcome people with new ideas. We will not be chained to ideas of the past. We resist conformity. We refuse to be crammed into a single narrow pattern.

These ideas, freedom and diversity, have survived and flourished here in the United States because we accept and practiced a third idea—and that is tolerance. We say and we believe, "My freedom, my right to be different, depends on yours. I can be free only to the extent that you are free too."

*   *   *

Soviet Communism does not permit diversity of ideas. Freedom, this doctrine says, is an evil thing. It says that people who exercise freedom of thought, people who dare to depart from the doctrine laid down in the Kremlin in Moscow are criminals. It puts such people behind bars or puts them to death.

Now this threat of Soviet Communism would be serious enough if it were just the old idea of tyranny that was challenging our idea of freedom. It is that, but it is infinitely more than that.

This fanatical doctrine dominates one of the greatest states in this world, a state which, with its satellites, controls the lives of hundreds of millions of people and which today possesses the largest military establishment in existence.

That would be serious enough. But it is even more serious than that, because those who hold and practice this doctrine pick out our country as the principal target of their attack. From their point of view they pick it out rightly. It is our country, with its belief in freedom and tolerance, its great productive power, its tremendous vitality, which stands between the Kremlin and dominion over the entire world. We must not forget that it is we, the American people, who have been picked out as the principal target of the Soviet Communists.

*   *   *

What do we mean when we say that our country is the principal target of Soviet Communism? We mean that the Soviet authorities would use, and gladly use, any means at their command to weaken and to alarm us. Although they have not thought it wise to use military force against us, they are trying other methods. One method is the attempt to confuse and divide the American people.

If the United States can be confused and divided, if it can be made to doubt the desirability of helping other free nations, if it can be brought to doubt the desirability of maintaining its own defenses, if we cease to be rational and resolute, if we can be brought to doubt one another—then we will be softened up. Then we will be too weak to stand up to Communist thrusts in other parts of the world, and too divided and confused to stand up to Communist infiltration at home. To create that situation is one of the main objectives of the people in the Kremlin.

They have another objective, which is to pick off members of the free community of nations one by one. They do that partly to add to their power. But they have another important purpose and that is to build up the idea that Communism is inevitable, that it is the "wave of the future."

They believe that that gives other countries a sense of fright and hopelessness. They think that, if they can spread this idea of a Communist world closing in on us, then we will begin to get rattled, and some people will move in one direction and others will move in another direction, and the United States will be torn apart.

The men in the Kremlin have another clear objective, and that is to change the balance of productive power in the world. At present, that balance is very strongly against them, but that would not be so if they could get control in Western Europe and in Japan.

* * *

Our first line of action—and this seems to me the basis of all the others I shall discuss—is to demonstrate that our own faith in freedom is a burning and a fighting faith. We are children of freedom. We cannot be safe except in an environment of freedom. We believe in freedom as fundamentally as we believe in anything in this world. We believe in it for everyone in our country. And we don't restrict this belief to freedom for ourselves. We believe that all people in the world are entitled to as much freedom, to develop in their own way, as we want ourselves.

If we are clear about this, if we are full of passion about this, then we have in our hearts and minds the most dynamic and revolutionary concept in human history and one which properly strikes terror to every dictator, to every tyrant who would attempt to regiment and depress men anywhere.

Why do I put a strong belief in freedom first in the order of an American program of action? Because it is fundamental, because the second line of action flows from it. As the President [has] said so forcefully, the United States must, with a thousand voices and with all the resources of modern science, preach this doctrine throughout the world. The world must hear what America is about, what America believes, what freedom is, what it has done for many, what it can do for all.

We must use every means we know to communicate the value of freedom to the four corners of the earth. Our message must go out through leaflets, through our free press, radio programs and films, through exchange of students and teachers with other countries, and through a hundred other ways. And this doctrine of freedom will carry conviction because it comes not out of the Government alone but out of the hearts and souls of the people of the United States. Because it is the authentic voice of America, freedom will ring around the world.

Thirdly, it is not enough that one should have faith and should make that faith articulate. It is also essential that we, and those who think like us, should have the power to make safe the area in which we carry that faith into action. This means that we must look to our defenses. It means that we must organize our defenses wisely and prudently, with all the ingenuity and all the methods in which we are best versed to make ourselves strong.

*   *   *

Fourthly, beyond faith and preachment and defense there lies the necessity of translating all of these into terms of the daily lives of hundreds of millions of peoples who live in this free world of ours.   I am talking about the effort we are now making to help create a better material life for ourselves and for other people in many parts of the world.

One part of this effort has to do with setting in operation again the great workshops of the free world.   Since the end of the war we have worked steadily at this problem and we have had a vast measure of success.   The chimneys of these factories are smoking again, raw materials are moving into them, finished goods are moving out.   Hundreds of millions of people see the specter of insecurity in their daily lives being pushed further back.

Another part of this effort to develop the economic conditions for freedom is to help create new workshops, new crops, new wealth in places where they have not existed before.   That is the purpose of the President's program of technical assistance for underdeveloped areas.

As you know, there are great areas of the world where people are living in a state of extreme poverty that is almost impossible for us to imagine. Millions of these people are not content any more to accept these conditions of poverty for themselves or their children.   They are looking for a way out.   That is a good thing.   The will to change is half the battle. But the question is whether these people will choose a way out that leads to freedom.   The question is whether they will move ahead in the free world with us.   If we want them to move in the direction of freedom, we must help them.

*   *   *

. . . [W]e have to do still another thing.   And that is to develop a sensible system of trade to exchange the goods which are being and will be produced.   This free world of ours can't operate if people are cooped up within narrow national limits, if they are not able to move about freely and exchange their goods, their services, and their ideas and knowledge.   Building up an orderly and free system of exchange is what we mean when we talk about expanding world trade. . . .

*   *   *

The fifth line of action is in the political field.   In this political field we have so far only scratched the surface of what can be done to bring the free world closer together, to make it stronger and more secure and more effective.

There are many ways of organizing the free world for common action and many different opinions on how it should be done.   But I think it is important in this hour of danger to concentrate our minds and our energies on using the machinery we have at hand, on expanding it and making it work.   When you look over the field, you will see that we now have created a great deal of good machinery.

There is the whole machinery of the United Nations which we are continually learning to use more effectively.   Within the framework of the United Nations we have other machinery, like the North Atlantic Treaty and the Organization of American States.

. . . What we need to do is to expand the machinery we have, to improve it, to use it with boldness and imagination, and, where necessary, to supplement it with new machinery.

Now our program of action would not be complete if I did not go on to a sixth field, and that is the area of our relations with the Soviet Union and the countries that have fallen under Communist control.   In this field, as in our relations with the free nations, we have the machinery of negotiation at hand.   In the United Nations we have a dozen or more conference tables at which our differences could be thrashed out . . . We shall go on trying to find a common ground for agreement, not perfect or eternal agreement, but at least a better arrangement for living together in greater safety.

But one thing is clear.   There can be no agreement, there can be no approach to agreement unless one idea is done away with, and that is the idea of aggression.   And that word "aggression" includes not only military attack but propaganda warfare and the secret undermining of free countries from within.

We do not propose to subvert the Soviet Union.   We shall not attempt to undermine Soviet independence.   And we are just as determined that Communism shall not by hook or crook or trickery undermine our country or any other free country that desires to maintain its freedom.   That real and present threat of aggression stands in the way of every attempt at understanding with the Soviet Union.   For it has been wisely said that there can be no greater disagreement than when someone wants to eliminate your existence altogether.

If, as, and when that idea of aggression, by one means or another, can be ruled out of our relations with the Soviet Union, then the greatest single obstacle to agreement will be out of the way.   As the results of our actions become clear and the free world becomes stronger, it will, I believe, become progressively easier to get agreements with the Soviet Union.

These, then, are the main lines of action by the Government and people of the United States in dealing with their present danger. . . .

Whittle Johnston

LITTLE AMERICA—BIG AMERICA

Current debates over American foreign policy are characterized by the tactics of guerrilla warfare. An antagonist, painstakingly mustering intellectual resources to deliver a decisive blow, discovers his opponent has slipped away before the power can be brought to bear. In this type of conflict the tactic of "factual saturation" is one of the most common, and one of the most disappointing. Each antagonist already feels himself in possession of more than enough factual ammunition to defeat his opponents —if only he can meet them on open ground. This is precisely the rub: the unwillingness of either side to fight on terrain considered acceptable by the other. The conflict, in short, is much more one over the meaning of the facts than it is over the facts themselves.

Take Vietnam, for example. The clearest thing about the Vietnam conflict is its ambiguity: The "fact" that it is a civil war directed against an existent order shot through with great weakness and corruption, and the "fact" that, at the same time, it represents resistance to willful aggression across a vital international border in which one regime attempts to subordinate another and humiliate its victim's protector. When some assign priority to the civil war rather than the external aggression while others give reverse priority, it is clear that very different principles of interpretation are being used to sift the "truth" from the ocean of fact.

American policy toward the Soviet Union provides another example. J. K. Galbraith recently expressed puzzlement over the simultaneous pursuit of two divergent approaches: on the one hand détente, on the other containment. It seems that a new approach is being created while an unwillingness to alter the old persists. One thinks of an artist who begins to paint a lion and then decides that he prefers a lamb, but out of infatuation with his original creation refuses to wipe the canvas clean, and fits the lamb's head onto the lion's body. . . .

. . . In a sense the situation today is the reverse of that a generation ago. Then the bulk of the population was committed to a strict limitation of America's role in world politics, while a reflective minority battled with the narrowness of the isolationist heritage. Today, the majority gives support to extensive foreign commitments, while a reflective minority expresses concern that America will overreach herself. Senator Fulbright's phrase, "the arrogance of power," gives symbolic expression to this anxiety over America's present place in the world.

Internationalists put forth two broad justifications to support a larger role for America in world politics: the argument from domestic virtue and

Abridged from *The Yale Review*, 48, 1 (October 1968), pp. 1–16. Copyright © 1968 by Yale University and used by permission of the publisher.

the argument from international necessity. The former was a continuation of the faith in the "American mission" characteristic of the nation from its birth; the latter, a response to the growing perception that fundamental changes in world politics made hazardous the continuation of policies once plausible under different conditions. Both justifications are newly called into question. The new position is that recent changes in world politics are not only compatible with, but call for, a reduced American role. The argument from American virtue is out of touch both with the enormous deficiencies of our domestic life and the limited relevance of a parochial experience for peoples beyond our shores. In their emphasis on domestic reform the critics are similar to an earlier generation of liberal isolationists who insisted that the most effective way for America to exert power internationally was through the influence of her good example domestically. In their view of world politics the critics also show frequent links with a more traditional conception, in terms of which the era of bipolarity since 1945 is seen as an aberration destined to give way to a more "normal" pattern, that is, a more pluralistic one governed by a more flexible balance of power. As the "abnormalities" come to an end, America's exaggerated role—a consequence of them—will also come to an end. . . .

Any judgment on the proper role for America in world politics presupposes a judgment on two interrelated questions: the nature and merit of American civilization, the nature and needs of the international system. Those with little faith in the merits of that civilization and much confidence in the orderliness of world politics will move toward a lesser role for America. Those with great faith in that civilization and little confidence in the international order will move toward a larger role for America. On questions of such enormity no two persons will stand at precisely the same place on the spectrum between lesser and larger commitment. Yet we cannot act effectively in foreign affairs unless the range of this divergence is confined.

*   *   *

The Peace of Westphalia registered the triumph of a new conception of world politics. The essence of the new conception was the sharp and reciprocal distinction between domestic and international politics: the one characterized by the existence of a sovereign state on a relatively cohesive social base; the other, by the very absence of any such sovereign authority or cohesive base. Westphalia was of crucial significance in the emergence of international law and the balance of power. It has been said that international law "really amounts to laying down the principle of the sovereignty of states and deducing its consequences"; with the official establishment of the principle at Westphalia, the "deducing of the consequences" began in earnest. Although the doctrine of the balance of power had antecedents before Westphalia, the phrase does not come into general usage until the half-century following. Its acceptance involved an explicit rejection of any vision of imperial order.   To put the matter briefly, the balance of power was a means to establish some control in a political world now irrevocably pluralistic.

The balance of power could not work without war, which made decisions possible in many situations where no other means of decision existed.   The connection between the balance-of-power system and war was not accidental.   The repudiation of imperial unity and the hard insistence on political pluralism clearly implied that, without any international sovereignty, war must be the ultimate arbiter.   We again run the risk of seeing the past through the lenses of current anxieties if we assume most statesmen of those times looked on war as a—much less *the*—primary evil of the human condition.   States clearly valued their independence more than they did peace, and they were willing to pay the price of periodic adjustments through war to preserve a system which allowed them very wide freedom of action. . . . War was also of the greatest significance in the shaping of national identities. Indeed, there was often a religious dimension to the link between the military life and the national identity: the ritual, symbolism, and pageantry; the patriotic call to sublimate individual egotism in the service of the common cause; the mystical union of the transitory self with the transcendent whole, sealed through blood sacrifice.

A failure to understand the centrality of war in the history of the Westphalia system does more than deprive us of an accurate understanding of ages past; it obscures to us the meaning of our own time, which is intimately related to the changed nature of war.   The crucial factor has been the exponential growth in destructive capacity. . . . The implications for the Westphalia system of the technical surprise were initially felt with the firing of "the guns of August"; they came to assume inexpressibly hazardous proportions with the brilliant flash over Hiroshima on that other August, a generation later.   A system taken as "natural" when the gains from freedom of action seemed always to outweigh the costs of adjustment through war now came to be seen in a very different light.   An irrepressible doubt arose: was it any longer rational, indeed possible, to preserve the free-wheeling pluralism of the Westphalia system?

Traditionalists had at hand a ready answer, for to them the system was unchanged, unchanging, unchangeable: a balance-of-power arrangement governed by the timeless rules of interest and equilibrium.   Any pretense that states saw their role in a different light was mere ideological window dressing concealing the "real" (i.e., traditionalist) bases of their behavior. But although there was a sense in which the old game was still being played, neither the rules nor the players were the same.   For now most states no longer thought of war—save at a limited level and under comprehensive restrictions—as a means of decision.   The situation was not unlike that of a classical economy in which member firms were in constant competition and refused to acknowledge any framework save the competitive market, but in which the historic sanctions for the market system—most particularly depressions—were no longer seen as operative.

Beyond this, there was a general shift in the scale of the participant units, and in the intensity of the ideological rivalry among them.   Both trends were intimately related to the deepening crisis of the Westphalia system which opened in 1914.   For in varying degrees that crisis brought home . . . to all states the radical insecurities consequent upon uncontrolled technological interdependence, in both its military and economic forms. The urge toward the creation of larger political units was rooted in the determination to bring the extended foundations of one's military and economic security under more effective political control.   The growth of ideological politics was the psychological parallel to the growth of continental-scale political units—a response at another level to the insecurities resultant from uncontrolled technological interdependence.   An expedient live-and-let-live attitude is possible only when people enjoy a considerable margin of security in their lives; the essence of the period which opened in 1914 was that this margin of security was vanishing, and it took with it the pattern of tolerance that had rested upon it.   The traditionalist doctrine which presupposed a non-ideological politics was *itself* an ideology, generalized from a body of experience that had now been overtaken by events.

The Westphalia tradition, dominant for some three hundred years, was thereafter challenged by two "transformative" orientations: a revolutionary perspective based in Russia, a liberal perspective based in America.   The circumstance which precipitated the revolutionary orientation was the collapse of the traditional Russia in the First World War; the figure who gave expression to it was Lenin.   With a dogmatic brilliance Lenin argued that the revolutionary tensions of Europe, manifested in the class struggle, had become intertwined with the revolutionary transformation of traditional societies around the world, manifested in imperialist rivalries.   From this perspective the First World War was seen not as an illustration of the timeless workings of the balance of power, but as a phase in the deep decay of a system which was itself a transitory historic phenomenon.   The task of the Communist movement was to harness the revolutionary momentum to its own purposes.   Thus was the "hard utopia" of the Communists generated: fiercely ideological, dogmatic in the certainty of its own end, unscrupulous in its means, intensely committed to the revolutionary transformation of the traditionalist system, shrewdly aware of the incongruities between technological interdependence and political particularism, naively insensitive to the stubborn strength of particularist forces resistant to its universalist vision.   After his somber encounter with Chairman Khrushchev at Vienna in 1961, President Kennedy indicated the enormous chasm between the Russian and the American outlooks: "The Soviets and ourselves give wholly different meanings to the same words—war, peace, democracy, and popular will.   We have wholly different views of right and wrong, of what is an internal affair and what is aggression, and, above, all, of where the world is and where it is going."

As the United States was drawn into deeper involvement in world politics it was caught up in a three-way debate over "where the world is and where it is going." It came to a clearer understanding of its own ideological preconceptions as a consequence of prolonged tension with approaches different from its own. As against the traditionalists, America stressed the need for change in a system it saw as profoundly unsatisfactory; as against the revolutionaries, America stressed different goals of change and different means for their accomplishment. In both respects America's position was a difficult one. For it is harder to undertake changes than it is to block them; negativism has a decisiveness that slow efforts at transformation cannot hope to have. And change is ordinarily easier to accomplish if one is dogmatic as to ends and ruthless as to means, than if one keeps an open definition of the end with scruples as to means.

. . . It would be a serious error to see traditional realpolitik as the central characteristic of the American approach to foreign policy. The central tradition has rejected reconciliation with the Westphalia system and dreamt of its transformation. To interpret American policy primarily in terms of European categories of realpolitik is not unlike the effort to interpret the American domestic tradition primarily in terms of European categories of class struggle. It was Tocqueville's great discovery that America is a society organized around the principles of democratic equality rather than aristocratic hierarchy. Marxist categories, of some relevance to societies where the inequalities of a technical age are superimposed on the inherited inequalities of a feudal age, have little relevance to American society, which was born free of the feudal inheritance. And so it is with foreign policy. . . .

The thinkers of the American Enlightenment shared with their European colleagues a profound dissatisfaction with the Westphalia tradition and a desire to transform it. . . . However, in Europe the conditions of political life gravely challenged the optimistic Enlightenment faith in international transformation. In America, by contrast, the privileged circumstances of insularity reenforced these optimistic expectations. The American outlook was similar to that of the British, for Britain was also an insular nation with a strong liberal tradition. But if British policy was at one remove from Continental realpolitik, American policy was twice removed, for the Americans lacked an experience central to the British: the prolonged balancing between two rival camps in which one was morally indifferent to the claims of either camp. Beyond this, when America came into intimate involvement with world politics its power relative to the challenges it faced was greater than had been that of Britain. As A. J. P. Taylor has suggested in *The Struggle for Mastery in Europe, 1848–1918,* the emergence of America marked the entry not so much of a new nation as of a new continent. This disparity of relative power is closely related to the American tendency to seek the *transformation* of a recalcitrant environment while the British are more inclined, through default, to stress *adjustment* to it.   Finally, ideology is more important as a basis of American cohesion than is the case with Britain, to say nothing of the great Continental states.

*   *   *

In contrast to most states of Europe, America has placed relatively little emphasis throughout its history on ethnic bond, state religion, or hierarchic class structure as a basis of cohesion. . . .

If the negative uniqueness of the American identity is seen in the relative weakness of ethnic, religious, and hierarchic class ties, its positive uniqueness is found in the centrality of the constitutional tradition.   To be sure America is not the only nation with a constitution; many other lands have long constitutional histories.   But the difference betwen the American constitutional tradition and that of, say, Britain or France, is of the utmost importance: in France or Britain constitutional history is an *aspect* of the history of the nation; in America, the history of the nation is a *consequence* of the Constitution. . . . In America, the nation's birth . . . is coeval with its legal incorporation, so to speak.   What, then, does it mean to be an American?   Since the identity lacks racial, religious, and class content, to define it in these terms is to restrict it falsely.   To be an American means to be a member of the "covenanting community" in which the commitment to freedom under law, having transcended the "natural" bonds of race, religion, and class, itself takes on transcendent importance.

The pragmatism of American life has one source in an intuitive fear that narrow definitions of the national identity will disrupt cohesion; emphasis on pragmatism represents a quest for the lowest common denominator of agreement among people of staggering diversities.   Another source is a by-product of the brute dynamism of modern technology which, given free rein in an open-class America, renders narrow codes irrelevant to the economic and social demands of the enormous market.   A third source is the common acceptance of the framework within which these diversities and this dynamism are to operate; and this has meant that, as Louis Hartz says in *The Liberal Tradition in America,* "American pragmatism has always been deceptive because, glacierlike, it has rested on miles of submerged conviction."   The acceptance of the framework itself is not pragmatic; it is axiomatic.   It is therefore easy to see why America, as she moved into more active involvement in world politics, would prove one of the least pragmatic of nations.   The essence of world politics is the absence of any overarching consensus.   And if pragmatism is the by-product of an axiomatic framework of consensus, the reverse is also true: where the framework is absent, ideological politics become inevitable.   The core of the American ideological policy is also clear: it is concern for the establishment of a framework within which the enormous diversities of world politics may operate safely.   Thus the United States came to speak of making the world safe for diversity; but this very goal presupposed prior agreement on the forms of diversity safe for the world.

What, then, is the proper role for America in world politics? It is as easy to rule out extreme answers to this question as it is difficult to know where to find the proper mean between them. It is not hard to see the hazards in a maximum American commitment to world politics, an effort everywhere to define and uphold a framework to make the world safe for diversity. The flaw in such a "big America" approach is intrinsic, its failure inevitable. Indeed, to attempt it is to repudiate politics itself which is, after all, the art of the possible. However vast the resources of the United States, they are finite, whereas the problems of world politics are without measurable limit. When one matches finite resources against infinite problems, it is only a matter of time until one faces practical ruin. If those who warn against the dangers of overcommitment do no more than make us aware of these hazards they serve an essential function.

Beyond this, there are grave limitations in America's domestic experience which handicap her in the assumption of such enormous responsibilities. At no time in any foreseeable future will Americans be able to harmonize the patterns of their domestic tradition with the necessities of their international responsibilities. And yet Americans will continue to see world politics very largely through the eyes of their own domestic experience. There is, after all, no way in which *any* people can wholly transcend their inheritance. . . .

It is, however, equally easy to see the limitations in the consistent pursuit of a minimalist policy—the preference for a "little America" which, to hear some contemporary critics, would undertake few commitments beyond the preservation of national territory. This policy is particularly weak when it takes for its justification the need to return to a more traditional balance-of-power policy. For the world in which such a policy had relevance is now dead beyond recall. It is also hazardous, in justification of a reduction of commitments, to assume that instabilities on the world scene will somehow reach a stabilization on their own. . . .

Kenneth Boulding describes this chanciness, in *The Meaning of the Twentieth Century*, by another metaphor:

We may dramatize the present world situation by saying that every day the hand of fate dips into a bag containing one black ball amid many white balls: the black ball of nuclear disaster. Up to now, every day, fate has brought up a white ball, and the world goes on, but the black ball is still in the bag, and as long as it remains there no one can feel very secure about his future.

Just beyond the "war trap" Boulding sees the "population trap" and the "entropy trap." These several dilemmas are part of the earthquake fault: the ongoing scientific and technological revolution which has produced largely unregulated and extremely hazardous conditions of interdependence. The United States is caught up in an enormous rolling revolution that cannot be stopped by an effort to withdraw from it. Nor can it be moved in a direction compatible with America's most basic interests except through sustained concentration of our energies upon the problem. In this period of history the greater danger for America is that, from an exaggerated diffidence toward herself and an unwarranted confidence in the possibilities of a "return to normalcy," she will be tempted to withdraw from international responsibility. Nations err in attempting too little as well as in attempting too much.

The risk of arrogance of power is implicit in the very situation the United States faces in world politics. What removes the charge of arrogance from the exercise of power in domestic politics is its legitimization; but there is no way in which the exercise of power in world politics can acquire the legitimacy it enjoys domestically. Those who would have us make the United Nations the central instrument of our foreign policy are haunted by the apparent illegitimacy of much that we do internationally. They seek, in an institution which gives expression to a rudimentary global will, justification comparable to what the democratic will confers domestically. There is probably no clearer sign of the inescapably ideological dimension in America's foreign policy than this persistent effort to find an international institution to serve as foster father to American policies and thereby remove from them the stigma of their illegitimacy. The quest is vain. The international institutions still lack effectiveness, and there is no ready way they can reform themselves. We demand too much of American—indeed of any—foreign policy if we measure it by the niceties to which we have grown accustomed in our domestic life. America's actions in world politics will have legitimacy conferred posthumously, so to speak, if in the larger history of mankind the American view of "where the world is and where it is going" is seen to have been justified.

The wish to escape from this dilemma through a reduction of external action and a focus on domestic needs is natural, but the prescriptions themselves are wrong. We err if we think of arrogance as a concomitant of action and humility as consequent upon the reduction of commitment. The essential source of the charge of arrogance is not to be found in any specific policy, but in the very *existence* of our power. To do nothing on the external scene, but to keep that power intact, would be another form of arrogance, the more insufferable because of the greater pretense of innocence. Other nations realize that we impinge on them at a thousand and one points, simply because we bulk so large on the world scene *whatever* we do. The possession of an arsenal capable of destroying all living things on the planet, of an economy that dwarfs its competitors, of an affluent democratic population with its *own* moral and political meaning in the history of mankind makes us a matter of concern to the world whatever our stance. The truth is that we intrude on others because we exist as one of the "enormous energy systems in history," to use Max Lerner's phrase. We are a part of the great liberal revolution and as such an inevitable affront to those who see human destiny as moving to very different ends by very different means. We cannot avoid giving offense to such critics unless America ceases to be America. But it is well to bear in mind that others also intrude on us, and not always with gentleness and humility. In truth, each nation has come to intrude in increasing degree on others simply because, through population growth and technological shrinkage, mankind lives in increasingly crowded quarters. The first item on the agenda of all peoples, and especially the great nations, must be concern with the means through which the vexations and hazards of life in common can be transformed into the satisfactions of a common life.

The notion that the nation can direct its primary energies to domestic affairs is also in error. All nations—and again the great nations in particular—must continue to work in *two* environments and devote a very large proportion of their resources to foreign policy. Any future significance of domestic programs is dependent . . . on more effective organization of the external realm. The dilemmas of the Johnson Presidency give poignant illustration of this dependency. And the assumption that if one could but tranquillize the Vietnam problem one could then turn with whole heart to the domestic scene is surely misleading. Many find Vietnam painful because here the enormous tensions of world politics have broken through the surface; they have become visible; one must acknowledge their existence.

The American approach to foreign policy—based on Enlightenment expectations, reinforced by the luxuries of insularity, given stubborn strength by the nature of the national identity—has always been directed toward the hope that the peace under law of its domestic community would come, gradually, to prevail in the world arena. Thus the tension between the two political worlds in which man has lived since Westphalia would be resolved, as the higher principles of the smaller world came to prevail over the lower principles of the larger world. Since the firing of the guns of August that hope has undergone a cruel transformation. The two worlds have, indeed, been brought into ever closer interdependence, but it has often seemed that the disorder of the larger world would undermine the order of the smaller world. America, frustrated in its earlier efforts to organize the world in accordance with the promise of law, now found the world organizing America in accordance with the necessities of war.

American policy over the last generation has been directed toward the triumph of the order of the smaller realm over the disorder of the larger realm. The nation has rightly sensed that the disintegration of the Westphalia tradition, and the emergence of revolutionary visions from that disintegration, have necessitated a larger, not a lesser, role for America. It's going to be a long voyage home.

THE SEARCH FOR A THIRD WORLD

Julius K. Nyerere

AFRICA MUST BE FREE

*   *   *

The slogan "Africa must be free" must not be confined to the idea of freedom from foreign rule. It must, if it means anything at all, mean freedom for the individual man and woman—freedom from every form of oppression, indignity, intimidation or exploitation. It must include the right of the individual citizen to re-elect or to replace the Government of his own country. It must also, of course, include the freedom of the Government to govern, without fear of any attempt to replace it by means other than that of the ballot box.

The African claims that his fight is for democratic rights. There are many, both in Africa and elsewhere, who believe in the sincerity of that claim. There are others who question whether, in fact, the African can really understand or practice democracy. It would be naive to think that African nationalists do not themselves sometimes question whether, once having established democratic institutions in their own countries, it will in fact be possible to use those institutions to maintain full democratic rights. But I have often wondered whether the people who question either the sincerity of the African's belief in democracy, or his ability to establish and safeguard democratic rights, are clear in their own minds as to what the essentials of democracy really are.

Too often the doubters of an African democracy have confined their idea of it to certain democratic institutions or forms which have been developed in particular countries and as the result of local circumstances and national characteristics peculiar to those countries.

For instance, the British critic when he speaks of "democracy" has a picture in his own mind of the Parliament buildings, a party in power within

Reprinted by permission of the publisher from *The New York Times,* March 27, 1960. Copyright by *The New York Times.* Adapted from a speech delivered at Wellesley College by Mr. Nyerere, who, on December 9, 1962, became President of the Republic of Tanganyika. Mr. Nyerere has been President of Tanzania since the Republic of Tanganyika and Zanzibar became federated in October 1964.

those Parliament buildings, and another party within the same imposing buildings, not actually in power but with hopes of getting into power if and when its turn comes to win a general election, and in the meantime enjoying the title of Her Majesty's Opposition.

So, to the Briton, democracy is an institution consisting of a debating house where one group is "for" and another "against" the motion, and each group is quite distinct from the other. Similarly, the American critic has his own picture of democracy. Each is confusing the machinery, or structure, with the essence. Each is, in fact, saying: "Can you imagine an African country where you have one party governing and another party in opposition?" To these critics an organized and officially recognized opposition has become almost the essence of democracy.

I may be oversimplifying the basis of the criticism and doubts, but that is certainly the way in which most people argue when they question Africa's ability to maintain a democratic form of government. They assume that if a country is governed by one party alone, the Government cannot be a "democratic" one. In doing so, I suggest, they ignore three important facts.

The first is this: that a country's struggle for freedom from foreign domination is a patriotic struggle; it leaves no room for difference. The issue, at that stage, is a simple one, and one which unites all elements in the country. As a result you find, in Africa and in other parts of the world that face a similar challenge, the growth not of a "political party" but of a nationalist movement. It is this nationalist movement which fights for, and achieves, independence; and it, therefore, inevitably forms the first Government of the independent state.

It would surely be ridiculous to expect a country—for the sake of conforming to a particular expression of democracy, which happens to be seen in terms of a Government party and an Opposition party, and midstream in a struggle that calls for the complete unity of all its people—voluntarily to divide itself in order to produce a ready-made Opposition at the moment of independence. Democracy has been described as a government of the people, by the people, for the people. Surely, if a Government is freely elected by the people, there can be nothing undemocratic about it just because nearly all the people, rather than only some of them, happen to have voted it into power?

Indeed, it appears to be natural that young nations which emerge as the result of a nationalist movement that has united their people shall be governed at first by a nationalist government as distinct from a party government; and no one should therefore jump to the conclusion that this means such a country is not democratic, or does not intend to remain democratic.

Another factor generally forgotten by these critics is that the presence of an organized Opposition as a visible symbol of "democracy" is not, in fact, universal. It is rather the Anglo-Saxon's symbolic demonstration of his own democracy. In particular, the two-party system one finds in countries with an Anglo-Saxon tradition implies something which Americans may not like, but which to my mind is nevertheless true—it implies the existence of a class struggle.

The third factor that is conveniently forgotten by some critics of African democracy is the history of Africa.   In traditional African society the African never was—nor thought himself to be—a cog in a machine.   He was a free individual in his own society.   But his conception of "government" was personal, not institutional.   When government was mentioned, the African thought of the chief; unlike the Briton, he did not picture a grand building in which a debate was taking place.

The colonizers of Africa did little to change this.   In colonial Africa you mention the word "government" and the average person immediately thinks of the district commissioner, the provincial commissioner or the governor. When, later, the mad African like myself reads Abraham Lincoln and John Stuart Mill, and demands that government should become institutional, what happens?   The district commissioner, the provincial commissioner and the governor—the very ones who have come to symbolize government in their persons—resist this demand.   We have to keep on insisting and "agitating" until, at the eleventh hour, our demands are granted, elections take place, and then government becomes, almost overnight, an institution.   But this happens only shortly before the country achieves independence.

In these circumstances, it would be surprising if the pattern of democratic government in Africa were to take on, immediately, the shape familiar to the United Kingdom or to the United States.   But it would be unfair to assume, therefore, that it was any less dedicated to the preservation of the rights of the individual.   Indeed, it is an injustice to African democrats when their fellow democrats in other parts of the world accept without thought the facile, and in fact illogical, criticisms of the very people who have delayed the establishment of democratic institutions in Africa.

It is important to emphasize the difference between democracy itself and the various forms it can take.   To my mind, there are two essentials of democracy.   The first of these is the freedom and well-being of the individual; the second is that the method by which the Government of a country is chosen must insure that the Government *is* freely chosen by the people.

When I say that Africa, today, seems to be in the best position to champion personal freedom and the democracy to preserve that freedom, I am not basing my claim solely on the moral strength which is hers because of her history.   There is another, though less lofty, factor.   In the world today there is a conflict between the advocates of the freedom of the individual and those who champion the primacy of the state.   When one examines the differences between the ideologies of the Eastern and Western powers, one can reduce them generally to this very conflict.

The West seems to have exaggerated its idea of freedom beyond the point where freedom becomes license; to have accepted a society in which, provided a man does not too obviously steal or murder, he can defend any form of self-indulgence by calling it "freedom of the individual." The Communist world—largely, I think, as a reaction against this exaggeration—has swung like a pendulum to the other extreme; the individual in a Communist society is secondary to something called the state.

Here, then, I think is the problem: where does society, or the state, draw the boundary of its rights and obligations; and where does the individual? It is a problem that has not yet been solved by either side in a way that can be accepted by the other.

In primitive African society this question of the limits of responsibility as between the individual and the society in which he lived was not very clearly defined. The traditional African community was a small one, and the African could not think of himself apart from his community. He was an individual; he had his wife, or wives, and children—so he belonged to a family. But the family merged into a larger "blood" family which, itself, merged into the tribe.

Thus he saw himself all the time as a member of a community; but he saw no struggle between his own interests and those of his community, for his community was to him an extension of his family. He might have seen a conflict between himself and another individual member of the same community, but with the community itself—never. He never felt himself to be a cog in a machine. There could not be this all-embracing, all-powerful modern concept of society which could "use" him as a cog.

That traditional "community" is still visible in Africa today; in a sense it is one of our problems. Having come into contact with a civilization which has overemphasized the freedom of the individual, we are in fact faced with one of the big problems of Africa in the modern world. Our problem is just this: how to get the benefits of European society—benefits that have been brought about by an organization based upon the individual —and yet retain Africa's own structure of society in which the individual is a member of a kind of fellowship.

Let me put this another way. One of the complaints of the European employer in Africa is that the African is paid a wage to which he has agreed, and then complains that it is not enough after all—usually because he does not use this wage merely upon himself and his family; there are others who lay claim upon his wage.

This is a fact, but one must not think that the African is therefore a natural "Communist." He is not. To him the wage is his wage, the property is his property; but his brother's need is his brother's need and he cannot ignore that need. He has not learned to ask, "Am I my brother's keeper?" The African is not "communistic" in his thinking; he is—if I may coin the expression—"communitary." He is not a member of a commune—some artificial unit of human beings; he is a member of a genuine community, or family.

Today, when there is this conflict between East and West—and I have said that I think this conflict is basically one between the rights of the individual and the rights of the state—Western Europe, which has had a much longer experience of its own pattern of society, is becoming self-critical. Africa is, in this sense, fortunate in that there is still to be found on our continent a form of organization of society which solves the fundamental conflict between the individual and society. It should be possible, therefore, for Africa to use both its own basic structure and the self-criticism of Western Europe to evolve a form of society that can satisfy both sides.

We are not so naive that we do not realize the problems new countries must face, and the anxious times through which such countries must pass. Nor are we unaware of the efforts, and even sacrifices, which people in new countries may be called upon to make in the national interest and in the process of consolidating the newly won freedom through economic reconstruction.

But, even when all this is granted, there should be no conflict between our commitment to freedom for the individual and our need for national effort. In fact, these can work together harmoniously as long as the emphasis is on the "national" interest, as implying the interest of the individuals who comprise the nation. What would need to be generated is a positive response on the part of the individuals and groups within the country.

The Africa we must create, the Africa we must bequeath to posterity, the Africa of our dreams, cannot be an Africa that is simply free from foreign domination. It must be an Africa that the outside world will look at and say: "Here is a continent that has truly free human beings." The outside world must be able to say: "If you really want to see how a free people conduct their affairs—if you want to see a people who live up to their ideals of human society—go to Africa! That is the Continent of Hope for the human race!"

I feel that Africa's own tradition, her moral strength, her lack of ties with one power bloc or another, and that sentiment of oneness which the centuries of suffering have built among all her peoples, can together fit her for the role I have suggested—the role of champion of personal freedom in the world today.

George Liska

THE "THIRD PARTY": THE RATIONALE
OF NONALIGNMENT

Nonalignment reflects the peculiar conditions of a world in which Communist power is rising and Western colonial empires have virtually disappeared in fact if not in memory. . . .

Nonaligned countries avoid alliances, refusing to add their power to that of others. If it were merely a matter of withholding their power from others, they would pursue a traditional policy of neutrality. In wartime, they would remain aloof, except when asked to mediate; under Cold War conditions, they would stay equally aloof. Not all the nonaligned countries have been pursuing such neutral policy. The militant neutralists have not been content merely to withhold their power from others as the traditional neutrals have done. Among those neutrals are Switzerland and nineteenth-century Belgium; countries that have been neutralized by treaty more recently, such as Austria; and those that have tried to virtually neutralize themselves, such as Burma. The "positive" neutralists have instead engaged in an active policy of playing the great powers against each other and offering unsolicited mediation between them.

The smaller the margin of power that favors either of two contending parties, the more relevant is the total power of an intrinsically weak third party. Such power need not be greater than the net advantage favoring one of the contending major powers, and it may be incommensurate in kind. Short of—and sometimes even despite—its manifest abuse, third-party influence is greatest with stalemated contestants. They are more than normally inclined to show respect for the forms (independence) and the fictions (impartiality and superior morality) upon which nonbelligerent or nonaligned countries base their claims to protection, function, and authority in the international arena.

In the annals of traditional diplomacy, there are two major counterparts to contemporary neutralists. One is a league of armed neutrals that actively seek to prevent forms of warfare, generally naval, that may injure its members' interests, principally its economic ones. The other counterpart is a former ally now bent on separate peace. The validity of this later grouping may be affirmed or denied, depending on how one judges the post-independence "defection" of the neutralist countries from the Western system, despite continued adherence, in many cases, to the principal values and

Reprinted by permission of The Washington Center of Foreign Policy Research and the publisher from Lawrence W. Martin, ed., *Neutralism and Nonalignment—The New States in World Affairs* (New York: Frederick A. Praeger, 1962), pp. 80–92. Copyright, The Washington Center of Foreign Policy Research, 1962.

aspirations of the West. A comparison of the actual behavior of the two groupings is less controversial.

The similarity between separate peace and neutralism is quite pervasive. It bears, first, on the salient reasons for separate peace in war: reaction to inferior status within an association, material inability to cope with the adversary, and desire for a special advantage for oneself, rather than for a more successful ally. For neutralist groups in firmly aligned and manifestly threatened countries, the desire to be released from struggle, typical of separate peace under duress, is aggravated by the apparent impossibility of leaving an alliance. To neutralist regimes situated in the zone between the two major alliances, the ease and profitability of the policy magnifies the desire for special advantage, typical of separate peace under inducement. The characteristic strategy of separate peace is to demand an impossible performance by the partner to be deserted, so that the anticipated failure to comply may make defection legitimate and reduce the danger of sanctions. The principal demand of the neutralists has been for instant and complete withdrawal of all vestiges of colonial control; a secondary demand has been for disarmament and diversion of resources into economic assistance. The latter demand coincides with the separate-peace-maker's typical ambition: to pacify the general conflict in such a way as to retain and consolidate previous gains. The characteristic technique is offering unsolicited mediation. Such mediation may be undertaken in good faith, when it is "armed" with the promise of behavior favorable to the complying side; or terms may be so defined as to ensure an apparent compliance of the favored party.

The attitude of the neutralists toward presently contending "blocs" is one thing; their position toward the institution of alliance as such is another. Traditionally, there have been two kinds of policy; neutralism has added a third. The three policies indicate degrees of increasing hostility toward alliances.

The first type of antialliance policy rules out alliance with a particular country while approving or condoning policies of alliance generally. Thus France, after 1871, would not consider an alliance with Germany unless the latter returned the conquered provinces. The rejection of this particular alliance, however, only intensified France's search for allies against the German enemy.

The second type of antialliance policy favors abstention from all alliances. Such a policy may be adopted after a dispassionate weighing of the gains and liabilities that could be expected from all feasible alternatives. Abstention was the policy pursued by England and the United States in periods of "splendid isolation" and has remained the policy of traditional neutrals. Incidentally, the abstaining country need not be opposed to alliances among other countries, for these often ensure its own position of aloofness. For instance, in the period before World War I, neutral Belgium favored an Anglo-French alliance that, at different periods, served as a restraint on France or as a counterpoise to Germany, or both. . . .

The third, or neutralist, antialliance policy opposes all alliances, including those among other powers. Antialliance ideology holds that competition for allies is a cause of tension and war. Alliances are concluded in anticipation of a test of strength; they increase the total power that statesmen can wield and encourage them to use it while the alliance holds together. Alliances might partially substitute for national armaments, but they also instigate an armaments race as states seek to attract new allies and to disrupt the alliance of the adversary. Armament efforts at least have the merit of absorbing national energies domestically; the race for allies takes place between countries and puts a high premium on prestige. Prestige is born of success, and the diplomatic success of one state entails the humiliation of another, which then seeks retribution. Since alliances are built on shared antagonism rather than on amity, they tend to fall apart. War is then welcomed as an alternative to disintegration of the alliance and isolation. The fear of isolation is viewed in the antialliance ideology as the *reductio ad absurdum* of the rationale for alliances. In the absence of alliances, all nations would be "isolated" and thus more amenable to universal law and its sanctions.

*   *   *

. . . [T]here are . . . many traditional reasons for the nonalignment of smaller powers. If only one issue or conflict is dominant, and the smaller state does not wish to be identified with the policy of either power center in a bipolar structure, it may elect to rely on almost automatic protection (assuming that one power group balances the other). In such a case, the danger of provoking one side by aligning with the other may well appear greater than the need for, or possibly of, protection. When more than one issue dominates the international system, a smaller state may hesitate to determine its alignment on the basis of only one of the issues. It might make common cause with the West against the East on the issue of Communist expansion, but not with the industrial, residually imperialist North, against the formerly colonial, preindustrial South, on the other dominant issue of today—economic development and political independence for the less developed countries. Similarly, as the number of particular conflicts increases, so does the fear of the smaller states that alignment may involve them with new antagonists. The political cost of alliance becomes extravagant when it entails not only an initial compromise with the ally, but the liability of adding his enemies to one's own as well. Such considerations would suffice to keep Afghanistan or Burma out of an alliance that included Pakistan and, consequently, antagonized India.

While following traditional antialliance patterns of thoughts and action, the nonaligned states and the neutralists have stressed two new factors in contemporary international relations to justify opposition to alliances. The first concerns modern weapons of mass destruction. According to the neutralist school of thought, no individual or collective effort by small countries can significantly increase a small country's security if security means capacity for defense against a nuclear power. So-called deterrence requires actions that are indistinguishable from provocation in the eyes of the target state. To parry the provocation, each great power will try to demonstrate that its nuclear opponent is unable to protect the small ally. The safest course for a small country is, therefore, to do nothing to attract the contending giants either as allies or as enemies. It should, instead, rely on the nuclear powers' reluctance either to initiate a major conflict over a small country or to antagonize other small countries by using force against any of them. Spontaneous solidarity of nonaligned countries to oppose great-power encroachments is the most effective "alliance" in a nuclear environment available to a small country.

The second factor that is working against alliance is the alleged relationship between Western alliance policy and Western colonialism. From the anticolonial viewpoint, the West has had two kinds of alliances. The more objectionable kind associates former colonies with former metropolitan or other Western powers; the other kind does not involve ex-colonial nations. The immediate victim of neocolonialism, which perpetuates Western presence and control, is the allied small country itself. The prototype of the neocolonial alliance is the Anglo-Iraqi alliance that replaced Britain's League of Nations mandate in the 1930's. Its military and political clauses can be read simply as devices to buttress a pliant oligarchy aligned with British interests and supported by the major ally's residual presence in the country. The government of the dependent ally cannot conduct its own foreign policy, and the people are not free to change the regime by force, if need be.

According to the same view, the dangers of neocolonial alliances may be only indirect, but less real, for other countries in the region. Colonialism thrives on conflict between indigenous forces. As long as smaller countries depend on their own resources, the argument might run, conflicts are nonexistent or inconclusive. But when lesser countries align with a major outside power, even if ostensibly against another major power, the ally acquires new resources and believes, rightly or wrongly, that it has gained additional support for pressing its claims on neighboring small states. . . . The affected states cannot but react by aligning with another power or by giving a militant slant to their nonalignment, to enhance its nuisance value, penalize the great-power ally of their local adversary, and secure countervailing outside assistance. In one way or another, the great-power adversaries secure new avenues of influence to the lesser states. By introducing arms and discord into the region, the alliance of a small state with a great power constitutes in Nehru's words, a "reversal of the process of liberation."

The other kind of Western alliance is that which does not include a former colonial dependent. NATO is such an alliance. The neutralists have objected to NATO only to the extent that, at least indirectly, it helped the metropolitan members resist the trend toward "decolonization" by reducing a colonial metropole's defense burden against the Soviet bloc in Europe. Alliances like NATO and, on the Communist side, the Warsaw Pact, are least "provocative" because they associate countries that are close to each other geographically and do not encircle the principal target state. Moreover, they are not "colonial" alliances, because they associate nations kindred in culture and color. Affinity in ideology and political organization among the members makes such groupings even more acceptable to the neutralists. They have been inclined to overlook the fact that such affinity has been forced upon the lesser allies in the Warsaw Pact, so long as the ideology can be considered "progressive" and the dominant Soviet ally manages to avoid overt repression within the alliance.

Seen from the neutralist viewpoint, the above criterion for differentiating between acceptable and unacceptable alliances has certain advantages. A big, unaligned country such as India may acceptably enter into security arrangements of her own with a small country like Nepal. And, as long as the areas included within the alliances of the major powers are kept at a minimum, the inbetween or unaligned area will be large. . . .

As reconstructed so far, the neutralist position on alliances has ignored the objective requirements of international equilibrium and security. The omission is not serious if one holds that a strategic parity would remain in existence between East and West even if the West withdrew from all bases in former dependent nations. All that is necessary is that the United States retain links with Japan, Australia, Turkey, and a few small island bases; it would need neither SEATO nor CENTO. . . .

In the long run, Soviet imperialism will not replace that of the West, the neutralists seem to believe. In this way, neutralist opposition to peacetime commitments can be bolstered with assumptions about the character of the two chief contestants and about the winners in the Cold War. The neutralists have inclined to discount the Western thesis that Communism is inherently aggressive; on the contrary, they have largely adopted the theory that internal expansion will absorb Communist efforts and that the Communists' bellicosity will subside when they have attained Western levels of mass consumption.

The assumptions about the West and particularly the United States, have been, in many ways, complementary. The United States may be deemed capable of deterring all-out war even without bases or allies on the Sino-Soviet periphery; but America has not been credited with the ability to defend small countries without destroying them, especially if these countries are close to the Sino-Soviet bloc. The neutralists have also seemed to assume that within the limits of American capability and resolution, the United States is tacitly committed to defend any country that is threatened by a Communist power, regardless of that country's previous policy. Therefore, it would be absurd to undertake the material and political liabilities of alignment.

* * *

The long-range neutralist ideal is the decline of both contending sides' power and influence relative to the new nations. This is what happened in both world wars and, unless a third destroys everything, it will, so the neutralists hope, happen again. The basic requirement is that the Cold War substitute for war be a competitive economic build-up of the less developed nations.

Meanwhile, however, concern about voicing fear has been very much a part of the universe of nonalignment and neutralism. There are nonaligned leaders who will privately admit that they fear Communist encroachments and resent Soviet "nuclear terror"; but the dogmatic neutralist rejects the very thought that he is swayed by the fear of anything and anyone. Fear makes for caution and has been a paramount reason for the nonalignment of Burma, Afghanistan, and Cambodia, countries close and vulnerable to the Sino-Soviet bloc. Absence of fear may be put forward as the reason for nonalignment when remoteness of the natural protection and vast size of a country like India apparently give a nation immunity.

Fear of an external threat often stimulates very pragmatic calculations. These may produce either alignment or nonalignment. The option will be affected by such intangibles as historical experience and political culture, as well as by specific, tangible threats. Thailand, for instance, chose alignment despite, and partly because of, her proximity to China. Burma opted for nonalignment. Unlike the Burmese, the Thai have long been independent and are impressed by the limitations of neutrality. And unlike the Cambodians, the Thai elite is familiar with the pitfalls of play-off policy. The Thai propensity for active diplomacy led, therefore, to initiative for and within a Western alliance. The Burmese tendency toward withdrawal found political expression in nonalignment. . . .

Much in the neutralist ideology of international security seems based on an optimistic degree of confidence in automatic protection. But seen in a second perspective, as a politics of compensation that reflects concern with internal problems, neutralism combines deep-seated emotions about the past with crudely pragmatic methods for coping with the present.

Many new nations have instituted a priority that the liberal, democratic West has more consistently preached than practiced—that of domestic over external conditions as determinants of foreign policy. This is not surprising. Domestic concerns tend to be preponderant in societies that are free from external security dilemmas or helpless to cope with them, and whose central authority is subject to factional opposition, rather than free for action abroad because of equipoised pluralism at home. In addition, many of the new states tend toward internationalization of domestic politics; this follows the essentially feudal pattern of internal factions aligning with, and receiving moral and material support from, different outside powers.   Even if the politically less developed countries manage to contain the internationalization of their internal troubles, their domestic politics still tend to resemble international politics.   Factional leaders fight to survive in governing positions without accepting the arbitrament of a successful performance of functions associated with the modern state.

The policies of nonalignment and neutralism are a means for counteracting these tendencies.   Nonalignment presumably enhances the international status and, consequently, the domestic authority of "national" leaders. This promotes short-run stability.   And the isolationist bias of nonalignment appeals to both traditionalist and nationalist factions, while it helps insulate factional and regional struggles against the strains of outside interference. The graver the internal troubles, the greater the temptation for leaders to go beyond nonalignment to militant neutralism.   Indonesia's militancy has intensified as internal tensions increased.   And underlying Indian "positive neutrality" is the leaders' concern with preventing the division of the country into several quarreling states.

This fear of domestic division is one of the reasons for the militancy of the neutralist governments in relatively nonintegrated new nations.   Neutralism, as an active foreign policy, provides a focus for domestic cohesion, and silences opposition to the government.   Moreover, to governing groups in many new nations militant neutralism appeals as a reaction against the passivity of former colonial status.   The hallmarks of dependency—lack of a separate foreign policy and of diplomatic access to third states that could counterbalance the metropole—seem perpetuated in today's "unequal alliances."   Any neutralist leader of a new nation is determined to avoid a relapse and to demonstrate his freedom and ability to create and use foreign policy alternatives.

*   *   *

Nonalignment and neutralism are international policies inspired largely by domestic concerns.   By the same token, they are political policies largely motivated by economic needs and interests.   The leaders of new and some not-so-new nations are committed to economic development as a means to the political stability that, among other things, would keep them in power. Many have come to believe that their countries cannot afford the cost in national unity or defense spending that a controversial alliance policy would entail.   The main reason, however, why the policy of nonalignment is economical is that it brings in material assistance from both sides.   The merely nonaligned leader seeks to demonstrate his impartiality by accepting assistance from both sides; the militant neutralist is seeking to prove his international importance in accepting such aid.   When the neutralist leader has to accept the West's conditions of aid, he pays the price for extending the tripartite game into the field of economics.   To have a Soviet alternative helps in relations with the West.   And the existence of a Western alternative has enabled some neutralists, such as India, to put economic relations with the Soviet bloc on a sound monetary basis. . . .

To sum up, the range of policies of small countries runs from biased neutralism through strict nonalignment to outright alliance membership.   Since the eclipse of the British-oriented ruling group in Ceylon, only some of the formally nonaligned French-speaking African elites have been openly critical of Sino-Soviet (and indigenous) imperialism; with such lone and, possibly, passing exceptions, the bias in neutralism has been against Western colonialism.   The typical nonaligned regime is primarily concerned with internal stability and, in some cases, with security against proximate powers. The militant neutralist invokes anti-imperialist ideological precepts while working to profit from the contest between old and new imperialisms.   Non-Communist Marxist that he often is, the neutralist actively seeks to employ the Soviet "antithesis" against the Western "thesis" to advance what he sees as the higher goal of his own nationalist and socialist synthesis.

David Esmond

THE NEW STUDENT LEFT IN INTERNATIONAL POLITICS

It is dangerous to oversimplify political movements which, of necessity, are themselves always somewhat oversimple.   Yet it is possible to summarize the style and focus of the "new left" by reference to its central ideal: the principle of community.

The rhetoric of community is nothing new to the left.   It always inspires brotherly feelings, connotes friendship, and appeals to a larger public than the left might otherwise reach.   Community rhetoric is an aggregating concept and also a good tactic, for few would have the temerity to attack it openly.   These pragmatic considerations have always played a role in left politics, but very often—indeed, almost always—the left in power has deserted the ideal, giving the impression that appeals to community are no more than a political device.

SNCC and ERAP,[1] most prominently among the new left organizations,

Reprinted by permission of the author from *The Activist* (November 1965).

[1] The Student Non-Violent Coordinating Committee and the Economic Research and Action Project of the Students for a Democratic Society (S.D.S.) respectively.

belie this interpretation.   Community, long merely a political noise on the left, has become part of an active program for domestic change.

That aspect of the new left style is pivotal, and all else revolves around it.   Like the Populists, to whom it gives an important place in its intellectual genealogy, the new left tends to subordinate foreign to domestic policy and doctrine.   Indeed, the tendency is so marked on the new left that it is possible to see its foreign policy as merely a *subsumptum,* a postscript added to its domestic teaching.

To understand the new left's concept of community and its implications for foreign policy it is necessary to go behind the more blatant of its political slogans: the equation of bureaucrat and automaton, or the analogy between the university student and the IBM card.   Such slogans evince a sort of elliptical exaggeration, a political poetic license.   Contrary to the expectations of its critics, the new left does not advocate throwing every computer, computer-operator, and college president into San Francisco Bay, nor does it believe that the establishment of anarchy would result in a society of permanent bliss and glee.   The new left are not Luddites; they are sophisticated enough to realize that the bureaucracies against which they inveigh, and the productive capabilities which those bureaucracies imply, are necessary for realizing their political goals.

To put it simply, community as a domestic ideal does not mean banishing civilization from the western hemisphere.   To the new left, community refers to a society in which people have the effective right to influence group decisions; it is, in other words, a subvariant in the long tradition of democratic thought.

Domestically, the left sees its role as that of redressing the social balance between community and isolation; of removing the impediments to participation, which it discerns in hierarchical structures which have usurped the right of decision belonging to the people as a whole.   Participation, to the new left, is the most critical aspect of justice.   Paul Potter has written that "the functional meaning of an idea or value is proportional to the extent to which an individual is challenged to make that idea a part of himself." Values must be lived, and can be lived only in community.   The student must experience democracy in the university to the greatest possible extent; the rural and urban poor must have some role in the political order other than that of a weary audience for the panegyrics of self-styled promoters; participation must be extended to those isolated because of race, lack of schooling, poverty, or any of the conditions stemming from hypocritical disregard of the "fundamental values" of American society.   Without participation, the new left insists, those values will always remain unreal.

Community also denotes the quality of social relations which will make total participation *possible*.   Part of the community-building of ERAP and SNCC seeks to mobilize new political forces in American politics.   Yet such efforts do not stop at the hope for renovation.   The new left seeks to build "parallel hierarchies," counter-communities, based on such institutions as the MFDP,[2] freedom schools, farm cooperatives and teachings which represent the new society in embryo.

If community is the goal, hierarchy is the enemy. The reaction against domestic hierarchy is partly psychological. Hierarchy is the milieu of fractured man, man the cog, the unit but never the participant. It implies specialization, and hence segmented relations between individuals. In a word, hierarchy is antithetical to community.

These domestic attitudes determine the new left stance on foreign policy. It carries them bodily into its analysis of international politics, and they lead directly to two criticisms of American foreign policy: (1) an attack by virtue of the *origin* of foreign policy and (2) an attack on its *aims*.

Foreign policy originates, as the left sees it, in a world of hierarchies. The State Department is unsavory enough; the CIA is intolerable. Primarily, however, the new left traces foreign policy decisions to a complex of corporate and military hierarchies, coordinated by the federal administration but outside any effective public control. Made by an inaccessible, insulated elite, foreign policy comes to symbolize all that the new left fears and hates: "Vietnam is a laboratory run by a new breed of gamesmen, who approach war as a kind of rational exercise in international power politics." The whole apparatus inspires a strange mixture of paroxysmic loathing and reverent terror.

That mixture can be explained. The new left never underrates the *technical* skill of the foreign policy hierarchies: if anything, it overrates that skill. The left fears, however, that such agencies, by nature instrumental, have become semi-autonomous if not entirely so; they have usurped the authority for setting the goals as well as the means of foreign policy. Participatory democracy, the left contends, is the sole means of returning the control of foreign policy to the people, and no decision in foreign policy will be legitimate until the rural and urban poor are enfranchised in an effective way, and until the military-industrial apparatus has been stripped of its present autonomy.

In this sense, participation is a goal in itself. The new left believes, however, that participation will also change the *aims* of foreign policy in ways which the left finds desirable. American foreign policy, in the eyes of the left, is not only suspect in origin but immoral or amoral in content: it is the chief compounder of injustice throughout the world.

Justice (which to the left includes freedom, equality, and the means for participation in community life) has several aspects in international politics. First, justice implies community and participation, and hence, national self-determination. American foreign policy in the Dominican Republic, in Vietnam, and elsewhere is an anathema for its acts to shore up

[2] Mississippi Freedom Democratic Party

reactionary and unpopular regimes. The war in Vietnam, an SDS poster asserts, is being fought to "prevent free elections," and if this is an extreme position it has nevertheless gained a wide following.

Second, justice implies individual freedom. The new left is offended by coercion, by the use of military power, by the "management" of news by Washington. It regards the draft with hostility as a violation of voluntarism and one which forces many to act against their conscience.

Third, justice implies an equitable distribution of resources. This, the left contends, is violated by hierarchic industries and corporations which exploit and extract the resources of the world which rightfully belong to its peoples. To be sure, the left concedes, such organizational structures may be essential to material progress, but hierarchies as now constituted continually introduce new and growing inequalities in distribution. Hence, such private cells of wealth must be continually broken into and their accumulations distributed to further justice in the international order.

To the new left, moreover, it is United States foreign policy which is the primary force behind distributive injustice. There is a certain political metaphysic in this equation. First, hierarchy is injustice ossified. The American foreign policy apparatus is the largest, most complex, most confusing network of hierarchies in the history of man, a staggering and grotesque eighth wonder of the world. It entails a giant defense budget, which underwrites private corporations and passes public resources into private hands, for the production of weapons which add nothing to the quality of human life. People are suffering from deprivations and the marvelous tricks and the interesting size and speed of military gadgets do nothing to assist them. To make matters worse, defense expenditure directs funds to industries which more and more use capital rather than labor intensively; it aggravates unemployment and the problem of poverty at home as well as abroad. American foreign policy supports military and other despots abroad. It forces the Soviet Union and other industrial states to devote a similar and unwarranted percentage of their resources to military expenditure. All these funds, the new left contends, could be used to increase justice through programs of flood control, fertilizer manufacture, farm machinery, road construction, birth control, and the like.

Yet all the new left's criticisms of foreign policy begin with its own domestic doctrines. It ignores altogether the question of whether the state system may not have properties which have no analogy in domestic politics. Its analysis of the economic implications of defense policy is interesting and possibly accurate, but it cannot refute, because it ignores, the continuing discussion of the dynamics and mechanism of the cold war.

The assumptions of the new left regarding the nature of international politics are real, if implicit, and debatable when they are not naive.

First, the new left shows no intention of changing the state system: that follows from its ecomium of national self-determination. Moreover, it shows no desire to eliminate centralized governmental structures, if for no other reason that they are needed to direct economic development.

Second, though the left values both peace and justice, like everyone else, it values *justice more than peace*. It is militant in the grand radical tradition. Yet, in its horror of war, it avoids the implications of this doctrine (which Mao, for instance, both understands and is willing to articulate) by its belief that *injustice is the primary cause of war*.

Though a movement as anti-monolithic and as vehemently pluralistic ideologically as the new left harbors a wide range of doctrines, certain themes are common, and those themes suggest that the new left views the world as directly analogous to domestic politics. It sees the world as a single state controlled by American bureaucracies.

From this viewpoint, the quest for justice—and for peace—is a matter of *internal* reform. Liquidate the military-industrial complex and convert the resources it consumes to public programs; enable the rural and urban poor to participate; use American capital to build the infrastructures of developing countries; achieve these goals and all will be, if not well, on the road to becoming so. The tactics of such an image of foreign affairs center on internal politics: they are identical with the domestic program of the "popgun" revolutionary: enfranchisement, counter-community, non-violence. Once radicals established Armies of the Lord or "organizational weapons": the new left has substituted more effective structures for the "scrapping" which spells day to day domestic politics, if they are less monolithic in structure. Yet in one sense, the new left is as monolithic as the old: it has one tactic, one set of aims, one strategy—and no distinct analysis of international politics.

The new left simply posits, on the international level, structures of hierarchy, with some central directive force comparable to those it has encountered domestically.

Yet if pluralism is a myth in domestic politics, as the new left would assert, it is hard to deny that the concept comes much closer to describing international reality. An alternative, more sophisticated model, which the new left employs in discussions of military policy and disarmament, assumes a system of states in place of a uniform international system, yet preserves the notion of a central will by assigning all initiative in the system to *one* state, the United States, to which all other states "react." Many of the policies adopted by the new left, such as the form of gradualism which argues that other states would reciprocate gestures in "tension-reduction" by the United States, reflect this alternative image of international affairs.

All of the new left assumptions, if valid, would maximize its ability to effect change on the international level, and one suspects this is the basis of their appeal and possibly the reason for their selection. Urgency is keenly felt, and students are eager to grapple with policy problems under which American officials seem to wilt. Urgency forces the left to assume that the hierarchies necessary to direct *economic* growth and development throughout the world will somehow be free of that arrogance of power which figures in the left's trenchant indictment of domestic hierarchies.   Urgency and the yearning for justice force the left to accept the doctrine of national self-determination with all its complexities and shortcomings, and with very little attention to the problem of the relation between state sovereignty and international order.

Tom Hayden once described the goal of the new left as a sort of "world Populism," a universal just community.   The central theme of its foreign policy is the yearning for that community, felt with a desperation which varies in degree but is always present, a yearning so inspired and so compelling that it determines the students' perception of those facts which support it and those tactics designed to produce it.   That limitation may be desirable in domestic affairs; it may eliminate much that is false, shoddy, and irrelevant in American life and thought.   Yet it is very doubtful that it serves to do more than obscure the understanding of international life and politics.

SUGGESTED READINGS

Apter, David E. (ed.), *Ideology and Discontent,* New York: Free Press, 1964.

Arendt, Hannah, *The Origins of Totalitarianism,* 2nd enlarged ed., New York: Meridian Books, 1958.

Draper, Theodore, *Castroism: Theory and Practice,* New York: Praeger, 1965.

Hoffmann, Stanley, *Gulliver's Troubles: or, The Setting of American Foreign Policy,* New York: McGraw-Hill, 1968.

Lyon, Peter, *Neutralism,* New York: Humanities Press, 1963.

Meinecke, Friedrich, *Machiavellianism; the doctrine of raison d'état and its place in modern history,* New Haven: Yale University Press, 1957.

Nolte, Ernst, *Three Faces of Fascism,* New York: Mentor, 1969.

Plamenatz, John, *Ideology,* New York: Praeger, 1970.

Schwartz, Benjamin L., *Communism and China: Ideology in Flux,* Cambridge, Mass.: Harvard University Press, 1968.

Tucker, Robert W., *The Soviet Political Mind,* New York: Praeger, 1963.

Waxman, C. I. (ed.), *The End of Ideology Debate,* New York: Funk & Wagnalls, 1968.

V. POWER AND CONFLICT

Power, for many contemporary political scientists, is virtually identical with politics. "International politics," Hans Morgenthau declares, "like all politics, is a struggle for power."[1] Such assertions, however, are not axioms and often conceal more than they reveal. There is more than "power" in politics, just as there are powers that are not "political." Power is the ability to achieve some result, to accomplish a work, or to reach an end. It is, consequently, as complex as human ambition and aspiration and as variable as the many paths that may lead toward the same goal.

A "natural history" of power must begin with its *sources*—land and resources, skills, capital, and human beings.[2] But a state may be extremely rich in the sources of power without being "powerful." The *supply* of power available to a state consists of those sources of power to which it has access. In a country with a strong belief in the sanctity of "private property," for example, the government may be unable to tap more than a tiny percentage of the national wealth. A medieval monarchy, however "absolute" its ruler might be in theory, was limited by its social and economic structure to control over a small fraction of its natural and human resources. Today, in many developing countries, government may have "dictatorial power" in the capital city but little or no access to the resources of the surrounding countryside. The supply of power, then, is critically dependent on the type of society, the form of government, and the beliefs and values that characterize a people.

Sources and supply, however, are internal considerations for an individual, group, or state. They define the tools we have, or might have, at hand. But power must be applied to be effective, and the *methods* by which power is used are critically dependent on the subject or person we hope to move. Money will not bribe a saint; a large navy may have little influence on Switzerland. We promise or threaten, punish or reward, based on our perception of the strengths and desires of others. It should be noted that reward is a form of power and of coercion no less than punishment, and often a more effective one.

[1] Hans J. Morgenthau, *Politics Among Nations,* New York: Knopf, 1967, p. 25.

[2] The term "natural history" is from Bertrand de Jouvenel, *Power: Its Natural History and Growth,* New York: Viking, 1949.

If I promise to make you rich for doing what I want, I threaten to leave you poor if you do not; your choice is constrained whatever decision you make. Mao Tse-tung's famous saying, "Whoever has an army has everything, for war settles everything. . . . Political power grows out of the barrel of a gun," is far too simple.[3] Mao himself began without an army and succeeded because the greater military strength of the Nationalists was unable to defeat him in the early years of the Chinese Revolution. War and power are not identical; war is only one method of power. In fact, since war always destroys resources it is less desirable than a method that leaves those resources intact. If war is the "last reason" of states, it is also a confession of weakness, an acknowledgement that other methods either do not exist or have failed.

A method of power, finally, can be evaluated only in terms of the gains it produces and the costs it entails. If the costs outweigh the gains, the method is worse than ineffective and we, using it, would be weaker than impotent. Gains and costs, in turn, can be assessed only in relation to our own *goals*. The United States might have "won" in Vietnam (or Korea) by launching a massive nuclear assault on its opponents, but—aside from the risks and possible costs of a world war—one deterrent was the damage Americans would have felt to their image of themselves. Moral beliefs and values are the ultimate determinants of power and impotence.[4]

In classical antiquity, for example, many political theorists argued that man had a place within the order of nature and that his desires were "by nature" fitted to that place. To want more—to desire to live forever or to rule the world, for example—was a self-delusion produced by a disease of the passions that required curing. Similarly man was only meant to have, and needed no more than, certain limited powers. Greater power, desired because of prideful illusion, would prove more than finite man could control and would, ultimately, be his ruin and destruction. The law of nature and justice according to that law, rather than power, occupied the central place in political science.

Power was raised in importance by a new political doctrine, associated with theorists like Machiavelli and Hobbes, which began with the premise that men have a "natural right" to whatever they desire but are restricted by a lack of power. An increase in power thus became equivalent to an increase in rightful liberty, and the mastery over nature became an aspect of justice in human affairs. In such a view of things, power became almost an end in itself.

All rational human endeavor consequently aimed at increasing the *substantive* power of men, their control over their own environment. But power is *relative* as well as substantive.[5] If our powers both increased, but yours grew faster than mine, you might be tempted to despoil me, increasing your own power and liberty at my expense. Thus, in order to protect justice while advancing liberty, it was necessary to allow substantive power to expand but to keep relative power "in balance."

[3] Mao Tse-tung, *Selected Works,* New York: International Publishers, 1956, II, 271.

[4] For a similar analysis of power, see Stanley Hoffmann, *Gulliver's Troubles: The Setting of American Foreign Policy,* New York: McGraw-Hill, 1968, pp. 26–33.

[5] See Carl J. Friedrich, *Constitutional Government and Politics,* New York: Harper, 1937, pp. 13–14.

As Alfred Vagts pointed out, the idea of "balance" has great political appeal for any time that faces "great upheavals, uncertainties and disappointments," seeming as it does to minimize the risk of decision.[6] But the doctrine of the "balance of power," as it developed in the seventeenth and eighteenth centuries, had even greater appeal. Theorists believed it would guarantee freedom, order, and progress by taking the major decisions of political life out of human hands. Men were often irrational and shortsighted, but the balancing of one force against another would produce a "self-regulating mechanism" that would, as Alexander Hamilton put it, "defy the little arts of little politicians to control, or vary, the irresistible and unchangeable course of nature." [7]

In a famous essay David Hume argued that the balance of power was a permanent rule of prudence in international politics.[8] A century later, most analysts still agreed. Writing in 1907 the British diplomat, Sir Eyre Crowe, saw the balance of power as the interest of every state in the international system, though only Britain was so situated as to follow, "immutably," policies designed to maintain the balance. In their different ways, Hume and Crowe were serene in the eighteenth-century faith that the "system" of the balance of power, founded on eternal laws of politics and grounded in the permanent "interest" of nations, would forever remain the basis of international politics.

But Ernst Haas demonstrates that the balance of power, far from being a law of politics, rested on (1) a particular political and technological environment; and (2) definite rules and procedures, maintained by a political and cultural consensus among policymakers. It was this consensus that changed the "balance" from a theoretical abstraction into the regulating principle of the international order. The attitudes of policymakers, not a self-regulating mechanism, formed the basis of the system. Haas calls attention to the fact that the balance depended on a political and moral climate in which conflict did not involve ultimate, or even very important, values. Though the French Revolution destroyed that environment, Haas notes, the balance of power persisted as a guide to policymaking because it remained the ideology of policymakers long after it had ceased to correspond to political reality.

Yet even in the nineteenth century, liberal politicians and statesmen were inclined to discard the balance of power as a guide to policy. Viscount Grey of Fallodon, British Foreign Secretary from 1905 to 1916, wrote:

I have never, so far as I can recollect, used the phrase "Balance of Power." I have often deliberately avoided the use of it, and I have never consciously set it before me as something to be pursued, attained and preserved. . . . I imagine it to mean that when one Power or group of Powers is the strongest "bloc" in Europe, our policy has been, or should be, that of . . . siding with some other combination of powers in order to make a counterpoise. . . . Now the Triple Alliance [9] . . . when Lord Salisbury and Lord Rosebery were Prime Ministers was indisputably the strongest political combination . . . in Europe. Nevertheless, the policy of friendship with

[6] "The Balance of Power: Growth of an Idea," *World Politics,* 1 (1948), 82–101.

[7] *The Federalist,* No. 11.

[8] David Hume, "Of the Balance of Power," in *Essays, Moral, Political and Literary* (1752), Part II, Essay VII.

[9] Germany, Austria-Hungary, and Italy. [Eds.]

it was followed by the British Government. . . . The most obvious reason was that the British Empire had occasions of acute friction with France and with Russia, friction more frequent and more acute than the countries of the Triple Alliance. . . . These are obvious, and some people will think, sufficient reasons, but underlying . . . them there was, I think, a belief that the power of the Triple Alliance made for stability and therefore peace in Europe. . . . The conclusion I would draw is that Britain has not in theory been adverse to the predominance of a strong group in Europe *when it seemed to make for stability and peace.* To support such a combination has generally been her first choice; it is only when the dominant Power becomes aggressive . . . that she, by an instinct of self-defense, if not by deliberate policy, gravitates to anything that can fairly be described as the Balance of Power.

Nevertheless, the concept of the balance of power has proved very durable among scholars even when statesmen reject it. Perhaps the appeal of the concept is that the vagueness in critical aspects of the theory, which Haas points out, allows theorists to discern order where none exists. Lord Grey was amused:

A Minister . . . must often be astounded to read of the carefully laid plans, the deep, unrevealed motives that critics or admirers attribute to him. Onlookers free from responsibility have time to invent . . . many things that Ministers have no time to invent for themselves, even if they are clever enough to be able to do it. If all secrets were known, it would probably be found that British Foreign Ministers have been guided by what seemed to them the immediate interest of this country, without making elaborate calculations for the future.[10]

No theorist, however, has failed to observe the changed character and meaning of power in international politics. First of all, power has become far less *stable* than it was in the past. Until the middle of the last century, territory and population were still the great sources of power, and rapid expansion of such assets was possible only through foreign conquest. It was, consequently, pardonable for theorists to equate preventing aggression with maintaining the balance of power. Today the great determinants of power are technological innovation and industrial productivity, and it is quite possible for a state to upset the international "equilibrium" by purely *internal* expansion and development. Moreover, as Talcott Parsons suggests, the dynamism of technological change threatens the stability of all political orders, and supplies of power grow more quickly and more unevenly than was ever true in the past.

Great powers like Germany and Japan emerged in a matter of years, while other states just as rapidly lost status and autonomy in world politics. Small states, for example, once suffered militarily only from being small. As technological innovation became more important, they found themselves unable to develop or afford the most advanced weapons. Countries like Greece or Poland in World War II did not only meet a German army that was *quantitatively* larger but one that was *qualitatively* better armed; subsequently, to avoid

[10] Both citations are taken from *Twenty-Five Years, 1892–1916*, by Viscount Grey of Fallodon, New York: Frederick Stokes, 1925, I, 5–8 (emphasis added). See also Ernst B. Haas, "The Balance of Power: Prescription, Concept or Propaganda," *World Politics*, 5 (1953), 442–477.

such a situation, small states have become dependent on assistance from a great power to an extent not true in the past. Even once-great powers, though they possess the scientific skills to develop new productive techniques or weaponry, lack the wealth needed by the "pace of obsolescence," which demands that old equipment be discarded every few years and replaced by the newest discoveries. Great Britain, for example, was forced to abandon the effort to maintain an "independent deterrent."

All of this emphasizes that *substantive* power has become radically distinct from *relative* power. Great increases in absolute power are insufficient to secure the position of a state. Either France or Britain, for example, is probably more "powerful" in absolute terms than any state in history before 1945, but both are at most secondary powers in world politics. The United States and the Soviet Union, often "paralyzed," as Gen. Pierre Gallois indicates, by the massive powers at their command, peer anxiously into the future, each fearful that some new development or some faltering in its own growth will cause it to "lose ground" relative to its opponent or to some third power. To keep power in balance, it is not enough to have equilibrium at any moment; states feel the need to guarantee that balance in the uncertain future. Belief about the future of power has become a vital element in the calculation of present power, and states have learned that nightmares may become realities with painful ease. Paradoxically, states have learned to be more fearful as they grow more strong.

Such anxieties about power have obvious consequences for international conflict. Logically, power and conflict are quite distant ideas, but conflict—real or imagined—is the source of our concern for *relative* power. And in turn, concern for relative power becomes a major source of conflict.

But conflict, of course, has innumerable sources in human affairs. To the theorists who shaped the modern political tradition, conflict was bound up in man's struggle against nature, and while most were concerned to prevent destructive conflict and war, they were equally convinced that conflict and competition were "natural" and a spur to human effort and invention. Sociologists, as late as the 1920s, often equated conflict with progress, science, and the growth of reason.[11]

Totalitarianism and total war have made social scientists less confident. In general the approach and aftermath of World War II inspired research on the ways in which conflict might be "resolved," based on an implicit theory that saw conflict as a kind of disease and a reflection of "irrational" qualities and emphasized stability, adjustment, and order.[12]

However understandable, this recent emphasis has serious defects, especially in underrating the extent to which conflicts between states involve real objects and rational differences. Nonrational elements contribute to, but are rarely the cause of, international contention.

The modern tradition, with its emphasis on the "war against nature," traces

[11] R. E. Park and E. W. Burgess, *Introduction to the Science of Society,* Chicago: University of Chicago Press, 1921, p. 578.

[12] Lewis Coser, *The Functions of Social Conflict,* Glencoe: Free Press, 1956, pp. 21–25.

many if not all conflicts to some form of economic scarcity, a doctrine that is reflected in many theories of the "economic causes of war." There is, of course, no doubt that economic conflicts are ubiquitous. In rich and poor states alike, men want more of the world's goods; states scramble for scarce resources like capital and seek to extract from one another more favorable terms of trade and aid; the coexistence of wealth and need results in envy, resentment, and exploitation. Yet the most serious forms of conflict rarely concern economic goods in any simple sense. Economic relations, however disadvantageous to one side, always involve some mutual benefit. Economic contests, consequently, are a natural field for bargain; when such conflicts involve violence, it is likely to be "economized," used with an eye to eventual compromise. As the psychoanalyst Dr. Robert Waelder put it, every economic gain has a price, and "the most critical conflicts concern goods which men deem priceless." [13]

Thomas Hobbes, though he discussed competition for material goods as a source of human conflict, emphasized fear and vanity as causes of the "state of war." Similarly, policymakers omit most economic considerations in defining the "vital interests" of a state, stressing three kinds of invaluable goods: (1) security, (2) morality, and (3) national dignity and honor.

Security, like "self-preservation," is an extremely complex idea because it depends on the definition that individuals or states give to the idea of "self," of those things that are rightfully their own. Economic goods, for example, may become vital if they are thought essential to our way of life, just as we may feel threatened if gains in wealth or relative power that we *expected* do not materialize. Security also involves our estimate of the intentions of our opponents and friends; for example, British power has not in this century seemed a menace to Belgium. And, as the discussion of relative power suggests, security increasingly is not a matter of present facts so much as it is a prediction about the future. Wilfrid Knapp points out the role of the desire for security in the origins of the cold war, arguing that Soviet fears, magnified by Stalin's personality, demanded so much "security" that the West could not satisfy the desire without endangering its own safety. It is no small part of contemporary international problems that security, never completely attainable, now seems almost hopelessly beyond the grasp of men and states.

Security, moreover, does not always comport with morality and honor. Pakistan's security might be advanced by friendly relations with India, but such relations would probably depend on abandoning the people of Kashmir. The Soviet Union, as Knapp indicates, might have improved its safety by "revising" Leninism or by breaking with Communist parties abroad—and indeed, it has made gestures in both directions—but doing so would have threatened its own moral foundation. America protected her security by refusing to intervene in the Czech (1968) and Hungarian (1956) crises and by making alliances with Franco and other dictatorships, but at some cost to her moral position and self-esteem. Radical differences in morality, similarly, are always a threat. The Soviet Union, Knapp points out, has challenged the moral

[13] "Conflict and Violence," *Bulletin of the Menninger Clinic,* 30 (September 1966), 270.

legitimacy of every Western government and the system of states as a whole; Western insistence on individual human rights threatens those who see collective goods as overriding individual claims. In fact, when political "realists" deprecated the role of morality in international conflict, they were *prescribing* as much as describing, hoping that conflicts could be made less intense if men concerned themselves only with the "realities" of power.

This is especially true in relation to the desire to preserve or assert national dignity and honor. Dignity involves the desire to "matter," to avoid helpless dependence, to assert the right of a state or a people to moral autonomy. And, as phrases like "the honor of the flag" suggest, honor and dignity may command resistance or rebellion even when there seems to be no chance of victory. Honor and morality complicate the equations of power; former Secretary of State Dean Rusk recently conceded that he had underestimated the North Vietnamese willingness to suffer and sacrifice in Vietnam, while the reluctance to "lose a war" for the first time has made it more difficult for the United States to contemplate withdrawal. There are times, of course, when a nation may be, as President Wilson asserted, "too proud to fight," but such a situation is normally associated with the sense of invulnerable security. And for most of humanity in the modern world, dignity is constantly threatened. Impersonal forces and distant peoples control much of the life of states, if they do not dominate it altogether. For poor and weak states, indignity has been the theme of political life, but even in the great powers, honor and security seem precarious. We may, like Hobbes, regard the desire for dignity as "vainglory," but we cannot deny its power in political life, especially in our times.

We must also recognize that conflict has a positive side. All of us, for example, have encountered the notion that a "common enemy" may unite a nation or a group of nations. This is not as simple as is often believed; in a divided state the external "enemy" may be perceived as the *ally* of one domestic faction. Britain was united by World War II, but in France, fascists and rightists saw the Nazis as potential friends; and communists, until the invasion of the Soviet Union, regarded the conflict as only another "imperialist war." Even when domestic conflict is not very severe, as in the United States at the beginning of the Vietnam War, the cost of a foreign embroglio in money and lives may heighten domestic disagreement and discord.[14] But the demands of conflict to compel and assist men, groups, and states to develop a sense of "identity," to discover their real commitments and values; no small attraction when so many feel confused and alone. Too, in all its forms, conflict is a form of communication. The appearance of stability and peace—in international and in domestic politics—may be an illusion in which resentment is driven into silence by hopelessness. Paradoxically conflict is often a sign that the powerful have grown more responsive to the weak; shouts of resentment may reflect a new confidence that such cries will be heard. If the expression of conflict is a danger to any political order, it also raises the possibility that

[14] Robin Williams, *The Reduction of Intergroup Tensions,* New York: Social Science Research Council, 1947.

215

old injustices may be remedied, that mutual complaints may be adjusted, and that a new and more stable order may result.[15]

But not all conflicts *can* be resolved or adjusted. "Peace" with Nazi Germany would have demanded the moral suicide of the rest of humanity. We may be able to explain the causes of evil in the conduct of men and of states, tracing it to fear or folly; we cannot deny that it exists. So long as this is true, war remains a possibility, and one required not only for physical survival but as a reflection of the justice we owe to our fellows and to ourselves.

[15] George Simpson, *Conflict and Community,* New York: T. S. Simpson, 1937.

Thomas Hobbes

MAN, POWER AND CONFLICT

. . . . (T)he felicity of this life consisteth not in the repose of a mind satisfied. For there is no *Finis ultimus* (utmost aim) nor *Summum Bonum* (greatest good) as is spoken of in the books of the old moral philosophers. Nor can a man any more live whose desires are at an end, than he whose senses and imagination are at a stand. Felicity is a continual progress of desire from one object to another, the attaining of the former being . . . but the way to the latter. The cause whereof being that the object of man's desire is not to enjoy once only and for an instant of time, but to assure forever the way of his future desire. And therefore . . . all men tend, not only to the procuring but also to the assuring of a contented life, and differ only in the way, which ariseth partly from the diversity of the passions in diverse men, and partly from the difference of the knowledge or opinion each one has of the causes which produce the effect desired.

So that in the first place, I put for a general inclination of all men a perpetual and restless desire of power after power that ceaseth only in death. And the cause of this is not always that a man hopes for a more intensive delight than he had already attained to, or that he cannot be content with a moderate power, but because he cannot assure the power and means to live well which he hath at present without the acquisition of more. And . . . hence it is that kings, whose power is greatest, turn their endeavors to the assuring of it at home by laws and abroad by wars; and when that is done, there succeedeth a new desire, in some, of fame from new conquest, in others, of ease and sensual pleasure, in others, of admiration or being flattered. . . .

Competition of riches, honor, command or other powers enclineth to contention, enmity and war, because the way of one competitor to the attaining of his desire is to kill, subdue, supplant or repel the other. . . .

Desire of ease and sensual delight disposeth men to obey a common power. . . . Fear of death and wounds disposeth to the same. . . . On the contrary, needy men and hardy, not contented with their present condition (as also, all men that are ambitious of military command) are inclined to continue the causes of war and to stir up trouble and sedition, for there is no honor military but by war, nor any hope to mend an ill game (but) by causing a new shuffle. . . .

To have received from one to whom we think ourselves equal greater benefits than there is hope to requite disposeth a man to counterfeit love, but really secret hatred, and puts a man into the estate of a desperate debtor. . . . For benefits oblige, and obligation is thralldom, and un-

Adapted by the editors from *Leviathan* (1651), Book I, Chapters 11 and 13.

requitable obligation, perpetual thralldom, which is to one's equal hateful. But to have received benefits from one whom we acknowledge for superior inclines to love. . . . Also to receive benefits . . . from an equal or inferior, so long as there is hope of requital, disposeth to love, for in the intention of the receiver the obligation is of aid and service mutual, from whence proceedeth emulation of who shall exceed in benefiting, the most noble and profitable contention possible. . . .

To have done more hurt to a man than he can or is willing to expiate inclineth the doer to hate the sufferer. For he must expect revenge or forgiveness, both of which are hateful.

Fear of oppression disposeth a man to anticipate or seek aid by society, for there is no other way by which a man can secure his life and liberty.

Men that distrust their own subtlety are in tumult and sedition better disposed for victory than they that suppose themselves wise and crafty. For these love to consult, the others . . . to strike first. . . .

Vainglorious men, such as without being conscious to themselves of great sufficiency, delight in supposing themselves gallant men, are inclined only to ostentation, but not to attempt. Because when danger or difficulty appears, they look for nothing but to have their insufficiency discovered.

Vainglorious men, such as estimate their sufficiency by the flattery of other men or the fortune of some precedent action, without assured ground of hope from the true knowledge of themselves are inclined to rash engaging and in the approach of danger or difficulty, to retire if they can, because not seeing the way of safety, they will rather hazard their honor, which may be saved with an excuse, than their lives. . . .

Men that have a strong opinion of their own wisdom in matters of government are disposed to ambition. Because without public employment in counsel or magistracy, the honor of their wisdom is lost. . . .

[M]en give different names to one and the same thing from the difference of their own passions. As they that approve a private opinion, call it opinion, but they that mislike it, heresy, and yet heresy signifies no more than private opinion but has only a greater tincture of choler. . . .

Ignorance of the causes and original constitution of right, equity, law and justice disposeth a man to make custom and example the rule of his actions [and] . . . to think it unjust which it hath been the custom to punish and that just, of the impunity and approbation of which they can produce an example or . . . a precedent, like little children that have no rule of good and evil manners but the correction they receive from their parents . . . save that children are constant to their rule whereas men are not so, because grown strong and stubborn, they appeal from custom to reason and from reason to custom as it serves their turn. . . . For I doubt not but if it had been a thing contrary to any man's right of dominion or to the interest of men that have dominion that the three angles of a triangle should be equal to two angles of a square, that the doctrine should have been, if not disputed, yet by the burning of all books of geometry, suppressed, as far as he whom it concerned was able.

Ignorance of remote causes disposeth men to attribute all events to the causes immediate and instrumental, for these are the causes they perceive. And hence . . . men that are grieved with payments to the public, discharge their anger upon the . . . Officers of the public revenue and adhere to such as find fault with the public government and when they have engaged themselves beyond hope of justification, fall also back upon the Supreme Authority. . . .

And they that make little or no inquiry into the natural causes of things . . . yet from the fear that proceeds from ignorance itself are inclined to suppose and feign unto themselves several kinds of powers invisible and to stand in awe of their own imaginations. . . . By which means it hath come to pass that from the innumerable variety of fancy, men have created in the world innumerable sorts of gods. And this fear of things invisible is the natural seed of that which every one in himself calleth religion, and in them that worship or fear that power otherwise than they do, superstition. . . . [S]ome . . . have been inclined . . . to nourish, dress and form it into laws, and to add to it, of their own invention, any opinion of the causes of future events by which they thought they should best be able to govern others and make unto themselves the greatest use of their powers. . . .

Nature hath made men so equal in the faculties of the body and mind, as that though there be found one man sometimes manifestly stronger in body or of quicker mind than another, yet when all is reckoned together, the difference between man and man is not so considerable as that one man can thereupon claim to himself any benefit to which another may not pretend as well as he. . . .

From this equality of ability, ariseth equality of hope in the attaining of our ends. And therefore, if any two men desire the same thing, which nevertheless they cannot both enjoy, they become enemies. . . . And from hence it comes to pass that where an invader hath no more to fear than another man's single power, if one plant, sow, build or possess a convenient seat, others may probably be expected to come with forces united to dispossess and deprive him, not only of the fruit of his labor but also of his life or liberty. And the invader again is in the like danger of another.

And from this diffidence of one another, there is no way for any man to secure himself so reasonable as anticipation, that is, by force and wiles to master the persons of all men he can . . . till he see no other power great enough to endanger him. . . . Also because there be some, that taking pleasure in contemplating their own power in the acts of conquest which they pursue farther than safety requires, if others, that otherwise would be glad to be at ease within modest bounds, should not by invasion increase their power, they would not be able, long time, by standing only on their defense, to subsist. . . .

Again. . . . every man looketh that his companion should value him at the same rate he sets upon himself, and upon all signs of contempt or undervaluing, naturally endeavors . . . to extort a greater value from his contemners by damage and from others by example.

So that in the nature of man, we find three principal causes of quarrel: first, competition, second, diffidence and third, glory. . . .

Hereby it is manifest that during the time men live without a common power to keep them all in awe, they are in a condition of war, and such a war as is of every man against every man. For war consisteth not in battle only or the act of fighting, but in a tract of time wherein the will to contend by battle is sufficiently known. . . .

Talcott Parsons

THE STRUCTURE OF GROUP HOSTILITY

*   *   *

The progress of science and related elements of rational thought is the core . . . of the process [of "rationalization."] Science is an inherently dynamic thing. Unless prevented by influences extraneous to it, it will continually evolve. Moreover, unless science is hermetically insulated from the rest of social life . . . this dynamic process of change will be extended into . . . philosophical and religious thought, and in the direction of practical application. . . . Hence through this dynamic factor, a continuing process of change is introduced, both into the primary symbolic systems which help to integrate the life of a society, and into the structure of the situations in which a large part of the population must carry on their activities.

The significance of this arises in the first place from the fact that there is much evidence that security . . . is . . . a function of the stability . . . of the socio-cultural situation. This is true especially because certain aspects of the situations people face are involved in the actual and . . . prospective fulfillment of their "legitimate expectations." These expectations are . . . apt to be highly concrete so that any change . . . is apt to be disturbing and arouse a reaction of anxiety. . . . [T]*echnological change inevitably disrupts the informal human relationships of the members of working groups* [1] . . . which have been shown to be highly important

Reprinted by permission of the author and the publisher from "Certain Primary Sources and Patterns of Aggression in the Social Structure of the Western World," *Psychiatry,* X (May 1947), 177–180.

[1] Italics added. [Eds.]

to the stability and working efficiency of the participants. . . . [T]he corresponding process of change on the level of ideas and symbols tends to disrupt established symbolic systems which are exceedingly important to the security and stability of the orientation of people.

. . . [T]he amount of such change to which even the best integrated personalities can adapt without the possibility of upsetting the smooth functioning of personality is rather limited. . . . [T]he continuing incidence of dynamic change through the process of rationalization is one major source of the generalized insecurity which characterizes our society. As such it should also be a major factor in maintaining the reservoir of aggressive impulses at a high level. It is a factor so deep-seated in our society that it must be expected to continue to operate on a major scale for the foreseeable future. . . .

*   *   *

It must be remembered that the incidence of the process of rationalization is highly uneven. . . . [T]here are always relatively "emancipated" and relatively traditional groups and sectors of the society. Certain of the emancipated groups, like the best of the professions . . . become relatively well institutionalized so that the dynamic process . . . is not so disturbing to them. They always . . . contain at least a fringe . . . where insecurity is expressed in . . . patterns of extreme emancipation which are highly provocative to the more traditionalized elements. . . .

The process is, however, always tending to spread into the relatively traditionalized areas of the society and thereby tending to threaten the security of the . . . elements most dependent on traditionalized patterns. . . . [T]he result is to stimulate what has . . . been called "fundamentalist reaction," a compulsively distorted exaggeration of traditional values. . . . This above all attaches to . . . religion, family, class attitudes, the informal traditions of ethnic culture . . . where non-logical symbolic systems are heavily involved.

The reverse side of the exaggerated assertion of these traditional patterns is the aggressive attack on . . . science as such, atheism . . . political and economic radicalism, and the like. The compulsive adherents of emancipated values . . . tend to brand all traditional values as "stupid," reactionary, unenlightened, and thus a vicious circle of mounting antagonism readily gets started. . . .

It is above all important that the values about which the fundamentalist pattern of reaction tends to cluster are . . . those of families, social class, socio-religious groups, ethnic groups, and nations. Many of these . . . are seriously in conflict with the explicit values of the Western world which largely stem from the rationalistic traditions of the enlightenment. They are hence particularly difficult to defend against rationalistic attack. Since, however, they are of fundamental emotional importance, the consequence more frequently than not is their "defensive" assertion rather than their abandonment.   This very difficulty of rational defense when rational values are in fact accepted favors . . . "unreasonable" aggression.

These circumstances seem to go far toward explaining the striking fact that aggression in the Western world tends to focus so much on antagonisms between solidary groups.   Some of these groups are, to be sure, those growing out of the . . . utilitarian structure of modern society, like . . . business and labor unions.   Probably more important, however, are the lines of conflict which cut across these groups, particularly those between religious and ethnic groups within nations and, above all, the conflict of nationalisms. . . .   [A]n antagonistic group is a peculiarly appropriate symbolic object on which to displace the emotional reactions which cannot be openly expressed within one's own group lest they threaten its solidarity. . . .   The "out group" should . . . be a group in relation to which one's own group can feel a comfortably self-righteous sense of superiority and at the same time a group which can be plausibly accused of arrogating to itself an illegitimate superiority of its own.   The Jews have . . . furnished almost the ideal scapegoat throughout the Western world.

. . . There are . . . potent reasons why nationalism should be the most important and serious focus of these tendencies.   The first is the realistic basis of it.   The organization of our civilization into nation states. . . . Above all, in the chronic tendency to resort to war in crisis situations the loyalty to one's government has had to be . . . the ultimate . . . loyalty, the one which could claim any sacrifice no matter how great if need be.

At the same time it is highly significant that *as between the fundamentalist and the emancipated poles . . . nationalistic loyalty . . . is largely neutral.*[2] . . .   [T]he "foreigner" is, moreover, outside the principal immediate system of law and order; hence aggression toward him does not carry the same opprobrium or immediate danger of reprisal that it does toward one's "fellow-citizen."   Hostility to the foreigner has thus furnished a means of transcending . . . immediately threatening group conflicts . . . at the expense of a less immediate but in fact more dangerous threat to security, since national states now command such destructive weapons that war between them is approaching suicidal significance.

Thus the immense reservoir of aggression in Western society is sharply inhibited from direct expression within the smaller groups in which it is primarily generated.   The structure of the society . . . contains a strong pre-disposition for it to be channeled into group antagonisms.   The significance of the nation state is, however, such that there is a strong pressure to internal unity within each such unit and therefore a tendency to focus aggression on the potential conflicts between nation-state units. ·. . .   Each state is . . . highly ambivalent about the superiority-inferiority question. Each tends to have a deep-seated presumption of its own superiority and a corresponding resentment against others' corresponding presumption.   Each

---

[2] Italics added.   [Eds.]

. . . tends to feel that it has been unfairly treated in the past and is ready on the slightest provocation to assume that the others are ready to plot new outrages in the immediate future.   Each tends to be easily convinced of the righteousness of its own policy while at the same time it is overready to suspect the motives of all others.   In short, the "jungle philosophy"—which corresponds to a larger element in the real sentiments of all of us than can readily be admitted even to ourselves—tends to be projected onto the relations of nation states at precisely the point where, under the technological and organizational situation of the modern world, it can do the most harm.

Ernst B. Haas

THE BALANCE OF POWER AS A GUIDE
TO POLICY-MAKING

*   *   *

Historically the balance of power has been held out as a means for planning policy in an intelligent and dispassionate manner.   It has been considered as a highly practical principle at once clarifying the nature of the state system and setting forth the operational rules whereby the survival of single states within that system might be assured.   Its merits lay in its objectivity, its detachment from ideology, its universality, and its independence from short-term considerations.   It stressed the essentials, timeless and inescapable, in international affairs: power and power relationships.

The eighteenth century advocates of the balance of power pictured Europe as a great "confederation" or "system."   Despite its division into sovereign states, eternally in competition with each other, Europe was held to be a "great family" of units characterized by similar institutions, similar value systems, and similar cultural traits.   Even the motivations of European rulers and statesmen were considered to be identical.   Politics, therefore, unfolded in a milieu characterized by an institutional and cultural consensus among the participants. . . .   In a Europe united culturally and institutionally, the balance of power was then regarded as a system in which state power was so distributed that no single state could acquire hegemony without calling into existence an alliance of all other states, an alliance strong enough to defeat the hegemony seeker.   Some saw in the balance

Reprinted by permission of the publisher from *The Journal of Politics* (August 1953).

system a roughly equal distribution of power between two "scales," while others insisted that one or several states must remain outside the match in order to act as "balancers," i.e., "throw their weight" into whichever scale proved to be the weaker in the actual or potential conflict.   In a milieu in which ideological, nationalist, and commercial motivations were held to be of no causative significance, the conflict of power—in terms of territory and populations—was the only criterion of international relations, the only source of hostilities between otherwise homogeneous ruling groups.

*   *   *

The institutional and cultural consensus in which such a system and its accompanying rules could gain intellectual acceptance was destroyed by the events of 1789.   The conflict for dominion as such ceased to be the common element in international politics, assuming that the earlier characterization had been the correct one.   Henceforth the "defense of the moral order," as Metternich liked to term the conflict between aristocratic and middle class ideology, entered the arena of international relations, and with it nationalism and national aspirations arose to confuse the earlier simple symmetry of interstate relations.   Even though Castlereagh, Talleyrand, Guizot, Metternich, and Gentz continued to apply the old terminology, even though Lord Salisbury could still speak of the Concert as the "federation of Europe" as late as 1897, the reality was otherwise.   No amount of lip service to an established concept could recreate the institutional consensus in which it had originated.

. . . Despite the changed conditions of the nineteenth and twentieth centuries the balance of power concept lost little of its popularity, with the exception of the period 1919–1939.   Writers continued to refer to it as the unifying system, first of European and then of world politics. . . .   The world was still pictured as the arena of power conflicts between sovereign states, eternally in competition with each other, with each state a potential hegemony seeker, unless checked in time with appropriate "counterweights." And the rules governing state behavior in the system underwent no change of principle. . . .

It is apparent that if the rules flowing from a balance of power system are to be applied to the making of foreign policy a number of operational or procedural assumptions inherent in the dispassionate approach can be isolated.   It is on the operational level that balance of power policies still bear the conditioning imprint of the monarchical era.   For the procedural watchwords are: rapid and secret decision-making, readiness to intervene, and the continuity of policy. . . .   [O]perational assumptions include the rough measurability of power, indifference to the merits of whatever issue demands participation in the conflict by the balancer, and the willingness to resort to war if judged necessary to preserve the balance.

Critics of the balance of power concept have at all times insisted that the notion of "balanced" power was a chimera primarily because there was no method of measuring power.   How was State A to know when and under what circumstances an alliance between States B and C would "threaten" the balance unless its statesmen had an accurate criterion with which they could measure the combined military and strategic potential of States B and C? . . . [T]he most mature and detached advocates of the balance as a guide to policy-making replied that there was no necessity for measuring power exactly.   They urged that a rough and approximate evaluation of strength and counterstrength was sufficient for the successful application of balancing rules. . . .

More important operationally than the necessity for an approximate estimation of relative power, however, is the requirement of flexibility.   Successful balancing policies assume the existence of maximum adjustability to external changes. . . .   [T]he degree of flexibility must be directly proportional to the degree of physical and technological interdependence in order to "preserve" the balance.   To balance power today more readiness to adjust to unforeseen changes is required than was true in 1914, for obvious technological reasons.   Failure to adjust implies failure to check power with power and is held to contain the seeds of national catastrophe.   Flexibility, moreover, calls for a number of qualities in the mechanics of government. Decision-making must be rapid if not instantaneous upon the receipt of intelligence reports containing news upsetting previous planning.   Furthermore it must be secret in order to keep the enemy in ignorance of the adjustments.   And the combination of secrecy and rapidity implies non-accountability for the decisions to organs and individuals outside the inner sanctum of ultimate responsibility.   Congressional committees thus cannot be consulted in advance on a sudden shift in policy if the shift is to be secret and instantaneous. . . .

Writers on the balance of power are unanimous in urging the need for "eternal vigilance" in external affairs.   Preserving the balance of power calls for incessant attention to all shifts of power everywhere and the continuous evaluation of these shifts with respect to the power position of the home state.   Operationally, therefore, a premium is put on armaments and military assistance policies, on continuous changes in the scale and quality of armaments to conform with the potential enemy's changes.   "Eternal vigilance" then implies no more and no less than the continuous expectation of rivalry and potential violence, supplemented with proper domestic and foreign policies to ensure the success of the home state in such a situation. Domestically, fiscal and industrial policies must be in tune with the possible need for hostilities.   Labor must be organized accordingly.   Conscription and mobilization policies must fit the pattern.   And the flexibility assumption calls for readiness to adjust these domestic policies on a moment's notice.   Externally, the need for eternal vigilance implies the readiness to intervene wherever and whenever the balance seems threatened.   Intervention may be undertaken either with or without the consent of the state at whose expense it takes place.   It may take the form of military occupation, economic assistance, military advice, leasing of bases, and even the removal of undesirable foreign governments and their replacement with more "suitable" groups. More commonly such intervention makes itself felt through participation in foreign elections through a variety of direct and indirect means perfected during the post-1945 era. In each case the choice of means is dictated, in theory, by the nature of the problem as viewed from the need for balanced power. . . .

Furthermore, all these policy operations are assumed to be continuous despite domestic changes. The replacement of one government by another is to have no influence on external policy or internal vigilance. The electoral victory of one party . . . is assumed to have no bearing on the continued application of its predecessor's approach. The relative strength of organized opinion groups and its variation in the domestic political process must be excluded from balancing operations if they are to be successful. . . .

An operational assumption of the highest significance is presented by the problem of how to view the nature of a given international dispute or tension. For the rôle of the balancer assumes that its commitment to the conflict be such as to preclude the examination of the dispute on its "merits." Balance of power rules assume that the end of state policy is the preservation of independence by averting the threatened hegemony of an expanding state. Hence the preservation of balanced power must be the only consideration . . . The rule demands that the weaker side be supported, no matter whether the stronger side is the military ally, the ideological sympathizer, or the best customer in international trade of the balancing state. Shifts in power alone are to be of determining significance in the selection of policy measures.

A final—and perhaps fatal—operational assumption of the balance of power as a guide for policy-making calls for the necessity of waging war under certain external circumstances. . . . Timely countermeasures, compensatory armaments, stable alliances—may all be used in the effort to persuade the hegemony seeking state to desist in time. But what if these measures should fail? If the expanding state remains indifferent to these measures war remains the only method of preserving the balance. Moreover, preventive war may be called for in order to maximize a momentary superiority in power if the long-run expectation is one of violent conflict in the first place. War, far from being excluded or banished by the application of balance of power rules, is in reality enthroned as the final method for preserving the balance as a system. . . .

It is on the level of concept that the most important assumptions of balance of power policies are found. The purpose of balanced power, it is held, is the safeguarding of the national interest. And the national interest, in turn, consists of assuring the preservation of the state in a world full of actual or potential enemy states, engaged in eternal competition for more power with each other. It is the common claim of balance of power theorists that there can be only one correct interpretation of the national interest. . . .

If the aim of foreign policy, based on the balance, is the preservation of the state's power position in a world of hostile states, the search for power must become an end in itself . . . The uses of power are altogether secondary in this approach. It is freely granted that power may be used for all kinds of ends other than the enjoyment of power for its own sake. But for purposes of understanding international relations, it is urged that these secondary usages are irrelevant and that it is the search for power in itself which is the fundamental factor of importance. . . . The preservation of the balance of power is the key motive of policy-making, to which all other possible motives must by nature be secondary, if not actually repugnant.

Unfortunately, "self-preservation" is a concept which does not lend itself to easy application in political analysis. . . . Preservation of existing frontiers, or of existing military, naval, and diplomatic jobs? Self-preservation is a term which may include the retention of the total institutional *status quo* in a given society, existing social stratification and deference patterns as well as private economic or ideological power. On the other hand it may imply merely the continuance in power of a given small group of individuals or a given ruler, irrespective of the larger sociological implications. The problem is confused further by the fact that there is little agreement at any one time as to what policies designed for self-preservation should involve in practice. . . .

. . . The national interest is the vital center piece of the entire intellectual structure from which balancing rules are derived. If in national interest no more is implied than self-preservation the questions which have been raised with respect to the latter concept are equally applicable to the former. On the other hand, if the national interest is defined merely as that portion of foreign policy aims which is acceptable to the whole national community, such as the preservation of peace, the attainment of national security or the protection of nationals, the concept becomes so vague as to lose its value as a guide to policy formulation. To others it has implied much more than these considerations and has been used to cover situations of what Professor Wolfers has called "goals of national self-extension." This did not necessarily call for policies of political expansion or even conquest but may have involved merely the championing of kindred ideological causes abroad or the principle of the open door in international trade. The key feature about the national interest as an objective principle is its alleged continuity and independence from socio-economic changes in the domestic political scene. Operative rules of flexibility, vigilance and preparedness, continuity over time, indifference to the nature of external issues except their power implications and the willingness to go to war if necessary, all depend on the central concept of national interest which they are to serve. For the protection of the balance of power is nothing but the protection of the national interest. . . .

What, then, is the national interest? Usually it is contended that the national interest includes all those features of state aspirations which bear a relation to the permanent and enduring needs of the state, thus in fact begging the question further. Geographical position is singled out frequently as containing the key to a particular national interest. Britain's insular position, America's command over Pacific and Atlantic approaches to her shores, Germany's central location between France and Russia, Russia's search for a warm-water port provide examples of this argument. The alleviation of population pressure coupled with the need for reliable sources of industrial raw materials and markets for manufactured goods are held out as the chief national interest in the case of Germany and Japan. The national interest of France, by contrast, seems to have called for the extension of French culture to the aborigines of the Upper Ubangi. Thus stated, the national interest concept acquires the sanctity of a fixed historical law for each state, immutable over long periods and always properly understood by intelligent and imaginative statesmen, misunderstood and bungled by those who did not really appreciate the position and interests of their country in world affairs. Balance of power policies are inconceivable unless they can be practiced with reference to some central principle defining the state's position in a world balance. . . .

. . . The vital question here is only: do all possible policy motivations fit the picture of a stable and immutable national interest?

. . . Little emphasis is required to show that the motivations of groups and individuals are as varied as they are conditioned by factors by no means immutable. Over a period of time British policy successively emphasized emancipating all overseas colonies and reducing imperial commitments, expanding imperial control, encouraging free trade and the tariff autonomy of the self-governing possessions, stressing protectionism and the closed nature of the Empire tariff system. Germany ignored overseas expansion and concentrated on armies and alliances for defensive purposes under Bismarck and sought overseas expansion as well as a powerful navy under Bethmann-Hollweg and Bülow. And the United States seemed to undergo marked oscillations in the permanence of its foreign policy motivations as well. Enthusiasm for expansion at the expense of Mexico alternated with indifference to such policies; "manifest destiny" in the Caribbean and the Far East had to compete with Wilson's withdrawal from China and Roosevelt's from the West Indies. Nor are differences in the conception of the national interest confined to successive periods. . . .

It is evident that various possible motivations appeal with varying amounts of intensity to given socio-economic groups. Imperial grandeur was a symbol of great appeal to Disraeli's Conservatives and Chamberlain's Unionists but was a much lesser symbol to Lloyd George's Liberals and a symbol of opposition to Arthur Henderson's Laborites. . . . The defense of Western Europe is a symbol of great magnitude to Fair Deal Democrats and Eastern Republicans though its appeal to Southern Democrats and

Midwestern Republicans seems to be quite another matter. . . .   The conception of the national interest, therefore, far from uniting these groups, seems to be but one element of major contention among them. . . .

. . . National interest to one may well be national lack of interest to another.   In fact, it may be concluded that the conception of national interest which prevails at any one time is no more than an amalgam of varying policy motivations which tend to pass for a "national" interest as long as the groups holding these opinions continue to rule.   These motivations may be homogeneous or conflicting, depending on the nature of the ruling group. . . .   All this implies not continuity but discontinuity in policy-making. . . .

Heterogeneity of motivations implies the absence of that very immutable central principle around which balance of power policies are to revolve.   It is for these reasons that writers on the balance of power have so frequently condemned the intrusion of ideological factors into policy-making, as well as any other motivation whose realization in terms of policy would be repugnant with balanced power.   The immediate result of their preoccupation with pure balanced power is the condemnation as fearful nonsense of any policy based on non-power considerations. . . .

The element of repugnancy may also occur when balance of power policies come into conflict with policies motivated by the need to appease public opinion or by the necessity of controlling a turbulent and dangerous minority in Parliament.   The balance of power assumes complete continuity despite changes of ministries, elections, party passions, and shifting majority coalitions, in the home state as well as abroad.   All these non-power considerations, internal as well as external, are equally irrelevant to the balancing policy.   Conversely, it follows that policy motivated and executed on grounds of economic desirability, ideological sympathy, or as a concession to parliamentary pressure is not in the national interest if it comes into conflict with power needs.   And the state which so ignored its power needs in deference to other motivations would be flirting with danger. . . .

*   *   *

In short, the rules of the balance of power assume rapid, consistent, secret, and dispassionate decision-making based on a reasoned analysis of abstract power needs, essentially amoral in nature.   "Intelligent" decision-making in terms of balance reasoning consists of obeying these injunctions.   "Unintelligent" policy-making ignores them or follows them only inconsistently. The fact that there cannot be any assurance of the presupposed objectivity of the basic national interest concept, however, renders it difficult to distinguish intelligent from unintelligent decisions since it is the nature of the motivations which tends to be the criterion.

*   *   *

Monolithic autocracies, whatever their inabilities in meeting the operational assumptions of balance of power rules may be, are able to satisfy the conceptual assumptions. The very nature of the régime implies one clear idea of the national interest which, to be sure, may vary over time, but which is dominant by definition at a given time. Not even this conceptual assumption applies in the case of democracy, if by democracy is meant the toleration of pluralism in the society constituting the state. And it is urged that modern democracy is inconceivable without such a toleration.

The very existence of the multi-group society poses the strong likelihood of co-existence of a variety of over-all policy motivations. . . . There is no assurance that a given foreign policy is more than the policy of the majority. Labelling it the "national interest" merely exposes it to the danger of having an entirely different but equally "national" interest substituted after the next election.

Existence of a consistent and widely accepted version of the national interest in a pluralistic society implies the existence of a consensus far beyond anything modern western history has demonstrated as reasonable. . . .

As long as pluralistic society recognizes the right of each group to pose its version of the national interest and to persuade other groups to accept it there can be no possibility of establishing a "general" national interest in the short run. . . . A given foreign policy will merely represent the compromise between the motivations entering the ruling group or coalition of groups. The very nature of pluralism precludes the possibility of unfailing agreement between ruling majority and the loyal minority.

On the operational level the consistent application of balance of power policies is even less practicable. If the absence of a consensus on the national interest makes impossible the adoption of one consistent foreign policy, consonant with the needs of balanced power, the operations entering the decision-making process in a democracy make such an approach a contradiction in terms. Thus the requirement for flexibility in attitudes toward foreign relations is bound to encounter serious obstacles. Secret and rapid decision-making may have been possible to the absolute rulers of the eighteenth century, but it is hardly a likely assumption under democratic conditions. It is possible, of course, for the executive to take action in secret and then confront the country with a *fait accompli* impossible to undo, as indeed the "revisionist" historians accuse Franklin D. Roosevelt of having done; but this procedure is not one any politician in a democracy is likely to indulge in for any length of time. It cannot, in short, be considered a standard rule of conduct in a democracy. The principle of non-accountability is equally unlikely to be practiced with any amount of consistency as the conduct of the Korean war should have amply demonstrated. Flexibility, in short, is the kind of quality which a democratic society does not and perhaps cannot possess in the sense required by the rules of balance of power diplomacy.

The principle of "eternal vigilance," no doubt, can be practiced by an autocratic régime with a considerable degree of success. It is dubious, however, that a democracy can do so. In its external aspects the assumption can be met without difficulty as far as intelligence activities and a certain amount of intervention are concerned. However, it is precisely the issue of intervention or non-intervention which may have serious domestic political implications if the opposition party chooses to make an issue of it, as indeed the Korean war has demonstrated once more. And the balance of power assumes the ready consent of all political groups to such policy measures whereas opposition to it implies conduct repugnant to balancing rules. The principle of eternal vigilance furthermore presupposes preparedness for war and willingness to expand or contract preparations as demanded by the external stimulus. Again the democratic framework is not such as to provide reassurance on this point. A policy of conscription considered essential by one party may not be so treated by the opposition. Fiscal, taxation, and economic control policies are subject to precisely the same limiting influences. Pluralism once more seems to obstruct the compatibility of motivations necessitated by consistent balance of power policies.

The potential rôle of the opposition party or parties is thrown into sharp focus by the remaining operational assumptions. Continuity in foreign policy is a virtue few democracies have permitted themselves to possess. While sharp reversals in policy are rare upon a change in the ruling party, minor changes are common and may in their implications be quite as important as more severe alterations. It is here that the problem of ideological disagreement assumes crucial importance. Continuity in policy presupposes agreement on essential ideological principles between all major parties. Such agreement is possible but it is by no means a feature which can be relied upon. . . .

If democratic pluralism makes continuity in foreign policy an unlikely assumption, indifference to the merits of a dispute is an even less realistic tenet. On the contrary, every foreign situation which might lead to "entanglement" is analyzed and misanalyzed and instead of prompt commitment on the basis of balance of power needs, commitment is usually delayed and decided upon only after the varying and perhaps clashing motivations of the ruling party are canvassed and sorted with respect to the disturbing foreign issue. The opposition party, furthermore, may be in a position to alter the government's policy in accordance with its motivations, i.e., inject further non-power and non-balancing considerations into a decision-making process already made difficult by the nature of the ruling groups. And in the final operational step presupposed by consistent balance of power policies, the waging of war if judged necessary, all these difficulties appear once more, often in a more acute form. Democracy certainly cannot be relied upon to go to war whenever its power position, as viewed by the group which happens to rule, seems to demand it. The confluence of clashing motivations is much too real a factor in democratic decision-making to permit such a hypothesis.

The inevitable mixture of domestic issues with foreign policy problems

makes the application of balance of power policies even more difficult.
The issue facing the foreign minister is not merely one of persuading his
following of the necessity of a given diplomatic *démarche* on abstract power
terms.   Every issue facing a cabinet is part and parcel of the total parliamentary picture.   Every issue can be made the beginning of an attack on
the government.   Every issue is potentially one of confidence or no confidence and therefore no issue can be met merely on the basis of its merits in
balance of power terms.   Governments stand or fall on the unity of the
total issue, and not on the foreign issue alone. . . .

Operationally as well as conceptually, therefore, democracy is characterized by the likelihood of the intrusion of policy motivations incompatible
with balance of power rules.   Commercial and economic interests of all
kinds, local military and naval considerations, clashing ideological aspirations unrelated to physical interests, varying conceptions of national security, not to mention the sudden and "irrational" foreign policy decisions
which may be attributable solely to the exigencies of domestic politics are
all present in democratic decision-making.   Consistent adherence to balance of power rules would seem to demand the relative isolation of the
policy-makers from the turmoil of day-to-day politics. . . .

*   *   *

A democratic society recognizes the validity of a variety of motivations.
The more pluralistic a society grows the greater the number of motivations
which enter the political process.   Consequently the definition of the national interest tends to grow more difficult and the practical application of
the national interest tends to vary more and more with every change in government or shift in party emphasis.   The power motivation is obscured; its
demands must constantly be compromised with the requirements of other
motivations, equally valid in democracy; and when these other motivations
happen to contradict the demands of power, the balance of power does not
and cannot act as a guide to policy-making. . . .

Pierre M. Gallois

POWER AND PARALYSIS

Undoubtedly it was the priority given to the affairs of Southeast Asia that masked from the U.S. State Department the important destabilizing effects of the Egyptian military preparations this spring. It was widely known in Europe that since the end of 1966 the Soviet Union had been building up the Egyptian arsenal and that, in quantity if not in quality, the equilibrium of forces in the Middle East was being upset. Moscow, seeking to appear as the protector of Islam, attempted to exploit American indifference toward both Middle East affairs and West European dependence on Arab oil. Profiting from American inattention, the Soviets proposed to increase their influence in the Middle East; to extend their existing military "facilities" in that part of the world; to invest first the eastern and then the western Mediterranean; and to control indirectly the sources of energy on which the East European economy depends.

In the Middle East the USSR had nothing to lose; on the contrary, she had everything to gain. A victory by the Arab forces would stand to her credit, and defeat could only push the vanquished into even further dependence on Moscow. Without the abettor taking any great risks, there were prospects that the status quo could be modified. The Kremlin, though remaining within the bounds of prudence as regards the risks inherent in its foreign policies, had no qualms about the strengthening of Egypt's military means.

Absorbed in Asia and negotiating with the Soviets at Geneva and elsewhere, the U.S. State Department could react only feebly. . . .

*   *   *

. . . After the outbreak of hostilities, it was not the United States' declaration of moral and material neutrality which modified the Soviet position, but rather the victorious turn that the Israeli High Command, its forces surrounded on all sides, was able to give to the military operations. . . .

. . . Today not a single Israeli citizen can be unaware of the isolation in which his country suddenly found itself. For him, it is clear that it is difficult to balance the addition of Soviet power to the strength the Arab masses represent, and that American good wishes and world power can only succeed in getting the *fait accompli* accepted, but not in forestalling it.

Thus the Middle East crisis confirmed a truth as old as the collapse of the U.S. nuclear monopoly and the truce between the two great "sanctuary" states: A confrontation between the two "Greats" on behalf of third parties

Reprinted by permission of the publisher from *Orbis,* 11, 3 (Fall 1967), pp. 664–676. ORBIS, a quarterly journal of world affairs, published and copyrighted by the Foreign Policy Research Institute, Philadelphia, Pa.

is excluded, and, paralyzed by the fear of one another, they can do nothing but accept *faits accomplis*.   In the Far East the two communisms, that of China and that of the USSR, preferring to avoid direct participation in the Vietnamese conflict, have decided to acquiesce in the large-scale destruction of North Viet Nam's military forces, industrial complexes and transportation arteries.   Of the natural, if not the formal, alliance between Moscow, Peking and Hanoi, little remains.   To the modification of the Middle East *status quo ante,* favored by the Soviets, Washington began by opposing an intellectual, verbal and material neutrality that could only encourage the relatively timid pro-Arab policy of the Soviets.   In the end, Israel supplied them both with the *fait accompli.*

II

Israel knows now that in order to prepare the way for her diplomacy—a case of vital necessity today—she must count, more than she expected, on her own moral, human and material resources.   Her area tripled, her population doubled, her frontiers finally conforming to the strategic conditions of her survival, she projects on the altered map the state she ought to be, if only she did not encompass such a strong Arab minority.   But despite the serious difficulties inherent in the fact that they are inhabited by Muslims, it is evident that Tel Aviv's trump cards are the territories Israel occupies.   This time the politics of the *fait accompli* and the helplessness of the two "Greats" when they are face to face worked in favor of Israel.

Does anyone seriously envisage Moscow taking up arms—or even sending "volunteers"—to dislodge the Israelis from the Gaza Strip, the West Bank territories, or the Sinai?   Such a direct armed intervention in the Middle East would be possible only if Washington declared that the events in Asia were monopolizing all its attention and resources, thus leaving Moscow free to act in the eastern Mediterranean. . . .   Its victory gives Israel possibilities for maneuver that the Arab governments do not have.   The latter know that the United States will intervene no more on the side of Israel than the USSR does on their side.   The situation evolves as if the two "Greats" had neutralized each other.   The trumps of future negotiations are naturally in the hands of the victors.

Taking into account their recent experiences, one can conceive that certain Israelis are seeking to establish the security of their country on a wholly new basis.   Where can oil be found if not in the Sinai?   And how can the defense of the State of Israel be assured—using conventional armaments—without disposing of important reserves of fuel?   Moreover, should it become necessary to renounce part of their recent territorial conquests, how could the Israelis carry the day a third time starting from a strategic situation as unfavorable as that prior to June 1967?   If the Arab air forces had been capable of striking by surprise, the fate of Israel would have been seriously compromised.   What government wants to depend uniquely on the errors and weaknesses of its adversaries?

Without much difficulty Israel should be able to create an atomic force capable of protecting its independence and its sovereignty over the entire country of Palestine.   Such an equilibrium could be easily established even in the eyes of the leaders of an Arab coalition.   These leaders—including the somewhat irrational ones among them—know quite well that there is no common scale of measurement for the risks one must take in sending armored divisions a few miles into enemy territory; despite Moscow's readiness to lend a helping hand in case of failure, an Israeli nuclear response would be instantaneous and devastating.   On her side, Israel is familiar with the inconveniences of her geographic situation.   Easily deprived of supplies, lacking the capacity to conduct lengthy conventional operations or sustain a war of attrition, Tel Aviv would have every interest in banking on the menace of taking recourse to weapons of mass destruction.   Everything urges Israel to endow herself with the means of pursuing a policy of nuclear deterrence: her concentration of brain-power, the smallness of her territory, the permanent Arab encirclement, and the devastating effects that a surprise attack directed against conventional forces, especially the Israeli Air Force, could have had in the spring of 1967.   Certainly, nuclear arms will be ineffective against internal guerrilla warfare and armed incursions from abroad on her soil.   To these menaces Israel must respond with analogous instruments.   But the existence of the State of Israel would be assured. The risk of menacing its survival would be exorbitant.

III

The recent events in the Middle East create a new situation.   In seeking above all to reach an accommodation with its former adversary, Washington has condemned to death—quite involuntarily, it is true—the nonproliferation of nuclear arms for which, elsewhere, the two "Greats" are willing to make such sacrifices.

Such a contradiction is inherent in the opposition that exists between the development of technology and traditional political concepts.   The statesmen who conduct the world's business have for the most part remained tradition-bound by virtue of the education they have received and the lessons they have been accustomed to draw from the observation of events. Because in America more than elsewhere scientific and technical progress is extremely rapid, the divorce between the real meaning of events and their common understanding appears to be most rending.   The confusion is great.   It is also shocking and paradoxical.

Within twenty years the Great Powers—beginning with the United States —have lost a monopoly of force that no one has even dreamed of contesting.   Yesterday, i.e., on the morrow of the Second World War, the numerical size of the population was militarily decisive. It permitted the mobilization of millions of combatants. Today, four thousand sailors on board a dozen Polaris submarines are capable of doing more damage than all the millions of Second World War soldiers. Yesterday, the arming of the mobilized masses gave heavy industry a determining role, and, in order to raise land, sea and air forces, one had to rely on a Pittsburgh, a Cleveland, a Magnitogorsk or Ruhr. Today, these huge industrial complexes are superfluous for constructing a dozen submarines and a few hundred missiles. Yesterday, the extent of one's territory was strategically the most important factor. Hitler found this out when he hurled his divisions against Stalingrad. Today, ballistic missiles annul distances. Yesterday, oceans or buffer states appeared to afford a protective glacis. This form of protection no longer exists.

Not by the irony of fate, but rather because their power permitted them to play the role of pioneers, the United States with the atom and the Soviet Union with the missile have bequeathed to the rest of the world a weapons technology that has partially destroyed the demographic, industrial and geographic advantages they alone possessed. It is not surprising that today they seek to limit the diffusion of a weapons technology capable of compromising the policy of hegemony to which their power naturally predisposed them. But it is no more surprising that other states attempt to exploit to their own profit the military and political possibilities of the new weapons. . . .

In the world as it is currently constituted no one doubts that only the United States and the Soviet Union can practice power politics (*politique de puissance*). According to the nature of their human or material means the other states have but two possibilities. Some can try to defend their neutrality. Others have no solution but to play out, in one form or another, the politics of subordination (*politique de dépendance*), whether political, diplomatic, technological or economic. Since Hiroshima, and especially since the advent of strategic missiles, the politics of power, of defense and of subordination have taken on a new meaning which must now be defined.

By power politics we mean the ability of the two "Greats"—and they only—to erect for themselves an inviolable "sanctuary" against each other and, a fortiori, everyone else too, while also commanding enough resources to intervene in areas beyond their own soil. This intervention they carry out with conventional arms in marginal conflicts to assure themselves advantages which are certainly important, but not vital, and which, if necessary, could be lost without compromising their existence as nations. The United States, like the USSR, constitutes a sanctuary. Moreover, in certain circumstances both Powers can intervene in force outside their homelands with conventional arms, as the Soviet Union did in Hungary in 1956 and as now—for entirely different reasons—the United States is doing in Viet Nam. For these two countries, provided that their vital interests are not in jeopardy, war remains that "continuation of politics by other means" which Clausewitz wrote about. Security of the homeland has devolved upon nuclear deterrence, while outside American territory—or Soviet territory—crises are "managed" or fought by the threat or use of conventional weapons.

IV

But as we have just seen in the Middle East, this kind of power politics has its limits. Face to face, the two "Greats" neutralize each other. Moscow has not intervened directly in support of its North Vietnamese ally and Washington was not able to prevent the Arab-Israeli war of June 1967 by seeking to secure Cairo's adherence to the 1957 agreement on freedom of navigation in the Strait of Tiran. Tacitly, the two Powers recognize some interests which they mutually want to respect, even if their respective allies pay the costs of this entente.

Neither Great Britain nor France has this dual capability of the "Greats": to safeguard the homeland and intervene militarily outside of it. They lack the necessary resources for intervention with conventional arms. The 1956 Suez affair showed that even together Great Britain and France are not able to interfere in "other people's business" without provoking an understanding between Moscow and Washington which is directed against them and their foreign policy interests. . . . On the other hand, the governments of London and Paris each have recourse to the atom in order to implement a minimum military policy: that of assuring the security of their national territory. The nuclear arms that each possesses guarantee their basic survival. At least that is the ostensible objective. Those who speak of a *politique de grandeur* (notably France's) have understood neither the political consequences of the coming of the new weapons nor the goals London and Paris wish to attain by forging their respective nuclear arsenals. As far as they are concerned, it is not so much a question of power politics as of the politics of defense.

The other states—insofar as they lack nuclear arms and take the proper measure of their resources, position on the map and ideological affinity—can practice only the politics of subordination, at least as long as they are not themselves theaters of the marginal conflicts in which the two "Greats" are indirectly opposed. Germany depends for the integrity of her territory on the United States, from which she buys her security. For the same reason Italy makes analogous concessions. India asks the assistance of three states in order to escape from the more severe exigencies of a single protector. Korea yesterday and Viet Nam today serve as jousting grounds for the adherents of two different ideologies.

It is normal that a government will try to pass from this last category into the second, thereby raising its status, thanks to the possession of a national nuclear arsenal, from a state of subordination to that of "sanctuary." This step compromises the Kennedy dream of a bipolar world, organized around Washington and Moscow. One can understand why the beneficiaries of this dream are still holding on to it and why the other states, moved by contrary interests, are seeking in multipolarity a solution which is more advantageous for themselves.

Even more than the USSR, the United States is at the origin of this geopolitical transformation of the world. In the forefront of scientific progress she bequeathed a technology to other countries which accelerates their transformation and modifies their position on the chessboard of world politics. However, America refuses to make allowance for the true international consequences of its own scientific and technological accomplishments. Thus, for example, in the domain of armaments the combination of nuclear explosives and the long-range missile has considerably increased the vulnerability of all civilian targets, while the decisive weapons are becoming more and more invulnerable. Consequently, the traditional goals of warfare are inverted. Yesterday, the objective of armed confrontations was the destruction of the enemy's armed forces and the conquest of his "valuables." Today, if there should be a war between nuclear powers, they could only destroy their respective "valuables" without annihilating their forces. The absurdity of such a form of fighting is so evident that an entente among nuclear powers is imperative. But this entente, while guaranteeing the vital interests of the atomic states, does not cover those of the others, even if they are friends and allies. That is why, since the new weapons have been forged, military alliances have hardly any meaning. This is as true for the East as it is for the West.

V

Insofar as its interests are concerned, the U.S. government has taken this new fact into account, notably since 1961. Yet one can reproach it for having sought to put its European allies on a false scent by leading them to believe that the new strategic situation has not altered the guarantee implicitly given them in 1950 and reaffirmed in 1956 in the NATO Council of Ministers. . . .

It was American experts themselves who, over the years, demonstrated to the Allied General Staffs in Europe the total incompatibility between conventional warfare and atomic warfare. They showed that in the same theater it was not possible to prepare for one form of war and wage the other; that the atom precluded the building up of men and matériel; that it is not necessary to possess considerable logistic facilities; that the conflict would take place in the space of a few hours, if not a few minutes; and that the aggressor, counting on surprise, would permit neither maneuvers nor mobilization. By contrast, conventional war demands large concentrations of men and matériel; requires a bulky logistical system; and unfolds as a function of time, permitting maneuvers on the field and also the mobilization of the belligerent's resources.   The two systems are mutually exclusive, like fire and water.

Several years after General Taylor's candid exposé, other American experts, striving to justify the strategic change-of-course of the United States, declared exactly the opposite.   They now hailed the role of naval surface fleets, which had been denigrated ever since Hiroshima: suddenly, with the unveiling of the MLF proposal, surface vessels became invulnerable.   The North Atlantic Treaty Organization could not stand up to these contradictions.   Washington's part of the responsibility for its discomfort was considerable.

But if the United States has not yet understood that the Europeans have clearly perceived the consequences of the strategic transformation wrought by the new weapons, the Europeans, for their part, have not grasped the American attitude in Southeast Asia.   Paris, London, Rome or Bonn should be aware of the analogy which might exist between Atlantic Europe of 1950 and, let us say, Pacific Asia of 1970.

In Europe, beginning in 1950 and for some years thereafter, the Soviet Union had a total atomic monopoly.   But the Russian nuclear arsenal was incomplete.   It would have permitted Moscow to intimidate its neighbors but not to attack American territory itself.   NATO, and especially the presence of American troops from Norway to Turkey, discouraged all thoughts of atomic blackmail until around 1962.   At that time the monopoly of long-range strategic weapons was broken, and the USSR and the United States began to come to terms, sometimes to the detriment of the interests of their respective allies.

Around 1970, China will have a monopoly of nuclear weapons in Asia. This monopoly will be meaningful with respect to the neighboring countries, but without effect against American territory, as was the case of the Soviet nuclear weapons from 1950 to 1962.   Just as in Europe, where the presence of American troops warded off atomic blackmail, so in Asia Washington might take recourse to the same policy of creating a "presence."   To its forces already installed in Korea, Taiwan, Viet Nam and Thailand the United States could add new contingents destined for countries it judged to be menaced by Peking.   Observers, advisers, administrators and constabulary would accompany these forces.   But the United States will find itself deeply involved in Asia in an unexpected and, for the American people, particularly distasteful way: America will become the protagonist of neocolonialism.

Within these perspectives, the war that is ravaging unhappy Viet Nam takes on another meaning.   To the earlier reasons for fighting, i.e., the struggle against communism and maintenance of a South Viet Nam independent of the Hanoi government, new reasons are added: limitation of Chinese expansionism and mastery of the Pacific.   Can the United States act otherwise?   To simplify a very complex situation, is not the United States facing alternatives of which pulling back on itself—isolationism—is one choice, and a policy of creating a "presence" and neocolonialism is the other?   When a country attains a certain degree of power its interests are worldwide, and no matter what its ethics may be, it uses force to protect these interests.   That is how the colonial powers of the eighteenth and nineteenth centuries acted.   In the modern world, by renouncing the dogma of "nonproliferation" and by furnishing certain Asian countries with the means of imposing the status quo on China, Washington would have a way of escaping from its dilemma.   But, and here is the other contradiction inherent in the U.S. position, the "proliferation" of the new weapons is no more admissible than the *de facto* colonialism from which this "proliferation" would permit the United States—partially—to escape.

*   *   *

VI

One of the characteristics of these times is that it is difficult for the government of a democratic country to conduct an intelligent foreign policy for want of being able to make its public understand the facts.   Totalitarian countries have a singular advantage in this respect.   Their governments do not have to give an account of themselves, and, if they do, it is before a small committee constituted generally of experts, and not before the masses whose reactions are more emotional than rational.   Some of the weaknesses of American diplomacy have certainly had their origin in the political and social system of the United States.

Nevertheless, if there is an important domain where government and public opinion should be in easy and complete accord, it is the necessity of winning the scientific and technological race that the Great Powers are running.   Everything depends on the outcome of this new form of competition.

The rate of "turnover" of modern weapons is essentially dependent on the scientific and technological environment of a country.   This "turnover," indispensable to the security and freedom of action of countries still able to engage in the politics of power, is marked by increasingly precipitous technological developments.   But what is more serious is the growing discrepancy between the lead time needed to develop a new weapons system and the diplomatic and political perspective that gives us foreknowledge of the conditions under which these new arms will be used.   Only yesterday governments were able to provide themselves with the instruments of a policy of force with a view toward using them under predictable circumstances. Hitler, as he began the rearmament of Germany in 1933, knew that he was creating instruments of combat that he would be able to use four or five years later—in a situation rendered particularly favorable by his diplomacy. Between political action and the turnover of weapons there could be a coincidence in time, the former preparing the way for the effective use of the latter.

Such a synchronization is impossible today. While technologically advanced weapons systems demand lead times of between six and ten years, a matching long-term political forecast is likely to be inexact or impossible. No matter how farfetched a political context may be, no matter how simple the means of actions envisaged to attain by force whatever ends a government may posit, it is no longer possible to synchronize the forging of arms for tomorrow with the prediction of conditions under which they might eventually be utilized.

Certain people in the United States have grasped this new fact perfectly. The Soviet Union has understood it as well. The resulting necessity is to substitute something new for the method of sequential political-military planning. This innovation is the cyclical development of weapons systems aimed at maintaining a constant superiority vis-à-vis the eventual adversary. Only material resources can limit the schemes of the developers. In short, maintaining this superiority depends on exploring everything that can be explored and on searching in all directions. By raising the level of a country's research, a scientific and technological establishment of the highest quality can be created, constantly kept up to date and available to the General Staffs. Their wishes will, of course, have to be reconciled with the financial resources of the moment.

This turnover of modern weapons contains the menace that new decisive weapons may be discovered. In the nuclear age we no longer have wars of attrition as in the past, with their slow and mutual adaptation of techniques and tactics on the part of the belligerents. Now, there could be at any time a breakthrough which destroys the validity of previous efforts and leads to a totally new orientation of the arms competition. The possibility of a technological breakthrough imposes a certain flexibility on armaments plans. One never commits oneself all the way before being assured—if such an assurance is possible—of the life-span and the value of a proposed weapon.

As infrequent as it was in the past, the succession of weapon after weapon is now integrated into the national life of the two superpowers. Heretofore, governments were able to create the means of pursuing a policy of force which they could foresee and for the execution of which they could plan. A similar initiative is no longer possible. Today, political strategy is conditioned by the current state of the weapons turnover. That is why a technological war involving the advanced industrial states has replaced the Cold War of the preceding period. In this new confrontation the most effective scientific and technological efforts are the surest guarantors of independent existence. It is not only imperative that the American people place this task in the front range of their preoccupations, but that they concede that other states, beginning with their friends, may do so as well. For thus these states, too, can affirm their right to existence.

Wilfrid Knapp

THE COLD WAR REVISED

Until recently the history of the Cold War was recounted in terms of an energetic defence on the part of the major western democracies—Britain and the United States, France, and later the Federal Republic of Germany—against the pressures and subversion of a Communist world bent on expanding its borders and influence. The revision of this thesis to which historians have invited us—since the appearance in 1959 of the first edition of W. A. Williams' *The Tragedy of American Foreign Policy* and, two years later, of D. F. Fleming's *The Cold War and Its Origins, 1917–1960*— puts American foreign policy in a different perspective, suggests that the Soviet Union was motivated in its foreign policy by fear and fear alone, and sometimes goes even further to suggest that all the evils which Westerners have seen in communism are the creation of their own misguided attempts to contain it.

The orthodox view rested on the assumption that the United States and its allies were status quo powers seeking no major extension of their own influence; that they were free societies which valued democratic government, uniting to preserve their own freedom (as they had signally failed to do before 1939) and ready to help others who were threatened by subversion or the possibility of invasion. The threat came from Russia and its satellite Communist states and parties: later (though here the story has never been so clear) from China. In varying degrees revisionists have questioned these assumptions, or at least their relevance to the conflicts of the Cold War. Louis Halle—though scarcely a revisionist—has argued that "The Cold War . . . represents an historical necessity to which the Communist movement is incidental rather than essential"; he . . . asserts that "what the Revolution of 1917 did was simply to reinvigorate the traditional principle of authoritarianism in Russia."[1] "Reinvigorate" is perhaps too weak a word. The difference between the way in which the Soviet Union conducts its affairs and the way any of the major democratic countries conduct their affairs is strikingly evident even on such a superficial level as the memoirs of two diplomats—very different in their abilities— which have recently been published.[2] Ivan Maisky moved in a free and open society even in wartime Britain. George Kennan, in contrast, returned to Moscow at the end of the war to find that the wartime alliance had changed nothing in the isolation of foreign diplomats. "We were sin-

Reprinted by permission from *International Journal*, 5, 23 Toronto (Summer 1968), pp. 344–356.

[1] Louis J. Halle, *The Cold War as History* (New York, 1967), pp. 11, 12.

[2] Ivan Maisky, *Memoirs of a Soviet Ambassador* (London, 1967); George F. Kennan, *Memoirs, 1925–1950* (Boston, 1967).

cerely moved by the sufferings of the Russian people as well as by the heroism and patience they were showing in the face of wartime adversity. We wished them nothing but well. It was doubly hard, in these circumstances, to find ourselves treated as though we were the bearers of some species of the plague." [3] Postwar Russia was a society deep-ridden with suspicion, one where the people were only told of V.E. day in the west the day after Britain and America accepted the surrender of German forces lest they should continue to fight in the east.

There are two levels at which this difference in the conduct of affairs affects the conduct of international relations. It makes the exchange of signals and communication between the two sides unusually difficult. The postwar settlement and the possibility of a reunification of Germany and Europe, which would require the highest arts of diplomacy, were set in the context of inordinately obstructed communication. But on a more fundamental level, and going back in time, the effect of the Bolshevik revolution was to undermine the presuppositions of the relations between states. Nothing is more basic to the conduct of such relations than an assumption of the legitimacy of national governments; but such legitimacy the Bolsheviks questioned from the start and, with decreasing optimism, devised their foreign policies on the assumption that their rivals would be overthrown. Apologists for the Bolsheviks maintain that tsarist autocracy could have been overthrown and a new society established only by a force as radical, ruthless, and determined as that of the Bolsheviks. They may or may not be right. But the Bolsheviks denied that other societies, such as the democracies of Western Europe, were any more capable of reform than tsarist Russia. It was an argument which Britain, France, and the United States had every reason to reject, just as they resisted the political activism, inspired and financed by Moscow, which went with it.

The point is relevant to the time scale of the new literature on the relationship between the Soviet Union and the West. Louis Halle believes that "from the beginning in the ninth century, and even today, the prime driving force in Russia has been fear"; but Denna Fleming places the origin of the Cold War in 1917. . .[4] Revisionists of the Fleming school may find fresh ammunition in the two scholarly works (certainly not written with this intention) by Arno Mayer and John M. Thompson.[5] A new perspective is given to the negotiation of the Versailles Treaty in detailed examination of the way in which "individually and collectively the Big Four spent more time on the Russian question than on any other major issue." [6] But the allied leaders scarcely emerge as the single-minded opponents of commu-

---

[3] Kennan, *Memoirs,* p. 195.

[4] Halle, *Cold War as History,* p. 12; Fleming, *Cold War and Its Origins,* chapters I and II.

[5] Arno Mayer, *The Politics of Peacemaking* (London, 1967); John M. Thompson, *Russia, Bolshevism and the Versailles Peace* (Princeton, 1967).

[6] Mayer, *Peacemaking,* p. 284.

nism that they have sometimes been depicted. . . . Opposed to the Bolshevik régime they certainly were; they neither wanted nor expected it to survive. Lenin's government was a double danger; it prevented the reestablishment of the balance of power in Europe, and it was the source of contagious ideas which could spread across the continent. But it was not a sufficient threat to bring a softer German treaty (as Lloyd George urged). The consequent failure to include Russia in a general settlement meant that Poland and Rumania achieved aggrandizement at Russia's expense. Revision of the German settlement twenty years later was bound to upset that in eastern Europe.

Although the Bolshevik government was thought to be weak and evanescent, there was constant debate on the best means to expedite its end. While help was given in an ill co-ordinated and ultimately ineffective way to the White armies, all the dilemmas of a more recent period, the arguments, and the rival positions were taken up—not the least of the dilemmas resulting from the absence of a moderate force, a middle way between Lenin and Kolchak. . . .

When World War II drew to an end the Soviet régime was undoubtedly very different. It had survived—and continued to survive—the aftermath of the foreign war which had been so fateful to the old monarchy. The contagion of its idealism was still a powerful force, enlisting the support of hard-core militants and more fickle followers in Western Europe and providing the stiff backbone of left-wing movements in Asia. Stalin was not much of an ideologist and had long since led his country away from a crusading revolutionary ideal. But he nonetheless remained at the head of a well-organized international Communist movement. He could no more ignore foreign Communist parties, and pretend that they did not exist, than an imperial ruler could disregard his colonies. . . .

Communism has always evoked phobias, which can be identified and put aside. The early ideology of the movement and its subsequent institutional organization still make its behaviour in international affairs different from that of Western governments. . . . On any count Stalin was a statesman nurtured in a system and ideology of which distrust was the centre and core; and his disposition exaggerated and deepened his suspicions to an infinite extent. . . . [T]he revisionist thesis states that Stalin sought security in the area of Europe closest to Russia's frontiers but does not relate his undoubted quest for security in the international area to the demands he made for his own safety, in terms of the great purges and terror of the 'thirties in the Soviet Union itself.

These considerations must be borne in mind when the new evidence—and equally important the new interpretation of old evidence—is examined, particularly in relation to the end of the war and the beginnings of the Soviet-American conflict. The examination is in any case like listening to one side of a telephone conversation—with a scrambler even on the side we can hear. United States government has never been noted for its clear lines of command and communication, and this is a period in which, we are told, a Russian request for a loan was lost by the State Department.   A high degree of scholarship is called for to interpret published United States documents and memoirs, to know for sure who was giving the orders and who was not only being listened to by the President but was actually influencing his policies. From the other, Soviet, side we still have no worthwhile background noise.   The point is important because of the two aspects of revisionism.   Gar Alperovitz . . . is scrupulously careful to point out that he has written about American foreign policy; his work "is not an attempt to offer a detailed review of *Soviet* policy" even though it "must inevitably deal with Soviet actions and reactions." [7]   Other writers are less cautious. They claim to interpret Soviet foreign policy on the basis of slender evidence; they go further and affirm or suggest that the harsh policies of the Soviet Union in Eastern Europe only came about in reaction to American pressures.

From the many points at issue in the present argument about the transition from World War II to the Cold War, those which stand out most clearly are the relation between Roosevelt's policy and that of Truman, the question of spheres of influence, atomic diplomacy, and the Polish question.

*   *   *

Gar Alperovitz has said that "Roosevelt's strong belief that co-operation was possible died with the President," and he has convincingly shown Truman's readiness to take a stand against the Russians, enhanced by the security and strength which the atomic bomb seemed to provide.   There is, however, evidence that Roosevelt's belief weakened before his death. He wrote to Stalin: "You are, I am sure, aware that genuine popular support in the U.S. is required to carry out any government policy, foreign or domestic.   The American people make up their own mind and no government action can change it.   I mention this fact because the last sentence of your message about Mr. Molotov's attendance at San Francisco made me wonder whether you give full weight to this factor."   Such references to public opinion were amongst the things that Kennan most deplored in the conduct of foreign policy, but they often form a means of conveying a warning of a politician's intentions in foreign policy. . . .   Roosevelt, it seems, expected conflict with Russia over China and had no intention of sharing atomic secrets with Russia.   It is thus an exaggeration to speak of "co-operation" between Roosevelt and Stalin.   There was little enough of it during the war.   As victory drew near Roosevelt's view was the more despairing one that Russia would dominate Europe after the war, that it

[7] Gar Alperovitz, *Atomic Diplomacy: Hiroshima and Potsdam* (New York, 1965), p. 13.

was in the American interest to make the best of a bad job and in the Europeans' (excluding Britain) to make the best of a worse one.   He is reported as saying: "European countries will have to undergo tremendous changes in order to adapt to Russia, but he hoped that in ten or twenty years the European influences would bring the Russians to become less barbarian." [8]

The point illustrates the gap between the re-examination of detail which Alperovitz has undertaken and the more sweeping comments of authors like David Horowitz and Fleming.   "Roosevelt and Hull had, throughout the war and in the structure of the United Nations, patiently constructed a basis for long-time collaboration with the Soviet Union." [9]   Thus Fleming; yet it was Roosevelt and Hull who, in the early days of the American war, had restrained the British in any recognition of one of the first requirements of Stalinist defence policy—the Baltic states—and thus contributed to the first misunderstanding over the opening of a second front.

Playing from weakness towards the end of the war Roosevelt fell into the contradictory policies of spheres of influence and the Yalta declaration on Eastern Europe.   Hitherto the United States had fluctuated between isolationism and a universalist foreign policy.   Now, drawn on by Churchill, it moved towards spheres of influence.   Alperovitz emphasizes Roosevelt's acceptance of the Churchill-Stalin agreement of October 1944. But while Stalin kept to his agreement with Churchill when the British intervened in Greece, Roosevelt dissociated himself from the British action.   So indecisive was the United States on spheres of influence that it could not even cash in on the credit side of Churchill's deal.

If the idea of spheres of influence was alien to traditional American foreign policy, it was also, in the Stalinist world, a new concept.   The secrecy of the closed society of Russia and the dominance of the Kremlin over the Communist parties of the world left no grey edges to Stalinist power.   It needed more than the brief experience of the armistice to convince Western leaders that Stalin's long-term policy was to install in Rumania, Bulgaria, or Hungary a government fundamentally different from that of the Soviet Union and of the international Communist world.

Only the more extreme revisionists have suggested that Russian policy in the Baltic states and Poland has been misinterpreted.   In this area Stalin gained most without having to overcome any resistance from his allies.   The Baltic states were incorporated into the Soviet Union—they receive scant treatment from the revisionists, as if they had little right to exist.   The western movement of frontiers was not seriously challenged. Stalin's insistence that Poland was a matter of life and death for the So-

---

[8] Printed in Robert I. Gannon, *The Cardinal Spellman Story* (New York, 1962) and cited by Geoffrey Warner, "From Teheran to Yalta: Reflections on F.D.R.'s Foreign Policy," *International Affairs*, XLIII (July, 1967), 533.

[9] Fleming, *Cold War and Its Origins*, I, 331.

viet Union was taken at its face value—and nowhere has a double standard been more often applied subsequently than in the assumption that Poland had to bow to Russian security needs rather than be protected from the historical rapacity of its neighbours.

Poland had not attacked Russia in 1939, whatever the follies of its foreign policies and its encroachments on Russia since the restoration of its independence at Versailles. But the occupation of eastern Poland by the Russians was accompanied by the deportation of hundreds of thousands of Poles into Russia—Vishinsky admitted a partial estimate of 387,932; Kennan estimated 1.2 million, the London Poles 1.6. Although the evidence will never be conclusive the Katyn graves seem attributable to the Russians. Arthur Schlesinger accepts that the Russians could not, for military reasons, give support to the Home Army in the Warsaw rising; but their failure to do so is consistent with the whole pattern of policy towards Poland (including Stalin's purge of the Polish Communist party in the 1930s). Their radio encouraged the Poles to rise against the Germans and they then made it difficult and costly for the British and Americans to air-drop supplies.

It was at this point that Kennan would have initiated the policy of "showdown": "this was the moment when, if ever, there should have been a full-fledged and realistic political showdown with the Soviet leaders: when they should have been confronted with the choice between changing their policy completely and agreeing to collaborate in the establishment of truly independent countries in Eastern Europe or forfeiting Western-Allied support and sponsorship for the remaining phases of their war effort." [10] It was the issue which most excited the anxieties of Churchill—the chief proponent of spheres of influence. Michael Howard's work [11] of "revisionism in reverse" has finally laid the legend of Churchill's attempt to influence the political outcome in Europe by a Balkan strategy (since he thought the Balkans were lost to the Russians anyway). And it also reiterates the importance of Poland in changing British attitudes. ("How, after the fall of Warsaw, any responsible statesman could trust any Russian Communist further than he could kick him, passes the comprehension of ordinary men" wrote Sir John Slessor,[12] who was responsible for the Warsaw airdrops.) Stalin could now afford the cat and mouse game which continued until Mikolajzcyk's escape from Poland after the war. The shift of frontiers to the west had given Russia territorial security and made a future Poland dependent on the Soviet Union in its relations with Germany. When Hopkins talked with Stalin in May 1945, Stalin said

[10] Kennan, *Memoirs,* p. 211.

[11] Michael Howard, *The Mediterranean Strategy in the Second World War* (London, 1966).

[12] Sir John Slessor, *The Central Blue: Recollections and Reflections* (London, 1956), p. 612.

that of course everyone understood about democratic government in Poland—but there must be limitations *in time of war* (so much for the fine promise of peace, three weeks after the war had ended). With magnanimity he reacted to Hopkins' request that the sixteen underground leaders be released by promising "lenient treatment."

Essentially the revisionist thesis is a simple one: that we hit the Russians first, and that such were their justifiable anxieties for their own security, especially after the atomic explosion, that they responded with the clamp-down in Eastern Europe and apparently aggressive policies elsewhere. Hence the infinite regress, back to 1917, or back ten centuries, to find a first cause. But the Polish example suggests how high the price had to be, even if it were paid, to make Russia feel secure. If in addition one had to pay for Communists to act against their nature—for the Ulbrichts and Gottwalds . . . not to behave as Communists then did, not to admire and copy the Soviet Union, not to accept and be themselves entrapped by the Russian secret police—how high would the price then have had to be to give Stalin the sense of security in international affairs that he had never succeeded in creating for himself within his own dominion?

The question is relevant to the new character of postwar diplomacy created by the atomic bomb. Alperovitz has stressed the relation of the bomb to the diplomacy of 1945—the prospect and then the actuality of having the Far Eastern war out of the way *and* the atomic weapon in hand. Scrupulously he avoids a firm conclusion as to the importance of the Russian question in the decision to use the bomb. In so far as he discusses the question he reads into the history of 1945 the moral attitudes and the fears of the present; once men were hardened to the bombing raids on Germany and Japan the arguments *against* use of the bomb would have had to be overwhelming to persuade the President to give up the possibility of ensuring victory without invasion and without the complications of Russian intervention. But equally the evidence does not show that the war was prolonged in order to permit the development of the bomb and its demonstration. For perhaps the only time the atomic weapon was used as a prelude to de-escalation.

Once the bomb existed it inevitably complicated the balance of power in international politics. Stimson—who in the 1930s had thought non-recognition would help limit Japanese expansion and then at the beginning of 1945 hoped that the success of the Manhattan project was worth waiting for because of the added strength it would bring to the American hand—now wanted (in September 1945) to offer the secret of the bomb as part of an approach to Russia to control and limit its use. He believed that "the only way you can make a man trustworthy is to trust him." A direct approach of the kind Stimson imagined was not made. For four years the United States retained its monopoly of the bomb. But it did not bring security, and it may be that the insecurity on both sides—the Soviet Union under the shadow of the bomb, the United States weak in ground forces—brought an acceleration of the momentum of the Cold War.   Only when the whiz kids entered the Pentagon were serious studies made of the real strength of Soviet forces in Europe; while their strength had been over-estimated so had the possibility of attack.

To the extent that the atomic bomb created this dual insecurity, frighten-ing the Russians without giving confidence to the Americans, it was a tragic development; it is hard to imagine that a major power would offer the secrets of its weapons to a rival in international affairs.   The extent to which the United States' possession of the bomb did accelerate the Cold War remains indeterminate.   There is no new evidence to change what ap-pear to have been Russian intentions in Berlin from the time when they entered the city—to establish exclusive control if the Western powers let them.[13]   Following Kennan, one may regret the crusading terms in which the Truman doctrine was enunciated; but the Marshall offer came between the Truman doctrine and the Czech coup. . . .   As Czechoslovakia was brought into the bloc, Yugoslavia was pushed out into the cold.   If Tito's Yugoslavia did not meet the demands which the suspicious Stalin and his police state made in the pursuit of their own security, could those demands conceivably have been met without weakening and destroying the whole of Western Europe?

In retrospect the Korean war remains a turning point, and one about which we are still uninformed; the kind of argument which David Horo-witz uses to explain its origin was used at the time and is no better sub-stantiated now than it was then.   It does not now seem that it was a pre-lude to Russian forward moves against Western positions in Europe—and at the time many of us believed that American insistence on German re-armament was an over-reaction which threatened the whole development of European unity.   Even more did scholars in Britain feel deeply anxious about a confrontation with the Chinese in Korea and never believed in "branding China as the aggressor."   Revisionism in this area is an Ameri-can phenomenon; many of us have no need of it.

By this time the policy of containment had acquired its own position and its own ideology—and the possibility of de-escalating the Cold War when it had "got us over a difficult time" was by no means easy.   In the United States it had proved impossible to create sufficient public commit-ment to finance the Marshall Plan without also invoking a more strident ideology.   In addition the reconstruction of Western Germany and Western Europe meant that much more was at risk in negotiations towards the un-certain objective of unification.   In spite of Soviet overtures after the death

[13] It is notable that David Horowitz (*The Free World Colossus: A Critique of American Foreign Policy in the Cold War* (New York, 1965), p. 84n) discusses the Berlin blockade in little more than the end of a lengthy footnote, concluding that the Russians "lifted the Blockade just at the time that the airlift would have ceased to be feasible."

of Stalin, the prospect of reaching a satisfactory reconciliation of Soviet and Western views on Germany seemed remote; and the perils of a weak Germany subject to Communist penetration or a strong Germany playing East against West loomed in the background even if negotiations were successful. Meanwhile Adenauer's democratic and prosperous Federal Republic was a bird in the hand. By this time Western and Eastern Europe had grown very different from each other; the events of 1956 showed how far the Western powers had gone in the acceptance *de facto* of a spheres of influence policy, but they also showed the resistance of the Soviet Union to any serious modification of the Communist system. These were the years in which Tito followed a Kennanist policy of seeking reconciliation and cooperation with the Soviet Union now that it had "mellowed"; he did not find it easy.

Thereafter, the record, especially in Asia and the Far East, is too complex to permit of brief review here. Except to stress its complexity. American Middle Eastern policy alone is a story with many facets; the tergiversations of the moralistic isolation of 1956 and the subsequent crusade of the Eisenhower doctrine, the support of Egypt from the last year of Dulles to the mid-sixties; the attempt to reach stability around Israel in the fact of Russian armament of the Arabs. In Southeast Asia the containment line of course could not easily be drawn; but success against the Communists in Malaya remains as one of the enterprises worth undertaking in the postwar world.

As scholars re-examine the history of the Cold War the record will undoubtedly be modified in detail, and it will certainly reveal mistakes and missed opportunities. Such re-interpretation has become more acceptable with the decline in the United States of that anti-Communist ideology which Europeans have long deplored. It is to be hoped that it is not replaced by a new unreason bred from guilt and self-reproach. It is worth remembering that the hardest of the old-time hardliners—men like Kennan and Harriman—have also been the most committed to pragmatism and negotiation.

SUGGESTED READINGS

Arendt, Hannah, *On Violence*, New York: Harcourt Brace, 1969.

Butterfield, Herbert, and Wight, Martin (eds.), *Diplomatic Investigations: Essays in the Theory of International Politics*, Cambridge, Mass.: Harvard University Press, 1966, Chapters 6, 7, and 11.

Claude, Inis L., Jr., *Power and International Relations*, New York: Random House, 1962, Chapters 1–3.

International Sociological Association, *The Nature of Conflict*, Paris: UNESCO, 1957.

Liska, George, *International Equilibrium*, Cambridge, Mass.: Harvard University Press, 1957.

Moore, Barrington, *Political Power and Social Theory*, Cambridge, Mass.: Harvard University Press, 1958.

Rapoport, Anatol, *Fights, Games and Debates*, Ann Arbor: University of Michigan Press, 1960.

Rosecrance, Richard N., *Action and Reaction in World Politics*, Boston and Toronto: Little, Brown, 1963.

Russell, Bertrand, *Power*, New York: Norton, 1938.

Schelling, Thomas, *The Strategy of Conflict*, Cambridge, Mass.: Harvard University Press, 1960.

Simmel, Georg, *Conflict* (K. Wolff, trans.), Glencoe, Ill.: Free Press, 1955.

VI. ARMS AND WAR

War is tragedy, but tragedy requires greatness as well as disaster. In war, nobility is mingled with brutality, self-sacrifice with self-assertion, and the paradox has challenged thinkers in all ages. Thucydides, pondering the human glories of Athens and the imperialist follies that were her doom, saw pride as the common thread that made the two inseparable. In Plato's *Republic,* the wealth necessary to civilized life and the small state demanded by justice inextricably exposed the best city to the risk of war. To theologians in the tradition of Saint Augustine, war was one reflection of man himself, made in the image of God yet tainted with original sin. "For none so good to man as man," wrote the American Puritan John Wise, "yet none a greater enemy."

That ancient wisdom discouraged any attempt to abolish war altogether, seeing it as a part of the limitations of human nature. The pride of the conqueror and the pride of the pacifist alike marched toward catastrophe, for, defying the restrictions that human nature imposed, both were fatally flawed by ignoring a vital element in the human equation. Man was not suited to total or final solutions.

But if war could not be eliminated, it was possible to limit it, to subject it to restraints and rules that might lessen its cruelties and destructiveness. Thus medieval scholars developed the idea of "just war" (*justum bellum*), a war fought in self-defense or to produce justice that did not aim at destroying an opponent but at reestablishing the conditions for peace and amity. The conduct of such a war, it was argued, was also necessarily limited by the object at which it aimed; force should be restricted to the smallest feasible amount, noncombatants should be spared wherever possible, men-at-arms should act with honor toward each other. And while a state that acted unjustly deserved censure, its victim should recognize that war would reveal a failure of its own policy, for it had failed to persuade its opponent to observe his highest duties *before* he resorted to violence.

Such theories did much to moderate and humanize war and helped to shape our own rules of international law. But even in theory, the doctrine permitted "crusades" that approached total war against heathens and infidels outside the Christian community, and in practice it did not prevent "Christian" states from engaging in almost continuous internecine war. Theorists like

Niccolò Machiavelli regarded such ideas as worse than unrealistic, seeing them as the hypocritical guise concealing the true interests of the Church, which sought to play one secular power off against another. "A certain prince, whom it is well not to name," Machiavelli wrote, "does nothing but preach peace and good faith, but he is really an enemy to both." [1]

Many early modern political thinkers were appalled by violence, especially civil and religious strife, and were preoccupied with the conditions for peace and domestic order. They distrusted any ideas of "natural community" or peace between men, paradoxically, for two reasons: (1) they thought such notions led to an underestimation of the *danger* of violence; and (2) they were concerned to begin with the secure, universal "hard facts" of the physical world and, as material beings, men are isolated and separate. But for whatever reasons, such theories tended to follow Thomas Hobbes in seeing war as the "natural condition" of man; even Immanuel Kant postulated that man in nature existed in a "state of war."

Order and peace, such theories contended, are contrary to the natural desire of human beings to satisfy their passions and to be free of the restraints imposed by nature and other men. But the "war of all against all" is futile, for no individual can hope to win it or to find security while it exists. Gradually men learned that lesson and also came to recognize that by combining with others they could gain both greater safety and greater power. The dangers of war, in this doctrine, are the great educator that teaches men the necessity of peace. Kant looked to the "cunning of nature," which used conflict to force combination, as a vital dynamic in the process that led toward human unity.

Not all theorists, of course, accepted the idea that man is naturally warlike. To Thomas Paine, war was the product of the monarchial system, which violated the natural equality of men by violence in the interests of the few and taught the many to fear and envy the warlike. "Man is not the enemy of Man," Paine proclaimed, "but through the medium of false governments." [2] When democracy became universal, Paine expected, war would disappear.

Both of these arguments, however, contained the germ of the idea that George Orwell satirized in *1984:* War is Peace. Paine's notion, for example, implied that a democratic state that waged war on a "reactionary" regime was speeding the day when war would be abolished and was probably only acting defensively. In our times, such conceits have been carried to extremes by governments that believed that their system of politics held the key to peace. The idea that conflict leads to peace, on the other hand, conforms to the nineteenth-century theory of a progressive tendency in history away from primitive, "military," political systems toward advanced, "industrial" states of society. The conquest of a "backward" state, in this doctrine, was not war at all but "pacification." [3] Some nationalists saw war as a means to unity and progress and followed the German historian, Heinrich von Treitschke, in his assertion that war "is the health of the state," but most theorists hated war's destructiveness. Their devotion to peace, however, only led them to see war

---

[1] *The Prince,* Chapter XVIII.

[2] *The Rights of Man,* London: Carlisle, 1819, Part I, p. 111.

[3] See John Stuart Mill in Chapter IV.

as a lapsing back to primitive or subhuman conditions. Peace and law existed on one side of the boundary; war, crime, and brutality were on the other, and all attempts to bridge them or to civilize war were almost certain to be futile. The only duty owed to the aggressor was that of destroying him by the most expeditious means. Some observers argued that chivalric or humanistic ideas toward the enemy could only prolong the war and, consequently, should be discarded. "You cannot qualify war in harsher terms than I will," General Sherman wrote the citizens of Atlanta, "war is cruelty and you cannot refine it." [4] Hatred and fear of war, paradoxically, contributed to total war.

The effect of such doctrines in removing the moral limitations on the conduct of war was, of course, made more deadly by the growing industrial and technological power that removed the material restrictions on warfare. As the horrors of our century make clear, the two factors were interrelated. The sheer destructiveness of war, once it broke out, called forth an outraged desire to punish the perpetrators, which made the moral restraint on war difficult; the costs of war made limited gains seem too small to be worth the sacrifice. It is not hard to understand the British crowds, after World War I, that cheered orators who pledged to "hang the Kaiser" and to "make Germany pay." Totalitarian ideologies raised the moral stakes of war further by making defeat intolerable to both sides. Almost all forms of violence became acceptable in war; the Allies, in World War II, eventually used the "terror bombing" they had condemned when the Germans used it in the early years of the struggle. The line between soldier and civilian disappeared. Treachery took on the qualities of heroism. Total war, it has become evident, makes total claims on the conscience as well as the life of the citizen.[5]

Appalling as these developments are, it is important to recognize that the *incidence* of violence has decreased as its *impact* has grown more dreadful. Social scientists who follow Max Weber in defining the state as the "monopoly of the legitimate use of force" rarely consider how recent that monopoly is, measured against the centuries when duels, blood feuds, and internal strife were the rule. Even the warrior has been displaced by the disciplined soldier; under all but the most unusual conditions, military power in industrial states is obedient to civilian authority.

It is such facts that Sigmund Freud had in mind when he argued that the growth of "civilization" tends to repress private hostilities and turns the human "instinct for aggression" back onto the individual himself. Several factors, however, work against Freud's hope that the antagonism of civilization toward violence might eventually make war impossible. As Freud knew, men resist turning aggression against themselves, and the repression of outlets *inside* the state may only increase the need for *external* objects of hostility. Furthermore the growth of a revulsion from violence may, as it did between the world wars, lead "barbarians" like the leaders of totalitarian states to expect

[4] William T. Sherman, *Memoirs,* Bloomington: University of Indiana Press, 1957, II, 126–127.

[5] Hans Speier, *Social Order and the Risks of War,* Cambridge, Mass.: MIT Press, 1969, pp. 263–278.

that "decadent" societies will offer no resistance toward aggression. Finally, and paradoxically, the turning of aggression onto the self, which Freud observed, is a source of guilt and self-hatred that can provide emotional support for war. For modern men, Nietzsche commented, "War is . . . a short-cut to suicide; it enables them to destroy themselves with a good conscience." [6]

But it is easy to overrate the irrational element in war. War, Karl von Clausewitz argued, is primarily a political act, the "continuation of policy by other means." A modern thinker who regarded ideas of international community as epiphenomenal, Clausewitz was nonetheless *prescribing* a subordination of war and military power to political control, insisting that war should be a rational act involving a calculus of ends and means but one that should never be allowed to become an end in itself. Military force should always be the servant of political ends. Clausewitz and the school he inspired also knew that states resort to war only when there is a serious conflict of goals, whence the appropriateness of the comment that "tensions, not weapons" cause wars.

In our times, however, the speed and power of weaponry have made it a major, if not primary, source of tension. Trust between nations was once a comparatively easy matter. The values and aims of states were not greatly different and neither the prospect of war nor the threat of defeat was unendurable. Neither condition exists today. Even without a conflict of values, moreover, there is always a finite possibility that another state *may* harbor hostile intentions or may change in that direction. In the nineteenth century, it was possible to overlook such a risk until it verged on probability; it took time for an enemy to arm and mobilize forces, and even then armies moved slowly and were easily checked by fortresses or natural barriers. Today, by contrast, a state can arm itself with nuclear weapons and deliver them on the homeland of its foe with frightening rapidity and unparalleled destructiveness. No time will be available to recover if trust is misplaced. The risks of trust seem prohibitive, and Frederick the Great's axiom, "skepticism is the mother of security," has become an imperative for modern political leaders in the world of international politics. [7]

Such facts make it difficult to devise any system of control for weapons of mass destruction; *any* inspection system is bound to overlook some weapons if there is a will to conceal them. In the nineteenth century, again, this might not have mattered, for concealed forces could not have been powerful enough to matter; not so today. As Jules Moch pointed out as early as 1955, the small number of existing nuclear weapons that might escape detection is so great in destructive power as almost to nullify the effect of disarmament. [8] And Seymour Melman, a strong advocate of disarmament, suggested that more moderate "arms control" agreements suffer from a defect no less serious: they would not control the technology that renders existing weapons obsolete at a bewildering rate. [9]

These obstacles have helped to fix attention on the means of "deterring"

---

[6] *The Gay Science,* No. 338.

[7] *Instructions to His Generals,* Harrisburg: Stackpole, 1944, p. 56.

[8] *Human Folly: to Disarm or Perish?* London: Gollancz, 1955.

[9] "The Arms Control Doctrine," *The Nation,* February 11, 1961.

potential aggressors from war through fear of the losses they would suffer themselves. A varied, complex body of theory has grown up that examines the relative efficacy of threats against the population or against the nuclear forces of an opposing state ("countercity" and "counterforce" strategies, as they are termed respectively). Great concern has been devoted to those situations where fear of vulnerability or hope for momentary advantage might lead a state to launch a preventive war (or "first strike"). Thornton Read's essay examines much of the literature in the field, hoping to clarify such concepts in the light of the contemporary military situation. Generally, however, strategic theory turns on a central proposition: only when, even granting an aggressor the most favorable conditions, it seems probable that he will suffer what are to him intolerable losses, have the conditions of deterrence been fulfilled.

All of the theories of deterrence, moreover, have an unreal quality. As Hans Speier argues, they are not premised on the *actual* effect that given weapons or strategies might have, but on the effects that another state may *believe* them to have.[10] The aim of massive war preparations is not to win a war, but to avoid one. To a very large extent, the aims of deterrence have been achieved in American-Soviet relations; neither state is likely to risk an attack on the other. Yet the threat of such a war also tempts the superpowers to believe that neither will risk total war to defend a local position. The Soviet Union would not go to war to defend Cuba in all probability, and many Germans have doubted whether the United States would fight to defend West Berlin. The threat of general war obviously encourages the superpowers to use force to maintain the solidarity of their alliance systems, as the U.S.S.R. did in both Hungary and Czechoslovakia. But as Speier points out, it also leads to the use of arms in the effort to split opposing alliances, whether by threats (implicitly or explicitly used by the Soviet Union in relation to Western Europe) or by extending protection to discontented states in the opposing "camp" (a policy at least partly followed by the United States in relation to Yugoslavia).

Similarly, of course, the success of deterrence has facilitated small wars and has given great credibility to theories like the doctrine of "national liberation war," which prescribes guerrilla combat as a means of making marginal gains against "imperialism." By keeping war confined to an area too small and a level of conflict too limited to justify general war, states or movements may hope to neutralize the massive arsenals of the great powers. This, in turn, has led to preoccupation with the "counterinsurgency" doctrine in countries like the United States. The military atmosphere in which such studies take place has often led to an overemphasis on strictly military concerns and too limited an attention to political aspects of guerrilla conflict, as has been evident in Vietnam. But as Chalmers Johnson notes, the same tendency has been evident on the side of insurgents; Mao's teaching, which stressed political power as a means to military victory, has become inverted in the "third generation of guerrilla war." Here, as elsewhere, war tends to escape its status as a means and to become an end.

[10] Hans Speier, *Force and Folly,* Cambridge: MIT Press, 1969, pp. 34–49.

Moreover, doubt of the ability or willingness of the superpowers to protect their allies may lead other states to seek nuclear weapons of their own. China may have developed her nuclear force for reasons of prestige and protection against outsiders and to win an element of autonomy in world affairs. (France's reasons were similar.) But other Asian states see such power as a threat, especially if they cannot count on American or Soviet protection. And the "nondiffusion" treaty may prove impotent in the face of such considerations. If so, as many observers have argued, a greater diffusion of weapons would greatly increase the likelihood of nuclear war.

It is hardly surprising that so many, considering the risks that war involves and the perils that armament entails, regard war and the arms race as lunatic, devoid of any rational purpose. But this attitude has a danger of its own. Sir Norman Angell "proved" that war no longer "paid" and was hence impossible, in his *The Great Illusion,* written in 1907—and the same fate could overtake similar works today. First, as Bruce M. Russett indicates, a technological breakthrough might invalidate the current nuclear stalemate by nullifying the defensive threat of effective retaliation (as a marked improvement in missile defense might do). It was such a development, after all, that enabled the Germans in World War II to nullify the "power" of the French system of defense and, with it, Allied strategies of retaliation. That, as Russett implies, indicates that a breakthrough may not be the result of an isolated scientific discovery but of a relaxation on the part of one side in the arms race.

Second, there is the danger that one state may calculate that another may not resist some threat or maneuver when in fact it *would* resist. The "credibility" of promises to fight is often a critical element in avoiding conflict. Hitler's decision for war in 1939 was partly based on his own, and his Foreign Minister Joachim von Ribbentrop's, error in discounting Chamberlain's pledge to go to war in defense of Poland.

In fact, some of the more elaborate theories of strategy developed by academics are not likely to be applied in actual political life. Political leaders are likely to insist on their right and responsibility to judge each situation. As the British physicist P. M. S. Blackett has argued, many theories of strategy are too precise to be used in the political world, where facts are always murky at the edges and situations uncertain.[11] Perhaps as important is the obvious fact that the old question "What is worth fighting for?" remains first and essential, even in a nuclear age. Always too important to be left to generals, war is too vital to be left to scientists, for it depends on our ultimate commitments and values as individuals and as peoples.

All too easily, as Russett shows, military concerns can acquire priority over and possibly even displace other goals. As Harold Lasswell argued in a famous essay, anxiety to defend themselves can easily make men over into the image of what they fear.[12] In fact, that may be the verdict on the effort of modern man to abolish war, especially given the common belief that doing so commanded victory in the "war against nature." War had its horrors, Rousseau

[11] "Critique of Some Contemporary Defense Thinking," *Encounter,* 16, 4 (1961), 9–17.

[12] "The Garrison State," *American Journal of Sociology,* 46 (1941), 455–467.

lamented, because of men's efforts to prevent it: "We have prevented particular wars only to start general ones which are a thousand times worse." [13] Certainly our condition is paradoxical at best. As Raymond Aron puts it, "Science helps men kill each other by mass production; it does not teach them wisdom. . . . the salient feature of the present phase of history . . . is that mankind, *for the first time in its history,* is preparing for a war it does not want to fight and looks to the common sense of statesmen to avoid it." [14] And that hope may fail unless mankind can gain common sense and a measure of wisdom.

[13] C. E. Vaughan, *The Political Writings of J. J. Rousseau,* Cambridge, England: Cambridge University Press, 1915, I, 295.

[14] *On War,* Garden City, N.Y.: Anchor Books, 1959, pp. 23 and 141.

Sigmund Freud

WHY WAR?

. . . [U]nder primitive conditions it is superior force—brute violence or violence backed by arms—that lords it everywhere. . . . [A] path was traced that led away from violence to law. But what was this path? Surely, it issued from a single truth; that the superiority of one strong man can be overborne by an alliance of many weaklings, that in union there is strength. Brute force is overcome by union. . . . Thus, we may define "right" (law) as the might of community. Yet it too is nothing else than violence quick to attack whatever individual stands in its path . . . but with one difference, it is the communal, not individual violence that has its way. But for this transition from crude violence to the reign of law, a certan psychological condition must first obtain. The union of the majority must be stable and enduring. If its sole *raison d'être* be the discomfiture of some overweening individual, and after his downfall it be dissolved, it leads to nothing. . . . [T]he cycle will repeat itself unendingly. Thus the union of people must be permanent and well organized; it must enact rules to meet the risk of possible revolts; must set up machinery ensuring that its rules—the laws—are observed and that such acts of violence as the laws demand are duly carried out. This recognition of a community of interests engenders among the members of the group a sentiment of unity and fraternal solidarity which constitutes its real strength.

So far I have set out what seems to me the kernel of the matter: the suppression of brute force by the transfer of power to a larger combination, founded on the community of sentiments linking up its members. . . . But such a combination is only theoretically possible; in practice the situation is always complicated by the fact that, from the outset, the group includes elements of unequal power. . . . The most casual glance at world history will show an unending series of conflicts between one community and another or a group of others, between large and smaller units, between cities, countries, races, tribes and kingdoms, almost all of which were settled by the ordeal of war. Such wars end either in pillage or in conquest and its fruits, the downfall of the loser. No single all-embracing judgment can be passed on these wars of aggrandizement. Some, like the war between the Mongols and the Turks, have led to unmitigated misery; others, however, have furthered the transition from violence to law, since they brought larger units into being, within whose limits a recourse to violence was banned and a new regime determined all disputes. Thus the Roman conquests brought that boon, the *pax romana*, to the Mediterranean lands.

Reprinted by permission of Sigmund Freud Copyrights Ltd. from a letter in answer to Albert Einstein (1932).

The French kings' lust for aggrandizement created a new France, flourishing in peace and unity. Paradoxical as it sounds, we must admit that warfare well might serve to pave the way to that unbroken peace we so desire, for it is war that brings vast empires into being, within whose frontiers all warfare is proscribed by a strong central power. In practice, however, this end is not attained, for as a rule, the fruits of victory are but short-lived, the new-created unit falls asunder once again, generally because there can be no true cohesion between the parts that violence has welded. Hitherto, moreover, such conquests have only led to aggregations which, for all their magnitude, had limits, and disputes between these units could be resolved only by recourse to arms. For humanity at large the sole result of all these military enterprises was that, instead of frequent not to say incessant little wars, they had now to face great wars which, for all they came less often, were so much the more destructive.

Regarding the world of today the same conclusion holds good, and you, too, have reached it, though by a shorter path. There is but one sure way of ending war and that is the establishment, by common consent, of a central control which shall have the last word in every conflict of interest. . . . [But] obviously such notions as these can only be significant when they are the expression of a deeply rooted sense of unity, shared by all. It is necessary, therefore, to gauge the efficacy of such sentiments. History tells us that, on occasion, they have been effective. For example, the Panhellenic conception, the Greeks' awareness of superiority over their barbarian neighbors, which found expression in the Amphictyonies, the Oracles and Games, was strong enough to humanize the methods of warfare as between Greeks, though it inevitably failed to prevent conflicts between different elements of the Hellenic race or even to deter a city or group of cities from joining forces with their racial foe, the Persians, for the discomfiture of a rival. The solidarity of Christendom in the Renaissance age was no more effective, despite its vast authority, in hindering Christian nations, large and small alike, from calling in the Sultan to their aid. And, in our times, we look in vain for some such unifying notion whose authority would be unquestioned. It is all too clear that the nationalistic ideas, paramount today in every country, operate in quite a contrary direction. Some there are who hold that the Bolshevist conceptions may make an end of war, but, as things are, that goal lies very far away and, perhaps, could only be attained after a spell of brutal internecine warfare. Thus it would seem that any effort to replace brute force by the might of an ideal is, under present conditions, doomed to fail. Our logic is at fault if we ignore the fact that right is founded on brute force and even today needs violence to maintain it.

I now can comment on another of your statements. You are amazed that it is so easy to infect men with the war-fever, and you surmise that man has in him an active instinct for hatred and destruction, amenable to such stimulations.   I entirely agree with you.   I believe in the existence of this instinct and have been recently at pains to study its manifestations.   In this connection may I set out a fragment of that knowledge of the instincts, which we psychoanalysts, after so many tentative essays and gropings in the dark have compassed?   We assume that human instincts are of two kinds: those that conserve and unify, which we call "erotic" (in the meaning Plato gives to *Eros* in his *Symposium*) or else "sexual" (explicitly extending the popular connotation of "sex"); and, secondly, the instincts to destroy and kill, which we assimilate as the aggressive or destructive instincts. . . .   Each of these instincts is every whit as indispensable as its opposite and all the phenomena of life derive from their activity, whether they work in concert or in opposition. . . .   Thus the instinct of self-preservation is certainly of an erotic nature, but to gain its ends this very instinct necessitates aggressive action.   In the same way the love-instinct, when directed to a specific object, calls for an admixture of the acquisitive instinct if it is to enter into effective possession of that object. . . .

If you will travel with me a little further on this road, you will find that human affairs are complicated in yet another way.   Only exceptionally does an action follow on the stimulus of a single instinct, which is *per se* a blend of Eros and destructiveness.   As a rule several motives of similar composition concur to bring about the act. . . .   Thus, when a nation is summoned to engage in war, a whole gamut of human motives may respond to this appeal; high and low motives, some openly avowed, others slurred over. . . .   Musing on the atrocities recorded on history's page, we feel that the ideal motive has often served as a camouflage for the lust of destruction; sometimes, as with the cruelties of the Inquisition, it seems that, while the ideal motives occupied the foreground of consciousness, they drew their strength from the destructive instincts submerged in the unconscious. . . .

You are interested, I know, in the prevention of war, not in our theories, and I keep this fact in mind.   Yet I would like to dwell a little longer on this destructive instinct which is seldom given the attention that its importance warrants. . . .   The living being . . . defends its own existence by destroying foreign bodies.   But, in one of its activities, the death instinct is operative *within* the living being and we have sought to trace back a number of normal and pathological phenomena to this *introversion* of the destructive instinct. . . .   Obviously when this internal tendency operates on too large a scale, it is no trivial matter, rather a positively morbid state of things; whereas the diversion of the destructive impulse toward the external world must have beneficial effects.   Here is then the biological justification for all those vile, pernicious propensities which we now are combating.   We can but own that they are really more akin to nature than this our stand against them, which, in fact, remains to be accounted for.

All this may give you the impression that our theories amount to a spe-

cies of mythology and a gloomy one at that!   But does not every natural
science lead ultimately to this—a sort of mythology?   Is it otherwise today
with your physical science?

The upshot of these observations . . . is that there is no likelihood of
our being able to suppress humanity's aggressive tendencies.   In some
happy corners of the earth, they say, where nature brings forth abundantly
whatever man desires, there flourish races whose lives go gently by, un-
knowing of aggression or constraint.   This I can hardly credit; I would
like further details about these happy folk.   The Bolshevists, too, aspire to
do away with human aggressiveness by ensuring the satisfaction of material
needs and enforcing equality between man and man.   To me this hope
seems vain.   Meanwhile they busily perfect their armaments, and their
hatred of outsiders is not the least of the factors of cohesion amongst
themselves.   In any case, as you, too, have observed, complete suppression
of man's aggressive tendencies is not in issue; what we may try is to divert
it into a channel other than that of warfare.

From our "mythology" of the instincts we may easily deduce a formula
for an indirect method of eliminating war.   If the propensity for war be due
to the destructive instinct, we have always its counter-agent, Eros, to our
hand.   All that produces ties of sentiment between man and man must
serve us as war's antidote. . . .

In your strictures on the abuse of authority I find another suggestion for
an indirect attack on the war-impulse.   That men are divided into leaders
and the led is but another manifestation of their inborn and irremediable
inequality.   The second class constitutes the vast majority; they need a high
command to make decisions for them, to which decisions they usually bow
without demur.   In this context we would point out that men should be at
greater pains than heretofore to form a superior class of independent thinkers, unamenable to intimidation and fervent in the quest of truth, whose
function it would be to guide the masses dependent on their lead.   There is
no need to point out how little the rule of politicians and the Church's ban
on liberty of thought encourage such a new creation.   The ideal conditions
would obviously be found in a community where every man subordinated
his instinctive life to the dictates of reason.   Nothing less than this could
bring about so thorough and so durable a union between men, even if this
involved the severance of mutual ties of sentiment.   But surely such a hope
is utterly utopian, as things are.   The other indirect methods of preventing
war are certainly more feasible, but entail no quick results.   They conjure
up an ugly picture of mills that grind so slowly that, before the flour is
ready, men are dead of hunger.

. . . Why do we, you and I and many another, protest so vehemently
against war, instead of just accepting it as another of life's odious im-
portunities? . . .   Because every man has a right over his own life and
war destroys lives that were full of promise; it forces the individual into
situations that shame his manhood, obliging him to murder fellow men,

against his will; it ravages material amenities, the fruits of human toil, and much besides. Moreover wars, as now conducted, afford no scope for acts of heroism according to the old ideals and, given the high perfection of modern arms, war today would mean the sheer extermination of one of the combatants, if not of both. This is so true, so obvious, that we can but wonder why the conduct of war is not banned by general consent. Doubtless either of the points I have just made is open to debate. It may be asked if the community, in its turn, cannot claim a right over the individual lives of its members. Moreover, all forms of war cannot be indiscriminately condemned; so long as there are nations and empires, each prepared callously to exterminate its rival, all alike must be equipped for war. . . . I pass on to another point, the basis, as it strikes me, of our common hatred of war. . . . We cannot do otherwise than hate it. Pacifists we are, since our organic nature wills us thus to be. Hence it comes easy to us to find arguments that justify our standpoint.

This point, however, calls for elucidation. Here is the way in which I see it. The cultural development of mankind (some, I know, prefer to call it civilization) has been in progress since immemorial antiquity. To this process we owe all that is best in our composition, but also much that makes for human suffering. Its origins and causes are obscure, its issue is uncertain, but some of its characteristics are easy to perceive. It well may lead to the extinction of mankind, for it impairs the sexual function in more than one respect, and even today the uncivilized races and the backward classes of all nations are multiplying more rapidly than the cultured elements. This process may, perhaps, be likened to the effects of domestication on certain animals—it clearly involves physical changes of structure— but the view that cultural development is an organic process of this order has not yet become generally familiar. The psychic changes which accompany this process of cultural change are striking. . . . They consist in the progressive rejection of instinctive ends and a scaling down of instinctive reactions. . . . On the psychological side two of the most important phenomena of culture are, firstly, a strengthening of the intellect, which tends to master our instinctive life, and, secondly, an introversion of the aggressive impulse with all its consequent benefits and perils. Now war runs . . . counter to the psychic disposition imposed on us by the growth of culture; we are therefore bound to resent war, to find it utterly intolerable. With pacifists . . . it is not merely an intellectual and affective repulsion but a constitutional intolerance, an idiosyncrasy in its most drastic form. . . .

How long have we to wait before the rest of men turn pacifist? Impossible to say and yet perhaps our hope that these two factors—man's cultural disposition and a well-founded dread of the form that future wars will take—may serve to put an end to war in the near future, is not chimerical. But by what ways or by-ways this will come about, we cannot guess. . . .

Karl von Clausewitz

ON WAR

War . . . is an act of violence which aims at compelling our opponent to do our will. . . . The goals of military violence, as well as the amount of effort to be made, will be determined by the political objective, the original motive for the war. . . . War is not a pastime; not a mere passion for venturing and winning; not the work of free enthusiasm; it is a serious business for a serious object. The war of a community, of entire nations and particularly civilized nations, is always called forth by a political motive in a political situation. It is, therefore, a political act, [and] . . . naturally this original motive . . . should continue to be the most important consideration in conducting it. Still, the political objective is not a despotic law-giver by that fact alone; it must accommodate itself to the nature of the means. . . . [C]hanges in those means may involve a modification in the political objectives, though the latter always must be given first consideration. Policy is intertwined in the whole course of war, and must continually influence it as far as the nature of the forces let loose by war will permit. . . . [T]hus war is not merely a political act but a political *instrument* . . . a method which must always include objectives as a part of itself. . . . *War is only a continuation of state policy by other means.*

* * *

War is only a part of political relations. . . . Interaction between governments does not cease simply because of war. . . . [I]t continues to exist whatever may be the forms or methods it uses. . . . [T]he chief lines on which the war develops . . . are only the general features of policy which run through the war until peace is made. How can we conceive it in any other sense? Does the mere cessation of diplomatic notes stop the political relations of different nations and regimes? Is not war merely another kind of writing and language [for the communication of] political thoughts? . . . War can never be separated from political intercourse and if, for whatever reason, this is done . . . it is merely a senseless thing, without purpose. . . . That politics should end completely when war begins is conceivable only in wars of life and death, based on pure hatred, for war is always the expression or manifestation of some policy.

The subordination of political perspectives to those of the military would be contrary to common sense, for policy has declared the war. . . . [I]t is the intelligent faculty, and war is its instrument, not the reverse. . . .

Translated by the editors from *Vom Kriege* (Berlin, 1832–1834), Book I, Section 1, and Book VIII, Section 3B.

In a word, the art of war in the highest sense is policy, although a policy which fights battles instead of writing notes.

According to this view, to leave the planning or the conduct of a great military enterprise to purely military judgment and decision . . . is foolish; indeed, it is an irrational procedure to ask professional soldiers for a "purely military opinion" on what the Cabinet ought to do with respect to a plan of war. . . . [N]otwithstanding the scientific character of contemporary military art, the leading outlines of the war are always determined . . . by a political and not a military agency.

This is perfectly natural. None of the major plans which are required for war can be understood without an insight into political relations [and objectives]. . . . [I]n reality, when people speak as they often do of the prejudicial influence of policy on the conduct of a war they are actually stating something else. It is not the influence, but the policy itself which is at fault. If policy is correct, that is, if it keeps its eye on the objective, then it can only act with advantage on the war. If it causes a divergence from the objective, the error is to be sought in a mistaken [conception of] policy.

It is only when policy promises itself a wrong effect from military means and measures, an effect which by their nature they cannot obtain, that it can exercise a prejudicial effect on the war. . . . Just as a person speaking a language in which he is not fluent may sometime say something he does not intend, so policy when intending right may order things which will not forward its aims.

This has happened countless times, and it shows that a certain knowledge of the nature of war is essential to the management of political intercourse [between states].

In summary, war is an instrument of policy; it must partake of the character [of policy]; it must measure with [policy] scale. . . . [T]he conduct of war in its major features is, therefore, policy itself, which takes up the sword in place of the pen but does not . . . cease to be guided by its own laws.

Thornton Read

NUCLEAR STRATEGY

MILITARY FORCES AND CIVILIAN HOSTAGES

In the classical doctrine of the just war a cardinal principle is the immunity of noncombatants from direct attack.[1] Force is to be used against force with no more collateral civil damage than can be helped. After the victorious army has occupied the contested territory, it may use force against civilians but only with discrimination and in order to establish governmental authority and maintain law and order. The classical concept of military forces fighting military forces and dealing with civilians in an essentially police role has been widely accepted, as a guiding ideal, and it has to a large extent been followed during the past several centuries despite extensive violations, especially in the Second World War. However, in recent discussions of military strategy and arms control, one school of thought explicitly reverses the classical doctrine, at least in regard to strategic forces, and proposes to establish a stable military balance based on invulnerable weapons which threaten vulnerable cities. This doctrine, which is sometimes called Finite Deterrence or Minimum Deterrence, would discourage the development of capabilities designed either to attack the opposing strategic weapons or to protect cities and civilians. Each side, in other words, would regulate the other's behavior by holding its people and civil substance in hostage.

The proponents of arms control and stable deterrence who argue against a counterforce strategy do so on the grounds not that a return to the ancient custom of exchanging hostages is desirable in itself but rather that modern technology leaves no other choice, or at least that the effort to maintain a counterforce doctrine and capability will increase the danger of war and accelerate the race to develop and procure the most destructive types of weapons. A remarkably sophisticated case can be made out for this viewpoint despite its apparent conflict with common sense and traditional morality.

Printed by permission of the author and the Center of International Studies, Princeton University. This paper was prepared for the Center of International Studies in August 1962. It was abridged by the editors and revised by the author for the present purpose in December, 1964. Copyright © 1966 Thornton Read.

The author is much indebted for helpful comment to James E. King, Klaus Knorr, William W. Kaufmann, Paul Ramsey, and especially to Donald G. Brennan.

[1] On the issue of noncombatant immunity in the classical just war doctrine and its relevance for the nuclear age see *War and the Christian Conscience* by Paul Ramsey, Duke University Press, Durham, N.C., 1961.

THE CASE AGAINST COUNTERFORCE

The objections to pursuing a counterforce strategy in the nuclear age can be broken down roughly into four arguments: (1) a counterforce posture increases the danger of war by creating an incentive to strike pre-emptively in a tense situation, (2) the pursuit of counterforce capabilities intensifies the arms race, (3) a counterforce strategy is not technically or humanly feasible, and (4) a strategic counterforce strike is not so much an alternative to attacking cities as a prelude to countercity threats in the form of what Herman Kahn has called *post-attack blackmail*.

It may be useful to begin the discussion by stating these objections more fully and as forcefully as possible. Later sections will examine them critically.

1. Reciprocal Fear of Pre-emptive Attack. In the past military engagements lasted through many exchanges of fire; men and weapons could expect to fire many rounds of ammunition during a war or even a battle. This is no longer the case: for example, a ballistic missile fires only once; so there is no point in shooting at it unless one shoots first by surprise and catches it on the ground. Thus counterforce warfare, which was once a natural consequence of the persistence of weapons through many exchanges of fire, is now confined to the special circumstance of a surprise attack. A balance of terror in which a clear advantage goes to the side striking first is dangerously unstable and could lead even a relatively unaggressive nation reluctantly to strike first simply from fear that the other side (perhaps acting from a similar fear) was about to do so. But, if both sides have invulnerable retaliatory forces, neither has to fear a surprise attack and neither has an incentive to launch one.

2. Arms Race or Stable Deterrence. If strategic weapons are intended only to threaten unprotected cities, the arms race will tend to level off as capabilities for civil damage approach the point of saturation. When destruction is nearly total, a superiority over the other side in destructive capability becomes relatively unimportant. It is sufficient that each be able to do enough damage to deter the other from attacking. The arms race may even go into reverse as each side realizes the futility of having more than enough capability to do unacceptable damage to the other. On the other hand, a capability to win a war by destroying the opposing weapons and protecting one's own civilians would require a formidable array of strategic weapons, surveillance systems and probably also an ambitious program of civil and active defense. Every advance in this direction made by one side increases the other's military requirements. In short, Minimum Deterrence allows the arms race to end in a stable balance where each side can achieve a sufficiency of military power which, within broad limits, is independent of the other's strength; but a counterforce strategy leads to endless competition and insatiable military requirements.

3. Feasibility of a Counterforce Strategy.   Not only is a counterforce strategy undesirable but it requires technical and human capabilities which do not exist and probably are not feasible.   For example, military targets would have to be located away from centers of population.   This has not been done in all cases even in the United States (as the case of Tucson, Arizona, illustrates) nor in the Soviet Union, and it may not be feasible in a densely populated area like Western Europe.   To maintain control of forces and fight a deliberate, discriminating war with military operations subject to civilian political direction places impossible requirements on the command and control system, which would be heavily damaged in a general nuclear war even if it were not a prime target.   And history offers little reason to believe that the surviving military and political leadership or the general public would maintain the self-restraint, discipline and organization necessary to carry through a rational strategy under the unprecedented conditions of a nuclear war, in which casualties would be frightful even if the other side tried to follow a counterforce strategy.

4. Counterforce As a Prelude to Nuclear Blackmail.   Finally the critic of a counterforce strategy would question the ultimate purpose of a counterforce exchange with modern strategic weapons.   How would the victorious side proceed to turn its victory to political account?   Unlike an occupying army, which can put pressure on individual people to submit to the established political authority and obey its laws, a strategic nuclear force which had destroyed its opposite could enforce a political settlement only by the threat to destroy cities.   In other words a strategic counterforce attack is not so much an alternative to a countercity threat as a prerequisite to it.   The ability to threaten cities cannot be renounced without renouncing the weapons themselves.   Short of nuclear disarmament, the most we can do is to give up the counterforce capability which would enable us to threaten cities with impunity, that is, without fear of reprisal.   Paradoxically, the closest we can come to renouncing a countercity strategy is to have *nothing but* a countercity capability.   But if, in the end, strategic nuclear weapons are useful only to threaten cities, would it not be better to cast them in that role from the beginning and outlaw strategic nuclear warfare by ruling that it, like the threat to shoot prisoners of war or civilians in occupied territory, is "off bounds" militarily?

COUNTERFORCE AND FIRST STRIKE

The debate over counterforce strategies and stable deterrence has been confused by various implicit assumptions which tend to restrict strategic vision and make the world of discourse a poorer approximation than it need be to the richness and complexity of the real world. For example, there is a tendency to confuse capabilities with doctrines or to confuse long term strategic choices as to what capabilities we should try to develop with short term choices as to how existing capabilities should be used to meet various contingencies that are considered to be probable enough—or, even if not very probable, serious enough—to be worth preparing for. In particular there is a tendency to confuse a counterforce capability with a first-strike capability, a first-strike capability with a first-strike doctrine, and a first-strike doctrine with a doctrine for the first use of nuclear weapons.

As a preliminary to a more fruitful discussion it may be useful to sharpen some definitions and to distinguish between things whose equivalence or necessary connection should be established as the *result* of analysis and not unconsciously assumed at the beginning.

A strategic counterforce capability may be defined as a capability to use strategic weapons against military targets, either tactical or strategic. The requirements for a counterforce capability include the ability to acquire targets (that is to locate and identify them) and to place a weapon sufficiently close to a target to destroy it or at least make it inoperable. The requirements for a first-strike capability include those for a counterforce capability plus additional requirements, namely (1) the intelligence or continuous surveillance capabilities to acquire a large number of targets at one time and (2) the firing discipline to launch a substantial fraction of one's weapons in a single coordinated attack or, in the case of missiles, in a more or less simultaneous salvo.

It is possible to have a good counterforce capability with a relatively modest first-strike capability—as the following example will illustrate: Suppose that our strategic deterrent consisted of mobile missiles, which move periodically, thus making it difficult for the enemy to know the location of all of them at any one time. Even if he had a satellite surveillance system which could locate mobile missiles throughout the country, some missiles would be hidden by cloud cover. Suppose further that, at any one time, he could locate 10 per cent of our missiles but that this 10 per cent varied so that over a period of several weeks every missile would at some time come under surveillance. He could then carry out a slow war of counterforce attrition, knocking out missiles as they came under surveillance. Thus an enemy with a negligible first-strike capability could nevertheless have a good strategic counterforce capability.

In short, when the protection of strategic forces depends on concealing their location and when there is a surveillance system able to keep a small but constantly changing fraction of them under surveillance, counterforce warfare becomes feasible, the advantage goes to the side with superior surveillance, but there is little advantage in striking first and so the situation is stable against the reciprocal fear of pre-emptive attack.

Furthermore, strategic weapons (such as long range bombers and

ICBM's) could be used to attack tactical targets such as POL (petroleum, oil and lubricants) depots, ammunition dumps, tactical air fields and transportation bottlenecks (especially bridges) and other targets which support ground operations. No matter how well strategic weapons are protected (by hardening, dispersal or mobility), there will probably always be some vulnerable military targets. Thus, so long as we have any strategic weapons, we will have some counterforce capability whether we want it or not. It is not certain that there will ever be "invulnerable" weapons which could not be hunted down and destroyed if sufficient effort were made. A world in which forces are invulnerable and only people can be attacked is a conceptual abstraction which it may be useful to analyze as a limiting case, but some caution should be exercised in basing strategic or arms control proposals on so oversimplified a model of the real world.

COUNTERFORCE SECOND STRIKE

Neither a counterforce capability nor strategic nuclear superiority need be destabilizing if there is no advantage in a simultaneous or salvo attack and hence no incentive to be the first to launch one. Even a first-strike capability is not necessarily destabilizing nor does it necessarily imply a first-strike doctrine. A first-strike *capability* may be inherent in the capability required to support a counterforce second-strike *doctrine*.

It has been argued that a counterforce second strike would not be feasible because missiles would already have been fired and bombers would be in the air so there would be no point in cracking up empty launching pads and runways which had served their purpose. But this again is an oversimplified view—a limiting case which may be easily and perhaps also usefully analyzed but which should not be taken as an accurate picture of the world as it is now or is likely to be in the years for which plans have to be made now.

If the enemy has more missiles than launching pads, that is, has a reload capability, it would be useful to knock out the pads before they can be reloaded. In the same way, a second-strike against airfields could prevent follow-on bombing attacks. To launch the whole bomber force in one attack would involve preparations which might be detected and thus give away the advantage of surprise. But still more important is the possibility that the missiles and aircraft which in principle could be launched simultaneously are not in fact likely to get off at the same time. There are problems of timing and coordination and missile countdown. In any case, it is hardly consistent to argue against a U.S. first-strike capability on the grounds that coordination of a large attack is difficult and at the same time oppose a U.S. second-strike counterforce strategy on the grounds that the enemy's coordination would be nearly perfect. . . .

FIRST-STRIKE CAPABILITY AND STABILITY

*   *   *

Admittedly a symmetrical balance where neither side can gain any advantage by striking first is preferable to the symmetrical case where either side can gain a decisive advantage by striking first, but is it preferable to the asymmetrical case where we wind up in a stronger position than the Soviets no matter who strikes first?   What is objectionable is not having weapons that are useful for a first strike but having weapons that are useful *only* for a first strike.   The Minuteman missile, for example, can be hardened and dispersed so as to survive a surprise attack but it also has the accuracy, potential reliability and salvo capability required for a first strike.   The danger of pre-emptive war comes from the *reciprocal* fear of surprise attack.   The cycle of mutual and mutually reinforcing fears (the Soviets are afraid that we are afraid that they . . . are about to strike) is broken if *one* side is well enough protected that it need not fear a surprise attack.

For example, consider the case that our fixed missiles are well enough protected that the Soviets would have to expend three of their missiles (on the average) to knock out one of ours and where they know only that our Polaris submarines are somewhere in the North Atlantic.   Thus an attack on our missiles would shift the strategic balance in our favor.   Indeed a salvo attack on the Polaris submarines would amount to lobbing missiles at random into the ocean, so a first strike against our strategic forces would be a form of unilateral disarmament and would be deterred even apart from the threat of retaliation.   This is the ideal second-strike posture, where a first strike is deterred not only by the fear of an unacceptable retaliatory blow but by the knowledge that the first strike, in itself, is militarily disadvantageous.

Of course such an ideal posture is not likely to be attained in fact—at least not soon.   There will remain some advantage in launching at least a fraction of one's strategic force at the more vulnerable enemy weapons before they can get off the ground.   At present,* however, enough of the American strategic forces could survive a Soviet first strike virtually to destroy the Soviet Union in retaliation.   Even though the Soviets would face a still worse outcome if they allowed us to strike first, the difference between the two catastrophes would hardly seem important enough to outweigh the hope of averting general war altogether.

The Soviets lived for years under overwhelming Western superiority and conducted their foreign relations with confidence rather than desperation. They have not done as much as they could to make their strategic forces less vulnerable to an American attack.   The Soviet leaders apparently feel confident that they control the risks of war and can stop their provocations

---

* [December, 1964—Eds.]

before the danger of an American strike reaches unacceptable levels. Even a remote possibility of an American first strike tends to reinforce the natural caution of the Soviet leaders. Far from increasing the danger of war, it discourages the kind of Soviet provocations which might lead to war. There is little historical evidence that the perception of danger makes the Soviet leaders reckless.

Since the United States now has a well protected retaliatory force, a proposal to establish a stable balance of mutual deterrence based on invulnerable weapons on *both* sides is really a proposal to remedy a Soviet weakness. American strategic superiority might better be regarded as a negotiable asset that could be given up in return for Soviet concessions, say in an arms control agreement. In the absence of such an agreement, we can pursue *both* a second-strike capability and a first-strike counterforce capability. This need not increase the danger of pre-emptive war provided we give the higher priority to a second-strike capability. Furthermore, the question of a first-strike capability is not one of either-or; nor is it a question of how good a capability we *require,* but rather of how much effort we should devote to improving the first-strike capability that can be inherent in a formidable second-strike force. The resulting strategic balance will depend on how technology develops and on how hard the Soviets try to protect their strategic forces.

RATIONALITY AND NUCLEAR WAR

To be sure, a well protected retaliatory or second-strike force would not in itself prevent an enemy from striking first against cities, but that would be a totally irrational thing to do. It has been argued that we ought not to assume rational conduct of warfare, that if nations were rational they would not have gone to war in the first place. But rationality is not something like virginity which one either has or does not have. There are all gradations of rationality and irrationality from normal foolishness to suicidal lunacy.

A somewhat more sophisticated view accepts the threat of suicidal war as a necessary deterrent. Walter Lippmann has expressed this view as follows:

Only a moral idiot with a suicidal mania would press the button for a nuclear war. Yet we have learned that, while a nuclear war would be lunacy, it is nevertheless an ever-present possibility. Why? Because, however lunatic it might be to commit suicide, a nation can be provoked and exasperated to the point of lunacy where only violence can relieve its feelings. This is one of the facts of life in the middle of the twentieth century. The nerves of a nation can stand only so much provocation and humiliation, and beyond the tolerable limits, it will plunge into lunacy.[2]

[2] "The Nuclear Age," *The Atlantic Monthly,* May, 1962, p. 46.

Whatever may be said for this passage as a *description* of the "facts of life," it could not easily be defended as a *prescription* for rational policy. No government could convincingly explain why it was cultivating weapons that could be used only by a madman to commit a massive atrocity. To admit that nuclear weapons have no other function than this if ever actually used is to concede much of the case for unilateral nuclear disarmament. So long as we must retain nuclear weapons and strategic delivery systems (even if ostensibly only to deter their own use), there is a moral imperative to devise rational ways of using them, or at least ways that are as little irrational and inhuman as possible, and to fashion our military power so as to make a rational and moral strategy possible.[3] We must do this despite the technical and human difficulties just as we must try to alter the political world in ways which will reduce and eventually remove the danger of nuclear war, no matter how poor the prospects of early success may seem.

COUNTERFORCE FIRST STRIKE FOLLOWED BY BARGAINING

It is possible to distinguish a spectrum of views concerning general war according to the relative emphasis placed on counterforce as compared with countercity attacks. The naive view envisions a spasm of mutual destruction with cities as primary targets. A slightly more sophisticated view recognizes that at least the side striking first should try to knock out as much as possible of the opposing striking power so as to minimize the damage done by the retaliatory blow. The next step is to recognize that a nation which destroys the enemy's cities is like a kidnapper who openly kills his victim, and thus destroys his bargaining power. Bargaining power (the power to secure favorable terms in the settlement of an issue which has erupted or threatened to erupt into war) is based on the threat posed to surviving assets by surviving weapons. To commit weapons against cities in an opening attack "wastes" weapons which could have been either withheld for bargaining or committed against the opposing weapons so as to reduce the counterthreat to one's own assets.

Thus we come to the concept of a spasm-like first-strike or counterforce exchange followed by threats and bargaining. At the beginning of a war both sides would have enough nuclear firepower to make countercity threats absurd and to make any difference in countercity destructive capability meaningless. One purpose of a counterforce first strike would be to establish strategic nuclear superiority at a low enough level of destructive potential that the superiority would be meaningful. The purpose, in other words, would be to destroy or drastically reduce the enemy's *capability* to hurt us and then to act on his *will* through our residual capability to hurt

---

[3] See Ramsey, *op. cit.* Also, *Nuclear Weapons and Christian Conscience,* Walter Stein (editor). London, Merlin Press 1961 and *Nuclear Weapons and the Conflict of Conscience,* John C. Bennett (editor). Charles Scribner's Sons, New York, 1962.

him.   Since a complete knockout blow against enemy weapons is extremely unlikely, this strategy requires a major program in both civil and active defense.   Western Europe presents an especially difficult problem in this respect because it is covered by Soviet short range mobile missiles which are the most difficult to target.   Furthermore, there is even less enthusiasm in Europe than in the United States for a massive civil defense program.

INTRA-WAR DETERRENCE, OR NO FIRST USE AGAINST CITIES

Finally one may take the next natural step in the direction of a counter-force strategy, carry the No-Cities doctrine to its logical conclusion, and recognize that attacks on cities would be hardly less pointless and immoral after a war was in progress than they were at the beginning—and for much the same reasons.   The basis for mutual deterrence of deliberate counter-population attacks can remain even after deterrence of war has failed. That is to say, we could have intra-war deterrence of countercity attacks in a counterforce nuclear war just as we could have intra-war deterrence of nuclear attacks during a local conventional war (as in Korea) or intra-war deterrence of Great Power intervention in an internal or sublimited war. Should deterrence fail, it need not fail all at once.   There are various pos-sible firebreaks in the spectrum of violence.   Of these, the break between conventional and nuclear warfare is probably the most important.   But the distinction between deliberate counterpopulation warfare and counterforce warfare (which may nevertheless entail severe civilian suffering) should not be too hastily dismissed even in the case of general nuclear war.   If current weapons and their deployment make this distinction fuzzy, that is more a reason for changing the deployment and the mix of weapons than for giving up what could be the last stopping place between a tragically destructive war on the one hand and an atrocity of global dimensions on the other.   In the nuclear age our margin for survival is not so great that we can afford to pass up any hopeful approach simply because it is difficult or doubtful.

In the concept of intra-war deterrence of countercity attacks (or No-First-Use-Against-Cities) the ability to threaten cities is not a means of bargaining over the settlement of the war.   It serves rather to neutralize the opponent's countercity capability so that countercity threats settle nothing at all.   They become a sanction for an international law against attacking noncombatants rather than an instrument of political conflict. Each side will retain during the war the ability to kill civilians, just as in the past a warring nation had the ability to execute prisoners of war or civilians in occupied territory but few nations in modern times have bar-gained with the lives of hostages.   Even the Nazis, for all their brutality, did not employ reprisals against occupied Europe to deter the Normandy invasion.

The willingness to make ". . . millions of women and children and noncombatants hostages for the behavior of their own governments" [4] comes from the curious standard according to which the morality of killing noncombatants depends on the physical distance between victim and executioner.[5]. . .

STRATEGIC NUCLEAR SUPERIORITY

There are two senses in which we could lose a general nuclear war: [6]

First, we could lose the assets we value, such as people, a way of life, wealth and the material basis of national power.

Second, we could expend our weapons and find ourselves at the mercy of an opponent who had retained a residual capability to threaten our assets, even though he might have lost much of his own.

It has been argued that strategic nuclear superiority is meaningless because, even on the most favorable assumptions, a first strike would leave the enemy in position to do great civil damage—that is, to make us lose in the first sense (above). But the danger is sometimes overlooked that a posture of Minimum Deterrence could put us in the position where, after a counterforce exchange or a controlled counterforce attack on us, the enemy would have a clear residual superiority. In other words, he would win in the second sense. To be sure, we might be able to spoil his victory by using our limited residual capability against his cities, so that he would lose in the first sense. But that would mean that we would suffer an even worse defeat in the second sense because using our weapons against his cities rather than against his forces would shift the balance of residual forces even farther in his favor. Although countercity attacks might make his victory meaningless, they would make our *defeat* even more painful. We would face an even stronger surviving government having even less incentive to spare our assets—in short, a tougher bargainer. Paradoxically, surviving assets are something of a liability in post-attack bargaining. The toughest bargainer would be a surviving government which had lost most of its assets except a powerful strategic force. To be sure, we would find little comfort in being this kind of "victor" but it would be hardly less comfortable to face such a "victorious" adversary after we had expended our own weapons against his cities. To actually carry out a countercity strategy is to commit not only the crime of indiscriminate slaughter but possibly also the blunder of losing the war and awaiting a reckoning at the hands of a powerful and outraged enemy.

[4] "Foreign Policy and Christian Conscience" by George F. Kennan, *The Atlantic Monthly,* May, 1959, p. 48.

[5] Bennett, *op. cit.,* p. 102. See also *The Irreversible Decision, 1939–1950* by Robert C. Batchelder, Houghton Mifflin, 1961.

[6] This distinction and the following argument are similar to those given by Paul Nitze in "Atoms, Strategy and Policy," *Foreign Affairs,* January, 1956, pp. 187–198.

Strategic nuclear superiority may be defined as the ability to win a strategic counterforce war—that is, to wind up with a residual strategic capability in the event that the war remained counterforce until the end, when the loser's weapons had been expanded or destroyed.

It may be argued that the chances of a general nuclear war's remaining counterforce are so small that strategic nuclear superiority does us little good. Yet it is widely felt that the Soviets derive *some* advantage from being able rapidly to mobilize several hundred divisions and arm them with modern heavy conventional equipment, including many tens of thousands of tanks and large caliber artillery, even though it is hard to imagine that warfare on a scale requiring such forces could remain conventional. There is little probability that either the Soviet conventional superiority or the American strategic nuclear superiority will ever be used to the full but, as George Kennan has remarked, "Armaments are important not just for what could be done with them in time of war, but for the psychological shadows they cast in time of peace." [7]

In discussing the Soviet attitude toward war, it is necessary to distinguish between their attitude toward (1) actual war, the possible destructiveness of which they recognize (2) the *risk* of war, which they are confident they control and can keep at a tolerably low level and (3) the *fear* of war, which they are prepared to exploit in order to intimidate other countries and to enlist the support of the "peace camp" within the Western world. Whatever may be said about thermonuclear war as an instrument of conflict, the fear of thermonuclear war is a powerful cold war weapon and one which the Soviets have used to their advantage. The well advertised development of a 100 megaton bomb shows how well the Soviets appreciate the psychological shadows cast by "unusable" capabilities.

If the Soviets can intimidate peaceful peoples by the development of counterpopulation weapons which it would be irrational to use under any circumstances, surely we should not hesitate to impress the Soviet leaders by the development of discriminating counterforce capabilities which it *would* be rational to use at least as a last resort.

To derive the most deterrent value from our nuclear superiority we should impress on the Soviets that: (1) It would be insane for them actually to attack cities, although, so long as they are inferior to us strategically, we can understand that they might want to make countercity threats as a matter of declaratory or deterrent policy. (2) We believe that the Soviet political and military leadership is entirely sane, rational and coolly calculating. Their past behavior has always been cautious. They have excellent self-discipline and have been no less ready to mitigate their demands when faced by superior power than to exploit weakness in an opponent. (3) Therefore, our strategic counterforce superiority is mean-

---

[7] George F. Kennan, *Russia, the Atom and the West*. New York: Harper and Brothers, 1957, p. 93.

ingful, and the Soviets must take it into account in their calculations, although they naturally cannot acknowledge it publicly.

The very real but also very limited value of our strategic nuclear superiority should not be either overemphasized or underrated, for example by arguments about whether an American President would respond to such and such a provocation by deliberately unleashing all-out war. Rather the question is how much advantage the West could obtain in a test of wills beginning say at the level of harassment and probing actions such as might occur around Berlin. At any level of escalation, would the West not gain *some* advantage from mutual recognition of what would happen if a counterforce exchange were carried to the limit? For example, suppose American counterforce strikes could reduce Soviet intercontinental capabilities to a level where they could only hurt us but not threaten our position as the world's leading power while we, on the other hand, could hold in reserve enough strategic capability to devastate the Soviet Union and China to virtually any desired degree. Even though the Soviets retained enough continental capability to hurt Europe badly, they would be unwise to do so in view of their vulnerability to attack by a much less vulnerable United States. *Having* a hostage does not entirely compensate for the disadvantage of *being* a hostage.

LIMITED RETALIATION

As discussed earlier, a massive attack against cities would be insane. However when strategic forces are well enough protected, there is no need to commit them all at once. Attacks could be carried out deliberately against one city at a time with each city being given warning in time to permit evacuation. Between attacks every effort could be made to settle the issue which had led to war. Cities chosen for destruction could be those with a high ratio of industrial to residential structures. Bombs with a minimum of fission yield could be detonated in the air to reduce fallout. Thus damage would be confined to property rather than people. This has been called the strategy of Limited Retaliation.[8]

The classical laws of war prohibit property damage except insofar as it is incidental to counterforce warfare. However, the moral basis for this rule is less clear today than it was in past centuries, when there was not a great deal of property over and above that required for human survival and the satisfaction of elementary physical needs. Today most property in a modern industrial nation is not necessary for survival or even for what past centuries regarded as normal comfort. Rather it supports national power and an affluent society of high mass consumption. An at-

[8] For a discussion and criticism of this strategy from several different points of view, see *Limited Strategic War* (Klaus Knorr and Thornton Read, eds.); F. Praeger, New York, 1962.

tack might be carefully designed to destroy much of a nation's industrial capacity while deliberately leaving enough for agriculture and the distribution of food. In short, the very modern technology that has made counterforce warfare obsolete can also make countereconomy warfare more humane than it has been in the past and perhaps more humane than a prolonged large-scale conventional war would be today.

Whatever its merits as a suggestive concept, the strategy of limited retaliation invites a number of practical questions: Would the enemy cooperate in carrying out such "set piece" warfare? Would he confine his own reprisals to evacuated cities and would he evacuate his own cities when warned? What would happen to an alliance like NATO if the Soviets chose to concentrate their threats or reprisals on one of the European nations?

Probably the least unfavorable circumstance for using limited retaliation would be in response to a deliberate, unprovoked aggression across a well defined boundary. If both sides recognized that the aggressor could back down without loss of face while the defender could not, the defender might come off better in a test of will, although the defender's position would be much improved if he had local forces capable of at least slowing down the aggressor's advance. An exchange of punitive reprisals at long range would be least promising in case a major war had grown out of a local incident or uprising (such as might occur in connection with Berlin) where both sides had been drawn in gradually in a series of small steps and without any major moves which could easily be reversed. The advantage of having stronger conventional forces on the spot is that they can serve political purposes directly and immediately. In a confused or ambiguous situation the locally superior side can "clarify" the situation to its own advantage.

Limited retaliation is not only a means of punishing the enemy (by destroying what he values); it is also a way of communicating resolve. An attack which did little physical damage could have a great psychological impact by crossing important symbolic barriers, and demonstrating a willingness to run risks, to enter on a dangerous and potentially painful test of will. Limited retaliation is one way of telling a generally cautious adversary that he has miscalculated and carried his provocations too far.

Since limited retaliation affects the opponent's will rather than his capability, it allows all gradations of violence down to purely symbolic acts. By contrast, a counterforce nuclear strike which was highly restrained in intensity would contribute little to a trial of strength since any relative degradation of the enemy's *capabilities* could be cancelled out by his reprisal. It may be possible, however, to combine the target system for a counterforce strategy with the purposes of limited retaliation. No matter how well strategic forces are protected, there will always be some vulnerable military targets, such as POL [9] depots and air bases. Attacks on such targets in the Soviet Union would be preferabe to attacks on Soviet cities. They would punish the enemy by destroying what he values. Presumably he does not like to see his military assets destroyed, even if in reprisal he destroys comparable assets on our side.

Instead of viewing nuclear counterforce attacks as a way of reducing enemy capabilities and incidentally doing extensive civil damage, we may think of them primarily as a way of acting on the enemy's will and only secondarily affecting his military capabilities. When our strategic forces are secure from attack, even if we have a superior counterforce first-strike capability, it may be better to use a strategy of limited counterforce retaliation as part of a bargaining strategy (at least at the beginning) rather than to launch a heavy strategic-tactical nuclear strike intended to compensate for our inferiority in conventional forces. However, our ability to limit Soviet reprisals and to secure favorable terms in a negotiated settlement would probably be improved by our having a counterforce superiority and if possible a good first-strike capability. As Arthur Burns [10] has argued, the Soviets could exploit a strategy of limited retaliation in an effort to destroy the NATO alliance by concentrating their reprisals on one of the European allies (say Germany). A war which was limited from the viewpoint of the Soviet Union and the NATO Alliance as a whole might not seem very limited from the viewpoint of the ally singled out for attack. The possibility of such an alliance-busting tactic by the Soviet Union may be the only contingency where the threat of a U.S. first strike has much residual validity.

Just as a first-strike capability, or at least a capability to win a controlled counterforce war, could serve to police limits on limited retaliation, so a strategy of limited harassment and property damage is one way of bringing to bear a residual strategic superiority following a counterforce exchange. The threat to do extensive property damage, including the destruction of evacuated cities, would be most credible when the victim was on the short end of a drastic strategic imbalance, so that he would be in an especially poor position to retaliate against *un*evacuated cities.

Finally, if it is accepted as a matter of moral principle that deliberate counterpopulation attacks are *never* justified, the threat to knock out evacuated cities could serve as the ultimate deterrent—even to attacks on occupied cities. The Soviets would hardly sacrifice their material wealth and power in order to kill hundreds of millions of noncombatants, even assuming they are totally insensitive to moral issues and public opinion, both domestic and foreign. Furthermore, the Soviets could not be certain how we would retaliate, no matter what we had said or sincerely believed beforehand.

[9] Petrol, oil, and lubricants. [Eds.]
[10] *Limited Strategic War,* Chap. VI.

CONCLUSIONS

This paper has tried to clarify issues, challenge common assumptions, highlight distinctions often blurred in debate, and lay out the alternatives for policy decisions rather than to wrap up a tidy solution. The purpose, in short, has been to expand rather than to narrow down the options open to a policy maker. Nevertheless, some definite conclusions have emerged, which may be summarized as follows:

The Fact of Uncertainty. The principal and overriding conclusion is that controlled counterforce nuclear war is not clearly infeasible but plans and forecasts as to how it should or would be conducted are highly uncertain and represent a fantastic extrapolation beyond historical experience. Our ability to deal with unfamiliar situations is limited at best. Millions of lives were sacrificed in the First World War through failure to adjust to so comparatively modest an innovation as the machine gun.

It would be irresponsible to underestimate what a fateful step is taken by crossing the nuclear threshold even in a limited way—let alone in a strategic trial of strength. Even with the most careful preparations including a determined effort to separate military targets from centers of population, we would still face great uncertainties in the actual conduct of the war. For example: Would both sides use only air bursts against soft targets in order to minimize fallout? Would targets such as bridges, which are near cities be attacked by fighter-bombers delivering small bombs with relatively high accuracy and at considerable risk to the lives of the pilots; or would larger bombs be delivered by less accurate missiles fired from a safer distance? How well do we know the location of Soviet missiles of all ranges? How heavy an attack could the Soviets accept and still maintain control of their response and fight a discriminating counterforce war? How much military effectiveness would be sacrificed to avoid collateral civil damage and could each side appreciate the restraint the other was exercising and reciprocate—from fear of reprisal if not from more worthy motives?

By thinking about these questions, making careful analyses and running war games, we may gain some insights and understanding which will be helpful in tactical planning, but overall military policy must be based less on an *estimate* of how the war would go than on the *fact* that even the best estimates are highly uncertain. The effort to fight a controlled counterforce war with a minimum of collateral civil damage might be relatively successful or it might fail and end in a catastrophe. Both possibilities have to be considered. Which should be emphasized depends on the context. Those responsible for developing capabilities and doctrines for strategic and tactical nuclear warfare must emphasize that counterforce nuclear warfare, however unpromising, is possible and that the effort to avoid civil damage is well worth making. Those, on the other hand, who are responsible for overall military policy should recognize that, although counter-force nuclear warfare is not impossible, it is a terribly dangerous expedient, likely to result in frightful civil damage and, as a means of defense, it is a singularly poor substitute for conventional combat forces.   So long as we have nuclear weapons and strategic delivery systems, we must make every effort to develop plans and capabilities for fighting a controlled general war even while recognizing how uncertain are the prospects for success.

The difficulties and dangers of a counterforce nuclear strategy are sufficient to justify reliance on a conventional strategy except as a last desperate resort.   It is one thing to recognize that nuclear warfare would probably involve heavy civil damage; it is another to develop forces and formulate war plans based on a strategy of deliberately doing civil damage.

*   *   *

Flexibility of Counterforce Strategy.   The real world is richer in pos-sibilities and options than is implied in much of the debate over strategy and arms control, which has tended to polarize around two views—one emphasizing stability, parity and Finite Deterrence based on a countercity capability, and the other emphasizing counterforce and strategic nuclear superiority.   As the preceding sections have shown, a counterforce strategy for general war is compatible with a wide variety of other options.   It can be combined with strategic nuclear superiority or with parity; with a first-strike capability and doctrine or with a symmetrical balance between two second-strike forces; with an effort to keep ahead in the arms race or with quite far-reaching arms control agreements; with a conventional strategy for local war or with several forms of limited tactical nuclear war including the use of well-protected strategic weapons against tactical support targets and the use of limited counterforce attacks as part of a bargaining strategy.

Nuclear Diffusion.   If countercity threats come to be regarded as in-decent, one motive is removed, or at least reduced, for small nations to acquire independent nuclear capabilities, which are often justified on the grounds that, although they would have no counterforce capability, the threat to destroy even a few cities would enable a small nation to deter any attack on itself without the support of a major ally.   This is a dubious rationalization in any case.   Ruling out countercity threats makes it even more so.

Unilateral Arms Control Initiatives.   There are a number of things we can do in our own interests which are also in the interests of the world at large including the Soviet Union.   We can by our declarations and example try to establish three rules: (1) military targets should be located away from cities, even at considerable extra cost (2) in case of war, attacks should be confined to military targets to the extent feasible (3) both sides should accelerate the phasing out, not necessarily of first-strike weapons, but of first-strike-only weapons.

Probably the Soviet Union would react (as they already have to similar initiatives) by claiming that we were trying to preserve war by inventing rules for its conduct while they are engaged in a crusade to abolish war through general and complete disarmament.   It should not be beyond our wit to handle this problem in public relations.   We could emphasize that our helpful and perfectly feasible measures are not put forward as a substitute for far-reaching solutions but as a means of making the world safer until more fundamental changes can be brought about.   If the Soviet Union can score propaganda points by *talking about* grandiose schemes which could be carried out only in a changed political world, we should be able to convey a favorable impression, at least to the discerning, by proposing mutually beneficial actions which we *are* carrying out in the present world.

Chalmers Johnson

THE THIRD GENERATION OF GUERRILLA WARFARE

During the past thirty years Asian Communist parties have helped instigate and have pursued five major guerrilla conflicts against Asian non-Communist, Western-allied, or Western colonial regimes.   Of these five struggles—China, 1937–49; Malaya, 1948–58; the Philippines, 1946–54; the Viet Minh Movement, 1946–54; and the Viet Cong Movement, 1959–present—two, Malaya and the Philippines, made no important contribution, except perhaps a negative one, to the developing body of Asian Communist theory on the strategy of revolution.   The Malayan and Philippine conflicts must be left out of account because their Communist leaders did not utilize directly the heritage of Mao Tse-tung's revolution and because both were defeated.   But the other three revolutionary wars—the Chinese Communist, the Franco-Vietnamese and the Vietnamese Communist—all show signs of mutual influence on the progressive development of what might be called an emerging Asian Communist "tradition" of revolutionary theorizing.   Of perhaps greater interest, the leaders of the third of these three successive generations of Asian Communist revolutionaries have

Reprinted by permission of the publisher from *Asian Survey*, 8, 6 (June 1968), pp. 435–447. © 1968 by The Regents of the University of California.

based their struggle on a strategy that is influenced by, but significantly different from, that of their revolutionary grandfathers.

"Guerrilla warfare," in the Asian Communist context, is an element of a concrete revolutionary strategy—that is, of a plan of coordinated behavior intended to bring a revolutionary association to power in a given social system. Our concern in the present discussion is neither with the sources of social disequilibrium that may have mobilized Asian revolutionaries (the "roots of revolution") nor with the particular ideological "future cultures" that Asian Communist revolutionaries hope to create. We are concerned not with why some Asian Communists are revolutionaries nor with what they propose to build on the ruins of the cultures that bred them, but with how they think they can defeat their enemies in order to begin their social rebuilding.

THE MAOIST TRADITION: MILITARY POWER THROUGH POLITICAL MEANS

Mao Tse-tung has been the primary strategic innovator in the Asian Communist revolutionary tradition. He began thinking about how to achieve a revolutionary victory after the Leninist strategic tradition had been decisively defeated in Asia—that is, after Chiang Kai-shek's 1927 defeat of the Chinese Communist Party and the Collapse of the Comintern-inspired united front. . . . Mao and later leaders inspired by him concluded that henceforth Communist revolutions could only take the form of revolutionary wars. Whether they knew it or not, they were responding to Trotsky's earlier gloss on Lenin's strategy of revolution: you can succeed without the army, but you cannot succeed against it. Mao's first axiom became that, in order to make a revolution in China (later generalized to include all of the allegedly neo-colonial nations and territories of the world), the Communist Party had to build an army and use it to defeat its enemies in military combat.

Despite many differing interpretations by foreign observers of the Chinese Communist revolution, the Chinese Communists themselves interpret it in exclusively military terms. For example, Lin Piao, Peking's Minister of Defense and "Chairman Mao's closest comrade in arms," * has said:

Comrade Mao Tse-tung's theory of and policies for people's war have creatively enriched and developed Marxism-Leninism. . . . The special feature of the Chinese revolution was armed revolution against armed counter-revolution. The main form of struggle was war and the main form of organization was the army which was under the absolute leadership of the Chinese Communist Party, while all the other forms of organization and struggle led by our Party were co-ordinated, directly or indirectly, with the war.

* Until 1971 when he was purged. [Eds.]

Since Mao does not admit of an alternative road to victory save the battle-field, the goal of all revolutionary Communist activity must be to prepare for success in battle: "The seizure of power by armed force, the settlement of the issue by war, is the central task and the highest form of revolution. This Marxist-Leninist principle of revolution holds good universally, for China and for all other countries." In short, "Every communist must understand this truth: political power grows out of the barrel of a gun." [1]

Chiang Kai-shek had demonstrated to Mao and the small band of military leaders and peasant rebels who fled to the countryside with him after the debacle of 1927 that a threatened regime defended by a professional army and willing to use that army against Communist rebels could thwart Leninist strategy. Mao therefore oriented his own revolutionary strategy, following upon his axiomatic definition of revolution as revolutionary war, to the solution of two problems: (1) the building of a Communist army, and (2) the development of tactics whereby an objectively weaker military force could defeat an objectively superior military force. His grand strategy, in its most fundamental military sense, was to obtain a decisive intelligence advantage over his otherwise invincible foes. If he could obtain near-perfect intelligence concerning his enemy's strength and movements—and at the same time deny the enemy such intelligence about his own forces—he could begin to correct the material and professional imbalance between the two antagonists. With intelligence, he could introduce the element of surprise, set ambushes, concentrate superior numbers at any selected point, choose the time and place of fighting, avoid all evenly-matched or un-favorable engagements, escape mopping-up campaigns, and contribute to the demoralization of the enemy's rank and file.

The fundamental dynamic problem of this strategy is how to create the web of intelligence upon which it is based. Mao found an answer to this problem in the Leninist doctrine of the united front. However, whereas Lenin saw the united front as a tactic for legitimatizing his party's activities, helping to position it within the target regime for purposes of carrying out a *coup d'état,* Mao conceived of a united front with the mass of the popula-tion so that the people could serve as the source of his army's manpower and as its intelligence-collecting network. In order to obtain this desired level of cooperation from the population, Mao argued, the revolutionary directorate had to discover some issue salient among the masses which the party could champion; the party thereby gains access to the people's sym-pathies and is able to organize the masses for guerrilla warfare.

As a revolutionary strategist with his own basic values and goals thor-oughly compartmentalized, Mao recognized the need to exploit oppor-tunistically *any* political issue that might bring about the desired level of mass organization. Most of the inner-party struggles during the revolu-

---

[1] Quotations from Lin and Mao are from Lin Piao, *Long Live the Victory of Peo-ple's War* (Peking: Foreign Languages Press, 1965), pp. 3, 26, 44.

tion concerned Mao's efforts to get his idea of the flexible use of a united front accepted by his party colleagues. Throughout the shifting alliances and political developments of the 1927–49 period, Mao remained committed to the goal of army-building, and he fought against those party members who confused the aims of this or that particular united front effort with the ultimate goal of a military victory by the Communist Party.

As early as 1930, Mao had identified the following issues as potentially exploitable bases for his guerrilla-oriented united front: (1) the contradictions between imperialism and the Chinese nation, and among imperialists themselves; (2) the contradictions within the counterrevolutionary ruling cliques; (3) the contradictions between rulers and the broad masses of the ruled; (4) the contradictions between the landlords and the peasantry; (5) the contradictions between the bourgeoisie and the working class; (6) the contradictions between warlords and their troops; and (7) the contradictions between the counterrevolutionary regime and the intellectuals and students.[2] At the outset of his guerrilla revolution, Mao chose number four—the contradictions inherent in the agrarian situation—as the most immediately promising basis for the united front, and he experimented with several different formulations of Red Army land policy in trying to exploit this issue. But he never forgot the other contradictions and always stood ready to shift his efforts to one or another in light of changing political realities.

From 1931, with the heightening of Japanese pressure on China, and particularly after 1935, when Mao became formal head of the Communist Party, he switched the party's united front policy to contradiction number one—that between imperialism and the Chinese nation. It was on this basis, in the context of the Japanese invasion of China, that Mao obtained the secure mass organization that ultimately allowed him to defeat the Kuomintang.

Mao's strategy is multifaceted and complex. There are, however, three aspects of it that are particularly relevant to a discussion of his successors' variations: first, what the Chinese Communists call the "mass line"; second, Mao's emphasis on "self-reliance"; and third, his three-phase periodization of the "protracted war."

The "mass line," despite its increasing ideological ossification in China after 1958, was one of Mao's key organizational insights; and during the revolutionary period, when it was relatively faithfully pursued, the mass line helped keep Mao's party free from the ideological dogmatism that has so often isolated Marxist-Leninist parties from popular political support. According to the mass line, the party must eschew a doctrinaire application of the Marxist-Leninist theory of social contradictions in formulating its policies. Instead, the party must conduct on-the-spot investigations into

[2] Mao Tse-tung, "A Single Spark Can Start a Prairie Fire" (January 1930), *Selected Works* (New York: International Publishers, 1954), I, pp. 119–21.

the social and political problems agitating the masses, and it must then interpret these findings in terms of Communist ideology, taking care not to run ahead of popular consciousness. By insisting on a rigid adherence to the mass line, Mao was able to forge a genuinely popular mass movement based on true sources of mass discontent; he thereby avoided the analytical and political sterility of so many Marxist movements when confronted with, for example, mass nationalism. Mao's development and adherence to the mass line is closely connected with the second important facet of his strategy, his emphasis on self-reliance.

Mao has preached self-reliance to successive generations of guerrillas partly because he himself won a military victory without any of the contemporary advantages enjoyed by Communist guerrillas, such as privileged sanctuaries, external sources of arms, or international champions seeking to obtain recognition or belligerent status for Communist forces. . . . During his own struggle for power, Mao was forced to stress self-reliance because external aid was never made available to him. However, later Communist guerrillas have used international political and military aid and the coordination of strategies in ways that Mao never dreamed of.

The third facet of Mao's strategy, protracted war, like the mass line and self-reliance, is linked to his lack of external assistance and to his assessment of the initial superiority of the enemy's armed forces. Mao wrote his famous and influential tract, *Lun Ch'ih-chiu Chan* ("On Protracted War"), during the first year after the Japanese invasion. Because of Japan's overwhelming power vis-à-vis China, Mao argued, it would take a long time for the Chinese guerrillas to equalize the military imbalance between the two; however, so long as his followers were willing to commit themselves to a long war of attrition, given the favorable conditions for a guerrilla united front created by the invasion, victory would ultimately be theirs. "Will China perish?" he asked. "No. She will have her final victory. Can China win a quick victory? No, this must be a protracted war. Is this conclusion correct? I think it is so."

In order to make his promise of eventual victory credible to party members during the dark days of May and June, 1938, Mao had to come up with an analysis that pointed to an ultimate Chinese triumph and at the same time offered practical guidelines during the early periods when victory was not in sight. He accomplished this by means of his famous three-stage periodization of the war: "the period of the enemy's strategical offensive, the period of the enemy's strategical defense and of our preparations for counter-offensive, and the period of our strategical counter-offensive." For each period, Mao set forth various combinations of tactics to be pursued, and although he was never too precise about this, the thrust of his analysis was clear: stages one and two were to be periods of guerrilla warfare and attrition, while stage three would be a period of victorious "strategic assault."

Mao's *On Protracted War* has become his most famous revolutionary military tract, and his three-stage blueprint is common knowledge today among Communist guerrillas throughout the world. This is an anomaly. In China, Mao's third stage never arrived during the period when Mao's forces were engaging a foreign foe, the Japanese army; and Lin Piao, in his 1965 reassertion of Maoist theory, refers only in passing to the three stages, placing much greater stress on the development of rural guerrilla bases than on the types of military operations that are appropriate to each stage of the war. Lin Piao accurately emphasizes that the importance of the Anti-Japanese War period was that it allowed the Communist Party to champion nationalistic resistance to the invader and thereby gain its first militarily significant mass following. *On Protracted War* itself should be read as a morale builder for the hard-pressed Chinese forces during the early phases of the war, and as Mao's realistic appraisal of the Japanese Army's strength and staying power. The Chinese Communist revolutionary victory is significant not because of any particular set of precepts advanced by Mao during its course (especially ones so abstract that they could not influence behavior significantly) but because it is the clearest example to date of a successful, internally derived, mass-based, militarily oriented strategy of revolution.

THE VIET MINH LEGACY:
DECISIVE VICTORY SHORTENS THE PROTRACTED WAR

Probably the single, most lasting contribution that Mao Tse-tung has made to the Asian Communist revolutionary tradition is his definition of revolution as revolutionary war. The Indochinese Communists who organized the Viet Minh movement against the French colonialists faced a comparatively easier task than Mao did, and one in which various nonviolent political options conceivably could have brought success. However, with the French resort to armed counterrevolution and with the precedent of Communist military victory emerging in China at precisely the same time, the Vietnamese movement for political independence took the form of a revolutionary colonial war. In retrospect, Asian Communist revolutionary theorists have tended to see this development as inevitable, as part of a Marxist law, proved by the Chinese and Viet Minh cases. One reason for the outbreak and exacerbation of the later Viet Cong conflict is that the Vietnamese Communists of the 1960s have never envisioned, nor are they organized for, any type of electoral or other nonviolent resolution of fundamental political problems (other than one that would ratify their own military victory).

The Viet Minh movement occupies a transitional position in the development of Asian Communist revolutionary strategy. It was explicitly influenced by Mao's victory, and Vietnamese Communist revolutionaries have analyzed their activities using concepts first formulated by Mao. For example, General Vo Nguyen Giap asserts:

1949 saw the brilliant triumph of the Chinese Revolution and the birth of the People's Republic of China. This great historic event which altered events in Asia and the world, exerted a considerable influence on the war of liberation of the Vietnamese people. Viet Nam was no longer in the grip of enemy encirclement, and was henceforth geographically linked to the socialist bloc.[3]

The Viet Minh revolution and the Chinese Communist revolution are actually far from similar. Guerrilla warfare in its relatively pure Chinese form is a strategy of poverty—both politically and militarily. The political operations that must precede the opening of guerrilla warfare, including adherence to united front principles such as the mass line, are dictated by the need to build a truly popular supporting structure, one that can sustain carefully controlled and slowly escalated military attacks on the target regime's forces. It is a strategy of military operations tailored to remain just under the threshold where professional armed forces could easily decimate the nascent revolutionary army. This strategy is delicate, painful, and slow in both its organizational preparation and actual implementation; no revolutionary party would voluntarily choose it if more direct alternatives were available.

In their struggle with the French occupiers, the Viet Minh Communists chose rather unthinkingly to follow Chinese precedents, just as they did a few years later with regard to land reform; but their revolutionary task was not as difficult as Mao's, and they enjoyed immensely greater military supplies than did the Chinese revolutionaries. The Viet Minh revolution was not a civil war but a colonial war of independence. Mass line investigations of popular grievances and trial-and-error testing of political programs were unnecessary because the revolutionaries could assume virtually universal anti-French sentiment and because the Viet Minh army was not totally dependent on the population for military support. The Viet Minh revolution contributed to the Asian Communist tradition of political violence, but it also began the reorientation of the tradition away from pure guerrilla warfare.

There is significant evidence of these Viet Minh modifications in guerrilla strategy. For example, the Viet Minh leaders considered the arrival in 1950 of Chinese Communist forces on Vietnam's borders more important than the continuing need to project a nationalistic image to the indigenous population: In November 1945, in response to united front demands, the Indochinese Communist Party had "dissolved" itself; however, on March 3, 1951, the Communists abandoned the "Viet Minh" facade (Viet Minh is an acronym meaning "League for the Independence of Vietnam") and emerged as the Vietnam Lao Dong (Workers) Party. By doing this they allied themselves more closely with the Socialist bloc, which was then supplying them with significant amounts of arms and technical assistance, but

[3] Vo Nguyen Giap, *People's War, People's Army* (Hanoi: Foreign Languages Publishing House, 1961), p. 22.

they also tended to turn the nationalistic struggle into a civil war. Even though the Lao Dong Party continued to fight against the French, many Vietnamese concluded that Communist Party "nationalism" did not have room for *all* persons of Vietnamese nationality. After 1954, some 800,-000 to 1,000,000 Vietnamese migrated to the south, while only some 30,000 to 100,000 went northward. Although it was probably unforeseen at the time, the creation of the Lao Dong Party contributed directly to the division of the country three years later and to the reopening of the civil war a decade later. Viet Minh revolutionary strategy placed more immediate value on its international alliances than it did on its popular infrastructure, and this constituted a departure from the guerrilla strategy of the Chinese Communists.

Another difference lay in the types of relationships the Viet Minh army maintained with the mass of the population. As in China, the revolutionary army was raised from peasant villages, whose inhabitants supported the struggle against the French, and the Vietnamese villages similarly supplied the revolutionary army with intelligence, logistic support, labor, guerrillas, militia and refuge. However, because the revolutionary army was not as dependent on the population as the Chinese Communist forces had been, the Viet Minh cadres began to use, on a small scale at this time, a tactic eschewed by the Chinese as counterproductive and contrary to the basic logic of guerrilla warfare—namely, terrorism. Although the elimination of traitors is to be expected in any revolutionary war, Vietnamese Communists displayed a much greater willingness to use terror against even potential traitors than had the Chinese, and they never showed the Chinese skill in developing methods of rehabilitation or reform of domestic opponents or wavering elements. Terrorism in this context served less to win the active support of the population than to raise the costs to the population of supporting the revolutionaries' enemies.

With regard to self-reliance, the Viet Minh revolutionaries did all of their own fighting, but they enjoyed secure sanctuaries across the Chinese border and a supply of military equipment unprecedented in the Chinese case until 1945 at the earliest. The key dates in the development of Viet Minh strategy are 1950 and 1953. In 1950 the Chinese Communists arrived on the Vietnamese borders, and in 1953 the Korean truce released large amounts of Chinese equipment for transfer to Vietnam. Chinese aid, consisting primarily of U.S. arms captured either from the Kuomintang armies or from U.S. forces in Korea, included ammunition, light arms, anti-aircraft guns, heavy mortars, 105 mm guns, and a few trucks of Russian manufacture. This equipment greatly enhanced the military capabilities of the Viet Minh army, but it also tended to give the army a more professional military orientation than had obtained in the Chinese People's Liberation Army. For example, the North Vietnamese army constituted an identifiable interest group within the post-revolutionary regime from the outset.

The enhanced military capability of the Viet Minh forces made possible the spectacular victory of positional warfare at Dien Bien Phu—the Viet Minh's most significant, and certainly most controversial, contribution to the evolving strategy of Asian Communist "people's war."   In *On Protracted War,* Mao cautioned against "decisive battles on which are staked the destiny of the nation."   He wrote:

The rash advocates of quick victory cannot endure the arduous course of the protracted war.   They want a quick victory, and whenever conditions turn slightly for the better, they clamor for a strategic war of decision.   If their wish were carried out, the entire resistance would be jeopardized, thus sacrificing our protracted war and falling into the vicious trap of the enemy.

Officers of most counter-guerrilla armies would agree with Mao; what they pray for most of all is a formal battle in which the rebels will "stand and fight."

The battle of Dien Bien Phu, contrary to Mao's advice, is an example of a patiently prepared, carefully launched, thoroughly successful assault against an enemy that according to some was overextended and according to others simply made a strategic mistake.   Although the defeat was not militarily "decisive" with regard to the enemy's entire war-making potential, it carried with it such a powerful psychological punch that it produced valuable reverberatory effects on the overall war-making *commitment* of the defending forces.

Vo Nguyen Giap himself is both candid and cautious in discussing the gamble he took in waging the battle of Dien Bien Phu . . .   The battle conceivably could have gone the other way, probably with equal if not greater impact on the morale of the revolutionary forces.   But it did not. Although "its main object was the destruction of enemy manpower, it took full advantage of the contradictions in which the enemy was involved," and herein lies a source of later modification of Maoist doctrine and a justification for trying shortcuts in Mao's long, arduous timetable.

The Viet Minh revolution partook formally of the basic aspects of the Maoist approach to the problems of revolution.   The Viet Minh Communists accepted the necessity of waging revolutionary war; they utilized guerrilla methods to overcome the enemy's professional military advantages; and they oriented their activities to the military defeat of the enemy's armed forces.   At the same time, they did not follow Mao's strategy closely.   As late as 1965, Lin Piao was arguing:

In order to win a people's war, it is imperative to build the broadest possible united front and formulate a series of policies which will ensure the fullest mobilization of the basic masses as well as the unity of all the forces that can be unified. . . .   To rely on the peasants, build rural base areas, and use the countryside to encircle and finally capture the cities—such was the way to victory in the Chinese revolution.

The Viet Minh did some of these things, although less thoroughly than had the Chinese, and they did other things that the Chinese thought risky and in violation of theory.   By producing the withdrawal of French forces, however, they too gained a victory—without being forced to annihilate the French Army.   The Viet Minh cut short the protracted war and thereby set their own successor generation to rethinking the problems of overall revolutionary strategy and to experimenting with a new definition of revolutionary "victory."

THE VIET CONG SYNTHESIS:
POLITICAL POWER THROUGH MILITARY MEANS

On February 20, 1962, Viet Cong guerrillas threw four hand grenades into a crowded village theater near Can Tho, South Vietnam.   A total of 108 persons were killed or injured, including 24 women and children.   On September 12, 1963, Miss Vo Thi Lo, 26, a school teacher in An Phuoc village, Kien Hoa province, was found near the village with her throat cut. She had been kidnapped by the Viet Cong three days earlier.   In June 1965, Saigon officials reported that 224 rural officials had been assassinated or kidnapped during the month, doubling the rate of April and May. On January 17, 1966, the Viet Cong in Kien Tuong province detonated a mine under a highway bus, killing 26 Vietnamese civilians, 7 of them children.   These types of revolutionary activities, undertaken systematically and over a period of several years, differentiate radically the Viet Cong strategy of revolution from that pursued by Mao Tse-tung.

On May 13, 1959, the Central Committee of the Lao Dong Party, meeting in Hanoi, declared that the time had come to begin the task of "liberating the South.   .   .   . to struggle heroically and perseveringly to smash the Southern regime."   In accordance with the basic orientation of Asian Communist revolutionary strategy, the Lao Dong Party determined that this task would require a revolutionary guerrilla war, and accordingly it began to build the political platform on which guerrilla military operations could be sustained.   Basing its united front appeal on propaganda directed against the policies of the Ngo Dinh Diem regime, on December 20, 1960 it created a united front organization, the National Liberation Front of South Vietnam (NLF), and it began both to mobilize the approximately 10,000 Viet Minh left behind in the South in 1954 and to infiltrate into the South guerrilla cadres of Southern origin.   NLF political workers undertook to organize peasant villages into a guerrilla infrastructure.

This approach appears familiar, but there was a fundamental difference between it and earlier precedents.   Ten years of development in military technology, particularly in the realm of air power and the use of helicopters, had made a purely military rationale for guerrilla warfare seem hopelessly unrealistic and time-consuming.   The Vietnamese Communists' former enemy, the French army, was itself proving at the time in Algeria that military answers to Mao's strategy could be developed. Moreover, the danger of American intervention against the rebels or against Hanoi itself was clearly recognized; the NLF served both as a focal point for building an indigenous united front in the South and as a lightning rod protecting Hanoi from the obvious danger of direct retaliation.

Other alternatives to a purely military approach were sought. "Contradictions" within the Saigon government suggested that the Viet Cong could isolate it politically and demoralize or win over its army without actually being forced to reverse the rebel-government military imbalance and defeat the defenders' armed forces in a Maoist "third-stage" positional war. The concept of three stages was retained in Viet Cong strategic planning, but the first two stages were reoriented away from steadily increasing guerrilla attrition and toward a political transformation of the target system through violent means. As Douglas Pike observes:

Not military but sociopsychological considerations took precedence. Military activities and other forms of violence were conceived as means of contributing to the sociopolitical struggle. . . . The two hundred to five hundred "guerrilla incidents" per week that went on in Vietnam week after week and month after month for five years had no purpose in themselves—and indeed when viewed in themselves often made no sense—except to serve the political struggle movement. Thus the primary purpose of the violence program was to make possible the political struggle movement.[4]

Selective terrorism not only terrorizes people; it atomizes them and causes them to make individual calculations of the relative costs and benefits in the short run of particular courses of behavior. In this sense it is somewhat comparable to the extortion rackets aimed at poorly protected, poorly socialized, ghetto dwellers and shopkeepers in American cities. The difference in Vietnam is that the Viet Cong not only institutionalized this type of daily cost-benefit analysis among the peasants of the South—which resulted in the peasants' growing disbelief in *any* policies promulgated by Saigon—but it also sought to legitimatize its activities by playing on impulses toward national unification, family and ethnic loyalties, religious differences, and hopes for peace and stability.

Viet Cong strategy, prior to the 1965 American intervention in force, differed from both Chinese and Viet Minh strategy in that military activity prepared the way for a political showdown, rather than political activity preparing the way for a military showdown . . . The Viet Cong assaults began in the villages and worked their way up toward district and provincial governmental levels, often enhanced by inept reactions from the central government but, in any case, carried out with a relentlessness not found in either Chinese or Viet Minh practice.

---

[4] Douglas Pike, *Viet Cong* (Cambridge: M.I.T. Press, 1966), pp. 32, 99. Pike first used the term "third generation of revolutionary guerrilla warfare" in this book, p. 36.

Because of differences in their basic conceptions of revolutionary strategy, the Viet Cong revolution also differed in detail from the Chinese and Viet Minh cases. There was no mass line investigation of popular grievances, except on a tactical basis to take timely advantage of particular developments. The Communist revolutionary effort, having been initiated from outside the embattled territory, was not dependent upon a critical level of political grievance for its sustenance. Similarly, the Viet Cong revolution was not self-reliant, either in terms of its equipment, core manpower or strategic inspiration. Equally significant, its front organization enjoyed international, coordinated efforts by Communist nations and organizations to advance its claim to a popular political existence separate from the Saigon government and allegedly preferred by the people of South Vietnam.

Since 1963, Viet Cong strategy has been undergoing various transformations in response to the changing reactions and capacities of the enemy. Although it is impossible to comment on this subject in any definitive way, we can indicate the lines along which Viet Cong thinking appears to have developed. Having defined the goal of the struggle in the South as a political rather than a military victory, the Viet Cong at first sought to make credible by violence the inability of the Saigon government to govern. In response to a growing American presence, they increased their military activity—but this time with the additional intention of exploiting "contradictions" in the American position. (There is no evidence that the Vietnamese Communists ever concluded that they alone could defeat the United States through guerrilla warfare over any realistic time period.)

The "contradictions" that the Viet Cong perceive in the American position include: (1) the falling out between the U.S. and some of its allies over the war in Vietnam; (2) the inability of the U.S. to match its extraordinary technical superiority to Viet Cong maneuverability and military intelligence; (3) America's domestic aversion to the war, producing opportunities for any ruling administration's political rivals (the Viet Cong do not generally predict a "collapse" of the American home front, but they do see the war as perhaps engendering in the U.S. an advantageous political competition—one that might bring to power a popular leader, such as General de Gaulle vis-à-vis Algeria, who would end the war on terms favorable to the rebels); (4) unintended consequences of the American style of large-scale operations in Vietnam, such as corruption in the distribution of American aid, which weaken the already attenuated stability and legitimacy of the Saigon government; and (5) the possible generation of a true, anti-American, nationalist reaction among the people of South Vietnam as a result of the large number of Americans sent there.

Like General Giap's "taking full advantage of the contradictions in which the enemy was involved" at the time of the battle of Dien Bien Phu, the Viet Cong revolutionaries (who of course include Giap) have tailored their military activities to exploit these perceived weaknesses. On the one hand, the Viet Cong have tried to create the impression that they are determined to wage a protracted (if need be, endless) war; on the other hand, they have aimed for "decisive victories" on the model of Dien Bien Phu (e.g., the Tet offensive of 1968). Both lines are intended to damage psychologically the U.S. commitment to the war, thus generating a negative cost-benefit analysis among American political leaders and thereby producing a victory more like that obtained by the Viet Minh than by the Chinese Communists. The essence of the strategy is not to defeat the U.S. and allied forces militarily but to convince the Americans through the use of violence, both pervasively and at selected points, that their position is hopeless.

Viet Cong revolutionary guerrilla strategy has thus come a long way from the doctrines of Mao Tse-tung. In a sense, Viet Cong strategy is a theory of neither "revolutionary" nor "guerrilla" war. It is not revolutionary to the extent that it creates social grievances rather than responding to them, and it loses its guerrilla characteristics to the extent that it no longer depends upon an overtly nonbelligerent but covertly engaged population to provide its army with an overwhelming intelligence advantage. Nevertheless, the strategies of Mao, the Viet Minh, and the Viet Cong are linked by their willingness to associate civilian populations with military activities and by their relatively undoctrinaire, opportunistic readiness to exploit any social "contradiction" in order to bring about the violent defeat of the enemy.

Bruce M. Russett

MAKING DEFENSE DEFENSIBLE

Evaluating and controlling military expenditures have become central concerns of American political life. High levels of defense spending are often laid to a quasi-conspiratorial "military-industrial complex," and the consequences of militarization are alleged to be economic waste, neglect of social priorities, and distortion of the political system. Yet discussion of a "military-industrial complex" is a symptom rather than a diagnosis. Very little solid information exists, and in any case there is no reason to think that the causes or consequences of all kinds of military spending are

Abridged by permission from *The Virginia Quarterly Review*, 46, 4 (Autumn 1970), pp. 529–551. Material drawn from Bruce M. Russett, *What Price Vigilance? The Burdens of National Defense* (New Haven: Yale University Press, 1971).

the same. If we are to control military spending so as to avoid excesses, yet to defend as much armed forces procurement as is necessary for our security, we must consider the matter with careful concern for objectivity, discrimination, and evidence. . . .

Military expenditures in the United States are now high by American standards. For the last twenty-five years they have regularly taken a greater share of the nation's produce than at any time in its history, other than in periods of all-out war. Since the Korean War the military budget has always been above 7 per cent of the country's G.N.P., with at least two and a half million men under arms. . . . The military effort also is high by international standards. In both defense expenditures as a proportion of G.N.P. and military manpower as a percentage of working-age males, the United States ranks, with Russia, among the most "militarized" of the world's nations. No American under fifty can recall a time in his adult life when our armed forces were small.

Yet during the past two and a half decades there has been, until recently, extremely little questioning of, let alone opposition to, the maintenance of a large military force by the United States. In a rich and expanding economy the burdens seemed tolerable, even demanded by the international situation. Presidential candidates campaigned against missile gaps; Congressmen almost never cut proposed military budgets, and indeed often increased them; in opinion surveys a large majority of the populace consistently expressed the view that the defense budget was either about right or too low.

The standard explanations are obvious enough: cold war, an arms race forced upon us by the Russians, and the need to defend weaker nations of the free world. Yet in our toleration of large armed forces as at worst a necessary evil we lost sight of some salient facts. One of the most intriguing is a standard pattern of wartime expansion and only partial postwar contraction of the military. Over the past century, the proportion of the budget devoted to military expenditures has never, after any war, returned to the prewar level. The figures on absolute numbers of military personnel are especially revealing. The Spanish-American War, World War I, World War II, and the Korean War each produced a virtual and permanent doubling of the armed forces over the size characteristic of the preceding years. It is not enough to invoke the image of American global responsibilities after each war. While that explanation surely has some truth, Parkinson's Law also comes to mind. So too does an image of a political system where each war weakened the restraints on the activities of military men and their civilian allies.

We are in an arms race with the Soviet Union, in the sense that many kinds of military procurements by one side demand some response by the other. But that race can be carried on at high or low levels of expenditure. A willingness to accept parity, or even inferiority, results in a much more limited set of interactions than does an insistence on predominance. So too does a readiness to accept a fairly wide margin of error in intelligence estimates in place of a rule always, when in doubt, to err on the side of exaggerating rather than underestimating the other side's capabilities and aggressiveness.   Thus even the arms race explanation requires attention to the prevalent images and expectations of domestic politics.   For instance, it is widely assumed that former President Johnson's 1968 decision to proceed with his Sentinel ABM system was to protect himself from rightwing political critics who were already unhappy about lack of progress in Vietnam—not out of any great sense of need for the system to protect the national security.   During the 1969 debate on ABM the critics argued that if the system were once begun, even on a small scale, it would set off Russian counter-measures that in turn would demand further American expenditures, and so on in an upward spiral.   By that logic, the arms race would force both us and the Russians into basically unwanted procurements—but only because of an initial erroneous and avoidable step by the United States.   Hence American domestic politics would greatly influence whether the arms race proceeded at a sprint or a creep.

Without minimizing the arms race pressures, and without ignoring the blindness of Russian domestic politics, we must look more closely at the confluence of interests among elements of the military, the civilian defense bureaucracy, Congress, and industry.   The armed services play bureaucratic politics in competing with one another for resources.   During the 1950's the Navy sought a strategic war capability, first in aircraft carriers and later in missile-carrying submarines, to avoid being submerged by the Air Force.   Likewise, Army personnel sought an anti-missile system, and within the Air Force advocates of manned bombers fought to keep the Air Force from being grounded, for strategic war purposes, in unglamorous missile silos deep below the Western plains.   Many industrial firms have become heavily dependent on Defense Department orders.   Their production methods are geared to the manufacture of a few units of hardware, each very expensive and requiring very high performance reliability. . . . Expense often is much less important than performance; the deliberate decision not to worry much about cost and to employ very high-quality components is quite different from the mass-production of automobiles . . . The development of modern weapons carries great uncertainties and risks to the firm requiring special contractual arrangements as compensation.   For all these reasons, defense contractors are often unenthusiastic about converting to civilian production, and make great efforts to keep their defense business by coming up with new weapons.

Finally, Congressmen too develop interests in maintaining the flow of defense contracts to their constituents, and in retaining military bases in their districts.   The consequence is an alliance among men from very different points in public and private life, each of whom supports military procurement programs in the classic tradition of American politics concerning public expenditure.   Businessmen support Congressmen's electoral campaigns; Congressmen roll logs for one another; and military and civilians in the bureaucracy seek and exchange favors with legislators and industrialists.

This is *not* to imply there is great waste in military procurement programs, or that political activities and favor-swapping in the military realm are dishonest or illegal. I would guess that the level of probity is at least as high as in the realm of purely civilian public expenditures. Nor is it surprising or censurable that the armed services and their suppliers should undertake political activities. Virtually all firms which sell to the government establish similar relationships, in other countries as well as in the United States. . . .

What *is* disconcerting, however, is the size of the American military establishment, and thus the enormous impact unavoidably made whenever generals, admirals, Congressmen, and businessmen combine to promote multi-billion dollar expenditures. The Defense Department's annual budget is larger than the total G.N.P. of all but six or seven of the world's countries. Its size is particularly disconcerting in light of the demonstrated staying power of the military establishment; that is, its ability to retain, after war, much of its wartime expansion. We cannot help but ask whether our armed forces are bigger than they need to be. If so, then what are the costs to the rest of the social and economic system? Among the often alleged offenses of defense are these:

1. There is a symbiotic relationship between spending and politics; for instance, Congressmen who support military expenditures benefit disproportionately from them in their constituencies. More important, this relationship has wider effects on the political system as military spending provides political support for legislators with "hard-line" positions across a spectrum of military and foreign policy issues, and some domestic matters as well.

2. The United States has failed, perhaps less for a lack of effort on its own part than from the "selfishness" of its allies, to use its system of military alliance as a means of reducing the American defense burden.

3. Military spending tends to come largely at the expense not of private consumption, but of investment and public expenditures for social needs such as health and education, thus endangering the long-run welfare of the country.

Here is some of the evidence on those questions.

II

The power of the purse has for centuries been the primary legislative instrument for restraining an extravagant or self-serving executive. In the United States, Congress must authorize and fund all Defense Department expenditures, yet its success, or even interest, in cutting military budgets has been unimpressive. The Defense budget is rarely scrutinized to evaluate many individual items; for every debate on ABM or manned bombers, hundreds of major programs are passed as proposed by the executive.

If items really were examined on their *individual* merits, we should see shifting patterns of alignment among Congressmen on defense issues. Some legislators would approve of bombers and others prefer missiles; still others would support needs of the Navy, or the Army, against any Air Force requests. But while each service and major weapons program does have its legislative champions, for the great majority of lawmakers the military effort is seen as a whole. A close study of the Senate shows that in the 90th Congress (1967–68) the alignments on virtually all Defense appropriation and authorization measures were very much alike, appearing as aspects of a more general attitude toward defense spending. Senators who voted to limit military research and development also voted, almost without exception, against the ABM in the preliminary skirmish over that system. Similarly, those who favored allocating $280,000 to a Charleston, South Carolina, Air Force base also virtually always favored the ABM.

One possible explanation for this behavior is logrolling; one Senator gets funds for the military base in his state while another, in exchange for his support, gets missile-manufacturing contracts for the aerospace firm in his constituency. Surely this happens. Another explanation, however, is that Senators have general convictions about the merits or perils of defense spending. Each may have a different cut-off point above which he would not approve more expenditures, but on either side of that point he implicitly ranks controversial spending measures in an order of desirability that agrees generally with the rankings of other legislators. The roots of these general convictions may lie in ideology, patriotism, intellectual evaluation, or partisan advantage.

In light of this second explanation, another and not entirely expected result is important: Senators' alignments on defense expenditure measures are very closely related to their alignments on a much wider spectrum of issues regarding defense and East-West relations. In the 90th Congress this broad spectrum included votes on the Vietnam war, money for the Arms Control and Disarmament Agency, various reforms in the Draft, aid to Communist countries, and conditions for ratifying the Consular Convention with the Soviet Union. These matters, unlike many defense appropriations measures, have little to do with direct economic gains for anyone's constituents; they are not subject to logrolling in the same way as are military expenditures. Thus the logrolling explanation, while doubtless partly correct, is incomplete. More general convictions are operating. The positions of Senators are fairly clear to anyone who has followed legislative debates in the past couple of years. The extreme conservatives or hawks are composed almost exclusively of Republicans and Southern Democrats; the liberals or doves are mostly Northern Democrats, though Senators Fulbright, Yarborough, and Hatfield are prominent.

This alignment, it must be noted, is not the same as those that appear for gun control, Space Agency appropriations, or foreign military assistance. . . . Thus the image of the "military-industrial complex" uniformly promoting weapons and aerospace expenditures is oversimplified. Rather, some procurement programs are outside the normal concerns of the preparedness advocates, who nonetheless give consistently "conservative" treatment to a variety of related but not strictly defense issues of foreign policy.

A time-perspective extending back to the first years of the Kennedy administration adds the following information: There is substantial continuity over time on the general cluster of defense and East-West relations matters. Senators who were proponents of heavy military spending and a hard line in the 90th Congress behaved much the same way six years earlier. But in the 87th Congress the defense expenditure issue was largely latent. Few military authorization or appropriation measures came to roll-call votes; if they did, the overwhelming majority of the Senate always favored them. Only more recently have military expenditures become controversial issues on which a large number of legislators were ready to take a critical stance. It may be no coincidence that in December, 1968, for the first time since the beginning of the cold war, the Gallup poll found a majority who thought the nation was spending too much for defense. Current partisan positions on defense have become reversed since the 1950's. When the Eisenhower administration was trying to hold down the defense budget, many Democratic Congressmen found "preparedness" a good vote-getting issue, and the Democrats as a group were more pro-defense than were Republicans. This was as true of Northern Democrats as of their Southern colleagues.

"Hawkishness" and "dovishness" are related to the distribution of some kinds of military spending around the country. Regardless of a Senator's party affiliation or whether he comes from a Northern or a Southern state, the greater the impact of Department of Defense spending on his state's labor force, the greater is the likelihood that he adopts a hard-line or hawkish stance in Congress. For example, six of the twenty Senators from the ten states which derived the largest proportion of their total payroll from direct Department of Defense employment (in descending order of defense dependence: Alaska, Hawaii, Virginia, Utah, Georgia, New Mexico, South Carolina, Oklahoma, Colorado, Kentucky) were among the most hawkish one-fifth of the Senate. These same states produced only two members of the most dovish fifth of the Senate.

. . . It is not obvious whether defense-dependence produces among voters a hard-line foreign policy attitude that is reflected by their legislative representatives, or whether hard-line Senators seek and find rewards in the form of defense installations for their districts. Probably some of both occur. In any case, it is rare to find an outspoken critic of recent American foreign policy from a state where the military employment impact is high.   Even the most prominent instance, Senator Gruening, proved not to be such an exception.   He was one of only three incumbent Democratic Senators not to be re-elected in 1968, perhaps because he had been more independent than his constituents would tolerate.   Defense expenditures for military installations go to support and reinforce, if not actually to promote, a set of hawkish and strongly anti-Communist postures in American political life.   This support may well be inadvertent rather than deliberate, but it does exist.   In turn, the Pentagon is supported, and its expenditures promoted, by those voters and political figures.

*   *   *

On the other hand, it is just as important to know that there seems to be no similar relation between hawkishness and a state's proportionate income from Defense Department contract awards.   This is contrary to some of the most common ideas about American politics, and demands notice just as does the above finding.   Some very slight association between foreign policy position and contract dependence exists, but its slightness is more striking than the fact of its existence.   A variety of possible explanations can be offered.   Perhaps because they are relatively enduring, military bases contributing direct employment to the state's economy exert a political influence on Capitol Hill that here-today, gone-tomorrow government contracts cannot.   Direct hire by the Defense Department may more strongly mold the attitudes of workers, both military and civilian, than does employment for a firm which in turn sells its products to the Pentagon.   Other possible explanations concern the likelihood that defense weapons and equipment contractors, unlike local suppliers of military bases, try to exert political influence on key Senators from other states as well as their own.   And there is some question about the reliability of the publicly-available data on the distribution of defense contracts—more accurate data might show a relationship that now eludes us.

Nevertheless, the difference between the political effect of direct employment and spending on contracts is clear.   If there is a "military-industrial complex," the industrial part, composed of the big manufacturing establishments, does not itself reinforce the hawkish or uncompromisingly anti-Communist forces in this country in any strong, simple, or direct way.   That is not to say that military spending on particular weapons systems is not promoted by industry.   Certainly Senators with defense industries at home do look out for them.   California, Colorado, and Washington represent three of the centers of the aerospace industry; on twenty specifically aerospace questions in the 90th Congress their Senators show exactly one vote (out of 120 possible) against the aerospace industry. But the political effect of that spending is not the same as that of money spent to maintain a large army of many men, with bases scattered freely around the country. . . .

III

United States military and political spokesmen have long complained that their allies provide less than a fair-share contribution to the joint defense of the West. This lament has focused primarily on the NATO allies where, despite their long-accomplished economic recovery, the European states spend very much less of their national income for defense than does the United States. In most cases, in fact, the Europeans' defense share of G.N.P. is half or less than America's. It appears that our allies are shirking their burdens by relying excessively on an American nuclear deterrent to which they do not contribute. . . .

But the difficulty is not specific to NATO, nor even to American alliances. For America it stems from a fundamental contradiction between two aims of postwar alliance policy. The United States sponsored NATO to achieve two goals. One, and probably the primary, was to protect the weak states by extending over them the umbrella of America's nuclear deterrent. The other was to augment American military strength with that of the European allies, and ultimately to reduce the burden of our commitments by creating strong local military capabilities in the path of any Soviet advance. Yet to the degree the former succeeds the latter is endangered. So long as the alliance organization is voluntary and the big power cannot coerce the smaller ones to build their armies, the smaller states are likely to regard the big country's armed forces as a substitute for their own. They will feel able to relax their own efforts because they have obtained great-power protection, especially if the external threat of attack is not considered very grave. Their effort will be less the greater is their confidence in the big power's guarantee. Moreover, the greater the size disparity between small powers and a big one, the less military effort the smaller ones make as a proportion of their income. This last rule varies where a small power is especially exposed to an external threat (for instance, Turkey) or where its military forces are used for some purpose other than defense against the common enemy (for example, Portugal with its colonial difficulties). Nevertheless, the general principle holds, that the smaller the nation relative to its big-power guarantor, the fewer sacrifices it will make to build a military force.

. . . Even in Eastern Europe, the Soviet Union has recently encountered the same dilemma. The Warsaw Pact is certainly no voluntary organization in the sense that members can enter or leave it at will, but in recent years at least the member states do seem to have developed considerable ability to determine for themselves what their levels of military effort will be. In the 1950's the Soviets were able to extract a fairly uniform military share of G.N.P. from each of them, but from the middle 1960's onward the East Europeans' proportionate contributions took on much the same shape as those of the NATO allies. All of them devote a much smaller share of G.N.P. to military ends than does the Soviet Union, and the defense proportion of G.N.P. varies closely with the size of the country. . . . Thus the Soviets, like the Americans, find that they have taken on alliance responsibilities and commitments, but without the accretion to their own military strength that they initially expected or were able to extract in the Stalinist days. . . .

The phenomenon tells us enough about what one can reasonably expect from various kinds of alliances to offer much guidance to Americans. In forming or keeping an alliance with other states and providing them with deterrence, a great power must expect that its allies will spend less on defense than they would do in the absence of the protective alliance. If the American goal is to bring other nations more effectively under its deterrent shield, then the United States should so judge the alliance's success. While it may still make every reasonable effort to persuade allies to do more for themselves, it would be short-sighted to slip into acrimony. Nor, from disgust, should it do anything to weaken its protective guarantee so long as it still places great value on preserving the independence and security of its allies. Perhaps paradoxically, it should actually be a bit worried when an ally persists in very heavy military expenditures of its own, as they may be a signal that the ally really does not have full confidence in the guarantee. American policy-makers must realize that efforts to reduce American defense spending by shifting major burdens to our current allies are most unlikely to succeed. Rather, each alliance must be evaluated in terms of the benefits it brings to us relative to the cost incurred by accepting a commitment to protect others. If the latter is too high, we will probably be able to cut our defense expenditures more by dropping the alliance than by trying to extract greater effort from the smaller state while the alliance is still in effect.

IV

There is a widespread myth in America that defense spending, even if higher than strictly necessary for national security, is not really a waste because the alternative use for resources would be equally frivolous civilian spending. That is, if the money were not going for weapons it would be turned back to the taxpayers for personal consumption, not used in the public sector for education, pollution control, urban development, or public health programs. If that were true, then the real price of defense would only be in the loss of some luxuries for middle and upper-class America, and we might well prefer always to err on the side of too much defense spending rather than too little. Certainly congressional behavior with the 1969 tax reform and tax reduction bill did little to ease the impression that among legislators tax cuts had higher priority than social needs.

The truth, however, differs substantially from the myth. When we look at patterns of spending over the past thirty years rather than just the most striking acts of recent congressional behavior, it is clear that public spending for domestic needs is in large part the real alternative to military expenditures.   In periods of rising defense needs in the United States, the resources to provide military goods have had to be extracted from various parts of the civilian economy.   The mirror-image of an increase in defense spending tells us what happens when military expenditures are reduced. Typically, the alternative uses for a defense dollar have been as follows: 42 cents from personal consumption, 29 cents from fixed capital formation (investment), 10 cents from exports, 5 cents from federal government civilian programs, and 13 cents from state and local governments' activities. . . .

Private consumption has indeed been the largest alternative use of defense money, at 42 cents to the dollar.   Personal consumption, however, always represents the largest segment of the economy anyway, usually almost two-thirds of the G.N.P. except in times of all-out war.   Fixed investment is normally only about a fifth of that amount.   Thus the absolute dollar shares are very deceptive if one wants to know what parts of the civilian economy bear *proportionately* heavy costs from defense.   For that we must take a model of the "average" American economy for the past thirty years and ask from where, on the basis of what actually did happen in a number of military ups and downs, would a hypothetical $25 billion defense increase come.   On that picture, private consumption would have been reduced by an amount equal to about 4 per cent of itself—but fixed investment would have declined by 14 per cent of its original level.   Expenditures of the federal government and state and local governments also would have suffered heavily, going down by 16 per cent and almost 11 per cent respectively.

Therefore investment and government civil spending are major casualties of high levels of defense expenditures.   So too is the balance of payments. The Vietnam war has imposed direct foreign exchange costs to maintain troops in Southeast Asia.   It has also imposed indirect costs, heavier ones. Exports have been hampered by the high level of demand, which diverts many products away from foreign markets.   From the other side of the coin, imports have been boosted to meet internal demand and because the inflation has made some foreign goods cheaper than those produced here. By my calculations, which are if anything conservative by comparison with those of many economists, the direct and indirect effects of the war account for very roughly three-quarters of the American balance of payments deficit in 1967.

The trade-off between defense spending and particular kinds of public expenditures over the past thirty years can also be identified.   Typically the proportionate change in spending for public education has been approximately the same as that for fixed capital formation, and for health and hospitals only slightly less—still about three times the relative effect on private consumption.   In both cases federal spending has been proportionately harder hit than has that of state and local agencies, as is not surprising since it is the federal budget that must immediately make room for an increased defense share.

Over the long run, the effects of this defense trade-off cannot help but be very great. The implication of past patterns is that if a cut could be achieved in the military budget, both fixed capital formation and social investments in health and education would benefit significantly. Or the reverse, the inability to cut defense spending deprives the nation of many of the long-term underpinnings of national strength. The economy's future resources and power base are damaged much more severely than is current indulgence. . . .

*   *   *

Certainly, there are important benefits, even in the civilian sector, from defense spending. The various spin-offs, and in some cases actual defense stimulation of certain kinds of public civil spending (for example, education after Sputnik) must not be ignored. Yet a careful evaluation points unavoidably to the conclusion that defense spending, with spin-offs, is hardly the most efficient way to achieve civilian benefits. Medical research still is more likely to produce medical breakthroughs than is weapons research, though occasionally the latter does help. Defense spending does hamper civil needs, and ultimately will leave us with a poorer, more ignorant, and less healthy population than if the military spending had not been thought necessary.

*   *   *

Past opportunity costs provide no perfect guide to what the costs will be for future military spending. Both the political system and the economy change, and the costs may be distributed differently. . . .

At the same time, we must recognize that there are many features of great stability and resistance in the political system. The pressures that have in the past directed the costs of defense so heavily toward investment and government civilian programs, rather than toward private consumption, are likely to retain most of their influence. . . . Any decision to maintain or increase military spending, therefore, probably will have effects not so very different from those in the past unless a very great effort is made to do things differently. It may well be easier to vary the level of military spending than to change drastically the distribution of trade-offs. If so, especially careful evaluation of military demands is essential, in terms of their probable actual if not always intended consequences.

V

The real and present problem with the armed forces in American politics is how to control spending for armaments, and how to limit the spill-over from alignments on defense expenditures into other issues of domestic and foreign policy. We should worry not about a sudden takeover of power by our soldiers, but about how to prevent slow accretions in the scope of military influence in the "normal" political system. Here we must concern ourselves as much with the military's civilian allies, who use arms spending for their own purposes, as with our soldiers and sailors.

We also need to limit arms spending because of the dangers of an arms race. So far, the arms race has not been rapidly run. While the absolute expenditure levels have risen, neither the United States nor the Soviet Union now devotes a larger share of its national resources to arms than it did in the mid-1950's. Were it not for Vietnam, the United States would show a clear decline in its defense share since the early 1960's. Also, the technology of the last decade has been kind to us, Russians and Americans alike—more kind than most of us realize in the face of awful weapons of death and pain. The kindness has been in the strength given to the defender. In a world of balance of terror, both superpowers have been able to build secure deterrents, making the initiation of nuclear war unattractive. The invulnerability of our deterrents, however, may not be a permanent gift. Technology is not autonomous; the hasty, ill-considered, or foolish procurement of new weapons could rapidly erode the invulnerability of one side or both. ABM systems, MIRV's, orbital bombs, and myriad other possibilities could destroy the contemporary balance that preserves the power which would reply to an attack but not initiate one. This is the greatest risk of the arms race; that we, and the Soviets, will do whatever is technologically feasible without properly considering its military and political implications. Like climbing mountains, trying to build new weapons just to see if it can be done has its attractions.

At the same time, we must not forget that a failure of deterrence can also come from a *neglect* of our weapons, both current and projected. Until there is an essential change in the international system, a failure to buy a needed new weapon could have effects as calamitous as a run-away arms race. For this reason too, money wasted on the wrong wars or the wrong weapons threatens our security, because after the waste we might then not have the resources for what we needed. Waste can provoke a wide reaction against all defense. For these reasons too, sound evaluation is required to make defense spending defensible. Not even the most ardent advocate of preparedness can favor a system that blinds rational choice, retains old programs beyond their usefulness, and selects new ones according to the accidents of political influence.

If we are to establish and maintain enlightened democratic control over defense expenditures, it is crucial that we understand both their causes and consequences. If we think that heavy military burdens are thrust upon us *solely* by the forces of international conflict, we shall never be able to evaluate properly the new military requests that will be made of American taxpayers. Nor if we fail to understand the consequences of such expenditures will we have the incentive to limit them.

SUGGESTED READINGS

Aron, Raymond, *A Century of Total War*, Garden City, N.Y.: Doubleday, 1954; Boston: Beacon, 1955.

Brennan, D. G. (ed.), *Arms Control, Disarmament and National Security*, New York: Braziller, 1961.

Halperin, Morton, *Contemporary Military Strategy*, Boston: Little, Brown, 1967.

Hoffman, Stanley, *The State of War*, New York: Praeger, 1965.

Johnson, Chalmers, *Revolutionary Change*, Boston: Little, Brown, 1966.

Kissinger, Henry, *Nuclear Weapons and Foreign Policy*, New York: Harper, 1957.

———, *The Necessity for Choice*, New York: Harper, 1961.

Knorr, Klaus, *The Uses of Military Power in the Nuclear Age*, Princeton, N.J.: Princeton University Press, 1966.

Nef, John U., *War and Human Progress*, Cambridge, Mass.: Harvard University Press, 1950.

Pruitt, D. G., and Snyder, R. C. (eds.), *Theory and Research on the Causes of War*, Englewood Cliffs, N.J.: Prentice-Hall, 1969.

Schelling, T. C., and Halperin, M. H., *The Strategy of Arms Control*, New York: Twentieth Century Fund, 1960.

Wright, Quincy, *A Study of War*, Chicago: University of Chicago Press, 1942: abridged ed., 1964, pb., 1965.

VII. THE BONDS OF WORLD COMMUNITY

It would be hard to argue that an international civilization or a "world community" exists, but it is difficult to deny that international politics is conducted, and largely directed, by civilized men. Certainly that is no automatic guarantee that world politics will be "civilized," despite the hope expressed in Sigmund Freud's essay in Chapter VI. Indeed we are far from the sunny optimism of Edward Gibbon, who believed that men need not fear the development of more terrible weapons since only civilized nations could develop them, and such nations would never employ weapons more terrible than those already in use in Gibbon's own eighteenth century.

Nonetheless, it cannot be denied that the civility of men exercises a "civilizing" effect on world politics. Not the least area of influence exists in terms of ideas of international morality. Man is, as the old philosophers would have it, a "moral being." He is never satisfied to be told that what he "ought" to do is utterly separate from "the reality" of things, because his feelings of what "ought" to be the case are part of that "reality." But if men must compromise their ideals in practice, they demand assurance that in so doing they are pursuing the "best possible" course in the given circumstances.

It has been fashionable in recent years to describe Machiavelli as a "value-free" social scientist who described what "is" and not what "ought to be." Yet nothing could be further from the case. Machiavelli believed that the right was so far separate from the existing state of things that it was folly to *begin* with the right and to endeavor to impose it on the world of events; one must rather begin with existing conditions in order to obtain a better state of affairs. Since all policies have their ambiguities, the policy we should choose, Machiavelli contends, is that which is "least harmful."

Machiavelli's great aim was to base political morality on politics itself; his key category is the morality or "reason" of the state (*raison d'état*), free from the control of norms and values "above" politics. Thus he admires a king like Ferdinand of Aragon, who can use the Church for the purposes of the state, and detests the Papacy ("a certain prince") for promoting in its own interest conflict and weakness among and within states. Machiavelli does not argue that the inner religious feelings or the beliefs about humanity of rulers are unimportant: his argument is that they are *politically* unimportant. What is important in politics is what men can see; a just man who has a reputation for injustice, Machiavelli would argue against Plato, may be a "good" man, but he is a political disaster. Moreover, Machiavelli's "reason of state" is morality of the *state,* not of the prince. The prince must act as the needs of the state command, not as his own desires dictate. Machiavelli's opposition to feudal nobles and to the Church would apply to the prince himself. Any group or individual within the state that prefers private interests to those of the whole ought to be sacrificed.

Machiavelli was concerned with what Sheldon Wolin has called "the economy of violence," which involves, for example, the use of some immediate violence to avoid greater evils or greater violence later.[1] But even Machiavelli relies on some rules of morality between states. Men, he argues, "are never so dishonest as to oppress you with such patent ingratitude" as to attack you when you have been their ally. Machiavelli relied on those rules because he recognized that there is no *certain* way to calculate the "economics" of violence, the more or less of policy; the influence of chance on human affairs being what it is, what seems wise policy may end in disaster. Morals are the rules of safety between states, which guarantee to some degree that defeat due to miscalculation is not fatal. The victor of the moment realizes he may be the loser the next: "Victories are never so prosperous that the victor does not need to have some scruples, especially as to justice."

Immanuel Kant, however, regarded Machiavelli's maxims as perverse. Kant was not "unrealistic"; he was fully aware of the problems of action in an imperfect world. But, he argued, the proper place to begin making a better world is with the moral standards *by which* we may judge a "better" policy better and a "worse," worse. Men cannot, Kant argues, accept conditions in the world as "givens." Education and action can change the conditions if policy is guided by moral norms. Machiavellians, he continues, do *not* argue that the "end justifies the means"—a position that Kant would himself largely accept—but rather that the "means justify the end." They are so bound up, he asserts, with technical skill and facility that they fail to see toward what ends such skill should be used; they become lawyers and not legislators. Kant is not upset that the great powers of his day accepted Machiavellian rules of *practice,* but rather that they accepted those rules as the ends and goals of states: the rules of Machiavellian practice had become the rules of international morality.[2]

David Hume, displaying his typical moderation and skepticism, took a position between Kantian and Machiavellian ideas of international morality. Such morality, he affirmed, is necessary and exists as part of the same "law of nature" that governs men as individuals. But, he argued, although the extent of moral obligation is as great in international as in any other politics, there is less to *compel* states and men to observe it. Hence we may infer that international morality rests more on the internal principles by which statesmen guide themselves than do domestic politics and morals.[3]

[1] *Politics and Vision,* Boston: Little, Brown, 1959, Chapter VII.

[2] See Norman Jacobson, "Political Science and Political Education," *American Political Science Review,* 57 (1963), 561–569.

[3] David Hume, *Treatise of Human Nature* (1739–1740), Book III, Part II, Section XI.

Prof. Hans Morgenthau applies this precept to his analysis of the "decline" of international morality. Morality between nations, he contends, was based on the governance of an international class, an aristocracy whose attitudes and manners were shaped by common standards and common institutions; however, he laments, democracy undermined rule by the traditional international aristocracy. It substituted the fictional "conscience" of states for the "concrete" conscience of individuals and placed national values and "will" above international standards of universal morality.

Two objections may be made to Morgenthau's otherwise excellent discussion. First, it tends to set up a "reactionary utopia," to regard the seventeenth and eighteenth centuries as examples of international virtue, something that Kant, who lived in those centuries, would not have done. To be sure, there was a *consensus* among nations, but that consensus, Kant indicates, was a consensus about means, which might be summarized in the phrase "international good manners." But states had accepted as ends the Machiavellian principle of adding to the power of the state, a principle that produced conflict even if all agreed that it was right and proper. And as has been noted in Chapters V and VI, if "manners" interfered with state policy it was policy that tended to prevail, especially in that "long term," of which today's "decline" of international morality is only a part. As Oliver J. Lissitzyn indicates, the "law of nations" arose in an international society that, while more and more interdependent in technical and economic terms, had grown more heterogeneous in *moral* terms. Unlike the "law of nature," which had been the keystone of medieval political thought,[4] the "law of nations" was a standard of *convenience* in the relations of states more than a standard of morality. Apparently the "decline" of international morality reaches further into the past than Morgenthau seems to believe.

Second, Morgenthau overlooks the fact that, as the traditional basis of international morality has declined, a new basis may have arisen. The social bases of consensus have passed, but the combination of destructiveness and interdependence in modern international society seem to *demand* and *compel* morality in a way that Hume and other traditional students could neither imagine nor foresee. Wendell Willkie's phrase "One world—or none" describes much about the moral climate of our times. Kant's criticism of Machiavelli has a timely ring: the present order of things can be changed; men can and *must* expand the area of morality in international politics. Lissitzyn, too, sees the problem of a new international law as far from hopeless, even though the U.S.S.R. stresses "struggle" and not "cooperation" in its view of law.

The greatest problem of law and morals in our times, Lissitzyn notes, is that rapid change tends to make any norms or rules of conduct and behavior obsolete and outdated. Under such circumstances even moral consensus on *ends* is not able to produce law. Lissitzyn notes, however, that states find in the General Assembly of the United Nations an agency that may be suited for making the rules of international law because it can change its norms and rules in conformity with the demands of an age of revolutionary change.

Change has been especially rapid in warfare and it has been hotly debated

[4] Ewart Lewis, "The Contribution of Medieval Political Thought to the American Political Tradition," *American Political Science Review,* 50 (1956), 462–474.

whether "the law of war," traditionally regarded as an effective restraint on man's ability to destroy his fellowmen indiscriminately, makes any sense at all. Some have argued that in practice legal restraints in wartime are nothing but "a collection of pious platitudes" to be brutally brushed aside by the norm of "military necessity." Maj. William Downey, Jr., however, asserts that no "military necessity" can "justify an act by a military commander which disregards a positive rule of law or which goes beyond the express limitation of a qualified rule of law." [5] That this theory is still applied, at least by the United States, can be proven by the much discussed trials that followed the revelation of the Mylai massacres.

Whatever may be said of morality, there is little doubt that in economic terms our world is far more interdependent than at any other time in history. Adam Smith, the great liberal economist (1723–1790), looked at such interdependence as a powerful "civilizing" factor:

The wealth of a neighbouring nation, . . . though dangerous in war and politics, is certainly advantageous in trade. In a state of hostility it may enable our enemies to maintain fleets and armies superior to our own; but in a state of peace and commerce it must likewise enable them to exchange with us to a greater value, and to afford a better market, either for the immediate produce of our own industry, or for whatever is purchased with that produce.[6]

Smith hoped that the desire for wealth would lead men to sweep away barriers to trade and to develop an international economy so integrated that war would be impossible, since the necessary war matériel and resources would always, in part, be located in foreign states. But while Smith's theories appealed to British merchants and manufacturers, who in the first half of the nineteenth century were much advanced in technology and foreign trade, they seemed much less attractive to countries who were trying to catch up with runaway Britain. So Alexander Hamilton in America and Friedrich List in Germany noted that wealth may be a source of conflict if by free trade some grow wealthier and wealthier and some poorer and poorer. Nations that have reached different stages in industrial development, Friedrich List maintained, cannot trade completely freely without the technologically less advanced nation sacrificing "its manufacturing power to foreign competition" and thereby binding itself to remain for all future time a poor agrarian country.[7] That this argument is by no means outdated is shown by James Weaver, who maintains that even technologically highly advanced nations, like the United States, will support free trade only in order to become richer to the detriment of its trading partners and will practice protectionism, for instance in oil, to the detriment of less developed nations.

Many economists of our time, however, will argue that the key to wealth is

---

[5] See W. G. Downey, Jr., "The Law of War and Military Necessity," from *The American Journal of International Law* (April 1953), pp. 251–262 and also Neil Sheehan, "Should We Have War Crime Trials?," *The New York Times Book Review*, March 28, 1971, pp. 1–3, 30–34, which includes a fairly complete bibliography of the Vietnam war crimes debate.

[6] *The Wealth of Nations* (1776), New York: Modern Library, 1937, p. 461.

[7] *The National System of Political Economy* (1841), Sampson S. Lloyd, trans., New York: Longmans, Green & Co., 1904, p. 258.

in amassing of capital. But to accumulate capital it may be necessary to forgo the immediate wealth that Adam Smith held out as lure in favor of growth and greater wealth in the long term. Smith describes an optimal condition among states satisfied with the existing division of land, labor, and capital; but the last two of these factors are subject to change, and even "land" (natural resources) may be added to by conquest. In an age of a "revolution of rising expectations," few states are satisfied with the existing order of economic affairs. For Barbara Ward, to provide such capital (and other aid) to the underprivileged masses of the earth is primarily a moral duty of the West. She regards the phenomenal "explosion" of "population, knowledge, communication, resources" as the fundamental challenge that faces mankind as a whole. She finds the answers to these challenges in a genuine willingness to sacrifice by those who are affluent, "in more creative experiments" of regional international organization and cooperation, and in greater and more serious concern with the increasing gap between the haves and the have-nots.

Her basic optimism is shared by the findings of the U.N. Commission on International Development, headed by former Canadian Prime Minister Lester Pearson, which, while admitting that the rich countries have grown richer, maintain that the poor countries have also become less poor absolutely, though in many cases not yet relatively. If the rich countries, the report asserts, would by 1975 approximate in their net aid 1 percent of their gross national product; would channel more of their aid through international agencies; would make longer commitments; and would extend loans at lower interests and more favorable conditions, the majority of the world's poorer countries could achieve self-sustaining growth in thirty years' time.[8]

The economics of development is a new and still vaguely defined field. Its problems lead to disagreement between those who are generally inclined toward socialist economic planning and international organization and those who believe that the free enterprise system has been more successful in creating economic growth and individual freedom than even the most intelligent governmental efforts. There are abundant pitfalls for the representatives of both schools. It is, for instance, often asserted that the sponsors of economic aid believe in unconditionally delivering the fruits of the work of generations of diligent Western peoples into the arms of the eagerly grasping leaders of uneducated, ignorant, and semibarbarous nations. But that Miss Ward feels the West has moral obligations to help economic growth in underdeveloped countries does not necessarily mean she does not believe that the recipient countries should also assume moral obligations in the use of these funds. Fruitful cooperation and genuine partnership are hardly imaginable unless such obligations are mutual. On a more technical level there are, of course, legions of difficult problems, the solution of which cannot be dismissed by glib phrases about "central planning," on the one hand, or "domestic capital accumulation," on the other. Nor are the problems of all underdeveloped countries the same. The theoretical and practical problems with which the West had been confronted once it decided to embark on economic, financial, and technical aid to the new nations were many and most complex.

[8] U.N. Commission on International Development, *Partners in Development,* New York: Praeger, 1969.

If material forces are no guarantee of world harmony and civility, it is natural that men should turn to spiritual and cultural factors in the hope of "civilizing" world politics. To those who have seen world politics as dominantly a "conflict of cultures" the solution to present dilemmas has seemed to lie in developing an international culture that might promote world "understanding" and avoid "fear and tension." Such an approach may be attacked from two positions. Culture, it can be argued, is in part the result of material conditions: it is pointless to strive for "understanding" in a world where some men are rich and others desperately poor, or where weapons of mass destruction become themselves sources of distrust. Others may argue that the gulf between cultures is too great to be "bridged," that an "irrepressible conflict" exists between them.

At least in the case of the United States and the Soviet Union, some scholars have argued, this is hardly the case. They have called attention to the great number of similarities between Soviet culture, especially Soviet Marxism, and the culture of the United States.[9]

Professors Samuel Huntington and Zbigniew Brzezinski have refuted this "theory of convergence," at least regarding governmental institutions and political processes.[10] But others have argued that while the industrial cultures of the two superpowers are similar, they are both cultures that lead to conflict, both part of one general mainstream that has led to today's seeming impasse in world politics. Technological, modern cultures, no matter whether communist or capitalist, the Spanish writer Francisco Ayala maintained, have been devoted to the "conquest of nature," the quest for material power, and the expansion of technology. These aims, he believed, subordinate man and his values to the demands of an impersonal process and lead inexorably to conflict.[11]

Undoubtedly if we are searching for cultural bonds for a future world community, we will have to reexamine the "cultural foundations" of the Western world.[12] "One world" exists in technical and military terms, and such a world makes the bonds of community seem a pressing imperative. International civility, if not community, may be the necessary condition for the survival of national and regional communities among men.

[9] See, for example, Glenn R. Morrow, "The Distinctive Contributions of Philosophy to the Issues of Peace," *Ethics*, 56 (1946), 273–279.

[10] *Political Power: USA/USSR*, New York: Viking, 1963.

[11] *Interrelations of Cultures, Unity and Diversity of Cultures*, Paris: UNESCO, 1953, pp. 240–244.

[12] John U. Nef, *The Cultural Foundations of Industrial Civilization*, Cambridge, England: Cambridge University, 1958.

Niccolò Machiavelli

THE END JUSTIFIES THE MEANS

* * *

A prince must take great care that nothing goes out of his mouth which is not full of these five qualities, and, to see and hear him, he should seem to be all mercy, faith, integrity, humanity, and religion. And nothing is more necessary than to seem to have this last quality, for men in general judge more by the eyes than by the hands, for every one can see, but very few have to feel. Everybody sees what you appear to be, few feel what you are, and those few will not dare to oppose themselves to the many, who have the majesty of the state to defend them; and in the actions of men, and especially of princes, from which there is no appeal, the end justifies the means. Let a prince therefore aim at conquering and maintaining the state, and the means will always be judged honourable and praised by everyone, for the vulgar is always taken by appearances and the issue of the event; and the world consists only of the vulgar, and the few who are not vulgar are isolated when the many have a rallying point in the prince. A certain prince of the present time, whom it is well not to name, never does anything but preach peace and good faith, but he is really a great enemy to both, and either of them, had he observed them, would have lost him state or reputation on many occasions.

* * *

Nothing causes a prince to be so much esteemed as great enterprises and giving proof of prowess. We have in our own day Ferdinand, King of Aragon, the present King of Spain. He may almost be termed a new prince, because from a weak king he has become for fame and glory the first king in Christendom, and if you regard his actions you will find them all very great and some of them extraordinary. At the beginning of his reign he assailed Granada, and that enterprise was the foundation of his estate. At first he did it at his leisure and without fear of being interfered with; he kept the minds of the barons of Castile occupied in this enterprise, so that thinking only of that war they did not think of making innovations, and he thus acquired reputation and power over them without their being aware of it. He was able with the money of the Church and the people to maintain his armies, and by that long war to lay the foundations of his military power, which afterwards has made him famous. Besides this, to be able to undertake greater enterprises, and always under the pretext of religion, he had recourse to a pious cruelty, driving out the Moors from his kingdom

Reprinted by permission of the publisher from *The Prince* (1513), Luigi Ricci, trans., revised by E. R. P. Vincent (London: Oxford University Press, 1935), Chapters XVIII and XXI.

and despoiling them. No more miserable or unusual example can be found. He also attacked Africa under the same pretext, undertook his Italian enterprise, and has lately attacked France; so that he has continually contrived great things, which have kept his subjects' minds uncertain and astonished, and occupied in watching their result. And these actions have arisen one out of the other, so that they have left no time for men to settle down and act against him.

*   *   *

A prince is further esteemed when he is a true friend or a true enemy, when, that is, he declares himself without reserve in favour of some one or against another. This policy is always more useful than remaining neutral. For if two neighbouring powers come to blows, they are either such that if one wins, you will have to fear the victor, or else not. In either of these two cases it will be better for you to declare yourself openly and make war, because in the first case if you do not declare yourself, you will fall a prey to the victor, to the pleasure and satisfaction of the one who has been defeated, and you will have no reason nor anything to defend you and nobody to receive you. For, whoever wins will not desire friends whom he suspects and who do not help him when in trouble, and whoever loses will not receive you as you did not take up arms to venture yourself in his cause.

*   *   *

And it will always happen that the one who is not your friend will want you to remain neutral, and the one who is your friend will require you to declare yourself by taking arms. Irresolute princes, to avoid present dangers, usually follow the way of neutrality and are mostly ruined by it. But when the prince declares himself frankly in favour of one side, if the one to whom you adhere conquers, even if he is powerful and you remain at his discretion, he is under an obligation to you and friendship has been established, and men are never so dishonest as to oppress you with such a patent ingratitude. Moreover, victories are never so prosperous that the victor does not need to have some scruples, especially as to justice. But if your ally loses, you are sheltered by him, and so long as he can, he will assist you; you become the companion of a fortune which may rise again. In the second case, when those who fight are such that you have nothing to fear from the victor, it is still more prudent on your part to adhere to one; for you go to the ruin of one with the help of him who ought to save him if he were wise, and if he conquers he rests at your discretion, and it is impossible that he should not conquer with your help.

And here it should be noted that a prince ought never to make common cause with one more powerful than himself to injure another, unless necessity forces him to it, as before said; for if he wins you rest in his power, and princes must avoid as much as possible being under the will and pleasure of others. The Venetians united with France against the Duke of

Milan, although they could have avoided that alliance, and from it resulted their own ruin. But when one cannot avoid it, as happened in the case of the Florentines when the Pope and Spain went with their armies to attack Lombardy, then the prince ought to join for the above reasons. Let no state believe that it can always follow a safe policy, rather let it think that all are doubtful. This is found in the nature of things, that one never tries to avoid one difficulty without running into another, but prudence consists in being able to know the nature of the difficulties, and taking the least harmful as good.

Immanuel Kant

THE CONFLICT BETWEEN MORALS AND POLITICS

Politics says: "Be ye wise as serpents"; morals adds as a limiting condition, "and guileless as doves." If these two cannot coexist in one commandment, then we really have a conflict between morals and politics. But if these two are to be united, the idea of a conflict is absurd, and the problem how to resolve it cannot even be presented as a task. Although the proposition, *Honesty is the best policy,* contains a theory which practice unfortunately (!) frequently contradicts, yet the equally theoretical, *Honesty is better than all politics,* is above all objections and is indeed the inescapable condition of politics. . . .

The practical man to whom morals is mere theory, even though he concedes that it *ought* and *can* be followed, bases his depressing rejection of our kind-hearted hope upon the idea that man by nature never *wants* to do what is required for attaining the goal of perpetual peace. . . .

It will then be said that he who has power in his hands will not let the people prescribe laws for him. A state, once under no external laws, will not be dependent on the judgment of other states in ' seeking its rights against them. Even a continent when it feels itself superior to another one, which may not actually interfere with it, will not neglect the opportunity to increase its power by robbing or conquering the other. Thus all

Translated by the editor from *Zum ewigen Frieden: Ein philosophischer Entwurf* (1795). *Collected Works,* E. Cassirer, ed. (Berlin: B. Cassirer, 1925), VI, 457–463. For recent editions in English see C. J. Friedrich, *Inevitable Peace* (Cambridge, Mass.: Harvard University Press, 1948), and L. W. Beck, *Perpetual Peace,* The Library of Liberal Arts (Indianapolis: Bobbs-Merrill, 1957).

theoretical plans for constitutional, international and world-law dissolve into empty, unworkable ideas.   On the other hand, a practice, based on empirical principles of human nature, and not feeling degraded by drawing its maxims from the ways in which the world is actually run, can hope to find a solid foundation for its edifice of political astuteness.

Of course, if there exists no freedom and no moral law based upon it, and if everything which happens and may happen is merely a mechanism of nature, then politics, the art to use this mechanism for governing men, is all of practical wisdom, and the concept of law an empty phrase.   But should one find it nevertheless necessary to connect the concept of law with politics, and even to raise the former to a limiting condition of the latter, then it must be conceded that the two can be united.   I can imagine a *moral politician,* that is a person who uses the principles of political astuteness so that they can coexist with morals, but I cannot imagine a *political moralist,* who forges his morals to the statesman's convenience.

The moral politician will adopt the principle that if unavoidable defects are found in a constitution or in the relations between states, it is his duty, especially if he be a head of a state, to see to it, that they be repaired as soon as possible, so that they conform to the law of nature, which is the model presented to us by the idea of reason.   This he will do, even if he has to sacrifice his own selfish interest.   But it would be unreasonable to demand that any defect be immediately and with impetuosity removed, since the disruption of a bond of national and world-community before a better constitution is ready to take its place, is contrary to all morals which in this respect agrees with political astuteness.   But it can be demanded, that those in power should seriously consider the maxim that such a change will be necessary, so that they may be continually approaching the goal of a constitution which is closest to right and law. . . .

It may well be true that despotic moralists, who blunder in practice, often violate political astuteness by prematurely taking or advocating measures, yet when they offend this way against nature, experience will by and by help them onto a better track.   But the moralizing politicians *make* reform *impossible* and perpetuate the violation of right by glossing over political principles which are contrary to right with the pretext that human nature is not *capable* of the Good as reason prescribes it.

Instead of the practice with which these politically astute men boast, they use *trickery;* they are intent to sacrifice the nation and, possibly, the whole world by flattering the ruling powers in order not to miss their private advantage.   This is the way of all professional lawyers (not *legislators*) when they go into politics.   Their task is not to argue about legislation but to carry the present commands of the law of the land, therefore every constitution in force at any time is for them the best, but when this is amended by higher authorities, then that too is regarded as the best.   Thus all goes on in its proper, mechanical order. . . .   They make a great show of understanding *men* (which one would certainly expect from them because they deal with so many) without however knowing *man* and what may be made of him, for which a higher point of view of anthropological observation is needed.   Equipped with such principles, they approach constitutional and international law as prescribed by reason but they cannot make this transition except in a spirit of trickery.   For they follow there, too, their usual course, the mechanism of despotically imposed coercive laws, even where the concepts of reason will permit lawful coercion only according to the principles of freedom, under which alone a lawful and durable constitution is possible. . . .

The maxims which he uses (though he does not pronounce them), are by and large the following sophisms:

1. *Fac et excusa.* Seize every favorable opportunity for arbitrarily appropriating the right of government over its people, or over the neighboring people.   The justification will be presented, and violence glossed over, much more easily and elegantly *after the accomplished fact,* than if one has to think up in advance convincing reasons and even wait for counterreasons.   This is particularly true in cases where the higher authority in the country is also the legislating authority which must be obeyed without arguing.   Such boldness itself gives the appearance of inner conviction of the righteousness of the deed and the god of success is afterwards its best advocate.

2. *Si fecisti, nega.* Whatever evil you have committed—for example, driving your people to despair and into rebellion—deny that it was *your* fault, but assert that it was due to the unruliness of the subjects.   Or if you have conquered a neighboring people, blame it on human nature, since one can count with certainty on being conquered if one does not meet force by force.

3. *Divide et impera.* This means: if there are privileged persons among your people who have merely made you their chief, as first among equals (*primus inter pares*), then sow discord among them and set them against the people.   Then, side with the people by pretending to give them greater liberties, and all will depend on your unconditional will.   Or, in case of neighboring states, it is a pretty safe way to create dissension among them, and under the pretense of protecting the weaker, to conquer them one after another.

No one is deceived by these political maxims; for they all are by now generally known.   Nor is it a case of embarrassment as if the injustices were too glaring.   For great powers are not ashamed of the judgment of the common crowd, but only of each other, and they are not ashamed that these principles become public but merely if they *fail to work,* since they are all agreed about the morality of these maxims.   What remains is *political honor* which they can count upon, namely *the aggrandizement of their power* by all available means.

One thing at least is clear: from all these twistings and turnings of an amoral doctrine of astuteness which seeks to derive a state of peace among men from the warlike state of nature, human beings in their private or in their public affairs cannot escape the concept of law, and they do not dare in public to base politics merely on the manipulation of astuteness and thus to refuse all obedience to a concept of public law. (This is particularly striking in the case of the law of nations.) On the contrary, they give [the concept of public law] all due honor, even if they invent a hundred subterfuges and camouflages in order to circumvent it in practice, and to impute to a crafty force the authority of being the source and bond of all law.

In order to end all this sophistry (although not the injustice which it glosses over) and to bring the false *representatives* of the mighty of this world to confess that it is not right but force which they plead for, let us . . . reveal that all the evil which stands in the way of eternal peace derives from the fact that the political moralist begins where the moral politician would properly leave off. The political moralist subordinates his principles to the end, i.e., puts the cart before the horse and thus vitiates his own purpose of bringing politics into agreement with morals.

Hans J. Morgenthau

THE TWILIGHT OF INTERNATIONAL MORALITY

A discussion of international ethics must guard against the two extremes either of overrating the influence of ethics upon international politics or else of denying that statesmen and diplomats are moved by anything else but considerations of material power. On the one hand, there is the dual error of confounding the ethical rules which people actually observe with those they pretend to observe as well as with those which writers declare they ought to observe. . . .

On the other hand, there is the misconception, which usually is associated with the general depreciation and moral condemnation of power politics prevalent in our culture, that international politics is immoral, if not amoral, through and through and in any case so thoroughly evil that it is no use looking for ethical limitations of the aspirations for power on the international scene. Yet, if we ask ourselves what statesmen and diplomats are capable of doing in furtherance of the power objectives of

Reprinted from "The Twilight of International Morality" by Hans J. Morgenthau in *Ethics*, 48 (January 1948), 77–99, by permission of The University of Chicago Press. Copyright 1948 by The University of Chicago Press.

their respective nations and what they actually do, we realize that they do less than they might be able to do and less than they actually did in other periods of history. They refuse to consider certain ends and to use certain means, either altogether or under certain conditions, not because of considerations of expediency in the light of which a certain policy appears to be impractical or unwise, but by virtue of certain moral rules of conduct which interpose an absolute barrier against a certain policy and which do not permit it to be considered at all from the point of view of expediency. Such ethical inhibitions operate in our time on different levels with different effectiveness. Their restraining function is most obvious and most effective in so far as the sacredness of human life in times of peace is concerned.

*   *   *

. . . With war taking on in recent times, more and more and in different respects, a total character, not only are ethical limitations upon killing observed to an ever lessening degree, but their very existence in the consciences of political and military leaders as well as of the common people becomes ever more precarious and is threatened with extinction.

*   *   *

The deterioration of moral limitations of international politics which has occurred in recent years with regard to the protection of life is only a special instance of a general and, for the purposes of this discussion, much more far-reaching dissolution of an ethical system which in the past imposed its restraints upon the day-by-day operation of the foreign offices, but which does so no longer. Two factors have brought this dissolution about: the substitution of democratic for aristocratic responsibility in foreign affairs and the substitution of nationalistic standards of action for universal ones.

In the seventeenth and eighteenth centuries, and to a lessening degree up to the first World War, international morality addressed itself to a personal sovereign, that is, an individually determined prince and his successors and to a relatively small, cohesive, and homogeneous group of aristocratic rulers. The prince and the aristocratic rulers of a particular nation were in constant intimate contact with the princes and aristocratic rulers of other nations through family ties, a common language (which was French), common cultural values, a common style of life, and common moral convictions as to what a gentleman was and was not allowed to do in his relations with another gentleman, whether of his own or of a foreign nation. As the princes competing for power considered themselves to be competitors in a game whose rules were accepted by all the other competitors, so the members of their diplomatic and military services looked upon themselves, as it were, as employees who served their employer either by virtue of the accident of birth, reinforced often, but by no means always, by a sense of personal loyalty to the monarch or because of the promise of pay, influence, and glory, which he held out to them.

It was especially the desire for material gain which provided for the members of this aristocratic society a common bond which was stronger than the ties of dynastic or national loyalty. Thus it was proper and common for a government to pay the foreign minister or diplomat of another country a pension; Lord Robert Cecil, the minister of Elizabeth, received one from Spain; Sir Henry Wotton, British ambassador to Venice in the seventeenth century, accepted one from Savoy while applying for one from Spain.

*   *   *

. . . However much transactions of this kind were lacking in nobility, those participating in them could not be passionately devoted to the cause of the countries whose interests were in their care, and they had obviously loyalties besides and above the one to the country which employed them. . . .

In that period of history the Austrian ambassador to France felt more at home at the court of Versailles than among his own nonaristocratic compatriots, and he had closer social and moral ties with the members of the French aristocracy and the other aristocratic members of the diplomatic corps than with the Austrians of humble origin. Consequently, the diplomatic and military personnel fluctuated to a not inconsiderable degree from one monarchical employer to another, and it was not rare that a French diplomat or officer, for some reason of self-interest, would enter the services of the King of Prussia and would further the international objectives of Prussia, or fight in the Prussian army, against France. . . .

It is significant for the persistence of this international cohesion of the aristocracy that as late as 1862, when Bismarck, on the occasion of his recall as Prussian ambassador to Russia, expressed to the czar his regret at the necessity of leaving St. Petersburg, the czar, misunderstanding this remark, asked Bismarck whether he was inclined to enter the Russian diplomatic service. Bismarck reports in his memoirs that he declined the offer "courteously.". . . Let us imagine that a similar offer were being made in our time by Mr. Stalin to the American ambassador or by an American president to any diplomat accredited in Washington, and let us visualize the private embarrassment of the individual concerned and the public indignation following the incident, and we have the measure of the profundity of the change which has transformed the ethics of international politics in recent times. Today such an offer would be regarded as an invitation to treason, that is, the violation of the most fundamental of all moral obligations in international affairs: loyalty to one's own country. When it was made and even when it was reported shortly before the close of the nineteenth century, it was a proposition to be accepted or rejected on its merits and without any lack of moral propriety attaching to it.

The moral standards of conduct with which the international aristocracy complied were of necessity of a supranational character. They applied not to all Prussians, Austrians, or Frenchmen but to all men who by virtue of their birth and education were able to comprehend them and to act in accordance with them.   It was in the concept and the rules of natural law that this cosmopolitan society found the source of its precepts of morality. It was, therefore, not by accident that the individual members of this society felt themselves to be personally responsible for compliance with those moral rules of conduct; for it was to them as rational human beings, as individuals, that this moral code was addressed. . . .   This sense of a highly personal moral obligation to be met by those in charge of foreign affairs with regard to their colleagues in other countries explains the emphasis with which the writers of the seventeenth and eighteenth centuries counseled the monarch to safeguard his "honor" and his "reputation" as his most precious possessions. . . .   A violation of his moral obligations, as they were recognized by his fellow-monarchs for themselves, would call into action not only his own conscience but also the spontaneous reactions of the supranational aristocratic society which would make him pay for the violation of its mores with a loss of prestige, that is, a loss of power.

When in the course of the nineteenth century democratic selection and responsibility of government officials replaced the aristocratic one, the structure of international society and, with it, of international morality underwent a fundamental change.   In the new age the place of the aristocratic rulers, who virtually until the end of the nineteenth century were responsible for the conduct of foreign affairs in most countries, has been taken by officials elected or appointed regardless of class distinctions. These officials are legally and morally responsible for their official acts, not to a monarch, that is, a specific individual, but to a collectivity, that is, a parliamentary majority, or the people as a whole.   An important shift in public opinion may easily call for a change in the personnel making foreign policy, who will be replaced by another group of individuals taken from whatever group of the population prevails at the moment.   Government officials are no longer exclusively recruited from aristocratic groups but from virtually the whole population. . . .   In countries such as Great Britain, France, or Italy, where the government needs for its continuation in office the support of a majority of parliament, any change in the parliamentary majority necessitates a change in the composition of the government.   Even in a country such as the United States, where not Congress but only general elections can put an administration into office or remove it, the turnover of the policy-makers in the State Department is considerable enough. . . .   The fluctuation of the policy-makers in international affairs and their responsibility to an indefinite collective entity has far-reaching consequences for the effectiveness, nay, for the very existence of an international moral order.

In one word, this transformation within the individual nations changed international morality as a system of moral restraints from a reality into a mere figure of speech.   When we say that George III of England was subject to certain moral restraints in his dealings with Louis XVI of France or Catherine the Great of Russia, we are referring to something real, something which can be identified with the conscience and the actions of certain specific individuals. When we say that the British Commonwealth of Nations or even Great Britain alone has moral obligations toward the United States or France, we are making use of a fiction, by virtue of which international law deals with nations as though they were individual personalities, but to which nothing in the sphere of moral obligations corresponds. . . .

The individual members of the electorate . . . may have no moral convictions of a supernational character at all . . . or, if they have such convictions, they will be most heterogeneous in content. . . . The fluctuating members of the policy-making group or of the permanent bureaucracy of the foreign office may or may not reflect these and similar divisions of opinion. In any case, the reference to a moral rule of conduct requires an individual conscience from which it emanates, and there is no individual conscience from which what we call the international morality of Great Britain or of any other nation could emanate.

. . . Ethical rules have their seat in the consciences of individual men. Government by clearly identifiable men, who can be held personally accountable for their acts, is therefore the precondition for the existence of an effective system of international ethics. Where responsibility for government is widely distributed among a great number of individuals with different conceptions as to what is morally required in international affairs, or with no such conceptions at all, international morality as an effective system of restraints upon international policy becomes impossible. It is for this reason that Dean Roscoe Pound could say as far back as 1923: "It might be maintained plausibly, that a moral . . . order among states, was nearer attainment in the middle of the eighteenth century than it is today."

While the democratic selection and responsibility of the government officials destroyed international morality as an effective system of restraints, nationalism destroyed the international society itself within which that morality had operated. The French Revolution of 1789 marks the beginning of the new epoch of history which witnesses the gradual decline of the cosmopolitan aristocratic society and of the restraining influence of its morality upon international politics. . . .

*   *   *

But even in 1914, at the eve of the first World War, there is in many of the statements and dispatches of statesmen and diplomats a melancholy undertone of regret that individuals who had so much in common should now be compelled to separate and identify themselves with the warring groups on the different sides of the frontiers. This, however, was only a feeble reminiscence which had no longer the power to influence the actions of men.   By then, these men had naturally less in common with each other than they had with the respective peoples from which they had risen to the heights of power and whose will and interests they represented in their relations with other nations.   What separated the French foreign minister from his opposite number in Berlin was much more important than what united them, and, conversely, what united the French foreign minister with the French nation was much more important than anything which might set him apart from her.   In other words, the place of the one international society to which all members of the different governing groups belonged and which provided a common framework for the different national societies had been taken by the national societies themselves giving to their representatives on the international scene the standards of conduct which the international society had formerly supplied.

When, in the course of the nineteenth century, this fragmentation of the aristocratic international society into its national segments was well on its way to consummation, the protagonists of nationalism were convinced that this development would strengthen the bonds of international morality rather than weaken them.   For they believed that, once the national aspirations of the liberated peoples were satisfied and aristocratic rule replaced by popular government, nothing could separate the nations of the earth and, conscious of being members of the same humanity and inspired by the same ideals of freedom, tolerance, and peace, they would pursue their national destinies in harmony.   Actually, the spirit of nationalism, once it had materialized in national states, proved to be not universalistic and humanitarian but particularistic and exclusive.   When the international society of the seventeenth and eighteenth centuries was destroyed, it became obvious that there was nothing to take the place of the unifying and restraining element which had been a real society superimposed upon the particular national societies. . . .

*   *   *

This fragmentation of a formerly coherent international society into a multiplicity of morally self-sufficient national communities which have ceased to operate within a common framework of moral precepts is but the outward symptom of the profound change which in recent times has transformed the relations between universal ethical precepts and the particular systems of national ethics.   This transformation has proceeded in two different ways.   It has weakened, to the point of ineffectiveness, the universal, supranational moral rules of conduct, which before the age of nationalism had imposed a system—however precarious and wide-meshed —of limitations upon the international policies of individual nations, and it has finally endowed in the minds and aspirations of individual nations their particular national systems of ethics with universal validity.

The crucial test of the vitality of an ethical system occurs when its control of the consciences and actions of men is challenged by another system of morality.   Thus the relative strength of the ethics of humility and self-denial of the Sermon on the Mount and of the ethics of self-advancement and power of modern Western society is determined by the extent to which either system of morality is able to mold the actions or at least the consciences of men in accordance with its precepts.   Every human being, in so far as he is responsive to ethical appeals at all, is from time to time confronted with such a conflict of conscience, which tests the relative strength of conflicting moral commands.   A similar test must determine the respective strength, with regard to the conduct of foreign affairs, of the supranational ethics, composed of Christian, cosmopolitan, and humanitarian elements to which the diplomatic language of the time pays its tribute and which is postulated by many individuals writers, and the ethics of nationalism which have been on the ascendancy throughout the world for the last century and a half.

Now it is indeed true that national ethics, as formulated in the philosophy of reason of state of the seventeenth and eighteenth centuries or in the concept of the national interest of the nineteenth and twentieth, has in most conflict situations proved itself to be superior to universal moral rules of conduct.   This is obvious from a consideration of the most elemental and also the most important conflict situation of this kind, the one between the universal ethical precept, "Thou shalt not kill," and the command of a particular national ethics, "Thou shalt kill under certain conditions the enemies of thy country."   The individual to whom these two moral rules of conduct are addressed is confronted with a conflict between his allegiance to humanity as a whole, manifesting itself in the respect for human life as such irrespective of nationality or any other particular characteristic, and his loyalty to a particular nation whose interests he is called upon to promote at the price of the lives of the members of another nation.   This conflict is resolved today and has been resolved during all modern history by most individuals in favor of loyalty to the nation.   Three factors distinguish, however, in this respect, the present age from previous ones.

First, there is the enormously increased ability of the nation-state to exert moral compulsion upon its members, which is the result partly of the almost divine prestige which the nation enjoys in our time, partly of the control over the instruments molding public opinion which technological developments have put at the disposal of the state.

Second, there is the extent to which loyalty to the nation requires the individual to disregard universal moral rules of conduct.   The modern technology of war has given the individual opportunities for mass destruction unknown to previous ages.   Today a nation may ask one single individual to destroy the lives of hundreds of thousands of people by dropping one atomic bomb, and the compliance with a demand of such enormous consequences demonstrates the weakness of supranational ethics more impressively than the limited violations of universal standards, committed in pre-atomic times, were able to.

Finally, there is today, in consequence of the two other factors, much less chance for the individual to be loyal to supranational ethics when they are in conflict with the moral demands of the nation.   The individual, faced with the enormity of the deeds which he is asked to commit in the name of the nation, and with the overwhelming weight of moral pressure which the nation exerts upon him, would require almost superhuman moral strength to resist those demands.   The magnitude of the infractions of universal ethics committed on behalf of the nation and of the moral compulsion exerted in favor of them affect the qualitative relationship of the two systems of ethics.   It puts in bold relief the desperate weakness of universal ethics in its conflict with the morality of the nation and decides the conflict in favor of the nation before it has really started.

It is at this point that this hopeless impotence of universal ethics becomes an important factor in bringing about a significant and far-reaching change in the relations between supranational and national systems of morality.   It is one of the factors which lead to the identification of both. The individual comes to realize that the flouting of universal standards of morality is not the handiwork of a few wicked men but the inevitable outgrowth of the conditions under which nations exist and pursue their aims. He experiences in his own conscience the feebleness of universal standards and the preponderance of national ethics as forces motivating the actions of men on the international scene, and his conscience does not cease being ill at ease.   While, on the one hand, the continuous discomfort of a perpetually uneasy conscience is too much for him to bear, he is too strongly attached to the concept of universal ethics to give it up altogether.   Thus he identifies the morality of his own nation with the commands of supranational ethics; he pours, as it were, the contents of his national ethics into the now almost empty bottle of universal ethics.   So each nation comes to know again a universal morality, that is, its own national one which is taken to be the one which all the other nations ought to accept as their own.   Instead of the universality of an ethics to which all nations adhere, we have in the end the particularity of national ethics which claims the right to, and aspires toward, universal recognition.   There are then as many ethical codes claiming universality as there are politically active nations.

*   *   *

The present period of history in which generally and, as it seems, permanently universal moral rules of conduct are replaced by particular ones claiming universality was ushered in by Woodrow Wilson's war "to make the world safe for democracy.". . .   A few months after the democratic crusade had gotten under way, in October, 1917, the foundations were laid in Russia for another moral and political structure which on its part, while accepted only by a fraction of humanity, was claimed to provide the common roof under which all humankind would once live together in justice and in peace. . . .   In the thirties the philosophy of naziism, grown in the soil of a particular nation, proclaimed itself the new moral code which would replace the vicious creed of bolshevism and the decadent morality of democracy and would impose itself upon mankind. . . .   With the termination of the second World War the two remaining moral and political systems claiming universal validity, democracy and communism, entered into active competition for the dominance of the world. . . .

It would be the most dangerous of illusions to overlook or even to belittle the depth of the difference which exists, in view of the moral limitations of international politics, between that situation and the condition of the modern state system from the end of the religious wars to the entrance of the United States into the first World War.   One needs only to pick at random any conflict which occurred in that latter period, with the exception of the Napoleonic Wars, and compare it with the conflicts which have torn the world apart in the last three decades in order to realize the importance of that difference. . . .   In the seventeenth and eighteenth centuries none of the contestants on the international scene aspired to impose his own particular system of ethics, provided he had one, upon the others. The very possibility of such an aspiration never occurred to them, since they were aware only of one universal moral code to which they all gave unquestioning allegiance. . . .

*   *   *

Only shreds and fragments survive of this system of supranational ethics which exerts its restraining influence upon international politics . . . only in isolated instances, such as killing in peacetime and preventive war.   As for the influence of that system of supranational ethics upon the conscience of the actors on the international scene, it is rather like the feeble rays, barely visible above the horizon of consciousness, of a sun which has already set.   Since the first World War, with ever increasing intensity and generality, each of the contestants in the international arena claims in his "way of life" to possess the whole truth of morality and politics which the others may reject only at their peril.   With fierce exclusiveness all contestants equate their national conceptions of morality with what all mankind must and will ultimately accept and live by.   In this, the ethics of international politics reverts to the politics and morality of tribalism, of the crusades, and of the religious wars.

*   *   *

Oliver J. Lissitzyn

INTERNATIONAL LAW IN A DIVIDED WORLD

"IN PARTES TRES"

Fifty years ago, echoing the optimism of the nineteenth century, the author of a standard British treatise on international law confidently asserted that "immeasurable progress is guaranteed to International Law, since there are eternal moral and economic factors working in its favour." [1] Today many Western jurists are asking, with varying degrees of pessimism, whether or not there is still something that can be properly called universal international law, and, if so, whether or not the universality of international law can long be maintained in the face of the cold war and the rise to statehood of an ever growing number of nations of non-Western antecedents.

As early as the inter-war period, some Western jurists saw a threat to international law in the rejection by the rulers of the Soviet Union of the fundamental values and premises of Western public order. At that time the Soviet Union was hardly strong enough to defy the West, and the Soviet challenge to the foundations of international law was soon overshadowed by that of the aggressive nihilism of the Axis powers, particularly Nazi Germany. The emergence of the Soviet Union after World War II as one of the super-powers, however, could not but increase the anxiety of Western observers, some of whom saw in the resulting "disunity" of mankind a threat to the very existence of international law.

The fear that the appearance of newly independent nations in Asia and Africa would destroy the universality of international law has been based partly on the notion that international law, created and nurtured in the culture of the West, cannot be fully understood and wholeheartedly accepted as a guide to conduct by nations whose cultural heritage is not Western. There is also some apprehension that the newly independent states, together with other less developed nations, may be disinclined to accept certain norms, developed mainly by the more advanced and stronger states of the West, that have served to protect Western public and private interests. The "expansion" of international law to Asian and African nations is said to be proceeding at the price of a "continuous dilution of its content, as it is reinterpreted for the benefit of the newcomers."

That the world is roughly divided today into three parts—the Communist states, the more advanced nations of the West, and the less developed countries—cannot be denied. But the division between the second and third parts, drawn in terms of levels of economic development, does not correspond to distinctions of cultural background and recency of emanci-

---

Reprinted from *International Conciliation* (March 1963).

[1] L. Oppenheim, *International Law: A Treatise.*

pation from colonial rule. Latin American nations are not highly developed economically, but share the Western cultural heritage and have been, for the most part, politically independent for more than a century. Japan, on the other hand, has a cultural background quite different from that of the West, but is highly developed economically and enjoyed, prior to World War II, great-power status. Before trying to appraise the impact of this tripartite division on international law and its universality, it is well to recall the origins of international law and its functions.

INTERNATIONAL LAW IN RETROSPECT

As a consciously recognized and practiced system of norms of interstate conduct deemed to be legally binding, international law is a product of modern Western civilization. Although in other ages and cultures some similar norms existed, they were never regarded as having the force of law and as being susceptible of interpretation and application by legal methods. The unique role of the West in the development of international law was associated with the peculiarly western European interaction of several historical factors. Among these factors were the decline of the authority of religion, the rise of relatively small nation-states in a balance-of-power system, exploration and conquest of distant lands, revival of the study of Roman law, and the "law habit" which had developed in the pluralistic feudal society, partly under the influence of the Roman legal tradition. Two other factors were more fundamental: an increasingly productive and complex economy based on technological innovation, and the growing emphasis—related to the rise of science—on rational thought and action. . . .

International law appeared and grew because it served the needs of the society that was developing in the West. Without a minimum of order, predictability, and stability, the private economic activity of modern society could hardly be carried on. On a continent divided into many small states and increasingly dependent on distant lands for supplies and markets, domestic law alone could not provide the necessary modicum of security. There was a need for standards of official conduct that would be recognized and normally followed by all governments. Without such standards, the movement of people, goods, and capital beyond national borders might be prohibitively risky. International law, furthermore, served to prevent unnecessary friction between governments and destruction of values and resources.

Large parts of the traditional law of nations—including norms delimiting the sovereignty and jurisdiction of states, the law of the sea, the norms of treatment of foreign nationals, and much of the law of war and neutrality—directly served all these functions. Other parts of international law, including diplomatic immunities and the law of treaties, indirectly served the same functions by facilitating contacts and the conclusion of agreements between governments.   The law of treaties eventually became the essential legal foundation of international organizations with all their manifold functions.   Treaties have become the principal means of creating new norms which are regarded as binding on the states that accept them and of entrusting rule-making powers to international organs.

International law has also been used as an instrument of policy, either of cooperation or of conflict.   It has served as a set of standards to which states appealed in disputes or conflicts of interest with other states, not only to persuade the other parties (or the arbitrators) to settle the conflicts in certain ways, but also as a symbol of rectitude to create or strengthen a consensus favorable to one of the parties and unfavorable to its opponents.   This use of the law is not new.   It may be recalled that the work of Grotius on the freedom of the seas, published in 1609, was written as a plea on behalf of a view of the law of the sea favorable to Dutch interests.

*   *   *

THE SOVIET UNION AND INTERNATIONAL LAW

*   *   *

The basic Soviet attitude toward international law was developed fairly rapidly under the combined pressure of practical need and Marxist doctrine.   The problem of reconciling the apparent acceptance of an international law binding on Communist and non-Communist governments alike with the Marxist conception of law has been a perennial source of difficulty for Marxist legal theoreticians; but it has not been allowed to stand in the way of the pragmatic use of international law in the interests of Soviet policy.   This pragmatic approach has remained substantially the same to this day, despite frequent variations in formulation and sometimes acrimonious discussion of the finer points by Soviet jurists.   All doctrines, formulations, and applications of international law are appraised in terms of their usefulness to the Communist cause.

*   *   *

A clue to the Soviet approach is the constant reference to "struggle" and "cooperation" in Soviet definitions of international law.   The idea that international law can be useful in struggles between states is a valid insight, for, in the past, states have often employed it to advance their own interests as against the interests of other states.   But the *order* in which the words "struggle" and "cooperation" appear in Soviet definitions of international law, as well as the Communist philosophy of history, symbolize the relative importance of the two in Soviet eyes.

A key Soviet definition of international law is that of A. Y. Vishinsky, who in 1948, called it "the sum total of the norms regulating relations between states in the process of their struggle and cooperation, expressing the will of the ruling classes of these states and secured by coercion exercised by states individually or collectively." The change in style of Soviet domestic and foreign policy that followed the death of Stalin was reflected in the tone, but not in the substance, of utterances of leading Soviet jurists. Vishinsky's definition survived Stalin and himself. In the textbook of international law published in 1957 by the Institute of State and Law of the Soviet Academy of Sciences, the only significant change in the definition is the addition of a reference to "peaceful coexistence," which reflects a new emphasis in Soviet foreign policy after the death of Stalin. . . .

It is this Soviet stress on antagonism rather than cooperation as the primary characteristic of the relations between the states of "the two systems" that sets narrow limits to the role of international law in world affairs. Some principles of international law of great generality and, hence, of uncertain content, have served Soviet leaders as slogans in their ideological struggle against the capitalist states. Among the more traditional of these principles are sovereignty, territorial inviolability and equality of states, and non-intervention. Other principles invoked, such as non-aggression and self-determination, for which Soviet spokesmen claim a major share of credit, are of more recent origin and are more controversial. All these principles, both old and new, have been used by the Soviet leaders both defensively and offensively.

* * *

. . . The Soviet tendency is to use the term "peaceful coexistence" to belabor any policy detrimental to Soviet interests, such as restrictions on trade with the Soviet Union and other Communist countries or support of anti-Soviet movements in these countries, and to justify Soviet policies. As Tunkin [2] points out, the 1961 Program of the Communist Party declares that "peaceful coexistence serves as a basis for the peaceful competition between socialism and capitalism on an international scale and constitutes *a specific form of class struggle between them.*" He adds that "in upholding the international law principles of peaceful coexistence and using them to support their foreign policy, the socialist states are striving for the constant strengthening of the positions of the world socialist system in its competition with capitalism.". . .

* * *

PERSPECTIVES

Despite the impact of Communist ideology and system of public order on international law and despite widespread distrust of Soviet motives and promises, "capitalist" countries, including the United States, continue to negotiate and conclude agreements with the USSR. . . .

[2] Head of the Treaty and Legal Department of the Soviet Ministry of Foreign Affairs in 1962. [Eds.]

*　　*　　*

It is possible, therefore, that if coexistence between the Soviet bloc and the "capitalist" world continues, and if the West maintains a healthy growth rate in all fields of human endeavor, the objective necessities of international life, the cumulative effect of cultural and other exchanges between the two, the disappearance of hostility-breeding feelings of inferiority with the succession of generations, and a breakdown in the unity of the "socialist camp," will bring about a gradual reinterpretation of Soviet doctrines to permit international law to play a greater role in the affairs of mankind.

*　　*　　*

The prospect is not for a sudden leap from anarchy into a world ruled by law, but for a very gradual erosion of the extreme hostility to other systems of public order implicit in Communist ideology and for a concomitant gradual expansion of the role of international law in the relations between the two camps. (However, the Chinese Communist elite, which has come to power more recently than the Soviet elite, which rules a country less advanced economically and scientifically than the Soviet Union, and which has been excluded from the activities of international organizations, is likely to remain at a peak of militancy and hostility toward the non-Communist world for a longer period than the Soviet elite.)

*　　*　　*

THE OUTLOOK

The sense of a "crisis" in international law experienced by many observers today is a product of the acceleration of the processes of change in the international community that is characteristic of our era. The factors that have caused this acceleration are well known. They include rapid technological progress; the rise of new ideologies and systems of public order, including militant communism; decolonization, itself spurred on by the Communist challenge to the West; the appearance of many new states of widely different cultural backgrounds and levels of development; rising demands for social reform; the fear of war and the growing reluctance of the more advanced states to protect their interests by coercive means; and the increase in the number and functions of international organizations. The processes of change have, on the one hand, tended to limit the operation or decrease the relevance of some traditional legal norms and, on the other hand, have created new areas of need for legal regulation. What then are the prospects for the future of international law in a divided, rapidly changing world?

At first glance . . . there appear to be many disturbing similarities between the attitudes of the Communist elites and those of the less developed nations, particularly the newly independent states, toward international law.   Both the Communist elites and the less developed nations emphasize, for example, self-determination, anti-colonialism, equality, non-intervention, and invalidity of "unequal" treaties.   The latter, like the Communist governments, tend to manipulate such highly general principles without much regard for consistency and reciprocity.   Spokesmen for the newly independent nations, like those for the Soviet Union, tend to reject the traditional doctrine that norms of general international law are automatically binding on new states (and on states ruled by new governments) and claim freedom to decide by which of the old norms they will be bound.   On the specific issues of "the international standard" and the three-mile width of the territorial sea, many of the less developed nations have ranged themselves with the Soviet bloc in opposing the traditional norms favored by the West and Japan.

Yet, on closer examination, the danger that the Communist elite and the less developed nations might form a coalition is seen to be illusory. The aims and motivations of most of the less developed countries diverge widely from those of the Communist elites.   A large number of these nations have not supported Communist proposals on expropriation of foreign investments and the width of the territorial sea.   Nor have they supported the Soviet bloc on the issue of sovereign immunity.   The posture of these nations toward judicial settlement of international disputes, despite considerable reluctance to accept the compulsory jurisdiction of the International Court, is by no means identical with the basic Communist hostility to such settlement—as the submission of several cases to the Court by Latin American, African, and Asian states indicates.   The Soviet Union has failed to gain the solid support of these countries for its position in the United Nations on many important political issues such as Korea, Hungary, Tibet, and the Congo.   Furthermore, the less developed nations have been far more willing than the Soviet bloc to participate in international regulatory organizations and arrangements such as ICAO, IMF, and GATT.[3]

Some of the attitudes of the less developed nations, particularly those related to the real or fancied vestiges of colonialism, will continue to trouble the West for a long time to come.   The relatively low level of economic development of most of the non-Western and Latin American states, and the continued dependence of these states on the industrial nations for capital and technical assistance, will tend to prolong feelings of inferiority and to breed suspicion that the more advanced nations are using their superior position to dominate the poorer countries.   To minimize resentment, the colonial powers should not exact, at the time of the granting of independence or subsequently, agreements that the less developed states are likely

---

[3] International Civil Aviation Organization, International Monetary Fund, and General Agreement on Tariffs and Trade.   [Eds.]

to regard as burdensome, unfair, and inconsistent with their best interests. The West cannot—and does not—disregard either the distinctive viewpoints of the less developed nations, or their claim to full participation in the international law-making process. Experience indicates that even on the seemingly most intractable of issues—that of protection of foreign investments—adjustment, compromise, and settlement on mutually acceptable terms will continue to be possible, at least so long as nations do not choose the path of complete elimination of private enterprise from their economic life.

It would be a mistake to discount as mere verbiage the often expressed concern of the less developed nations for the strengthening and development of international law. Weak in material power, these nations must seek protection and assistance in international law and organization. This does not mean, of course, that the less developed nations will have no distinctive points of view or will not attempt—as all nations have done—to use international law to promote their own real or fancied interests. Moreover, the less developed countries will insist on having their voices heard in the formulation and development of the law, and will utilize their collective numerical strength to maximize their influence in this process.

Customary international law has at times developed with considerable speed to provide for the regulation of new transnational needs and activities. The twentieth century has witnessed, for example, the rapid development of the doctrines of air sovereignty and the continental shelf. Nevertheless, the acceleration of the processes of change in the international community and the detailed nature of the regulation required for many new activities render custom an inadequate instrument for the formation of legal norms in response to all the new needs and expectations.

The less developed nations may be expected to use their influence to strengthen the trend toward law-making by multilateral treaties, particularly on subjects of special interest to them, such as racial discrimination. Nations with a close community of interest or with similar attitudes and institutions will continue, as in the past, to devise special norms to regulate their mutual relations. The network of multilateral and bilateral treaties will continue to increase in complexity. Regional legal institutions, such as those of Europe, will continue to be created by states with special common interests.

The conclusion of treaties embracing limited numbers of states may seem to be a further impairment of the "universality" of international law. But such treaties continue to be made and to operate within the framework of the more basic and general rules that constitute "universal" international law. Among these general rules, those of the law of treaties—the rules concerning the conclusion, validity, interpretation, performance, revision, and termination of treaties—will continue to be of fundamental and perhaps increasing importance.

There will be sustained efforts to formulate and develop the basic customary rules in negotiated conventions similar to those on the law of the sea and on diplomatic intercourse and immunities.

Here, again, the fact that such conventions deal with general norms which in principle are "universal" and yet are unlikely to be adhered to by all states—and thus formally to bind all states—might indicate a further breakdown in the universality of international law. Nevertheless, the necessities of international life will continue to demand a large measure of uniformity of basic rules, and many, if not all, of the rules formulated in the conventions may be expected to be universally accepted in practice.

The numerical strength of the less developed nations may also lead them to favor efforts to formulate and develop the law by declarations, adopted as resolutions by the [U.N.] General Assembly. Such declarations are not formally binding. However, they have the appearance of expressing a world consensus and cannot be totally disregarded by national and international decision-makers. They may be employed to confirm and strengthen existing precedents and trends in international law, or to initiate new trends. General Assembly resolutions have already been so used.[4] The actual effect of such declarations depends, of course, on several factors, including the extent to which they express a real consensus, the number and importance of the states supporting and opposing them, and the degree to which they correspond to the requirements of international life. There are many indications that the less developed nations are becoming aware of the fact that a resolution opposed by the more powerful states, or by some of them, does not carry as much weight as one that is not so opposed. The influence of the more advanced states may be expected to continue to offset, in some measure, the numerical preponderance of the less developed nations in the General Assembly, thus preventing the appearance of too large a gap between the purported content of the law and the realities of material power.

Thus, international law will continue to be "universal" in the sense that there will be a substantial number of concepts and norms understood, invoked, and followed—despite occasional violation—by all states. The scope and complexity of international law, furthermore, will continue to expand, especially in the form of treaties, in keeping with the expansion in the number and complexity of transnational activities and interactions in a shrinking world.

International law will still be viewed by many observers as inadequate and fragmentary, since it will not constitute, for a long time to come, a

[4] See, for example, General Assembly Res. 95 (I), 11 Dec. 1946, by which the Assembly unanimously reaffirmed the principles of international law recognized in the Nuremberg Tribunal's Charter and judgment, and Res. 1721 (XVI), 3 Jan. 1962, in which the Assembly unanimously declared, *inter alia,* that outer space and celestial bodies are free for exploration and use by all states in conformity with international law and are not subject to national appropriation.

comprehensive order in which the most important aspects of the relations between states—including resort to violent forms of coercion—are effectively regulated by law. But legal institutions can never guarantee lasting peace and security. Even in the best organized national societies, they are often ineffective in resolving major conflicts of interest and power. In the United States, the federal Constitution and the Supreme Court did not prevent civil war a hundred years ago. The excellent British legal system did not make impossible a twentieth century civil war in Ireland. Contemporary international law, of course, is not nearly as adequate or effective as the national legal systems of well-organized states. But its role in world affairs, although not as important as the role of national law in most states, is far from negligible. In fact, it is an essential framework for many aspects of international relations, as shown by the measure of its acceptance in practice even by the Communist states.

The absolutist dichotomy between the presence and absence of worldwide agreement on values is false. In the world community, as in national societies, there is a broad spectrum of values and of degrees of consensus on them. A large measure of agreement on values does, of course, strengthen the cohesiveness of a community and the efficacy of its legal order. But it is not a question of all or nothing.

A black-and-white contrast between a world in which common ideological values prevail and in which peace rests securely on law, on one hand, and a world in which lawlessness and naked force rule, on the other, is out of place here. These are but non-existent extremes of a continuum in which, as history suggests, international law will play varying roles in different periods and in relations between states with different interests and systems of public order.

Side by side with conflicting values and interests are many common or mutual interests. It is the existence of the latter that makes possible the regulation and adjustment of the conflicts of interest by law. Virtually all human beings agree on the importance of such basic material needs as survival, health, food, clothing, and shelter. Even antagonistic systems of public order such as "socialist" and "capitalist" have a common stake, for example, in the avoidance of general war, the maintenance of diplomatic relations and of facilities for international transport and communication, the conservation of certain national resources, and the exchange of certain goods and services on a mutually advantageous basis. In the relations between the advanced and the less developed nations, the number of common or mutual interests is even greater.

As already indicated, the conflicts of interest—and particularly those caused or reinforced by the Communist ideology and system of public order—today prevent a rapid expansion of the role of law in international affairs. The more exacting demands addressed to international law are not likely to be fully satisfied in the immediate future. A world public order comparable in scope and effectiveness to the public order of a well-organized nation is still far away. In the international community there are, as yet, no formally established special institutions for orderly modification of the law and of existing legal rights without the consent of the states concerned. But the conflicts of interest do not prevent mutually acceptable regulation of transnational activities in the areas of international relations where there is some community of interest, however limited. Since all stages engage in such activities, there is a basis for the existence of "universal" international law in the sense of a number of concepts and norms understood, invoked, and honored by all states, as well as of "particular" international law—norms that apply to some but not all states. Both universal and particular international law may be expected to grow in scope and complexity as the volume and variety of transnational activities increase. Universal agreement on ideological goals and ethical values is not a prerequisite for the existence—or even the growth—of international law.

Barbara Ward

A NEW DIRECTION FOR THE WEST

"If we could first know where we are and whither we are tending, we could then better judge what to do and how to do it." The words are Abraham Lincoln's but the dilemma is our own. Over the last decade, we in the Western world have become more and more aware of being under steady, undermining attack. We have felt our institutions threatened, our aims thwarted, our pretensions mocked. After 300 years of world-wide dominance, nothing in our experience prepares us for this sense of insecurity; our temptation is to lash out at it blindly and angrily. But there is no safety in such reactions. We must know "where we are and whither we are tending." Otherwise, we shall fight against symptoms, not causes, and battle with shadows whereas our real struggle is with the angel of history itself.

The point can be quickly illustrated. Just over a hundred years ago, Western power in the Far East began to seem virtually irresistible. The Western merchants with their new goods and vessels, the Western soldiers with their new weapons moved inexorably in. It was the first rising, in

Reprinted by permission of the author and the publisher from *The Saturday Review,* January 27, 1962, pp. 10–12, 59.

the China Sea, of the great tide of modern science and technology. In China, the Westerners were dismissed as "barbarians" and blamed for all the disruption they brought with them. Their techniques were ignored while a passionate rear-guard action was fought to keep old Mandarin society unaltered down to its last ceremonious particular. Within fifty years, Chinese society all but collapsed and then entered on another fifty years of anarchy.

In Japan, on the contrary, the West had been studied by leaders and soldiers long before Commodore Perry arrived to demand the opening of the Hermit Kingdom. Westerners were seen not as "barbarians" but as representatives of a new type of society which, to resist, Japan would need in some measure to assimilate. Heroic readjustments—including profound structural changes such as the abolition of feudal land tenure—were made, and within fifty years the West regarded Japan as an equal. In short, the Chinese suffered history; the Japanese controlled it. A similar choice confronts the West today.

Communist pressure on our contemporary society to some degree resembles Western pressure on the Far East a century ago. We can, like the Manchu dynasty in China, regard our adversaries as "red devils" and attribute all the disruption they cause to an immoral and violent conspiracy. Or we can, like the Japanese, look at the pressure not so much as a pressure exercised by malevolent enemies but rather as a deeper historical pressure of change and upheaval which they simply project and exploit.

Which of these interpretations should we choose? Let us look at three areas in which we are most keenly aware of Communist competition and challenge. They force us to confront the issue of a working world order for mankind, in part by their boasts that it will be Communist ("We will bury you"), in part by the frightful dangers of the arms race in which both sides are engaged. Again, they compel us to consider the future allegiance of the "uncommitted" third of humanity by their claim that capitalism simply exploits the underdeveloped peoples whereas Communism offers them the way to both equality and abundance. And this claim is in turn part of their more fundamental credo—that only Communism has the secret of long-term economic expansion and can confidently promise its people standards of living which by 1980, so goes the boast, will be half as high again as those in stagnant, inhibited, self-contradictory capitalist economies.

Clearly in this confrontation between Communism and the West, none of the basic conditions has been created by the Communists. We need some form of coherent world order because science has annihilated space, opened up instant communication, and made the world a single neighborhood of potential destruction. Equally, the Communists did not create the desires and tensions of the emergent peoples. Modern industry and technology drew them into the web of world trade and set their feet on the first rung of the ladder of a modern economy. Communists or no Communists, they would try to climb the rest of the way.

As for the dream of abundance, science and technology are making it not a dream, but a fact. In the developed world of the West, living standards are higher than ever before; yet some $60 billion is spent on arms each year. An American road program can swallow up as much money in a few years. A space program will do the same. Yet men are unemployed, food is in surplus, oil is in surplus,[1] aluminum threatens a surplus, steel capacity is not fully used, most colonial products are in surplus. In spite of the immensity of demand, science keeps supply ahead of it. If, therefore, the Communists say they will increase their national income by 5 or 6 percent a year, there is no reason to doubt their ability. They have been doing so for years. So have Italy and West Germany and, more recently, France. And the reason is the same. Science and technology have created the preconditions and the materials for abundance. All that is needed is the community's decision to mobilize them, by one means or another, to the full.

Nor is the picture any different in other areas of Communist challenge. We may become aware of the need for more widespread, vigorous, and scientific education . . . The need for such education is inherent in our growing technological sophistication. We may reach out into space to answer a Soviet challenge. But the decision to explore the upper air was in fact made when the new technology first took Orville Wright a few feet off the ground. Soviet competitiveness does no more than underline in more violent colors challenges and upheavals that are inherent in the fact that we are living through the greatest revolution humanity has ever known —the revolution of scientific change.

Nothing like it has ever happened before. When mankind moved from hunting and fishing to settled agriculture and the city-state, the change stretched over millennia. Even so, it modified every human habit and institution. Today, changes of infinitely greater magnitude are occurring in decades, not even in centuries. Everything is exploding—population, knowledge, communication, resources, cities, space itself. These are the forces of change which we have to understand and master. Communism is in a sense incidental. It exploits a revolution it did not create, and its pretension to produce satisfactory human solutions is answered by the wall across Berlin.

Communist success or failure is not the point. The fundamental question is whether we in the West are able to confront the challenge of our times. And here we face the agonizing difficulty that some of the creative

---

[1] By 1971, however, it was generally believed that the demand for oil was outracing the exploration and development of new resources. [Eds.]

responses we need to make run deeply against the grain of our traditional thinking. . . .

Today, in each of the major areas of challenge—international order, the developing world, the use of our abundance—we are inhibited by attitudes inherited from our prescientific past. The attitudes are dear to us. We can modify them only with great distress and questioning. But these are precisely the pains of any great historical transformation. History does not offer men only the easy options. It tends to come up on their blind side and challenge them precisely where their interests and beliefs are most deeply engaged.

We instinctively distrust the idea of an organized international society because our emotional allegiance is still to our own isolated, independent, sovereign nation. We instinctively question the idea of a special effort or program to speed the development of the emergent peoples, for we inherit the belief that "normal" trade and investment should govern the relations between sovereign states, developed or otherwise. And we tend to reject the idea of a sustained program of economic growth—by whatever percentage a year—because our instincts still regard "big government" as a menace and private activity as the really legitimate tool of economic expansion.

Now, as we have seen, Communism rejects all these reactions. What is more serious is that the facts of our scientific age belie them too. No nation can be isolated in the atomic age. Fallout rains down on the committed and uncommitted alike. The underdeveloped areas cannot speed up their growth without special long-term assistance since "normal" investment tends to go to wealthy countries, while in "normal" world commerce the price of manufactured goods produced in emergent territories goes down. The national circuit is making the rich richer while the poor lag further behind.

Above all, the experience of the last decades underlines the fact that private demand alone does not unlock the full range of modern scientific production. It took a vast arms effort to jerk American industry to double its size after 1940. It took the Marshall Plan to push Europe into the new pattern of the mass consumption economy. American food production, maintained by government aid, so far outstrips American—or Western—demand that the surpluses, grown on less and less land, could feed a hungry world. And Europe's farming now promises to show the same surge. In short, the astonishing secret of the modern scientific economy is that, after a certain stage of development, we can have what, as a community, we decide to have. Imagination is not limited by scarce resources. On the contrary, resources are limited by scarce imagination. Yet it is broadly true to say that in the West today this freedom of imagination comes only when—as with arms or the space race—fear is involved. Even education has had to beg for funds under the guise of national security.

This, then, is the agonizing confrontation of needs and policies in the West today. It is possible to plan purposefully—through public agencies, through private agencies, through the cooperation of both—for an abundant world. But to many Western minds planning is seen as the abdication of freedom to total government. This is their core of orthodoxy. Here, as with the Manchus and their ancient tradition, they are more willing to face defeat than to compromise.

Happily, however, the choice is not in fact so stark. To opt for purposive policies aimed at abundance does not involve slavery or totalitarianism or total government control. . . . [T]here are now creative experiments to show how abundance can be organized in freedom. The Common Market proves that free nations can concert their politics and policies and achieve greater cooperation. . . . [T]he West must go to closer and international cooperation in the Atlantic area, as the nucleus of world order, to Western support for quicker economic growth in new common markets in Latin America, in Africa, in Asia, to consistent Western programs for higher, steadier domestic expansion, for bolder aims in education, in culture . . . urban living, and for prosperous free economies rolling forward on the two essential wheels of lively private expansion and vigorous public investment.

These are not pipe dreams. They have been partially achieved. What is needed now is that we should generalize them . . . into an accepted grand strategy, and then challenge Communism at its most vulnerable point, saying to the world: We can give you cooperation, abundance, growth, and more equal sharing—and we can give you freedom too.

Above all, alone in human history, our tradition of freedom is based on the belief that all men must share its benefits and that the foundation of true freedom can be found only in justice. The rights and woes of the disinherited have thundered out in our society from the days of the first Jewish prophet down to the last of them, Karl Marx. That salvation for the rich depends upon compassion for the poor has been the inescapable lesson of the Gospels through two millennia. Today, for the first time in human history, our Christian duty—to feed the hungry, to clothe the naked —can be physically and actually fulfilled. Modern science provides the material resources to do precisely this. Therefore to leave disease, starvation, and misery untended is now, for the rich nations, a matter of choice. They have a new freedom added to the dimensions of their liberty—they can choose to end or not to end the servile poverty of their fellow men.

It is no coincidence that Communism claims each of these Western traditions for its own. It claims to remake heaven and earth, it claims a universal brotherhood, it claims to offer abundance and equality to all the children of men. We may know how much is specious and corrupted in its claims. But what will our claim to freedom look like if the world sees it to be uncreative, isolationist, and locked up in its own selfish wealth? The Western citizen of today, if he is to face the world's crisis of freedom, cannot ignore the deepest ideals of his own free tradition. He must wish to "recreate the face of the earth." He must see the human race as one brotherhood. He must set his abundance to work to end other people's misery and want. In this spirit, freedom will conquer. Without it, freedom hardly deserves the name.

James H. Weaver

HOW TO STAY THE RICHEST COUNTRY IN THE WORLD

"There are three billion people in the world and we only have two hundred million of them. We are outnumbered 15 to 1. If might did make right they would sweep over the United States and take what we have. We have what they want."
                    —*President Johnson, Camp Stanley, Korea, Nov. 1, 1966.*

In 1964, the United States had 6 percent of the world's population and 34 percent of the world's income. If all countries, developed and underdeveloped alike, were to achieve a per capita income equaling America's —the announced goal of the Soviet Union—then the U.S. would have 6 percent of the world's population and 6 percent of the world's income. We could hardly be said to enjoy leisure class status (or power, or prestige, or influence) in such a situation. No country with only 6 percent of the world's income would have the impact in the world that the United States has today. And American economic policies are carefully tailored to preserving this privileged position. Observe:

1. *The U.S. supports free trade—when it works to our advantage—but frequently practices protectionism to the detriment of developing nations.*

Textiles, for example, have historically been the primary industry used to develop country after country. This pattern was established by England and has been followed by the northeastern United States, the American South, Japan, etc. Once the currently underdeveloped countries started following the pattern, however, the U.S. imposed textile import quotas through the Long Term Arrangement in cotton textiles. The value of our imports of cotton textiles grew at a rate of 30 percent a year from 1958 to 1960, before the quotas were imposed. After the imposition of the textile arrangement the annual rate of growth fell to 14 percent. If

Reprinted by permission from *Commonweal*, April 4, 1969, pp. 67–68.

the value of our imports had continued to grow from 1960 to 1966 at the earlier rate, the total value of imports in 1966 would have been $1.3 billion. This compares to actual imports of $449 million in 1966. Thus, the probable cost to the underdeveloped nations of the Long Term Arrangement has been approximately $850 million a year in foreign exchange earnings.

Another striking example of U.S. policy toward underdeveloped countries is the oil import quota program. In the period 1950 to 1957 (just prior to the imposition of this program) the value of U.S. petroleum imports was increasing 15.1 percent a year. Since the program came into effect in 1957, petroleum imports increased 2.3 percent a year to 1964. If the previous growth rates had prevailed through 1964, petroleum imports would have been valued at $2.6 billion in that year as opposed to the actual import value of $1.1 billion. This program costs underdeveloped nations approximately $1.5 billion per year.

The United States has also historically opposed commodity agreements, having relaxed this policy only briefly in the early '60s to accept the coffee agreement. However, it has recently become fairly clear that the U.S. will fail to continue its support for the coffee agreement. We have also clearly torpedoed the cocoa agreement. The U.S., actually, follows a dual policy in this regard. We regulate, supervise, and control the production of cotton, wheat, tobacco, soybeans, and peanuts at home, but we insist on a free market internationally.

2. *Foreign aid is designed to serve the political and economic needs of the United States rather than the development needs of the recipient nations.*

With certain exceptions (the Peace Corps, for example), U.S. foreign aid does not help underdeveloped countries to develop. Our Public Law 480 program, which ships surplus agricultural products to underdeveloped countries, has been a program primarily to benefit domestic agriculture, rather than to help underdeveloped nations. The program has even allowed the landlord-peasant relationship (feudalism) to continue in many of those countries where aid has been given.

Other aid programs subsidize lagging U.S. exports, or lay the groundwork for future U.S. economic gains. A 1965 AID statement declared that "development loan dollars, now spent in large preponderance in the U.S., contribute substantially to employment in our export industries, and have created important footholds for future U.S. export markets after U.S. assistance is phased out." Meanwhile, interest on loans has risen sharply since the '50s, and underdeveloped nations must devote a large part of new aid to servicing past debts.

Let's look at the countries which the U.S. aided from 1953 to 1965. The countries which received the largest amount of aid per capita were: 1. Taiwan, which received $324 per capita, totalling $3.5 billion, of which

65% was military; 2. Jordan, which received $299 per capita, totalling $.5 billion, of which 7% was military; 3. Laos, which received $295 per capita, totalling $.5 billion, of which the military portion was classified; 4. Korea, which received $221 per capita, totalling $5.6 billion, of which 39% was military; 5. Vietnam, which received $208 per capita, a total of $3.0 billion, of which the military portion was classified. We can see the types of countries that the U.S. has tended to favor—reactionary or military regimes whose principal virtues have been either militant anti-Communism or a location next to the Communist bloc. In 1966–67, 25% of our aid went to South Vietnam.

The United States has not supported the expansion of United Nations aid programs, has not been enthusiastic about expanding the International Development Association, and successfully opposed the Stamp plan for international monetary reform, which would directly help underdeveloped countries.

3. *Underdeveloped countries lose out on direct private investment from the U.S.*

If one examines the data for the period 1950 to 1964, one sees that U.S. direct private investment outflows from the United States to underdeveloped countries amounted to $10 billion. The United States repatriated from these same countries $21 billion during this period. The U.S. brought $2 out for every $1 that went in. If we look at the rates of return on American direct investment abroad, we see that in 1964–65 Americans earned 23 percent on investments in Africa, 36 percent in Asia, and 12 percent in Latin America.

But won't the U.S. assist the development of the rest of the world simply because, in the long run, such development is necessary for America's own well-being? Both liberals and conservatives alike fall back on this assumption to reassure themselves that, whatever our present shortcomings, the story will have a happy ending because it *must* have one.

First, it is argued that the U.S. needs the rest of the world to develop to serve as markets. But this is not true today. With the introduction of Keynesian economics and the techniques of demand management, it is possible for any developed country to have, at home, the level of effective demand it needs in order to provide for full employment. It can reduce taxes or increase government spending to create a demand for whatever it is capable of producing. In 1964, the U.S. cut taxes by some $10 billion and increased demand by approximately $30 billion. Therefore, it is obvious that we do not need the rest of the world for markets. One of the points about the *General Theory* of which Keynes was most proud was that it made imperialism unnecessary and ended the need to have other countries buying a country's excess products.

Secondly, it is argued that the United States needs the underdeveloped countries because it needs their raw materials. But this argument does not stand up under careful scrutiny either. The United States is the world's largest producer of almost all types of raw materials. We are capable of supplying ourselves with necessary natural resources. Those which cannot be produced at home can be synthesized—natural rubber was unavailable in World War II and the United States developed synthetic rubber. With the introduction of plastics in the 1950's it became possible to substitute for any number of metals and other products which we needed before. It is not denied that our standard of living would suffer if we did not have imports of raw materials from underdeveloped countries. But the United States could live very well—could be very rich indeed—without the raw materials that we get from underdeveloped countries.

The third argument that is made is that the United States needs the rest of the world to develop for the sake of world peace. But this ignores all past history. Most developing countries have always been expansionistic, militaristic, and aggressive. England developed first and took over half the world. After England came France and Napoleon, then Germany and its expansionism, then the United States which took over a large part of Mexico, the Philippines, Puerto Rico, etc. Russia followed the pattern and now China is showing symptoms of doing the same. Developing countries are, at least in the short run, belligerent and prone to expand.

In fact, of course, most underdeveloped countries are *not* developing, or if they are developing and growing it is at a much slower pace than that of developed countries. The data on this subject are clear. From 1950 to 1964 the GNP of the poorest 60 percent of the countries in the world grew from 82 percent to 166 percent. The wealthy countries grew much faster than the countries at the bottom of the scale. In 1950 the poorest 60 percent of the world's population received 13.2 percent of world income and in 1964 they received 11.1% of world income. The richest 40 percent of the world's population, which had received 86.8 percent of world income in 1950, received 88.9 percent in 1964.

The United States has no desire to share its privileged status in the world. We do not want "them" sweeping over us and taking what "we" have. U.S. policy does not assist development, nor is there any necessity which might require this policy to change. And—obviously—U.S. policy has been a grand success.

THE GREAT FOREIGN AID FRAUD

In 30 years' time, the majority of the world's poorer countries can achieve self-sustaining growth.   That is the judgment of the Commission on International Development headed by Mr. Lester Pearson, which includes such hard heads as those of Mr. Douglas Dillon, Sir Arthur Lewis and M. Robert

RICHER NATIONS' 1968 AID PERFORMANCE

| | Net aid as % of gnp | Grants as % of commitments | Average loan terms: | | |
			Rate of interest	Years to maturity	Years grace
Switzerland	0.10	48	4.9	13.5	2.0
Japan	0.25	57	3.9	18.0	5.4
Canada	0.28	75	1.1	43.5	8.6
Sweden	0.28	75	2.5	34.0	9.6
United States	0.38	45	3.5	30.0	7.8
Britain	0.42	46	1.3	24.8	6.3
Germany	0.42	36	3.9	21.2	5.9
Holland	0.54	56	3.9	29.7	6.6
Australia	0.57	100	—	—	—
France	0.72	70	3.7	18.0	0.8
Average for 15 DAC countries *	0.39	50	3.3	24.8	6.5

* The ten shown plus Austria, Belgium, Denmark, Italy and Norway.

BRITAIN'S RECORD IN THE 1960s

	1961	1968
Gross aid disbursements (£mn)	170	210
Net aid (deducting loan repayments and interest) (£mn)	151	150
Net aid as % of gnp	0.55	0.42
Grants as % of aid commitments	52	46

The latest studies indicate that the balance-of-payments cost of aid is less than £50 million a year.   Each £100 allotted to bilateral aid has brought £63 of orders to British firms.   And for each £100 channelled through multilateral agencies, orders worth as much as £116 have been placed in Britain.

Britain's one notable advance during the 1960s was the switch in 1965 to interest-free loans.   In 1968 these loans made up 89 per cent of its aid disbursements.

Reprinted from *The Economist* (November 1, 1969), p. 29.

HOW THE MAIN AID RECIPIENTS
HAVE BEEN DOING

Gnp growth (annual average 1960–67)	Gnp per head, 1967			
	Under $100	$100–200	$200–300	$300 and over
Over 6%	—	S. Korea 7.4	Taiwan 5.2 Jordan 31.9	Mexico 2.0 Peru 5.1 Spain 2.0
5–6%	Pakistan 4.2	Egypt 3.7	Turkey 5.7	—
4–5%	—	Kenya 6.4 Philippines 2.8	Brazil 2.7 Colombia 5.2	Chile 14.5
3–4%	India 2.4 Nigeria 2.1	Congo 7.1 Morocco 6.9	Ghana 7.7 Tunisia 18.9	—
Under 3%	—	Indonesia 1.0	Algeria 12.3 Senegal 13.9	—

Figures after each country show, in dollars, annual aid received per head of population (1964–67 average). Each country shown received over $50 million aid per year in 1964–67. So did Israel, Jugoslavia, Laos and South Vietnam.

Marjolin. They justify their judgment by the record of recent years. These countries already show an average annual real growth rate of 5 per cent. A rate of 6 per cent would do the job by the year 2000.

The commission's report [1] shows how this rate can be generally attained if the community of nations would actually do some of the things its members have lately talked of doing. The report is wholly realistic. Of the population explosion, it says that: "No other phenomenon casts a darker shadow over the prospects for international development." It notes that massive family planning programmes have now been launched in countries that contain 70 per cent of the poor world's population; and it shows the need to sustain and extend this work. It is very specific about action required to increase the poorer countries' earnings from exports. It insists on the role of private capital in development, and prescribes means of encouraging investment.

But it is most revealing when it discusses aid; and it may have most im-

[1] "Partners in Development." Pall Mall Press. 400 pages.

pact here.   "Aid" is the word that leaps into the average man's mind when he reads something about international development.   His current cynicism reflects the prevalent idea that, after years of generous aid-giving, the poorer countries are as poor as ever, mainly because they are inept, prolific, and ungrateful.   The Pearson report shows this belief to be grotesquely false.

When President Kennedy launched the United Nations into its first "development decade" in 1961, two main targets were set.   The poorer countries (roughly, those where average annual incomes were less than $500) were each to aim at achieving at least 5 per cent annual growth by 1970. The richer ones (including communist states) would undertake to channel to the poorer ones, in aid and investment, at least 1 per cent of their national incomes.   Later, it was agreed to raise this target to 1 per cent of their gross national products—an increase of over a fifth.

The less developed countries, on average, now show an annual rate of gross investment equal to 17.8 per cent of gnp; and 85 per cent of this has come from domestic savings.   In the face of worsening terms of trade, they have raised their export earnings by an annual average of 6.1 per cent. In the face of the population explosion, they have raised average production per head by 2.5 per cent per year.   Even in the huge "hard case" of India, the new farming breakthrough leads the Pearson commission's staff to envisage a steady annual gnp growth rate of 6 per cent in the 1970s.

If the richer countries had fulfilled their part of the compact, they might now have more right to carp at the poorer ones' performance.   But carp they do.   The commission is obliged to speak of "aid weariness" and to record that "international support for development is now flagging."   And one reason is that "the real economic burden of foreign aid to wealthy countries is often considerably exaggerated."

This exaggeration largely arises from the habit of seeing "the total flow of resources to developing countries . . . as something that the rich countries 'give' to the poor.   Nothing could be farther from the truth."   The report shows that the developing countries are now paying back to the richer ones over $4,000 million a year in servicing their debts (quite apart from paying dividends on investments), and that in the 1960s these debt service payments have mounted by 17 per cent per year.   If present trends continue, there would by 1977 again be a large net flow of money from the poor to the rich countries.

Far from approaching their own target, the richer countries as a group have receded from it.   At the start of the decade, the net flow of resources to the poor world from the non-communist richer nations equalled 0.89 per cent of their combined gnps.   By 1968 it had sunk to 0.77 per cent.   Its composition had also deteriorated.   By 1968, nearly half consisted of investment and commercial credit.   This, the Pearson commission points out, can in no sense be termed "aid"—though it too often is.   Of the remaining half (now equal to only 0.39 per cent of the gnps), the proportion taking the form not of grants but of loans tripled during the 1960s. The proportion "tied" to purchases in one country rose until only a sixth of the aid was untied. Tying, the commission notes, usually reduces the aid's value by over 20 per cent. A fifth of the aid took the form of surplus food and commodities. The commission questions whether in such cases there is any real cost to the supplier.

During the 1960s the richer non-communist nations doubled their combined gross national products to a total of $1,700 billion in 1968. Yet the aid they provided in grant (or "grantlike") form fell from $4.5 billion in 1961 to $4.1 billion in 1968. The fall in real value was much sharper. This performance can be favourably viewed in only one perspective: in comparison with that of the communist states. These states' tranfers to the poorer countries still run at only about $350 million a year. No wonder Russia has excused itself from joining in the preparations for a second UN development decade.

The Pearson commission, regretting its inability to get information about the communist states' activities, does not prescribe for them. For the others, its primary recommendation is that they should each aim at making an aid contribution equal to 0.7 per cent of gnp by 1975 (without abandoning the 1 per cent target for all resource flows). It urges them to channel at least a fifth of their aid (instead of the present tenth) through multilateral agencies, and to make commitments for periods of at least three years at a time. Its 20 proposals for making aid more effective include a plan for gradually (and painlessly) untying the greater part of it. It is also urged that aid loans should bear no more than 2 per cent interest and provide for grace periods of 7 to 10 years, with maturity at between 25 and 40 years.

What the main recommendation on aid means is that nations which will by 1975 have probably increased their combined annual gnps by $600 billion (at 1968 prices: the nominal increase being doubtless much greater) should earmark for aid something like a sixtieth part of that increase. Is this absurdly visionary?

SUGGESTED READINGS

Brierly, James L., *The Law of Nations: An Introduction to the International Law of Peace,* 6th ed., New York: Oxford University Press, 1963.

Deutsch, Karl, and Hoffmann, Stanley (eds.), *The Relevance of International Law,* Garden City, N.Y.: Anchor Books, Doubleday, 1971.

Falk, Richard A., *Legal Order in a Violent World,* Princeton: Princeton University Press, 1968.

Johnson, Harry G., *The World Economy at the Crossroads,* New York: Oxford University Press, 1965.

Myint, Hla, *The Economics of the Developing Countries,* New York: Praeger, 1965.

Myrdal, Gunnar, *Asian Drama: An Inquiry into the Poverty of Nations,* New York: Pantheon, 1968, 3 vols.

———, *International Economy: Problems and Prospects,* New York: Harper & Row, 1956, 1969.

Niebuhr, Reinhold, *Christianity and Power Politics,* New York: Scribner's, 1940.

Northrop, F. S. C., *The Meeting of East and West,* New York: Macmillan, 1946.

Pincus, John A. (ed.), *Reshaping the World Economy: Rich Countries and Poor,* Englewood Cliffs, N.J.: Prentice-Hall, 1968.

Rostow, W. W., *Stages of Economic Growth: A Non-Communist Manifesto,* New York: Cambridge University Press, 1960.

VIII. DIPLOMACY AND FOREIGN POLICY

"An ambassador," wrote Sir Henry Wotton, "is an honest man sent to lie abroad for the good of his country." That statement, written in the early seventeenth century, still describes the attitude of many men toward diplomats and diplomacy. The terms are inextricably connected to a whole set of symbols and meanings: the tailed coat, the ribbon and star of an order of knighthood, crystal palaces and fountained gardens, the rapier finesse of men equally at home at conference or in the boudoir. Even the waltz is not exempt: "All the delegates dance," wrote one observer of the Congress of Vienna in 1815, "save Mr. Talleyrand, who has a club foot." Diplomacy still seems a cloak-and-dagger world, where the figures of Machiavelli and Metternich merge with the three musketeers and the Count of Monte Cristo.

But there was a reality behind the myths of the old diplomacy. Its skills and style, its unfailing good manners and social grace, were appropriate to an age of aristocracy when the image of chivalry still hung over the courts of Europe and the age of mass politics was far away. One need not romanticize the great age of diplomacy to recognize as much. It had follies, but its follies were those of aristocracy itself; in 1635, to cite one example, a Venetian offer to mediate the Thirty Years' War was rejected by Sweden because the Venetians had omitted "Most Powerful" from the lengthy list of titles of the Swedish Queen Christina. To many of the analysts and observers of the nineteenth century, diplomacy seemed less sinister than foolish.

There is no doubt, however, that the influence of diplomacy was great. In the days when the only means of communication between states were painfully slow, governments at home could not hope to supervise the conduct of foreign relations; often months away from the capital of his state, the diplomat had to be allowed discretion and be trusted to his own resources. Often the result of his labors was not that which domestic leaders would have preferred; for example, John Jay's treaty with England in 1794 was greeted by a storm of protests at home. Karl Marx, in his *Secret Diplomatic History of the Eighteenth Century,* argued that the "economic" arguments made to support British foreign policy were almost entirely developed after the fact, to justify to Parliament and the commercial classes policies arrived at by the aristocracy on its own terms.

But although traditional diplomacy endured for many a year, the world that gave it birth began to die with the Industrial Revolution and the revolution in France, at the beginning of an age of technology and of mass mobilization. Increased speed in communication made it possible for governments to exercise an almost day-to-day surveillance of diplomatic offices abroad; increased speed and destructiveness of weapons made such control seem necessary. The increasing centralization of diplomacy in the hands of the Foreign Offices at home deprived the diplomat of much of his autonomy. So long as men believed, with the optimism of the nineteenth century, that foreign policy was becoming less vital, that war was disappearing, that the age of crisis had passed, diplomacy was allowed to operate largely on its own terms. To be sure, the democratic revolutions made it necessary for diplomats to give increasing attention to mass sentiments, but the means of conducting and controlling foreign policy remained in the hands of diplomatic professionals, trained in the ethics of traditional diplomacy.

The seeming inability of diplomacy to avert the disaster of World War I, the new realization of the peril and menace in foreign policy, and the discovery of an unsuspected network of secret treaties and understandings between states all contributed to the end of mass indifference toward the conduct of foreign policy. Woodrow Wilson denounced secret treaties as likely to lead to war and proclaimed the end of the old diplomacy:

It is this happy fact, now clear to the view of every public man whose thoughts do not still linger in an age that is dead and gone, which makes it possible for every nation whose purposes are consistent with justice and the peace of the world to avow, now or any other time, the objects it has in view.[1]

Wilson's proclamation of the principle of "open covenants, openly arrived at" heralded an age in which democratic nations more or less sincerely attempted to conduct their foreign relations without secrecy.

"Open" diplomacy, however, proved no more successful at averting war and crisis than had the old "secret" diplomacy. In some ways, in fact, it proved decisively inferior. Nor should this have been unexpected. Alexis de Tocqueville would have shared Wilson's faith in the excellence of the intentions and values of democracy; but, he argued, the people, however strong their moral judgment, are unable to choose policies adapted to those ends. That would require the technical and professional skill of an elite, Tocqueville argued, and nowhere more than in the complex areas of foreign policy. The tendency to judge complex political issues in terms of simple moral categories is a dangerous one, perilous, in fact, to the moral ends that policy seeks to attain.[2]

In our world of economic complexity, of the "balance of terror" brought about by weapons of mass destruction, and of rapid political change, the times seem to make speedy decisionmaking, secrecy, and the expert's command of technical data all the more necessary. Wilson's view proved oversanguine, as

[1] Albert B. Hart (ed.), *Selected Addresses and Public Papers of Woodrow Wilson,* New York: Boni & Liveright, 1918, pp. 247–248.

[2] *Democracy in America,* New York: Vintage, 1957, I, 246–248.

he himself came to realize: the *age* of the old diplomacy may have died, but the *need* for it has not. Sir Harold Nicolson realized this, and in large measure lauds the virtues of the old diplomacy as opposed to the new. One would surmise that a latter-day practiser of the art, Henry Kissinger, would not disagree either.

The question is not simply one of lament for the past, nor even of developing a new diplomatic "elite." Citizens may leave foreign policy to the "experts" as long as they believe the professionals are getting results. But it is too much to expect that the calm atmosphere of former times will return; the leisurely pace of the old diplomacy and of an age that nurtured it are far removed from our own. Too much is at stake: civilizations, ways of life, the existence of entire peoples and nations. Citizens will demand some assurance that the efforts of experts are being lent to good ends, that the technicians are guided by a moral goal.

But the very nature of the modern world makes the developing of a new cosmopolitan diplomatic elite difficult. Modern professionals do not form one group of like-minded diplomatists; the foreign policymaking elite is a complex group of several many-tiered bureaucratic pyramids with shifting, seldom clear relationships between them. The various organs of government of the modern state, be it democracy or dictatorship, are usually in competition, often in rivalry, and sometimes even in internecine struggles with one another. As Adam Yarmolinsky shows, the American military establishment approaches and handles foreign policy quite differently from the Department of State. They are the two most important bureaucratic organizations guiding and implementing the foreign policy of the United States, yet they significantly differ in their respective basic outlooks, their sizes and resources, their relationships to action, their attitudes to domestic pressures, and their planning for the future. True enough, the Office of Management and Budget (with a helping, correcting, or hindering hand from Congress) allocates to them their resources, and the National Security Council discusses top policy-decisions while its staff, in Henry Kissinger's language, "sorts out the options" for the President. Nevertheless, rivalries and power balances between the departments remain. Bureaucratic earthquakes may lead to a thorough reassignment of responsibilities among all foreign policy agencies, but this will merely result in a redistribution of functions and powers and not in the creation of either monolithic discipline or cooperative harmony. Much of policymaking, therefore, can be traced back today to the nature of the respective policymaking organizations and the relationships of the exponents of the individual bureaucratic organizations to each other and to their respective influences on the persons or councils that make the vital decisions at the top.

Graham T. Allison has shown the insufficiency of analyzing foreign policy as a chain of rational actions by an "actor," the traditional method of the realistic school of international politics. Such actions, after all, depend to a large extent on the performances of specific bureaucratic organizations, while the complete decisionmaking process can only be understood if, in addition, one also pays due attention to "bureaucratic politics," that is, the combination of bargaining and negotiation that often results in compromises incomprehensible to an analysis based on pure logic and reason. Therefore Allison advanced the thesis that foreign policy analysis built on the "rational model" should be followed by analyses based respectively on the "organization model" and on the "bureaucratic politics model," and that only a fusion of these three studies will result in complete understanding of the behavior of a government in a serious and complex crisis.[3]

Allison's models may explain the making of foreign policy in a dramatic crisis where fast action is imperative. But much of foreign policy is incremental,[4] and the huge foreign policy programs necessitate constant congressional support and therefore sustained public backing. To obtain congressional support for foreign policy programs, however, requires special techniques that differ from those used in the usual democratic process, at least in America. As Dean Acheson, a deft practitioner of the art, points out in his memoirs, "foreign policy has no lobby, no vested interest to support it, no constituents. It must be built on a broad conception of the national interest, which lacks the attraction and support that can be generated by, say, a tax reduction, a tariff increase, or an agricultural subsidy." Yet, as Yarmolinsky has shown, while domestic politics look as irrelevant to the "Chief Lobbyist" for the State Department, the Department of Defense is deeply involved in domestic politics by the very fact that it moves vast numbers of men and goods. Not only does the draft directly affect the whole citizenry, but the procurement of the instruments of war affects the economic welfare of American communities and companies. When such a large part of the department's aircraft is purchased from West Coast companies, can it be said that foreign policy has "no constituents"? Moreover in a Middle Eastern crisis, for example, the oil interests will have different constituents from those who demand more support to Israel.

This task of winning confidence and loyalty from people and professionals appears to be a very difficult one. The professionals obsessed with the dangers and complexities of contemporary world politics find it difficult to tolerate the intrusion of "amateurs" or of "political" considerations derived from areas other than international politics. Recent developments in American political life show that, in an age when foreign policy has assumed such vast dimensions that domestic politics have become dependent on it, traditional processes may be insufficient for both democratic control of the government and the obtaining of public consensus for the government's actions. The prescription of the Roosevelt-Truman-Acheson era of a "bipartisan," or rather "extrapartisan," foreign policy coalition bridging the gap between the professional elite and the public (so well described by Dean Acheson) has definitely broken down. It resulted in an immobilisme, not unlike the one that caused the collapse of the French Fourth Republic. Whatever remains of the old coalitions is undermined by the protest movements. It has become clear that at least in a democracy, not even the vast resources of a superstate can be mobilized by the elite without durable and dedicated public support.

But public support cannot be obtained by "charisma" alone; it also involves information to and education of the public, or else the accusations of "decep-

[3] "Conceptional Models and the Cuban Missile Crisis," *American Political Science Review* (September 1969), pp. 689–718.

[4] See especially David Braybrooke and Charles E. Lindblom, *A Strategy of Decision: Policy Evaluation as a Social Process,* New York: Free Press, 1963, pp. 61–79.

tion" will ring loud in the land, as the case of the *Pentagon Papers* has proven. Yet, as the London *Economist* asserts, President Johnson was by no means unique in exercising "dissimulation" while leading the United States deeper and deeper into the quagmire of the Vietnam War. Did not Wilson and Roosevelt, Grey and Chamberlain do similar things when they led their respective nations into two world wars? Or is the "question of war and peace" different from "the other business democratic publics entrust to their governments"? The *Economist*'s answer is that democratic governments "sidle up to the question of war—crabwise, eyes averted, hand over mouth"—largely because they fear the criticism of the liberal intelligentsia that represents a significant section of the public and, moreover, has a great influence over the information *media*. Yet, so says the writer writing for this very liberal paper, liberals "understand the misery of war, but . . . do not possess a matching intellectual grasp of the way cause and effect continuously operate among the powers of the world." [5]

The late C. Wright Mills was in many ways such a liberal observer, though of a rather radical persuasion. He was convinced that the professionals, while grasping the "way of cause and effect" only too clearly, are prevented by their preoccupation with immediate problems from thinking seriously about the goals of policy. Mills seemed to imply in fact that the more expert the elite became, the more specialized its skills, the less able it was to see the whole of the political picture, including the future. The elites, he argued, are prisoners of the drift of world politics, incapable of guiding it. The "drift" of events, he concluded, was dominated by a "military metaphysic" leading to war, and those who did not seek to avert it were "crackpot realists" whose narrow concern for the immediate realities of politics led them to overlook its equally real tendencies. In 1958 Mills feared a drift into World War III; today, if alive, he might perhaps regard Vietnam as a way station in this macabre process.

But if elites seemed to have assumed such an omnipotent grip of the great powers today, who guides the foreign policies of the scores of new states that have emerged from colonial subjection into the arena of world politics? The small elites that led these people to freedom and indeed, to often incomplete nationhood, threw themselves with great fervor into international activity, not only in order to change international society through the entrance of the teeming postcolonial masses, but also for psychological reasons. Independence, as Nehru once defined it, "consisted fundamentally and basically of foreign relations." The foreign policy style of these new elites was characterized by moralizing and rhetoric. Only in that way could they properly dramatize the justification of foreign policy to the inexperienced home publics that were expected to rejoice in the consciousness that their representatives, after centuries of ignominious oppression, were now heard by the people of the world. At the outset these new elites presented to the world policies very different from those the polished old diplomacy, which Nicolson describes, used to work with. While insisting on equality the new elites of the third world demanded obligations from the advanced states that they themselves, in the name of sovereignty and independence, were not willing to assume. But, as Oliver J. Lissitzyn has shown,[6] in accepting the norms of traditional international law, the new states

[5] "The Way We Go to War," *The Economist* (London), June 26, 1971, pp. 15–16.
[6] See Chapter VII.

became gradually socialized into the existing system, though undoubtedly their presence in such large numbers also changed the very nature of this system. Sizable gaps developed, however, in many new states between the enthusiasm of their leaders for foreign politics and the inability of their peoples, still at an early stage of developing national consciousness, to follow them. The problems that the elites of new countries are facing today are therefore not completely different from those facing the United States: how can foreign policy become a legitimate popular endeavor?

But should such efforts to influence the people stop at one's border or should the "new diplomacy" turn directly to the peoples of other nations? There may be even less hope in the prescription of the new diplomacy that turns from the professionals to the people and substitutes "communication" for "negotiation." Hans Speier indicates that the effort to use mass communication as either a weapon or a diplomatic instrument was a severely limited one during World War II and became increasingly more so in the cold war.[7] Not only in the totalitarian states did individual men feel themselves insignificant and find they were unable to act effectively to change the political order; even where such action might be possible, private citizens tended to be unsure of the bases on which they ought to have acted and the ends they should have striven for. World politics seemed more and more incomprehensible and complex. More important, the most unexpected effect of the new diplomacy was that individual men had lost faith in words and had become suspicious of ideas. The new diplomacy encouraged states to turn to propaganda to effect their aims; ideas became "weapons" measured by utility and not their truth. Once bit; twice shy: too many battlecries have proved false, too many promises have been broken, too many moral exhortations proved hollow. The age of disillusionment with ideas, of cynicism about words, had set in.

Psychological warfare in peacetime could easily develop into what is termed "subversion," though the expression has been used too often to describe any form of encouragement to violent dissent. However, when a foreign power systematically appeals to an indigenous rebel group to seize power from a government inimical to its goals and when these appeals are combined with the supply of weapons and instructions in organizational techniques, we may well be confronted with an increasingly popular method of the "newest diplomacy." Used formerly by totalitarian and colonial powers for their own imperialistic purposes, it is increasingly pointed to by the New Left as a legitimate and effective method of fomenting revolutions of "liberation" in countries regarded as under the repressive rule of neocolonialists. Such revolutionary subversion usually leads to guerrilla warfare.[8] Guerrilla fighters may or may not serve the purposes of a foreign power. If they do, the foreign power in question may assert that these purposes are entirely idealistic and altruistic, aiming at world revolution rather than at the aggrandizement of, let us say, Chinese or Cuban power. Whether the treatises of Mao Tse-tung, Che Guevara, General Giap, and others will serve in the next generation as part of the equipment of the "compleate diplomatist" or whether a quite different kind of novel diplo-

[7] Hans Speier, "International Communication: Elite vs. Mass," *World Politics* (April 1952).

[8] On guerrilla war, see Chalmers Johnson's article in Chapter VI.

macy, based on the highly institutionalized and civilized processes initiated by the United Nations and by regional organizations, will give new form to some of the principles of international civility, upheld by the admirers of "old diplomacy," only the future can tell.[9]

[9] On the "novel diplomacy" of international organization see the essays in the next chapter.

Sir Harold Nicolson

THE OLD DIPLOMACY

Let me . . . consider five of the chief characteristics of the old diplomacy.

In the first place Europe was regarded as the most important of all the continents. Asia and Africa were viewed as areas for imperial, commercial or missionary expansion; Japan, when she arose, appeared an exceptional phenomenon; America, until 1897, remained isolated behind her oceans and her Doctrine. No war, it was felt, could become a major war unless one of the five great European Powers became involved. It was thus in the chancelleries of Europe alone that the final issue of general peace or war would be decided.

In the second place it was assumed that the Great Powers were greater than the Small Powers, since they possessed a more extended range of interests, wider responsibilities, and, above all, more money and more guns. The Small Powers were graded in importance according to their military resources, their strategic position, their value as markets or sources of raw material, and their relation to the Balance of Power. There was nothing stable about such categories. Places such as Tobago or Santa Lucia, at one date strategically valuable, lost all significance with the invention of steam. At one moment Egypt, at another Afghanistan, at another Albania, would acquire prominence as points of Anglo-French, Anglo-Russian, or Slav-Teuton rivalry: at one moment the Baltic, at another the Balkans, would become the focus of diplomatic concern. Throughout this period the Small Powers were assessed according to their effect upon the relations between the Great Powers: there was seldom any idea that their interests, their opinions, still less their votes, could affect a policy agreed upon by the Concert of Europe.

This axiom implied a third principle, namely that the Great Powers possessed a common responsibility for the conduct of the Small Powers and the preservation of peace between them. The principle of intervention, as in Crete or China, was a generally accepted principle. The classic example of joint intervention by the Concert of Europe in a dispute between the Small Powers was the Ambassadors Conference held in London in 1913 at the time of the Balkan Wars. That Conference, which provides the last, as well as the best, example of the old diplomacy in action, prevented a Small-Power crisis from developing into a Great-Power crisis. I shall consider it under my next heading.

The fourth characteristic bequeathed by the French system was the es-

Reprinted with permission of the publisher from *The Evolution of Diplomatic Method* by Harold Nicolson (New York: Macmillan; London: Constable & Company, 1954), pp. 99–107. First published by The Macmillan Company in 1954.

tablishment in every European country of a professional diplomatic service in a more or less identical model. These officials representing their Governments in foreign capitals possessed similar standards of education, similar experience, and a similar aim. They desired the same sort of world. As de Callières had already noticed in 1716, they tended to develop a corporate identity independent of their national identity. They had often known each other for years, having served in some post together in their early youth; and they all believed, whatever their governments might believe, the purpose of diplomacy was the preservation of peace. This professional freemasonry proved of great value in negotiation.

The Ambassadors, for instance, of France, Russia, Germany, Austria and Italy, who, under Sir Edward Grey's [1] chairmanship, managed to settle the Balkan crisis of 1913, each represented national rivalries that were dangerous and acute. Yet they possessed complete confidence in each other's probity and discretion, had a common standard of professional conduct, and desired above all else to prevent a general conflagration.

It was not the fault of the old diplomacy, by which I mean the professional diplomatists of the pre-war period, that the supremacy of Europe was shattered by the First World War. The misfortune was that the advice of these wise men was disregarded at Vienna and Berlin, that their services were not employed, and that other non-diplomatic influences and interests assumed control of affairs.

The fifth main characteristic of the old diplomacy was the rule that sound negotiation must be continuous and confidential. It was a principle essentially different from that governing the itinerant public conferences with which we have become familiar since 1919. The Ambassador in a foreign capital who was instructed to negotiate a treaty with the Government to which he was accredited was already in possession of certain assets. He was acquainted with the people with whom he had to negotiate; he could in advance assess their strength or weakness, their reliability or the reverse. He was fully informed of local interests, prejudices or ambitions, of the local reefs and sandbanks, among which he would have to navigate. His repeated interviews with the Foreign Minister attracted no special public attention, since they were taken for granted as visits of routine. In that his conversations were private, they could remain both rational and courteous; in that they were confidential, there was no danger of public expectation being aroused while they were still in progress. Every negotiation consists of stages and a result; if the stages become matters of public controversy before the result has been achieved, the negotiation will almost certainly founder. A negotiation is the subject of concession and counter-concession: if the concession offered is divulged before the public are aware of the corresponding concession to be received, ex-

---

[1] British Foreign Secretary, 1905–1916.   [Eds.]

treme agitation may follow and the negotiation may have to be abandoned. The necessity of negotiation remaining confidential has never been more forcibly expressed than by M. Jules Cambon,[2] perhaps the best professional diplomatist of this century. "The day secrecy is abolished," writes M. Cambon, "negotiation of any kind will become impossible."

An ambassador negotiating a treaty according to the methods of the old diplomacy was not pressed for time. Both his own Government and the Government with whom he was negotiating had ample opportunity for reflection. A negotiation that had reached a deadlock could be dropped for a few months without hopes being dashed or speculation aroused. The agreements that in the end resulted were no hasty improvisations or empty formulas, but documents considered and drafted with exact care. We might cite as an example the Anglo-Russian Convention of 1907, the negotiation of which between the Russian Foreign Minister and our Ambassador in St. Petersburg occupied a period of one year and three months. At no stage during those protracted transactions was an indiscretion committed or a confidence betrayed.

*   *   *

. . . I am fully conscious of the many faults that the system encouraged. The axiom that all negotiation must be confidential did certainly create the habit of secretiveness, and did induce men of the highest respectability to enter into commitments which they did not divulge. We must not forget that as late as 1914 the French Assembly was unaware of the secret clauses of the Franco-Russian Alliance or that Sir Edward Grey (a man of scrupulous integrity) did not regard it as wrong to conceal from the Cabinet the exact nature of the military arrangements reached between the French and British General Staffs. Confidential negotiations that lead to secret pledges are worse even than the televised diplomacy that we enjoy today.

Nor am I unaware of the functional defects which the professional diplomatist tends to develop. He has seen human folly or egoism operating in so many different circumstances that he may identify serious passions with transitory feelings and thus underestimate the profound emotion by which whole nations can be swayed. He is so inured to the contrast between those who know the facts and those who do not know the facts, that he forgets that the latter constitute the vast majority and that it is with them that the last decision rests. He may have deduced from experience that time alone is the conciliator, that unimportant things do not matter and that important things settle themselves, that mistakes are the only things that are really effective, and he may thus incline to the fallacy that on the whole it is wiser, in all circumstances, to do nothing at all. He may be a

---

[2] Governor-General of Algeria, 1891–1897. French Ambassador at Washington, 1897–1902; at Madrid, 1902–1907; and at Berlin, 1907–1914. [Eds.]

stupid man or complacent; there are few human types more depressing than that of Monsieur de Norpois [3] or the self-satisfied diplomatist.   He may be weak of character, inclined to report what is agreeable rather than what is true.   He may be vain, a defect resulting in disaster to all concerned.   And he often becomes denationalised, internationalised, and therefore dehydrated, an elegant empty husk.   A profession should not, however, be judged by its failures.

Adam Yarmolinsky

BUREAUCRATIC STRUCTURES AND POLITICAL OUTCOMES

The most immediate if not the most important domestic influences on United States foreign policy are the institutions responsible for carrying out that foreign policy, principally the Department of State and the Department of Defense.   What an institution does and what it is are alternatively cause and effect.   An examination of the significant differences between the two departments may throw some additional light on the processes by which foreign policy is shaped at home and specifically on the relative roles of the military and non-military components of United States foreign policy today.   The thesis advanced here is that the policy-makers in the Department of Defense have a number of advantages in the internal political contests that determine the shape of American foreign policy apart from the merits of their own views, and indeed largely apart from the strength of their constituencies, on budgetary issues, and that these advantages are a major domestic influence on U.S. foreign policy.

The most obvious and perhaps the most important difference between the Department of Defense and the Department of State is one of sheer size.   Expenditure for defense is running at a rate some twenty times the rate for all other international activities, including foreign aid and USIA (if Vietnam expenditures are excluded, the ratio might be down to 15-to-1, although a large part of foreign aid expenditures also go to Vietnam).   Defense employs millions of men, in and out of uniform; employees of the State Department are measured only in tens of thousands.   Defense also

Reprinted by permission from *Journal of International Affairs,* 23, 2 (1969), pp. 225–235.

[3] A fictitious character representing the smooth but unimaginative French diplomat of the late nineteenth century who appears in Proust's *Remembrance of Things Past.* [Eds.]

provides employment for an additional three million in defense industry (as well as more millions in industries dependent in part on the defense establishment), for which there is no counterpart in the operations of the Department of State. . . .

The sheer size of the military establishment not only provides economies of scale, but also makes resources available at the top in manpower, in expertise, and in the variety of services that makes the difference between crisply executed operations and constantly cramped and curtailed operations. It may not be true that overseas commercial telephone conversations between State Department officials and embassies abroad have been cut off in midstream because appropriations were exhausted; but it is true that only the Defense Department (and through it the White House) has effective immediate voice communications throughout the world. United States ambassadors abroad have to ask for rides on their military attachés' aircraft, and State Department officials at home have to ask for rides in their Pentagon colleagues' official automobiles.

Not only is the Defense Department much bigger, but it is much more pervasive as well. The State Department has embassies and consulates girdling the globe, and in most of those posts foreign service officers are matched by members of United States military missions. The military presence, however, extends also into the heartland of the United States. Where the State Department has established only a few toe and fingerholds in the local councils on foreign relations in the larger urban centers, the length and breadth of the country is dotted with military bases and defense plants. Thus the influence of the Defense Department as measured by its presence and its spending power, is diffused throughout the United States somewhat unevenly, but very widely; while the much more limited potential influence of the State Department and its ancillary agencies is limited to the nearly voteless District of Columbia and to its voteless constituencies overseas.

The Defense Department's extensive domestic involvement gives it an advantage apart from the relative strengths of constituencies; it sensitizes the Department to domestic political realities. Most of the time the Defense Department is acting within the physical limits of U.S. sovereignty. It is spending taxpayers' dollars. It is drafting the sons of citizens and voters. It is making decisions that affect the economic climate of American communities and the economic welfare of American companies. Most of the time, the State Department is observing and reporting on a bewildering jumble of activities beyond the reach of the sovereign power of the United States.

What the Defense Department does plants it hip-deep in domestic politics. What the State Department does tends to involve it in a fictitious construct called foreign policy: only in the areas of commercial and economic policy is it brought face to face with the reality of domestic interest group pressures.

The State Department's detachment from domestic realities is wholly understandable if not wholly excusable. Foreign affairs business, as it is conducted, exposes its practitioners to more crises per minute than any other walk of life except perhaps that of the university president. At any time of the day or night the State Department Message Center is receiving a signal of more or less distress from at least one of the 119 countries in which the United States maintains missions. In the wee hours the cables marked NIACT, or "night action," are rushed to a duty officer who must decide whether to call and wake the appropriate assistant secretary, remembering that the assistant secretary may already have been wakened once before. Early in the morning last night's take of cables is culled over, digested and circulated in innumerable copies, and several times during the day overflowing in-baskets are topped off with a new sheaf of paper.

Like Pavlov's dog, people learn to react to cables, and too often their reflexes are conditioned so that they react to little else. . . . Sooner or later, the faithful cable reader imbues the governments he reads about in the cables with an existence of their own, quite apart from the flesh-and-blood human beings whose continuing quarrels and occasional agreements are dimly reflected in the statements (and the rumors) emanating, like so much ectoplasm, from the anonymous mouths of their foreign office spokesmen.

Anyone concerned with foreign policy is conditioned to react to cables. The great majority of those concerned with foreign policy are actually trained to react to cables as the primary data in their experience. The members of the United States Foreign Service, as decent and dedicated a corps of men as one could hope to find, are systematically educated to believe that the processes of communication among the chanceries of the world, the construction and interpretation of formal and informal notes, communiqués, aides-memoires and assorted démarches, are skills which, taken together, constitute a profession. As mathematicians communicate among themselves with and about mathematical formulae, so foreign service professionals communicate among themselves with and about diplomatic formulae.

* * *

None of this is to suggest that what old foreign service hands like to call "old-fashioned diplomacy" is unimportant. Quite the contrary. It may make the difference between a minor crisis heating up into a major one or cooling off until next time. What is emphatically suggested is that constant communications among foreign affairs professionals about what they believe to be their common concerns may sometimes put them quite out of touch with reality. They may become so absorbed with diplomatic moves and countermoves that they lose sight of what motivates the individual players. They may even come to believe that foreign policy controls domestic politics rather than vice versa.

There is a popular image of the Pentagon riding roughshod over the Congress and political domestic interests.   Certainly it is true, at least until recently, that Defense has had a good deal less difficulty with its enormous budget than State has had with its tiny one.   But the Pentagon's budgetary victories are as much a measure of its involvement in domestic politics as the State Department's budgetary defeats are a measure of its estrangement from domestic politics.   Pentagon policy-makers are much less likely than State Department planners to ignore the primacy of U.S. domestic politics in making calculations about the political behavior of their own govern- ment.   It is paradoxical that by far the stronger of the two departments should be the more responsive to domestic political pressures.

*   *   *

Perhaps the most salient characteristic of the Defense Department is its orientation towards action.   This is not to suggest an organization strain- ing at the leash to involve the United States in foreign wars.   It is rather to point out that the business of Defense is to recruit, to select, to train, to feed, and to equip large numbers of men; to move them rapidly over great distances; and, when directed, to engage them against a resistant opponent. The business of the Department of State and its supporting agencies, on the other hand, has been mainly to observe, to report, to negotiate, to advise, to assist, and to propagandize.   In short, the function of the Defense De- partment is to act, and the function of the State Department is largely to find ways to avoid or postpone action, at least by the United States.   For Defense, action is the object; for State, it is the danger to be avoided.

The orientation of the Defense Department towards the management of men and machines in turn puts an emphasis on speed and efficiency in de- fense operations which the State Department fails to match, even making allowances for the relative strengths in resources available to management. Somehow the responsible officials in Defense have tended in recent years to learn about the new crisis before the State Department officials get the word; the State Department memorandum reaches the White House a day or two after the Defense Department memorandum arrives—and the staff work in the memorandum is just not as crisply or effectively done.   These are differences that do not affect the merits or the wisdom of the recom- mendations emanating from the two departments.   They do affect the likelihood that the recommendations will be acted on.   If the voice of the Pentagon has been heard more clearly in recent years in the highest coun- cils of the Republic, it is at least in part because it is more audible.

The fact that the Defense Department is primarily responsible for the management of its own very large resources gives it still another advantage over the State Department.   Its management responsibilities inoculate its officials against the most serious disease that afflicts State Department officialdom: the disease of heliotrophism.   The Secretary of State under at least three Presidents has seen it as his primary responsibility to advise the President rather than to direct the affairs of his department.   The under secretaries and the assistant secretaries see their primary role as furnishing policy advice to the Secretary rather than carrying out the policies that he and the President establish.   The bureau chiefs, the section chiefs and the branch chiefs in turn see themselves primarily as policy advisors looking up towards their own shops.   In consequence, it sometimes appears that everyone is advising the President on foreign policy and no one is running the Department of State.   Whatever criticisms can be made of Defense management—and current evidence indicates that criticism is warranted— it must be recognized that Defense Department officials, military and civilian, regard the management of the defense establishment as their primary and ultimate responsibility.

It is paradoxical that by far the richer of the two departments is also in a sense the more cost-conscious.   This is not to ignore the fact that the Defense Department probably wastes more money than the State Department spends.   By the same token, a large supermarket may waste more than the total sales value of the corner grocery store.   The corner grocery store proprietor works longer hours and scrimps and saves on things the supermarket proprietor can afford to and does overlook.   But the supermarket management faces choices on location, on selection and organization of merchandise that are simply not available to the corner grocery store.   Because it must make these choices, the management develops an awareness of the cost of not pursuing a particular course—what economists call an opportunity cost—which the corner grocer has no opportunity to discover.

*   *   *

One more significant point of difference between the working styles of the two departments is to be found in the relationship that has existed for some time between planning and operations.   In the Defense Department the essential planning tool is the budget.   When Secretary McNamara introduced the concepts of functional budgeting (the overall organization of the budget under headings based on like objective rather than like object) and the five-year program and force structure (projecting the current year budget over the next five years with accompanying projections for numbers and sizes of military units), he gave the responsibility for the five-year program to the organization within his office that controlled the current year budget, thus integrating the planning function with day-to-day management.   When the Systems Analysis shop was split off from the Comptroller under a new Assistant Secretary so that more extensive special studies could be undertaken, ultimate responsibility for program and budget still remained with the Comptroller.   In the area of direct relations with State, the planning function was similarly integrated with operations. Within the Office of the Assistant Secretary of Defense for International Security Affairs, the Assistant Secretary set up a policy planning staff as a kind of free-wheeling adjunct to the regional and subject-matter specialized units within the office to work on whatever problems might be assigned to it from time to time.   This staff examined the long-range planning implications of immediate decisions facing the department, but it did so always in the context of a matter that was very much at the top of the Assistant Secretary's immediate priority list.   It did not produce policy papers *in vacuo,* but rather made recommendations for action in areas where the Assistant Secretary and the Secretary were prepared to act.

By contrast the policy planning function in the State Department has been lodged in a policy planning council, a group of senior foreign service officers assigned for this purpose, who have largely generated their own agenda, but whose work product has had very little visible impact on the decision-making that goes on at the other end of the building.

The Defense Department approach to policy planning in the foreign policy area has the obvious defect of limiting the opportunities for the planning staff to raise questions that are wholly outside the current concerns of decision-makers.   But this function is one that, realistically, must be performed outside government if it is to be performed effectively and if the result is to draw the attention of busy men at the top of any government structure.   On the other hand, the Defense Department approach to the planning process reinforces the effectiveness of the department in generating immediate policy proposals, and particularly in taking a more active and less reactive position on matters that are on the joint State-Defense agenda.

*   *   *

Both State and Defense planning suffer from the inadequacies of overseas information gathering.   The various components of the intelligence community, military and civilian, each reflects its own bureaucratic biases. But since information is pooled within the community, the intelligence consumer's problem is likely to be one of penetrating beyond the bureaucratic compromises and waffle language to identify the conflicts in data and interpretation.

To attribute to Defense advantages in size, speed, efficiency, and cost-consciousness, and better integration of the planning function is not to suggest that its recommendations are wiser or more appropriate than those that emanate from the State Department.   It does appear, however, that there are reasons why Defense may receive a more favorable hearing quite apart from any military bias in U.S. foreign policy decision-making. Whether this imbalance tends to lead foreign policy decision-makers to choose military over non-military alternatives is not at all clear.   One might advance the hypothesis that the ready availability of military alternatives makes them somewhat more likely to be chosen and that certain military habits of mind—a tendency to see issues in black-or-white, we-or-they terms—may even infect civilian policy-makers within the Department.

Non-military alternatives are generally more difficult both to plan and to execute than military alternatives. This is not to minimize the complexity of military operations nor to denigrate the skills of the military planner. But doing without the instruments of force and violence creates new opportunities as well as new constraints. The United States intervention in the Dominican Republic in 1965 was an extraordinary example of the skillful use of limited force, but if the United States foreign policy apparatus had been better prepared to report and to understand what was happening in Santo Domingo, through eyes other than those of military attachés, it might have avoided intervention, and it would thereby have made possible other policy initiatives which were effectively barred or at least delayed by military intervention.

Once a course of action involving military action has been chosen, other non-military actions are necessarily subordinated to military considerations, if not to military control. It was probably inevitable that control of U.S. civilian programs of agricultural assistance in Vietnam should come under the control of the military. But in the absence of a civilian organization that could argue effectively for additional bombing restraints and more rapid transfer of control to the Vietnamese, the program continued to fall far short of its stated goals.

There are some functions that cannot be effectively performed by one department on behalf of another. Defense Department civilians may be better equipped than their State Department colleagues to undertake a critical examination of the overseas base rights required by the military establishment. But no element in the Defense Department can give effect to this kind of critical analysis without a clear statement of overall foreign policy priorities coming from the Department of State. And if the process of critical analysis in Defense gets ahead of the process of policy formulation in State, it may be effectively stymied until State catches up.

Organizations have their own internal priorities too, even apart from the pursuit of their fundamental purposes. When analytic processes of the Defense Department resulted in a decision to abandon development of the Skybolt missile, on which the Royal Air Force pinned great hopes of rejuvenating its own strategic bomber force, the resultant diplomatic crisis took the United States government by surprise because the State Department had not examined the decision as a foreign policy problem. Whether or not State was kept properly briefed on the effect of the Skybolt decision on British defense planning, it would have been unreasonable to expect Defense to take full account of the foreign policy implications in what Defense regarded as a weapons development issue.

*   *   *

There is a somewhat over-simplified view of the foreign policy process in which the military-industrial complex is seen as arming us to the teeth in order to impose the American way of life on an unwilling world. But as outlined above, it may be that the explanation for the tone of U.S. foreign policy is actually to be found in the structural and behavioral differences between the two institutions most responsible for foreign policy, the Department of State and the Department of Defense; and that the impulses generated by these differences are relatively insulated from the influence of relative constituency strengths and budgetary controls.

The relative positions of State and Defense are constantly changing, particularly with the advent of the new administration. What will be the effect of the new management in the Office of International Security Affairs in Defense and the ambitious plans for a central staff on the seventh floor of the State Department remains to be seen. The new dimensions of the National Security Council staff also have direct bearing on the internal power balance. But any National Intelligence Estimate of the current situation as between State and Defense must begin with the assumption that in any contest between the two, Defense still has a considerable advantage, in what is called in defense planning jargon M-Day resources—or resources immediately available at the moment when the contest begins.

The effects of any imbalance can to some extent be countered by the work of the National Security Council staff in monitoring the departmental work products and in reaching out for information and advice for the NSC and the President. But the NSC staff cannot itself alter the power balance between the departments. Only changes in their internal management, or shifts in the distribution of responsibility among all the foreign policy agencies can do that.

Dean Acheson

CHIEF LOBBYIST FOR STATE

THE PLAN OF CAMPAIGN

We laid out a busy schedule for the first session of the Seventy-ninth Congress.* The Senate Committee on Foreign Relations would start with the Mexican Water Treaty, while on the House side the Ways and Means Committee would take up the renewal of the Reciprocal Trade Agreements Act, and the Banking and Currency Committee an act authorizing participation in the Bretton Woods International Monetary Fund and Development

Reprinted by permission of the publisher from *Present at the Creation*, by Dean Acheson (New York: Norton, 1969), Chapter 12, pp. 95–101. Copyright © 1969 by Dean Acheson.

* The 79th Congress served from 1945 to 1947. During the period described in this essay, Acheson was Assistant Secretary of State for Congressional Relations. [Eds.]

Bank. With these well started on their legislative course, we would feed into the Senate the United Nations Charter (not yet negotiated) and two tax treaties, and, into the House, bills authorizing continuation and enlargement of the authority and funds of the Export-Import Bank (which I had fathered in 1933) and our participation in the Food and Agriculture Organization. This work would keep us all busy until after midsummer.

One reason for leading off with the Mexican Water Treaty was to broaden and popularize the idea that foreign policy should be nonpartisan, outside of politics. If the opposition were brought into the formulation of policy—so the doctrine ran—they would be guilty of a foul in attacking it later on. Mr. Hull had put forward the idea in 1934 in the most political of all areas of foreign policy—tariff making—but it had not flourished. He revived it in his talks with selected members of Congress during 1943 and 1944 about a world organization to enforce peace and, in the campaign autumn of 1944, by his arrangement with Dewey through Dulles that the war should be kept out of election issues. On a minor scale we had succeeded in taking postwar relief—UNRRA—out of the political arena.

THE THEORY OF NONPARTISAN FOREIGN POLICY

We now wanted to go further. Plainly, no effective postwar foreign policy could emerge from political controversy. The idea of a nonpolitical foreign policy was the holy water sprinkled on a political necessity. The perhaps apocryphal sign in the Wild West saloon—"Don't Shoot the Piano Player"—was the basic idea of nonpolitical foreign policy. Foreign policy has no lobby, no vested interest to support it, and no constituents. It must be built on a broad conception of the national interest, which lacks the attraction and support that can be generated by, say, a tax reduction, a tariff increase, or an agricultural subsidy. The Constitution makes the President the piano player of foreign policy, but unless his immunity from assault with intent to kill is extended to members of either party who work with him in the legislative branch, no consistent foreign policy is possible under the separation of powers. The doctrine, of course, aids the Administration, but its immediate beneficiaries are in the Congress.

This beneficent attitude has its limitations. As Senator Vandenberg would often wryly point out, it did not bring him Democratic support on election day. In his more reflective comments he was quite aware that "common action does not mean that we cease to be 'Republicans' or 'Democrats' at home." It meant that in foreign policy cooperation could be purchased at the price of "consultation and mutual decision from start to finish." This was not Senator Robert Taft's view. "The purpose of an opposition," he said, "is to oppose"; and oppose he did, from start to finish.

By virtue of intelligence, convictions, and force of character, Senators Vandenberg, Taft, and Eugene Millikin of Colorado exerted the greatest influence on Republican policy in the Senate. By tacit understanding,

Vandenberg took the lead in foreign affairs and the others led in fiscal and domestic matters. Where the currents crossed, as in tariff and trade policies, the sea was always rough. Gene Millikin insisted that he was the most honest of the triumvirs, adducing as proof that although all three were bald, he let a shining pate proclaim the fact, while the other two, in a vain effort to mislead onlookers in the Senate gallery, brushed hair from the side of their heads over their arid crowns.

The notion that cooperation in a nonpartisan foreign policy could be purchased by consultation is too broad. "Historically," wrote Vandenberg, "this [nonpartisanship] has not been the case in China, Palestine or Japan." He attributed the exceptions to lack of consultation, a plausible but disingenuous explanation. There was endless consultation. The true explanation was wholly understandable Republican unwillingness to take on the responsibility for what looked like thoroughly messy and probably losing ventures. It is interesting to note that Vandenberg mentioned Japan as one of the countries outside the nonpartisan-policy sphere in August 1948. Three years later greatly improved prospects and the appointment of a Republican, John Foster Dulles, to conduct the negotiations leading to the Japanese peace treaty brought the treaty within the nonpartisan-policy area and led to its overwhelming ratification by the Senate in the midst of the presidential election campaign of 1952. The possibility of this happy result did not escape President Truman in his consideration of the Dulles appointment.

In short, the doctrine and practice of nonpartisanship in foreign policy is a very practical political expedient, designed to moderate asperities inherent in our constitutional system. "The doctrine of the separation of powers," Justice Brandeis has explained, "was adopted by the Convention of 1787, not to promote efficiency but to preclude the exercise of arbitrary power. The purpose was, not to avoid friction, but, by means of the inevitable friction incident to the distribution of the governmental powers among three departments, to save the people from autocracy." Today, in the determination of our policies toward "the vast external realm" with all its complexities and dangers, there is a superabundance of friction to save the people from the autocratic imposition of courses of action. The purpose of nonpartisanship is to ease the difficulties in the way of maintaining continuity and predictability in action. To borrow a phrase of Woodrow Wilson's, it is the essential "oil of government."

THE PRACTICE OF NONPARTISAN FOREIGN POLICY

The nonpartisan oil of government lubricated the machinery of legislation through the leadership. In the Seventy-ninth Congress this operated in the Senate out of the Secretary of the Senate's office, and in the House out of Speaker Rayburn's "Board of Education" room in the basement of the Capitol. Here "Mister Sam" presided at a large desk over a select company ensconced in overstuffed sofas and chairs and refreshed from an immense refrigerator. The Secretary of the Senate's quarters, west of the Senate chamber, were equally secluded from public view and inquiry, approached from a dead-end corridor and through a busy document-and-record office. A long narrow room lined with chairs along two sides ended with Leslie Biffle's desk. A door to the left of it led into his private dining room, served from the Senate restaurant. Here the power structure of the Senate met and decided what, at first, appeared to be largely matters of procedure—what should be taken up, when, how long it should be discussed, when voted on, and so forth. But with experience, and recalling Justice Holmes's dictum that "legal progress is secreted in the interstices of legal procedure," one came to realize that legislative achievement was secreted in the interstices of these procedural decisions and the attitude of the Senate hierarchy that they embodied.

At the committee stage, nonpartisan foreign policy was a *sine qua non*. There we worked with Tom Connally and Arthur Vandenberg in the Senate and their equally colorful counterparts in the House, Sol Bloom of New York and "Doc" Eaton, once the pastor of John D. Rockefeller's Baptist church in Cleveland and later of the Madison Avenue Church in New York, and in 1945 representative of the Fifth New Jersey district and senior minority member of the Foreign Affairs Committee. With adequate "consultation and mutual decision" they could bring most of their colleagues through the marking-up and committee-report stages of the legislative process. But this only launched the vessel with a fair wind. The hazards of the cruel sea lay ahead. If the bill happened to deal with trade agreements, Senators Taft and Millikin would deny it a fair wind in the Finance Committee, and in the Ways and Means Committee of the House going was heavy on both sides to begin with. On the floor of both chambers any foreign affairs legislation needed strong support. This was arranged in Les Biffle's dining room and in the "Board of Education."

In the former the gay, genial Majority Leader, Alben Barkley of Kentucky, presided while Biffle, the silent, smooth, friendly Secretary of the Senate, the most knowledgeable operator on the Hill, acted as chief of staff. Solemn, courteous, and kindly Walter George of Georgia, the Nestor of the gathering, usually put the seal on a decision by his pronouncement at the end of a rambling discussion over "bourbon and branch water" or lunch. Barkley and Biffle invited those who might be especially wanted, and others wandered in more or less regularly from the Senate floor at about noon. Sometimes Biffle, I, or one of the senators gave a luncheon. Membership in the group was bipartisan though heavily weighted on the Democratic side. Vandenberg, Robert M. LaFollette, Jr., of Wisconsin, and Wallace H. White, Jr., of Maine were always welcome. Membership seemed to emerge from personality—congeniality, good humor, willingness to compromise and get on with the Senate's business, and general friendliness to the Administration, in varying degrees. Some who had many or all of these qualities I never saw there—for instance, Mr. Truman either before or after he became Vice President, doubtless because he was too occupied with more specific interests.   In other instances absence might be due to the angularity of nature or sharpness of tongue, which often made Tom Connally an uncomfortable colleague.   The habitués included Ernest W. McFarland and Carl Hayden of Arizona, George L. Radcliffe and sometimes Millard E. Tydings of Maryland, Burton K. Wheeler of Montana, Theodore Francis Green of Rhode Island, Carl A. Hatch of New Mexico, Burnet R. Maybank of South Carolina, Lister Hill of Alabama, and Scott W. Lucas of Illinois.   The effectiveness of decisions by this group came not from its sheer power to put them through the Senate but from its knowledge of how to put them through and the willingness to put its knowledge to use.

In the House, leadership was more compact and authoritarian—the Speaker; the Majority Leader, John W. McCormack of Massachusetts; the Majority Whip, Robert Ramspeck of Georgia; and the Chairman of the Rules Committee, Adolph J. Sabath of Illinois.   In the Rules Committee resided the all-important power of determining when and under what procedural conditions a bill might come before the House.   After a preliminary talk with the Speaker, and then with the rest of the leadership, the time would be ripe for a slightly larger group to meet in "Board of Education" to set the stage.   Sam Rayburn, a man of few words (once asked about General Eisenhower's qualifications for the Presidency, he is said to have replied, "Good man; wrong job"), was a loyal and true friend. Earlier a small service had earned me McCormack's favor.   Mrs. McCormack had been awarded a papal decoration, but under war conditions difficulty arose in getting it from Rome to Washington.   A little negotiation succeeded in its being brought over in the diplomatic pouch of Myron C. Taylor, President Roosevelt's Personal Representative at the Vatican. Bob Ramspeck, a most courteous and helpful gentleman, never failed us. Sabath I left entirely to the Speaker; he was not amenable to any persuasions of mine.

The leadership in both houses helped those who helped themselves. Self-help included not only the basic committee work, the hearings, and work with the committee staffs on their reports but the initial canvassing of members' voting predilections.   Here one needed both strong feet and patience.   At this time and later, as Sam Rayburn would tell our weaker successors, day after day Will Clayton * and I would take corridor after corridor of the House office building—Will on one side and I on the other— calling at every office, making our sales talk, and keeping a record of the responses we got for Skeeter Johnston's always-current voting lists.   Our weapons were reason and eloquence.   The leadership worked on the waverers' hope of favors or fear of penalties to come.   It also divided the

* Then Assistant Secretary of State for Economic Affairs. [Eds.]

labor of debate, allotting, according to skills and with an authority that we could not command, exposition and guerrilla warfare against the opposition.

REFLECTIONS ABOUT CONGRESS

All through this book runs the thread of my multifarious relations with the Congress, sometimes tumultuous, sometimes calmly cooperative, sometimes framed in the adversary ritual of committee hearings. To make specific episodes more understandable, I have pulled together here a few reflections of a broader character on the nature of the institution, its actual role in our scheme of government as against the constitutional theory of it, and my actual relations with its members, much warped through the myth popularized by press and commentators.

Long ago Henry Adams pointed out that the chief concern of the Secretary of State—the world beyond our boundaries—was to most members of the Congress only a troublesome intrusion into their chief interest—the internal affairs of the country, and especially of the particular parts of it they represented.

Two aspects of this basic fact should be stressed. First, the principal consequence of foreign impact upon particular districts is trouble; rarely is it, or is it seen to be, beneficial. Second, the legislative branch is designed with a constitutional purpose of making each legislator the representative of a specific and limited area. Reapportionment does not affect this fact. The President is the only elected official with a national constituency. Senators, since their direct popular election, are the ambassadors of states, concerned with their parochial interest. The focus and representation of members of the House of Representatives are even more narrowly circumscribed. Almost every time they legislate they affect foreign interests, but this concerns them only indirectly and seemingly distantly, for the familiar aspects of foreign affairs are war, relief, and trade; and trade more often appears as a threat of foreign competition than as potential markets for American goods. Even producers of commodities historically dependent on export matters, like wheat and cotton, have long been conscious of surplus problems and the increasing foreign production of these staples.

For the most part, then, the Secretary of State comes to Congress bearing word of troubles about which Congress does not want to hear. Furthermore, the members of the legislative branch not only represent narrower constituencies and interests than does the President and those he has chosen to aid him in dealing with the broadest national and international affairs, but largely they share the narrower interests and attitudes which they represent. That this should be so is wholly natural and proper, since under our system they must be residents of the state, in the case of the Senate, and of the district, in the case of the House. Those who live long enough among their constituents to win confidence, support, and the responsibility of representing them are pretty likely to share prevalent views.   To say this invites criticism, but it is a simple and obvious fact.

The result is a built-in difference in the point of departure between the legislative and executive branches when problems of foreign policy are considered.   Furthermore, the wide difference in their duties creates differences in the time that each can and must allot to foreign affairs and the amount of recent intelligence and deeper background that each has available.   This is no different from the relation between a parent and a physician in considering a medical problem of a member of the family; each brings something different and important to the discussion.

What the executive brings is initiative, proposal for action; what the legislature brings is criticism, limitation, modification, or veto.   In foreign affairs the tendency toward this division of function has always existed; since the second quarter of this century it has become true of nearly all domestic as well as foreign policy.   Once it was thought that Congress would press forward with popular initiatives and the President could hold back with more conservative caution.   To aid him he was given a negative veto in each house equal to a third of the total.   However, today both the complexity and urgency of matters calling for action and the difference in the nature of the constituencies have made the President the active and innovative initiator and the legislators the more conservative restrainers. They are powerfully armed to perform this role by the complicated annual procedures with which they have surrounded and often whittled down such policies, for instance, as foreign aid, requiring four committee hearings a year accompanying an authorizing act of Congress and an appropriation.

The most publicized weapon of Congress—and one which as often as not proves frustrating to those who employ it—is the investigation.   One cannot improve upon Woodrow Wilson's comment upon it: "Congress stands almost helplessly outside of the departments.   Even the special, irksome, ungracious investigations which it from time to time institutes . . . do not afford it more than a glimpse of the inside of a small province of federal administration. . . .   It can violently disturb, but it cannot often fathom, the waters of the sea in which the bigger fish of the civil service swim and feed.   Its dragnet stirs without cleansing the bottom."

These experiences induce an attitude of exasperated frustration in many members of Congress, which may be expressed in the kind of sulky opposition that characterized the last two years of relations between the Senate Committee on Foreign Relations and the Johnson Administration, or the destruction that flowed from Congressman John J. Rooney, of the Appropriations Committee, when he acquired a distaste for the State Department's cultural relations program, which doubtless his Brooklyn district shares, or Senator Allen Ellender's hostility to foreign aid, which his constituents in Louisiana would probably agree was "pouring good money down a rat hole."

To bridge these and other gaps in values and understanding required hours of tramping the halls of the House and Senate office buildings, innumerable gatherings and individual meetings, social occasions of all sorts at which all the arts of enlightenment and persuasion were employed. My years as Assistant Secretary were generously given over to these efforts and brought me a large and pleasant acquaintance and some warm friendships at both ends of the Capitol. The much-publicized political attacks on me in 1950 and 1951 were accompanied in only a few cases by personal animosity. For instance, Senator William F. Knowland, who later criticized and opposed me strongly, in private always remained most courteous and friendly.

In making our calls, particularly in the Senate, we learned to bear the irrelevant with more than patience as it ate up precious time. Those who assert that I do not suffer fools gladly—and I have seen that view in print— do me less than justice for these anguishing hours. Despite current folklore, one could and did learn to suffer, if not gladly, at least patiently when, as often happened, doing so paid dividends. This recalls a story that Sir Robert Menzies, the former Prime Minister of Australia, has told on himself. At a party victory celebration a particularly crashing and somewhat inebriated bore, poking his grubby finger in Menzies' shirtfront, announced, "The trouble with you, Bob, is you don't suffer fools gladly."

"What," asked Sir Robert coldly, "do you think I am doing now?"

Wilson Carey McWilliams

DEMOCRACY, PUBLICS AND PROTEST: THE PROBLEM OF FOREIGN POLICY

*   *   *

For the American of earlier generations it seemed right and proper to dispute a foreign policy decision with all one's might *until* a commitment was finally made. Once the country was engaged, however, debate should be suspended until the conflict came to an end. . . .

Lincoln, who believed with his party that the war with Mexico was "unnecessarily and unconstitutionally commenced by the President," declared in 1848 that:

Reprinted by permission from *Journal of International Affairs*, 23, 2 (1969), pp. 189–209.

When the war began, it was my opinion that all those who, because of knowing too *little* or because of knowing too *much,* could not conscientiously approve the conduct of the President in the beginning of it, should, nevertheless,
as good citizens and patriots, remain silent on that point, at least till the war
should be ended.[1]

Nothing could be more foreign to the spirit of our recent years, and it
is naturally no surprise that some should lament the change and others,
seeing a new politics of conscience, should exult.   Delight or regret, however, serve badly to inspire understanding.   The meaning and the impact
of the present change in American political life are to be found in three
developments: first, the fact that domestic politics have become decisively
dependent on foreign policy; second, the decay of democratic control
over and commitment to government; and third, the failure of political
leadership to respond to this difficult and changing situation.   Protest is a
portent—both protester and policy-maker would be advised to read its
omens rightly.

I

* * *

Plato knew what recent analysts are discovering, that any distinction between foreign and domestic policy is no more than one of degree, that is
at most, a distinction of feeling and not of fact.   In the first book of the
Laws, his Athenian stranger is made to demonstrate that a state founded
on the principle that "every state is, by a law of nature, engaged perpetually
in an informal war with every other state" so shapes the life and expectations of its people as to produce (at best) "informal" conflict between
villages, between households, and within the individual himself.   Foreign
politics influences the life of states; the life of states influences foreign
policy.
    Mutual influence is a fact; the only issue is the relative importance of
each factor in the life of the polity.   Classical thought insisted that, for a
good state, foreign policy is a necessity only; domestic life was the prime
value.   A state which moulds itself to achieve success in relation to outsiders is, properly speaking, only an alliance.   State, village or self are all
secondary phenomena; such unity as they possess is defined by the "common enemy" whose power each envies or fears.   The foreign is ubiquitous;
domesticity does not truly exist; a friend is only one who has not yet
become a dangerous enemy.
    The danger in this situation, the classics knew, was the sense in which
man, set apart by unyielding barriers of flesh, is a foreigner to every other

[1] Cited in Carl Sandburg, *Abraham Lincoln,* New York: Harcourt Brace, 1954,
p. 95.

man. That isolation is the universal foundation of human life, the fearful egoism to which the child is born. First loyalties to parents and kinsmen are given only because these men seem less threatening than the rest of the world. As we have reason to know, this "domestic" world only conceals and postpones the "state of war."

Postponement is crucial, for the time of development allows society to seduce the emotions out of the self, attaching them by shared joys to social things, while the growing mind is freed to discover the visions and values which can unite men across the walls of physical difference. Political society, for Aristotle the result of a slow ascent, personal as much as historical, from household and association, is defined by these bonds and by the common life. The attention of political society turns inward because civic community is the primary symbol. Foreign policy is always the derivative phenomenon; men will defend the city because they value what it is and what they have, not because they envy outsiders.

The highest good . . . is neither war nor civil strife—which things we should pray to be saved from—but peace with one another and friendly feeling. So, with regard to the well-being of polity or an individual that man will never make a statesman who pays attention primarily and solely to the needs of foreign warfare, nor will he make a lawgiver unless he designs his war legislation for peace rather than his peace legislation for war.[2]

Plato was far from suggesting that external circumstances might not compel a state to adopt policies undesirable in themselves. In fact, it was because the foreigner was always a consideration in domestic life that all states were imperfect—the legislator's alloy of the metals was perpetually flawed with "foreign bodies." Plato argued only that external pressures should be met grudgingly and reluctantly, and that external involvements should be entered into only when they could not be avoided.

Modern political theory differs precisely on this point. Accepting "original nature" as human nature, it takes the psychology of the child as that of man. The self-referential emotions which lead man to seek untrammeled "liberty" are his "by right of nature," and if a prudent response to conflict and weakness leads him to restrict his desires, it is only in the interest of a greater fulfillment of those desires. The purpose of society, apart from order, becomes the mastering of nature and an expansion of human power to enhance the ability to enjoy one's "natural right."

Not only did this theory make nature something foreign to men and states, it elevated conflict and the desire to expand power to a first place in human affairs. That desire, in part, shaped modern history: the tangled contentions of Secretary Laird are only a drab and juiceless version of Machiavelli's axiom that "good arms make good laws."

The "liberal tradition" made the modern creed a part of American

---

[2] Plato, *Laws,* Book I, 626A–627E.

politics from the beginning. Government exists, the authors of *The Federalist* declare, to impose order on anarchic men and beyond that very negative aim, to expand power. Calling a prohibition of "offensive war founded upon reasons of state" a "novel and absurd experiment," Hamilton asserted that the "fiery and destructive passions of war reign in the human heart with a much more powerful sway than the mild and beneficent sentiments of peace." His moral, like that of Crete's legislator, was not that America should strive to check or weaken that tyrannous sway, but that the expectation of conflict should be the "model" of our political system:

By a steady adherence to the Union, we may hope, erelong, to become the arbiter of Europe in America . . . a vigorous government . . . would baffle all the combinations of European jealousy to restrain our growth. . . . We might defy the little arts of little politicians to vary the irresistible and unchangeable courses of nature.

Hamilton's theory was never unopposed in America, and the traditional argument that democratic states would be inferior to others in the conduct of foreign policy was sometimes interpreted as a moral compliment. It presumed that democracy would put its domestic goals first, conducting its foreign policy as it did domestic life: acting by the slow processes of discussion and debate, avoiding secrecy, distrusting experts, and always subjecting its policy to change. (The last, obviously, is a mixed "vice": it is hardly a virtue to persevere in stupid policy.)

Similarly, the fear, common to the Left and to foreign policy elites, that democratic states would *project* their domestic problems into foreign policy presumes the primacy of domestic things. The only difference between the two arguments lies in their respective assessments of the fact. Elites have feared that such projection would be irrational and destructive of policies designed to further the interests of the state; Left critics have argued that this projection would be "functional" for the established order, diverting discontent abroad without touching the real problem at home. The latter critique, which formed the basis of the old Left-isolationism, insisted that almost all foreign involvement was either a mask for suspect interest or an attempt to quiet domestic dissent.

The case against isolationism is weak on moral grounds and, for years, was not much better on grounds of prudence. Isolationism helped keep us from annexing the Dominican Republic during Grant's term and fought a hard battle against imperialism after the Spanish War (though, unfortunately, one which was often tinged with racism and the idea of "unassimilable" peoples). In the 1920's and the 1930's, isolationists were the spearhead of the "good neighbor" policy, and if they made a dubious coalition with Henry Cabot Lodge . . . to defeat Versailles, their case that the treaty's vindictiveness contained the seeds of the next war is hard to fault.

The case against isolationism rests on the fact that the technical and economic realities of the modern world—desirable or not—have made it impossible for a state to stand aside. As we have been told with tiresome iteration, the range, speed and power of modern technology have destroyed the old basis of the state; and modern organization, designed to use if not to harness that technology, passes over the old boundaries.

The isolationist debacle of the 1930's and 1940's was partly due to the failure to realize that the crisis of the depression had to be seen as a world crisis, and that once that crisis had produced the Third Reich, "keeping hands off" would cost more lives and men in the long run. . . . [I]solationism was unable to see further than formal political acts of intervention, nor did it recognize the intervention which America was engaged in through economic expansion, technological growth and the psychological impact on others of American wealth and power.

That failure would, if anything, be more serious today. As we surely know, communication and change have drawn masses of men into international awareness, shattered old communities and created new hopes. "Peaceful competition" is itself an intervention in the lives of men. Often, like all competition, it results in strange irrationalities like the race to the moon; often, its effects are positive. (Even Herbert Marcuse comments that the reason the Soviet Union cannot retrogress into neo-Stalinism is the need to show the Soviet public some signs of success in competition with the United States.[3]) Always and everywhere, however, modern economic and technical life involves an "intervention," one which is two-sided: when it brings America into the life of other states, it brings those states into our own.

*   *   *

For contemporary America the overriding problem of maintaining peace is an external one. It is a situation which many states, especially those of the third world, have confronted all their lives; for us, it is fairly new, with unfamiliar results. There is still a danger that we will project domestic difficulties into foreign policy, but that danger has lessened greatly relative to the danger (which before we scarcely knew apart from war) that foreign and international problems will be *injected* into national life; that we will *create domestic difficulties* in order to avoid or avert the foreign problems that policy-makers see.

This is a possibility which Leninism, for example, did not foresee; yet surely there are many examples. Unconsciously, McCarthyism was such a response; fearing the U.S.S.R. but unwilling to fight her, we vented fear and frustration on our own citizens. Vietnam and Korea were conscious decisions, though in both cases policy-makers underrated the domestic costs, to pay a price at home for stability abroad. The "currency crisis"

---

[3] Herbert Marcuse, *One-Dimensional Man*, Boston: Beacon, 1968, pp. 44–45.

and the resulting pressures for unpopular deflationary policies are the result of aid and other political disbursements combined with the problem created by use of the dollar as the world's currency. Even our comparative willingness to permit the nationalization of American companies abroad—which certainly has costs at home—obviously results from international considerations. . . .

When David Esmond wrote that New Left theories of foreign affairs were shaped by the fact that foreign policy is the "nemesis of community" he touched a vital point.[4] However bizarre or simplistic these theories may be, they are partly a response to the fact that the old "nemesis" is increasingly predominant in American life and that any hope of community and any hope of controlling domestic policy now requires the ability to control foreign policy. Without such control political democracy will become little more than an epiphenomenon, pleasantly diverting, perhaps, but little more.

It only compounds the problem that the injection of foreign problems demands sacrifice of kinds which Americans before 1945 were willing to make only in time of war and that since 1945 they have made only under the threat of war. Now, in fact, we may have to ask for greater sacrifices, in pride as well as in material things, precisely at a point where our resources of political commitment have run thin.

II

Political democracies, while hardly models of success, have done far better with foreign policy than nineteenth century critics expected. That moderate achievement is partly due to a change in the position of democratic states relative to others. The aristocratic case against democratic foreign policy presumed an elite which could effectively ignore the mass, an assumption which was always limited but which had some truth during the *ancien régime*. That truth has long since disappeared and it is as pointless to be bemused by the fact that in some states there are few manifestations of public pressure as it is to presume that in the United States *all* pressures *have* public manifestations. Internal change and total war have joined hands to mobilize and organize most social forces and, consequently, to involve them deeply in national political decision. This "fundamental democratization of society" results in pressures which limit and affect foreign policy whatever the nominal political character of the state.

Modern organization makes industrial states, at least, slow to make and slow to change foreign policy or, for that matter, domestic policy. In an inter-connected economy based on complex agreements and understandings the economic rule is that costs are "inflexible downward." Translated into political terms, policies are "inflexible backward," that is, difficult to

4 See Chapter IV. [Eds.]

change in the (very long) short term except at costs which states are unwilling to pay. Aware of the costs of making commitments, leaders in the great states often hesitate to make them and qualify those they do make. A bold leader like Khrushchev appears as an "adventurer" to many of his colleagues, and the Soviet Union, burdened now with a collegial system, may be even slower to change than the United States.

To those who have lived through the Johnson years this characterization may seem inaccurate. In spite of exceptions like the Dominican intervention, however, the semblance of rapidity is only the eternal deceit of policy which, when it acts, often seems bold because we do not know the prolonged period of inaction which preceded it. If, for example, the Soviet leaders had not allowed themselves to hope that the developments in Czechoslovakia would take care of themselves, military intervention might not have been needed; if the United States had made its military commitment in Vietnam before the political situation in Saigon had collapsed, it might have dissuaded Hanoi from hoping for national re-unification. This is not to argue that either outcome would have taken place; only that a case can be made for either course with the aid of hindsight. Consider the disastrous effects of hesitancy with respect to the Bay of Pigs, when we lacked the daring to cancel *or* to carry through effectively. . . .

An additional element of the organizational complexity of our times is that more groups and individuals are now involved in the making and conducting of foreign policy. Once foreign policy was the prerogative of the state ministries, foreign affairs and defense. Now virtually every governmental agency has some role, as do great numbers of "private" groups (a fact attested by the C.I.A.'s use of such groups for its own purposes), and even the shift of tourism from an elite to a mass phenomenon has its effects. Control, then, is less effectively centralized; a foreign policy becomes a massive effort at coordination and of bargain, and it is probably a misnomer to speak of states as having *a* foreign policy at all.

The policies of the great states tend to be uninspiring, even boring. Confused, hesitant, slow-moving, they lend themselves to little idealism and moral passion and those leaders who try to introduce these values do little more than disillusion their followers. . . .

The real "success" of democracy in a world where foreign policy bulks large lies, however, in the changes that have taken place and been effected in the internal life of democracies themselves. Put bluntly, democratic states—and the nation-state was never more than an approximation of democracy—have become less democratic in the making of policy. It has always been a war-time device in America to resolve the republic into a "constitutional dictatorship" if not a totalitarian state, vesting massive extra-constitutional powers in the executive. That necessity has become permanent, though Congress has more than once struggled with the trend and still fights continual and often pointless skirmishes. Increasingly power lies in administration, and the old government of laws relies more and more for what political constraint it possesses on the personality of the President.

Similarly, growth in population has effectively restricted those who have access to the public to a small percentage of the populace. Political action, save in rare instances, is the prerogative of those who act as secondary governments over men: those who command the media and those great organizations which combine and concert the actions of masses of insignificant individuals who are "voluntary" only in the laughing language of law.

Political life only deprives the individual of the illusion of dignity and importance which he can feel in the narrow circle of his family. Rousseau pointed out that while sovereignty is always a unit, as population grows the citizen's fractional share declines, and one seventy-millionth of the electorate is, in simple mathematical terms, statistically insignificant. The existence of polling, after all, confirms the *personal* unimportance of the voter . . . The question is not, does the voter feel *any* effective connection with the political world, but how much does he feel *relative* to the affection he feels for his family or other less-than-political groups? Only that is a measure of estrangement, for only that is a measure of the willingness to sacrifice for the common good.

Men will sacrifice from love or from hope, and while love leads men away from politics, hope offers men less than it once did. The old historical vision is weaker than in the past; survival, not merely progress, is threatened at every turn and the pace of change makes men cling desperately to what they have, for the gains already achieved are the stimuli to fear of loss. Political leaders have fallen back more and more on the appeal to fear, the negative hope which is only the desire to retain. Yet fear is a limited weapon; men become dulled to old fears and new ones are required, and there are few fears which can move men who have already learned to live with the threat to life itself.

It is potentially a world of economic and material abundance—potentially only, for few Americans, even, share it—but it is a world of massive *political* scarcity. The great resources of politics, feelings of duty, obligation, even of loyalty are in short supply. . . . It is this which inspires fears of a neo-isolationism which continually reappears in high places. The isolationism which is feared is not one of a polity whose members do not need the world; it is one of isolated *men,* not states, without devotion to much beyond themselves.

Liberal and radical criticism of American foreign policy is not new but until recently it did not touch the chord of mass response, simply because it has tended to ask for *more* and not less sacrifice. Foreign economic assistance has been far from wise in all cases, but the growing opposition to it is hardly a matter of philosophy. The phrase "win or get out," which describes the attitude of the largest number of Americans toward Vietnam, bespeaks the "millennial" or "moralistic" aspects of our culture—those serviceable excuses for political ignorance in political science—[less] than it does a desire to pay *no* costs. Read accurately, the phrase is win *and* get out; certainly, there is little moral grandeur in the wish that "South Vietnamese boys fight their own wars."

* * *

III

Kenneth Waltz's comment is apposite: "It was Plato who said in effect: the people are sick; their rulers must be cured. The question of leadership lies beneath the problem of the people's willingness to sacrifice. . . ." [5] If the many are debased, their elevation becomes the task of the few, and if the few will not attempt it, their own "elevation" becomes suspect. . . . Certainly, failure to lead convicts a man of want of courage, for seen rightly, a public which cannot find its way is a challenge, and the American public is large enough to be flexible and more than once has revealed an almost pathetic willingness to be led.

Criticism of the people has always been a convenient excuse for political men, able to excuse themselves for following their own inclinations by citing "pressure," eager to blame their failures on lack of support, willing to accept the laurel for what they could have avoided only at political cost. It is this, in fact, which makes the whole question of public influence on policy so difficult beyond the simple statement that X group did Y or poll A showed B, and policy Z resulted, an even simpler form of behaviorism, since the stimuli are multifarious, than the S-R theory. Beyond that, our "hard" data consists of the comments of the public men and the memoirs of statesmen, both about as reliable as tests of fact as toothpaste advertising. . . . [W]e are left with the traditional tools: introspection, comparison, and interpretation.

Public men, common sense tells us, are neither such fools as to ignore opinion altogether nor are they its creatures, if for no more noble reason than the knowledge that whatever the public may think at the moment, it is readily persuaded by success and ready to disavow failure. Starting with some idea of the public good, policy makers can be limited by pressures which do not change their intent. Beginning with the raw material of opinion and interest, policy makers seek to build a supportive coalition and each unit of the coalition has its own cost. The weighing of cost against gain is rather too mechanical a standard. The process is closer to the eternal problem of art: the effort to use recalcitrant materials and the fallible hand of man to produce a result which, while imperfect, bears the greatest possible likeness to the artist's vision. And the arts of politics, as Plato knew, are more difficult than many; the painter can remove a mistake and try again, the author may discard a first draft, but political errors may be irrevocable.

---

[5] Waltz, *Foreign Policy and Democratic Politics,* Boston and Toronto: Little Brown, 1967, p. 270.

*   *   *

Roosevelt was . . . a master of political theatrics. He differed from many among the policy-making elite in viewing the public as a *resource,* not only something which was a limiting, if manipulable given, but something which could be changed and upgraded. He was, perhaps, the supreme master of political translation, the difficult art of explaining complex things in a simple way, the soft deceit which is always a necessary element of mass political education. (After all, political men *live* political things; others will and can spend only a short time on them.) Hence the great series of homilies: "if your neighbor's house is afire . . . ," or "if you see a rattlesnake coiled to strike. . . ." In many ways, these were Socratic *questions* which appealed to the everyday life of men and asked them if their practice did not contain a more general lesson. And, as events succeeded, men found it so. Contrast the argument that we are fighting so that "we will not have to fight in Wichita": it presumes that we would fight for Wichita, dubious in itself unless we live there; second, it presumes that we can see a connection between Khesanh and Wichita, which is hard to perceive except that they are on the same planet. Between the two cases lies the measure of the teacher's art.

Political education, however, requires a faith in the educability of the public. The combined events of the twentieth century have undermined much of our older confidence. . . . Yet among policy-makers and political scientists alike, that doubt of the public has become a deep anxiety, a fear of mass involvement which almost amounts to regarding the people as the enemy of sound political life, and which has generated—if only in comparison—a new confidence in elites and the leaders of groups in the "pluralistic process."

Thus, the social scientific description of McCarthyism as a "mass movement" is paralleled by Richard Goold-Adams' belief that much can be forgiven John Foster Dulles in view of the McCarthyite pressures under which he operated. Even so devoted a group theorist as David Truman, however, saw McCarthyism as the result of a failure of certain elites to defend the "rules of the game," and Michael Rogin has demonstrated beyond much doubt that McCarthy's support was rooted in a section of the elite—one in which Dulles had some standing—and that it was a "mass" phenomenon in only a very limited sense.

Even if the analysis of the "mass" were beyond question, it would not prove ineducability, but only that the teaching task may be difficult. Korea and Vietnam do, certainly, reveal a public distaste for prolonged, indecisive and limited conflict; but even in these cases, the facts are ambiguous. Initially, both conflicts were greeted by a *rise* in support for the administration. Dissent was bound to grow, for each day provides a new opportunity to quarrel with the execution of policy while approving its "ends." In both cases, however, real dissension seems to have resulted in large part from elite confusion as to the ends of policy, the result of radical disagreements at higher levels; if the public could not discern a "reason" for the conflict and its sacrifices, it is in part because there was no reason, only reasons which were often contradictory.   In Korea, the ostensible aims of the war went from restoration of the boundary to reunification and back to restoration again.   In Vietnam, if the tangled course of policy is not yet clearly traced, no one doubts that it has been and is labyrinthine. . . .

Leadership in America has sometimes succeeded, often strikingly; if it had not, we should have taken a more searching look at it without the stimulus of Vietnam.   As it is, failure is marked enough and frequent enough to move us to seek causes.

A simple cause lies in the character of our professional policy-making elites themselves.   First, the "national security managers" (the phrase is Richard Barnet's [6]) are, like all bureaucrats, concerned to protect themselves against outside interference and jealous of their expert standing. Their claims have a plausibility that is denied to others; when George Kennan wrote that the mistakes of the past were the result of "democracy as practiced in this country" and argued that "the external problems of the country should be given precedence over the internal ones" there was a persuasiveness in his argument which a career official in the Post Office or Agriculture could hardly have mustered for analogical statements.   In other words, rationalization of hostility to interference comes more easily to the national security bureaucracy.

Second, expertise is extrinsic and not intrinsic: its techniques are rooted in a series of assumptions about man and politics.   In a rapidly changing world all expertise is dangerous: today's wisdom is tomorrow's obsolescence, and bureaucracies respond very slowly to that dictum.   Knowledge of this fact, or at least, knowledge that others believe it, makes bureaucracies unusually sensitive to and defensive about their assumed knowledge. . . .

Finally, our career elites tend to be drawn from distinct social strata (these differ among the foreign service, the military, and the C.I.A., but there is considerable homogeneity to each) and, like all bureaucracies, they tend to be socialized into distinct assumptions even if they did not initially share them.   Also, foreign policy elites live separately from the rest of Americans, either in military cantonments or abroad for long periods of their lives.   The friendship groups and social circles in which they move are more distinct from others than are those of the domestic bureaucracy.   Since foreign policy elites *choose* to spend their lives in this way, they are likely to be recruited from men who feel estranged from their fellow citizens and from our national life and politics. . . .

All of these factors accentuate resistance to the public, suspicion of politics and doubt of democracy.   They imply that foreign policy is ac-

---

[6] Richard J. Barnet, *Intervention and Revolution: the United States and the Third World*, New York and Cleveland: World, 1968.

corded a guiding role in national life, dubious enough in itself.   Second, they put foreign policy elites outside the normal rule of political pressure in the country.   Leaders in elective politics, whatever else may be charged to them, value the allegiance, affection and admiration of the people: the most serious charge is that they do so too much.   The rule of pressure is that . . . [o]ne gives to one's friends what one *can,* and to one's enemies, what one *must.* . . .

Isolated, intellectually and socially autonomous and suspicious, the friends of foreign policy bureaucrats, to a degree unequalled in other bureaucracies, are *inside;* outside there are only enemies.   Hence, the rule: when involvement in domestic politics is unavoidable, give what one must to the most dangerous enemy.   The lingering effect of McCarthyism, consequently, was and remains serious.   It taught that the Right can and will hurt.   Responsible and even supportive Liberal-Left dissent was not to be feared and could, for the most part, be safely ignored; it was the Right that needed conciliating and must not be offended. . . .

That alone suggests a major argument for the techniques of protest: they are needed to shock the unwilling into noticing one's claims and to compel one's likely allies to take up the advocacy of one's cause.   The leadership problem of elites, moreover, is made more severe by the increasing maladaptation to contemporary life of the traditional politics of American foreign policy.

The foreign policy coalition which governs American foreign policy grew out of the debate between interventionist and isolationist, the last great foreign policy debate before Vietnam.   Buttressed by the peculiar structure of American party politics, the Right retained national strength after the public had come to think in new terms, and, especially in the early Cold War, continued into the post-war world the political structure of the late thirties.   Roosevelt's carefully "bipartisan" coalition, shaped in that period, was, as Bradford Westerfield writes, really "extrapartisan," uniting the internationalist wings of both parties.[7]

Obviously, this meant that foreign policy was insulated against domestic party politics and debate, and many have indicated this as an advantage, presuming a real debate would have been "extreme" and "ideological." Certainly, there was a case for this view in the early post-war world, but it had dangerous long term effects.   First, it is responsible in part for the monolithic anti-communist emphasis of the early Cold War, one of the few principles common to "internationalists" of the Left and Right center. Second, if one accepts the principle that the "extremes" were irrational . . . they do not grow more rational by exclusion.   Rather the reverse: in a two-party debate, as we have reason to know from domestic contention, moderate elements exert powerful "domesticating" influence on their

[7] H. Bradford Westerfield, *Foreign Policy and Party Politics,* New Haven: Yale University Press, 1955, p. 16.

cohorts. Exclusion simply frustrates both extremes and isolates the moderates themselves. In a democracy there is no guarantee that the extremes will remain permanently excluded; the long term result has simply been to weaken established partisan loyalties and faith in the political system.

The policy was not without frustrations for others. It added the world of politics to those forces making for an inflexible, slow-moving policy. . . . [I]n *foreign policy* the United States has been governed by a coalition not unlike those of the Fourth French Republic, where *immobilisme* was a way of life because any change was likely to offend groups which were critical to coalition support. The "center" can keep balance and little more. . . .

IV

The old mechanisms of constitutional control over foreign policy have broken down; the machinery of public control is, by the most minimal democratic standards, equally if not more defective. Aware of ignorance, painfully conscious of impotence, and eager—like all men—to escape the burden of moral responsibility when it is tied to no benefit and when an excuse is ready at hand, the public has lapsed into a passivity at once reverential and resentful, and remains unable to activate itself. Reverence and resentment are always the twin offspring of passivity, the natural sentiments of men when reduced to children's status as much as they are to the child.

The leaders of the great private governments, uneasily aware of the narrow base of commitment among their membership, confine themselves to an equally narrow definition of "group interest" supposed to be the safe base of support. Left out of account are those broadly shared values which are the core of democratic commitment and which—if only because those abstractions alone are values common to Americans generally—constitute the only useful definition of the "national interest." Political leadership, equally fearful of the public in matters of foreign policy, has done little better. One finds a politics of drift: left to itself, the public can, at best, judge new conditions with old ideas, and few attempt to teach it better. . . . The "arrogance of power" has been less characteristic than many believe. . . . More pervasive has been the *peril of responsibility:* the need to achieve *some* result immediately, and the willingness to accept the means at hand even at the cost of long term problems. Of course, no time has ever been faced with more short term danger, but no time has been surer of threatening change—change which makes the dangers of the past which were thought sufficient to justify its compromises look small, and which reduces that once seemingly prudent statecraft to the dimensions of petty opportunism or worse.

The claim of the protest movements is simply that the tactics of radical dissent and direct action can, at least, by their dramatic quality, capture the

attention of the media, and through the media, the public. By such a
capture, they can at least *make* an issue, initiate a new question, compel
some kind of choice. In that, they have been strikingly successful. The
early peace movement, like the marcher who "supported Kennedy's reluctance" to test nuclear weapons, was surely instrumental in creating the
climate for the beginnings of *détente*. . . . The Vietnam protests . . .
did more than force the abdication of an incumbent president and the initiation of talks. They began the activation of the liberal internationalist, and
created, in fact, a situation in which liberal leaders were enabled or compelled to rise to the moment.

These protests began—hopefully not too late—to undermine the old
foreign policy coalition from the Left. Its erosion from the Right . . . was
already well underway. Moderate and liberal Republicans are under increasingly successful challenge, and the old internationalist South of the
Walter Georges has progressively yielded to a militantly conservative South,
less agrarian and more tied to space and defense industry. Left dissent on
foreign policy forced Democratic leaders to make choices, sometimes painful ones, but which certainly play their role in compelling a serious debate
over ABM. . . .

Protest, however, is issue-creating, not issue-resolving. Policies still
depend on the public's reaction *to* the issue and on the creative ability of
political men. Protest is weak as a public educator, for the media will be
captured only at the price of the drama and violence necessary to appeal
to the public's titillated sense of horror. Public *fears* will grow with time
precisely because the appeal of resistance is so great to resentful men who
must still cling to respectability. Protest is an easy scapegoat for the age;
the great interests and organizations that change our lives and influence
policy do their work privately, not on TV screens. The successes of protest
have been based on the conscience that the public of old possessed.

*   *   *

When the movements began to command attention of the mass media,
however, the media became the primary recruiting agent, and the "message"
became that which the media, a very distorted mirror at best, chose to
convey. There is, after all, a difference between Port Huron and "Hey,
Hey, LBJ" or the obscenities of the recent S.D.S. convention in Chicago.
The massive increase in membership and followership is particularly serious
in a student movement which faces a new "generation" every four years.
Sophistication declined to the level of cheap sloganeering, and the network
of personal relations and socialization which had enabled S.D.S. in particular to make a reasonably workable thing of its wildly decentralized
structure, collapsed. . . . [T]he need for formal controls of ideology and
membership purge becomes an "organizational need" and not a matter
for choice.

There is nothing very new in this; the revolution devours its own, and many have felt sympathy for Marx's "I am not a Marxist." It may serve, however, to teach movements of protest a lesson, just as it is hopeful that the movements will teach policy-makers a corresponding truth.

V

Policy-makers, it is to be hoped, will learn that *neither* Left nor Right can be ignored safely and that those political devices and procedures designed to avoid introducing the public and politics into political decision have out-lived their usefulness. The sullen passivity of the Cold War, which allowed policy-makers much latitude provided that they did not ask for much, is now hardly adequate. Vietnam is only the symbol: many long-postponed, long-decaying problems will demand decision, and decisions which cannot be made cheaply. Certainly, policy-makers must learn—must *know*—the truth that for the states of today's world, especially the industrial powers, the scarcity of resources is not so much a matter of material powers as of *political* powers, the power which comes from devotion and loyalty. This dearth implies, at least, that America should not be committed abroad until the state and the cause to which we commit ourselves are worthy of Ameri-can devotion. If the people must learn to lower their standards, it is the task of political leaders to prove that this is needful. The burden of proof lies with the policy and not the value; can anyone who has read the *Laws* ask less even in this time?

*   *   *

C. Wright Mills

WE CAN'T TRUST THE POWER ELITES

The history of modern society may most readily be understood as the story of the enlargement and centralization of the means of power. In feudal societies, these means are decentralized; in the modern age they have become centralized. The rise of industrial society has involved the development and the centralization of the means of economic production, as peasants and artisans are replaced by private corporations and govern-

Reprinted by permission of Simon and Schuster from *The Causes of World War Three* (New York: Simon and Schuster, 1958), pp. 15–16, 37–38, 40, 47–50, 86–89. Copyright © 1958, by C. Wright Mills.

ment industries.   The rise of the nation-state has involved similar developments in the means of violence and political administration, as kings control
nobles and self-equipped knights are replaced by standing armies and
military machines.   The climax of all three developments—in economics,
politics, and in violence—is now occurring in most dramatic form in the
U.S.A. and in the U.S.S.R.

Before World War II several nations made international history; when
that was the case, war was easier to explain as the blind result of their
fatal interplay.   But now when there are only two—and everything between them is practically a political vacuum—the making of history is
more centralized and more open to the politics of explicit decision.

In the two superstates the history-making means of power are now
organized.   Their facilities of violence are absolute; their economic systems are increasingly autarchic; politically, each of them is increasingly a
closed world; and in all these spheres their bureaucracies are world-wide.
These two continental behemoths of our epoch have gone "beyond
nationalism" to become the centers of blocs of previously sovereign power.
They have relegated the European scatter of nations to subsidiary importance; they control the pace, and even the possibility, of industrial
development among the underdeveloped peoples of the world.   International power, in short, has been centralized.

* * *

. . . Given the scope and the centralization of the means of power now
organized in these two superstates, the role of explicit decision is enlarged.   Those who have access to these new means of history-making have
become explicitly strategic in such matters as the causes of war and the
perpetuation of conditions that are cumulatively leading to war.

This situation increases the weight of those causes of war which lie
within nations and which influence the decisions made and the defaults
committed by elites in their sovereign names.   The enlargement and the
centralization of the means of power is a symptom of the chance of men
really to make history; it is a signal of their opportunity to transcend fate
and to allow decision—and so, possibly, reason—to make a difference in
the shaping of this epoch.

Surely these developments mean that if those who now occupy the new
command posts are not capable of avoiding World War III, then they are
legitimate and accessible targets for intellectual examination, for moral
debate, and for political action. . . .

* * *

To believe in political responsibility is to recognize that there may be
power elites who are irresponsible because of general incompetence or because they are possessed by dogmas which incapacitate them for certain
uses of the power available to them.   And of course it means that they may
be both dogmatic and incompetent.   The ready inference from the procla-

mations of the U.S. elite and from their decisions and lack of decisions is that this is indeed the case. . . .

* * *

. . . [I]n both Russia and America, the ruling circles are possessed by the military metaphysic.

Confronted by the buzzing confusion of the world in which they live, decision-makers regularly seize upon the threat of violence as "the real factor." The deciding point in the conflict between Soviet communism and American capitalism is held (especially, it now must be admitted, by the elite of the U.S.A.) to be the state of violence and the balance of fright. The pivotal decision made by the elite is in accordance with this military metaphysic. . . . It rests upon the dogmatic view—held, I am sure, with sincerity and good intention—that only by accumulating ever new and ever greater military peril can a condition of peace be created. The key moral fact about it is the virtual absence within ourselves of opposition to this definition of world reality, to the elites' strategy and policies. The key political and intellectual result is the absence within Russia and within America, among publics and masses, of any truly debated alternatives.

* * *

The arms race is the master line of action followed by the power elites of the continental states. It is not subordinated to and made an instrument of any economic and political goal. What is the economic and political goal of the U.S., to which its military actions are a means? The accumulation of military power has become an ascendant end in itself; economic and political maneuvers and hesitations—from imperialist action in the desert to diplomatic coyness in the drawing room—are subordinated to and judged in terms of military forces and potentials. The spokesmen of each side say they know that war is obsolete as a means of policy, yet they search for peace by warlike means. The strategic outlook is not decisively, and certainly not permanently, changed by any one or another turn of the arms race. We are both beyond that. The equipment in combat readiness on both sides is already devastating. The development of this equipment is cumulative: One "ultimate weapon" follows another in geometric progression, and the base for the acceleration in both war camps is quite adequate for the end in view. Never before has there been an arms-race of this sort —a scientific arms race, with a series of ultimate weapons, dominated by the strategy of obliteration. At every turn of this "competition," each side becomes more edgy and the chances become greater that accidents of character or of technology, that the U.S. radar man in Canada or his Russian counterpart in Siberia, will trigger the sudden ending.

But the strategic outlook is the idiot's outlook. It is the fact of this idiot's race that is important, not the score at any given moment, not the alarmist cries which would frighten men from examining its deadly assumptions. . . . Both the Russian and the American elites, and intellectuals in both societies, are fighting the cold war in the name of peace, but the assumptions of their policies and the effects of their interactions have been, and are, increasing the chances of war. War, it is assumed in their military metaphysic, is the most likely outcome of the parallel existence of the two types of political economy. Such is the official lay of the land, the official definition of reality, the contribution to peace of the nationalist spokesman among the power elite.

*   *   *

The thrust toward World War III is *not* a plot on the part of the elite, either that of the U.S.A. or that of the U.S.S.R. Among both, there are "war parties" and "peace parties," and among both there are what can be called crackpot realists. These are men who are so rigidly focused on the next step that they become creatures of whatever the main drift—the opportunist actions of innumerable men—brings. . . .

. . . Lacking a program, the opportunist moves short distances among immediate and shifting goals. He reacts rather than inaugurates, and the directions of his reactions are set less by any goals of his own than by the circumstances to which he feels forced to react out of fear and uneasiness. Since he is largely a creature of these circumstances, rather than a master of independent action, the results of his expedient maneuvers and of his defaults are more products of the main drift than of his own vision and will. To be merely expedient is to be in the grip of historical fate or in the grip of those who are not merely expedient. Sunk in the details of immediate and seemingly inevitable decisions to which he feels compelled to react, the crackpot realist does not know what he will do next; he is waiting for another to make a move.

*   *   *

For those who would quietly attain modest goals in a short while, and who are acting within a main drift that is generally beneficent, crackpot realism is quite fitting. They need neither enduring means nor orienting programs of scope. But for those who are in the main drift toward World War III and who would stop that drift and attain a world condition of peace, opportunism is merely a series of cumulative defaults. Short-run pursuits are leading to long-run consequences that are not under the control of any program. The absence of an American program for peace is a major cause of the thrust and drift toward World War III.

In the meantime, and in the absence of such a program, elites of political, military, and economic power are at the focal points of the economic, political, and military causes of war. By their decisions and their indecisions, by their defaults and their ignorance, they control the thrust of these causes. They are allowed to occupy such positions, and to use them in accordance with crackpot realism, because of the powerlessness, the apathy, the insensibility of publics and masses; they are able to do so, in part, because of the inactionary posture of intellectuals, scientists, and other cultural workmen. In both the U.S. and the U.S.S.R., and in the frightened zones that lie between them, there is a political vacuum, and an intellectual vacuum. In both, the thrust toward World War III is accelerated by elite behavior in the name of the sovereign state and in accordance with the military metaphysic.

SUGGESTED READINGS

Albrecht-Carré, René, *A Diplomatic History of Europe Since the Congress of Vienna,* New York: Harper & Row, 1958.

Frankel, Joseph, *The Making of Foreign Policy: An Analysis of Decision-making,* New York: Oxford University Press, 1967.

Hoffmann, Stanley, *Gulliver's Troubles, or the Setting of American Foreign Policies,* New York: McGraw-Hill, 1968.

Iklé, Fred C., *How Nations Negotiate,* New York: Praeger, 1965.

Kennan, George F., *Memoirs, 1925–1950,* Boston: Little, Brown, 1967.

Macridis, Roy C. (ed.), *Foreign Policy in World Politics,* 3rd ed., Englewood Cliffs, N.J.: Prentice-Hall, 1967.

Nicolson, Sir Harold, *Diplomacy,* 3rd ed., New York: Oxford University Press, 1963.

Qualter, Terence H., *Propaganda and Psychological Warfare,* New York: Random House, 1962.

Rosenau, James N. (ed.), *International Aspects of Civil Strife,* Princeton: Princeton University Press, 1964.

―――― (ed.), *Domestic Sources of Foreign Policy,* New York: Free Press, 1967.

Waltz, Kenneth N., *Foreign Policy and Democratic Politics,* Boston: Little, Brown, 1967.

IX. GOVERNING THE WORLD COMMUNITY

From antiquity to the present, the perception that mankind is a single species has suggested to many that human beings should share a common world government as they share a common nature. Stoics conceived of a world-city, the *cosmopolis,* which alone was worthy of human devotion. Saint Augustine saw in the City of God the true reality to which sinful men were blind, and Christians and Jews alike shared an apocalyptic vision of a world at peace, obedient to God's law, in which all men would be brothers. Dante, in his *De Monarchia* (1317), combined the abstract logic of the Schoolmen with the fervor of his poetic imagination to argue for a world empire that could abolish war and permit man's true nature to emerge.

The moral arguments of ancient and early modern thinkers, however, could never overcome the *practical* limitations on their ideal. The daily life and attention of men was fixed on a locality or some other limited sphere. Alexander and Marcus Aurelius dreamed of world harmony and governed empires that imposed military and political rule over millions, but neither they nor others like them could overcome the dominantly local character of life and personal loyalty. And even such unity as they could enforce fell short of the unity of mankind.

The technological revolution of the modern age, however, has progressively removed such limitations. It has created what is in larger measure a world economy; it permits and encourages relations between individuals across state boundaries; it has generated international associations and political movements. And, of course, it has augmented the peril and destructiveness of war. Men in the nineteenth century were willing to trust the balance of power and the free play of historical forces, confident that these would enlarge and perfect the sphere of international order. In the thunder of 1914, however, such trust and optimism almost disappeared. A multitude of voices began to demand international government or at least a "collective security" organization to prevent the recurrence of war.

Men like Woodrow Wilson acted from a sense of desperation that led them to spurn the practical objections that seemed to remain in the path of international government. If the League of Nations will not work, Wilson declared, "it must be *made* to work," for the forces shaping international politics demanded it.

But, of course, the League was not "made to work." As A. F. K. Organski indicates, the hope for a "collective security system" shared one essential premise with the doctrine of the "balance of power": the belief that the "system" would be self-regulating. While the advocates of collective security felt it necessary to channel political forces through rationally designed institutions, they still hoped that such institutions would have an automatic logic of their own. But as Organski shows, collective security depends on the policies of states no less than the balance of power. In fact, it demands a moral agreement that peace is *always* preferable to violence, the conviction that there is nothing "worth fighting for," and the corollary preference for order as opposed to change. Especially in the League of Nations, the weakness of that assumption was evident. Advocates of collective security underrated the resentment of poorer and disadvantaged states and the strength of the demand for justice as forces arrayed against the "status quo" that collective security was to maintain.

The moral and political consensus required by the "assumptions" of collective security, in other words, did not exist. Many, like Reinhold Niebuhr, became disenchanted with their former beliefs about the immediate prospects of world unity. Technical forces had created an interdependent world, Niebuhr argued, but human loyalties had remained parochial; world government, consequently, was an "illusion."

Disillusionment with the first experiments in collective security, however, only led to more modest claims and hopes for international organization. Even the most somber "realists" have tended to hope that limited experiments may lead in the direction of stronger political community at the international level.

The framers of the United Nations, for example, recognized the limits of international community. They had little confidence, unlike Wilson, that "world opinion" and "moral suasion" would deter aggression, and consequently, greatly expanded the role of armed enforcement of the U.N. Charter. Yet they were also aware that enforcement could prevent conflict only when the great powers agreed. As the veto demonstrates, the framers of the Charter also *expected* the great powers to disagree, but were willing to settle for collective security in those cases—however few—where agreement was possible because only in such cases was effective action possible. And finally, they moved beyond the League of Nations in attempting, though very cautiously, to encourage and establish procedures for peaceful change.[1]

But as James P. Sewell observes, even the limited hopes of the framers of the Charter proved excessive given the tensions and conflicts of the cold war. Although the United States attempted, for a time, to use the United Nations as an instrument for containment, the United Nations gradually abandoned the idea of "enforced peace." Peaceful change became one new focus of attention, and new nations found themselves able, as David A. Kay indicates, to develop an "anticolonial" consensus and a new definition of human rights within the U.N. In relation to conflict, the U.N. increasingly emphasized "balancing" between blocs and the pacific settlement of disputes. Early successes in the role of mediation encouraged U.N. officials and enthusiasts, like

[1] Inis L. Claude, Jr., "The Management of Power in the Changing United Nations," *International Organization*, 15 (1961), 219–235.

the late Secretary-General Dag Hammarskjöld, to envision a broad role for "preventive diplomacy" and "peace-keeping" forces. But as Sewell points out, crises like those in the Congo and the Middle East reveal that the U.N. cannot act preventively or keep the peace unless there is a peace to keep, a condition that requires at least minimal agreement between the superpowers and the combatants themselves. The U.N. may perform important tasks, but only within the structure of international relations imposed on it by the conflicts and attitudes of states in general and the great powers in particular.

This result would not have surprised the "functionalist" theorists, who always argued that the attempt to govern the world by controlling violence was too difficult and too limited in the international order that emerged after World War II. As Prof. Inis L. Claude, Jr., observes, David Mitrany and others wished to avoid direct conflict with national loyalties or concern with "political" contests. By building organizations to serve "pragmatic" economic and social ends, they hoped to win support for international organization, and by the indirect route of filling man's economic and social needs, for international community.

The cold war never permitted functional organizations to develop very far within the U.N., but a new theory of functionalism has developed in relation to regional organization. Many, like Ernst Haas, who hope for the growth of international community but recognize the near impossibility of achieving it in the face of superpower conflict, turned to regional organizations as a practicable first step. Regional organizations, restricted to areas of greater community of interests and values, might pave the way for regional government.

Haas, as Roger D. Hansen indicates,[2] argues that economic and political matters form a "continuum." It is impossible, for example, to regulate coal and steel without affecting national defense. If regional economic organizations were developed, their activities would necessarily "spill over" into broader and political spheres. And if they were successful, they would create new group support and pressure for expanding their authority to deal with those additional areas as well, eventually culminating, by an almost autonomous process, in regional government.[3] So far, such predictions have not been verified; in Europe, the "process" of integration has been stalled if not stopped. As Hansen points out, theorists like Stanley Hoffmann have argued that political goals and gains are radically different from economic goods, that politics is separate from—rather than part of a continuum with—economics. In Hoffmann's view, no "automatic" transition can ever take place from one to the other. Moreover, Hoffmann contends, "regions" are autonomous only in very limited ways; in an integrated world, the conflicts and opportunities of the international system as a whole impinge on them at every point. This is especially important because the hostility between the superpowers, combined with the "paralysis" of the nuclear standoff, gives individual nations great chances for independent maneuver and possibly for greater gains than would

[2] Roger D. Hansen, "Regional Integration: Reflections on a Decade of Theoretical Efforts," *World Politics,* 21 (January 1969), pp. 242–271.

[3] Ernst B. Haas, *The Uniting of Europe,* Stanford, Calif.: Stanford University Press, 1958.

be possible in regional contexts. "Regions," in other words, may be "out-dated." They, no less than individual states, have only flimsy boundaries, and new technological and organizational forces cross over them with comparative ease, endangering regional solidarity by forging inseparable bonds of inter-dependence between individuals, groups, and states and the international order as a whole. And regions, unlike nation-states, have no important political resources with which to defend their unity; few regions inspire much allegiance and fewer offer significant rewards in the quest for dignity.

As Hansen points out, other theorists, like Amitai Etzioni, had never seen regional organization as more than a "stage" in political development, foresee-ing the eventual breakup of regions under the impact of transregional forces.[4] Etzioni, among others, argued that the "dialectic" process of destruction and growth would lead toward still larger, international, units of government. There is little encouragement for this theory in recent events. In fact, Profes-sor Etzioni's argument is very similar to the doctrine of eighteenth-century thinkers who sought to prove that history was guided by forces that impelled it toward world community. Immanuel Kant, for example, saw a "cunning of nature" that used the warlike dispositions of men to further perpetual peace by forcing them to form ever larger political units to deal with ever more powerful enemies. In one sense, moreover, these early theorists were more "realistic" than their modern counterparts: they recognized that each "stage" of development was an occasion for violence between those tied to the old order and those committed to the new. Similarly, Niebuhr wrote in the 1930s (in his *Reflections on the End of an Era*) that no "new age" could come into being without the violence of "barbarians" who alone could destroy the old. Obviously, such possibilities have few attractions in the era of atomic weapons.

Yet all of these theories, plans, and policies have been based on a core of common values and goals: the hope for expanding international community government. Can one assume, however, that world government is desirable even if practicable? Ancient political thinkers would have answered in the negative. Plato, as Prof. Leo Strauss has noted, believed firmly that peace was essential to the development of what is excellent in man's nature, and this doubtless demanded a world regime.[5] Equally, however, Plato believed that a world regime could not be just, for it could not give sufficient attention to, and would lack knowledge of, the needs of men as individuals. Man has a com-mon nature and a diverse existence, and between the two exists a dilemma that led Plato and others to a belief in the small state, incapable of massive destructiveness and capable of giving due attention to individual personalities. Such arguments may seem irrelevant, at best, in the atomic age. They add a doubt, however, to the discussion of international organization, a restraint to enthusiasm, a recognition that a world tyranny would certainly be the worst of governments, even if it were a peaceful one. In addition the classical argu-ment may suggest an inherent limitation to international community (though not necessarily to international government). Men demand a sense of per-

[4] Amitai Etzioni, *Political Unification,* New York, Holt, Rinehart & Winston, 1964.

[5] *Natural Right and History,* Chicago: University of Chicago Press, 1953, pp. 148–149.

sonal worth and of importance to those who rule them, which is best summarized in the word "dignity." Large groups and societies make each individual *qua* individual seem smaller, though his importance as a member of an aggregate may increase. On the whole men have been reluctant to yield their highest devotion to large groups in place of small; even inside states, many or most of us consider our loyalty to friends and family as ranking above patriotism. The pressure of dangers or the hope of benefits may lead to larger organizations and governments, but never without some reluctance and nostalgia. And it is difficult to find that such reluctance and nostalgia are entirely misplaced. Even in an age of superpowers and atomic weapons, one may feel the appeal and power of the case made by philosophers as diverse as Plato, Jefferson, and Rousseau in favor of the moral excellence of the small state.

A. F. K. Organski

COLLECTIVE SECURITY

The idea of collective security rests upon five assumptions that must prove to be correct if the idea is to work out in practice. They are:

1. In any armed combat, all nations will agree on which combatant is the aggressor. What's more, they will reach this agreement immediately, since rapid and united action is necessary if aggression is to be brought to a halt before extensive damage is done.

2. All nations are equally interested in stopping aggression from whatever source it comes. Preventing aggression is a value which overrides all others in international relations. Neither friendship nor economic advantage will stand in the way of action against an aggressor.

3. All nations are equally free and able to join in action against an aggressor.

4. The combined power of the collectivity, i.e., of all the nations in the world except the aggressor, will be great enough to overwhelm the aggressor.

5. Knowing that overwhelming power stands ready to be used against it, an aggressor nation will either sheathe its sword or go down in defeat.

As we shall see, the fourth and fifth assumptions are essentially correct, but the first three are in error, and for this reason the system has never worked in practice.

ASSUMPTION ONE:
AGREEMENT ON THE IDENTITY OF THE AGGRESSOR

Unfortunately for the operation of collective security, there is rarely unanimous agreement on which nation is the aggressor in an international squabble. The accused nation, itself, almost invariably denies the charge, claiming that it was provoked by the aggressive action of others. Friends of the aggressor agree. Friends of the victim protest. The final verdict of history is liable to depend upon who writes the account of the event. Historians have argued and will continue to argue who was the aggressor in World War I. Most of the nations in the world have no doubt whatever that the Communist North Koreans started the Korean War by invading South Korea, but the Communist nations insist that the initial attack came from South Korea. It seems quite likely that if a major war occurs between East and West, the ultimately accepted version of who was the aggressor will depend upon who wins the war.

Reprinted by permission of the publisher from A. F. K. Organski, *World Politics* (New York: Alfred A. Knopf, 1958), pp. 373–384. Copyright 1958 by A. F. K. Organski.

Apart from the possibilities of falsifying history, there is an even more basic problem in the fact that there is no clear definition of aggression. It is frequently assumed that aggression is synonymous with the first use of military force by one nation against another. This diminishes but does not eliminate the difficulty of identifying the aggressor in many cases. In the past few decades we have witnessed a number of instances in which nations obviously spoiling for a fight have launched armed attacks so unprovoked, so open and so brutal, so lacking in regard for both the rules of warfare and the principles of human decency, that identification of the aggressor proved no problem. It was the Japanese who attacked the Americans in World War II and not the other way around. American forces were at breakfast and in church that morning in 1941 when Japanese planes without warning bombed and strafed the American fleet at Pearl Harbor. It was Germany that started the war in the first place by attacking Poland on the flimsiest of pretexts. It was Fascist Italy that attacked Ethiopia, Albania, and Greece and stabbed a dying France. It was the Russians who attacked the Finns. In all these cases, the practice of labelling as aggressor the first to use armed force seems to lay the blame at the proper door, but other cases are not always so simple.

What, for example, are we to make of Israel's attack on Egypt in 1956? Israel was certainly the first to launch a major attack, but before that attack there had been almost nightly raids across the Israeli border by Egyptian commandos and a series of retaliatory raids by the Israelis. Who was the first to use force, then? Apparently Egypt. But the amount of force was small, for the raiders did not do much damage, and they returned home after each foray. How *much* force must be used before it is to be considered aggression? A single border incident involving half a dozen raiders is clearly too small. An organized attack by a division is probably enough. But where is the dividing line? How many raids equal the attack of a division? There are no easy answers.

In this particular case, the question was complicated by the fact that Israel steadily insisted that she wished to live in peace with her neighbors, while Arab leaders stated officially and categorically that their aim was to erase Israel from the map. Do stated intentions count?

To complicate matters even further, Egypt was at that time in the process of building up a force, armed with Russian planes and weapons, that would have been capable of putting the threats of her leader, Col. Nasser, into effect. Is it aggression to attack a neighbor who is arming to annihilate you? The common sense answer would be: "No, not if it is certain he plans to attack as soon as he is strong enough. Yes, if there is a possibility that he may not attack." But how are we to read the future? In a world where collective security was in full operation, we would wait until the aggressor actually attacked, knowing that the collectivity could turn him back with ease. Any previous action against him would, itself, be aggression. But in a world where collective security is by no means certain and every nation must defend itself, who can say with certainty that Israel was the aggressor?

Other problems are posed by the possibility of threatening force without using it. Suppose one nation threatens another and the weaker nation gives in without a fight. Hitler did not use force in taking over Czechoslovakia. His threats were enough to frighten the Western allies, and resistance on the part of little Czechoslovakia alone would have been suicidal. The Germans marched in unopposed, but was that not aggression?

*   *   *

The Communist nations have devised other techniques that escape legal definition as aggression, although the effect may be the same. It is extremely difficult to detect aid that is given to revolutionaries in other countries to enable them to overthrow their own governments, particularly if such aid is largely in the form of military training and ideological indoctrination for a small number of leaders. Weapons and supplies can be identified, but can we classify the sale of arms to revolutionaries as aggression? Was China an aggressor in Indo-China because she gave material aid to the rebels in their fight against the French? Was Russia an aggressor in Korea because she supplied the North Koreans with arms to attack their neighbors to the south?

*   *   *

And what about the use of so-called "volunteers," the latest technique to plague those seeking a simple definition of aggression? Whole divisions or even armies that are called "volunteers" fool no one, but what about a relatively small number of high officers or specialists such as bomber pilots or submarine commanders? Does the nation that supplies these to another nation share in any aggression it commits? It becomes clear that even the identification of military aggression is by no means simple.

How much more difficult is our task if we consider economic and ideological aggression as well as the use of military force. . . . A nation can be strangled by an economically more powerful nation just as surely as she can be conquered by a nation that is more powerful militarily. Iran was brought to her knees by the Western refusal to buy her oil after she nationalized the industry and threw out the British. Hitler attacked the Balkans economically long before his armies began to cross their frontiers, and Russian penetration of the Middle East to date has not involved a single soldier.

Even ideological attack may be highly effective. Joseph Goebbels, Hitler's minister of propaganda, demonstrated how deadly such attacks can be in developing home-grown traitors and in weakening a victim's will to fight once military aggression occurs. Russia daily beams propaganda broadcasts to large areas of the world urging the undermining of pro-Western governments, and we, for our part, broadcast to the Russians and the satellite peoples, urging them to throw off Communist rule. Such actions are not customarily considered aggression, but their military value in case of an armed conflict may turn out to be substantial.

One final problem: under collective security no nation is prejudged to be guilty. Only after the aggressor has actually struck can the collectivity act in its turn. Such procedure seems necessary if the system is to be absolutely fair and impartial, but it greatly decreases the efficiency of the scheme. Of course, if the aggressor is a small one, no harm is done. No preparation is required to deal with such an aggressor; one stern warning by the combined great powers will be sufficient to stop the small nation dead in its tracks and make it consider. However, if the aggressor is a major power that can be stopped only by great armed strength, it is necessary to know which nation is the aggressor some time in advance of any aggression it actually commits. Nations need time, perhaps even years, to weld their separate armies into one mighty fighting force. Germany defeated one nation after another and wrecked most of Europe before she was brought down in defeat, because all the nations that eventually combined against her were not prepared to enter the fight at the start.

*   *   *

The assumption that all nations will agree on the identity of the aggressor is false. In the absence of a clear definition of aggression, aggressive acts can be disguised, and even when they are committed openly, claims and counterclaims can be launched as to which side started it all. It is unfair to identify an aggressor as such before he strikes, but once a major aggressor strikes, it may be years before he can be put down again, even with the combined fighting strength of a united collectivity of nations. The first assumption simply does not stand up.

ASSUMPTION TWO:
UNIVERSAL INTEREST IN STOPPING AGGRESSION

The second assumption underlying the concept of collective security is that all nations are equally interested in preventing or stopping aggression. This, too, is belied by the facts, for in the course of recent history, aggressors have never found themselves friendless. It is curiously contradictory to assume on the one hand that all nations are equally capable of becoming aggressors and on the other that they are all equally interested in stopping aggression when it occurs. Nations that are contemplating aggression—or acts that other nations may consider aggression—obviously will not support schemes that will insure their own future defeat. Nor will the friends who would benefit from their aggression turn against them.

Nevertheless, the belief that aggression is equally deplored by all is a popular belief, particularly in the periods immediately following wars, when the world hungers for perpetual peace, when the defeated lie punished and even the victorious are tired of combat. . . .

. . . We must not forget that to nations that are fundamentally satisfied with the existing order, i.e., to the dominant nation and its major allies, peace and security mean the preservation of the privileges they have.   As long as peace is preserved, the losses they suffer will be minimized and the tempo of their decline slowed down.   To the dissatisfied, on the other hand, international peace means peace without justice.   If such a nation becomes strong enough, it may become a challenger with much to gain from up-setting the existing order, by force of arms if no other way is possible.   For the dissatisfied of little power, initiating the aggression against larger nations is out of the question.   Such nations must wait for the opportunity provided by the aggression of a larger challenger.   Thus when a powerful and dissatisfied challenger strikes, it runs interference for many nations that are dissatisfied with their place in the existing order.   For this reason, a major aggressor seldom fights alone.

Not even the dominant nation can be counted upon to oppose all acts of aggression with equal vigor.   Unfortunately for collective security, the old refrain that peace is indivisible and that aggression anywhere threatens all nations everywhere is not really true.   All nations are not equally afraid of being attacked.   Appeals to the self-interest of nations, a major argument of those who favor collective security, miss the point.   A major nation need not fear attack from any but a small handful of nations.   Such a nation is understandably unwilling to make *a priori* commitments that it will fight on the side of anyone attacked anywhere in the world even if its own in-terests are not at stake.

*   *   *

It is obviously mistaken to believe that peace and security are universal goals of all nations, overriding all others.   When nations are immediately and severely threatened, security may in fact take precedence over all other concerns, but in the normal run of events, security can be taken for granted, and peace is only one of many national goals.   It is a sad fact but true that when the interests of the great powers are not directly threatened, aggressors may be left to devour their victims undisturbed.

ASSUMPTION THREE:
UNIVERSAL ABILITY TO OPPOSE AGGRESSION

The successful operation of collective security assumes not only that all nations are *interested* in stopping aggression but also that they are *able* to do so, that is, that they are free to join with other members of the col-lectivity in taking action against the aggressor.   This, too, is incorrect.

A small nation bordering on a potential aggressor will think twice before joining any move against its more powerful neighbor, for battles "to stop the aggressor" are quite likely to be fought upon its territory, destroying its industries and its homes as well as those of the aggressor.   Such fears quite naturally may cool its ardor for seeing collective security work.   It is true that such nations, because of their location, are most exposed to aggression, themselves, and one might think that they would have the most to gain from the successful operation of collective security. But such nations are too weak to defend themselves successfully, and other nations are too distant to prevent their fall if the aggressor attacks. The most that other nations can promise is liberation after the conquest is completed, and liberation is likely to prove even more destructive than the initial conquest.

Because of this, these nations frequently attempt to take refuge in neutrality. Even great powers may resist lending a hand to stop aggression because of such fears. . . .

There are other reasons why nations sometimes cannot join in action against an aggressor. Their troops may be committed elsewhere, far from the scene of aggression. At the time of the Korean War, France was heavily engaged in trying to defend her colony in Indo-China from Communist rebels and could not spare many troops for the Korean conflict. More recently, France, in trying to hold another rebellious colony, Algeria, withdrew from Europe troops that were committed to the North Atlantic Treaty Organization. . . .

Sometimes a nation requires the help of an aggressor to defend itself against possible aggression from other quarters. Again, France provides an example. At the time when Fascist Italy attacked Ethiopia, France was reluctant to move against her, for she still hoped that Italy might be won to her side in the coming battle against Germany. The facts turned out to be otherwise, but the hope is understandable.

When aggression is committed by one of a nation's most valued allies, the choice is even more difficult. Could the United States afford to oppose aggression committed by either England or France, whose help she requires in the struggle against Russia? Events appear to prove she can afford it, for when England and France attacked Egypt in an effort to seize back the nationalized Suez Canal, the United States opposed them and forced their withdrawal, much to the detriment of Allied relations. Perhaps the dominant nation in the world can afford to antagonize anyone. But could England or France afford to oppose aggression committed by the United States? Probably not. . . .

Finally, we must not overlook the strength of economic ties in binding nations together, even when one commits unwelcome aggression. Nations that are economically tied to an aggressor may not be able to sever their ties without great hardship. In addition to the initial hardship of having to rearrange an entire economy on short notice and convince the population to tighten its belts for the duration of the crisis, there is the danger that once the crisis is ended, it may prove impossible to reestablish the broken economic ties, for the aggressor may have shopped around and found more secure sources of supply or better markets elsewhere. The plan for collective security stresses the fact that an aggressor is economically dependent upon other nations and thus can be punished by economic sanctions. Once economically isolated, he will find it difficult to go on fighting. This is probably true. However, we must not forget that interdependence is a two-way street with nations also dependent upon the aggressor and thus unable to break away completely.

The first three assumptions, then, are incorrect. It cannot be assumed that nations will agree on what constitutes aggression or on which nation is the aggressor. Nor can it be assumed that all nations are either interested in stopping aggression or able to join in action against the aggressor. Under these circumstances, collective security cannot be expected to work, even though the remaining two assumptions are correct.

ASSUMPTION FOUR:
PREPONDERANT POWER OF THE COLLECTIVITY

All against one, the basic formula of collective security, is neither sporting nor heroic but it guarantees success in any trial of strength. The assumption that the collectivity, once united and once intent on preventing aggression, is strong enough to keep the peace, is essentially correct. It seems fairly obvious that no single nation is strong enough to win a victory against the combined strength of all other nations in the world.

However, some nations can come closer to achieving such a victory than others. Should the aggressor be a small nation, no great problem is posed. The intervention of a single great power will be enough to send its troops scurrying for home. But stopping aggression by one of the great powers is more difficult. Germany, for example, came close to victory in World War II. However, the case of Germany proves our point. Germany did not fight alone, nor did she fight all her enemies at once. Particularly at the beginning, she picked off her victims one at a time, and her early successes rested on the fact that before the kill, she isolated each victim. For Austria and Czechoslovakia, Germany did not fight at all. The conquest of Poland did require the use of force, but Hitler was careful to neutralize Russia before he attacked. Then, with the Eastern front secure, he turned to the West and conquered all of Europe to the Channel. Only then, did he turn and attack Russia. The combined strength of England, the United States, and Russia eventually defeated Germany but not without a mighty and costly struggle.

Today, with the possible exception of the United States and Russia, there is no nation that could successfully resist a coalition of other great powers, surely not France or England, who withdrew from Suez rather than stand up to American opposition, surely not China, who dares not attack Formosa. In truth, the United States is so powerful today that its strength alone guarantees any area in which it is interested against the aggression of any nation except Russia, and even in the case of Russia, a firm and public American commitment to defend an area must give the Russians pause.

However, even the two super-powers, America and Russia, probably could not stand up against the rest of the world combined. Russia, today, is not even as strong as the United States. Compared to the whole Western alliance, she is by far the weaker party. Deserted by China and the satellites, she would not stand a chance. Collective security, then, could take care of Russian aggression, for with the whole world against her, Russia would not be half as dangerous as she appears today. Russia is dangerous precisely because the whole world is *not* combined against her and because the *potential* power of Russia *and* her allies is so great.

That leaves the United States. Could she defy the world? We think not. The matter will never be put to the test, so we cannot be sure, but the concern with which the United States tends her alliances with Western Europe, the energy she spends trying to win new allies from among the neutral nations, and the consternation with which she views the fall of any new nation to Communism, are clear enough indication that she fears to stand alone in any battle against world Communism. The collectivity is also stronger than the United States.

Collective security is not really necessary unless the aggressor is one of the two great super-powers. The combined might of all the nations in the world is not required to put down aggression by lesser nations. Indeed, there is no nation on earth that dares to risk the severe displeasure of these two giants. Continued acts of aggression by small and medium-sized nations cannot be blamed upon a lack of collective security. Even without collective security, they would not be possible unless the two great powers both looked the other way *or* unless one of the great powers protected the aggressor against the other.

The assumption that no nation could successfully resist the combined might of all the others is correct. The difficulty is that in cases of small aggressors, this combined might is not necessary, and in the only cases where it *would* be necessary, i.e., aggression by either the United States or Russia, such a force could not be gathered. One of these nations is the dominant nation in the existing international order, the other the major challenger. Each has its own group of followers who would never admit that their leader was an aggressor and who would be neither interested nor able to oppose it if it were.

ASSUMPTION FIVE:
PEACE BASED ON PREPONDERANT POWER

The fifth and final assumption underlying the concept of collective security is that a would-be aggressor faced with the certainty of united opposition from the rest of the world, would give up its plans for aggression as hopeless. This assumption, too, is probably correct. . . .

*   *   *

The preponderant power of the collectivity would, indeed, be sufficient to prevent aggression *if* it could be mobilized on the side of peace, but it is here that the error of the first three assumptions is most telling, for as long as nations are governed by national interest rather than by principle, as long as they refuse to recognize that their friends may be aggressors and are disinterested or unable to oppose them, so long it will be impossible to mobilize the kind of united force that would be necessary to make collective security work.   We must conclude that the plan is fundamentally unworkable, noble though it may be in inspiration.

Dag Hammarskjöld

PREVENTIVE DIPLOMACY IN THE UNITED NATIONS

*   *   *

Fundamental though the differences splitting our world are, the areas which are not committed in the major conflicts are still considerable. Whether the countries concerned call themselves non-committed, neutral, neutralist or something else, they have all found it not to be in harmony with their role and interests in world politics to tie their policies, in a general sense, to any one of the blocs or to any specific line of action supported by one of the sides in the major conflict.   The reasons for such attitudes vary.   That, however, is less important in this special context than the fact that conflicts arising within the non-committed areas offer opportunities for solutions which avoid an aggravation of big Power differences and can remain uninfluenced by them.   There is thus a field within which international conflicts may be faced and solved with such harmony between the power blocs as was anticipated as a condition for Security Council action in San Francisco.   Agreement may be achieved because of a mutual interest among the big Powers to avoid having a regional or local conflict drawn into the sphere of bloc politics.

With its constitution and structure, it is extremely difficult for the United Nations to exercise an influence on problems which are clearly and definitely within the orbit of present day conflicts between power blocs.   If a specific conflict is within that orbit, it can be assumed that the Security Council is

Reprinted from the *Introduction to the Annual Report of the Secretary-General on the Work of the Organization,* June 16, 1959–June 15, 1960, General Assembly, Official Records: Fifteenth Session, Supplement No. 1A (New York, 1960), pp. 4–5.

rendered inactive, and it may be feared that even positions taken by the General Assembly would follow lines strongly influenced by considerations only indirectly related to the concrete difficulty under consideration. Whatever the attitude of the General Assembly and the Security Council, it is in such cases also practically impossible for the Secretary-General to operate effectively with the means put at his disposal, short of risking seriously to impair the usefulness of his office for the Organization in all the other cases for which the services of the United Nations Secretariat are needed.

This clearly defines the main field of useful activity of the United Nations in its efforts to prevent conflicts or to solve conflicts. Those efforts must aim at keeping newly arising conflicts outside the sphere of bloc differences. Further, in the case of conflicts on the margin of, or inside, the sphere of bloc differences, the United Nations should seek to bring such conflicts out of this sphere through solutions aiming, in the first instance, at their strict localization. In doing so, the Organization and its agents have to lay down a policy line, but this will then not be for one party against another, but for the general purpose of avoiding an extension or achieving a reduction of the area into which the bloc conflicts penetrate.

Experience indicates that the preventive diplomacy, to which the efforts of the United Nations must thus to a large extent be directed, is of special significance in cases where the original conflict may be said either to be the result of, or to imply risks for, the creation of a power vacuum between the main blocs. Preventive action in such cases must in the first place aim at filling the vacuum so that it will not provoke action from any of the major parties, the initiative for which might be taken for preventive purpose but might in turn lead to counter-action from the other side. The ways in which a vacuum can be filled by the United Nations so as to forestall such initiatives differ from case to case, but they have this in common: temporarily, and pending the filling of a vacuum by normal means, the United Nations enters the picture on the basis of its non-commitment to any power bloc, so as to provide to the extent possible a guarantee in relation to all parties against initiatives from others.

The special need and the special possibilities for what I here call preventive United Nations diplomacy have been demonstrated in several recent cases, such as Suez and Gaza, Lebanon and Jordan, Laos and the Congo.

A study of the records of the conflicts to which I have just referred shows how it has been possible to use the means and methods of the United Nations for the purposes I have indicated. In all cases, whatever the immediate reason for the United Nations initiative, the Organization has moved so as to forestall developments which might draw the specific conflict, openly or actively, into the sphere of power bloc differences. It has done so by introducing itself into the picture, sometimes with very modest means, sometimes in strength, so as to eliminate a political, economic and social or military vacuum.

The view expressed here as to the special possibilities and responsibilities of the Organization in situations of a vacuum has reached an unusually clear expression in the case of the Congo.   There, the main argument presented for United Nations intervention was the breakdown of law and order, the rejection of the attempt to maintain order by foreign troops, and the introduction of the United Nations Force so as to create the basis for the withdrawal of the foreign troops and for the forestalling of initiatives to introduce any other foreign troops into the territory with the obvious risks for widening international conflict which would ensue.

Whether the Congo operation is characterized as a case of preventive diplomacy, or as a move in order to fill a vacuum and to forestall the international risks created by the development of such a vacuum, or as a policy aimed at the localization of a conflict with potentially wide international repercussions, is not essential.   Whatever the description, the political reality remains. It is a policy which is justified by the wish of the international community to avoid this important area being split by bloc conflicts. It is a policy rendered possible by the fact that both blocs have an interest in avoiding such an extension of the area of conflict because of the threatening consequences, were the localization of the conflict to fail.

Those who look with impatience at present day efforts by the United Nations to resolve major international problems are inclined to neglect, or to misread, the significance of the efforts which can be made by the United Nations in the field of practical politics in order to guide the international community in a direction of growing stability.   They see the incapacity of the United Nations to resolve the major bloc conflicts as an argument against the very form of international co-operation which the Organization represents.   In doing so, they forget what the Organization has achieved and can achieve, through its activities regarding conflicts, but which, unless solved or localized, might widen the bloc conflicts and seriously aggravate them.   Thus the Organization in fact also exercises a most important, though indirect, influence on the conflicts between the power blocs by preventing the widening of the geographical and political area covered by these conflicts and by providing for solutions whenever the interests of all parties in a localization of conflict can be mobilized in favour of its efforts.

The Organization in this way also makes a significant contribution in the direction of an ultimate solution of the differences between the power blocs, as it is obvious that it is a condition for an improvement in the situation that the area to which those differences apply, as a minimum requirement, is not permitted to expand and, so far as possible, is reduced.

It is with this background that the initiative for United Nations intervention in the Congo conflict was taken under Article 99 of the Charter, for the first time applied fully, according to its letter and in the spirit in which it must have been drafted.   It is also in this light that one has to view the fact that not only the first but also the subsequent decisions in the

Security Council regarding the Congo have been taken by votes in which the power bloc conflicts have not been reflected.

*   *   *

James P. Sewell

KEEPING THE PEACE: SOVIET AND AMERICAN SECURITY POLICIES

*   *   *

This essay endeavors to interpret Soviet and American initiatives and United Nations outcomes in keeping the peace. Eventually the focus is "peacekeeping," which can be defined inductively as the dispatch of internationally authorized personnel from relatively disinterested third-party states to a holding action, physically or symbolically, between two belligerents who acquiesce in this arrangement and in the cease-fire necessary for its initiation and its continuation. "Preventive diplomacy," in its use by Dag Hammarskjöld, is a comparable notion which shares with peacekeeping the empirically unsubstantiated implication that open hostilities are thereby averted, not merely suspended. Though less exalted, "truce-keeping" more tellingly describes actual cases. Peacekeeping has not forestalled wars; wars have sometimes triggered peacekeeping.

Peacekeeping, a high United Nations official once remarked, lies between Chapters VI and VII of the United Nations Charter. . . . Peaceful settlement, or peacemaking, is the subject of Chapter VI; preventing war and enforcing peace is the declared purpose of Chapter VII.

Peacekeeping outcomes are more modest than those expected from either Chapter VI peacemaking or Chapter VII peace maintenance. Peacekeeping is directed into a situation of conflict in order to freeze it or keep it frozen, quite possibly along lines of a forcibly revised *status quo,* whereas in principle peacemaking would yield a lasting political settlement demanding no continued third-party activity between disputants, and Chapter VII sanctions would either deter entirely or reverse gains resulting from a threat, breach, or act of aggression against the *status quo.*

Like peacemaking, peacekeeping conjures up a vision of third-party

Reprinted in abridged form by permission of New York University Press from Alvin Z. Rubinstein and George Ginsburg, eds., *Soviet and American Policies in the United Nations* (New York: New York University Press, 1971), pp. 125–163. © 1971 by New York University.

mediation between two antagonistic parties.   A continuum of U.N.-sanctioned forcefulness might establish peacekeeping (with peacemaking) at one extremity, peace maintenance or enforcement at the other.   Actual cases would then range from virtually figurative or token peacekeeping instances such as U.N. "presences" and perfunctory individual investigation of complaints, through observation corpsmen, passively interpositioned forces, and more active policing of temporary agreements or even of volatile situations as such, then on to forcible application af a U.N. judgment upon a duly found aggressor.   In the same direction across this continuum the perceived third-party attributes of "U.N." action fade and disappear.   The Secretary-General's personal representative as U.N. presence is apt generally to be regarded as disinterested in the best sense of that word; Secretary-General-directed peacekeeping contingents, such as those in the Congo, are more suspect in the eyes of some U.N. participants, if only because their presence as such tips the scales in someone's favor; the Secretary-General-anointed Korean operation was a second-party action supporting one of two belligerents, the putative innocent.

It is no great exaggeration to state that the first quarter century of United Nations security featured actions undertaken by governments outside the U.N.; ex parte enforcement precipitating a façade of collective legitimation; a series of largely unsuccessful attempts at peacemaking; and a few varied peacekeeping operations shaped by the expectations acknowledged above and other constraints surveyed below.

I

No concern among wartime United States policy makers bent on transforming the United Nations from an alliance into a postwar international security organization outweighed the resolve that World War III must not be allowed to happen.   This resolve was shared by the American people. Alongside the commitment to peace, however, operated a domestic political premise.   After the war, Franklin Roosevelt and various other public figures believed, Americans would not abide continuing international commitments if these demanded stationing their boys across the oceans and shouldering heavy military tax burdens at home. . . . Growing overseas military commitments, especially from the late nineteen-forties to the present, seem to belie one of the initial premises.   Peacekeeping and other security developments must be seen against the background of these stable and shifting assumptions.

Peace on the cheap, or "effortless security" in Eugene Rostow's phrase, was hardly a new political problem for American leadership.   Collective security, championed by Woodrow Wilson, offered an alluring formula for international society to avoid war without depriving states of their sovereign autonomy.   The surety of collective action by all on behalf of any one victim against any other transgressor would restrain or if necessary repel acts violating the victors' armistice settlement. Before and after such an exceptional mobilization of the multinational fire brigade . . . national life would go on much as always. Collective security was a scheme with apparent gains for everyone and no evident costs for anyone.

During World War II, however, the notion of collective security in effect underwent severe practical modification. Disarmament as a complement to collective security did not receive the attention in United Nations' blueprints for permanent peace that it had had during the League of Nations era. While the public advent of the atomic bomb following the San Francisco conference of 1945 caused some rethinking, the management of force, not the elimination of forcible implements, remained the operative premise—protestations later rising from a politics of disarmament notwithstanding. Force for enforcement in United States planning now assumed a kinetic quality superseding the potential energy implicit during bygone days when a vision of polyglot minutemen, responsive if called but otherwise engrossed in normal peacetime activities, held sway. More important, this force-in-being was to be managed, singly or jointly, by the powerful leaders of a prevailing grand alliance of United Nations.

The United States would, in wartime prevision and in fact, emerge as the strongest of the victors. Great Britain, her war-precipitated weaknesses momentarily hidden from American and Soviet discernment by lion-hearted Churchillian posturing, was taken as a second pillar of the new framework of international security. Britain was foreseen initially as a stout ally in peace as in war, an ally strong enough to carry sustained responsibility for stability in much of the world. . . . The Soviet Union was apprehended as the third pillar necessary for any lasting peace. Maintaining an Anglo-American alliance with the Soviet Union in order to defeat all the Axis powers and preserve the ensuing settlement constituted a major priority of American and British wartime diplomacy. China was conceived by Roosevelt as a promising check, with American support, against Japanese resurgence; Churchill and Stalin tolerated what they considered a harmless illusion. These powers would become FDR's "Four Policemen." France was later included as a mainstay in United Nations' security designs, partly at the behest of the British.

In official United States expectations, then, the emergent great powers would prevent World War III by enforcing the peace they would establish —and the American contribution to this enforced peace would consist not of American boys stationed indefinitely abroad but of highly mobile, widely based naval and air units capable of deterring or suppressing threats and breaches. . . .

Soviet assumptions about security in the postwar world differed in important respects, although certain early expectations seem remarkably similar to those of U.S. planners. While Americans were inclined to treat peace as a normal condition whose disruption by aberrant war might thenceforth be prevented by inventing the right devices or merely by setting up known mechanisms, Soviet theory regarded struggle at all social levels as the natural state of mankind in each historic phase short of a distant and undefined human destiny.   On the other hand, wartime circumstances presented common Axis foes and suggested a dire menace to future Soviet security; no immediate Allied disagreements arose over whose aggressions the United Nations were meant to frustrate.   Rather like U.S. planners, although drawing different inferences, the Soviets initially saw Japanese and particularly German threats offset by a preponderant armed concert of the Allied powers.

Gazing backward, no single guiding conception of the postwar world appears to explain the actions either of American or Soviet policy makers. . . .

Spheres of influence explain more than designs for global hegemony when approaching the evolution of United Nations peacekeeping.   No doubt many Americans find distasteful the thought of an extra-national expanse . . . over which a great power stands ascendant, whether such a sphere of influence be Soviet or other.   But however odious the idea and however tacit or even confused any early Soviet-Anglo-American understandings on its application, a number of subsequent events are illuminated by viewing them as phenomena that occur either within or outside a domain or preserve effectively overseen by the Soviet Union or the United States.

That this notion was not alien to all American founding fathers of the United Nations security scheme is apparent from contemporary records. . . .

. . . "I think," said Secretary of War Henry Stimson to his assistant John McCloy, "that it's not asking too much to have our little region over here which never has bothered anybody."   Since the Soviet Union was establishing just such a realm in Eastern Europe, it would be in no position to object.   Without disagreeing on implications for the Western Hemisphere, McCloy urged more flexibility elsewhere: "We ought to have our cake and eat it too; . . . we ought to be free to operate under this regional arrangement in South America, at the same time intervene promptly in Europe; . . . we oughtn't to give away either asset."

Roosevelt's exchange with Stalin at Teheran over a United Nations framework for postwar security suggests how, at one point in time, the American leader dealt with (or failed to deal with) the tricky relationship between his Four Policemen plan and great-power spheres of influence. Churchill had favored regional councils or committees for Europe, the Far East, and the Americas, a proposal that Stalin also liked.   While pressing his own argument for a concert of great powers capable of acting anywhere, if necessary, to crush even a major peacebreaker, FDR was asked if this meant that American troops would be sent overseas. The President immediately balked.   Roosevelt admitted that in the event of another threat to Europe and a nonproductive ultimatum to the aggressor, he foresaw only the possibility of U.S. naval and air detachments to support British and Soviet ground forces.

Euphemisms render more palatable or more obscure the facts of global condominium.   Around the Soviet Union, earlier "safety zones" have ripened into a "Socialist commonwealth."   In the West, "collective self-defense" arrangements (nominally obliged to U.N. Charter Article 51) may disintegrate but "regionalism" and what President Nixon calls "preventive diplomacy" among governments and regimes goes on.   Scholars discern a "tight bipolar" international system which loosens as the imperial realms of two lesser great powers, and of other traditional colonialists, break off into nonaligned statehood.

Finally, on the significance for maintaining peace accorded a permanent organization of the United Nations, official spokesmen for the United States and the Soviet Union initially took positions not far apart.   For both, from the outset, a United Nations organization was secondary as a means to security.

A United Nations organization was secondary in the sense that its writ would enter into practical effect only after a passage of time.   After the postwar *status quo* had jelled, U.S. policy makers foresaw, the United Nations as an organization might become a useful operative agent in maintaining peace.   On the face of the matter, similarly, there is no indication that Soviet planners wished an enforcement-fitted U.N. before peacetime lines came into being. . . .

Even when fully established as an instrumentality in keeping the peace, the organization was expected by both Americans and Soviets to remain limited as to the scope of action authorized by the United Nations. . . . Article 33, introducing Chapter VI on peaceful settlement, invites disputants to "seek a solution" first *themselves;* Article 52(2) enjoins Members to try "regional arrangements" before trying the Security Council. It is difficult to escape an inference that by its three founding powers the United Nations organization was meant to serve as a forum of last resort.

*   *   *

In no way was Soviet-American mutuality on U.N. limitations more evident than in establishing the Security Council great-power unanimity rule, or "veto."

The unanimity requirement appeared to many as merely a frank admission that no effective collective action could be taken by the United Nations without the agreement of all the great powers.   This, of course, was true, as far as it went.   However, to Roosevelt, Churchill, and Stalin—and, to a lesser extent, even to such men as Stettinius and Hull—the concept went further than that.   They felt not only that the Organization *could not* act without great power unanimity but also that the Organization *should not try* to act when unity was lacking.[1]

In a similar vein Stalin concluded: "Can one trust that the role of the United Nations will be sufficiently effective? . . . It will be effective if the Great Powers that carried on their shoulders the main burden of war against Hitlerite Germany will act afterward in a spirit of unity and collaboration. It will not be effective if this necessary condition is absent." [2] And in his diary Arthur Vandenberg, Republican U.S. Senator from Michigan, confided that what struck him about the American position prepared for Dumbarton Oaks was its conservatism "from a nationalist standpoint. It is based virtually on a four-power alliance. . . . and no action looking toward the use of force can be taken if any one of the Big Four dissents. [Cordell] Hull's whole theory is that there must be continued agreement between the Big Four or the postwar world will smash anyway. Also, to his credit, he recognizes that the United States will never permit itself to be ordered into war against its own consent." [3]

*   *   *

If expansion was the Soviet . . . key to postwar security, kinetic force was in American planning the chief device to guarantee peace. Should it later prove possible to negotiate terms under which nuclear-capable American forces would stand ready to engage in collective enforcement operations with other United Nations' troops, this would of course be a welcome outcome from every standpoint. If not, or at least in the interim, the United States Navy, Air Force, and mobile ground forces would be prepared for action jointly with the British, with others, or if it came to that, alone. Domestic proposals for United Nations enforcement were joined by other proposals for United States enforcement, with or without others' assistance. . . . During the same period Senator Harry Truman scored the Republican platform as "ambiguous" and called upon his own party to pledge "that the United States will take part in world affairs this time and maintain the peace by using the Army and Navy, if necessary." [4]

*   *   *

II

The shifting postwar international system, profoundly shaped by the objectives and means of the two superpowers and by the existing character and degree of tension between them, has in turn conditioned govern-

[1] L. D. Weiler & A. O. Simons, *The United States and the United Nations,* New York: Manhattan, 1967, p. 40.

[2] Quoted from S. B. Krylov, *The History of the Founding of the United Nations* (Moscow, 1960), by A. Ulam, *Expansion and Coexistence,* New York: Praeger, 1969, p. 412.

[3] Weiler and Simons, *op. cit.,* p. 32.

[4] Quoted in Robert A. Divine, *Second Chance,* New York: Atheneum, 1967, p. 212.

ments' strategic choices of the United Nations or alternative channels, their tactics in getting those things they want and avoiding those things they do not want through the United Nations, and outcomes from the interplay of these policies. While most Soviet and American assumptions manifested during the U.N.'s origins remain surprisingly stable throughout this quarter century, subsequent events and developments have contributed to changes in relationships among the organization's members and to certain innovations, notably peacekeeping, in the ubiquitous yet often mutually self-denying national quest for security internationally. Given the incipient organization's tangential relationship to Soviet and American designs for their security in the postwar world, it is hardly illogical that the United Nations has since its founding counted for relatively little in keeping the peace. In mitigating war the U.N. has not, however, been altogether negligible.

The United Nations organization as an available security instrumentality soon received even lower priority in the strategic policies of both superpowers. Soviet control of "buffer" areas to its west and elsewhere, and especially the *de facto* dismemberment of Germany, lessened the officially defined value to the U.S.S.R. of any further great-power security agreements through United Nations auspices. Hence Soviet expansion, in this respect as well as because of its impact upon the United States and other Western Governments, lowered the probability of such agreements. Soviet intentions for Iran, intimated earlier to the Americans, were thereafter rebuffed, in part by exposure in the Security Council. The Greek civil war—initially brought to the same forum by the Soviets, along with the Greek regime, on the former's demand that British troops be withdrawn—was in Western media treated as directed from Moscow. Russia's great-power allies thwarted her claim to Libya and to warm water access, an historic push. While containment of Soviet expansion had already begun, Russian security demands vis-à-vis Germany, reckoned the gravest threat, were in process of fulfillment without necessity of the United Nations.

Britain's weakness from the war, so openly demonstrated by the Labour Government's leadership, softened Anglo-American discord over the future of Britain's imperial estates. Churchill's "iron curtain" speech of 1946, the frantic American assumption of what one participant later called "the job of world leadership . . . with all its burdens and all its glory" [5] by way of U.S. aid to Greece and Turkey, and British determination, in Truman's view, "to wash their hands of the whole matter" of Palestine,[6] were landmarks along the way to hardened lines between two antagonistic global powers. Collective self-defense arrangements such as NATO and the Warsaw Treaty Organization would subsequently confirm

[5] Joseph M. Jones, *The Fifteen Weeks,* New York: Viking, 1955, p. 7.

[6] Harry S Truman, *Memoirs,* New York: Doubleday, 1956, v. II, p. 157.

the tendency to bipolarity and the growing resort to alternative modes rather than the U.N. for concerting, or legitimizing, security policies.

This was the setting for negotiations on national "armed forces" to stand in readiness for Security Council/Military Staff Committee disposal in case of United Nations "action with respect to threats to the peace, breaches of the peace, and acts of aggression." With success, one or more "special agreements" would have allowed Charter Article 43 implementation to end the security transition envisaged in Article 106. The talks failed. Probably neither the Soviet nor American representatives badly wanted military contingents available to the United Nations, though neither wished the public onus for failure. Mutual suspicions were further aroused by the United States and U.S.S.R. proposals and in turn by their rejection.

*   *   *

Force level proposals implied the purposes to which peace maintenance operations might be devoted. Inis Claude observes that "the United States was curiously unwilling to recognize the fact that the terms of reference of the projected international force excluded the possibility of its being used, and therefore the necessity of its being usable, for the purpose of taking enforcement action against major powers. In view of the fact that United States officials had previously recognized and accepted —indeed, insisted upon—this restriction of the organization's capability, it was extraordinary to find a United States spokesman arguing that the Security Council should be equipped to 'bring to bear, against any breach of the peace anywhere in the world, balanced striking forces drawn from the most powerful and best equipped forces that could be provided by the Members,' so that the United Nations could 'enforce peace in all parts of the world.' " [7] . . .

As to the composition of forces, the Soviet Union insisted upon equal or identical national contingents, while the United States, United Kingdom, France, and China urged comparable forces supplied in accordance with the special military strengths of each participant. The nuclear-capable United States joined by Britain and China and, insofar as this bore upon deterrence of a rejuvenated and vengeful Germany, by France, favored forces poised around the world for swift reprisal; the Soviet Union adamantly opposed this, contending they should remain at home unless called. . . .

The Soviets, Claude concludes,

feared that an authorization for the stationing of United Nations contingents on foreign bases would provide ideological cover to encircle the Soviet Union. They suspected that the Western powers sought a provision permitting one

[7] Inis Claude, "United Nations and the Use of Force," *International Conciliation,* March, 1961, pp. 349–350.

state to assist others in equipping the contingents assigned to the Security Council in order to gain "an opportunity to influence the policies of these States and thus to occupy a dominant position with regard to the armed forces to be placed at the disposal of the Security Council." Their insistence upon establishing a more rigid rule than the Western powers wished regarding the withdrawal of United Nations forces reflected the suspicion that the West sought to gain "a pretext for the continuous presence of foreign troops in territories of other States." [8]

On the other hand, some Americans suspected that the Soviet plan, if accepted, would (as one observer expressed it) "preclude the possibility of United States forces ever being employed by the Security Council outside the Western Hemisphere." [9]

U.N. Secretary-General Trygve Lie attempted to establish a small emergency "United Nations land force" for violence-ridden Palestine on the limited great-power consensus. Both the American and British Governments, whom he had approached privately, turned him down. Thus ended serious efforts, at least during the U.N.'s first twenty-five years, to create Article 43 agreements conceived variously as the "heart" or the "teeth" of United Nations maintenance of international peace and security.

It was not, however, the end of political contrivance. Unrequited if shy attempts at peacemaking led to continuing U.N. presences in troubled areas beyond the superpowers' spheres of influence, often in decolonizing areas. The Middle East, the Indian subcontinent, and what might be called the Greater Archipelago of Indonesia all contributed to the art of settling for the readily possible. From touring field missions staffed and financed by U.N. member governments—sometimes national representatives already on the scene—these presences gradually came to include U.N. secretariat personnel and persons answering to the U.N. Secretary-General whose extended field duty was financially underwritten at least in part through the United Nations. . . .

Often these initiatives emanated from the secretariat or from various middle powers. Almost invariably American representatives welcomed and supported them. "Executive capacity" or, in Dag Hammarskjöld's phrase, the U.N. as "dynamic instrument" was a cherished American aim, especially during the years of clear-cut U.S. dominance. By now the Soviet veto had become the standard explanation of U.N. impotence to an American public always more prepared than its elected representatives to bank on this last best hope for peace. It was the United States, not the Soviet Union, that had remained true to United Nations ideals. . . . For Americans the U.N. was an idealized alter ego, and if "it" had thus far not lived up to the faith therein invested, "it" had at least not yet turned

[8] Inis Claude, *ibid.,* p. 353.

[9] Joseph E. Johnson, "The Soviet Union, the United States, and International Security," *International Organization,* February, 1949, as quoted in Weiler and Simons, *op. cit.,* p. 132.

against its master.   To expand the authority of the Secretary-General and General Assembly was to strengthen the United Nations in much the same pragmatic fashion the political system of the United States had developed.   From the Government's shorter-run standpoint, the U.N. was a bully rostrum to impress upon American constituents its vigilance against Communist encroachment and a handy dumping-ground for issues domestically too hot to handle.

For the same objective reasons the institutional inventions added to conventional U.N. diplomatic auspices were anathema to Soviet officialdom. . . . The secretariat appeared to be stacked against the Soviets. Russian nationals were cut out of the internal communications networks on political matters.   A "mechanical majority" delivered General Assembly legitimacy, for what that was worth in Soviet eyes, to United States policy, and the Interim Committee threatened to become even more pernicious to defined Soviet interests.   Field personnel for U.N. presences were generally drawn from North America and Western Europe, not from the Soviet sphere. . . .

Yet the Soviets acquiesced in measures they could not stop by voicing strict constructionist views of the Charter.   When they felt the appropriateness of the tactic, like others from time immemorial to the present, they walked out.

The Korean episode, so often told, retold, and reinterpreted, was at once a logical extension of these tendencies and a sharp break.   [Secretary-General Trygve] Lie banished any doubts that may have remained about his activism—or, in Soviet perspectives, his "neutrality."   Some months after the military operation had been mounted, "Uniting for Peace" capped the effort to remodel the General Assembly as a security organ.   And a "United Nations" field presence had reached new magnitudes.   But substituting massive force for benign observation, itself a departure, set in motion other developments as well.

Most obviously, it reaffirmed with a vengeance to the Soviet Union that there was no safety in dropping out of United Nations participation, even as a gesture.   Later, as the approach of the American/United Nations forces toward the Yalu River triggered restiveness by the representative of India and other . . . members . . . , the Assembly arena's potential for influencing the governments of politically independent new United Nations members began to enter into Soviet estimates.   Two years after Stalin's death, with a package deal leading to sixteen new memberships, the Assembly as a forum attended by Asians and others became even more inviting; with subsequent African admissions its prominence for Soviet purposes would rise even higher.   The two-camp thesis yielded to a thesis of two camps plus.

*   *   *

III

The golden years of peacekeeping, in the sense of ersatz arrangements that fall within the definition offered early in this essay, were those of Dwight Eisenhower's Presidency and Dag Hammarskjöld's Secretary-Generalship. This period coincided with growing Soviet confidence, sparked by Sputnik and by successful testing of intercontinental ballistic missiles and represented by Nikita Khrushchev's claim of a shift in the correlation of world forces. But the Soviet part in U.N. peacekeeping was essentially reactive, and as catalytic policy makers neither the leader of the other superpower nor the new U.N. Secretary-General initially played a role as important as did Britain and France.

Despite growing symptoms during 1956 of another eruption in the Middle East, the Eisenhower Administration failed to act in ways other than those that hastened the explosion. "I really don't know how much we can do," said Secretary of State Dulles to Emmet John Hughes early in September. "Every day that goes by without some outbreak is a gain, and I just keep trying to buy that day. I don't know anything to do but keep improvising." [10] . . .

The Israeli attack mobilized U.S. leadership to hand-wringing and to invocation of the United Nations. A Security Council draft resolution demanding an immediate cease-fire and withdrawal of Israeli troops was rejected by the twin negatives of Britain and France. French and British air strikes hit Egyptian airfields. . . .

. . . Called to emergency session by the United States among others, the Assembly endorsed a cease-fire and authorized steps by the Secretary-General to secure and supervise it. Lester Pearson of Canada, solicitous of Britain and perhaps of France and Israel, was a prime mover on behalf of an international corps, later christened the United Nations Emergency Force (UNEF). "We have to get them off the hook," he said.[11] Reversing the anticipations of great-power action expressed by U.N. founders, Pearson urged that UNEF be composed of units from middle and smaller states. In these steps U.S. policy makers willingly concurred. Ten states volunteered troops numbering up to 6,000 at one point; these patrolled on Egyptian territory, though not in Israel, until ordered out by Nasser in 1967.

Consequences of the . . . events of 1956 are almost imponderable for subsequent Franco-Anglo-American relations, for Soviet influence in the Middle East, and for decolonization. The bitterness already felt toward United Nations "meddling" in British and French affairs was compounded by the experience and by these Governments' tendencies to blame the

[10] Hughes, *Ordeal of Power,* New York: Atheneum, 1953, pp. 177–178.

[11] Andrew Boyd, *United Nations: Piety, Myth and Truth,* Baltimore: Penguin, 1964, pp. 105–106.

U.N., rather than the United States or other U.N. members, for "its" blundering intervention.   But given the train of events leading through October 1956, the outcome could have been far worse for all hands without interposed U.N. peacekeepers.

Until the muffled American outrage at Franco-British intervention . . . the United States was by Soviet proclamation the chief villain in these pieces.   Noteworthy shifts in Soviet tactics occurred. . . .

In August and September the United States was castigated as the leader of an attempt to reinstate imperialism through an international administration of the Canal and an Association of Suez Canal Users to pressure Egypt into concessions by threatening a Canal boycott.   The Republican administration, it was maintained, wished support from American oil companies in the coming election; the prospect of a Canal boycott would delight them, and if it were actually effected, foreign oil sales financed from borrowed dollars would enslave purchasers.

By mid-October Soviet observers had detected "sharp contradictions . . . between the Western partners" on whether to try "new tactical methods of implementing the old policies." [12]   The brazen behavior of the British and French in Egypt—and in the Security Council—called for extraordinary measures: "Since Britain and France have sabotaged the work of the Security Council the responsibility for solving the problem rests with an emergency session of the U.N. *General Assembly*.   [Emphasis added.]"   "The situation in Egypt requires immediate and vigorous action by the United States," wrote Bulganin to Eisenhower; "If such action is not taken, the U.N. will lose its prestige in the eyes of all mankind and will thus collapse."   The Soviets suggested that the United States and the U.S.S.R. combine military operations to secure the withdrawal of the British and French.   Bulganin upbraided Ben-Gurion for taking retaliation into his own hands rather than using U.N. channels.

Within a few weeks the United States again was first on the Soviet firing line.   The United States vote in the Assembly was held to be hypocritical because it did not back specific steps to achieve Anglo-French withdrawal. Egyptians were warned that the Americans intended to use UNEF to aid implementation of U.S. schemes.   Later the Americans were accused of just this.   Meanwhile the Soviet Union, which had joined so eagerly in Assembly attempts to resolve the immediate crisis, subsequently refused to share the financial burdens of UNEF.

Suez can stand as a bench mark against which to compare peacekeeping continuity and change in the subsequent period.   Hammarskjöld quickly set about enunciating a doctrine of filling dangerous vacuums and elaborating a series of multiple-purpose precedents.   United Nations peace forces became a favored topic in discussions of the Lebanon, the Congo, Yemen, Cyprus, and the renewal of overt hostilities between India and

[12] G. Ratiani, "New Threats Against Egypt," *Pravda,* October 18, 1956.

Pakistan offered opportunities to put some of these ideas to work, though invariably on an *ad hoc* basis underpinned by fragile consent and tentative acquiescence.

*   *   *

Like their original responses to the Suez episode, Soviet and American reactions to the Congo incidents of July 1960 moved both Governments toward early endorsement of intervention underwritten by the U.N. Eisenhower turned down a Congolese invitation for U.S. military assistance, urging instead an appeal to the U.N. Both Kasavubu and Lumumba promptly initiated such requests. The Soviets, with the Americans, backed Security Council resolutions in July and August leading to the establishment of the U.N. Operation in the Congo (ONUC) (Opération de Nations Unies au Congo).

But Soviet-American agreement on the uses of United Nations instrumentalities soon proved illusory. Unlike Suez, which temporarily shifted the focus of both Governments to the forcible intervention of others, the Congo vacuum rapidly drew attention to the moves and motives of the rival superpowers. Each originally deemed U.N. action "the least costly way to prevent the other from realizing its objectives," [13] perceived as the establishment of itself or its system in the heart of Africa. Thus, in the absence of congruent objectives, if not inevitably because of mutual suspicion, only one of the two could regard outcomes with equanimity.

The confused Congo situation contributed to a growing Soviet-American rift over U.N. action. Though UNEF peacekeepers patrolled Middle East cease-fire lines, ONUC peacekeepers found no Congolese peace to be kept. Efforts to make such a peace, or for that matter simply to fashion a truce, unavoidably favored certain Congolese and international participants over others. Even when Soviet and American aims apparently converged, as for instance upon the continuation or restoration of a Katanga integral to the Congo, the complexities of implementation led to new accusations regarding the partiality of the U.N. Secretary-General and those under his direction.

Political opposition buffeted both American and Soviet policy makers. Official France and Britain, lobbyists for Belgian and other financial interests, and U.S. Senator Thomas Dodd, the "Ambassador to Katanga," among others, bedeviled those in the Eisenhower and Kennedy administrations who wanted a strong U.N. stance. Soviet officials sought to heed both the sensitivities of emerging Africans (themselves of divided counsel) and, from another quarter, attacks from the Chinese People's Republic. The Soviet spokesman time and again demonstrated his distress that a draft United Nations directive failed to excoriate the capitalist-imperialist aggressors. . . .

---

[13] Ernest W. Lefever, "The Limits of U.N. Intervention in the Third World," *Review of Politics,* Jan. 1968, reprint p. 4.

Without question United Nations auspices served United States objectives in the Congo, as officially defined, more than those of the U.S.S.R. —over the short run.   In the words of Jonathan Bingham, then an American representative at the U.N., this operation was "a notable example of a situation where the policy and actions of the United Nations have been generally in accord with our thinking, while the Soviet view has been consistently overriden." [14]   If certain premises are accepted, the Congo today likewise suggests that the United States got the better of the Soviet Union through ONUC and its diplomatic and logistic context. . . .   But some Americans are wondering whether military regimes such as that of General Mobutu are the best achievable outcomes of United Nations or any alternative intervention.

In other respects, too, the returns are incomplete.   While the Soviets failed in their troika *démarche,* they have apparently succeeded in making a successor Secretary-General yet more circumspect about U.N. security measures than he might otherwise have proved.   The Congo denouement further served to restrict the General Assembly as a feasible avenue to internationally legitimated intervention, and American postures, approximating the standard Soviet position, seem increasingly to face away from this plenary arena.

Most visibly to Americans, the Congo expedition saddled the United Nations with a large financial deficit.   ONUC costs about $10 million per month compared to UNEF's $1.5 million.   At mission's end in 1964, ONUC's bill totaled $411 million.   The Soviet Union refused to support either "illegal" operation, and U.S. efforts to force the issue, besides failing to change the Soviets' stand, have probably served to make other U.N. members more reluctant to endorse potentially costly peacekeeping without strict procedures which would assure the active consent of all great powers represented in the Security Council.   Subsequent peacekeeping operations have reflected this new awareness.

Thus, the Yemen observation mission was authorized by the Security Council and financed by "parties at interest."   Both were points Soviet representatives had long pressed.   In the field UNYOM achieved a very limited success. . . .

Cyprus' troubles aroused Soviet concern that the Mediterranean island was earmarked for service as the base for a NATO multilateral force (MLF) equipped with nuclear weapons.   Since this NATO plan has been abandoned, Soviet fears seemingly have subsided.   UNFICYP is subject to frequent Security Council reauthorization and to voluntary financial support. Criticized for not joining in this financial support, a Soviet spokesman reportedly responded that the U.S.S.R. contribution consists of allowing the West to utilize the U.N. so as to avoid embarrassment.   The "occupiers," as the Soviets call them, include, along with the peripatetic

[14] *New York Times Magazine,* September 16, 1962, p. 86.

Scandinavians and Canadians, observers from a permanent Security Council member—Britain.   Soviet officials show little interest in closer involvement, and with the relative isolation of Cypriot from Greek-Turkish affairs—for the moment, at least—American officials likewise are less intimately engaged.   Quiet talks have occurred between individual representatives of the Greek and Turkish communities, and UNFICYP has been reduced somewhat in size, but to date the political situation remains unsettled and murky.

For a better understanding of Soviet and American policies and United Nations peacekeeping during this period, several noncases are also pertinent.   Guatemala and Hungary in the fifties and the Dominican Republic and Czechoslovakia in the sixties further illuminate the unwritten spheres-of-influence and no-man's land substratum of contemporary peacekeeping.   Each protest of superpower intervention reached a United Nations forum.   The latter two were adorned by some of the trappings, if not the substance, of collective legitimacy.   All four interventions provided the cold war opposition with some big moments before friendly media. Yet none occasioned serious resistance by the other superpower.   Regarding the Hungarian revolution, for instance, Dulles transmitted a clear message to the Soviets that the United States would not intervene. . . .

IV

Two major objectives, one short and one longer in range, have informed authoritative U.S. postures in peacekeeping situations: (*a*) stop Communism; (*b*) establish stable (i.e., Communist-resistant) systems.   Other objectives, such as economic benefit (or avoidance of economic loss) and amicable relations with governments who feel strongly about particular controversies, are secondary to the extent they are not subsumed beneath the first and second objectives. Setbacks on economic matters and the disgruntlement of friendly governments may have uncomfortable repercussions, but losses to Communism lead to electoral defeat and retirement to private penitence and public obloquy, if not to the spread of the Red scourge over this and planets yet uncontested.

"The minimum aim of Soviet United Nations policy," writes William Kintner, "is to identify the Soviet Union with the 'wave of the future' and the hopes of underdeveloped countries and to paralyze action in the United Nations unless it furthers Soviet objectives." [15]   Obstruction, however, must be weighed against the possibility that the aborted U.N. action would on balance have proved preferable to action mounted beyond Soviet-neutralist surveillance.   Beyond survival and security within an expanded realm, the Soviets seek to extend their influence and ways (Russian culture as well as

[15] "The United Nations Record of Handling Major Disputes," in Gross, ed., *The United States and the United Nations,* Norman: Oklahoma University, 1964, p. 122.

Socialism) through all available means, including United Nations activities that promise net gains. . . .

Whether the Soviet Union or the United States has benefited more from United Nations peacekeeping operations and their side effects, on the assumption that both do not gain equally, must remain a question partly unanswered. Two summary evaluations can serve as boundary judgments for any such assessment. According to William Kintner, "American power has often been neutralized in United Nations disputes, whereas Soviet power has been rendered effective beyond its normal reach." [16] Conor Cruise O'Brien, to the contrary, maintains that the "major decisions of the United Nations on Iran, on Palestine, on Korea, on keeping China out of the United Nations and keeping Formosa [sic] in China's Security Council seat, on Suez, on Hungary and on the Congo have one thing in common: they were all in line with United States . . . policy. . . ." [17] Immediate outcomes, at least, have thus far generally favored U.S. preferences. The absence of global conflagration benefits both leading protagonists, though the exact contribution of peacekeeping firebreaks to this status is disputable. Future peacekeeping proposals are likely to appear palpably beneficial to both American and Soviet leadership—the latter bearing a higher threshold of skepticism—or else fail to achieve U.N. sanction beyond that accorded the volunteer peacekeepers and facultative finance characterizing recent instances.

* * *

Political hostility between the superpowers has meant failure to date on the original, and still the soundest, Charter foundation for a broad range of security measures in keeping the peace. However, the use of lesser power field personnel, an achievement due more to the qualified forbearance than the policies of these two, is an innovation to be reckoned with if ever it is fitted to the political support implicit in piecemeal Soviet-American détente. With troubles along the Soviet and American peripheries of the global condominium, problems at home, a common recognition of the danger of accidental war, and premonitions of a Chinese People's Republic increasingly active upon the stages of the world, the international temperature may be right to forge understandings that will permit future peacekeeping engagements to be joined to negotiated political settlements instead of mutual recriminations and United Nations bankruptcy.

Past peacekeeping missions have been dispatched in lieu of genuine *rapprochement* among antagonists. Future missions may depend upon concurrent if embryonic political settlement. In the Middle East, for instance, blue berets are unlikely to find acceptance unless Israel relinquishes territory it occupied in 1967, and this, in turn, is unlikely to occur

[16] *Ibid.*, p. 121.
[17] Cruise O'Brien, Montague Burton Lecture at Leeds.

unless Arab governments extend to representatives of the Israeli people the recognition of that right to survive that is implicit in face-to-face negotiations.   The welfare of Palestinians likewise demands recognition. Given such auspicious circumstances, peacekeeping interposition would become more plausible though less important.   Without such circumstances, even peacekeeping along recognized boundaries seems impossible. . . .

If political composition with or without peacekeeping is to obtain, here as elsewhere Soviet-American symmetry in restraining local allies and in reminding them of their abiding interests is imperative.   Given sufficient concord on details and timing, the Security Council resolution of November 22, 1967, establishes an ample framework for lasting settlement, including demilitarized zones to guarantee "the territorial inviolability and political independence of every State in the area" and a Special Representative—Gunnar Jarring during the years following 1967—to facilitate mutual accommodation.

Is there a future for U.N. peacekeeping in Southeast Asia?   Short of containing Chinese influence, there would seem to be little Soviet incentive for a U.N. mission, though one might be tolerated under the formula of silent acquiescence and financial nonparticipation.   If it is true, as Bernard Gwertzman divines, that a central Soviet aim is "the isolation of the United States and the gradual erosion of its influence on the world scene," [18] continued American involvement in Indochina probably furthers this aim. Should the Nixon administration decide to initiate in this area the "spheres of restraint" . . . commended by Under Secretary of State Elliot Richardson—thereby terminating what the President has called the American role of "peacekeeper in the Asian world"—it might find, difficulties due to U.N. nonmembers notwithstanding, that United Nations peacekeeping can facilitate orderly extrication by absorbing some of the political liability for a redeployment of American forces.   Here too the lasting way is also the more difficult: serious negotiations by all interested parties leading to a political settlement.

[18] New York Times, May 13, 1970, p. 2.

David A. Kay

THE POLITICS OF DECOLONIZATION: NEW NATIONS IN THE U.N.

The fifteenth session of the General Assembly of the United Nations which convened in New York in September 1960 marked an important turning point in the history of the Organization. The United Nations had been created primarily through the efforts of states with a European or European-derived political and social culture possessing a common history of political involvement at the international level. During its first ten years the Organization was dominated by the problems and conflicts of these same states. However, by 1955 the process of decolonization which has marked the post-1945 political arena began to be reflected in the membership of the United Nations. In the ten years preceding the end of 1955 ten new nations devoid of experience in the contemporary international arena and struggling with the multitudinous problems of fashioning coherent national entities in the face of both internal and external pressures joined the Organization. By 1960 the rising tide of decolonization had reached flood crest with the entry in that one year of seventeen new Members—sixteen of which were from Africa.

The growth in the proportion of Members which have achieved independence since 1945 is impressive. Whereas in 1955 only 13.2 percent of United Nations Members fell in this category, by the end of 1966 this figure had leaped to 45 percent. Equally important in terms of their impact on the Organization was the fact that the size of the influx of new nations in 1960–1961 was largely unexpected as late as 1958.

Despite all the discernible distinctions between the new nations—and there are many—they possess a common core of characteristics that vitally affects their participation in the United Nations' political process. These new nations are generally ex-colonial, nonwhite—in the 1960 influx predominantly black—and possessed of a compelling desire to eradicate speedily the remaining bastions of European colonialism. Closely associated with their demands for an end to colonialism is their personal commitment to eradicating that variant of racialism which maintains white superiority over black. In terms of social and economic criteria many sectors of their societies are premodern, a fact that is only thinly disguised by the polite diplomatic euphemism "developing countries" which is currently in vogue to describe this aspect of their condition. In terms of the lodestar of post-1945 international relations, the East-West conflict, the preponderant majority of these new nations, with varying degrees of

Reprinted by special permission from *International Organization,* 21, 4 (Autumn 1967), 786–811. Copyright 1967, World Peace Foundation, Boston, Massachusetts.

consistency, attempt to follow the lesson of the African proverb, "when two elephants fight, it is the grass that suffers."

*   *   *

For the new nations the traditional concern of the United Nations with human rights has been but another vehicle for advancing their attack on colonialism and associated forms of racial discrimination. Traditionally, the promotion of human rights has been viewed from the perspective of protecting the citizens in the fullest possible exercise, compatible with organized society, of those rights which flow from the dignity and worth of the individual. For this perspective, centered as it is on the individual, the new nations have substituted a perspective centered on the evils of Western colonialism with its domination of black by white. . . .

The extent to which the new nations' concern with eliminating all vestiges of colonialism dominated the perspective from which they viewed the human rights activity of the Organization was pointedly demonstrated at the Assembly's seventeenth session. In preparation for the fifteenth anniversary in 1963 of the adoption of the Universal Declaration of Human Rights the United States joined with six other states at the seventeenth Assembly in requesting the Secretary-General to appoint a special committee to draft plans for the anniversary. During the Third (Social, Humanitarian, and Cultural) Committee's consideration of this draft Guinea, Mali, and Mauritania joined in offering an amendment expressing the hope

that all States will implement General Assembly resolution 1514 (XV) [Declaration on the Granting of Independence to Colonial Countries and Peoples] so that the fifteenth anniversary of the Universal Declaration of Human Rights may be celebrated in an atmosphere of independence and freedom.

For the new nations self-determination and national independence, rights of political groupings and not of individuals, head the list of human rights which the Organization should promote. This redefinition of the traditional individual-centered concept of human rghts has gained acceptance with the entry of the new nations into the Organization, and both the Third Committee and the Assembly adopted this amended version of the draft.

At the seventeenth session the Assembly approved a draft sponsored by 34 states requesting the Commission on Human Rights to prepare a draft declaration and a draft convention on the elimination of all forms of racial discrimination. Using the draft declaration prepared by the Commission as a basis for discussion, the eighteenth Assembly proceeded to draft the final text of the Declaration on the Elimination of All Forms of Racial Discrimination. During the course of the Third Committee's consideration of the draft Declaration three of the nine paragraphs were successfully amended by various new nations. One new paragraph each was added to the preamble and the operative paragraphs. The net effect of these successful maneuvers of the new nations was to impose a sense of stridency on the draft and sharpen its application to the remaining white colonial regimes of Africa and particularly South Africa.   It declared that

an end shall be put without delay to governmental and other public policies of racial segregation and especially policies of *apartheid,* as well as all forms of racial discrimination and separation resulting from such policies.

And finally, every state

shall fully and faithfully observe the provisions of the present Declaration, the Universal Declaration of Human Rights and the Declaration on the granting of independence to colonial countries and peoples.

With seventeen states abstaining the Third Committee approved the amended draft which the Assembly adopted unanimously.

In assessing the role played by the new nations on human rights questions [Louis] Henkin's appraisal seems sound.

The anticolonial atmosphere of the Assembly and the increasing and confident majorities of "new nations" led to the injection of anticolonial issues into the human rights covenants.   Self-determination was added to the roster of human rights as an additional weapon against colonialism although there was no suggestion that this was a right of the individual, that the individual could claim it against an unrepresentative government, or that minorities could invoke it to support secession. . . .   Human rights was being used as a political weapon against colonialism or economic imperialism, not to enhance the rights of all persons against all governments.[1]

A systematic analysis of the Assembly's voting record is a significant tool in measuring the success with which the new nations have wielded political influence on colonial issues.   Such an analysis is particularly well suited to determining publicly acknowledged shifts in positions and the number of battles won or lost.   For the purpose of this study 23 roll-call votes on colonial issues taken during the sixteenth, seventeenth, and eighteenth plenary sessions of the General Assembly have been selected for analysis.   Selection was based on the importance of the issues involved and was designed to provide as representative a grouping as possible. Where multiple votes, i.e., paragraph-by-paragraph votes, were taken on a draft, an attempt was made to select the vote which best represented the issue involved.   In general, the plenary vote was used in this analysis. However, in a few cases where the only roll-call vote on a draft resolution was in committee or where the committee vote reflected an element not present in the plenary vote the committee vote was selected.

One indication of the extent of influence exercised by the new nations on colonial issues can be provided by determining the extent of their concurrence with the United Nations majority on these issues.   While it is true that frequent concurrence with the majority cannot prove that effective

[1] *International Organization,* Vol. 19, No. 3, p. 513.

influence was exercised—it may only indicate a slavish following of the majority—the lack of such agreement wou'd demonstrate the absence of effectively applied influence. The certainty with which a high degree of concurrence with the majority can be used as one index of effectively applied political influence increases when the states concerned are found to have actively engaged in initiating and pushing the proposals voted upon. Such intimate involvement with the issues of parliamentary diplomacy is largely incompatible with a blind desire to be always on the winning side regardless of the merits of the question at stake. As the central focus of the diplomacy of the new nations in the United Nations colonialism certainly qualifies as an area in which they have been actively engaged. Thus, if it is found that the new nations have a high majority agreement voting score on the colonial questions analyzed, it would be at least presumptive evidence of the effective exercise of political influence on their part.

On those colonial votes analyzed for the sixteenth through the eighteenth sessions in which 50 percent or more of the new nations voted together they were in agreement with the Assembly majority on 87 percent of the votes. A majority of the new nations found it necessary to oppose the Assembly majority on only 4.3 percent of these votes and abstained on 8.7 percent of them. The two issues on which the majority of the new nations abstained were rejected by the Assembly. This majority agreement score is particularly impressive as an index of the effective exercise of political influence when it is noted that 91.3 percent of the votes were on items initiated and sponsored in whole or in part by the new nations. The possibility of servile fellowship yielding a specious index is considerably reduced by this intimate involvement with the issues.

*　　*　　*

However, the most striking fact revealed in this analysis is the extent to which it has become exceedingly unfashionable to oppose the anticolonial thrust of the new nations. While the majority of the Latin American nations supported the new nations on 76.2 percent of the 23 analyzed colonial votes, not once did a majority of the Latin American Members oppose the new nations on these issues. Even the Western European states have found the sanctuary of abstention more alluring than outright opposition to the new nations on colonial issues. On only 22.7 percent of the analyzed roll-call votes did a majority of the Western European states vote in opposition to the new nations. The extent to which states are unwilling to publicly record through the medium of a roll-call vote their opposition to the anticolonial measures advanced by the new nations in the United Nations is a convincing demonstration that at least with respect to this issue category the new nations have successfully used their political influence to delegitimize colonialism. It is no longer respectable or politic to vote against such measures, and the only prudent means of registering opposition in the Assembly has become abstention.

Certainly one element of the success of the new nations in regard to colonial issues is the cohesion of the group on this issue. Of the 23 votes analyzed for the sixteenth through the eighteenth sessions of the Assembly there are only six instances in which states voted in an opposite direction from that of the group and all six of these instances were on the two roll calls where a majority of the group abstained. On the other 21 votes there was not a single case of a state voting in the opposite direction from that of a majority. Even more impressive as an index of cohesion is the failure of any of the new nations to resort to abstention on any of the twelve votes from the seventeenth and eighteenth sessions. At least on colonial issues the new nations form a cohesive group that has an impressive record for initiating and obtaining the adoption of a wide range of anticolonial measures.

One must view as an outstanding achievement of the new nations their successful forging between 1960 and 1966 of an international moral consensus against the continuation of Western colonialism. By 1966 the impropriety of any defense of the continued existence of colonialism was apparent to all except the retrograde regimes of southern Africa. Within the United Nations itself the new nations succeeded during this period in making their own uppermost concern, colonialism, the uppermost concern of the Organization. At the behest of the new nations the Assembly has moved from general pronouncements of moral and legal rights, such as the 1960 Declaration on Colonialism, to condemnations of specific nations accompanied by requests for diplomatic and economic sanctions and threats of military sanctions. The Special Committee of Twenty-Four has maintained a constant surveillance of the remaining colonial areas while its anticolonial directorate has kept up a steady stream of reports and recommendations to other organs of the United Nations. As frustration grew over the recalcitrant attitude of the remaining colonial powers, the new nations sought Security Council endorsement of mandatory enforcement programs designed to eliminate these regimes. By the end of 1966 such sanctions had been adopted only with regard to Rhodesia, and in that case the precipitous action of the Rhodesian regime played a large role in forcing the Security Council to take such a course. The greatest success of the new nations' wielding of political influence during these years remained the success in shifting their concern and outlook on colonialism over to the Organization.

Much of the success of the new nations in effectively exercising political influence in the United Nations in the decolonization process is owed to a propitious world political situation. One product of the Cold War has been the creation of an environment in which either of the two major antagonists, the United States and the Soviet Union, views a gain in support for the other as a defeat for itself. This attitude on the part of these two Great Powers has been reflected in active campaigns on their part to cultivate the support of the new nations. This great-power competition for support provided the new nations with numerous opportunities to advance their interests by playing off the East and the West against each other. Well aware of the bargaining advantages offered by the circumstances of the Cold War, the new nations have not hesitated to employ this advantage to the fullest. Repeated warnings were issued by the new nations that the obstinate attitude of the West on colonial questions was rapidly diminishing its influence with these new states and aiding the East in its courting of these states.

Another advantageous aspect of the political situation facing the new nations during this period was that their major goal, the independence of the remaining colonial areas, was largely under the control of the West. Most of the Western nations were more sensitive to public pressure than many other states and also found the role of colonial master a profoundly disturbing one to play. Reinforcing the disquietude of the West over its role as colonial master were the remarkably successful indigenous nationalist movements which were threatening if not to evict the colonial powers at least to make their continued rule extremely expensive in both blood and treasure.

The extent to which the new nations were able to make their own perspective of the proper concerns of the Organization the perspective of the Organization itself decisively demonstrates its hyperdependency upon the Member States. At least at its present stage of development the United Nations is more an arena than an actor in the international scene. It provides a convenient forum for the assertion of conflicting national policies and demands and even in some instances for multilateral collaboration in the settlement of disputes. One consequence of the ease with which the dominant concern of the United Nations can be altered by a shift in the concern of a significant group of Member States or the entry of new Members is the disillusionment and bitterness that such shifts cause among the advocates of the previous dominant concern. Witness, for example, the melancholy remarks of the Earl of Home [2] upon the rise of decolonization as the major concern of the United Nations.

Resolutions have been persistently passed by the Assembly in particular on colonialism, which could only be described as reckless and careless of peace and security. Everyone has seen the chaos in the Congo and knows that it derives from a premature grant of independence to a country whose people were totally unprepared for their new responsibilities. Yet many Delegates were instructed by their Governments to sponsor and vote for resolutions which could only multiply and magnify that chaos in other places.

*   *   *

[2] British Foreign Secretary, 1960–1963; changed his name to Sir Alec Douglas-Home as prime minister, 1963–1964; became foreign secretary again in 1970. [Eds.] The speech below, given December 18, 1961, is reprinted in Raymond A. Moore, Jr. (ed.), *The United Nations Reconsidered*, Columbia: University of South Carolina Press, 1963, pp. 128–130.

Such a resolution [the Declaration on Colonialism] and others like it reveal an almost total lack of responsibility, and certainly pay no heed to the main purpose of the United Nations which is to ensure order and security of peace.

*   *   *

The severity of such resulting "crises of confidence" could perhaps be lessened if there were a general realization that at its present stage of development the United Nations is primarily an arena for the interaction of conflicting national policies. This is not to deny that it may perform valuable tasks in areas of peace and security, decolonization, or economic development but rather to argue for a realization that the performance of such tasks rests on the approval or acquiescence of the Member States and does not have a significant life apart from their attitudes. Thus, the shift after about 1955 in the primary emphasis of the Organization away from collective security and toward decolonization efforts is a natural result of its hyperdependency on the attitudes of the Member States.

In connection with this phenomenon it seems also to be a characteristic of United Nations politics that secondary concerns either are recast in terms similar to the predominant emphasis or else gradually atrophy. Thus, the traditional human rights activities of the Organization have lost their individual-oriented perspective and have become to a considerable extent only an adjunct to the decolonization struggle. On the other hand, collective security has ceased for the present to be a meaningful concern of the Organization. As is strikingly indicated in the activities of the new nations the politics of the United Nations is a politics of successive approximation toward goals involving a variable mix of private negotiations, public oratory, and voting. . . . Of course, compromise is the very heart of this political process of successive approximation. The compromises are intra- as well as inter-group accommodations and often involve issues remote from the immediate concern of the negotiations. Thus, the United States during the 1960's was forced to balance its support for its European allies in the military-political confrontation with the East against hoped-for influence with the new nations.

Inis L. Claude, Jr.

THE FUNCTIONAL APPROACH

* * *

The functional theory rests upon a very complex conception of the nature and causes of war, and promises a correspondingly elaborate set of results bearing upon the establishment and maintenance of peace. The basic assumptions and prescriptions of functionalism in regard to the problem of peace may be divided into three broad segments.

In the first place, war is regarded as the product of the objective conditions of human society. It is the result neither of man's native instinct nor of his acquired sinfulness, neither of the state's inherent nature nor of its irrational policy; war is a disease of global society, caused by grave deficiencies in the economic and social circumstances of mankind. Poverty, misery, ill-health, illiteracy, economic insecurity, social injustice, exploitation, discrimination—these are the factors which create the desperation, apathy, frustration, fear, cupidity, and hatred which make the world susceptible to war. This diagnosis owes much to the Marxian insistence upon the significance of material determinants for political conditions, but its popularity has not been confined to representatives of any particular school of thought. The notion that war is traceable to deep-seated causes in the economic and social realm has become part of the standard intellectual currency of the twentieth century.

Given this assumption, functionalism sets out to treat the basic ailments of mankind. It proposes to elevate living standards in backward areas, reduce the interference of national frontiers with the working of the complex global economy, minimize the factors that make for economic instability, and promote the attainment of higher levels of health, literacy, culture, and social justice. This is not merely a program for aiding the poor by enlisting the altruistic, or the enlightened selfish, assistance of the rich; much of the business of functionalism relates to the solution of problems which affect the most highly developed sector of the world, precisely because it is highly developed. Functionalism undertakes to grapple with the effects of both the excessive primitiveness of underdeveloped regions and the excessive intricacy of economic and social relationships in the intensely industrialized parts of the world. Thus, it hopes to extirpate the roots of war.

In the second place, functionalism attributes the phenomenon of war to the institutional inadequacy of the national state system. The state is at fault, not because it is intrinsically a fighting organism, as the power politician would have it, but because it is increasingly an inappropriate

Abridged by permission of Random House, Inc., from *Swords into Plowshares*, 3rd ed., by Inis L. Claude, Jr. (New York: Random House, 1964), pp. 347–367. © Copyright 1956, 1959, 1964, 1971 by Inis L. Claude, Jr.

and ineffectual agency for doing what has to be done in order to promote the economic and social health of the human family.   The state system imposes an arbitrary and rigid pattern of vertical divisions upon global society, disrupting the organic unity of the whole, and carving the world into segments whose separateness is jealously guarded by sovereignties which are neither able to solve the fundamental problems nor willing to permit them to be solved by other authorities.   Peace requires solutions of economic and social problems which can be achieved only by problem-solving agencies coterminous in territorial competence with the problem areas.   The appropriate administrative unit varies with the nature of the problem, but it only accidentally corresponds to the boundaries established by the state system; more and more, the problems which are crucial to the fitness of human society for sustaining a peaceful regime are becoming bigger in scope than national states.   Hence, the mission of functionalism is to make peace possible by organizing particular layers of human social life in accordance with their particular requirements, breaking down the artificialities of the zoning arrangements associated with the principle of sovereignty.

Beyond this, functional theory purports to provide an indispensable laboratory for the experimental development of organizational patterns and techniques which may serve as models for the ultimately necessary machinery of internationalism on the highest political levels.   In the long run, the world requires a replacement for the state system.   The essential process of institutional invention can be expected to gain momentum by being put into operation first in the areas of recognized common interest.

Finally, functionalism envisages its task in terms of the alteration of the subjective conditions of mankind.   War is caused by the attitudes, habits of thought and feeling, and allegiances which are fostered by the state system.   Functional organizations may, by focusing attention upon areas of common interest, build habits of cooperation which will equip human beings for the conduct of a system of international relations in which the expectation of constructive collaboration will replace that of sterile conflict as the dominant motif.   Working international agencies will create a system of mutual advantages which will assume too great a value in the eyes of its beneficiaries for them to contemplate disrupting it by permitting resort to war.   Men will recognize international organization as the giver of good gifts which their states are no longer able to provide; they will cease to regard the derogation of sovereignty as a dubiously permissible national sacrifice, and come to think of it as a transfer of authority which is essential to the attainment of desirable results, a profitable investment in the good life. Thus, fundamental loyalties will be increasingly shared by the state and the agencies of the world community, the sentiment of human solidarity will be deepened, and the subjective basis will be prepared for progressively broader and more effective cooperation among the peoples of the world.

This concept involves not only the notion of transforming the international outlook of particular human beings, but also that of transferring competence from one set of human beings to another. So far as the traditional ruling classes of international affairs, the diplomats and the military men, are concerned, functionalism is perhaps a project for *evasion* as much as for *conversion*.

For all its emphasis upon the underlying economic and social roots of war, it does not altogether avoid the concoction of a devil theory; its villains are those gentlemen—perhaps more properly described as inveterate sinners in the national interest than as genuine devils—who have long held something approaching a monopolistic control of the conduct of relations among states. Functionalism comes very close to regarding these officials as incorrigible. Long habituated to the treatment of international affairs as an area of conflict and competition, they are unlikely to be swayed by the new mode of thought. Hence, functionalism envisages a process of circumvention, described hopefully by H. G. Wells as the evolution of "a comprehensive world control in the presence of which Foreign Offices would fade out, since, by reason of the conditions of their development, they are themselves incapable of establishing peace," and sarcastically by Georg Schwarzenberger as a project by which the "vicious dragons" who are presumed to inhabit Foreign Offices are to be "cleverly outwitted by gallant reforming knights."

More seriously, the expectation of functionalism is in line with the concept of multilevel interpenetration of governments which was brilliantly formulated by J. A. Salter after World War I. The development of specialized international agencies dealing with problems outside the scope of traditional diplomacy will result in making virtually every department of government a kind of Foreign Office, and bring into the active conduct of international relations a host of national officials whose professional training and interests give them a predisposition to concentrate upon the pragmatic issues of how to solve common problems for the common advantage, rather than to focus upon questions of national prestige and sovereign authority. Internationalism will well up from the collaborative international contacts of officials in labor, health, agriculture, commerce, and related departments, eventually endangering the citadels in which diplomatic and military officials sit peering competitively and combatively at the world outside the state.

In summary, functionalism proposes to promote peace by eliminating objective conditions which are deemed conducive to war, introducing new patterns of organization which may transform the global institutional system, and initiating the development of subjective trends which may cause the "erosion" of sovereignty, thereby assisting "states to work together and so gradually develop a sense of community which will make it psychologically more difficult to press the claims of sovereignty in ways that are antisocial."

*   *   *

The concept of functionalism . . . may appear to be an easy way out of the dilemma which confronts modern civilization. Men who have come to regard the directly political approaches as nothing better than prescriptions for humanity's beating its bloody head against the stone wall which guards national sovereignty may be heartened by the notion that there are poorly watched backdoors through which access may be gained. Functionalism may be regarded as a device for sneaking up on sovereignty, full of hopeful possibilities for establishing the groundwork of international community.

It has the great merit of appealing both to humanitarian idealism and to national self-interest. . . .

Functionalism proposes not to squelch but to utilize national selfishness; it asks governments not to give up the sovereignty which belongs to their peoples but to acquire benefits for their peoples which were hitherto unavailable, not to reduce their power to defend their citizens but to expand their competence to serve them. The realist who repudiates the expectation that altruism can become a major factor in international politics may find much to hope for in a system of organization which invites states to the common pursuit of common interests.

*   *   *

On the other hand, the student of international organization will do well to keep his critical wits about him when he is confronted with the functional answer to the problem of world order. . . .

The central thesis that war is a product of unsatisfactory economic and social conditions in the global community should arouse a bit of skeptical eyebrow-arching. . . .   The recent history of the world clearly fails to confirm the existence of a direct correlation between national economic backwardness and aggressiveness; it was advanced Germans, not primitive Africans, who shattered world peace in 1939. The debate concerning the role of economic factors and motivations in world politics is an involved and quite possibly an interminable one, certainly not one to be settled here. The point is that the analysis of the causes of war and the conditions of peace falls into the category of unfinished business, and that the assumptions which underpin the functional approach should be regarded as hypotheses, not established verities.

*   *   *

Assuming the feasibility of marking off a distinctively nonpolitical sector of human affairs, it is not self-evident that work in this area should or can be assigned first place on the international schedule. In objective terms, it may be that "the elements of order are the prerequisite of economic and social progress," and that "to forward the world's material welfare and human rights the peoples must first be freed from the scourge of modern war." Reverting to the subjective sphere, we may ask whether states can in fact be induced to join hands in functional endeavor before they have settled the outstanding political and security issues which divide them. Functionalism's insistence upon putting first things first does not settle the matter of what things are first.

*   *   *

The assumption of the rational transference of human loyalties is also a fit subject for skeptical scrutiny. How malleable is human allegiance? Do men actually shift their emotional bonds so as always to keep them connected with the entities from which their real blessings flow? Can functional agencies do enough, fast enough, conspicuously enough, to capture the imagination of peoples and elicit from them the rational recognition of, and consequent emotional dedication to, the values of an organized international community? Functional activities are likely to be helpful, but unlikely to be stirring and sensational; international agencies are likely to find themselves stimulating and facilitating the provision of services and solution of problems by national states, with the credit redounding to the states rather than being entered to the account of internationalism. If this were not so, governments could be expected to arrange that it should become so, since the responsible agents of national states are not likely to wax enthusiastic about the sponsorship and subsidization of projects for undermining the normative foundations of the state system. There is room for doubt that functionalists have found the key which infallibly opens the doors that keep human loyalties piled up in sovereign warehouses, thereby permitting those loyalties to spill out into the receptacles of internationalism.

Finally, it must be noted that functionalism is not in a hurry, and its claim to offer hope to the world is implicitly based upon the supposition that a long period is both necessary and available for working out solutions to the problems of the world. How much time does man have at his disposal for building the foundations of peace? The honest answer probably is that no one can say, and the urgent insistence of doctrinaires that the sand is running out and that quick solutions are certainly possible because they are obviously necessary is no more worthy of uncritical acceptance than the smug assumption of functionalists that there is a long run and their stodgy insistence that there is no satisfactory substitute for the methods of gradualism. Nevertheless, there is ample justification in the atomic age for giving serious thought to the question of time limits; as Carlos Romulo suggested at the tenth anniversary meeting of the United Nations, "Our clients are the next generation . . . but there may be no next generation unless we do today what has to be done for the two billion clients who are now alive."

What makes our age unique, I suppose, is that the immediate questions and the ultimate questions are locked together.

*   *   *

A major feature of the United Nations system in operation has been the steady enlargement and diversification of its functional program. The central organization itself and most of the Specialized Agencies have devoted particular attention to the promotion of economic and social progress in the underdeveloped areas, and the leading components of the organizational system have combined their efforts most notably in the Expanded Technical Assistance Program and the collateral operations of the Special Fund. This development has doubtless been in some measure a compensatory reaction, like that of the League, to the frustration of organizational endeavors in the most sensitive political fields. It has been stimulated by the conversion of the first Secretary-General, and of many other international officials and national leaders, to the view that "poverty remains mankind's chief enemy," when confronted with the reality that misery, disease, and ignorance are the chief facts of life for more than half of the world's population. It has been facilitated by the fortuitous circumstance that the American conception of how best to combat the spread of Communism has largely coincided with the functionalist conception of how best to build the foundations of a peaceful world society; as a result of this contingency, the critical portion of the financial support for the developing program has been provided by a government which is much more deeply committed to anti-Communism than to functionalism. Its political dynamics have been supplied primarily by the newly emergent peoples of the non-European world, whose conception of what is needed to achieve the goals of national advance has tended to coincide with functionalism's doctrine of what is needed to achieve the purpose of international order; thus, the effective political demand for expansion of the program has emanated mainly from states which are more deeply committed to specific national interests than to the general propositions of functional theory.

*   *   *

The clearest lesson of United Nations experience is that functionalism's assumption of the preliminary separability of political and nonpolitical matters does not hold true—not in this generation, at any rate. We are not vouchsafed the privilege of warming up the motors of international collaboration in a sheltered area of concordant interests, getting off to an easy start and building up momentum for crashing the barriers of conflicting interests that interpose between us and the ideal of world order. The dilemma of functionalism is that its ultimate impact upon politics may never be tested because of the immediate impact of politics upon functionalism.

*   *   *

The two great political struggles which have developed in the United Nations, the cold war between the Soviet Communist bloc and the anti-Communist bloc led by the United States, and the separate but closely intertwined conflict between the non-European attackers of colonialism and the heirs of the colonial system, have both impinged sharply upon functional operations. Separately and in combination, they have decisively affected the answers to basic questions of national participation, of the uses to which the machinery of collaboration can and should be put, and of the scope and distribution of the functional effort. In general, they have decreed that the United States should lead and direct the enterprise, making it primarily an element of the anti-Communist program and secondarily a device for alleviating the tensions of the struggle over colonialism. The Soviet Union has shifted from an initial policy of virtually complete abstention to one of general, but yet relatively small-scale, participation in functional activities. The underdeveloped states, a group which largely coincides with the anticolonial bloc, has tended to resent the anti-Communist orientation determined by the United States, and to demand the appropriation of a greater share of a much larger functional budget to meet the needs of their aspiring peoples.

The crucial political fact of the United Nations functional system is the dominant position assumed by the United States, for reasons which include the unrivaled economic stature and the general political importance of this country as well as the disinclination of the Soviet Union to compete for the role of leadership in this realm. This fact carries with it a tendency for the agencies of economic and social action to become excessively reliant upon the support, and particularly the financial support, of the United States. Such heavy dependence upon a single power inevitably minimizes the international flavor of the functional program. Stated differently, the unique position held by the United States serves as the basis for excessive American control. This control is in the first instance negative; the United States has a financial veto power which it has used to accomplish such purposes as the termination of the United Nations Relief and Rehabilitation Administration and the International Refugee Organization, and the blocking of efforts to establish "SUNFED," the Special United Nations Fund for Economic Development so avidly and persistently advocated by spokesmen for the less developed states. It extends also to the positive direction of policy. As Paul G. Hoffman innocently put it in Congressional testimony, he maintained such personal relations with the successive Presidents of the International Bank for Reconstruction and Development during his service as head of the Marshall Plan administration that

we had no problem, because we discussed all these loans they were thinking of making and they were always good enough to come to us and say, "What about the impact of this loan to Turkey? Do you think we ought to go ahead with it?" That was informal and that is one of the best ways of control. . . .

American predominance not only has the effect of permitting the harnessing of international cooperative mechanisms to the objectives of United States foreign policy, but it also exposes them to the internal political peculiarities of the American scene.

*   *   *

The functional experiment of the United Nations represents the laying of the groundwork for the first systematic global attack upon basic economic and social problems, the beginning of the definition of the assignment which devolves upon the organized international community, and the initiation of the process of learning how to tackle the job. The actual achievements thus far are substantial and significant, even though not spectacular, world-shaking, or world-saving. Above all, the record to date indicates that functional activity is, at least in the short run, more dependent upon the political weather than determinative of the political weather. In the long run, however, it may be that the economic and social work of international organization will prove to be one of the means of developing a system whereby man can control his political climate.

SUGGESTED READINGS

Bloomfield, Lincoln P., *The United Nations and United States Foreign Policy*, Boston: Little, Brown, 1967.

Claude, Inis L., Jr., *Power in International Relations*, New York: Random House, 1962, Chapters 4–8.

——— *The Changing United Nations*, New York: Random House, 1967.

Deutsch, Karl W., *Political Community at the International Level*, Garden City, N.Y.: Doubleday, 1954.

Etzioni, Amitai, *Political Unification: A Comparative Study of Leaders and Forces*, New York: Holt, Rinehart and Winston, 1965.

Goodspeed, S. J., *The Nature and Function of International Organizations*, New York: Oxford University Press, 1967.

Haas, Ernst B., *Beyond the Nation-State*, Stanford: Stanford University Press, 1964.

———, *Tangle of Hopes: American Commitments and World Order*, Englewood Cliffs, N.J.: Prentice-Hall, 1969.

Nye, Joseph S., Jr. (ed.), *International Regionalism*, Boston: Little, Brown, 1968.

Sewell, James P., *Functionalism and World Politics*, Princeton: Princeton University Press, 1966.

Stoessinger, John G., *The United Nations and the Superpowers: United States-Soviet Interaction at the United Nations*, rev. ed., New York: Random House, 1969.

X. TOWARD A NEW WORLD ORDER

Visions of the future are rarely bright in our times. Ideas and ideals seem either discredited or impotent; the hopes of a Woodrow Wilson, reflected in the mirror of contemporary analysis, are reduced to neurosis or naiveté. This was already true, to some extent, in the nineteenth century, the "nothing but" era when theorists argued consistently that politics was nothing but economics, or geography, or race, or history. It has become even more true in the post-war world as bewildering transformations, appalling threats, and human enormities make us feel like so many leaves swept along by the flood toward some cataclysmic waterfall, happy enough if we can find some private back-water.

Of course, there is no safe haven for any of us. But equally, we should recognize that events and environments, harsh and demanding though they may be, never determine more than a part of politics. Politics includes policy, the human response to conditions, which includes resistance, adaptation, imagination, and creativity. In the world of politics, human beings strive to unite the physical world they are *in* with the psychological and intellectual world they are *of*. That task is certainly difficult, probably impossible in ultimate terms, but its very challenge justifies the belief that politics ranks high among the human arts and commands our study of the successes and failures of those who have attempted the art before us.

At the end of World War II, the victorious nations in the West confronted the world in a mood of sober optimism. During the dark days of the war even the conservative Churchill had envisioned a future of "broad, sunny uplands," and the sacrifices of the war and the triumph of the "freedom-loving" allied coalition over the "freedom-hating" fascists and militarists seemed to permit and insist that such an ideal be realized. Learned and dedicated groups, both private and official, took up the task of "planning the peace" and charting the future direction of the world. But it soon became clear that most such plans were destined only for dusty archives. The defeat of old enemies had only created new dangers.

In the wake of German defeat came the Soviet armies invading the countries of central and southeastern Europe; and in the wake of the Soviet armies came a new form of imperialism. Partly through direct annexation (camouflaged in some cases by faked plebiscites à la Napoleon), partly through indirect rule by native Communist elites and exiles, buttressed by Soviet occupation forces, civilian "experts," and police agents, Stalin succeeded in building a new empire of more than a hundred million souls.

But indigenous revolutions led by intellectuals who were both socialists and nationalists were condemned in Moscow as "counterrevolutionary" or "revisionist" and either brutally suppressed as in Hungary (1956) and Czechoslovakia (1968) or deflected by a largely short-range compromise as in Poland (1956). Grass-roots workers' revolts, in some ways even more embarrassing to those who assert they represent the "workers of the world," as in East Germany (1953) and Poland (1970), had even less of a chance. The "Brezhnev Doctrine," intended to justify the suppression of the "Prague spring," makes it quite clear that "peaceful coexistence" must not guide relations *among* the socialist states and that collective security within Moscow's communist family must involve armed intervention in domestic affairs as well. The Soviet occupation of Czechoslovakia [1] was a late but grim reminder that even in Europe the cold war was not yet dead and buried though the lines of demarcation between East and West, once regarded as temporary, had been long ago accepted by both sides as lasting, if not final.

In the early postwar years, however, that boundary seemed terribly fragile, little more than a line at which, temporarily, the Soviet armies had stopped for breath. Western Europe was prostrate and eastern and central Europe were little more than armed camps. Moreover, it soon became evident that the Soviet challenge was complicated by the unexpected strength and pace of anticolonial revolutions in Asia and Africa. The old world was ruined by the war, and in the new, emerging world the West, as Barbara Ward put it, found itself "at bay." [2]

Certainly, in the late forties the challenge of Soviet totalitarianism seemed both more fearful and more urgent than to the hindsight of even the most objective observer a quarter of a century later. With France and Italy facing social and economic crisis bordering on chaos, and with Greece and Turkey apparently in the direct frontline of Soviet expansionism, and with England too exhausted by the war even to play her traditionally dominant role in the eastern Mediterranean, America was "catapulted" by events more than by her own initiative to become a guarantor of the European *status quo*.

The most generally accepted doctrine of American foreign policy during this period was formulated by George F. Kennan:

. . . the Soviet pressure against the free institutions of the Western world is something that can be contained by adroit and vigilant application of counter-force . . . corresponding to the shifts and maneuvers of Soviet Policy . . .[3]

[1] For the best short analysis of events in Czechoslovakia in 1968, see Richard Lowenthal, "The Sparrow in the Cage," *Problems of Communism* (November–December 1968).

[2] *The West at Bay,* New York: Norton, 1948.

[3] *American Diplomacy, 1900–1950,* Chicago: University of Chicago, 1951, p. 120. First published anonymously as "The Sources of Soviet Conduct," *Foreign Affairs* (July 1947), pp. 566–582.

Yet originally at least Kennan and many of those who shared his views hoped that "containment" would be an only temporary policy. He hoped that "if the Western world finds the strength and resourcefulness to contain Soviet power for a period of ten to fifteen years," the Kremlin would change its policy of aggression and the coming into power of a younger generation in Russia would lead to a new period of negotiation, adjustment, and even fruitful cooperation.

Kennan's timetable was probably still colored by the optimism of the postwar period. Even though with the Korean War and the change of administrations in Washington, the policy of containment became reformulated and applied globally, it was not basically changed. John Foster Dulles promised a "roll-back" of Soviet power during the presidential campaign of 1952, yet once in office, he continued to "contain" rather than to "roll back" and "liberate."

The great change in Soviet-American (or East-West) relations, which the original architects of containment had not foreseen, came about because of changes in the overall military situation, in which Western monopoly of nuclear weapons was replaced gradually by a rough parity. The question of whether effective "mutual deterrence" could be imagined without the actual risk of a nuclear holocaust became the subject of much serious soul-searching in the West.[4]

By 1962 the hope for a pluralistic world order had replaced the anticommunist crusading of the 1950s. And yet the logic of commitments along the famous "perimeter" that resulted in the building of "situations of strength" precisely where no solid preconditions for "strength" (let alone Truman's and Kennan's "free peoples" and "free institutions") ever existed, combined with much political optimism and wishful military thinking of many, though not all, American leaders, led to the tragedy of Vietnam. If there was deception, there was even more self-deception, and it is self-deception that is the real nemesis of power. As so often before, in Raymond Aron's words, "the power to destroy" was not tantamount to the "power to control."

It is, therefore, no wonder that not even the harshness of the Brezhnev doctrine could prevent a continuing relaxation of East-West relations in Germany and central Europe, of which Willy Brandt's *Ostpolitik* may only be a more explicit expression. And even though Soviet expansion in the Mediterranean and the regular presence of Soviet naval vessels in such faraway regions as the Indian Ocean and the Persian Gulf are anxiously watched by Western experts, the necessity of Soviet-American cooperation in dealing with the perilous Middle Eastern situation became paramount.

Yet, as Robert Conquest reminds us, there are limits to a Soviet-American *détente* that must be perceived more like a stable truce between suspicious but sensible neighbors than genuine peace between like-minded partners. It is up to the United States, Conquest believes, to conduct a policy that will thwart expansionist adventures, which extremists in the Kremlin can still be expected to launch, without, however, pushing the Soviet Union into a situation of despair in which its leaders may be tempted to think of nuclear confrontation.

[4] See the articles by Thornton Read and Bruce Russett in Chapter VI.

The limits of American power in the third world, so flagrantly demonstrated by the Indochinese debacle, are realized by the rather haltingly advanced Nixon Doctrine. Perhaps President Nixon, fearing that a disillusioned public will overreact toward neo-isolationism, was trying to show that he was indeed disengaging himself according to plan not only from Vietnam but from the whole of Asia and the third world. But as Zbigniew Brzezinski asserts, the contradictions of the Nixon Doctrine can be explained by the fact that it is not a doctrine at all but rather "a continuous process of redefinition of American foreign policy in the light of new domestic and international circumstances." But a wider vision and more convincing common goals are needed for really effective international leadership that a "doctrine" seems to imply. By the spring of 1971, however, the "new modes of partnership," which the President proposed, seemed far from realization. In the economic field particularly, as Brzezinski reminds us, "old forms of economic relations" began to lag badly behind the emerging new realities. President Nixon's surprising announcements in August 1971 regarding the devaluation of the dollar by cutting its ties with gold and resorting to ill-concealed protectionism were certainly prompted by serious threats to the American economy. But as they were not preceded by international negotiations or even consultations, they represented the kind of unilateral action that shocks old friends and frightens potential new ones away.

Unfortunately the continuous debate on Vietnam that often saturated American thinking on international affairs after 1965 has not yet produced much consensus beyond general condemnation. According to William Pfaff, the chief enduring factor in a badly split American public opinion is an inclination toward moralizing and a seeking for "final solutions." This, if true, would of course make for "tone-deaf diplomacy." Others, like Jeremy Stone, believe that "telling the truth" by American Presidents, supported by a "vigilant public and press," will clamp healthy limits on American and even on Soviet-American joint power. "Self-restraint" is also Stanley Hoffmann's remedy, a self-restraint that would lead to less intervention and to a more realistic analysis of local realities. Nation-states are after all not arranged in tidy rows of dominoes, and when one state falls, maintains Hoffmann, "nationalism, national self-determination, formal sovereignty" may prevent the others from tumbling down. But for Carl Oglesby and the New Left, such judicious pragmatism is wholly inadequate; indigenous revolutions everywhere, and especially in America, are the precondition for a better international order.

Yet, on the plane of international diplomacy, signs are multiplying that the world is emerging from the ideological framework that since the early 1950s has often beclouded the underlying power realities of the bipolar cold war. New poles of power are appearing and new checks and balances between these will have to be worked out. In Asia, for instance, we cannot speak in the abstract about "treaty commitments" and "military assistance" without thinking in terms of concrete power adjustments. The Chinese Peoples Republic may welcome the reduction of American military involvement, particularly on the Asian mainland, and will therefore regard this aspect of the Nixon Doctrine a contribution to the new Asian order. The President's visit to China in 1972 seems to confirm such a view. On the other hand, the same Chinese leaders fear that the Nixon Doctrine is encouraging Japan to rearm and that Japan's stupendous economic expansion, once her political sights are changed, will be followed by a military expansion of the same proportion.[5]

Thus while the later 1960s presented to sinologists and sovietologists the fascinating spectacle of an apparently lasting split between the two communist giants, the 1970s have started with more food for speculation regarding the coming of a triangular or even quadrangular balance in Asia and the Pacific. It became clear that in the case of strongly ideological nations a common doctrinal heritage may aggravate rather than reconcile fundamental differences in interests. Whether a workable modus vivendi can be arranged between Russia and China, joined by the longest common frontier in the world, will not depend on the unsurpassed sophistry of Soviet and Chinese neo-Leninist ideologists but rather, as Richard Lowenthal points out, on "the measure of rationality of the leadership on both sides." Lowenthal believes that given this measure of rationality, "the continuation of limited and controlled conflict" between the two communist poles "remains a far more plausible prospect than its end by either reunion or catastrophe." He predicts the development of "triangular politics" in which, with the participation of the United States, "different combinations of cooperation and conflict are possible at different periods." That even slight movements of rapprochement between two of the three powers in the triangle will be watched with anxiety and suspicion by the third power became quite clear from the cautiously ambiguous comments the Soviet Union released when, in July 1971, President Nixon's projected journey to Peking was announced.

Moreover, the Australian scholar and strategist Hedley Bull draws our attention to the fact that the emerging triangular politics—which already characterizes the new balance of power in Asia and in the Pacific—will suffer from "the principal uncertainty" of whether it will become quadrangular by the entrance of Japan as a full-fledged great power.[6] Nor will it be possible to ignore the increasing significance of some of the middle powers in that region (or, for that matter, in Europe). If India could be discounted because of her economic and military weakness and perplexing domestic problems, would the Soviet Union have reacted to the first signs of a serious Sino-American rapprochement by signing a twenty-year friendship pact with New Delhi? The degree of Australian alliance may considerably strengthen America's position in the Pacific, while, some years ago, the cataclysmic anticommunist military coup in Indonesia greatly weakened China's hopes of influence in Southeast Asia. Bull wonders whether the security of the less powerful states, such as Japan, India, Indonesia, and Australia, may not be furthered in the future by the creation of a regional organization, which would not be directed against

[5] See, e.g., Chou En-lai's interview with James Reston, *The New York Times,* August 10, 1971.

[6] According to Herman Kahn, Japan by 1975 will have the world's third largest gross national product for about six years; it also will probably have been a major net source of capital for international investment for about five years, and will probably pass the Soviets in per capita product as well. Kahn conjectures that in the year 2000 Japan may have surpassed the most advanced Western country in development. *The Emerging Japanese Superstate,* Englewood Cliffs, N.J.: Prentice-Hall, 1970, pp. 4–6 and *passim.*

China but would nonetheless exclude all the three superpowers. One may also speculate whether the constellations and configurations of major and middle powers in this region will not come to resemble the European balance of power of a bygone age.

Yet scholars and commentators, entranced with the fascinating possibilities of multilateral balances of power forming new alliances and alignments, tend to forget that those who direct the fortunes of nations may be guided by other considerations. The stringent imperatives of domestic conditions, the tenacious clinging to power of discredited elites, and the very limitations of human capacities to deal with delicate relations on five continents and seven seas simultaneously may still drag us into the world of George Orwell's 1984. With terrible prescience Orwell foresaw the multibloc world in which an atomic stalemate made total war or total victory impossible but in which peaceful cooperation, or even amicable adjustments, were no longer attempted in good faith. He foresaw what we in fact have experienced in the last decade: armed conflicts limited to the periphery of politics, in areas like the Congo, Indochina, or the Middle East, around vague frontiers for purposes seemingly obscure. Orwell predicted a world in which ideology would lose its moving power; a world in which the crusading zeal of governments and peoples would lapse. Only one abiding motive for conflict would remain: the need of leaders within blocs to find some outlet for the frustrations of their subjects. In a complex world of industrial technology and complex organizations, Robert Michels demonstrated, it is an "iron law" that some command and many obey. It is an equally iron law that the many will resent being forced to obey, and a stable regime must find an object for that resentment. Orwell blamed the desire of leaders for power; a conservative might affix the blame to the turbulent desires of the masses. Either, however, would expect the "Great Hate" and perpetual war at the periphery as the logic of the new era.

The nations most likely to suffer and even to lose their identity, if anything like Orwell's catastrophic vision became full reality, would be those who from time to time gather under the designation of "nonaligned." More than a few of them today happen to have all sorts of ties not only to regional blocs formed among themselves, but also to some of the great powers. India, for instance, still regards itself nonaligned, yet her security and economic survival depend on the friendship and assistance of not one but actually two superpowers. Be it as it may, the heads of government of as many as fifty-three non*aligned* states met at Lusaka for the third time in September 1970 to confer on the problems of "peace, independence, development, cooperation and democratization of international relations." As in Bandung in 1955, and in Belgrade in 1961, they agreed in blaming the superpowers and their military blocs for most of the ills of the world: intervention in the internal affairs of other states, wars of aggression, the arms race, presence of foreign military forces in small countries, and the prolongation of colonialism, particularly in southern Africa.

"The balance of terror," the Lusaka Declaration asserts, "has not brought peace and security to the rest of the world." The lofty principles of the United Nations, the declaration maintains, could be brought closer to realization if the role of the nonaligned countries would be strengthened within and without the United Nations. Moreover the nonaligned and militarily weak nations desire, more ardently than any others, "the dissolution of great power military alliances" and genuine disarmament, particularly of the great atomic powers.

One way of progress toward the kind of international community that the nonaligned nations (and many others) desire may be found in the United Nations' addressing itself to novel and timely concerns that have arisen in both the most and the less advanced countries, the solution of which cannot depend merely on arms control and generally accepted political power balances. Malthusian anxieties are strong again in our world, though they vary in intensity and are approached in different countries and by different groups of scholars in widely differing ways. Growth-minded governments and growth-minded economists are chiefly interested in the quantitative development of economic resources; others find that the gist of the problem is a fairer distribution of what we produce rather than the piling up of goods and gold in a few advanced countries. Modern demographers, however, agree that no matter how much we produce and no matter how just the distribution of these goods, only a slowing down of the stupendous population explosion can avoid a global catastrophe. Recently Malthusians—and in one sense or another, we are all such—have become ecological. Thus George Kennan proposed an international agency with far-reaching powers for the conservation of the world's resources.[7] This agency would order a halt to economic development and distribution wherever long-range considerations demand the curbing of short-range zeal or greed. Many complex questions are raised by Kennan's proposal: will the bonds of world community be furthered more by emphasis on development, by aid to poor nations, or by the conservation of resources? If scientists become our ecological guardians, who will guard *them* and how? And how will they assume their fateful authority over problems that, on a smaller scale, have perplexed men in recurrent periods in many civilizations, for instance in the Egypt of the biblical Joseph?

Such questions of political adjustment and management, which must be settled before scientists could assume authority or even wield influence, should be uppermost in the minds of those who believe that the great problems of the world can be solved only when the most advanced and powerful nations decide not only to coexist peacefully, but also to cooperate in great constructive tasks without the reservations and suspicions that even nonbelligerent adversaries harbor. The noted Soviet scientist, Andrei Sakharov, a member of that remarkable group of intellectual dissenters whom latter-day totalitarian controls have not silenced completely, believes and even predicts that an increasing liberalization of communist countries and an inevitable trend toward socialism in capitalist nations will lead to a *convergence*, first of all, of the Soviet Union and the United States. Once truly allied, they will succeed in solving the problems of the poor countries, after which the road will be free toward world government. He takes it for granted that scientific expertise and the highest moral and ethical qualities will grow evenly in the elites of the future. Characteristically, although Sakharov's plan was published and is widely read in the West, it was circulated only privately among a small number of Russian intellectuals, and not at all in China. There is, indeed, little indication that a transition from peaceful coexistence to genuine convergence will develop in

[7] See George F. Kennan, "To Prevent a World Wasteland," from *Foreign Affairs,* 48 (April 1970), pp. 401–413.

the foreseeable future. The stark facts of the "limits" of *détente"* that Robert Conquest discussed are still with us. If, however, Sakharov and his friends can undermine in some way the stubborn tyranny of a self-perpetuating political elite in their own country, the specter of Orwell's 1984 may at least lose some of its terrifying reality.

From conceptions of the future Kenneth Waltz redirects our attention to the present. The bipolar world, he contends, is by no means dead, and its foundations are stabler than many analysts have imagined. The basis of bipolarity is the technological and economic supremacy of the United States and the U.S.S.R., and the increased activity and assertiveness of third powers is possible only because the "Big Two" are in conflict. The bipolar structure of the international system, Waltz contends, has been—and is likely to continue to be—a system that produces general international stability while allowing an area of autonomy and freedom to third powers unwarranted by their comparative strength. The system in this sense combines flexibility with some measure of security. "Multi-polarity," Waltz maintains, will be for the foreseeable future a secondary fact *within* the general structure of relations established by the bipolar world.

Yet Waltz is far too perceptive to extend his analysis far into the future. Europe already has most of the requirements which go to make a superpower; technological and political changes may provide similar opportunity to others. Unlike such writers as Prof. Hans Morgenthau, Waltz notes that a three-power world would almost certainly be less stable than the bipolar order. Indeed, even the limited flexibility created by the growth of Chinese and European influence has destabilized some, still largely peripheral, issues in international politics. It would not be too much to say that to the extent that the world becomes truly "multipolar" Waltz sees a prospect that is, if anything, grimmer than Orwell's.

Ours is not a time that lends itself to high enthusiasms or to bright visions of international harmony and human fraternity. For many, a stoic endurance seems the only alternative to blank despair. Yet the darkest moments of human life are as impure as the brightest, and the logic of events never entirely governs men. The faiths and goals, the values and ideals of men and of political communities, contribute something to the meaning of events—indeed they are inseparable from a *political* event, as differentiated from a physical fact. There remains always the possibility that men will find the wisdom and charity necessary to avoid the terrifying and realize the hopeful possibilities of our time and of the world's future.

Morton A. Kaplan

LOOSE BIPOLARITY: A MODEL OF AN
INTERNATIONAL SYSTEM

. . . [T]he loose bipolar system . . . differs in many important respects from the "balance of power" system. Supranational actors participate within the international system. These supranational actors may be bloc actors like NATO or the Communist bloc or universal actors like the United Nations. Nearly all national actors belong to the universal actor organization and many—including most of the essential national actors—belong to one or the other of the bipolar blocs. Some national actors, however, may be non-members of bloc-organizations.

In distinction to the "balance of power" international system, in which the rules applied uniformly to all national actors, the essential rules of the loose bipolar system distinguish, for instance, between the role functions of actors who are members of blocs and those who are not.

In the "balance of power" system, the role of the "balancer" was an integrating role because it prevented any alliance from becoming predominant. In the ideal form of the system, any national actor is qualified to fill that role. In the loose bipolar system, however, the integrating role is a mediatory role. The actor filling it does not join one side or the other, but mediates between the contending sides. Therefore, only non-bloc members or universal actor organizations can fill the integrative role in the loose bipolar system.

The functioning of the loose bipolar system depends upon the organizational characteristics of the supranational blocs.[1] If the two blocs are not hierarchically organized, the loose bipolar system tends to resemble the "balance of power" system, except that the shifting of alignments takes place around two fixed points. Such shifting is limited by the functional integration of facilities, since a shift may require the destruction of facilities and the reduction of the capabilities of the shifting national actor. Shifting in alignment tends also to be limited by geographic and other logistic considerations. Nevertheless, the bloc actors constitute relatively loose organizations and the international system itself develops a considerable flexibility.

Reprinted by permission of the author and publisher from *The American Political Science Review* (September 1957). (This is another part of an article, the first part of which is included in Chapter V as "Balance of Power: A Model of an International System.")

[1] Extensional definitions would identify NATO as relatively non-hierarchical and the Communist bloc as mixed hierarchical. If the Communist bloc were to be so integrated that national boundaries and organizational forms were eliminated, it would become fully hierarchical.

If one bloc has some hierarchical organizational features and the other is not hierarchically organized, a number of consequences can be expected. The hierarchical or mixed hierarchical bloc will retain its membership, since functional integration will be so great that it would be difficult for satellite members to withdraw or to form viable national entities if they did.   The relative permanence of membership in the bloc constitutes a threat to non-members.   Therefore, such a bloc is unlikely to attract new members except as a consequence of military absorption or political conquest by a native political party which already had associate membership in the bloc through the medium of an international party organization. The irreversible characteristics of membership in such a bloc constitute a threat to all other national actors, whether associated in a bloc or not.

The non-hierarchical bloc has a looser hold over its members but is more likely to enter into cooperative pacts of one kind or another with non-bloc members.   The pressure emanating from the hierarchically organized bloc, however, is likely to force the non-hierarchically organized bloc to integrate its bloc activities more closely and to extend them to other functional areas, or alternatively to weaken and undermine the bloc.

If both blocs subscribe to hierarchical integrating rules, their memberships become rigid and only uncommitted states can, by choosing an alignment, change the existing lineup.   Any action of this sort, however, would tend to reduce the flexibility of the international system by eliminating nations not included in blocs.   Non-bloc member actors therefore would be more likely to support one or the other of the blocs on specific issues rather than to support either in general.   If both blocs are hierarchically organized, their goals are similar—hierarchical world organization— and incompatible, since only one can succeed in leading such a world system.

With only two major groupings in the bipolar system, any rapid change in military capabilities tends to make this system unstable.   For this reason, possession of a larger stockpile of atomic and thermonuclear weapons by both major blocs is a factor for stability within the system.

The rules of the loose bipolar system follow:

1. All blocs subscribing to hierarchical or mixed hierarchical integrating principles are to eliminate the rival bloc.

2. All blocs subscribing to hierarchical or mixed hierarchical integrating principles are to negotiate rather than to fight, to fight minor wars rather than major wars, and to fight major wars—under given risk and cost factors—rather than to fail to eliminate the rival bloc.

3. All bloc actors are to increase their capabilities relative to those of the opposing bloc.

4. All bloc actors subscribing to non-hierarchical organizational principles are to negotiate rather than to fight, to increase capabilities, to fight minor wars rather than to fail to increase capabilities, but to refrain from initiating major wars for this purpose.

5. All bloc actors are to engage in major war rather than to permit the rival bloc to attain a position of preponderant strength.

6. All bloc members are to subordinate objectives of universal actors to the objectives of their bloc but to subordinate the objectives of the rival bloc to those of the universal actor.

7. All non-bloc member national actors are to coordinate their national objectives with those of the universal actor and to subordinate the objectives of bloc actors to those of the universal actor.

8. Bloc actors are to attempt to extend the membership of their bloc but to tolerate the non-member position of a given national actor if the alternative is to force that national actor to join the rival bloc or to support its objectives.

9. Non-bloc member national actors are to act to reduce the danger of war between the bloc actors.

10. Non-bloc members are to refuse to support the policies of one bloc actor as against the other except in their capacities as members of a universal actor.

11. Universal actors are to reduce the incompatibility between the blocs.

12. Universal actors are to mobilize non-bloc member national actors against cases of gross deviation, *e.g.,* resort to force by a bloc actor. This rule, unless counterbalanced by the other rules, would enable the universal actor to become the prototype of a universal international system.

Unlike the "balance of power" international system, there is a high degree of role differentiation in the loose bipolar system. If any of the roles is pursued to the exclusion of others, the system will be transformed. If one bloc actor eliminates another, the system may be transformed into a hierarchical system. If the universal actor performs its function too well, the system may be transformed into a universal international system. Other variations are possible.

The tight bipolar international system represents a modification of the loose bipolar system in which non-bloc member actors and universal actors either disappear entirely or cease to be significant. Unless both blocs are hierarchically organized, however, the system will tend toward instability.

There is no integrative or mediatory role in the tight bipolar system. Therefore there will tend to be a high degree of dysfunctional tension in the system. For this reason, the tight bipolar system will not be a highly stable or well integrated system.

The universal international system might develop as a consequence of the functioning of a universal actor organization in a loose bipolar system. The universal system, as distinguished from those international systems previously discussed, would have a political system as a subsystem of the international social system. However, it is possible that this political system would be of the confederated type, *i.e.,* that it would operate on territorial governments rather than directly on human individuals.

The universal international system would be an integrated and solidary system. Although informal political groupings might take place within the system, conflicts of interest would be settled according to the political rules of the system. Moreover, a body of political officials and administrators would exist whose primary loyalty would be to the international system itself rather than to any territorial subsystem of the international system.

Whether the universal international system is a stable system or not depends upon the extent to which it has direct access to resources and facilities and upon the ratio between its capabilities and the capabilities of the national actors who are members of the system.

The hierarchical international system may be democratic or authoritarian in form. If it evolves from a universal international system—perhaps because the satisfactions arising from the successful operation of such a universal international system lead to a desire for an even more integrated and solidary international system—it is likely to be a democratic system. If, on the other hand, the hierarchical system is imposed upon unwilling national actors by a victorious or powerful bloc, then the international system is likely to be authoritarian.

The hierarchical system is a political system. Within it, functional lines of organization are stronger than geographical lines. This highly integrated characteristic of the hierarchical international system makes for great stability. Functional cross-cutting makes it most difficult to organize successfully against the international system or to withdraw from it. Even if the constitution of the system were to permit such withdrawal, the integration of facilities over time would raise the costs of withdrawal too high.

The unit veto international system is one in which all actors possess such great capabilities that an aggressor—even if it succeeded eventually in destroying an actor—could be destroyed in return. Within this system, each actor relies upon itself exclusively for its own protection, rather than upon alliances.

The unit veto system is maintained by mutual threat. Therefore the dysfunctional tension within it is likely to be quite high. For this reason, actors may succumb to threats, *i.e.,* they may lose nerve, or they may launch an aggressive venture simply because they cannot stand the tension. As a consequence, the unit veto international system is not likely to have a high degree of stability.

THE "BREZHNEV DOCTRINE"

In connection with the events in Czechoslovakia the question of the relationship and interconnection between the socialist countries' national interests and their internationalist obligations has assumed particular urgency and sharpness. The measures taken jointly by the Soviet Union and other socialist countries to defend the socialist gains of the Czechoslovak people are of enormous significance for strengthening the socialist commonwealth, which is the main achievement of the international working class.

At the same time it is impossible to ignore the allegations being heard in some places that the actions of the five socialist countries contradict the Marxist-Leninist principle of sovereignty and the right of nations to self-determination.

Such arguments are untenable primarily because they are based on an abstract, nonclass approach to the question of sovereignty and the right of nations to self-determination.

There is no doubt that the peoples of the socialist countries and the Communist Parties have and must have freedom to determine their country's path of development. However, any decision of theirs must damage neither socialism in their own country nor the fundamental interests of the other socialist countries nor the worldwide workers' movement, which is waging a struggle for socialism. This means that every Communist Party is responsible not only to its own people but also to all the socialist countries and to the entire Communist movement. Whoever forgets this in placing sole emphasis on the autonomy and independence of Communist Parties lapses into one-sidedness, shirking his internationalist obligations.

The Marxist dialectic opposes one-sidedness; it requires that every phenomenon be examined in terms of both its specific nature and its overall connection with other phenomena and processes. Just as, in V. I. Lenin's words, someone living in a society cannot be free of that society, so a socialist state that is in a system of other states constituting a socialist commonwealth cannot be free of the common interests of that commonwealth.

The sovereignty of individual socialist countries cannot be counterposed to the interests of world socialism and the world revolutionary movement. V. I. Lenin demanded that all Communists "struggle *against* petty national narrowness, exclusivity and isolation, and for taking into account the

Sergei Kovalev, "Sovereignty and the International Obligations of Socialist Countries," *Pravda,* September 26, 1968. This translation is from "Czechoslovakia and the Brezhnev Doctrine," prepared by the Subcommittee on National Security and International Operations of the Committee on Government Operations, U.S. Senate, 91st Congress, 1st Session (Washington, D.C.: Government Printing Office, 1969), pp. 14–18.

whole, the overall situation, for subordinating the interests of the particular to the interests of the general."

Socialist states have respect for the democratic norms of international law. More than once they have proved this in practice by resolutely opposing imperialism's attempts to trample the sovereignty and independence of peoples. From this same standpoint they reject left-wing, adventurist notions of "exporting revolution" and "bringing bliss" to other peoples. However, in the Marxist conception the norms of law, including the norms governing relations among socialist countries, cannot be interpreted in a narrowly formal way, outside the general context of the class struggle in the present-day world. Socialist countries resolutely oppose the export and import of counterrevolution.

Each Communist Party is free in applying the principles of Marxism-Leninism and socialism in its own country, but it cannot deviate from these principles (if, of course, it remains a Communist Party). In concrete terms this means primarily that every Communist Party cannot fail to take into account in its activities such a decisive fact of our time as the struggle between the two antithetical social systems—capitalism and socialism. This struggle is an objective fact that does not depend on the will of people and is conditioned by the division of the world into two antithetical social systems. "Every person," V. I. Lenin said, "must take either this, our, side or the other side. All attempts to avoid taking sides end in failure and disgrace."

It should be stressed that even if a socialist country seeks to take an "extrabloc" position, it in fact retains its national independence thanks precisely to the power of the socialist commonwealth—and primarily to its chief force, the Soviet Union—and the might of its armed forces. The weakening of any link in the world socialist system has a direct effect on all the socialist countries, which cannot be indifferent to this. Thus, the antisocialist forces in Czechoslovakia were in essence using talk about the right to self-determination to cover up demands for so-called neutrality and the C.S.R.'s withdrawal from the socialist commonwealth. But implementation of such "self-determination," i.e., Czechoslovakia's separation from the socialist commonwealth, would run counter to Czechoslovakia's fundamental interests and would harm the other socialist countries. Such "self-determination," as a result of which NATO troops might approach Soviet borders and the commonwealth of European socialist countries would be dismembered, in fact infringes on the vital interests of these countries' peoples, and fundamentally contradicts the right of these peoples to socialist self-determination. The Soviet Union and other socialist states, in fulfilling their internationalist duty to the fraternal peoples of Czechoslovakia and defending their own socialist gains, had to act and did act in resolute opposition to the antisocialist forces in Czechoslovakia. . . .

People who "disapprove" of the actions taken by the allied socialist countries ignore the decisive fact that these countries are defending the interests of worldwide socialism and the worldwide revolutionary movement. The socialist system exists in concrete form in individual countries that have their own well-defined state boundaries and develops with regard for the specific attributes of each such country. And no one interferes with concrete measures to perfect the socialist system in various socialist countries. But matters change radically when a danger to socialism itself arises in a country. World socialism as a social system is the common achievement of the working people of all countries, it is indivisible, and its defense is the common cause of all Communists and all progressive people on earth, first and foremost the working people of the socialist countries.

The Bratislava statement of the Communist and Workers' Parties on socialist gains says that "it is the common internationalist duty of all socialist countries to support, strengthen and defend these gains, which were achieved at the cost of every people's heroic efforts and selfless labor."

What the right-wing, antisocialist forces were seeking to achieve in Czechoslovakia in recent months was not a matter of developing socialism in an original way or of applying the principles of Marxism-Leninism to specific conditions in that country, but was an encroachment on the foundations of socialism and the fundamental principles of Marxism-Leninism. This is the "nuance" that is still incomprehensible to people who trusted in the hypocritical cant of the antisocialist and revisionist elements. Under the guise of "democratization" these elements were shattering the socialist state step by step; they sought to demoralize the Communist Party and dull the minds of the masses; they were gradually preparing for a counterrevolutionary coup and at the same time were not being properly rebuffed inside the country.

The Communists of the fraternal countries naturally could not allow the socialist states to remain idle in the name of abstract sovereignty while the country was endangered by antisocialist degeneration.

The five allied socialist countries' actions in Czechoslovakia are consonant with the fundamental interests of the Czechoslovak people themselves. Obviously it is precisely socialism that, by liberating a nation from the fetters of an exploitative system, ensures the solution of fundamental problems of national development in any country that takes the socialist path. And by encroaching on the foundations of socialism, the counterrevolutionary elements in Czechoslovakia were thereby undermining the basis of the country's independence and sovereignty.

The formal observance of freedom of self-determination in the specific situation that had taken shape in Czechoslovakia would signify freedom of "self-determination" not for the people's masses and the working people, but for their enemies. The antisocialist path, the "neutrality" to which the Czechoslovak people were being prodded, would lead the C.S.R. straight into the jaws of the West German revanchists and would lead to the loss of its national independence. World imperialism, for its part, was trying to export counterrevolution to Czechoslovakia by supporting the antisocialist forces there.

The assistance given to the working people of the C.S.R. by the other socialist countries, which prevented the export of counterrevolution from the outside, is in fact a struggle for the Czechoslovak Socialist Republic's sovereignty against those who would like to deprive it of this sovereignty by delivering the country to the imperialists.

Over a long period of time and with utmost restraint and patience, the fraternal Communist Parties of the socialist countries took political measures to help the Czechoslovak people to halt the antisocialist forces' offensive in Czechoslovakia. And only after exhausting all such measures did they undertake to bring in armed forces.

The allied socialist countries' soldiers who are in Czechoslovakia are proving in deeds that they have no task other than to defend the socialist gains in that country. They are not interfering in the country's internal affairs, and they are waging a struggle not in words but in deeds for the principles of self-determination of Czechoslovakia's peoples, for their inalienable right to decide their destiny themselves after profound and careful consideration, without intimidation by counterrevolutionaries, without revisionist and nationalist demagoguery.

Those who speak of the "illegality" of the allied socialist countries' actions in Czechoslovakia forget that in a class society there is and can be no such thing as nonclass law. Laws and the norms of law are subordinated to the laws of the class struggle and the laws of social development. These laws are clearly formulated in the documents jointly adopted by the Communist and Workers' Parties.

The class approach to the matter cannot be discarded in the name of legalistic considerations. Whoever does so and forfeits the only correct, class-oriented criterion for evaluating legal norms begins to measure events with the yardsticks of bourgeois law. Such an approach to the question of sovereignty means, for example, that the world's progressive forces could not oppose the revival of neo-Nazism in the F.R.G., the butcheries of Franco and Salazar or the reactionary outrages of the "black colonels" in Greece, since these are the "internal affairs" of "sovereign states." It is typical that both the Saigon puppets and their American protectors concur completely in the notion that sovereignty forbids supporting the struggle of the progressive forces. After all, they shout from the housetops that the socialist states that are giving aid to the Vietnamese people in their struggle for independence and freedom are violating Vietnam's sovereignty. Genuine revolutionaries, as internationalists, cannot fail to support progressive forces in all countries in their just struggle for national and social liberation.

The interests of the socialist commonwealth and the entire revolutionary movement and the interests of socialism in Czechoslovakia demand full exposure and political isolation of the reactionary forces in that country, consolidation of the working people and consistent fulfillment of the Moscow agreement between the Soviet and Czechoslovak leaders.

There is no doubt that the actions taken in Czechoslovakia by the five allied socialist countries in Czechoslovakia, actions aimed at defending the fundamental interests of the socialist commonwealth and primarily at defending Czechoslovakia's independence and sovereignty as a socialist state, will be increasingly supported by all who really value the interests of the present-day revolutionary movement, the peace and security of peoples, democracy and socialism.

THE NIXON DOCTRINE

The postwar era of American foreign policy began . . . in 1947 with the proclamation of the Truman Doctrine and the Marshall Plan, offering American economic and military assistance to countries threatened by aggression. Our policy held that democracy and prosperity, buttressed by American military strength and organized in a worldwide network of American-led alliances, would insure stability and peace. In the formative years of the postwar period, this great effort of international political and economic reconstruction was a triumph of American leadership and imagination, especially in Europe.

For two decades after the end of the Second World War, our foreign policy was guided by such a vision and inspired by its success. The vision was based on the fact that the United States was the richest and most stable country, without whose initiative and resources little security or progress was possible.

This impulse carried us through into the 1960's. The United States conceived programs and ran them. We devised strategies, and proposed them to our allies. We discerned dangers, and acted directly to combat them.

The world has dramatically changed since the days of the Marshall Plan. We deal now with a world of stronger allies, a community of independent developing nations, and a Communist world still hostile but now divided.

*   *   *

Compiled by the editors from President Richard M. Nixon's televised speech to the nation, "The Pursuit of Peace in Vietnam," on November 3, 1969, and his report to Congress, "A New Strategy for Peace," February 18, 1970 (*Department of State Bulletin,* November 24, 1969 and March 9, 1970).

Let me briefly explain what has been described as the Nixon doctrine. . . .

We Americans are a do-it-yourself people. We are an impatient people. Instead of teaching someone else to do a job, we like to do it ourselves. And this trait has been carried over into our foreign policy.

In Korea and again in Viet-Nam, the United States furnished most of the money, most of the arms, and most of the men to help the people of those countries defend their freedom against Communist aggression.

Before any American troops were committed to Viet-Nam, a leader of another Asian country expressed this opinion to me when I was traveling in Asia as a private citizen. He said: "When you are trying to assist another nation defend its freedom, U.S. policy should be to help them fight the war, but not to fight the war for them."

Well, in accordance with this wise counsel, I laid down in Guam three principles as guidelines for future American policy toward Asia:

—First, the United States will keep all of its treaty commitments.

—Second, we shall provide a shield if a nuclear power threatens the freedom of a nation allied with us or of a nation whose survival we consider vital to our security.

—Third, in cases involving other types of aggression, we shall furnish military and economic assistance when requested in accordance with our treaty commitments. But we shall look to the nation directly threatened to assume the primary responsibility of providing the manpower for its defense.

*   *   *

America cannot live in isolation if it expects to live in peace. We have no intention of withdrawing from the world. The only issue before us is how we can be most effective in meeting our responsibilities, protecting our interests, and thereby building peace.

A more responsible participation by our foreign friends in their own defense and progress means a more effective common effort toward the goals we all seek. Peace in the world will continue to require us to maintain our commitments—and we will. As I said at the United Nations, "It is not my belief that the way to peace is by giving up our friends or letting down our allies." But a more balanced and realistic American role in the world is essential if American commitments are to be sustained over the long pull. In my State of the Union Address, I affirmed that "to insist that other nations play a role is not a retreat from responsibility; it is a sharing of responsibility." This is not a way for America to withdraw from its indispensable role in the world. It is a way—the only way—we can carry out our responsibilities.

Zbigniew Brzezinski

HALF PAST NIXON

The title above is not a forecast but a statement of fact. Whether President Nixon is reelected or not, his first administration has passed its halfway mark. His foreign policy is on the record—both in words and in deeds.

*   *   *

Nonetheless, it is also a fact that doubts and uncertainties about the Administration's foreign policy persist. They are reflected in public opinion polls at home, and even more in the searching questions that one encounters from America's true friends when traveling abroad. . . .

Indeed, one is even tempted to say that never before has an administration said so much so often and in so many words about its foreign policy—and yet has been so little understood. Why is this so, given the undeniable effort by the President and his associates to articulate a coherent, understandable, and relevant foreign policy?

To attempt an answer, some analysis of the essential components of the Administration's foreign policy is first in order. That foreign policy has been labeled—not by historians but, rather immodestly, by its chief architect—as the Nixon Doctrine. . . .

THE NIXON DOCTRINE

Essentially, the Nixon Administration sees American foreign policy during the preceding two decades as having been determined by one overriding reality: that it was the United States alone that could conduct a policy designed to stem the tide of Communist aggression and to build a reasonably stable framework of international cooperation. This reality shaped U.S. global involvement and eventually gave rise even to a subconscious bureaucratic vested interest in the maintenance of a variety of political and military commitments.

This situation prevails no longer. Many traditional nations have regained their energy and their position in the world, the Communist bloc has become fractured, and at the same time a new relationship of nuclear parity with the Soviet Union has emerged. All of this compels a basic reassessment, all the more so since the war in Vietnam has prompted widespread domestic dissatisfaction with the scale, character, and thrust of American global involvement. Indeed, as the President emphasized in his

Reprinted by permission from *Foreign Policy* (Spring 1971), pp. 3–21. Copyright 1971 by National Affairs, Inc.

465

presentation of the second (1971) State of the World message,[1] dissatisfaction has reached such a level that the major danger today is no longer over-involvement but rather isolationist underinvolvement. The President thus sees himself as engaged in an effort to strike a proper balance, correcting both the excesses of the past and the overreactions of the present.

In that context, Nixon's Presidency is the beginning of an era and his predecessors, Johnson and Kennedy, are demoted to transitional figures. It was under them that American global involvement reached its peak and then began to recede, and it was under them (and perhaps even because of them) that domestic support began to fracture. The Nixon Doctrine is, therefore, in the eyes of its framers, a historical watershed.

Although the doctrine addresses itself to the American relationship with the world as a whole, it is possible to isolate its chief components and emphases. . . . As a broad generalization, the principal foci of that doctrine can be said to include Vietnam as an immediate problem, the American-Soviet relationship, relations with our principal partners, both in Western Europe and Japan, and finally the question of American-Chinese relations. Other issues and regions are clearly of secondary importance.

VIETNAM AND THE SOVIET UNION

With regard to Vietnam, the Nixon Doctrine is in effect the U.S. functional equivalent of Lin Piao's concept of people's revolutionary war: a "people's revolutionary war," says the Nixon Doctrine, can be suppressed only by the people concerned. Accordingly, the objective of the President is to achieve the essential—though not necessarily the complete—U.S. military disengagement by the end of 1972, with that disengagement not linked causally to the eventual outcome of the Vietnamese war. It would appear that the Administration hopes that that outcome will become apparent only later, say by 1975 or 1976. If it turns out to have been a successful one, i.e., the political survival of a non-Communist South Vietnam, the war, the U.S. engagement in it, as well as Nixon's Vietnamization will become, retroactively, victories. If the eventual outcome is the collapse of the Saigon government, its immediate cause—it is hoped—will be ascribed to the ineffectiveness of the South Vietnamese rulers.

To attain the above objective, the President has sought to keep his options open, and has therefore rejected repeated proposals that he indicate a terminal date for U.S. military involvement in the war. His spokesmen have argued that to do so would give Hanoi an excessive degree of certainty concerning U.S. intentions. Moreover, he has repeatedly hinted that the United States might adopt more forceful measures (presumably massive and unrestricted bombing of North Vietnam) if the North Viet-

[1] Dated February 25, 1971.

namese place U.S. forces in South Vietnam in jeopardy during the latter phases of the withdrawal process.

With regard to the Soviet Union, initially the Administration's point of departure was the oft-repeated slogan "from an era of confrontation to an era of negotiation." Indeed, in the 1970 message the section dealing with the Soviet Union was even entitled "an era of negotiation." The 1971 message is considerably less Pollyannaish: it abounds in warnings that "in certain fundamental aspects the Soviet outlook on world affairs is incompatible with a stable international order," that "intransigence remains a cardinal feature of the Soviet system," and several times points to the possibility of a U.S.-Soviet confrontation.

Nonetheless, the broad objective of the Nixon Administration, rather like that of its predecessors, remains unchanged: it is to stabilize, regularize, and eventually transform the U.S.-Soviet rivalry into a somewhat less antagonistic relationship. To that end, the Administration has proceeded with a triad of negotiations which the White House sees, according to the linkage theory,[2] as being interdependent: they involve the strategic arms issue, certain regional conflicts, and the development of functional ties. (The linkage theory, by the way, is held by the Administration to be a fact of life: it is argued by its spokesmen that the requirement of "parallel progress" has been borne out by experience.)

The first of the above negotiations involves an effort to minimize the insecurities that both parties feel because of the arms race, and an attempt to contain that race. It is no secret that these talks have been moving extremely slowly and that they may have been further delayed by political division both within Washington and Moscow; moreover, technological developments are continuously introducing new complexities into an already extraordinarily complex relationship.

The second aspect of U.S.- Soviet diplomacy has involved an effort to create some accommodation on a regional basis in areas of political contention. The Four-Power talks on the Middle East are in essence Two-Power talks; they are an example of an attempt to create some bilateral understanding of common stakes in regional stability. Similarly, talks on Berlin fall into the same category, and it is possible that the scope of these discussions will eventually be enlarged to deal with the broader matter of European political and security issues.

Most progress has been made in the third field of U.S.-Soviet negotiations, namely, the promotion of what might be called functional cooperation. This includes such things as common undertakings or mutual acceptance of limitations with regard to outer space, seabeds, pollution. and ecological problems, not to speak of even more specialized scientific

---

[2] *This theory holds that U.S.-Soviet relations at different points around the globe are sufficiently interrelated so that U.S. policy in one place, e.g. the Middle East, will have direct impact on Soviet behavior in other places, e.g. Berlin.*

cooperation.   The Administration has also continued the effort, initially launched in 1966 as part of "building bridges," to involve the Russians in a special new institute, designed to study problems of the post-industrial society, the applications of systems analysis, and the like, thus hoping to induce in the Russians a somewhat less ideological perspective on future social trends.

EUROPE, CHINA, AND MILITARY SECURITY

With regard to a more equal alliance relationship with Western Europe and Japan, a matter which is clearly uppermost in the longer-range thinking of the White House, the President has sought to reduce friction (by cultivating President Pompidou of France and by pledging the return of Okinawa to Japan), to stimulate a greater sense of independent responsibility on the part of our allies (e.g., the Nixon-Sato communique, referring to Japan's security stake in South Korea and Taiwan, and the December 1970 NATO Council decision pledging a European effort to strengthen NATO infrastructure), without at the same time stimulating fears of an American disengagement. . . .

With regard to China, it would appear that the Administration is guided primarily by two considerations, one tactical and one strategic.   On the level of tactics, Washington has been clearly jolted by the sudden rush of recognitions of the Peking government and by the high probability that Peking may soon be seated in the United Nations, at the expense of the Nationalist Chinese government.   How to devise a stratagem which avoids the latter without preventing the former has been the Administration's major concern since the second half of 1970, especially given the Administration's longer-range desire to take advantage of the triangular relationship now prevailing among Washington, Peking, and Moscow.

The various unilateral gestures so far adopted by the Nixon Administration can therefore be seen as an effort to obtain eventually some flexibility in that triangular relationship, even if these gestures by themselves do not materially improve the American-Chinese relationship in the short run. The Administration certainly realizes that in such a triangular relationship intense hostility between any two automatically benefits the third.   This puts a premium on restraint on the part of all three towards one another while benefiting particularly the one which attains a lower level of antagonism towards the remaining two. (Incidentally, one can therefore believe the Administration when it affirms in the 1971 message that "it is absurd to believe that we could collude with one of the parties against the other," but it strains one's credulity, and doubtless Mao's and Brezhnev's as well, to read that "we, therefore, see no advantage to us in the hostility between the Soviet Union and Communist China.")

To back up the foregoing central four pillars of the Nixon Doctrine, the Administration has been devising a somewhat new strategic posture and security policy. In its essence, it postulates a lower U.S. capability for conventional warfare, it assumes a lesser probability of a major confrontation simultaneously in the West and in the East, and it appears to favor (although with some ambiguity) an earlier reliance on nuclear weapons in the event of a grave crisis. The ambiguity with regard to the last point is due largely to the simultaneous recognition *and acceptance* of a situation of relative parity in non-survivability with the Soviet Union, a situation which makes increased reliance on nuclear weaponry somewhat less appealing.

As far as more specific commitments in the security field are concerned, it appears likely—short of a significant accord soon in SALT—that the Nixon Administration will place more emphasis on longer-range delivery systems in more complex configurations, and perhaps more emphasis on underwater systems, in order to offset the loss of bases and increased Soviet strategic capability. Similarly, major refinements and innovations will be required in regard to detection systems. Finally, more low-yield tactical nuclear weaponry may become needed to compensate for lower troop levels and for the apparent inclination to rely on tactical retaliation at the point of aggression (in contrast to Dulles' strategic retaliation at the source of aggression). More broadly, it might be said that in the fifties President Eisenhower, in his security policy, emphasized air; in the sixties President Kennedy shifted the focus of attention to land; in the seventies, President Nixon is stressing the seas.

A CRITICAL APPRAISAL

. . . There is first of all the question of emphasis. While it is difficult to fault the Administration's general priorities, one is struck by Washington's extremely limited interest in what is commonly described as the Third World. It may be true that the Kennedy Administration occasionally overdid its wooing of third-rate statesmen and fourth-rate countries, but the Nixon Administration, far from establishing a balance, appears to be turning its back on most of mankind.

* * *

. . . [T]he priorities of the Administration appear to be right, but the absence of any serious concern and, perhaps even more important, of any systematic analysis of longer-range trends in those parts of the world where the majority of the globe's population resides, is especially troubling, for it seems to reflect a curiously conservative and static vision of the world. It is true that international stability, as well as mankind's general progress, depend in the first instance on the successful resolution of the problems identified as the Nixon Doctrine's principal concerns. But it is also true that progress on that "higher" priority must be supplemented and accompanied by a wider conceptual recognition of the increasing interdependence of the world, of the growing transformation of what used to be international politics (conducted by distinct nation-states) into a highly intimate global political process, permeated by a highly sensitive global nervous system.

That global political process is bound to be very sensitive to revolutionary changes even in the economically or militarily less important regions, prompting a direct feedback into the relations between the most powerful states. Thus, in the years to come, the radicalization of Latin America will inevitably create opportunities, temptations, and even imperatives for Soviet involvement, however cautious, thereby dangerously taxing U.S.-Soviet relations. Leaving hemispheric interests aside, that consideration alone should prompt more attention to Latin American problems. The argument that the Alliance for Progress was a harmful mirage does not justify a policy of passive indifference to a revolution of continental dimensions.

More broadly still, the Nixon Doctrine seems to be insufficiently concerned with what might well emerge as the central threat to international stability in this and the next decade: the contagious spread of global anarchy. Social and political fragmentation appear to be the likely prospects for both Pakistan and India, as well as for parts of Africa and Latin America. This may prompt in turn new ethnic and religious, as well as ideological conflicts, and perhaps even an anti-modernist, inward-looking escapism, which would further inhibit collective efforts to cope with poverty and backwardness. As one Malaysian scholar recently put it: [3]

It is no wonder that the new nations feel insecure and are beginning to find that race and religion, things already well known in the past, are the only certainties. Although they are aware that the trend towards political fragmentation is itself dangerous, it does appear that they are preparing themselves to sacrifice the universalist features of modernization for a return to the uniqueness of their respective national experience. There is cause for their anxiety, the uphill battle for national survival will be exhausting, the new nations might become more negative and backward looking than before, and whatever creativity their more brilliant minds may have is likely to produce work within an increasingly narrower cultural and social framework. Unless there is a fresh and firm commitment to the wider framework of international cooperation, world organizations, multilateral trade and undreamed of advances in communications at all levels, this will be the destiny of most Asian nations. It is not surprising therefore that many educated Asians now feel, rightly or wrongly, that for Asia to continue to share in the modernizing parts of the Western experience, it may be necessary to keep the West from withdrawing from Asia.

But to prevent the advanced world from such a withdrawal, it, too, needs a common vision and a framework. It is here that the Nixon Doctrine is

[3] *Professor Wang Gungwu, "Asia and the Western Experience,"* Quadrant, *December 1970, p. 14.*

most deficient.   It is essentially a negative concept reacting to the excesses of the past; it offers little leadership and historical direction.   Yet the basic reality of international affairs is that some leadership is needed, that only America can provide it, and that even our friendly foreign critics expect it. Thus, efforts to repair and renovate alliance relationships will come to naught, unless both Western Europe and Japan come to share common goals and common responsibilities.   The fifties saw the vision of the Atlantic alliance as a binding concept; the seventies require something broader still, and the Nixon Doctrine—though occasionally inching up to it—fails to provide such a larger goal.   It recognizes the "great intellectual challenge" involved in the effort "to define and assume new modes of partnership," but it fails to seize the opportunity to postulate a larger community of the developed nations, spanning Japan, Western Europe, and the United States, as the historically relevant response to that challenge.

WHAT KIND OF PARTNERSHIP?

It is doubtful that without such a larger effort and a more compelling goal global stability can be promoted, or even existing alliance relations significantly enhanced.   Indeed, without a challenging goal, the advanced nations may themselves become victims of an increasingly widespread social *anomie,* while alliance relations could even atrophy, especially if Western Europe flirts with neutralism or if American-Japanese economic tensions mount.   This is why the correct emphasis placed by the Nixon Administration on the pre-eminent importance of alliance relationships needs to be grounded on a broader foundation, translating into a political vision the evident organic growth of closer economic ties between the most advanced states.

That growth, however, is not without its tensions and it has already produced some painful conflicts.   The mishandling by both the United States and Japan of the textile issue is in some ways reminiscent of the Skybolt snafu in U.S.-British relations.   The Administration simply appears not to have done its homework in the economic field, and the gap between the emerging interdependence and old forms of economic relations is creating difficulties which could eventually prompt a major crisis in the advanced world's economy.

The absence of a larger theme for alliance relations also affects political relations.   This is most marked in the discussion of the U.S.-Japanese relationship, where the need for adjustment is acknowledged but where no effort is made to spell out what the substance of that new, more balanced relationship might be.   As a result, the Japanese have been particularly perplexed by the meaning of the Nixon Doctrine, while Indonesian and

Korean anxieties have been aroused by the possibility that the United States desires to have Japan replace the United States in Asia.[4]

CREDIT WHERE CREDIT IS DUE

In regard to Europe, it does appear that NATO consultations have been given deeper meaning, and the Administration has been meticulous in briefing its allies about SALT. At the same time, however, there is reason to believe that the Nixon Administration harbors strong reservations concerning Chancellor Brandt's *Ostpolitik;* and its warnings against permitting Moscow to pursue a differentiated detente appear to be as much directed at Bonn as at Moscow. That may be fair enough, except that the Administration itself has been rather passive with regard to East-West relations within Europe (although wisely it has demonstrably supported both Tito and Ceausescu). . . .

Perhaps the soundest part of the Administration's policy concerns the Soviet Union. . . . It speaks in sober and realistic terms, especially when pleading with the Soviet leaders not to succumb to the temptation of seeking nuclear supremacy over the United States. The fact that the Administration recognizes the possibility that some Soviet leaders may be tempted to exploit SALT to establish such superiority is significant, and one can only hope, first, that the Kremlin will heed the warning and, second, that if it does not the Congress will recognize in time the dangers involved.

Similarly, the discussion of arms control represents an unusually measured effort to strike a balance between obvious American interests and the interests of the principal antagonist. One suspects that portions were deliberately drafted in order both to educate and influence the otherwise inaccessible Soviet leadership. It is, therefore, a cause for regret that the Administration did not see fit to pursue a somewhat more flexible negotiating strategy: step-by-step limitations might have created a greater climate of mutual confidence and widened the reciprocal interest of both states in reaching eventually a comprehensive agreement. A more forward approach could have also had the added advantage of establishing sooner whether the Soviet leaders are exploiting SALT primarily in order to improve the Soviet military position vis-a-vis the United States.

With regard to regional issues, the Nixon Administration deserves credit for a subtle and skillful approach to the Middle Eastern question, both as it pertains to U.S.-Soviet relations and to the region itself. While not jeopardizing the basic commitment of the United States to the preservation of Israel, it has been sound in seeking to subordinate the territorial issue to the security issue, thereby keeping open the possibility of an eventual

---

[4] *For a characteristic expression of this anxiety, see Hahm Pyong-choon, "The New Japan: The Chrysanthemum and the Transistor?" The Pacific Community, April, 1970, especially p. 436.*

peace of reconciliation and not of conquest between the parties involved.

A somewhat more critical appraisal seems warranted in the case of the Administration's handling of the China issue. . . .   Although it is true that no fundamental normalization of U.S.-Chinese relations is likely until the Taiwan issue is somehow resolved, and that issue in its turn is not likely to be resolved until after the death of both Mao and Chiang, an earlier adoption by the United States of a more flexible position on the issue of U.N. membership might have averted the crisis which now seems likely.   Salvaging a seat for Nationalist China is now bound to be more difficult, while the expulsion of Nationalist China might leave the United States isolated in its view that the mainland Chinese do not have the right to resolve the Formosan issue as their own domestic affair and therefore by whatever means they choose.

PERSISTING UNCERTAINTIES

It is extremely difficult to judge whether a strategy different from the one pursued by the Administration might have been more effective in bringing the Vietnamese war to a speedier conclusion.   A solution through negotiations seems extremely unlikely, unless by that is meant a thinly disguised acceptance of defeat by one of the parties involved.   Civil wars do not end in compromise and coalition governments.   At this stage, neither side seems prepared to capitulate to the other and for good reason: the South Vietnamese, thanks to American efforts and lately their own, are stronger than five years ago, while the North Vietnamese know that the Americans will soon be gone.

*   *   *

Finally, with regard to the defense posture of the United States, one cannot suppress the feeling that it is being shaped primarily by a combination of domestic political and fiscal calculations, and not even by the logic of the Nixon Doctrine itself.   As a result, the combat readiness of ground forces is being cut back, while the absence of an integrated concept imposed from above is again permitting service interests to dictate individual allocations.   This could prove particularly serious in the new setting of Soviet-American parity.   In that new context, the President has defined his basic defense objective as the maintenance of "sufficiency," i.e. "enough force to inflict a level of damage on a potential aggressor sufficient to deter him from attacking" as well as "the maintenance of forces adequate to prevent us and our allies from being coerced."

In other words, the former objective means enough power to influence the will of the potential aggressor, and the latter means enough power to prevent one's own will from crumbling.   In large measure, these are psychological intangibles, and one can only speculate, somewhat uneasily, as to whether the margin of safety is wide enough.

The Nixon record . . . is thus uneven. It is also, however, creditable. There is no contradiction between the two propositions. To shape and conduct a global foreign policy, in the midst of unprecedented domestic changes and of a highly unpopular foreign war, and to do so with longer-term objectives clearly in sight, is an almost superhuman task. On some issues the Nixon Administration has done, in this writer's opinion, extremely well; on others it has been the prisoner of both history and of its somewhat narrow horizons, especially in regard to the novel conditions likely to confront America during the seventies.

THE HISTORICAL SETTING

It is time to return to the question raised at the outset: Why is the Administration's foreign policy so little understood? Two partial answers are possible. Much of the skepticism and doubt surrounding the Nixon Doctrine is due not to any intrinsic contradictions in that doctrine but to the general division in the United States concerning the goals and means of foreign policy. The war in Vietnam has been a catalyst for growing public disenchantment with massive U.S. involvement abroad, a disenchantment that began in the early sixties as the felt danger to the United States seemed to decline. The divisions at home which the war produced fractured the domestic consensus on foreign policy which had existed since the days following World War II, when Senator Vandenberg aligned himself with President Truman on the key question of America's relationship to Europe.

President Nixon is the first postwar President to conduct a foreign policy in the setting of domestic dissent. None of his predecessors labored under a similar handicap. In large part, therefore, the Nixon Doctrine is an attempt to respond both to changed international as well as domestic conditions. Its object is to preserve as well as give some new meaning to America's continued involvement in the world, even while satisfying some of the critics of the policies pursued in the sixties, especially in regard to Vietnam. A measure of ambiguity is thus inherent and even desirable, lest foreign policy issues further polarize American public opinion and limit the President's freedom of action.

Secondly, but closely related to the above, it is important to note that some of the difficulty with the Nixon Doctrine is due to a misnomer. In its eagerness to carve out a historical niche for itself, the Administration has gone out of its way to stamp its foreign policy as "the Nixon Doctrine," a historical milestone initiating a new era. Yet there is no such doctrine. What passes for the Nixon Doctrine is essentially a continuous process of redefinition of American foreign policy in the light of new domestic and international circumstances. That is as it should be, and the differences in emphasis and nuance between the first and the second Presidential messages are proof that the Administration is creatively engaged in such a process.

The Truman Doctrine was a doctrine because it crystallized in a few simple propositions a process of change that had preceded it and which cumulatively meant the assumption of altogether novel responsibilities by the United States. The Nixon "Doctrine," in spite of frequent references to it and lengthy efforts to spell out what it means, is not a doctrine because it marks the beginning of a probably lengthy and difficult process of defining new patterns of America's relationship to the world and of a similarly lengthy process of building up a new domestic basis for that relationship. It is, therefore, above all else, part of a transitional phase and a symptom of that transition.

William Pfaff • *Jeremy J. Stone*
Carl Oglesby • *Wilson C. McWilliams* • *Stanley Hoffmann*

AFTER VIETNAM, WHAT?: A SYMPOSIUM

WILLIAM PFAFF

*   *   *

We will experience a reasonable calm if there are no more Vietnams. I do not think that it will take an American "Algeria" to discredit interventionism, but I may be wrong. There are many in and out of government who insist that a "bad" settlement (and they would consider bad almost any settlement remotely possible) will have calamitous results. Since these are mostly the same people who, as Hawks, have steadily worked to create a situation in which anything less than victory is calamity—and to convince the world of this—they may be right.

There certainly will be domestic bitterness. The American public has never really experienced failure. My suspicion is that we have more than adequate defense mechanisms—that America's introversion and national optimism will muffle reality. We will barely acknowledge what has happened, repressing the truth, grateful that the war is over. But if that should not happen, and the terms of the settlement (or its outcome) come as a shock, we could turn bitterly isolationist—and resume tearing ourselves apart in controversy. That seems more likely than renewed interventions. Most likely of all is a fairly slow and baffled inward-turning. . . .

What will happen in American foreign policy itself will be less a matter of intellectual choice and resolute revisions than a slow and disorderly retreat. The battle among the theorists has been going on for years without decisive effect. Policy follows theory—if at all—by erratic leaps, when

Reprinted by Permission from *Commonweal*, March 21, 1969, pp. 7–14.

a bright formulation of ideas coincides with an appropriate crisis. (The ideas may be good or bad, "containment," "collective security," "stages of growth." Eventually each is irrelevantly inflated by the policy process into a general principle of action, a universal problem solvent. Containment, a specific policy addressed to the specific problems presented by Stalin's Russia in Central and Southern Europe in 1947–48, is still—in the teeth of George Kennan's protests—being applied in Southeast Asia today.) Or policy shifts crab-wise under the buffeting of events. We have become a neo-isolationist nation in mood without knowing what neo-isolationism might mean, or caring very much.

But let me attempt to name the themes in the debate. There is *conservative interventionism:* arguing that ours is the decade of penultimate battle with Communism. The struggle is ideological; the very divisions within Communism make it the more dangerous, multiplying its appeals. There is *liberal interventionism:* the penultimate battle really is with world poverty and disorder. We and the Communists provide warring "models," to one or the other of which the rest of the world must conform, eventually providing either liberalism or Communism the palm of historical victory. There is *liberal legalism:* avoid unilateral interventions; build cooperation with Russia; build up collective security alliances and regional organizations; build up the UN; extend arms control. The UN will police the world. Or regional organizations will do it. Or we and Russia will do it together (several versions of this theory exist). There is *neo-isolationism:* what happens in much of the world, and certainly on the Asian mainland and in Africa, is of little direct relevance to American national interests and (or) beyond our power to do much about. There is the *"realist"* position: foreign policy is the art of staying afloat; history is bloody-minded; the Third World's troubles have very little essentially to do with the ideologies of Russia or America. The United States chiefly has reason to worry about Russia, a great power and a hostile one, and about Europe and Japan—the societies which can make a difference in the world. Keep relations stable among these and we—and the Third World—may all manage to stay afloat. There is the (American) *radical left* position: the West and Russia alike are in the last stages of bureaucratic industrial despotism; revolution is required here and in the Third World. What revolution means for the Third World can be described. What it means for us we don't know, nor much care since it inevitably will be an improvement (history is benign; man progresses).

*   *   *

More important to the long-run policy of this country are certain enduring factors in the American world-view. . . . moral isolation, a certain messianism, an apolitical ambition to find "final" solutions (legal, organizational, or military). This country does change its foreign policy, and periodically it has been forced back onto limited, "realistic," programs.

But we always drift back again towards the tantalizing absolutes—towards total withdrawal from the world, or totally making the world over. (In this respect, the New Left's apocalyptic goals are, like bombing, as American as cherry pie.)

We have, I think, no great talent for foreign politics. Like imperial Germany, we are tone-deaf in diplomacy, and not really very interested in the rest of the world. We are uneasy about the opinions of others, yet defiantly righteous—are we not God's New Israel? We are chastened now, and turning inward. We could reverse, if Paris goes badly, and that would be very bad for us, and assuredly for Vietnam. If things go well, ours will not really have been an intellectual conversion, but only that we—whose national virtue, after all, is pragmatism—have tried the other way and it didn't work.

*   *   *

JEREMY J. STONE

In Vietnam, we practiced to deceive; the web we wove is the measure of that deception. We started from the premise that South Vietnam was a sovereign state, a vital interest, and a free society. By a policy of gradual escalation, we tried to make caution seem implacable tactics in a war of nerves. We pretended that the aggression was clearer in fact and law than it was. We pretended that the South Vietnamese were more unified in resistance than they were. We lied about body counts. We pretended Khe Sanh and Tet were victories and distorted the events in the Tonkin Gulf. We pretended we could not be held responsible for South Vietnamese torture of prisoners or political repression of dissidents. We pretended the U.S. Senate had freely given its authority to the war. We pretended repeatedly that the war could be won rapidly, and bemused ourselves with statistics.

With each deception, fewer and fewer people could keep themselves fooled, until finally even the highest officials had to search for historical analogies to maintain their confidence.

The thing to do "after Vietnam" is to tell the truth. Presidents need to be franker about the trap they find themselves in. Cabinet officers must be a little readier to resign. Senators must risk a bit more. And to maintain these standards, integrity must be rewarded and the absence of it condemned. A vigilant public and press have to notice and support acts of political courage so that politicians can survive them.

Because everyone is soberer about peace, a term that covers ambiguously the problems of Vietnam, the Arms Race, and the Middle East, we might get unprecedented support for arms agreements or Middle East settlements after Vietnam. Because the dollar had a scare, we might get world monetary reform. Because the Senate is frustrated and guilty, we might get a revolt against the Armed Services Committee.   We are entering a period in which much is possible and little, *a priori,* impossible.

But for some of this, the Vietnamese war must be liquidated in a way that leaves no doubt in the minds of Americans that the war was disaster. This requires no particular outcome, but it does require restraint in post-negotiation claims of victory.   Americans still do not understand why Peking thinks it taught us a lesson in Korea; after being pushed back to the Korean "waist" we simply denied that we had entertained hopes of reuniting Korea.   The same kind of reevaluation could still lose a hard won lesson.

Even assuming that America has been badly burnt in Vietnam, avoiding a repetition may still require a Senate primed to assert its war powers. The domestic fears of Communist takeovers in Southeast Asia or Latin America are still too strong for any one president.   And just as the costs of Korea were ignored in the Vietnamese involvement, a Madison-Avenued compromise in Vietnam might not be an obstacle to another intervention somewhere else.

If we have learned in Vietnam the limits of our power, the next lesson may be the limits of U.S.-Soviet power combined.   The Russians and the Third World are even more prone to anticipate a U.S.-Soviet coalition than we are.   A joint attempt at political intervention, as for example in the Middle East, might expose a new kind of impotency.   As the Russians may be learning in Czechoslovakia, modern-day intervention gets more and more complicated every day, and less and less likely to produce the desired results.

The most dramatic opportunity produced by Vietnam is the live chance to secure a comprehensive U.S.-Soviet arms treaty.   Both we and the Russians see a swollen U.S. defense budget being reabsorbed by now traditional strategic weapons industries as men are brought home from Vietnam. And both tend to think that only Vietnam has prevented the conclusion of an agreement.   Thus, stored-up expectations for progress may now support unprecedented efforts at cooperation—at least for a time.   In terms of the weapon deployment cycles also, both sides are better able to contemplate agreement than ever before in the Cold War. . . .

CARL OGLESBY

The underdeveloped world is starving to death, and the disaster which this protends for us all draws upon us at an accelerating rate.

How is it to be deflected or postponed, not even to say averted?   What are the starving people of the world supposed to do?

The characteristic response of the underdeveloped world to its own predicament is socialist revolution, this being the means by which an entire population can achieve collective self-modernization.

The advanced world's characteristic response to revolution is Vietnam and the Alliance for Progress. With the first, it announces its refusal to sur-render its dominance over the global south. With the second, it confesses that centuries of this dominance have converged upon this half of this century to produce an intolerable social order.

Vietnamism has failed. Generalizing the violence of domination forces the militant unification of the entire victim people. From that point on-ward, the revolution can only be mauled, not defeated, for the structure of world power relations is such that to invest sufficient energies to destroy the revolution is to open the attacker's flank to other modes of counterattack. Through the mediations of the world structure of power, Vietnam counter-attacked through Europe by means of a Vietnam-induced weakness in the dollar-gold relation, triggering not only Basel, but also sparking the politics of *le défi,* the days of May, etc.

Concurrently, the Alliance fails. More people, less food; higher import prices, lower export earnings; rising debt, shrinking ability to finance the debt; more "crash" programs, more wasted money; more American eco-nomic penetration, more big American corporations, more U.S.-trained and U.S.-equipped counterinsurgency forces. . . . Very well, everyone knows throughout Latin America, hungrier and more fascist today than when the great *Alianza* adventure began, the appalling melodrama of the "minute-to-midnight" situation has only deepened.

Meanwhile, it has become indubitable—repeat, *indubitable*—that the only Third World countries which stand even a chance of surviving, of pushing themselves into the imperative modernization, are those which have taken the path of violent socialist revolution. Compare the Soviet Union with Eastern Europe, China with India, or Cuba with Hispaniola.

Any human being who is at all interested in staving off the forthcoming defeat of the species must therefore acknowledge one overriding responsi-bility. *He must do whatever he can to make the revolution more possible.* The irony we must live with lies in this: Failing in this project, we will only have made that revolution inevitable. Succeeding, we will have made it less necessary.

WILSON CAREY MC WILLIAMS

. . . If one fault stands out in American foreign policy in Vietnam and elsewhere, it is the absence of prematurity, the heavy-handed pragmatism which calls itself "realism" and which, in fact, is a euphemism for drift.

*   *   *

We began and proceeded badly in Vietnam, but not because we "inter-vened" in the affairs of another state or even because we intervened in a civil war. Intervention is not a policy; it is a fact. American wealth and power are constant invaders of other lands, psychologically if not physi-cally; our currency is the world's medium of exchange; our military potential a constant threat for some and a partial protection for others.

Nor can we simply, by some self-denying ordinance, relieve ourselves of the responsibility to use all our powers to produce the ends we hope to achieve[:]

. . . a comparatively peaceful, pluralistic and stable world which affords a maximum of satisfaction and justice to all men and nations.

National insurgency, romanticism aside, *is* a menace to that sort of world, and not simply because it could be a way for the great powers to sneak around the nuclear stalemate. Rather, the vogue of national insurgency requires that all governments in developing states spend more on their military establishments than they can afford, for if the primary means of stopping insurgents lies in removing economic and social causes of discontent, a secondary means is the ability to confront the sniper and the dynamiter with more effective weapons than a land reform bill and persuasive rhetoric. If the developing states spend their substance on arms, there is less to deal with precisely the economic and social needs which can, if frustrated, fuel a serious uprising. And frustration is, in any case, the logic of the new states. Hence the tendency, which has shattered one new democracy after another, to put primary emphasis on a government which can keep order, whatever its other virtues, or want of them. . . .

All of which means that American military assistance may be a necessity for many states if they are to escape the cycle of military requirements. That may also demand personnel from the U.S. to train new armies in tactics and organization and use of equipment, and that kind of involvement *can* create a situation where we may become involved again.

To avoid the mistaken involvements like Vietnam—not to avoid involvements at all—thus becomes the test of policy. A first, and simple, recommendation is that the United States must cease dealing with Asia as a colonial appendage and, as we did with Europe, both require more participation by Asians and concede more to Asian desires for dignity and participation in decision-making. America may, for example, have a global "interest" in Vietnam, but Japan has a very empirical one and Japan is a great power—as much as any state other than the Soviet Union and the United States can be. Japan may have to be conceded the dominant voice in Asian policy, and certainly an equal one. It is high time that at least civilian sovereignty was returned to Japan in Okinawa, and time to consider phasing out our military presence there as well. America has "special relations" with certain Asian states—the Philippines, Australia and New Zealand (at least peripherally part of the continent) and, horribly but inevitably, with Formosa. That demands no more of us than our "special relation" with Britain does on the Continent, a role which involves us as at most *primus inter pares*.

More importantly, we must not allow ourselves to become the psychological and political captives of a regime which is bent on its own political destruction. If—as we always knew in Vietnam—reforms are needed to have any chance of success, we must insist on those reforms being instituted *before* any assistance is made available and we must reserve the right to remove ourselves if the regime backslides at some later date.   This is hard; it is an admission of a mistake, and security planners are loath to concede one, yet it is surely safer than our policy in Vietnam.   We refused, there, more than one real chance to either escape honorably or to compel the South Vietnamese to make those changes which we were vainly urging with the frail tongue of reason.

This only states a truth of morals and tactics alike: it is foolish to contest—or to be forced to contest—a war of national liberation on behalf of a government which is not worth defending.   In the past, we have often elected to support *any* government because of the realization that few states ever "emerged" from Communism and the secondary fear that the American public would become irrationally militant if they felt we were consistently "losing."   (Actually, it might have suggested that we might try a few wars of liberation ourselves—as in Korea or East Germany; fortunately, we have been a bit too responsible for that, though not, alas, in Latin America.)   That policy, however, simply allowed our local opponents to pick the time and place for a contest, a dangerous advantage to concede even weak opponents.

Nor, it is clear, will that policy work any more.   The greatest "lesson" of Vietnam is that the State Department and other policy planners can no longer ignore the values and ideas of the American liberal-left.   In the post-war world, the left was rational and responsible, the right, lunatic and dangerous.   Badly burned in the "who lost China?" imbroglio and the McCarthyite aftermath, the policy-makers became unduly sensitive to right-wing irrationalities, assuming—oddly enough—that there was no serious "enemy to the left."   It may seem a faint defense of the Vietnam protests to say that whatever their irresponsibilities and irrationalities, they have changed that.   Policy-makers will not again assume that only the right's possible reactions are to be feared.   At worst, that will produce a healthy caution; at best, it may be a step toward a sunny common-sense policy in which America neither intervenes by reflex nor abstains from dogma, but judges each case by asking whether those we are requested to defend represent a cause worthy of American devotion.   Dollars and weapons may be abundant, but guerrilla war has helped to remind us, even in this age, that devotion is still both the strongest and most fragile resource of nations.

STANLEY HOFFMANN

The main lesson we should learn from Vietnam is self-restraint.   The policy of world-wide anti-Communist containment we have pursued since the end of World War II did not *have* to get us ensnared in Vietnam; there was no fatality here: our involvement in Vietnam resulted from discrete decisions.   But the whole thrust of our policy was to make of the United

States the world-wide champion of anti-Communist "stability"; to make us overlook the fundamental distinction between military expansion or subversion by our chief adversaries—Russia and China—and essentially domestic developments in which indigenous Communist or pro-Communist forces quite independent from Moscow or Peking play a part; to make us apply a policy of containment through massive military and economic aid even in parts of the world where it was likely to lead to more, not less, trouble for us and our protégés, because it had worked so well in the special circumstances of Western Europe.   Even though we had a choice we acted as if we had had none.

What went wrong in Vietnam? Everything. Given our definition of our objectives—to free South Vietnam of organized Communist penetration— we never had a chance of succeeding at a cost that would not have amounted to the very destruction of the people we were assumed to protect.   Our analysis, based on a false analogy with Korea, did not correspond to the political realities of South Vietnam.   Even if we had recognized that we were faced with a rebellion rather than an invasion, "counter-insurgency" can succeed only when the insurgency is still in its early phases, and when the challenged government still has enough authority and effectiveness to lead its own battle.   Otherwise, it becomes a battle between the native rebels and the foreign protector of the challenged government; in such a battle, to quote Raymond Aron, the rebel wins if he doesn't lose, the foreigner loses if he doesn't win.   And we couldn't win in Vietnam, both because the costs of victory *in* the South would have meant the destruction *of* the South, and because the costs of massive escalation *outside* the South entailed global risks of large-power confrontation we did not want to face.   We didn't, because, in the final analysis, our national interest in Vietnam was not so vital.   The superiority of our military might did not compensate for the more compelling quality of the "other side's" interest, i.e., for the greater resolution of the other side, which we consistently and arrogantly minimized.

The lesson we should learn is not only to analyze local realities more realistically, with fewer myths and illusions, so as better to assess our chances of success.   It is *also* to curtail drastically the interventionist tendencies of our foreign policy, even in areas where these chances look better.   We must revise our national interests.   A great power cannot afford to treat every tremor as major threat.   We have an interest in preventing a change in the balance of power obtained by our chief adversaries either through aggression or through their strategic policies; but we have no interest in preventing or crushing insurgencies in countries whose flawed political and social systems foster such rebellions.   Even if the rebels are Communist or pro-Communist, intervention by the United States is guaranteed only to increase their nationalist, anti-imperialist appeal; only if they are authentically national do they have a chance to succeed; but then, however much of a nuisance their victory may be for us, it would neither change the overall balance of power, nor simplify the task of our main adversaries, already plagued by too much diversity in their fragmented "camp."

This is a world in which nationalism, national self-determination, formal sovereignty, invalidate domino theories. Had we not intervened in Vietnam, Saigon would probably have fallen to the NLF. The result would have been unpleasant for us, but a Communist South or a Communist reunified Vietnam would not have been a Chinese satellite, nor a guarantee of collapse for the rest of Southeast Asia. Indeed, other Southeast Asian countries, rather than strengthening their own societies and defenses, have tended to rely far too much on us. The loss of American prestige due to the failure to prevail in Vietnam will not be any smaller than the loss that would have resulted from a failure to get trapped. . . .

In the final analysis, the most important lesson of Vietnam is that moral and political considerations cannot be separated. Self-restraint is today a political as well as a moral imperative for all states, and particularly for the superpowers. The United States, partly by accident, partly through the exuberance of overwhelming power, global and activist principles, and a heady sense of "world responsibility," has ended by acting as an empire, despite all intentions to the contrary. In the process, it is the sense of responsibility, indeed the self-respect of smaller nations, that has been atrophied. We cannot impose on others our inevitably parochial and often disembodied notions of world order and domestic stability. A "realism" that is based, implicitly, on a notion of America's capacity to shape the destiny of others whatever the obstacles is not only unrealistic, it is also derived from moral considerations that are unacceptable. Our good intentions are not what matters; it is our behavior that counts.

Our first task now is not to replace the old crusade of the late 1940s with an anti-crusade that would take the United States out of world affairs, as some people on the New Left seem to want it, but to overcome the old cycle of over-activism followed by retreat, and to aim at a scheme of world order based on true diversity, even at the cost of domestic turbulence. To seek world order by curtailing both wars and revolutions is to court disaster, political and moral. It is inter-state conflict that has to be moderated; this is what we should concentrate on now. New balances of power will have to be encouraged in various parts of the world, with bigger responsibilities for middle-size powers; regional inter-state disputes that could embroil the superpowers will have to be kept under control; the rivalry between the United States and its two chief adversaries will also have to be dampened, especially in the arms arena. The United States must think of its *impact* on others, instead of relying on its material power to *move* others. It is a large enough task, one which requires the substitution of what Pascal called the spirit of finesse for the spirit of geometry (or engineering) that we have exhibited so often.

Richard Lowenthal

RUSSIA AND CHINA: CONTROLLED CONFLICT

* * *

. . . In trying to evaluate the prospects of the conflict, it may be useful to start by separating its components. The first striking fact is that the basic power rivalry between the two communist giants has survived the disappearance of many of the original policy issues of the late 1950s—issues that were linked to the situation of China's material dependence on a richer and more powerful ally. As a nuclear power with an independent role in world affairs, China is clearly determined never again to rely on Soviet economic or military aid for achieving its policy aims; nor has the Soviet Union any more grounds to fear that it might be drawn against its will into risky adventures by the now defunct alliance. What has remained, however, is the power rivalry itself—the interest of Russia in slowing down the growth of the industrial and military might of its eastern neighbor, and the determination of China to overcome the obstacle.

At present, the rivalry manifests itself above all as a struggle for influence in Asia. That struggle takes the form of political competition in North Korea, which has become independent of both, and in North Vietnam, which both have supported without ever coöperating directly. It takes the form of primarily economic competition with Japan. It appears as a direct clash in the Mongolian Peoples' Republic, where China is trying to undermine Soviet control, and in South Asia, where the Soviets are objectively aligned with the United States for the protection of India and have profited from the collapse of Chinese influence in Indonesia.

The importance of the frontier issue in the wider power conflict remains highly controversial among outside observers. The nature of China's overpopulation is not such as to constitute an urgent compulsion to expand her territory: China remains short of capital rather than land. Nor is there the slightest evidence of a Chinese inclination to engage in dangerous military adventures at the present stage—rather it is the contrast between wild language and cautious behavior that continues to impress the student. Even for the longer run, assuming an absolute and relative growth of China's military power and an eventual exhaustion of the reserves of arable land with a further increase of her population, it is by no means "fatalistically inevitable" that she must seek to expand at Russia's expense, at the risk of nuclear war, rather than move south against weaker neighbors or seek peaceful economic solutions. But neither can the possibility of such a development be excluded from the Soviet point of view in the light

Abridged by permission from *Foreign Affairs* (April 1971), pp. 507–518. Copyright by the Council on Foreign Relations, Inc., New York.

of the growth of Chinese armaments, of her present hostility, and of her insistence on the illegitimate origin of the present frontier. Seen from Moscow, the rise of China to the full status of a modern world power, which may be slowed down but is unlikely to be prevented, remains a potential long-term threat to Soviet territorial security—by now presumably the only serious threat of that kind.

If we now turn to the ideological aspects of the conflict, the struggle for control of the nonruling communist parties has lost much of its earlier importance because of the comparative failure of Chinese efforts in this field. . . . The Chinese themselves seem to have come to realize their failure as an international doctrinaire center: there is evidence that for the propagandist struggle against the West and the Soviets, they are relying more and more on supporting militant movements of an outright nationalist character, like the Palestinian guerrillas, rather than left-wing ideological sects.

By contrast, the ideological legitimation of divergent roads of domestic development has remained a far more vital element in the conflict; but it is also far more liable to be affected by changes in the leadership and domestic policy of either country. Among the latter, changes in China are likely to have a more far-reaching impact on Sino-Soviet relations. A Soviet turn toward a new effort at modernizing reform could now only produce an intensification of Chinese ideological invectives, while a turn toward a wholesale rehabilitation of Stalin's memory and methods, from which its more primitive advocates are said to expect an ideological reconciliation with the Chinese, would leave the basic differences unaffected and only deprive the Maoists of the tactical pretext that they are defending the Stalinist tradition. In fact, the basic feaures of Soviet society which form the counterfoil to Mao's vision, such as its reliance on highly differentiated material incentives and its rigid bureaucratic stratification, go back to Stalin's own decisions, as Mao knows perfectly well; and they are unlikely to disappear through any change in the Soviet leadership conceivable at this stage.

On the other hand, a turn on China's part in a more "materialist" and therefore more Soviet-like direction, with more stress on material incentives and continuity of production and less reliance on revolutionary enthusiasm, is conceivable after the disappearance of Mao. Indeed the signs are not lacking that forces favoring such a "pragmatic" turn have increased their influence in the Chinese leadership since the end of the cultural revolution, and that they are the same who have pressed for a normalization of state relations with the Soviet Union. . . . In that sense, a decline in bitterness of China's ideological hostility toward the Soviet Union and a move toward a climate of peaceful coexistence between independent communist powers building different types of "socialism" would be a possible development after Mao's demise. But it would not, of course, end the power rivalry between them; it might even, by speeding the success of China's modernization, make her a more formidable rival for Russia at a quicker pace. The power rivalry, then, will continue to be decisive for the substance of the conflict, while ideological factors may influence its more or less acute and intensive forms at particular times. That substance excludes a true "reconciliation" between the two leading communist powers in the sense of a return to a stable alliance based on the primacy of common ideological convictions and goals. But given a measure of rationality of the leadership on both sides, the fact of a serious conflict of power interests makes nuclear war between them no more inevitable than between either of them and the United States.

The continuation of limited and controlled conflict between Russia and China thus remains a far more plausible prospect than its end by either reunion or catastrophe. But in an increasingly triangular world, that leaves unanswered a question of decisive practical importance for the West: the question of priorities. In a triangular constellation, different combinations of coöperation and conflict are possible at different periods, with two of the major powers combining on different issues against the third. Yet it is in the nature of such a constellation that the combination that will become effective at any particular time is not predetermined, and therefore not predictable. It will be decided by the choice of the most urgent issues at any given moment, and that depends on the political skill of the leaders of each of the new Big Three—including the United States.

Hedley Bull

THE NEW BALANCE OF POWER IN ASIA AND THE PACIFIC

In the 1950s a balance or pattern of power grew up in Asia and the Pacific, the central feature of which was the conflict between the Sino-Soviet bloc and the American alliance system. It is obvious that this pattern has been disintegrating in the course of the last decade, and that in the 1970s it will be replaced by something quite new. What this new balance will be we cannot say with any assurance, but certain propositions may be tentatively advanced.

The new balance will rest primarily upon an equilibrium among three

Abridged by permission from *Foreign Affairs* (July 1971), pp. 669–681. Copyright by the Council on Foreign Relations, Inc., New York.

great powers—the United States, the Soviet Union and China—and the principal uncertainty is whether they will be joined by a fourth, Japan. Each of the three present great powers gains from the conflict between the other two (although only up to a point: it is unlikely that any of them wishes to see the others embroiled in a nuclear war). Each fears that the other two will combine against it. Russia and China express this fear of collusion in strident terms; while the United States does not voice its concern in any comparable way, it does not wish to see a restoration of Sino-Soviet solidarity.

In fact, the tensions on all three sides of this triangle seem likely to persist and to exclude an enduring and comprehensive combination of any two against the third for the foreseeable future. A Sino-American understanding has been made more likely by the evident willingness of the Nixon Administration to seek an improvement in relations with China, and the presumed interest of China in influencing United States policy against an understanding with Russia; moreover, the disengagement of the United States from mainland Southeast Asia will remove one important source of friction. . . .

A Sino-Soviet understanding might be facilitated by changes of régime in Moscow, Peking or both, but the border dispute is likely to outlive particular governments and the ideological claims and counterclaims of the last decade to leave a legacy of bitterness. The restoration of a working partnership between Russia and China on particular issues is a real possibility, but it would not be a return to the close-knit alliance of the 1950s; for the present the relationship between Russia and China remains the principal point of friction among the great powers.

The Soviet-American side of the triangle, unlike the other two sides, already rests upon firm foundations of mutual understanding. The United States and the Soviet Union recognize common interests in the avoidance of nuclear war, and are involved in an extensive network of negotiations covering SALT, Berlin, the Middle East and many other issues. They have developed a habit of tacit coöperation in relation to China on the Indian subcontinent, in relation to non-nuclear nations in the context of the non-proliferation treaty and in relation to economic have-nots in the context of the United Nations Conference on Trade and Development. But the Soviet-American relationship does not contain the makings of an alliance directed against China, still less of a system of joint hegemony or condominium designed to preserve their privileged position against all comers. The United States and Russia each values China as a check on the power of the other, as the Americans demonstrated by their neutrality in the Sino-Soviet border dispute and the Russians by helping to defend China's strategic frontier in North Vietnam. The United States and the Soviet Union by virtue of their strategic preëminence still have more to fear from each other than from any third party; if it is the Sino-Soviet relationship that is the principal point of *friction* among the great powers, it is the Soviet-American relationship that remains, in Stanley Hoffmann's phrase, the relationship of major *tension*.

Changes in the pattern of relations among these great powers are possible, even likely, especially in the relationship of China to each of the others. Even a partial mending of the fences between China and the Soviet Union, or between China and the United States, might have major consequences for the area as a whole. But these changes are likely to take the form of limited coöperation for particular purposes and to fall short of any general alliance. They are also likely to be unstable in nature. Whatever proves to be the pattern of power relationships, it is unlikely to reproduce the stable alliances and antagonisms of the cold-war period, the sources of which lay in conditions—the polarization of power and the ideological schism—which have long been in decay and may soon disappear altogether.

II

The position of the United States in the Asian and Pacific balance is also likely to decline drastically. In the 1970s America's military capability to exert influence in the area will be qualified by a number of factors that have not operated in the past: the achievement by the Soviet Union of parity with the United States in strategic nuclear arms; the presence of significant Soviet naval power in the Indian and Pacific Oceans; the emergence of China as a strategic nuclear power; and the emergence of Japan as a potential military great power.

To this decline in America's military ability to sustain the role she has played in the past there must be added a no less striking decline in her will to sustain it. Three years ago it was possible to argue that after the United States completed her withdrawal from mainland Southeast Asia this would not necessarily lead to an abandonment of other positions in the area. On the contrary, the result might be a reinforcement of them; the new American policy would be not so much a retreat as a strategic withdrawal to defensively superior positions on the Asian periphery; Walter Lippmann, for example, argued in favor of an American redoubt in Australia. It is now clear that America's withdrawal from Indochina will not be accompanied by new commitments or deployments elsewhere; on the contrary, the pattern of American force deployments in Japan, Okinawa, Taiwan, Thailand, Korea and the Philippines is already one of reduction.

The pattern of United States withdrawal, indeed, is not local or regional but global, although Europe has so far been less affected than other areas. Moreover, it reflects loss of confidence in the ends of United States foreign policy as well as in the means. This is why the present revulsion against the Vietnam war is not comparable with the revulsion against mainland Asian involvement that followed the Korean War, a revulsion that brought with it only a resolve to change the means by which America's purposes in the world were pursued, from local conventional action to global nuclear. Since the time of the Truman Doctrine the United States has been viewed by its leaders, rightly or wrongly, as a country dedicated to resistance to aggression and to the containment of communism on a global scale. These goals are now rejected by large sections of American public and Congressional opinion.

It is true that the United States will remain vitally interested in the global balance of power, and therefore in its relations with Russia, China and Japan. But concern for the global balance of power does not necessarily require United States intervention to resist aggression or to contain communism in particular areas. The American interventions in Korea and Indochina were motivated not only by concern about the global balance but also by those legalistic and ideological purposes which are now losing their grip on the American public mind.

The Nixon Doctrine, however, seeks to preserve the essentials of the older policy while taking account of the new public mood. . . . In his report to Congress of February 25, 1971, President Nixon claimed that the operations in Cambodia and Laos, conducted with American military assistance but without American ground forces, are a concrete illustration of the principles of the Nixon Doctrine.

The new formula, however, cannot disguise the fact that United States policy is undergoing a change not merely of means but of ends. It now seems likely that the United States, unconvinced that the global balance of power is at stake, will be prepared to allow aggression to succeed, and communism to expand, in Indochina and possibly in other areas of Asia and the Pacific, rather than intervene directly to prevent it. Treaty commitments may be kept as Britain, France and Pakistan may claim to have kept their commitments under the Manila Treaty. But how will they be interpreted? A nuclear shield will be available; but how credible will its use be after China has developed an intercontinental ballistic missile (ICBM) capability? What if, in cases of conventional aggression, the country directly threatened is not able to meet the challenge? The withdrawal of American forces will be a fact, whereas "local self-reliance" will be merely a hope; "the Vietnamization of the war" may or may not enable a non-communist government to survive in Saigon, but in either case the American forces, once they have gone, will not return.

The Nixon Doctrine, moreover, is not a sacred text defining the possibilities of American involvement for all time, but merely a milestone on a road that may lead to more radical disengagement. . . .

III

In the course of the next decade a strategic nuclear stalemate or relationship of mutual deterrence is likely to develop between China and the United States, and between China and the Soviet Union. Indeed, in view of reports that a limited deployment of Chinese medium-range ballistic missiles (MRBMs) has already taken place, China may well be able to threaten the Soviet Union, as well as U.S. forces in Asia. It is true that when China develops its ICBM force there will be some who will say that it will be unable to penetrate Soviet and U.S. anti-ballistic missile (ABM) screens, and that the United States and the Soviet Union will each still be in a position to eliminate or cripple the Chinese strategic nuclear force in a disarming strike. But China will be able to create sufficient apprehension in Soviet and American minds as to her capacity to retaliate effectively to bring to an end the situation in which each of the superpowers has felt confident that it can make nuclear threats against China with impunity.

By any of the various yardsticks of nuclear strength, China will not in the foreseeable future command "parity" with the superpowers. Nor should it be assumed that in bargaining with them in a crisis situation China will necessarily be able to make up by superior will or resolve for her inferiority in strategic capacity. Nevertheless, the Chinese nuclear force will be a new source of strength to China's diplomatic position. Moreover, it will help further erode confidence in the reliability of American commitments to allied and friendly states, and strengthen the forces making for proliferation in India, Japan and Australia. Just as in Western Europe in the late 1950s the emergence of a Soviet-U.S. nuclear stalemate led to the raising of questions about the credibility of American nuclear threats on behalf of allies, so in the Pacific in the 1970s the emergence of a Sino-American nuclear stalemate will pose the same questions. In Europe the American alliance has survived despite these questions; the same may obtain in the Pacific. Nor will the Chinese nuclear force be sufficient in itself to cause countries in the area to seek to acquire nuclear weapons: too many other factors are involved in the debate about nuclear weapons in each of the countries concerned. But in each of these countries the hand of the pro-nuclear party will be strengthened.

The United States itself may come to revise its attitude toward nuclear proliferation in the area, as it balances the costs of the latter against those of continued nuclear commitment. "Local self-reliance," taken to its logical conclusion, implies the existence of independent nuclear capabilities. For the present the United States remains opposed to the spread of nuclear weapons and has made clear that disengagement does not include withdrawal of the nuclear umbrella. But the nonproliferation treaty does not enjoy the status, in the hierarchy of American priorities, that it had under the Johnson Administration; and pressure on non-nuclear countries to adhere to it has been relaxed along with America's "tutelary" role. No

Asian or Pacific country bent upon the acquisition of nuclear weapons is likely in the near future to receive encouragement from the United States, but such a country might already be justified in concluding that if it were to "go nuclear" the United States would accommodate itself to the situation soon enough.

IV

By the end of the decade the Asian balance may be further complicated by the emergence of Japan as a fourth great power. Already Japan's position as the third richest country in the world has brought with it an increased political stature: certainly the agreement of the United States to the return of Okinawa and the generally more independent stance of Japan within the framework of the Japan-United States security agreement reflect this increased bargaining power which derives from the recognition of economic potential. Even if Japan's growth rate does not average over 11 percent in the next decade, as it did in the last, Japan's economic position relative to other major states is likely to go on improving. Moreover, even if defense expenditure were to be no more than about one percent of GNP as envisaged in the Fourth Defense Build-Up Plan for 1972–76, Japan's likely rate of growth will ensure very substantial absolute increases (the expansion of the Self-Defense Forces over the last decade has actually been accompanied by a decline in defense expenditure as a proportion of GNP). A number of factors make for the treatment of defense as a higher priority: the reëmergence of nationalist feeling, the growing importance in Japanese life of a generation less affected by the memory of defeat, the emergence of defense as a subject of public discussion and study, and the actual problems of security posed for Japan by the disengagement of the United States, the nuclear armament of China and the growing Japanese economic stake in other parts of the region whose security is in doubt.

But if by a great power we mean—following Ranke—a country that can maintain itself against any other single power without allies, Japan is not yet one. Nor can she become one without acquiring the military accoutrements of a great power, which at the present time include a strategic nuclear force. In his address to the United Nations in October 1970, Japanese Prime Minister Eisaku Sato said that whereas history had shown that countries with great economic power were tempted to possess commensurate military forces Japan had no intention of using any major portion of its resources for military purposes; in a speech to the Diet in November the same year he spoke of Japan's path in this respect as "a completely new experiment in world history." The idea that Japan can be such a new kind of great power may be thought to chart a wise and prudent course for Japan, and even to contribute a constructive precept to the international debate. But there is no reason to believe that Japan, or any other country, can attain the status of a great power without providing itself with the military means that have been a necessary condition of such a status in the past.

It is true that military force as an instrument of foreign policy is now circumscribed by powerful inhibitions and is of diminished utility in relation to some of the ends, such as the promotion of economic gain, for which it has traditionally been employed. It is also true that questions of trade, aid, investment and multi-national enterprise now occupy a large place on the agenda of diplomatic discussion, and that Japan's position as an economic colossus places her at the center of this discussion. Finally, it is true that Japan's economic strength provides her with powerful leverage in dealing with other countries over a range of non-economic issues.

But Japan, while she retains only her present armed forces, cannot guarantee her own security and enjoys only that amount of freedom of diplomatic manœuvre that is consistent with reliance upon the United States. Japan does not now perceive any direct threat to her security. But if this were to change, her position of dependence would quickly become apparent. Nor can Japan, simply by relying upon economic strength, play the role of a principal party in the range of politico-strategic issues in dispute in the area, even those—such as the future of Korea and Taiwan—that vitally affect her. The political stature that Japan has already attained, moreover, does not derive solely from her economic performance; it reflects other countries' assessments of Japan's potential military power—their knowledge of the speed with which Japan could become a great military power and memory of her past performance as such.

It is not inevitable that Japan will elect to become a great power, in this decade or later. Japanese leaders are well enough aware of the opposition that would be generated in the area and the problems that would be created for Japan in her economic as well as political relations with other states by a premature move in this direction. Nor is it worth speculating as to how, in detail, if Japan were to become a great power, this would affect what would then be the quadrilateral of great-power relations in the area. It is clear, however, that in the calculations of foreign offices in the area the possibility of Japan's emergence as a major political and strategic as well as economic force there is already taken very seriously into account.

V

The middle powers of the region, to different degrees and in somewhat different ways, are likely to view their own interests as best served by the preservation of an equilibrium among the three or four great powers. They are likely to feel threatened by the domination of the region by any one great power, and to regard some measure of checking or balancing of each by the others as the condition of their own security and freedom of manœuvre.

Take the case of Australia, which in the past 20 years has seen its interests as lying in the maximization of U.S. presence and influence in the area and the minimization of that of Russia and China. In August 1969 the Australian Minister for External Affairs at that time, Gordon Freeth, made a speech about Soviet penetration of the Indian Ocean in which he argued that the Soviet presence was not necessarily prejudicial to Australian interests, that Australia and the Soviet Union had common interests in the containment of China, and that there might even be opportunities for coöperation. . . .

It may be argued not only that the new perspective suggested by Freeth is the correct one but also that it is likely to become part of the orthodox Australian foreign policy of the future. The point, however, does not concern simply Australia's interest vis-à-vis the Soviet Union but is a more general one. China, Japan, and indeed the United States are also likely to be assessed by Australia according to the contribution they make to the equilibrium among the great powers of the area, the effect of their presence or influence in checking the encroachment of the others. Australia, of course, will not regard the competition of the great powers as if it were indifferent to the outcome. As an ally of the United States, Australia will continue to consider that its interests are bound up with a continuing American presence and influence, in a way in which they are not bound up with the political fortunes of the others. But Australian assessments will at least include the recognition that *any* of the great powers is capable of contributing positively to the equilibrium or balance of the area. This is an element that was not present in Australian thinking of the previous period.

The same theme may be illustrated with reference to Indonesia. Indonesia under its present government is absorbed in economic reconstruction and pursues a very correct policy toward its neighbors. But the ambition to assert leadership within peninsular Southeast Asia is still an aspect of its foreign policy, reflected in its sponsorship of the Association of South East Asian Nations (ASEAN), from which powers external to the region have been excluded. Indonesia has a naturally dominant position among the states of peninsular Southeast Asia, but this could be threatened by the encroachment upon the area of China, Japan, the Soviet Union or the United States. Given that the influence of these powers cannot be excluded from the peninsular region, Indonesia's perceived interests are likely to lie in a situation in which no one of them achieves a preponderant position.

Equilibrium among the great powers depends on the existence of conflict among them; it can be threatened in certain cases by understandings among the great powers bringing this conflict to an end in particular areas.

An understanding between the United States and China might have grave implications for Taiwan, South Korea and the non-communist states of Indochina.   A rapprochement between China and the Soviet Union might deprive India of its chief prop against China, and might be regarded as potentially menacing by Japan as well.   An understanding between the United States and the Soviet Union, so long an objective of India's foreign policy in the era of Nehru, has in fact weakened India's diplomatic position now that it has come about.   India's increased dependence on the Soviet Union for security against China, at a time of declining U.S. interest in the subcontinent, has provided India with a new motive for seeking a settlement with China, as well as for forming closer relations with middle powers in the Asian and Pacific region.

VI

Finally, the American alliance system in Asia and the Pacific is likely to continue to decay.   But it is unlikely to be replaced by a new alliance of regional powers along any of the lines that have been suggested.   The true theme of international politics in the area is likely to be that of self-reliance.   With some exaggeration it may be said that the situation is like that which Canning described when, at the time of the breakdown of the Holy Alliance, he wrote: "Things are getting back to a wholesome state again: every nation for itself and God for us all."

Though it does appear to be in decay, the American alliance system in Asia and the Pacific does not seem likely to disappear in the next decade. Within each of the alliances linking the United States to a country in the region there is a diminished sense of community of interest, a tendency on the part of the regional country to question the value of the American commitment, reinforced by a tendency on the part of the United States to question the extent of the present commitment, if not the commitment itself.   The most important element in the system, the U.S.-Japanese security treaty, even if it survives, is likely to go on being slowly modified to take account of Japan's increased political stature and capacity for self defense.   The American commitments to Taiwan and South Korea could not be abrogated without producing convulsions in East Asia, and their termination could hardly take place except as part of wider settlements. But the possibility of these settlements is now for the first time the subject of serious attention in Washington.

The United States commitment to Thailand, through the Rusk-Thanat interpretation of the obligations of the Manila Treaty, seems likely to survive only on a limited liability basis.   The South-East Treaty Organization (SEATO), after the withdrawal of American forces from Indochina, may come to mean as little to the United States as it does to Britain and France.   Even the alliances with the Philippines, Australia and New

Zealand, which have a more enduring basis, are subject to this sense on both sides of a diminished community of interest.

The movement of the United States and Britain toward disengagement from Southeast Asia has been accompanied by suggestions, emanating chiefly from Washington and London, that new alliance arrangements comprising countries of the region might take over the tasks which the external powers are in process of laying down.   A few years ago Alastair Buchan suggested an alliance between India, Japan and Australia.[1]   There have been suggestions that an alliance might arise on the foundation of the nine-power Asian and Pacific Council (ASPAC), or on that of the five-power ASEAN.   The idea is sometimes broached of an alliance centered upon coöperation between Japan and Australia.

These projects reflect the desire of the external powers to rationalize their own withdrawal by demonstrating that their presence in the area is no longer necessary since local elements are at hand to accomplish the common task.   They are not founded upon the realities of the area.   India, Australia and Japan do not share a common perception of external threats to their security; still less do the members of the unwieldy ASPAC.   It is difficult to regard ASEAN as a potential military alliance, the chief anxieties that some of its members have about their security being those that they entertain in relation to one another.

*   *   *

If no new military alliance appears to be in process of formation, it may not be wholly unrealistic to think of a new association of regional states that would not be a military alliance directed against an outside power such as China, but a regional collective security organization in the strict sense of one concerned with relations among its own members.   It is anomalous that there does not exist, in the Asian and Pacific area, an association that is able to perform the mediating and peacekeeping role in relation to disputes within it that may be played in other areas by the Organization of American States (OAS) and the Organization of African Unity (OAU).   At the same time it seems unlikely that in the next decade there will be any expansion of the role of the United Nations in the area, particularly if, as seems likely, the possibility of consensus within the Security Council is further limited by the entry of China into the organization.

Such an Asian and Pacific regional security group, excluding both the United States and the Soviet Union but containing Japan, India, Indonesia and Australia, would not reflect the cultural unity and aspirations to ultimate political unity that underlie the OAU.   Its role in security matters might be no more than to provide mediation and good offices, and to

[1] "An Asian Balance of Power?" *Australian Journal of Politics and History*, August 1966.

symbolize aspirations for regional peace and security. It would be in no sense a principal source of security for its members, which they could treat as a substitute for their own arms and alliances. But it might serve to mitigate, however slightly, the factors making for international tension in the area. Today this may not be a realistic or negotiable proposition, but in the course of the decade it could become one.

George Orwell

TRIANGULAR PERPETUAL WAR

. . . On the sixth day of Hate Week, after the processions, the speeches, the shouting, the singing, the banners, the posters, the films, the waxworks, the rolling of drums and squealing of trumpets, the tramp of marching feet, the grinding of the caterpillars of tanks, the roar of massed planes, the booming of guns—after six days of this, when the great orgasm was quivering to its climax and the general hatred of Eurasia had boiled up into such delirium that if the crowd could have got their hands on the two thousand Eurasian war criminals who were to be publicly hanged on the last day of the proceedings, they would unquestionably have torn them to pieces—at just this moment it had been announced that Oceania was not after all at war with Eurasia. Oceania was at war with Eastasia. Eurasia was an ally.

There was, of course, no admission that any change had taken place. Merely it became known, with extreme suddenness and everywhere at once, that Eastasia and not Eurasia was the enemy. Winston was taking part in a demonstration in one of the central London squares at the moment when it happened. It was night, and the white faces and the scarlet banners were luridly floodlit. The square was packed with several thousand people, including a block of about a thousand schoolchildren in the uniform of the Spies. On a scarlet-draped platform an orator of the Inner Party, a small lean man with disproportionately long arms and a large, bald skull over which a few lank locks straggled, was haranguing the crowd. A little Rumpelstiltskin figure, contorted with hatred, he gripped the neck of the microphone with one hand while the other, enormous at the end of a bony arm, clawed the air menacingly above his head. His voice,

Reprinted by permission of Brandt & Brandt and Martin Secker & Warburg from *Nineteen Eighty-four* (New York: Harcourt, Brace, 1949), pp. 180–182, 186–200. Copyright 1949 by Harcourt, Brace and Company, Inc.

made metallic by the amplifiers, boomed forth an endless catalogue of atrocities, massacres, deportations, lootings, rapings, torture of prisoners, bombing of civilians, lying propaganda, unjust aggressions, broken treaties. It was almost impossible to listen to him without being first convinced and then maddened.   At every few moments the fury of the crowd boiled over and the voice of the speaker was drowned by a wild beastlike roaring that rose uncontrollably from thousands of throats.   The most savage yells of all came from the schoolchildren.   The speech had been proceeding for perhaps twenty minutes when a messenger hurried onto the platform and a scrap of paper was slipped into the speaker's hand.   He unrolled and read it without pausing in his speech.   Nothing altered in his voice or manner, or in the content of what he was saying, but suddenly the names were different.   Without words said, a wave of understanding rippled through the crowd.   Oceania was at war with Eastasia!   The next moment there was a tremendous commotion.   The banners and posters with which the square was decorated were all wrong!   Quite half of them had the wrong faces on them.   It was sabotage!   The agents of Goldstein had been at work!   There was a riotous interlude while posters were ripped from the walls, banners torn to shreds and trampled underfoot.   The Spies performed prodigies of activity in clambering over the rooftops and cutting the streamers that fluttered from the chimneys.   But within two or three minutes it was all over.   The orator, still gripping the neck of the microphone, his shoulders hunched forward, his free hand clawing at the air, had gone straight on with his speech.   One minute more, and the feral roars of rage were again bursting from the crowd.   The Hate continued exactly as before, except that the target had been changed. . . .

WAR IS PEACE [1]

The splitting-up of the world into three great superstates was an event which· could be and indeed was foreseen before the middle of the twentieth century. With the absorption of Europe by Russia and the British Empire by the United States, two of the three existing powers, Eurasia and Oceania, were already effectively in being. The third, Eastasia, only emerged as a distinct unit after another decade of confused fighting. The frontiers between the three superstates are in some places arbitrary, and in others they fluctuate according to the fortunes of war, but in general they follow geographical lines. Eurasia comprises the whole of the northern part of the European and Asiatic land-mass, from Portugal to the Bering Strait. Oceania comprises the Americas, the Atlantic islands including the British Isles, Australasia, and the southern portion of Africa.

[1] This excerpt is from a fictitious work, "The Theory and Practice of Oligarchical Collectivism," by Emmanuel Goldstein, who in the novel is the leader of an underground opposition. Orwell used this device to explain the genesis and nature of the world of 1984. [Eds.]

Eastasia, smaller than the others and with a less definite western frontier, comprises China and the countries to the south of it, the Japanese islands and a large but fluctuating portion of Manchuria, Mongolia, and Tibet.

In one combination or another, these three superstates are permanently at war, and have been so for the past twenty-five years. War, however, is no longer the desperate, annihilating struggle that it was in the early decades of the twentieth century. It is a warfare of limited aims between combatants who are unable to destroy one another, have no material cause for fighting, and are not divided by any genuine ideological difference. This is not to say that either the conduct of war, or the prevailing attitude toward it, has become less bloodthirsty or more chivalrous. On the contrary, war hysteria is continuous and universal in all countries, and such acts as raping, looting, the slaughter of children, the reduction of whole populations to slavery, and reprisals against prisoners which extend even to boiling and burying alive, are looked upon as normal, and, when they are committed by one's own side and not by the enemy, meritorious. But in a physical sense war involves very small numbers of people, mostly highly trained specialists, and causes comparatively few casualties. The fighting, when there is any, takes place on the vague frontiers whose whereabouts the average man can only guess at, or round the Floating Fortresses which guard strategic spots on the sea lanes. In the centers of civilization war means no more than a continuous shortage of consumption goods, and the occasional crash of a rocket bomb which may cause a few scores of deaths. War has in fact changed its character. More exactly, the reasons for which war is waged have changed in their order of importance. Motives which were already present to some small extent in the great wars of the early twentieth century have now become dominant and are consciously recognized and acted upon.

To understand the nature of the present war—for in spite of the regrouping which occurs every few years, it is always the same war—one must realize in the first place that it is impossible for it to be decisive. None of the three superstates could be definitely conquered even by the other two in combination. They are too evenly matched, and their natural defenses are too formidable. Eurasia is protected by its vast land spaces, Oceania by the width of the Atlantic and the Pacific, Eastasia by the fecundity and industriousness of its inhabitants. Secondly, there is no longer, in a material sense, anything to fight about. With the establishment of self-contained economies, in which production and consumption are geared to one another, the scramble for markets which was a main cause of previous wars has come to an end, while the competition for raw materials is no longer a matter of life and death. In any case, each of the three superstates is so vast that it can obtain almost all the materials that it needs within its own boundaries. . . .

All of the disputed territories contain valuable minerals, and some of them yield important vegetable products such as rubber which in colder climates it is necessary to synthesize by comparatively expensive methods. But above all they contain a bottomless reserve of cheap labor. . . . The inhabitants of these areas, reduced more or less openly to the status of slaves, pass continually from conqueror to conqueror, and are expended like so much coal or oil in the race to turn out more armaments, to capture more territory, to control more labor power, to turn out more armaments, to capture more territory, and so on indefinitely. It should be noted that the fighting never really moves beyond the edges of the disputed areas. The frontiers of Eurasia flow back and forth between the basin of the Congo and the northern shore of the Mediterranean; the islands of the Indian Ocean and the Pacific are constantly being captured and recaptured by Oceania or by Eastasia; in Mongolia the dividing line between Eurasia and Eastasia is never stable . . . but the balance of power always remains roughly even, and the territory which forms the heartland of each super-state always remains inviolate. Moreover, the labor of the exploited peoples round the Equator is not really necessary to the world's economy. They add nothing to the wealth of the world, since whatever they produce is used for purposes of war, and the object of waging a war is always to be in a better position in which to wage another war. By their labor the slave populations allow the tempo of continuous warfare to be speeded up. But if they did not exist, the structure of world society, and the process by which it maintains itself, would not be essentially different.

The primary aim of modern warfare . . . is to use up the products of the machine without raising the general standard of living. Ever since the end of the nineteenth century, the problem of what to do with the surplus of consumption goods has been latent in industrial society. At present, when few human beings even have enough to eat, this problem is obviously not urgent, and it might not have become so, even if no artificial processes of destruction had been at work. The world of today is a bare, hungry, dilapidated place compared with the world that existed before 1914, and still more so if compared with the imaginary future to which the people of that period looked forward. In the early twentieth century, the vision of a future society unbelievably rich, leisured, orderly and efficient —a glittering antiseptic world of glass and steel and snow-white concrete— was part of the consciousness of nearly every literate person. Science and technology were developing at a prodigious speed, and it seemed natural to assume that they would go on developing. This failed to happen, partly because of the impoverishment caused by a long series of wars and revolutions. . . .

But it was also clear that an all-round increase in wealth threatened the destruction—indeed, in some sense was the destruction—of a hierarchical society. In a world in which everyone worked short hours, had enough to eat, lived in a house with a bathroom and refrigerator, and possessed a motorcar or even an airplane, the most obvious and perhaps the most important form of inequality would already have disappeared. If it once became general, wealth would confer no distinction.   It was possible, no doubt, to imagine a society in which *wealth,* in the sense of personal possessions and luxuries, should be evenly distributed, while *power* remained in the hands of a small privileged caste.   But in practice such a society could not long remain stable.   For if leisure and security were enjoyed by all alike, the great mass of human beings who are normally stupefied by poverty would become literate and would learn to think for themselves; and when once they had done this, they would sooner or later realize that the privileged minority had no function, and they would sweep it away.   In the long run, a hierarchical society was only possible on a basis of poverty and ignorance. . . .

*   *   *

The essential act of war is destruction, not necessarily of human lives, but of the products of human labor.   War is a way of shattering to pieces, or pouring into the stratosphere, or sinking in the depths of the sea, materials which might otherwise be used to make the masses too comfortable, and hence, in the long run, too intelligent.   Even when weapons of war are not actually destroyed, their manufacture is still a convenient way of expending labor power without producing anything that can be consumed.   A Floating Fortress, for example, has locked up in it the labor that would build several hundred cargo ships.   Ultimately it is scrapped as obsolete, never having brought any material benefit to anybody, and with further enormous labors another Floating Fortress is built.   In principle the war effort is always so planned as to eat up any surplus that might exist after meeting the bare needs of the population.   In practice the needs of the population are always underestimated, with the result that there is a chronic shortage of half the necessities of life; but this is looked on as an advantage.   It is deliberate policy to keep even the favored groups somewhere near the brink of hardship, because a general state of scarcity increases the importance of small privileges and thus magnifies the distinction between one group and another. . . .

War, it will be seen, not only accomplishes the necessary destruction, but accomplishes it in a psychologically acceptable way.   In principle it would be quite simple to waste the surplus labor of the world by building temples and pyramids, by digging holes and filling them up again, or even by producing vast quantities of goods and then setting fire to them.   But this would provide only the economic and not the emotional basis for a hierarchical society.   What is concerned here is not the morale of the masses, whose attitude is unimportant so long as they are kept steadily at work, but the morale of the Party itself.   Even the humblest Party member is expected to be competent, industrious, and even intelligent within narrow limits, but it is also necessary that he should be a credulous and ignorant fanatic whose prevailing moods are fear, hatred, adulation, and orgiastic triumph.   In other words it is necessary that he should have the mentality appropriate to a state of war. It does not matter whether the war is acually happening, and, since no decisive victory is possible, it does not matter whether the war is going well or badly. All that is needed is that a state of war should exist. The splitting of the intelligence which the Party requires of its members, and which is more easily achieved in an atmosphere of war, is now almost universal, but the higher up the ranks one goes, the more marked it becomes. It is precisely in the Inner Party that war hysteria and hatred of the enemy are strongest. In his capacity as an administrator, it is often necessary for a member of the Inner Party to know that this or that item of war news is untruthful, and he may often be aware that the entire war is spurious and is either not happening or is being waged for purposes quite other than the declared ones; but such knowledge is easily neutralized by the technique of *doublethink*. Meanwhile no Inner Party member wavers for an instant in his mystical belief that the war is real, and that it is bound to end victoriously, with Oceania the undisputed master of the entire world.

All members of the Inner Party believe in this coming conquest as an article of faith. It is to be achieved either by gradually acquiring more and more territory and so building up an overwhelming preponderance of power, or by the discovery of some new and unanswerable weapon. The search for new weapons continues unceasingly, and is one of the very few remaining activities in which the inventive or speculative type of mind can find any outlet. . . .

. . . What is more remarkable is that all three powers already possess, in the atomic bomb, a weapon far more powerful than any that their present researches are likely to discover. . . . [S]ome hundreds of bombs were dropped on industrial centers, chiefly in European Russia, Western Europe, and North America. The effect was to convince the ruling groups of all countries that a few more atomic bombs would mean the end of organized society, and hence of their own power. Thereafter, although no formal agreement was ever made or hinted at, no more bombs were dropped. All three powers merely continue to produce atomic bombs and store them up against the decisive opportunity which they all believe will come sooner or later. And meanwhile the art of war has remained almost stationary for thirty or forty years. . . .

None of the three superstates ever attempts any maneuver which involves the risk of serious defeat. When any large operation is undertaken, it is usually a surprise attack against an ally. The strategy that all three powers are following, or pretend to themselves that they are following, is the same. The plan is, by a combination of fighting, bargaining, and well-timed strokes of treachery, to acquire a ring of bases completely encircling one or other of the rival states, and then to sign a pact of friendship with that rival and remain on peaceful terms for so many years as to lull suspicion to sleep. During this time rockets loaded with atomic bombs can be assembled at all the strategic spots; finally they will all be

fired simultaneously, with effects so devastating as to make retaliation impossible. It will then be time to sign a pact of friendship with the remaining world power, in preparation for another attack. This scheme, it is hardly necessary to say, is a mere daydream, impossible of realization.
. . . It is absolutely necessary to their structure that there should be no contact with foreigners except, to a limited extent, with war prisoners and colored slaves. Even the official ally of the moment is always regarded with the darkest suspicion. War prisoners apart, the average citizen of Oceania never sets eyes on a citizen of either Eurasia or Eastasia, and he is forbidden the knowledge of foreign languages. If he were allowed contact with foreigners he would discover that they are creatures similar to himself and that most of what he has been told about them is lies. The sealed world in which he lives would be broken, and the fear, hatred, and self-righteousness on which his morale depends might evaporate. It is therefore realized on all sides that however often Persia, or Egypt, or Java, or Ceylon may change hands, the main frontiers must never be crossed by anything except bombs.

Under this lies a fact never mentioned aloud, but tacitly understood and acted upon: namely, that the conditions of life in all three superstates are very much the same. In Oceania the prevailing philosophy is called Ingsoc, in Eurasia it is called Neo-Bolshevism, and in Eastasia it is called by a Chinese name usually translated as Death-worship, but perhaps better rendered as Obliteration of the Self. The citizen of Oceania is not allowed to know anything of the tenets of the other two philosophies, but he is taught to execrate them as barbarous outrages upon morality and common sense. Actually the three philosophies are barely distinguishable, and the social systems which they support are not distinguishable at all. Everywhere there is the same pyramidal structure, the same worship of a semi-divine leader, the same economy existing by and for continuous warfare. It follows that the three superstates not only cannot conquer one another, but would gain no advantage by doing so. On the contrary, so long as they remain in conflict they prop one another up, like three sheaves of corn. And, as usual, the ruling groups of all three powers are simultaneously aware and unaware of what they are doing. Their lives are dedicated to world conquest, but they also know that it is necessary that the war should continue everlastingly and without victory. Meanwhile the fact that there *is* no danger of conquest makes possible the denial of reality which is the special feature of Ingsoc and its rival systems of thought. Here it is necessary to repeat what has been said earlier, that by becoming continuous war has fundamentally changed its character.

*   *   *

. . . [W]hen war becomes literally continuous, it also ceases to be dangerous. When war is continuous there is no such thing as military necessity. Technical progress can cease and the most palpable facts can be denied or disregarded.   As we have seen, researches that could be called scientific are still carried out for the purposes of war, but they are essentially a kind of daydreaming, and their failure to show results is not important. Efficiency, even military efficiency, is no longer needed.   Nothing is efficient in Oceania except the Thought Police.   Since each of the three superstates is unconquerable, each is in effect a separate universe within which almost any perversion of thought can be safely practiced.   Reality only exerts its pressure through the needs of everyday life—the need to eat and drink, to get shelter and clothing, to avoid swallowing poison or stepping out of top-story windows, and the like.   Between life and death, and between physical pleasure and physical pain, there is still a distinction, but that is all.   Cut off from contact with the outer world, and with the past, the citizen of Oceania is like a man in interstellar space, who has no way of knowing which direction is up and which is down. . . .

. . . In our own day they are not fighting against one another at all. The war is waged by each ruling group against its own subjects, and the object of the war is not to make or prevent conquests of territory, but to keep the structure of society intact.   The very word "war," therefore, has become misleading.   It would probably be accurate to say that by becoming continuous war has ceased to exist.   The peculiar pressure that it exerted on human beings between the Neolithic Age and the early twentieth century has disappeared and has been replaced by something quite different.   The effect would be much the same if the three super-states, instead of fighting one another, should agree to live in perpetual peace, each inviolate within its own boundaries.   For in that case each would still be a self-contained universe, freed forever from the sobering influence of external danger.   A peace that was truly permanent would be the same as a permanent war.   This—although the vast majority of Party members understand it only in a shallower sense—is the inner meaning of the Party slogan: WAR IS PEACE.

*   *   *

Andrei D. Sakharov

SCIENTIFIC COOPERATION AND SOCIALIST CONVERGENCE

Having examined in the first part of this essay the development of mankind according to the worse alternative, leading to annihilation, we must now attempt, even schematically, to suggest the better alternative. (The author concedes the primitiveness of his attempts at prognostication, which requires the joint efforts of many specialists, and here, even more than elsewhere, invites positive criticism.)

1. In the first stage, a growing ideological struggle in the socialist countries between Stalinist and Maoist forces, on the one hand, and the realistic forces of leftist Leninist Communists (and leftist Westerners), on the other, will lead to a deep ideological split on an international, national, and intraparty scale.

In the Soviet Union and other socialist countries, this process will lead first to a multiparty system (here and there) and to acute ideological struggle and discussions, and then to the ideological victory of the realists, affirming the policy of increasing peaceful coexistence, strengthening democracy, and expanding economic reforms (1960–80). The dates reflect the most optimistic unrolling of events.

The author, incidentally, is not one of those who consider the multiparty system to be an essential stage in the development of the socialist system or, even less, a panacea for all ills, but he assumes that in some cases a multiparty system may be an inevitable consequence of the course of events when a ruling Communist party refuses for one reason or another to rule by the scientific democratic method required by history.

2. In the second stage, persistent demands for social progress and peaceful coexistence in the United States and other capitalist countries, and pressure exerted by the example of the socialist countries and by internal progressive forces (the working class and the intelligentsia) will lead to the victory of the leftist reformist wing of the bourgeoisie, which will begin to implement a program of rapprochement (convergence) with socialism, i.e., social progress, peaceful coexistence, and collaboration with socialism on a world scale and changes in the structure of ownership. This phase includes an expanded role for the intelligentsia and an attack on the forces of racism and militarism (1972–85). (The various stages overlap.)

Reprinted by permission of the publisher from Andrei D. Sakharov, *Progress, Coexistence and Intellectual Freedom,* translated by *The New York Times* (New York: Norton & Co., 1968), pp. 81–89. © 1968 by The New York Times Company.

3. In the third stage, the Soviet Union and the United States, having overcome their alienation, solve the problem of saving the poorer half of the world. The aforementioned 20 per cent tax on the national income of developed countries is applied. Gigantic fertilizer factories and irrigation systems using atomic power will be built [in the developing countries], the resources of the sea will be used to a vastly greater extent, indigenous personnel will be trained, and industrialization will be carried out. Gigantic factories will produce synthetic amino acids and synthesize proteins, fats, and carbohydrates. At the same time disarmament will proceed (1972–90).

4. In the fourth stage, the socialist convergence will reduce differences in social structure, promote intellectual freedom, science, and economic progress and lead to creation of a world government and the smoothing of national contradictions (1980–2000). During this period decisive progress can be expected in the field of nuclear power, both on the basis of uranium and thorium and, probably, deuterium and lithium.

Some authors consider it likely that explosive breeding (the reproduction of active materials such as plutonium, uranium 233 and tritium) may be used in subterranean or other enclosed explosions.

During this period the expansion of space exploration will require thousands of people to work and live continuously on other planets and on the moon, on artificial satellites and on asteroids whose orbits will have been changed by nuclear explosions.

The synthesis of materials that are superconductors at room temperature may completely revolutionize electrical technology, cybernetics, transportation, and communications. Progress in biology (in this and subsequent periods) will make possible effective control and direction of all life processes at the levels of the cell, organism, ecology, and society, from fertility and aging to psychic processes and heredity.

If such an all-encompassing scientific and technological revolution, promising uncounted benefits for mankind, is to be possible and safe, it will require the greatest possible scientific foresight and care. and concern for human values of a moral, ethical, and personal character. (I touched briefly on the danger of a thoughtless bureaucratic use of the scientific and technological revolution in a divided world in the section on "Dangers," but could add a great deal more.) Such a revolution will be possible and safe only under highly intelligent worldwide guidance.

The foregoing program presumes:

(a) worldwide interest in overcoming the present divisions;

(b) the expectation that modifications in both the socialist and capitalist countries will tend to reduce contradictions and differences;

(c) worldwide interest of the intelligentsia, the working class, and other progressive forces in a scientific democratic approach to politics, economics, and culture;

(d) the absence of insurmountable obstacles to economic development in both world economic systems that might otherwise lead inevitably into a blind alley, despair, and adventurism.

Every honorable and thinking person who has not been poisoned by narrow-minded indifference will seek to insure that future development will be along the lines of the better alternative. However only broad, open discussion, without the pressure of fear and prejudice, will help the majority to adopt the correct and best course of action.

A SUMMARY OF PROPOSALS

In conclusion, I will sum up some of the concrete proposals of varying degrees of importance that have been discussed in the text. These proposals, addressed to the leadership of the country, do not exhaust the content of the article.

1. The strategy of peaceful coexistence and collaboration must be deepened in every way. Scientific methods and principles of international policy will have to be worked out, based on scientific prediction of the immediate and more distant consequences.

2. The initiative must be seized in working out a broad program of struggle against hunger.

3. A law on press and information must be drafted, widely discussed, and adopted, with the aim not only of ending irresponsible and irrational censorship, but of encouraging self-study in our society, fearless discussion, and the search for truth. The law must provide for the material resources of freedom of thought.

4. All anticonstitutional laws and decrees violating human rights must be abrogated.

5. Political prisoners must be amnestied and some of the recent political trials must be reviewed. . . . The camp regime of political prisoners must be promptly relaxed.

6. The exposure of Stalin must be carried through to the end, to the complete truth, and not just to the carefully weighed half-truth dictated by caste considerations. The influence of neo-Stalinists in our political life must be restricted in every way. . . .

7. The economic reform must be deepened in every way and the area of experimentation expanded, with conclusions based on the results.

8. A law on geohygiene must be adopted after broad discussion, and ultimately become part of world efforts in this area.

With this article the author addresses the leadership of our country and all its citizens as well as all people of goodwill throughout the world. The author is aware of the controversial character of many of his statements. His purpose is open, frank discussion under conditions of publicity.

Kenneth N. Waltz

THE BALANCE OF WORLD POWER

Balance of power is the hoariest concept in the field of international relations. Elaborated in a variety of analyses and loaded with different meanings, it has often been praised or condemned, but has seldom been wholly rejected. . . .

Balance-of-power theory assumes that the desire for survival supplies the basic motivation of states, indicates the responses that the constraints of the system encourage, and describes the expected outcome. Beyond the survival motive, the aims of states may be wondrously varied; they may range from the ambition to conquer the world to the desire merely to be left alone. But the minimum responses of states, which are necessary to the dynamics of balance, derive from the condition of national co-existence where no external guarantee of survival exists. Perception of the peril that lies in unbalanced power encourages the behavior required for the maintenance of a balance-of-power system.

Because of the present narrow concentration of awesome power, the question arises whether the affairs of the world can any longer be conducted or understood according to the balance-of-power concept, the main theoretical prop of those traditionally called realists. Even many who share the realist concern with power question its present relevance. They do so for two reasons.

It is, in the first place, widely accepted that balance-of-power politics requires the presence of three or more states. Political thought is so historically conditioned that the balance of power as it is usually defined merely reflects the experience of the modern era. In Europe for a period of three centuries, from the Treaty of Westphalia to the Second World

Reprinted by permission from *Journal of International Affairs,* 21, 2 (1967), pp. 215–231.

War, five or more great powers sometimes sought to coexist peacefully and at other times competed for mastery. The idea thus became fixed that a balance of power can exist only where the participants approximate the customary number. But something more than habit is involved. Also mixed into ideas about necessary numbers is the notion that flexibility in the alignment of states is a requirement of balance-of-power politics. The existence of only two states at the summit of power precludes the possibility of international maneuver and national realignment as ways of compensating for changes in the strength of either of them. Excessive concentration of power negates the possibility of playing the politics of balance.

Second, war or the threat of war, another essential means of adjustment, is said to be of only limited utility in the nuclear age. In balances of power, of course, more is placed on the scales than mere military force. Military force has, however, served not only as the *ultima ratio* of international politics but indeed as the first and the constant one. To reduce force to being the *ultima ratio* of politics implies, as Ortega y Gasset once noted, "the previous submission of force to methods of reason." [1] Insufficient social cohesion exists among states and the instruments of international control are too weak to relegate power to the status of simply the *ultima ratio*. Power cannot be separated from the purposes of those who possess it; in international politics power has appeared primarily as the power to do harm. To interdict the use of force by the threat of force, to oppose force with force, to annex territory by force, to influence the policies of other states by the threat or application of force—such uses of force have always been present at least as possibilities in the relations of states. The threat to use military forces and their occasional commitment to battle have helped to regulate the relations of states, and the preponderance of power in the hands of the major states has set them apart from the others. But, it is now often said, nuclear weapons, the "best" weapons of the most powerful states, are the least usable. At the extreme, some commentators assert that military force has become obsolete. Others, more cautious in their claims, believe that the inflated cost of using military force has seriously distorted both the balance between the militarily strong states and the imbalance between the strong and the weak ones. National military power, though not rendered wholly obsolete by nuclear weapons, nevertheless must be heavily discounted. The power of the two nuclear giants, it would seem, is then seriously impaired.

A weird picture of the political world is thus drawn. The constraints of balance-of-power politics still operate: each state by its own efforts fends for its rights and seeks to maintain its existence. At the same time, the operation of balance-of-power politics is strangely truncated; for one es-

---

[1] Quoted in Chalmers Johnson, *Revolutionary Change* (Boston: Little, Brown, 1966), p. 13.

sential means of adjustment is absent, and the operation of the other is severely restricted. In the nineteenth-century liberals' vision of a world without power, force was to be banished internationally by the growing perfection of states and their consequent acceptance of each other as equals in dignity. The liberal utopia has reappeared in odd form. The limitation of power—or in extreme formulations, its abolition—is said to derive from the nuclear armament of some states; for nuclear armament makes at once for gross inequality in the power of states and for substantial equality among all states through the inability of the most powerful to use force effectively. Those who love paradox are understandably enchanted. To examine the ground upon which the supposed paradox rests is one of the main aims of this essay.

I

The first reason for believing that balance-of-power politics has ended is easy to deal with, for only its relevance, not its truth, is in question.

If the balance-of-power game is really played hard it eventuates in two participants, whether states or groupings of them. If two groupings of states have hardened or if the relation of major antagonism in the world is simply between two nations, the balance-of-power model no longer applies, according to the conventional definition. This conclusion is reached by placing heavy emphasis on the process of balancing (by realignments of states) rather than on altering power (which may depend on the efforts of each state).[2] In a two-power world, emphasis must shift from the international process of balancing to the prospect of altering power by the internal efforts of each participant.

Admittedly, the old balance-of-power model cannot be applied without modification to a world in which two states far exceed all others in the force at their disposal. Balance-of-power analysis, however, remains highly useful if the observer shifts his perspective from a concentration upon international maneuver as a mode of adjustment to an examination of national power as a means of control and national effort as a way of compensating for incipient disequilibria of power. With this shift in perspective, balance-of-power politics does not disappear; but the meaning of politics changes in a manner that can only be briefly suggested here.

In a world of three or more powers the possibility of making and breaking alliances exists. The substance of balance-of-power politics is found in the diplomacy by which alliances are made, maintained, or disrupted. Flexibility of alignment then makes for rigidity in national

[2] See, for example, Inis L. Claude, Jr., *Power and International Relations* (New York: Random House, 1962), p. 90; and Morton A. Kaplan, *System and Process in International Politics* (New York: John Wiley & Sons, 1957), p. 22.

strategies: a state's strategy must satisfy its partner lest that partner defect from the alliance. A comparable situation is found where political parties compete for votes by forming and reforming electoral coalitions of different economic, ethnic, religious, and regional groups. The strategies (or policies) of the parties are made so as to attract and hold voters. If it is to be an electoral success, a party's policy cannot simply be the policy that its leaders may think would be best for the country. Policy must at least partly be made for the sake of party management. Similarly in an alliance of approximately equal states, strategy is at least partly made for the sake of the alliance's cohesion. The alliance diplomacy of Europe in the years before World War I is rich in examples of this. Because the defection or defeat of a major state would have shaken the balance of power, each state was constrained to adjust its strategy and the deployment of its forces to the aims and fears of its partners. This is in sharp contrast to the current situation in NATO, where de Gaulle's disenchantment, for example, can only have mild repercussions. Though concessions to allies will sometimes be made, neither the Soviet Union nor the United States alters its strategy or changes its military dispositions simply to accommodate associated states. Both superpowers can make long-range plans and carry out their policies as best they see fit, for they need not accede to the demands of third parties. That America's strategy is not made for the sake of de Gaulle helps to explain his partial defection.

Disregarding the views of an ally makes sense only if military cooperation is relatively unimportant. This is the case in NATO, which in fact if not in form consists of unilateral guarantees by the United States to its European allies. The United States, with a preponderance of nuclear weapons and as many men in uniform as all of the Western European states combined, may be able to protect her allies; they cannot possibly protect her. Because of the vast differences in the capacities of member states, the approximately equal sharing of burdens found in earlier alliance systems is no longer conceivable. The gross inequality between the two superpowers and the members of their respective alliances makes any realignment of the latter fairly insignificant. The leader's strategy can therefore be flexible. In balance-of-power politics, old style, flexibility of alignment made for rigidity of strategy or the limitation of freedom of decision. In balance-of-power politics, new style, the obverse is true: rigidity of alignment in a two-power world makes for flexibility of strategy or the enlargement of freedom of decision.

Those who discern the demise of balance-of-power politics mistakenly identify the existence of balances of power with a particular mode of adjustment and the political means of effecting it. Balances of power tend to form so long as states desire to maintain their political identities and so long as they must rely on their own devices in striving to do so. With shrinking numbers, political practices and methods will differ; but the number of states required for the existence and perpetuation of balance-of-power politics is simply two or more, not, as is usually averred, some number larger than two.

II

The reduction in the number of major states calls for a shift in conceptual perspective. Internal effort has replaced external realignment as a means of maintaining an approximate balance of power. But the operation of a balance of power, as previously noted, has entailed the occasional use of national force as a means of international control and adjustment. Great-power status was traditionally conferred on states that could use force most handily. Is the use of force in a nuclear world so severely inhibited that balance-of-power analysis has lost most if not all of its meaning?

Four reasons are usually given in support of an affirmative answer. First, because the nuclear might of one superpower balances that of the other, their effective power is reduced to zero. Their best and most distinctive forces, the nuclear ones, are least usable. In the widely echoed words of John Herz, absolute power equals absolute impotence.[3] Second, the fear of escalation strongly inhibits even the use of conventional forces, especially by the United States or the Soviet Union. Nuclear powers must fear escalation more than other states do, for in any war that rose to the nuclear level they would be primary targets. They may, of course, still choose to commit their armies to battle, but the risks of doing so, as they themselves must realize, are higher than in the past. Third, in the nuclear age enormous military power no longer ensures effective control. The Soviet Union has not been able to control her Asian and European satellites. The United States has found it difficult to use military force for constructive purposes even against weak opponents in Southeast Asia. Political rewards have not been proportionate to the strength of the states that are militarily most powerful. Finally, the weak states of the world, having become politically aware and active, have turned world opinion into a serious restraint upon the use of force, whether in nuclear or conventional form. These four factors, it is argued, work singly and in combination to make the use of force more costly and in general to depreciate its value.

Never have great powers disposed of larger national products, and seldom in peacetime have they spent higher percentages of them on their military forces. The money so lavishly expended purchases more explosive power and more varied ways of delivering it than ever before in history. In terms of world distribution, seldom has military force been more narrowly concentrated. If military force is less useful today, the irony of history will have yet another vivid illustration. Has force indeed

[3] John Herz, *International Politics in the Atomic Age* (New York: Columbia University Press, 1959), pp. 22, 169.

so depreciated as to warp and seriously weaken the effects of power in international relations? The above arguments make it seem so; they need to be re-examined. The following analysis of the use of force deals with all four arguments, though not by examining them one by one and in the order in which they are stated.

E. H. Carr long ago identified the error of believing "in the efficacy of an international public opinion," and he illustrated and explained the fallacy at length.[4] To think of world opinion as a restraint upon the military actions of states, one must believe that the strong states of the world—or for that matter the weak ones—would have used more military force and used it more often had they not anticipated their condemnation. Unless in a given instance world opinion can be defined, its source identified, and the mode of its operation discerned, such a view is not plausible. . . . With "world opinion," as with Adam Smith's "invisible hand," one must ask: What is the reality that the metaphor stands for? It may be that statesmen pay their respects to world opinion because they are already restrained by other considerations.

Are such considerations found, perhaps, in changes that have taken place in the nature and distribution of force itself? If the costs of using military force have lessened its value, then obeisance paid to world opinion is merely a cloak for frustration and a hypocritical show of politeness. That the use of force is unusually costly, however, is a conclusion that rests on a number of errors. One that is commonly committed is to extend to all military force the conclusion that nuclear force is unusable. After listing the changes effected by nuclear weapons, one author, for example, concludes that these changes tend to restrict "the usability and hence the political utility of national military power in various ways."[5] This may represent merely a slip of the pen; if so, it is a telling one. A clearer and more interesting form of the error is found in the argument that the two superpowers, each stalemated by the other's nuclear force, are for important political purposes effectively reduced to the power of middle-range states. The effective equality of states apparently emerges from the very condition of their gross inequality. We read, for example, that "the very change in the nature of the mobilizable potential has made its actual use in emergencies by its unhappy owners quite difficult and self-defeating. As a result, nations endowed with infinitely less can behave in a whole range of issues as if the difference in power did not matter." The conclusion is driven home—or, rather, error is compounded—by the argument that the United States thinks in "cataclysmic terms," lives in dread of all-out war, and bases its military calculations on the forces needed for the ultimate but unlikely crisis rather

---

[4] Edward Hallett Carr, *The Twenty Years' Crisis, 1919–1939,* 2nd ed. (New York: Harper & Row, 1964), p. 140.

[5] Knorr, *On the Uses of Military Power,* p. 87.

than on what might be needed in the less spectacular cases that are in fact more likely to occur.[6]

Absolute power equals absolute impotence, at least at the highest levels of force represented by the American and Soviet nuclear armories. At lesser levels of violence many states can compete as though they were substantially equal. The best weapons of the United States and the Soviet Union are useless, and the distinctive advantage of those two states is thus negated. But what about American or Soviet nuclear weapons used against minor nuclear states or against those who are entirely without nuclear weapons? Here again, it is claimed, the "best" weapon of the most powerful states turns out to be the least usable. The nation that is equipped to "retaliate massively" is not likely to find the occasion to use its capability. . . . Instruments that cannot be used to deal with small cases—those that are moderately dangerous and damaging—remain idle until the big case arises. But then the use of major force to defend a vital interest would run the grave risk of retaliation. Under such circumstances, the powerful are frustrated by their very strength; and although the weak do not thereby become strong, they are, it is said, nevertheless able to behave as though they were.

Such arguments are often made and have to be taken seriously. In an obvious sense, part of the contention is valid. When great powers are in a stalemate, lesser states acquire an increased freedom of movement. That this phenomenon is now noticeable tells us nothing new about the strength of the weak or the weakness of the strong. Weak states have often found opportunities for maneuver in the interstices of a balance of power. This is, however, only part of the story. To maintain both the balance and its by-product requires the continuing efforts of America and Russia. Their instincts for self-preservation call forth such efforts: the objective of both states must be to perpetuate an international stalemate as a minimum basis for the security of each of them—even if this should mean that the two big states do the work while the small ones have the fun. The margins within which the relative strengths of America and Russia may vary without destroying the stalemate are made wide by the existence of second-strike retaliatory forces, but permissible variation is not without limit. In the years of the supposed missile gap in America's disfavor, Khrushchev became unpleasantly frisky, especially over Berlin and Cuba. The usefulness of maintaining American nuclear strength was demonstrated by the unfortunate consequences of its apparent diminution.

Strategic nuclear weapons deter strategic nuclear weapons (though they may also do more than that). Where each state must tend to its own security as best it can, the means adopted by one state must be geared to the efforts of others. The cost of the American nuclear establishment, maintained in peaceful readiness, is functionally comparable to the costs

[6] Hoffmann, "Europe's Identity Crisis," *Daedalus* (Fall 1964), pp. 1279, 1287–88.

incurred by a government in order to maintain domestic order and provide internal security.   Such expenditure is not productive in the sense that spending to build roads is, but it is not unproductive either.   Its utility is obvious, and should anyone successfully argue otherwise, the consequences of accepting his argument would quickly demonstrate its falsity. Force is least visible where power is most fully and most adequately present.[7]   The better ordered a society and the more competent and respected its government, the less force its policemen are required to employ.   Less shooting occurs in present-day Sandusky than did on the western frontier.   Similarly in international relations, states supreme in their power have to use force less often.   "Non-recourse to force"—as both Eisenhower and Khrushchev seem to have realized—is the doctrine of powerful states.   Powerful states need to use force less often than their weaker neighbors because the strong can more often protect their interests or work their wills in other ways—by persuasion and cajolery, by economic bargaining and bribery, by the extension of aid, or finally by posing deterrent threats.   Since states with large nuclear armories do not actually "use" them, force is said to be discounted.   Such reasoning is fallacious.   Possession of power should not be identified with the use of force, and the usefulness of force should not be confused with its usability. To introduce such confusions into the analysis of power is comparable to saying that the police force that seldom if ever employs violence is weak or that a police force is strong only when policemen are swinging their clubs.   To vary the image, it is comparable to saying that a man with large assets is not rich if he spends little money or that a man is rich only if he spends a lot of it.

But the argument, which we should not lose sight of, is that just as the miser's money may grossly depreciate in value over the years, so the great powers' military strength has lost much of its usability.   If military force is like currency that cannot be spent or money that has lost much of its worth, then is not forbearance in its use merely a way of disguising its depreciated value?   Conrad von Hötzendorf, Austrian Chief of Staff prior to the First World War, looked upon military power as though it were a capital sum, useless unless invested.   In his view, the investment of military force was ultimately its commitment to battle.[8]   It may be permissible to reason in this way, but it makes the result of the reasoning a foregone conclusion.   As Robert W. Tucker has noted, those who argue that force has lost its utility do so "in terms of its virtually uncontrolled use."   But, he adds, "alter the assumption on which the argument proceeds—consider the functions served by military power so long as it is not

[7] Cf. Carr, *The Twenty Years' Crisis*, pp. 103, 129–32.

[8] Quoted in Alfred Vagts, *Defense and Diplomacy: The Soldier and the Conduct of Foreign Relations* (New York: King's Crown Press, 1956), p. 361.

overtly employed or employed only with restraint—and precisely the opposite conclusion may be drawn." [9]

In the reasoning of Conrad, military force is most useful at the moment of its employment in war. Depending on a country's situation, it may make much better sense to say that military force is most useful when it deters an attack, that is, when it need not be used in battle at all. When the strongest state militarily is also a status-quo power, non-use of force is a sign of its strength. Force is most useful, or best serves the interests of such a state, when it need not be used in the actual conduct of warfare. Again, the reasoning is old-fashioned. Throughout a century that ended in 1914, the British navy was powerful enough to scare off all comers, while Britain carried out occasional imperial ventures in odd parts of the world. Only as Britain's power weakened did her military forces have to be used to fight a full-scale war. By being used, her military power had surely become less useful.

Force is cheap, especially for a status-quo power, if its very existence works against its use. What does it mean then to say that the cost of using force has increased while its utility has lessened? It is highly important, indeed useful, to think in "cataclysmic terms," to live in dread of all-out war, and to base military calculations on the forces needed for the ultimate but unlikely crisis. That the United States does so, and that the Soviet Union apparently does too, makes the cataclysm less likely to occur. But not only that. Nuclear weapons deter nuclear weapons; they also serve as a means of limiting escalation. The temptation of one country to employ larger and larger amounts of force is lessened if its opponent has the ability to raise the ante. Conventional force may be used more hesitantly than it would be in the absence of nuclear weapons because it cannot be assumed that escalation will be perfectly regulated. But force can be used with less hesitation by those states able to parry, to thrust, and to threaten at varied levels of military endeavor.

Where power is seen to be balanced, whether or not the balance is nuclear, it may seem that the resultant of opposing forces is zero. But this is misleading. The vectors of national force do not meet at a point, if only because the power of a state does not resolve into a single vector. Military force is divisible, especially for the state that can afford a lot of it. In a nuclear world, contrary to some assertions, the dialectic of inequality does not produce the effective equality of strong and weak states. Lesser states that decide to establish a nuclear arsenal by slighting their conventional forces render themselves unable to meet any threat to themselves other than the ultimate one (and that doubtfully). By way of contrast, the military doctrine of the United States, to which the organiza-

[9] Robert W. Tucker, "Peace and War," *World Politics,* Vol. XVII (Jan. 1965), p. 324 fn.

tion of her forces corresponds, is one of flexible response. Great powers are strong not simply because they have nuclear weapons but also because their immense resources enable them to generate and maintain power of all types, military and other, at different technological levels.

Just as the state that refrains from applying force is said to betray its weakness, so the state that has trouble in exercising control is said to display the defectiveness of its power. In such a conclusion, the elementary error of identifying power with control is evident. Absence of control or failure to press hard to achieve it may indicate either that the would-be controller noticed that, try as he might, he would have insufficient force or inappropriate types of force at his command; or it may indicate that he chose to make less than a maximum effort because imposition of control was not regarded as very important. One student of international relations has remarked that "though the weapons of mass destruction grow more and more ferociously efficient, the revolutionary guerrilla armed with nothing more advanced than an old rifle and a nineteenth-century political doctrine has proved the most effective means yet devised for altering the world power-balance." [10] But the revolutionary guerrilla wins civil wars, not international ones, and no civil war can change the balance of power in the world unless it takes place in the United States or the Soviet Union. Enough of them have occurred since the Second World War to make the truth of this statement clear without need for further analysis. Even in China, the most populous of states, a civil war that led to a change of allegiance in the cold war did not seriously tilt the world balance.

Two states that enjoy wide margins of power over other states need worry little about changes that occur among the latter. Failure to act may then not betray the frustrations of impotence; instead it may demonstrate the serenity of power. The United States, having chosen to intervene in Vietnam, has limited the use of its military force. Because no realignment of national power in Vietnam could in itself affect the balance of power between the United States and the Soviet Union—or even noticeably alter the imbalance of power between the United States and China—the United States need not have intervened at all. Whether or not it could have safely "passed" in Southeast Asia, the American government chose not to do so; nor have its costly, long-sustained efforts brought success. If military power can be equated with control, then the United States has indeed demonstrated its weakness. The case is instructive. The People's Republic of China has not moved militarily against any country of Southeast Asia. The United States could successfully counter such a move, one would expect, by opposing military force with military force. What has worried some people and led others to sharpen their

[10] Coral Bell, "Non-Alignment and the Power Balance," *Survival*, Vol. V (Nov.–Dec. 1963), p. 255.

statements about the weakness of the powerful is that the United States, hard though it has tried, has been unable to put down insurrection and halt the possible spread of Communist ideology.

Here again old truths need to be brought into focus. As David Hume long ago noted, "force is always on the side of the governed." [11] The governors, being few in number, depend for the exercise of their rule upon the more or less willing assent of their subjects. If sullen disregard is the response to every command, no government can rule. And if a country, because of internal disorder and lack of coherence, is unable to rule itself, no body of foreigners, whatever the military force at its command, can reasonably hope to do so. If Communism is the threat to Southeast Asia, then military forces are not the right means for countering it. If insurrection is the problem, then it can hardly be hoped that an alien army will be able to pacify a country that is unable to govern itself. Foreign troops, though not irrelevant to such problems, can only be of indirect help. Military force, used internationally, is a means of establishing control over a territory, not of exercising control within it. The threat of a nation to use military force, whether nuclear or conventional, is pre-eminently a means of affecting another state's external behavior, of dissuading a state from launching a career of aggression and of meeting the aggression if dissuasion should fail.

Dissuasion or deterrence is easier to accomplish than "compellence," to use an apt term invented by Thomas C. Schelling.[12] Compellence is more difficult to achieve than deterrence, and its contrivance is a more intricate affair. In Vietnam, the United States faces not merely the task of compelling a particular action but of promoting an effective political order. Those who argue from such a case that force has depreciated in value fail in their analyses to apply their own historical and political knowledge. The master builders of imperial rule, such men as Bugeaud, Galliéni, and Lyautey, played both political and military roles. In like fashion, successful counterrevolutionary efforts have been directed by such men as Templer and Magsaysay, who combined military resources with political instruments.[13] Military forces, whether domestic or foreign, are insufficient for the task of pacification, the more so if a country is rent by faction and if its people are politically engaged and active. To say that militarily strong states are feeble because they cannot easily bring order to minor states is like saying that a pneumatic hammer is weak because it is not suitable for drilling decayed teeth. It is to confuse the purpose of in-

---

[11] "Of the First Principles of Government," in *Hume's Moral and Political Philosophy*, ed. by Henry D. Aiken (New York: Hafner, 1948), p. 307.

[12] Thomas C. Schelling, *Arms and Influence* (New Haven: Yale University Press, 1966), pp. 70–71.

[13] The point is well made by Samuel P. Huntington, "Patterns of Violence in World Politics," in *Changing Patterns of Military Politics,* ed. by Samuel P. Huntington (New York: The Free Press of Glencoe, 1962), p. 28.

struments and to confound the means of external power with the agencies of internal governance.   Inability to exercise *political* control over others does not indicate *military* weakness.   Strong states cannot do everything with their military forces, as Napoleon acutely realized; but they are able to do things that militarily weak states cannot do.   The People's Republic of China can no more solve the problems of governance in some Latin American country than the United States can in Southeast Asia.   But the United States can intervene with great military force in far quarters of the world while wielding an effective deterrent against escalation.   Such action exceeds the capabilities of all but the strongest of states.

Differences in strength do matter, though not for every conceivable purpose.   To deduce the weakness of the powerful from this qualifying clause is a misleading use of words.   One sees in such a case as Vietnam not the *weakness* of great military power in a nuclear world but instead a clear illustration of the *limits* of military force in the world of the present as always.

III

Only a sketch, intended to be suggestive, can here be offered of the connections between the present structure of the global balance of power, the relations of states, and the use of force internationally.

Unbalanced power is a danger to weak states.   It may also be a danger to strong ones.   An imbalance of power, by feeding the ambition of some states to extend their control, may tempt them to dangerously adventurous activity.   Safety for all states, one may then conclude, depends upon the maintenance of a balance among them.   Ideally, in this view, the rough equality of states gives each of them the ability to fend for itself.   Equality may then also be viewed as a morally desirable condition.   Each of the states within the arena of balance will have at least a modest ability to maintain its integrity.   At the same time, inequality violates one's sense of justice and leads to national resentments that are in many ways troublesome.   Because inequality is inherent in the state system, however, it cannot be removed.   At the pinnacle of power, only a few states coexist as approximate equals; in relation to them, other states are of lesser moment. The bothersome qualities of this inevitable inequality of states should not cause one to overlook its virtues.   In an economy, in a polity, or in the world at large, extreme equality is associated with instability.   To draw another domestic analogy: where individualism is extreme, where society is atomistic, and where secondary organizations are lacking, government tends either to break down into anarchy or to become highly centralized and despotic.   Under conditions of extreme equality, the prospect of oscillation between those two poles was well described by de Tocqueville; it was illustrated by Hobbes; and its avoidance was earnestly sought by the authors of the *Federalist Papers*.   In a collection of equals, any impulse ripples through the whole society.   Lack of secondary groups with some cohesion and continuity of commitment, for example, turns elections into auctions with each party in its promises tempted to bid up the others. The presence of social and economic groups, which inevitably will not all be equal, makes for less volatility in society.

Such durable propositions of political theory are lost sight of in the argument, frequently made, that the larger the number of consequential states the more stable the structure of world politics will be.[14]   Carried to its logical conclusion, the argument must mean that perfect stability would prevail in a world in which many states exist, all of them approximate equals in power.

The analysis of the present essay leads to a different conclusion.   The inequality of states, though not a guarantee of international stability, at least makes stability possible.   Within the structure of world politics, the relations of states will be as variable and complex as the movements and patterns of bits of glass within a kaleidoscope.   It is not very interesting to ask whether destabilizing events will occur and disruptive relations will form, because the answer must always be yes.   More interesting are such questions as these: What is the likely durability of a given political structure, whether international or domestic?   How does it affect the relations of states, or of groups and individuals?   How do the relations of constituent units and changes within them in turn affect the political structure?   Within a state, people use more violence than do governments. In the United States in 1965, 9,814 people were murdered, but only seven were executed.   Thus one says (with some exaggeration, since fathers still spank their children) that the state enjoys a monopoly of *legitimate* violence.   Too much violence among individuals will jeopardize the political structure.   In international relations it is difficult to say that any particular use of violence is illegitimate, but some states have the ability to wield more of it.   Because they do, they are able both to moderate others' use of violence and to absorb possibly destabilizing changes that emanate from uses of violence that they do not or cannot control.   In the spring of 1966, Secretary McNamara remarked that in the preceding eight years there had been "no less than 164 internationally significant outbreaks of violence. . . ."[15]   Of course, not only violence is at issue. To put the point in more general terms, strong structures are able to moderate and absorb destabilizing changes; weak structures succumb to them.

No political structure, whether domestic or international, can guarantee stability.   The question that one must ask is not whether a given distribu-

---

[14] By "structure" I mean the pattern according to which power is distributed; by "stability," the perpetuation of that structure without the occurrence of grossly destructive violence.

[15] *The New York Times,* May 19, 1966, p. 11.

tion of power is stable but how stable different distributions of power are likely to be. For a number of reasons, the bipolar world of the past two decades has been highly stable.[16] The two leading states have a common interest in stability: they would at least like to maintain their positions. In one respect, bipolarity is expressed as the reciprocal control of the two strongest states by each other out of their mutual antagonism. What is unpredictable in such a two-party competition is whether one party will try to eliminate the other. Nuclear forces of second-strike capacity induce an added caution. Here again force is useful, and its usefulness is reinforced in proportion as its use is forestalled. Fear of major war induces caution all around; the Soviet Union and the United States wield the means of inducing that caution.

The constraints of duopolistic competition press in one direction: duopolists eye each other warily, and each is very sensitive to the gains of the other. Working in the opposite direction, however, is the existence of the immense difference in power between the two superpowers and the states of middle or lesser rank. This condition of inequality makes it unlikely that any shifts in the alignment of states would very much help or hurt either of the two leading powers. If few changes can damage the vital interests of either of them, then both can be moderate in their responses. Not being dependent upon allies, the United States and the Soviet Union are free to design strategies in accord with their interests. Since the power actually and potentially at the disposal of each of them far exceeds that of their closest competitors, they are able to control in some measure the possibly destabilizing acts of third parties or to absorb their effects. The Americans and Russians, for example, can acquire the means of defending themselves against the nuclear assaults that the Chinese and French may be able to launch by the mid-1970's. Anti-ballistic-missile systems, useful against missiles launched in small number, are themselves anti-proliferation devices. With considerable expectation of success, states with vast economic, scientific, and technological resources can hope to counter the armaments and actions of others and to reduce their destabilizing effects.[17] The extent of the difference in national capabilities makes the bipolar structure resilient. Defection of allies and national shifts of allegiance do not decisively alter the structure. Because they do not, recalcitrant allies may be treated with indifference; they may even be effectively disciplined. Pressure can be applied to moderate the behavior of third states or to check and contain their activities. The Suez venture of Britain and France was stopped by Ameri-

[16] For further examination of the proposition, see Kenneth N. Waltz, "The Stability of a Bipolar World," *Daedalus,* Vol. XCIII (Summer 1964), pp. 881–909. On the possibility of exercising control, see Waltz, "Contention and Management in International Relations," *World Politics,* Vol. XVII (July 1965), pp. 720–44.

[17] On the limitations of a small nuclear force, see Waltz, *Foreign Policy and Democratic Politics* (Boston: Little, Brown, 1967), pp. 145–48.

can financial pressure. Chiang Kai-shek has been kept on a leash by denying him the means of invasion. The prospective loss of foreign aid helped to halt warfare between Pakistan and India, as did the Soviet Union's persuasion. In such ways, the wielding of great power can be useful.

The above examples illustrate hierarchical control operating in a way that often goes unnoticed because the means by which control is exercised are not institutionalized. What management there now is in international relations must be provided, singly and occasionally together, by the duopolists at the top. In certain ways, some of them suggested above, the inequality of states in a bipolar world enables the two most powerful states to develop a rich variety of controls and to follow flexible strategies in using them.

A good many statements about the obsolescence of force, the instability of international politics, and the disappearance of the bipolar order are made because no distinction has been clearly and consistently drawn between international structure, on the one hand, and the relations of states on the other. For more than two decades, power has been narrowly concentrated; and force has been used, not orgiastically as in the world wars of this century, but in a controlled way and for conscious political purposes. Power may be present when force is not used, but force is also used openly. A catalogue of examples would be both complex and lengthy. It would contain such items, on the American side of the ledger, as the garrisoning of Berlin, its supply by airlift during the blockade, the stationing of troops in Europe, the establishment of bases in Japan and elsewhere, the waging of war in Korea and Vietnam, and the "quarantine" of Cuba. Seldom if ever has force been more variously, more persistently, and more widely applied; and seldom has it been more consciously used as an instrument of national policy. Since the war we have seen, not the cancellation of force by nuclear stalemate, but instead the political organization and pervasion of power; not the end of balance of power owing to a reduction in the number of major states, but instead the formation and perpetuation of a balance *à deux*.

SUGGESTED READINGS

Badgley, John, *Asian Development: Problems and Prognosis,* New York: Free Press, 1971.

Burton, J. W., *Systems, States, Diplomacy and Rules,* Cambridge, England: Cambridge University Press, 1968.

Cooper, Chester, *The Lost Crusade: America in Vietnam,* New York: Dodd, 1970.

Ehrlich, Paul, and Ehrlich, Ann, *Population, Resources, Environment,* San Francisco: Freeman, 1970.

Goulet, Denis, *The Cruel Choice: A New Concept in the Theory of Development,* New York: Atheneum, 1971.

Haas, Ernst B., *Tangle of Hopes: American Commitments and World Order,* Englewood Cliffs, N.J.: Prentice-Hall, 1969.

Herz, John, *International Politics in the Atomic Age,* New York: Columbia University Press, 1959.

Quester, George H., *Nuclear Diplomacy: The First Twenty-five Years,* New York: Dunellen, 1971.

Rapoport, Anatol, *The Big Two: Soviet-American Perceptions of Foreign Policy,* New York: Pegasus, 1971.

Stoessinger, John G., *Nations in Darkness: China, Russia and America,* New York: Random House, 1971.

BIOGRAPHICAL NOTES

ACHESON, DEAN, 1893–1971
U.S. Secretary of State, 1949–1953. Author of *Power and Diplomacy* (1958).

BANKS, MICHAEL H., 1936–
Lecturer in International Relations, London School of Economics and Political Science. Contributor to *Foreign Policy of the Powers* (F. S. Northedge, ed., 1969).

BRZEZINSKI, ZBIGNIEW, 1928–
Born in Poland, educated in Canada and at Harvard; taught at Harvard University (1953–1960); now Professor of Public Law and Government and Director of the Research Institute on Communist Affairs, Columbia University. Author of, among other works, *The Soviet Bloc: Unity and Conflict* (2nd ed., 1961), *Political Power: USA/USSR* (with S. P. Huntington, 1964), *Dilemmas of Change in Soviet Politics* (1969), and *Between Two Ages: America's Role in the Technetronic Age* (1970).

BULL, HEDLEY, 1932–
Professor of International Relations, Australian National University, Canberra; Director, Arms Control and Disarmament Research Unit, British Foreign Office, 1964–1967. Author of *Strategy and the Atlantic Alliance* (1964) and *The Control of the Arms Race* (2nd ed., 1965).

CARR, EDWARD HALLETT, 1892–
British historian, Fellow of Trinity College, Cambridge University. In the Foreign Service (1916–1936); Assistant Editor of *The Times* (1941–1946). Among his many works are *Nationalism and After* (1945), *A History of Soviet Russia, 1917–1926* (8 vols., 1950–1969), *German-Soviet Relations Between the Two World Wars* (1951), and *What is History?* (1961).

CLAUDE, INIS L., JR., 1922–
Professor of Government and Foreign Affairs, University of Virginia. Author of *Power and International Relations* (1962), *Swords into Plowshares* (4th ed., 1971), and *The Changing United Nations* (1967).

CLAUSEWITZ, KARL VON, 1780–1831
Prussian general. His writings were regarded for generations as the most authoritative works on war. Published posthumously in ten volumes, 1832–1837.

COBBAN, ALFRED, 1901–1968
British historian. Author of *Dictatorship: Its History and Theory* (1939), *Ambassadors and Secret Agents* (1954), *History of Modern France* (4 vols., 1957–1961), and others.

CONNOR, WALKER F., 1926–
Teaches political science at the Rensselaer Polytechnic Institute. Author of the forth-coming *Ethnic Nationalism: the Path of Political Disintegration*.

EMERSON, RUPERT, 1899–
Professor of International Relations (Emeritus since 1970), Harvard University. Au-thor of *From Empire to Nation* (1960), *Self-Determination Revisited in the Era of Decolonization* (1964), *Malaysia* (1966), and *Africa and U.S. Policy* (1967).

ENGELS, FRIEDRICH, 1820–1895

ESMOND, DAVID, 1944–
Graduate student at the School of Public Affairs, State University of New York, Albany, and examiner with the Budget Division of the State of New York.

FIELDHOUSE, D. K., 1925–
Teaches history at Oxford University. Author of *The Colonial Empires* (1966) and editor of *The Theory of Capitalist Imperialism* (1967).

FREUD, SIGMUND, 1856–1939

GALLOIS, PIERRE M., 1911–
General of the French Air Force (retired). Author of *The Balance of Terror: Strat-egy for the Nuclear Age* (1961) and *Paradoxes de la Paix* (1968).

GONCHAROV, LEONGARD V.
Deputy Director, Africa Institute, U.S.S.R. Academy of Sciences, Moscow. Author of several books (in Russian) on African economic conditions and international relations.

HAAS, ERNST B., 1924–
Professor of Political Science, University of California, Berkeley. Author of *The Uniting of Europe* (1958), *Beyond the Nation-State: Functionalism and Interna-tional Organization* (1964), *Human Rights and International Action* (1970), and *U.S. and International Organizations* (1970).

HAMMARSKJÖLD, DAG, 1905–1961
Swedish economist and diplomat. Became Secretary-General of the United Nations in 1953. Killed while on U.N. mission to the Congo.

HOBBES, THOMAS, 1588–1679

HOFFMANN, STANLEY, 1928–
Professor of Government, Harvard University. Editor of *Contemporary Theory in International Relations* (1960), *The State of War* (1965), and *Gulliver's Troubles, or the Setting of American Foreign Policy* (1968); coauthor of *The Relevance of Inter-national Law* (1968).

HUNT, ROBERT N. CAREW, 1890–1959
On retiring from the British Foreign Office he became a Fellow of St. Anthony's

College, Oxford University. Author of *Marxism, Past and Present* (1955) and *The Theory and Practice of Communism* (5th ed., 1957).

JOHNSON, CHALMERS, 1931–
Professor of Political Science, University of California, Berkeley. Author of *Peasant Nationalism and Communist Power* (1962) and *Revolutionary Change* (1966); editor of *Change in Communist Systems* (1970).

JOHNSON, HARRY G., 1923–
Professor of Economics at the University of Chicago and the London School of Economics. Author of *The World Economy at the Crossroads* (1965), *Economic Policies Toward the Less Developed Countries* (1967), *Economic Nationalism in Old and New States* (1967), *New Trade Strategy for the World Economy* (1969), and others.

JOHNSTON, WHITTLE
Professor at the School of International Service, American University, Washington, D.C.

KANT, IMMANUEL, 1724–1804

KAPLAN, MORTON A., 1921–
Professor of Political Science, University of Chicago. Author of *System and Process in International Politics* (1959) and *Macropolitics* (1968); coauthor of *Political Foundations of International Law* (with Nicholas Katzenbach, 1961); editor of *New Approach to International Relations* (1968).

KAY, DAVID A., 1940–
Teaches political science at the University of Wisconsin. Author of *The New Nations in the United Nations, 1960–1967* (1970); editor of *The United Nation's Political System* (1967).

KHRUSHCHEV, NIKITA SERGEIEVICH, 1894–1971
Became head of the Communist Party of the U.S.S.R. in 1953 and Chairman of the Council of Ministers in 1958. Resigned from all offices in October 1964.

KNAPP, WILFRID, 1925–
Fellow of St. Catherine's College, Oxford University. Author of *A History of War and Peace, 1939–1965* (1967), *Unity and Nationalism in Europe since 1945* (1969), and *Tunisia* (1970).

LISKA, GEORGE, 1922–
Professor of Political Science, Johns Hopkins University. Author of *International Equilibrium* (1957), *Nations in Alliance* (1962), *Imperialist America* (1967), *Alliances and the Third World* (1968), *War and Order* (1968), and others.

LISSITZYN, OLIVER J., 1912–
Professor of Public Law, Columbia University. Author of *The International Court of Justice* (1951) and *International Law Today and Tomorrow* (1965).

LOCKE, JOHN, 1632–1704

LOWENTHAL, RICHARD, 1908–
Professor of International Relations, Free University of Berlin. Born and educated in Germany, he went to England after 1933 and became a well-known newspaperman and writer, specializing in the Soviet area. Author of *World Communism: The Disintegration of a Secular Faith* (1964) and *Issues in the Future of Asia* (1969).

MACHIAVELLI, NICCOLÒ, 1469–1527

MARX, KARL, 1818–1883

McWILLIAMS, WILSON C., 1933–
Teaches political science at Livingston College, Rutgers University. Author of *The Dilemma of Atomic Power in a Divided World* (1963) and of *The Idea of Fraternity in America* (1972). Coeditor of this volume.

MILL, JOHN STUART, 1806–1873

MILLS, C. WRIGHT, 1916–1962
Was professor of Sociology, Columbia University. Author of *The Power Elite* (1956), *The Sociological Imagination* (1959), *The Marxists* (1962), and others.

MORGENTHAU, HANS J., 1904–
Professor of Political Science, University of Chicago and City College of the City University of New York. Born and educated in Germany, he came to the United States in 1937. Since 1948 widely regarded as the leader of the realist school in international relations. Author of *Scientific Man vs. Power Politics* (1946), *Politics Among Nations* (5th ed., 1972), *The Purpose of American Politics* (1961), *A New Policy for the United States* (1967), *Truth or Power* (1970), and others.

NICOLSON, SIR HAROLD, 1886–1966
In British diplomatic service, 1909–1929; Member of Parliament, 1935–1945; author of political and literary biographies. Among his writings on international affairs are *Peacemaking 1919* (1933), *Curzon, The Last Phase* (1934), and *Diplomacy* (1939).

NYERERE, JULIUS K., 1922–
President of Tanganyika, 1962, and since October 1964, President of the Republic of Tanzania.

OGLESBY, CARL, 1935–
Former leader of Students for a Democratic Society (SDS). Coauthor of *Containment and Change* (1967); editor of *The New Left Reader* (1969).

ORGANSKI, A. F. K., 1923–
Professor of Political Science, University of Michigan. Author of *Population and World Power* (with Katherine Organski, 1961), *The Stages of Political Development* (1965), and *World Politics* (2nd ed., 1968).

ORWELL, GEORGE, 1903–1950
English novelist and essayist.

PACHTER, HENRY M., 1907–
Professor of History, City College of the City University of New York. Author of *Collision Course: the October Crisis of 1962* (1963).

PARSONS, TALCOTT, 1902–
Professor of Social Relations, Harvard University. Author of *The Social System* (1951), *Structure and Process in Modern Societies* (1960), *Theories of Society* (1961), and many more.

PFAFF, WILLIAM, 1928–
Writer and columnist. Author of *Power and Impotence: the Failure of America's Foreign Policy* (with Edmund Stillman, 1967).

READ, THORNTON, 1921–
Research scientist, Bell Telephone Laboratories. Author of numerous scientific papers. Since 1957 engaged in research on tactics and deployment for active antimissile defense, and more recently on nuclear strategy. Consultant to many high-level government agencies, among them the Office of the Special Assistant to the President for Science and Technology and the Office of the Assistant Secretary of Defense for International Security Affairs. Member of the Center of International Studies, Princeton University, 1960–1963. Coeditor of *Limited Strategic War* (with Klaus Knorr, 1962).

RUSSETT, BRUCE M., 1935–
Teaches political science at Yale University. Author of *Community and Contention: Britain and America in the Twentieth Century* (1963), *World Handbook of Political and Social Indicators* (1964), *Trends in World Politics* (1965), and *International Regions and the International System* (1967).

SAKHAROV, ANDREI D., 1921–
Leading Soviet nuclear scientist, author of many important papers in theoretical physics. Developed the Soviet hydrogen bomb. Member of the Soviet Academy of Sciences. Proponent of reforms in Soviet education and scientific policies; one of the leaders in the struggle for intellectual freedom.

SETON-WATSON, HUGH, 1916–
Professor of Russian History, University of London. Author of *The Decline of Imperial Russia* (1952), *The East European Revolution* (3rd ed., 1961), *Neither War nor Peace* (rev. ed., 1962), *The Russian Empire, 1801–1917* (1967), and others.

SEWELL, JAMES P., 1930–
Teaches political science at Yale University. Author of *Functionalism and World Politics* (1966).

STONE, JEREMY J., 1935–
Specializes in arms control and disarmament research. Author of *Containing the Arms Race* (1966), *Strategic Persuasion* (1967), and *The Case Against Missile Defense* (1968).

TSOU, TANG, 1918–
Professor of Political Science, University of Chicago. Author of *Embroilment Over Quemoy* (1959) and *America's Failure in China* (1963).

WALTZ, KENNETH N., 1924–
Professor of Political Science, University of California, Berkeley. Author of *Man, the State and War* (1959) and *Foreign Policy and Democratic Politics* (1967).

WARD, BARBARA (Lady Jackson), 1914–

English journalist, writer, and lecturer. Author of *Five Ideas That Changed the World* (1959), *The Rich Nations and the Poor Nations* (1962), *Nationalism and Ideology* (1966), *Lopsided World* (1968), and many more.

WEAVER, JAMES H., 1933–

Professor of Economics, American University, Washington, D.C. Author of *The International Development Association: A New Approach to Foreign Aid* (1965) and *The International Bond Market in the Nineteen Sixties* (1965).

YARMOLINSKY, ADAM, 1922–

Professor of Law, Harvard University. Deputy Assistant Secretary of Defense for International Security Affairs, 1965–1966; Special Assistant to the Secretary of Defense, 1961–1964. Author of *Recognition of Excellence* (1960) and *Military Establishment: Its Impacts on American Society* (1971).

SUGGESTED CORRELATION OF READINGS WITH TEXTBOOKS

Chapters in Textbooks:

Chapters of Readings	Hans Morgenthau, Politics Among Nations (1972)	A. F. K. Organski, World Politics (1968)	John Stoessinger, Might of Nations (1969)	R. J. Holsti, International Politics (1967)	Donald Puchala, International Politics Today (1971)	Vernon Van Dyke, International Politics (1966)
I Theories of World Politics	1–2	1	1	1	1, 15	1
II Nations and Nationalism	8	2–3	2	3	2, 9	4, 9
III Imperialism and After	5	10–11	4		3	4, 6, 9
IV The Role of Ideology	7		3		3	5
V Power and Conflict	3–5, 11–14	6, 12	3	5, 7	8	10–12
VI Arms and War	22–23	13	6, 12	12	12	7–8, 18–19
VII The Bonds of World Community	15–18, 20		7–9, 13	13–14	13	10, 14
VIII Diplomacy and Foreign Policy	31–32	5, 15	8	6–11	10	2, 13, 15–17
IX Governing the World Community	24, 26–28, 30	16–18	10–11	15–16	6–7, 14	20–21
X Toward a New World Order	20–21	14, 19	14		11	22